The Politics of Civil Society Building

Kees Biekart

The Politics of
Civil Society Building

European Private Aid Agencies
and Democratic Transitions
in Central America

International Books and the Transnational Institute, 1999

© Kees Biekart, 1999

Cover design: Marjo Starink, Amsterdam
Cover photo: 'Encuentro de dos mundos', Daniel Hernández © Daniel Hernández, 1993
Maps: Jan Vos, Medio, Amsterdam
DTP: Henk Pel, Zeist
Printing: Haasbeek, Alphen aan den Rijn

Keywords: Development Aid / NGOs / Democracy / Latin America
ISBN: 90 5727 025 0

International Books, A. Numankade 17, 3572 KP Utrecht,
tel.: ++ 31 30 273 18 40, fax: ++ 31 30 273 36 14,
e-mail: i-books@antenna.nl, http://www.antenna.nl/i-books
in cooperation with
Transnational Institute, Paulus Potterstraat 20, 1071 DA Amsterdam,
tel.: ++ 31 20 662 66 08, fax: ++ 31 20 675 71 76,
e-mail: tni@worldcom.nl, http://www.worldcom.nl/tni

Contents

Tables, Figures and Maps   7
Preface   9

Charity and Solidarity
Introduction   13

Part I: Civil Society Building

1 *Mixing Poverty and Democracy*
  Democratic Transition, Civil Society and the International Context   21

2 *Between Compassion and Survival*
  The Relevance of Private Aid Agencies   59

3 *Learning from Failure*
  Civil Society Building and Impact Assesment   93

Part II: Central America

4 *The Absence of a Third Option*
  Democratic Transitions in Central America   135

5 *A Tacit Consensus*
  Private Aid Intervention Strategies in Central America   181

6 *Four Aid Chains in Central America*
  Assessing Civil Society Building Performance   221

The Paradox of Private Foreign Aid
Conclusions   295

Notes   303
Interviews   355
References   363
Acronyms and Abbreviations   397
Index   411

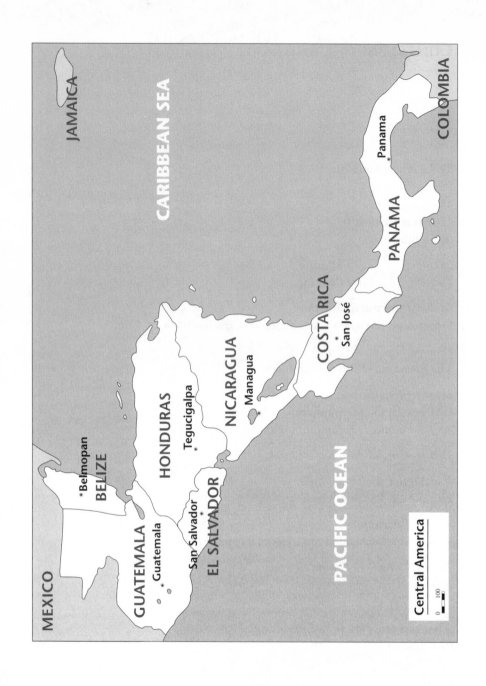

Tables, Figures and Maps

	Map Central America	6
1.1	State, civil society and political society	34
1.2	The balance between the state and civil society	42
1.3	Changing relations between the state and civil society during stages of democratic transition	46
1.4	International actors and democratisation	50
2.1	Overview of the largest European private aid agencies	61
2.2	Actors and aid flows in a simplified private aid chain	79
2.3	Four types of private aid intervention strategies	88
2.4	Stakeholders and aid flows in multiple aid chains	90
3.1	Private aid chains and civil society building	98
3.2	Points for assessing achievement of development initiatives	107
3.3	A framework for assessing civil society building performance	129
	Map Central America 1980-84	155
4.1	Stages of democratic transition in Honduras	157
4.2	Stages of democratic transition in El Salvador	161
4.3	Stages of democratic transition in Guatemala	166
5.1	Official development assistance to Central America (1985-95)	212
6.1	The three FUNDADESE offices (1994-96): Aid chains and linkages with the Civil Society Assembly (ASC)	261

PREFACE

In early November 1998, just before this book went to press, hurricane Mitch passed through Central America. Tropical storms and heavy rain wrought destruction and despair throughout the region. Especially in Nicaragua and Honduras the human tragedy was enormous, leaving over 25,000 casualties, nearly two million homeless and considerable areas destroyed by floods and buried under mud. Suddenly, Central America was back in the headlines of the international press, after an *absence* of nearly a decade. The international donor community responded quickly with large emergency relief operations, while governments and multilateral institutions postponed debt service obligations in order to facilitate the reconstruction of these highly indebted countries.

As with most natural disasters that have struck the Central American countries in the past, the poorest layers of society were most affected. But the difference with earlier earthquakes and hurricanes is that these countries are no longer ruled by military regimes. Civil society has become better organised and the new (civilian) governments have been made more accountable to their citizens. However, democratic rule still remains fragile, not least because the level of poverty and social inequality is still very high. The inflow of additional international aid can possibly contribute to keeping the process of democratic transition on track and prevent a return to the decades of polarisation and deteriorating impoverishment. Fortunately, there are also lessons that can be learned from the recent past when international solidarity with the Central American people in their struggle against authoritarian rule flourished.

This study examines how European private aid agencies have contributed to democratic transition in these countries and what lessons can be learned for future policies to confront social injustice. It is the product of innumerable encounters in Europe and Latin America with people who have shaped and sharpened my thinking about social justice, political transformation and the search for alternative strategies. Those who were interviewed for this study are listed in the last section of the book, but several others deserve to be specially mentioned here. The person who encouraged me to start this research in the first place was Daniela Mangelschots, a Belgian solidarity worker living in Nicaragua and Honduras, with whom I shared many long and inspiring discussions. Another source of inspiration was Víctor González, a Salvadoran sociologist with whom I coordinated the initial stage of the fieldwork as part of a TNI-sponsored research project. Víctor's death in 1993 and Daniela's sudden dying in 1995 left a great emptiness. The book is dedicated to these two special *compañeros*, in memory of their commitment to the struggle for social justice in Central America.

I am grateful to many others who provided key support and advice, among them Wilson Campos and the staff of ASOCODE, John Nielsen and the staff of *Ibis*-Denmark, Abelardo Morales, Rolando Rivera, Isabel Román, Danuta Sacher, Carlos Sojo, Edelberto Torres Rivas and the staff of FLACSO (Costa Rica); Xabier Gorostiaga, Finn Hansen, Els van Poppel, Jesper Ravn, Ivana Ríos and the staff of CRIES, Welvin Romero, Klaus-Dieter Tangermann, Martha Thompson (Nicaragua); Deborah Barry and the staff of PRISMA, Stefan Declerq, Dorte Ellehammer, Ina Eriksson, Alfonso Goitia, Merete Hansen, Arnd 'Paolo' Luers, Allan Martell, Edgar Palacios and the staff of CPDN, René Ramos, Karin Urschel (El Salvador); Doris Melisa Cardozo, Jorge Irías and the staff of CODEH, Ineke Jansen, Piet Schuijt, Carlos Talavera, Xiomara Ventura (Honduras); Hans Petter Buvollen, Maribel Carrera, John Contier, Manolo García, Rachel Garst, Carmen Rosa de León, Alberto Mazariegos and the staff of FUNDADESE, Oscar Maldonado, Amanda Rodas, Mario Silvestre, Ulrik Sparre, Helmer Velásquez and the staff of CONG-COOP (Guatemala); Xavier Declerq, Monique Muntingh, Nan Valckx (Belgium); Hans Peter Dejgaard, Gitte Hermansen (Denmark); Henny Helmich (France); Klaus Linsenmeier, Barbara Lucas (Germany); Sally O'Neill (Ireland); Frank Amalric (Italy); Theo Bouma, Chris Bransz, Henk Dielis, Kees Hudig, Dineke van den Oudenalder, Karel Roos, Holke Wierema, and the library staff of CEDLA and the Royal Tropical Institute (the Netherlands); Vegard Bye (Norway); Christian Freres, Mariano Aguirre, José Antonio Sanahuja (Spain); Stephen Baranyi, Alun Burge, Mandy Macdonald and Pauline Martin (United Kingdom).

Research for this book was undertaken between 1990 and 1996 as part of several research projects at the *Transnational Institute* (TNI) in Amsterdam and the Political Science Department of the University of Amsterdam. I am grateful to TNI director Fiona Dove and Professor Gerd Junne of the International Relations section of the Political Science Department for their encouragement and for providing the conditions to facilitate the completion of the manuscript. Fieldwork in Central America and Europe was partly financed with grants from *Buntstift*, *Christian Aid*, NOVIB, SCIAF and *Trocaire*. Although these private aid agencies were aware that the research would critically examine their own activities, it is greatly appreciated that they never interfered in any stage of the project. The publication of the manuscript was supported with grants from the Jurriaanse Stichting, the Research Centre for International Political Economy (RECIPE) and the Social Sciences Faculty of the University of Amsterdam.

Fellows and colleagues of the *Transnational Institute* have been important sources of stimulation throughout the research process. Joel Rocamora and Anjali Sundaram encouraged me to continue my research on European private aid agencies from a Central American perspective. Marcos Arruda, Hanneke van Eldik Thieme, Jan Willem van der Raad, Jochen Hippler and Saul Landau gave me valuable input at the early stage of the research and the staff of the Amsterdam office provided an inspiring working environment. I would particularly like to thank Martin Jelsma for his unconditional support at critical moments, and David Sogge for providing many ideas and resources in the framework of TNI's Private Aid Agencies project.

Discussions and encounters with other 'NGO watchers' at a number of international workshops and during private meetings were another source of inspiration. I would like to thank Mark Edelman, Mike Edwards, Alan Fowler, Martin Köhler, Laura Macdonald, Geraldine MacDonald, Stefan Mair, María Luz Ortega, Jenny Pearce, Laura Renshaw, Roger Riddell, Mark Robinson, John Saxby, Ian Smillie, Alison Van Rooy, Fons van der Velden, Frits Wils and Simon Zadek for giving valuable suggestions and exchanging (unpublished) manuscripts. The quality of the book was greatly improved by stimulating comments on draft chapters by Chris van der Borgh, Jean Carrière, Jolle Demmers, Alex Fernández, Gerd Junne, Hans van Heijningen, Barbara Hoogenboom, Martin Jelsma, Ans Kolk and David Sogge. The manuscript was edited and corrected for language by Lisa Chason. Jan van Arkel and Trees Vulto of International Books efficiently prepared the manuscript for publication.

The key source of stimulation throughout these years has been Alex Fernández Jilberto of the Political Science Department of the University of Amsterdam. He has become a close friend and never lost confidence in a positive outcome. I am also deeply grateful to my parents, and to my *compañera* Wilma den Uijl with whom I could share the *encanto* for Latin America. Experiencing the confidence, patience and commitment of all those who supported me over the past decade made the whole project a pleasant and rewarding undertaking. I hope their spirit also is reflected in the book.

Kees Biekart
Amsterdam
November 1998

CHARITY AND SOLIDARITY

Introduction

> '*In order to have the continued opportunity to express their*
> *"generosity", the oppressors must perpetuate injustice as well.*
> *An unjust social order is the permanent fount of this "generosity",*
> *which is nourished by death, despair and poverty.*'
>
> Paulo Freire (1972: 26)

The international aid system has apparently reached its saturation point: the golden era of development aid, which started in the 1970s, is over. For over a decade, official development assistance as a percentage of donor nations' GNP has been declining and has also dropped in real terms. In addition, the majority of private aid agencies in the North is experiencing budget cuts and stagnating income from public fund-raising. A qualitative shift parallels these signs of growing 'compassion fatigue': solidarity with the poor and the oppressed (which had been one of the driving forces behind foreign aid) is becoming a remnant of an obscure past. Solidarity has been replaced by charitable donations, which are cultivated by assertive public fund-raising campaigns for emergency relief in the South. Private aid agencies seem to expect declining income unless they appeal to the 'gut feelings' of the well-nourished Northern public. Meanwhile, the system of global injustice driven by market-based principles is perpetuated, less challenged than it ever has been in the post-colonial period. Maybe solidarity with the poor was, after all, constrained by the logic that eradicating global poverty and inequality would seriously affect Northern living standards. Hamelink (1997: 18) identifies this as the essential moral choice in development cooperation: 'The rich are only willing to act in accordance with such moral principles as human solidarity as long as their own interests are not threatened by these acts.'

A popular argument to justify the reduction of development aid flows to the South is to question whether development aid really contributes to reducing poverty. Cassen's (1986) well-known question 'Does aid work?' received many answers, probably as many as there are opponents and supporters of development aid. But concrete claims about aid effectiveness so far have not been convincing and should be treated with caution as they are often based on dubious evidence and phrased in a polemical tone. The point is that the development aid community has been obsessed with the question about aid effectiveness for quite some time now, which is understandable if one realises that the long-term survival of aid donors depends on an affirmative answer. However, the question whether aid works probably deserves only one simple reply: nobody really knows, nor is it likely that anybody will ever provide a satisfactory answer. This has to do with the problem that achievements of development interventions cannot be easily empirically tested, for these are shaped by a broad variety of factors fundamental to the complexity of social processes. This makes it very difficult to determine the 'added value' of external aid. For all donor agencies this is a serious dilemma, as they are pressured to show results of their aid interventions in order to sustain their annual levels of income from tax-based budgets or private donations. After all, in a market-oriented culture the rules are simple: you either perform, or you perish.

This pressure to show results is one of the key dilemmas faced by those aid donors most committed to addressing poverty at the grassroots level: private aid agencies. Also known as 'international' or 'Northern' NGOs, they were amongst the pioneers of development aid, acting as key innovators of donor strategies to tackle poverty and oppression. Although only handling about ten percent of total aid flows, private (non-governmental) aid agencies are believed to have several advantages over official (governmental) aid agencies because they maintain direct and more participatory relationships with organisations supporting the Southern poor. Although the bulk of private aid is still oriented toward addressing the symptoms of poverty, many private aid agencies also advocate strategies for social and political change, by defending human rights, supporting democratisation and enabling marginalised sectors to actively decide about their own development needs. While representing a minority of the total number of agencies, these change-oriented private aid agencies (such as OXFAM and NOVIB) are amongst the largest in terms of aid budgets. They often receive the lion's share of their income from governments, who consider private aid agencies to be key complementary channels for delivering aid to the poor.

However, a number of recent studies suggest that private aid agencies have not been as successful in alleviating poverty as was often assumed. Not only did they seldom reach the very poorest, their contribution to empowering the poor in many cases was actually not demonstrated. This generated questions in the early 1990s about the effectiveness of private foreign aid; questions that Cassen and others had asked earlier about official aid performance, but again without generating satisfactory answers. Assuming that it is indeed difficult to determine aid effectiveness, it could be questioned whether the results of aid interventions say anything about the quality of aid. Instead of asking whether aid works, it might therefore be more relevant to explore *how* aid works in practice, or *why* it has often failed, as Smillie (1995a) and others have suggested.

❖

This book examines how European private aid agencies have contributed to the recent democratic transitions in Central America. The roots of this project go back to August 1987, when I discussed with Honduran friends the potential consequences of the Esquipulas peace agreement which had just been signed. At that time, civil wars were raging all over the region and prospects for peace were bleak. As one of the last battlegrounds of the Cold War, Central America had become a top US foreign policy priority under President Reagan. The US government perceived the revolution in Nicaragua and the growth of armed opposition movements in El Salvador and Guatemala as a serious 'communist threat' to its traditional sphere of influence. European governments used diplomatic channels to support a peaceful settlement, for which a basis was laid with the 1987 Esquipulas agreement. Meanwhile, opposition movements in El Salvador, Guatemala and Honduras were advocating an end to authoritarian rule and US intervention, with support from a broad variety of external non-governmental actors: churches, labour unions, human rights organisations, solidarity committees and private aid agencies.

My initial intention was to make a comparative study between Chile and Central America, examining the role of private aid agencies in the Chilean transition to democracy and their role in Central America in the same period. However, after spending four months in Chile to monitor the activities of the Chilean opposition in their campaign to win the 1988 plebiscite against Pinochet, I was no longer convinced that this was a good idea. The Chilean research *centros* (which took the lead in this campaign) appeared to be controlled by the moderate centre-left opposition parties and were financed by European and Canadian private aid agencies. Not only did they play a decisive role in achieving a victory over the military regime, they also simultaneously managed to neutralise (and marginalise) popular organisations and the more radical left-wing opposition parties. Indirectly, private aid agencies thus contributed to the scenario prioritised by the US government: a smooth democratic transition without challenging the neoliberal economic model that was introduced by Pinochet's 'Chicago boys'.

With the Chilean experience in mind, I prepared my research in Central America to examine the role of private aid agencies during the complex regional crisis of the late 1980s. Apparently, the role of European and Canadian private aid agencies was very similar, as in Central America these agencies also financed local development NGOs linked to the opposition. But I gradually became aware of having overlooked a fundamental difference between the political transformations in Chile and Central America: while Chile was going through a process of 'redemocratisation', democracy had been absent in Central America and was actually still in the process of being 'constructed'. Political parties of the opposition were not temporarily restricted as in Chile, but were weak or absent in Central America. The key role of political parties, mediating and articulating demands between civil society and the state, was actually performed by local development NGOs or by coalitions of popular organisations, all with substantial support from private aid agencies. In other words, political opposition parties still had to be consolidated, as they often emerged out of underground political movements. European private aid agencies were not just reaffirming the legitimacy of a former political elite, but seemed to be really concerned with strengthening new political expressions of the poor and the oppressed. A further difference with Chile was that the majority of European private aid agencies clearly opposed US counter-insurgency policies in Central America and generally refused to work with quasi-democratic regimes controlled by US-sponsored armed forces.

The guiding question for the current study emerged in 1990, a few months after the historical changes in Eastern Europe and amidst rapid changes in the Central American political landscape: how and to what extent were European private aid agencies contributing to democratic transitions in Central America? In Nicaragua, the Sandinistas were unexpectedly defeated during the February 1990 elections. One month later, informal negotiations started between armed opposition groups in El Salvador and Guatemala and their governments. Suddenly, democratic transitions were accelerating in a region that had been prioritised by private aid agencies for almost a decade. Would it be possible to attribute these political transformations, in one way or another, to the interventions of private aid agencies? It was clear that my focus would not be on official aid agencies, in spite of the fact that these had been very important for Nicaragua throughout the 1980s. But it was private aid agencies that were the key supporters of oppositional groups in civil society in neighbouring countries. Deliberately, I chose to examine European private aid agencies, and not their counterparts in the United States, as the latter (with some exceptions) often were part of US counter-insurgency programmes in Central America. Although my focus initially was on private aid programmes 'supporting democratisation', the civil society discourse entering the (official) donor community in the early 1990s attracted my attention, and turned out to be a very useful tool for analysing 'the politics of civil society building'.

Due to my research activities for the *Transnational Institute*, I had the opportunity to make regular field trips to Central America between the 1987 Esquipulas agreement (providing the framework for the regional peace process) and the final 1996 Guatemalan peace agreement. Given the rapid changes in the region (and the world in general) it proved to be critical to interview the key actors in Central America and Europe several times within a broad time frame. Fieldwork for this book started in 1990 with a first survey among European private aid agencies, followed by several visits to Central America to narrow the research focus. The early stage of field research in Central America was facilitated by three local research teams in El Salvador, Guatemala and Honduras who attempted to map the vast range of private aid interventions in these countries. Four case studies were eventually selected for a more detailed analysis of the dynamics between donor and recipients in the process of civil society building. This fieldwork in Europe and Central America was completed in 1996, one month before the Guatemalan peace agreement formally concluded the last civil war in the region.

The book is structured in two parts, each containing three chapters. The first part examines conceptual and methodological issues that are then empirically applied to the Central American context in part two. The two separate parts are 'horizontally' linked, in the sense that elements discussed in Chapter 1 are elaborated for Central America in Chapter 4, just as the analytical issues of Chapters 2 and 3 are matched by the empirical evidence of Chapters 5 and 6. In addition, two main themes are interwoven throughout the book. One is a discussion about the dynamics of democratic transition and changing relations between the state and civil society. Although this is a debate largely generated by the democratic transitions in Southern Europe in the 1970s and the Latin American 'Southern Cone' in the 1980s, it gained new momentum in the 1990s after the political transformations in Eastern Europe, Central Asia and Africa. Surprisingly, Central America never figured as a source of empirical evidence for these 'transitologist' analyses by scholars such as O'Donnell, Schmitter, Stepan and Linz. Therefore, a theoretical framework was required to understand the process of incipient democratisation in societies *without* democratic traditions, in which civil society was highly exclusive and external forces extremely influential. To analyse the forces shifting the balance between the state and civil society, Chapter 1 examines and defines key concepts in understanding the dynamics furthering or obstructing the strength of civil society. The purpose is to pin down what is actually meant by 'democracy', 'civil society' and 'democratic transition'. This chapter also explores the popular concept 'NGO' and explains why this term is better avoided in relation to democratic transition.

The second theme addressed throughout the book is the assumption that private aid agencies increasingly have become key actors in 'global civil society'. The analysis focuses on their (changing) position in the international donor community and their potential to contribute to democratic transition. Until recently, the international dimensions of democratic transition have only received marginal attention and were generally considered part of the official rhetoric promoting democracy and human rights. But support to democratisation by 'third governments' appears to be rather different than private aid agencies' policies to strengthen civil societies. In Chapters 2 and 3 a framework is developed to examine these strategic choices and to map the range of private aid intervention policies.

A wide variety of international actors have intervened in Central America over the past two decades, with foreign aid one of their most powerful instruments. The main external actor without any question has been the United States, which channelled over US$ 7.5 billion dollars in military and humanitarian aid to the region during the 1980s (Sanahuja 1992). Although their contribution in monetary terms was much smaller, European and Canadian private aid agencies also became key external actors as they were the principal source of support for opposition groups in Guatemala, El Salvador and Honduras. Private aid agencies are generally singled out as a group of international actors that combine aid donations with international advocacy. However, little is known about the character and scope of their interventions or about their policy intentions, topics that are analysed in detail in Chapter 2. It is not sufficient to demonstrate that private aid agencies have been relevant external actors during democratic transitions; the challenge is to demonstrate *why*, *how* and *to what extent* they have been relevant. This raises one of the most critical questions in current aid debates to which I referred earlier: how to assess the impact of (private) aid interventions? This generates a number of other questions which barely have received satisfactory answers. For example, what is exactly meant by the 'impact' of foreign aid? And how to assess private aid impact on local processes of democratic transition? How to attribute local achievements to the interventions of external agencies? These questions are addressed in Chapter 3, which also discusses methodological dilemmas related to impact assessments.

The second part of the book is entirely dedicated to the complex arena of Central American politics of the past decade, which has been profoundly influenced by external actors. Concepts and frameworks developed in the first part are used to examine the role of private foreign aid in the region, with particular emphasis on Honduras, El Salvador and Guatemala. Chapter 4 provides a historical context to understand the shifting balances between the state and civil society in these countries and to identify key stages in the processes of democratic transition. Chapter 5 examines the policies and priorities of European private aid agencies during the Central American crisis, and how these changed in the post-Cold War period. This provides a framework for Chapter 6, in which four private aid-supported organisations that played a key role in strengthening civil society are examined in more detail. Findings of these Central American case studies will be used in the Conclusions to discuss some general lessons about the politics of civil society building and to explore the future prospects of private foreign aid.

It was a deliberate choice to focus my analysis on private aid agencies striving for social change, as they have shown in the past to take sides with the oppressed and the marginalised, acting in the spirit of international solidarity. It is therefore regrettable that these 'progressive' private aid agencies often lack the capacity to critically examine their own strategic choices and that they tend to dismiss any criticism from outsiders. It will repeatedly be argued in this book that this defensive attitude is counter-productive to what they actually want to achieve, that is, to carry out their legitimate role as key allies of those groups in the South struggling for social justice. While the tone of my analysis often may be critical concerning the choices that these private aid agencies make, the book is not meant to support criticism that aid is not working. It was argued earlier that this easy critique generally lacks any substantiation. The purpose of this book is different. It tries to identify the main lessons that can be learned from private aid agency strategies aimed at changing unequal power relations in Southern civil societies. But it also examines how (and why) many private aid agencies committed to social change in the 1990s have shifted away from solidarity aid and appear to have surrendered to a market-driven culture in which solidarity has been replaced by the safer route of simple charity provision.

PART I

Civil Society Building

1 Mixing Poverty and Democracy

Democratic Transition, Civil Society and the International Context

There are two potential problems with democracy in Latin America, according to Jorge Castañeda (1993: 338). Democracy is either meaningless as a result of electoral fraud and massive manipulation, or it is explosive: 'Giving the poor the vote, and allowing their votes to be counted when they represent the majority of a society's inhabitants, leads to demands, policies and ruptures that in Latin America have historically tended to provoke military coups and the end of representative democracy.' The lesson from Latin America appears to be that 'poverty and democracy do not mix easily', and that, more generally, the 'Western' notion of democracy apparently does not work in countries in which the majority of the population lives under the poverty line. It is useful to start an examination of democratic transitions in Latin America with Castañeda's provocative observation for it raises the question whether democracy is at all viable in poor societies. What does democracy mean in these societies that have been ruled, and sometimes are still ruled, by authoritarian regimes?

The present chapter discusses the 'problem' of democratic transition in Latin America and the meaning of democracy in order to provide an analytical framework for understanding the dynamics of democratisation in Central America. Several key concepts – such as democracy, citizenship and civil society – are explored and explained to avoid the semantic confusion that often dominates debates on democratisation. Especially the concept 'civil society' has been explained in so many ways, and for different purposes, that it often becomes a meaningless concept and part of the 'problem' it is supposed to tackle. While trying to avoid this caveat, civil society is critically analysed in its various dimensions and in its historically changing balance with the state. At the end of the chapter, the analysis focuses on the role of the international context for democratic transitions, as the ultimate purpose of this book is to examine the interaction between transnational private aid agencies and key domestic actors during democratic transitions.

1.1 Democratic transition in Latin America

One of the central topics in recent debates about political transformations is the concept of *democratic transition*. As this will be one of the key issues in the present study on Central America, the concept will be further examined in the following pages. Democratic transition could be defined as a complex process of shifting relations between the state and civil society, in which authoritarian rule is gradually replaced by political democracy. However, this definition is hardly satisfactory without explaining what is meant by 'civil society' and 'democracy'. To start with the latter: few concepts have been more contested in political science theory than the concept of democracy. Outsiders would be surprised to learn that there is virtually no discussion about its meaning: democracy simply means 'rule by the people'. However, as this could be explained in many different ways, a clear working definition is needed. In contemporary debates two theoretical approaches to the concept of democracy can be identified, a narrow and a comprehensive approach.[1]

The most important representative of the narrow approach is Joseph Schumpeter, who proposes a very practical understanding of democracy. In his critique of classical democracy doctrine, Schumpeter (1943: 269) suggests a definition of 'modern' democracy, which is still very popular with (North American) political scientists: 'The democratic method is that institutional arrangement for arriving at political decisions in which individuals acquire the power to decide by means of a competitive struggle for the people's vote.' In its many variations, this represents the liberal (or pluralist-elitist) tradition of democratic thought, in which public accountability of rulers by citizens through regular competitive elections has become the central characteristic of a system for organising relations between the rulers and the ruled. As there are many types of democracy, depending on socio-economic conditions and state structures, several scholars have tried to expand the definition by capturing all those elements that might affect a democratic outcome. In the Latin American discussion, baroque definitions have emerged – generally inspired by Schumpeter and Dahl (1971) – trying to incorporate this rich variety of democratic practices into an all-embracing one-liner. For instance, Diamond, Linz and Lipset (1989: xvi) define democracy as 'a system of government that meets three essential conditions: meaningful and extensive *competition* among individuals and organised groups (especially political parties) for all effective positions of government power, at regular intervals and excluding the use of force; a highly inclusive level of *political participation* in the selection of leaders and policies, at least through regular and fair elections, such that no major (adult) social group is excluded; and a level of *civil and political liberties* – freedom of expression, freedom of the press, freedom to form and join organisation – sufficient to ensure the integrity of political competition and participation.' The merit of this approach is that the pluralist-elitist conceptualisation of democracy often has been abused to legitimise authoritarian regimes which properly organised fair elections, but simultaneously obstructed processes of democratic transition. Although understandable, adding these properties to the definition of democracy could make the definition unwieldy (Karl 1990).[2]

The more comprehensive approach to the concept of democracy prefers to stick closer to its classical meaning of 'rule by the people' in which not elections but 'political participation' is the central focus. Out of its many variations, the definition by Schmitter and Karl (1993: 40) is particularly useful: 'Modern political democracy is a system of governance in which rulers are held accountable for their actions in the public realm by citizens, acting indirectly through the competition and cooperation of their elected representatives.' The advantage of such a comprehensive approach is that it contains all necessary concepts required to discuss democratic transitions in Latin America. The *system of governance* points at the regime type, which determines the way in which access to public offices is organised, who is included or excluded, which strategies are applied to get access, and what the rules of decision-making are. Most Latin American countries have experienced either oligarchic, dictatorial or authoritarian regimes, preceding democratic ones. Regimes have *rulers,* those who have the authority to give legitimate commands over others. The *public realm* is the sphere where collective norms are exhibited and choices are made, which are binding for society and guaranteed by the state.

One of the key concepts in this definition is that of *citizens*: 'All regimes have rulers and a public realm, but only to the extent that they are democratic do they have citizens' (Schmitter and Karl 1993: 41). In the Athenian city-state, citizens were at one and the same time subjects of political authority and the creators of public rules. As citizen-governors they made no distinction between the state and society. In modern 'liberal' (representative) democracy, citizens have been granted rights and duties by the nation state. *Citizenship* is therefore a key concept to explore, as it refers to the membership of the political community: the organic link between the state and its citizens. Citizenship as it is known today is a product of struggle: 'Throughout the formative phase of the modern state, the struggle for membership in the political community has largely been synonymous with the attempt to establish a form of popular sovereignty through the entrenchment of civil and political rights' (Held 1995: 67).

Civil rights guarantee individual autonomy of citizens, such as freedom of speech and thought, or the right to be treated equally to others before the law. The struggle for civil rights starting in eighteenth century Britain and the United States preceded the struggle for political rights of the late nineteenth and early twentieth centuries. Only after decades of struggle and pressure from excluded sectors of the population (because of race, gender, age, class or literacy) political rights – basically the right to vote and to run for public office – were granted to all native-born adults. By the second half of this century, European and Latin American democracies formally had abolished all restrictions to citizenship. However, in Latin America this often did not lead to the effective protection and full exercise of citizens' rights. Therefore, another dimension should be added to understand democratic transition in Latin America: a variety of implicit *restrictions* have been posed upon the full exercise of citizenship. The existence of formal democratic rights did not automatically guarantee political freedom for all citizens.

Rueschemeyer, Huber Stephens and Stephens (1992) acknowledge that the exercise of civil rights does not in itself constitute the exercise of democratic power. Although it is a necessary condition of stable democracy, it limits state power to the guarantee of both individual and collective liberties either under democratic or non-democratic regimes. They argue that the essence of democracy is embodied in two dimensions: universal suffrage, and responsibility and accountability of the state. The protection of civil rights is a necessary third dimension to guarantee the stability of a democratic regime. Based on the degree to which these three dimensions are met, they differentiate between 'democratic' and 'non-democratic' (oligarchic or authoritarian) regimes, and between 'full' and 'restricted' democracies. Karl (1990) adds a fourth dimension to describe democracy (in addition to contestation, accountability and inclusion): civilian control over the military. This is an essential dimension for the Latin American situation, which is not implicit in the narrow definitions previously mentioned.

Therefore, I would prefer to follow the comprehensive definition of Schmitter and Karl and suggest that 'real existing democracy' needs to be analysed in terms of the extent to which it is 'restricted'. Three key restrictions should be mentioned. First, in Latin America (and this applies to most other regions in the world) free and fair elections did not lead to democratic governance, often caused by the lack of civilian control over the armed forces. Elections formally broadened political participation of citizens, but in practice this only applied to particular civil society sectors and generally only for limited periods of time (Booth 1989). Second, unfavourable social and economic conditions have seriously weakened the effective exercise (and even the protection) of both civil and political rights. Existing barriers to freedom of speech and association, or the right to cast a vote in free and fair elections are deeply rooted obstacles to social and economic reform. Cammack (1994a: 189) points at the need to remove these obstacles in order to realise political citizenship in Latin America, but in line with Castañeda warns of the potentially explosive consequences: 'if citizenship and democratic participation become a reality, they will inevitably lead to demands for long overdue social and economic change'. A third restriction on exercising full citizenship in Latin America has been a general absence of autonomy by the polity from external constraints. Without exception, the sovereignty of (Southern) nation states has been (and still is being) challenged by geo-political interests of other (Northern) nation states, which is enhanced by the asymmetry of the global economy.

These three restrictions underline the need to analyse democratic transition in Latin America beyond the boundaries of narrowly defined concepts of democracy derived from Western political history. The slow process of Latin American democratisation was generated by a series of social struggles taking place over a long period of time, basically aiming to establish full citizenship without restrictions. Efforts to understand these struggles thus require a structural analysis of the main actors involved and of the national and historical contexts in which they evolved. This long historical perspective – which will be elaborated for Central America in Chapter 4 – potentially also explains why processes of democratic transition in South America were essentially different from Central America.[3]

– *Lessons from democratic transitions in South America*

The concept 'democratic transition' became popular among academics to explain the return to democratic rule in Southern Europe in the 1970s and in South America in the 1980s. Much of the analytical framework on democratic transitions – which was developed in a large number of studies[4] – also was applied to the political shifts that occurred in Eastern Europe at the end of the Cold War. Except for Costa Rica, democratic transitions in Central America received virtually no attention in these studies, although taking place in the same period.[5] This raises the question whether the 'transition framework' and the lessons from South America (and to a lesser extent from Eastern Europe) are at all relevant for Central America. After all, the Central American transitions were quite different from South America, as the latter only were dealing with *temporary* authoritarian rule. Or were the driving forces behind re-establishing democratic rule in South America possibly similar to the forces that 'constructed' democracy in Central America? In other words, is it possible to generalise about the context and the conditions that determine the (re)emergence of democratic rule?

The answer is probably not very encouraging. For instance, looking at democratic transitions in South America, and only considering the major domestic forces in these transitions, one could broadly identify two positions on this issue. One is that of O'Donnell and Schmitter (1986: 19) who argue: 'there is no transition whose beginning is not the consequence – direct or indirect – of important divisions within the authoritarian regime itself, principally along the fluctuating cleavage between hard-liners and soft-liners.' These internal divisions gave way to a series of negotiations, either induced by the regime itself or by oppositional elites, leading to peaceful 'pacted' transitions. In response to O'Donnell and Schmitter, Diamond *et al.* (1989) and Stepan (1990) argue that too little credit has been given to the role of opposition forces. They maintain that the principal force that led to regime transition was a change in the strength and mobilisation of civil society. When core supporters of the military regime realised that perpetuation of military rule was no longer in their interest, they switched to become part of the (passive) opposition to the military regime. As soon as members of other key groups of civil society, such as the clergy and academics, joined the 'growing numbers of defectors from authoritarianism', they were able to effectively pressure the military regime for change. As Stepan (1990: 44) puts it: 'The passive opposition will grow much larger as people no longer need constantly to fear savage repression. Passive opponents will also lose some of their passivity as they become willing to participate in anti-regime actions orchestrated by the active opposition. Under the right conditions, the passive and active opposition will coalesce and expand to the point where the idea of redemocratisation wrests hegemony away from authoritarianism.'

The point of the polemic is of course: what are these 'right conditions'? Under which conditions are authoritarian regimes forced to make 'strategic choices', or under which conditions does an opposition forge a coalition capable of delegitimising an authoritarian regime? Before democratic transitions in Latin America

started, theoretical discussions had focused on the character of necessary preconditions for stable democracy. But the polemic did not lead to any consensus about
the principal preconditions. Was it the level of capitalist development (or 'socio-
economic modernisation') at that particular moment, as Lipset and others argued?
Was it the quality of the 'civic culture' (Almond and Verba 1963) or of the 'political
culture' (Wiarda 1981) that determined the probability of democratic transition?
Were these conditions primarily domestically determined (Moore 1966) or chiefly
induced by external influences as Cardoso and Faletto (1969) and other scholars of
dependency theory argued? After the experiences of democratic transitions in the
1980s, all these preconditions proved to be insufficient to explain the end of military rule. It appeared that no single precondition could explain the dynamics of
democratic transition, since much contradictory evidence was generated by the
transitions in South America (Karl 1990). In fact, most of these preconditions were
the outcomes of democratic transitions rather than their causes.

After studying in detail the dynamics of democratic transition in Latin America
(and later in Eastern Europe) some 'transitologists' – notably Diamond, Linz,
Lipset (1989) and Huntington (1991) – tried to refine the modernisation approach
by listing the whole variety of factors and preconditions that could influence or
determine the establishment of democracy in these countries. Diamond *et al.*
suggested a comprehensive theoretical framework consisting of ten theoretical
dimensions (political culture, regime legitimacy, historical development, class
structure, national structure, state structure, political and constitutional structure,
political leadership, development performance and international factors), based on
twenty-six selected case studies. These dimensions covered dozens of specific variables and questions from which they derived forty-nine tentative propositions
about the likelihood of stable democratic government. Huntington, in a similarly
empiricist way, selected thirty countries that became democracies after the mid-
1970s and focused on five factors that could have determined these transitions:
legitimacy problems, global economic growth, the Catholic Church, changing
policies of external actors and demonstration effects.

These attempts to construct a new theoretical framework for democratic transition were criticised from various angles. Remmer (1995: 110) pointed at the fundamental difficulty of generalising about such a diverse and complex framework
of causal paths and conditions: 'Most reasonably parsimonious frameworks, such
as modernisation theory, provide limited insights into empirical variations through
time and space, while richer and more comprehensive explanatory efforts tend
to yield complex and untestable case-by-case historical accounts of political democracy.' Cammack (1994a: 177) also pointed at the problematic implications of
analysing democracy as a general phenomenon, as no general laws of democracy
or homogenous patterns exist that can explain the causes of democracy: 'Liberal
democracy is a conjunctural historical phenomenon, explicable in terms of its
structural conditions of emergence and reproduction, and their interaction with
its own institutional dynamics. As such it can be understood only if the histor-

ical context in which it emerges and is reproduced can be theorised.'

Another group of theorists therefore tried to tackle these problems (implicitly linked to generalisations about the causes of democratic transition) either by looking at 'contingent choice' (O'Donnell *et al.*, Przeworski), path-dependent analysis (Karl and Schmitter), centring on elite compromise (Higley and Gunther) or taking a structuralist approach (Cammack, Rueschemeyer *et al.*). From these approaches, Rueschemeyer *et al.* is particularly relevant as they have been one of the few to include both South and Central America in their empirical analysis. They extended Moore's (1966) paradigmatic argument that 'past conflicts and institutional structures have long-term effects and are of critical importance for later developments. Any attempt to explain current change without attention to these continuing effects of past history – any "presentist" analysis – is doomed to fail' (Rueschemeyer *et al.* 1992: 23).

Implicitly they criticise those studies that focus on shorter term changes (O'Donnell, Huntington or Przeworksi) with their emphasis on voluntaristic factors (leadership or choice) with little attention for structural constraints. Rueschemeyer *et al.* suggest a theoretical framework to explain why capitalism (economic development) has contributed to the development of democracy. Crucial dimensions in explaining the emergence of democracy (and authoritarianism) are the balance between class power, the nature of the state and the impact of transnational structures of power. The primary agents of democratisation in their analysis are not new dominant classes, but subordinate classes: 'Capitalist development is associated with democracy because it transforms the class structure, strengthening the working and middle classes and weakening the landed upper class. It was not the capitalist market, nor capitalists as the new dominant force, but rather the contradictions of capitalism that advanced the cause of democracy' (1992: 7).

After comparing historical patterns of democratisation in Europe, South America, Central America and the Caribbean, they conclude that the urban working class was the driving force of democratisation in the advanced capitalist societies (Europe), whereas in South America the middle classes played a more prominent role in democratisation.[6] However, these middle classes had an ambivalent attitude towards democracy, as they allied both with the oligarchy and the military to accept restricted democracy, or with the working class to struggle for full democracy.[7] The formation of class alliances and the relationship between the state and civil society in the various Latin American countries was determined by their integration in the world economy and by their position in the global state system. What made democratisation in Central America different from the South American experience was the absence of consolidated mass-based unions and political parties capable of countering economic elite and military interests. This was in turn caused by systematic repression of these organisations by the oligarchy and the military, beginning in the 1930s and actively supported by US economic and military intervention. By comparing Central America with the British Caribbean,

Rueschemeyer *et al.* (1992: 263) show that external influence potentially was a key element in furthering democracy: 'The [British] colonial state, by allowing the formation of organisations of subordinate classes, contributed to a strengthening of civil society and a shift in the balance of class power which was favourable to democratisation. The dictatorial states in Central America did the opposite in that they used their coercive capacity to partially surpress the development of civil society, particularly the organisation of the rural and urban lower classes.' With US support, the state in Central America for many decades was able to act autonomously from civil society and repressed efforts for political articulation and participation of subordinate sectors in civil society.

The history of 'postponing' democratic rule in Central America for several decades appears to be a fundamental difference with democratic transitions in South America and Southern and Eastern Europe.[8] However, this does not imply that the rich debate of transitologists is useless for the present analysis. The previous overview generates at least three questions about the conceptual tools used in this debate and how these could be elaborated for the Central American experience. The first question is: what could be the meaning of 'democratic transition' for a region that has not experienced democratic rule before? This question becomes even more relevant now that the transition literature in the mid-1990s is shifting its attention towards the conditions for 'democratic consolidation', in which the incomplete democratic transitions in Central America are again ignored.[9] A second important question is related to the meaning of civil society and the impact of key social sectors during democratic transitions. On this issue the analysis of Rueschemeyer *et al.* is not very explicit, as it focuses more on explanations for why Latin American states are strong and civil societies have been weak. This also touches upon the problem that interests of various social groups cannot simply be aggregated as is often done in the analysis of regime change. A third question addresses the role of international actors during democratic transition (or during democratic consolidation). The key role of the United States was already mentioned, but particularly transnational influences countering US intervention also should be carefully analysed to understand how political openings were forged by opposition groups in the 1980s. Rueschemeyer *et al.* do point to the important role of the Catholic Church, but unfortunately do not elaborate on these and other forces any further. This last issue will be examined later in this chapter; the first two questions are the central topic of the following pages.

– Identifying stages of democratic transition

To understand differences between patterns of democratisation, such as between South and Central America, Karl (1990) points at the need to look carefully at 'modes of transitions', and thus at the arrangements being made by key political actors during regime change. These negotiated agreements might establish (or restrict) the parameters for democratic consolidation in the future. For example, accords between political parties and the armed forces about future delimitations of civilian and military spheres – that might look temporary at the initial stage of transition – could become serious barriers for future transition to unrestricted democratic rule. To understand what actually happens during transitions, several stages, or 'sequences', have been identified to map the various (irreversible) steps in regime change. In the transition literature these have been identified as 'regime breakdown', 'liberalisation' and 'democratic consolidation' (O'Donnell *et al.* 1986). These stages could be confusing if the last transition stage ('transition to what?') is not clearly specified. Linz and Stepan (1996: 5-6) argue that the stage of 'consolidated democracy' is achieved when 'democracy has become "the only game in town"', a stage in which 'the overwhelming majority of the people believe that any further political change must emerge within the parameters of democratic formulas'. Others have argued that this is too minimalistic as it resembles the criteria for 'formal democracy', and that democratic transition is not completed unless it passes through the stages of 'participatory democracy' (high levels of participation among all social categories) and 'social democracy' (increasing equality in social and economic outcomes) (Huber *et al.* 1997). In a similar way, democratisation could be considered as an ongoing process of improving political equality and popular control, which implies that a stage of 'consolidated democracy' is not a final stage, but instead part of the transition process itself.[10]

Although the formal definition of consolidated democracy as was proposed by the 'transitologists' is not very accurate for the Central American situation, as will be illustrated in Chapter 4, it is still analytically useful to identify various democratic transition stages. However, there are several reasons to be more accurate about these stages in Central America's democratisation process. One is that several transitions (from war to peace, and from authoritarianism to democratic rule) became interlinked during the political transformations of the 1980s. It appeared to be necessary to specify subsequent transition stages, instead of using the broader stage of 'liberalisation' which was very much geared towards the Southern European and the South American experiences. The period after 'authoritarian rule' will therefore be split up in three stages: 'early transition', 'mid-transition' and 'late transition'.[11] Another reason to be cautious about the complex process of democratic transitions is the assumption that there is not one (authoritarian) regime, but several coexisting ('partial') regimes (Schmitter 1992). This implies that democratic transition should be disaggregated and analysed as a combination or an accumulation of several regime transitions, which Karl (1995) has called 'hybrid transitions'. This suggestion is helpful to understanding democratisation in Central America, in which several 'imposed' or 'authoritarian' transitions in the mid-1980s occurred without substantial regime changes. For example, the elections in El Salvador (1982, 1984) and Guatemala (1984, 1985), convened amidst civil war and state repression, were typical elements of 'authoritarian transitions' and a result of external pressure by the United States (Torres Rivas 1987). Moreover, these transitions were not followed by a 'resurrection of civil society' or a 'popular upsurge' as O'Donnell and Schmitter described in the South American transitions.[12]

– *The meaning of civil society*

Earlier debates on the causes of regime transitions – in which the breakdown of authoritarian regimes was explained as a result of internal splits in the regime (O'Donnell) or by a regrouping of oppositional forces in civil society (Stepan) – suggested an artificial state-civil society dichotomy. It was perceived that although during initial stages of transition *liberalisation* generally came from 'above' and during stages of consolidation *democratisation* came from 'below' (Weffort 1993), the potential roles of powerholders and opposition were closely interconnected during regime transition. As Mainwairing *et al.* (1992: 299) observe: 'Many transitions involve complex interactions between regime and opposition forces from an early stage.' Central to the understanding of the dynamics of democratic transition is therefore to analyse changes in the relations between the state and civil society, or more precisely: the political relations between the state and its citizens. The quality of relations between the state and civil society ultimately determines the quality of democracy. Diamond, Linz and Lipset (1989: 35) concluded after reviewing ten cases of democratic transition in Latin America that there is a strong correlation between the strength and autonomy of associational life and the presence and vitality of democracy: 'Just as democracy requires an effective but limited state, so it needs a pluralistic, autonomously organised civil society to check the power of the state and give expression democratically to popular interests.' But what is exactly meant by *civil society* and by *associational life*?

The concepts 'associational life' and 'civil society' are often used as synonyms, as both refer to the organisational density of society as a condition for democracy. However, the origins of the two concepts are quite different. Associational life stems from the analyses of De Tocqueville and Durkheim, who concluded that social mobilisation and the development of an ever expanding web of relatively autonomous organisations facilitates democracy. The idea of an 'associational revolution' is closely linked to the notion of pluralism as a necessary condition for democracy. Civil society in its modern conception, however, primarily refers to citizenship and to a distinct 'societal public sphere' of social relations between the family and the state.[13] Civil society can be defined as the totality of social institutions and associations, both formal and informal, that are not strictly production-related, governmental or familial in character.[14] But this definition needs more elaboration if it is used in relation to democratic transition.

In Latin America, thinking about civil society was strongly influenced by Antonio Gramsci and interpretations of his writings by progressive Italians, notably Norberto Bobbio. Although Gramsci's conceptualisation of civil society and the state is not always consistent, he argued that a strong and dense civil society was closely connected to the development of capitalism, as the terrain of struggle of the people against the hegemony of the market and the state. The capitalist state maintained its hegemony through 'consent' by ideologically dominating a dense civil society, combined with its hegemony by 'coercion'. In this way, the ruling classes made minority rule and democracy compatible. One of the most important implications of his thinking was that the right of any elite to exercise state power would be ultimately dependent upon popular acceptance. As Bratton (1994: 59) puts it: 'As long as civic actors grant consent, civil society exists in a complementary relationship to the state; its social institutions serve the hegemonic function of justifying state domination.' This opened the way for perceiving of a counter-hegemonic project which could be created within a civil society that had been functional to capitalist hegemony. Gramsci thus considered a counter-hegemonic project within civil society as a *means* to transform capitalist society, and not as an end in itself. However, due to interpretations by Bobbio (1987) and others, for the Latin American left in the 1980s 'the essential point was that it offered a new rationale for a more multi-faceted struggle against dictatorship and militarism rather than capitalism as a whole' (Pearce 1997a: 63). After the establishment of military regimes, they realised that revolutionary struggles (whether peaceful or armed) needed a new perspective, and many used Gramsci as a way to abandon Marxism, notably in Chile after the defeat of Allende's Popular Unity.[15]

While Gramsci undoubtedly contributed to broadening the concept of civil society by separating it from the political and economic sphere, he also contributed to the interpretation of civil society as an essentially 'good thing' (Cohen and Arato 1992).[16] Civil society became an idealised counter-image to counterpoise social virtue and political vice, the realm of freedom versus the realm of coercion, making the term serviceable to political struggle but thereby losing its analytical value. White (1994: 378) shows how the (re)discovery of civil society by political pluralists, modernisation theorists and others contributed to convert 'civil society' into a political slogan for a wide variety of purposes: 'Neo-populist development theorists and practitioners extol the virtues of grassroots NGOs as paradigms of social participation and the potential building blocks of democracy; economic liberals bolster their case for deregulation and privatisation by emphasising how these measures contribute to the emergence of a business class to counterbalance and discipline wayward states; treasury based cost-cutters see devolution of governmental functions to voluntary organisations as an ideologically palatable way of reducing state expenditure; conservative thinkers see it as a way of preserving traditional social solidarities in the face of disruptions caused by markets; and radical socialists zero in on the potential role of social organisations based on community, group or issue in transforming society or providing an alternative form of social governance.' White vividly illustrates here that the term civil society in its precise meaning could become elusive.[17]

However, just as was earlier argued with the concept of democracy, the confusion about the meaning of the concept civil society should not be overstated. Although civil society is a theoretical concept, and not an empirical one, it can be a useful tool for analysing the practice and meaning of recent processes of democratisation in Latin America (Pearce 1997a).[18] Two interrelated questions seem to be central to the confusion about the concept: what are the properties of civil society, and who belongs to it? Particularly the last question points to *which* civil society one has in mind. It could be helpful to start from the (obvious) notion that civil society can only be analysed in relation to the state, and that 'society' as such becomes 'civil' both in its separation from and implicit relation to the state (Bratton 1994). In others words, civil society should be defined both in terms of *society* (as opposed to, autonomous and separate from the state), and as *civic* (being part of the political system). This still leaves room for different interpretations about which organisations actually belong to civil society. For example, are those social organisations not directly related or opposed to the state, such as remote local self-help organisations, also part of civil society? And what about organisations not directly aiming at political participation, such as sports clubs?

Taking up the first question about the properties of civil society might help us move forward. The complexity of the concept civil society is not least of all the result of its multiple interpretations by political philosophers over the past two hundred years. Bratton (1994) and others[19] have shown that these thinkers empha-sised different *dimensions* of civil society: *material* (Hegel, Marx and Engels), *organisational* (Ferguson, De Tocqueville) and *ideological* (Gramsci). Instead of emphasising one of these dimensions, Bratton argues that each dimension is critical for the emergence of civil society. The material dimension is determined by the nature of the dominant economic system, the organisational dimension is deter-mined by the structure of relationships between social organisations, and the ideological dimension by the dominant values and attitudes that in turn determine the material and institutional realms.[20] Reducing civil society to one of these dimensions will not only generate confusion, but allow the concept to lose its quality as a rich tool for analysing state-society relations. In Bratton's words (1994: 57): 'Although political resources, organisations, and ideas may be observed, none alone can capture the quality and complexity of civil society as a whole. Civil society is a composite concept.' By stressing the need to analyse linkages within each dimension and the synergy between them, it becomes clear that civil society is broader than just the sum of its constituent parts.

This still leaves the second question unanswered: which organisations belong to civil society? Van Rooy (1996) suggests that non-civic associations such as sports clubs only belong to civil society if they contribute to 'social processes critical to development', for instance if politics is discussed internally or if it enhances (polit-ical) leadership. However, this implies a very complicated definition of civil society which is probably difficult to handle. Whitehead (1997: 107) points at the existence of 'uncivil associations' (such as fundamentalist sects) that 'may have to be tolerated in a democracy, but cannot be regarded as part of a modern liberal civil society.' Others (such as Bayart) only include those organisations that actively interact with the state, making a sharper definition possible, but giving a rather restricted interpretation of civil society. I agree with White (1994: 379) when he proposes to use the more common, broader sense of the concept, instead of defin-ing it away. Both for practical reasons (it prevents confusion) as well as to under-line the social complexity. He defines civil society as 'an intermediate associational realm between state and family populated by organisations which are separate from the state, enjoy autonomy in relation to the state and are formed voluntarily by members of society to protect or extend their interests or values.' Sports clubs thus belong to civil society, even if they do not discuss politics internally. So do self-help organisations operating in remote areas.

But with this definition the 'state' and the 'market' are not yet delimited in relation to civil society. For example, does a shoe factory belong to civil society, and what about a state-owned shoe factory? The first is an economic institution, belonging to 'economic society' and is thus not part of civil society. However, the employers' association of shoe manufacturers indeed is part of civil society. The state-owned factory, for its economic activity, also belongs to 'economic society', but in terms of its political character one could argue that it is part of the state. The distinction between the state and civil society cannot always be clearly marked. Civil society thus has to be explained in its relationship with the state and with society more in general. White (1994: 281) notes that civil society 'derives much of its specific political character from the deeper socio-economic structure and the distribution of interests, social norms and power resources which society embodies.' This implies that social relationships in civil society potentially contain 'social power' that in turn is determined, as Bratton already noted, by these interests, norms and power resources. The relevance of this specification is to underline that a weak civil society is not only weak in relation to the state, but also because some sectors are weaker (or stronger) than others.

To define the relationship between the state and civil society, it can be helpful to disaggregate civil society and add the notion of 'political society'. Gramsci used the term to refer to organisations that normally belong to civil society, but are in fact part of the political superstructure.[21] Political society is a separate sphere of actors and institutions mediating, articulating and institutionalising the relations between the state and civil society.[22] Political parties (and legislatures) are the key institutions of political society. But when their function of mediation and articulation is performed or complemented by other organisations in civil society – such as broad multisectoral coalitions – these could also (temporarily) be included in political society. Stepan (1988) used this distinction between civil and political society to analyse the political dynamics of the Brazilian opposition to authoritarianism and to differentiate between the opposition in the civil arena and opposition in the political arena. The point is of course, if this distinction is not made, where should political parties be located? They are not part of the state, although the state conditions the operation and structure of parties. They could be conceived as part of civil society, albeit with the special function of organising and articulating organised interests within civil society *vis-à-vis* the state. It is therefore more appropriate to locate political parties in political society, depicted in Figure 1.1 as an intermediary sphere between the state and civil society. This introduces the issue that has become a growing concern of development aid agencies in recent years: what is the function of civil society during democratic transition?

– *The shifting balance between the state and civil society*

It is widely believed that a crucial relationship exists between civil society and democratisation. Not only is a strong (diverse, dense, autonomous) civil society considered to be a prerequisite for democracy, it can also play a crucial political role in undermining authoritarian regimes and in the establishment and mainten- ance of a democratic polity. However, there is less agreement about *how* civil society can be conducive to democratisation, and at *which stage* of democratic transition this is most crucial. Diamond (1994) suggests that a vibrant civil society is probably more essential for consolidating democracy than for initiating it.[23] He notes that the primary goal in the struggle for democracy is the establishment of a viable and democratic political society, and that a vibrant civil society is a condi- tion for further developing and securing democracy. In this view, the role of civil society becomes important in the stage of *consolidating* democracy, after electoral norms and procedures have been established in political society. Along the same line O'Donnell (1988: 283) writes: 'If political democracy is to be consolidated, democratic practice needs to spread throughout society, creating a rich fabric of democratic institutions and authorities.'

But what is the role of civil society when democracy is not yet consolidated, that is, when political society is still weak? Stepan has argued in the Brazilian case that the military regime took advantage of the suspicious attitude of the Church and the labour movement towards political parties that wanted to serve as intermediaries between civil society and the military regime. The result was that links between opposition groups in civil society and those of political society were weak, giving the military regime the possibility to exploit this sharp separation between the two 'arenas' of the opposition. The liberalisation of the regime ('*abertura*') was wel-

Figure 1.1   *State, civil society and political society*

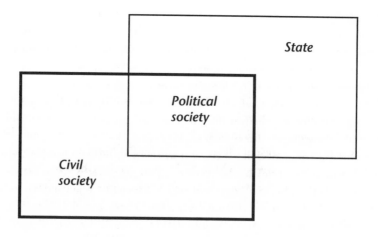

comed by the opposition in civil society, although it did not change the rules for political parties of the opposition. Stepan (1988: 6) uses this example to explain the difference between 'liberalisation' and 'democratisation': 'Democratization entails liberalization but is a wider and more specifically political concept. Democratization requires open contestation for the right to win control over the government, and this in turn requires free elections, the results of which determine who governs. Using these definitions it is clear there can be liberalization without democratization. Liberalization refers fundamentally to civil society. Democratization involves civil society, but it refers fundamentally to political society.' Following the earlier mentioned discussion between O'Donnell and Stepan, it could be asked again whether the priority in democratic transitions should be to strengthen civil society first, and then political society, or the other way around. However, this suggests that a strategic choice could be made between a top-down approach of elite transitions 'forging political society', and a bottom-up approach of increasing popular pressure and participation from below, by 'strengthening civil society' (Weffort 1993; Nunnenkamp 1995). Both processes are of course interdependent and take place simultaneously, and should therefore be studied in their complexity. This topic will come back in Chapter 3 when donor approaches to strengthening civil society are examined.

One crucial question has not yet been tackled: how is civil society supposed to play a role during democratic transition, and how does this apply in practice? The pluralist notion holds that civil society 'represents a reservoir of resources – political, economic, cultural, moral – to check and balance the power of the state' (Diamond 1992: 7). It follows the assumption that the 'autonomy' of a broad spectrum of interest groups can limit the power of the state, making control of the state by society possible. Generally, this idea is based on experiences of Western political democracies where civil society plays an important role in sustaining 'unrestricted' democratic political systems. A 'vibrant' and 'autonomous' civil society is usually understood in terms of its *pluralism* (number, size and variety) of interests that are organised; its *democratic orientation* (the civic values that are pursued) and its *political participation* (active use of civic rights and duties, and the formation of new leadership). However, it does not say very much about causal links between civil society and democratisation, other than that civil society is either 'resurrecting' or 'newly emerging' 'to resist the domination of an authoritarian regime and hasten its exit to power' (Diamond 1992: 11-12). The 'density' of civil society certainly is important, but obscures the fact that there are differences in power and interests between the constituent parts of civil society.[24]

The pluralist notion of civil society, as it was used in the Latin American context in the 'transition literature', has been criticised for not differentiating between the forces that occupy either civil society or political society. Cohen and Arato (1992: 56) question whether there is still anything left of a 'resurrected' civil society 'after selective repression, co-optation, manipulation, internal conflicts, fatigue, disillusionment, and the channelling of opposition into the party and electoral systems

take their toll and demobilise the "popular upsurge".'[25] The question is whether
actors in civil society are at all able to define their role *vis-à-vis* either political
society or the state, when (as happened during many transitions) traditional political elites appear to be immune to pressures from civil society. Pearce (1997a: 62)
thus suggests that the 'transitologists' ultimately were not truly interested in the
sphere of civil society *per se*: '"Civil society" is not conceptualised in relationship
to democracy itself, as in any sense necessary to it, and there is no apparent reason
why associational, organizational and movement life amongst the population
should be conceptualized as "civil society" at all.' In other words, it is not convincingly argued how a 'stronger civil society' would necessarily weaken the power of
traditional elites and increase social and political equality, unless civil society is
considered 'as an arena of contestation, a space which reflects the divisions of
society as a whole'.[26]

White (1994) has argued that a strong civil society can contribute to democratisation in four complementary ways: (i) when organised forces in society attain
enough strength to weaken the authoritarian state, the balance between civil
society and the state can be altered; (ii) particular sectors of civil society can enforce standards of public morality and performance upon the state, playing a
disciplinary role in relation to the state; (iii) civil society can articulate interest
group demands, as an alternative channel of representation, serving as an intermediary between state and society; (iv) civil society can play a constitutive role by
redefining the rules of the political games along democratic lines. Although White
was primarily concerned with the improvement of the quality of governance, his
categories can also be applied to stages of democratic transition as demonstrated
later in this chapter.

Still, it is necessary to be more explicit about how the balance between the state
and civil society could be changed and who are the main actors capable of shifting
this balance. Again, Bratton (1994: 58-59) is helpful as he emphasises the need to
analyse civil society in relation to the state: 'Because civil society is a theoretical
concept, it is best apprehended deductively, by deriving it in conjunction with the
concept of the state. The state, civil society and political society together exhaust
the scope of public life, and none of these concepts can be fully understood in
isolation from the other.' Along Gramscian lines, he conceives of the state as 'the
realm of the politics of force (domination), and civil society as the realm of the
politics of consent (hegemony)'. Although each of the realms is based on different
sources of political power, neither of the two can claim to monopolise public life
without provoking a reaction from the opposite realm to retain political space.
This movement of what Bratton calls the 'centre of gravity of political life' between
the state and civil society is continuously alternating. In periods of state domination of political life, social actors in civil society will try to find new independent
forms and channels to recover the political initiative and balance state power
through political society. The composition and legitimacy of political society is
therefore a crucial indicator for determining this 'centre of gravity' and the dy-

namics of political change. Even if political society is either banned or absorbed by the state, this will provoke a reaction from civil society to occupy new autonomous positions of contestation. This continuously shifting balance between the state and civil society is possibly a key to explain the various stages of democratisation. The alternation of political initiative reconfirms what was argued earlier: civil society is sovereign. In Bratton's words (1994: 59): 'The right of any elite to exercise state power is ultimately dependent upon popular acceptance. This acceptance – the key political resource for those who wish to rule – is manufactured by the institutions of civil society. For as long as civic actors grant consent, civil society exists in a complementary relationship to the state; its social institutions serve the hegemonic function of justifying state domination.'

The potential role of civil society in democratisation has two further dimensions that should be examined. The first was already mentioned: democratisation is more than just a matter of shifting the balance between the state and civil society, it also depends on patterns of conflict and cooperation between various parts (or sectors) that make up civil society. Rueschemeyer *et al.* call it 'the balance of power between classes and class coalitions', although this should be extended to include also gender and ethnic balances. These patterns are determined by material, organisational and ideological conditions. The other dimension is that the strength and the role of civil society is contingent upon the structure, strength and autonomy of the state, and on the international political environment (White 1994; Robinson 1995a). The following section focuses on the contending forces inside civil society and their relation with the state. In other words, what does a 'stronger' civil society mean in practice, and who are the crucial actors contributing to its strength?

1.2 Civil society: actors, roles and stages

The composition of any civil society is a product of *social struggle*, as Fowler (1996b) and others have argued. The structure and strength of any civil society is determined by the slow historical process of nation-building. The evolving character of the nation state determined the composition of civil society, and vice versa. The term social struggle is emphasised to underline the often violent way in which civil society has been constructed, and to stress the implicit *uniqueness* of civil society in each country. Even within the same nation state various patterns of civil society configurations have developed as a result of local power struggles (Putnam 1993). Major differences can be traced between the development of the state and civil society in former colonial powers and former colonies, for example between Europe and Latin America. European nations have grown more or less organically from their own social struggles and wars, whereas the formation of Latin American nations was permanently disrupted by Spanish colonialism, US imperialism or Cold War rivalry. The result is a weaker sense of common interests or common identities, often visible in weak citizenship, or even a duality in civicness.[27] These unique national histories and the consequences of non-organic nation-building should be included in an assessment of the constituent parts of civil society.

From the theoretical considerations of the previous section it could be concluded that 'civil society' can be defined as a normative and a teleological concept, as a value, but also as an 'observable reality' in which a wide variety of social actors and organisations often pursue opposing goals (Pearce 1997a; Van Rooy 1998). This section will look at who the constituent parts in civil society actually are, which interests they represent, and what their potential role in democratisation could be. This is an important issue in relation to aid policies of donor agencies who often prefer to work with non-governmental organisations (NGOs) in their efforts to strengthen civil society. However, 'NGO' is a blurry concept in a discussion of state-society relations: it should be specified what 'non-governmental' means in relation to other organisations of civil society and in relation to 'governmental' institutions. As with 'civil society', the concept 'NGO' has become a buzzword in development policy circles, meaning very different things to various constituencies (Smillie 1995b). This section will briefly discuss the meaning of NGOs in civil society and to what extent the concept is useful for the present analysis. The key purpose of the following pages is to develop a practical framework for analysing changing relations between the state and civil society during democratic transitions.

– NGOs and civil society

Non-governmental organisations often are equated with 'voluntary organisations', belonging to the 'third sector' of organisations in society that serve personal and social interests based on shared values. The third sector together with the 'second sector' (private enterprise) are understood as the private realm, as opposed to the public realm of the state ('first sector').[28] This implies that all organisations in the private realm by definition are 'non-state' and 'non-governmental' organisations (NGOs). Development discourse, however, generally assigns NGOs to the 'third sector', as these private organisations delivering services to the poor pursue social values instead of profits. NGOs should therefore not be equated with business organisations that primarily pursue profit, but that does not mean they do not belong to the (economic) private sector. 'Their relationships with the persons whom they serve – clients and customers – exhibit essential similarities' writes Uphoff (1995: 19). He argues that most NGOs belong to the service-subsector of the private sector: they primarily service persons who are not members of their organisation. As a result, NGOs formally cannot be held accountable for the services they deliver, whereas membership organisations are formally subject to accountability by their members. The category 'third sector' can generate confusing questions, such as: if most NGOs are not part of the third sector, do they belong to civil society? As far as their civic function is concerned – to contribute to voluntary collective action and self-help – they certainly do. But if it is their economic function that is considered, they probably do not belong to civil society.[29]

Official aid agencies, such as USAID, tend to consider most organisations of civil society as 'NGOs' on the conditions that these are concerned with influencing state policies, and are autonomous from the state and political parties (Blair *et al.* 1995). Supporters of this view call this subset of the NGO-community *civil society organisations* (CSOs), which excludes those NGOs that are only concerned with service delivery, relief or productivity functions. However, this vague notion of CSOs is problematic because the two conditions (influencing state policies and autonomy from state and parties) for NGOs are difficult to apply in Latin America. The first would include virtually all social organisations in a given civil society, as most organised social interest in Latin America has been concerned with influencing state policy. Ironically, the condition of autonomy from either the state or political parties would practically exclude all organisations in civil society. The concept CSO is not only too broad, it also contains a strong smell of anti-statism – which might explain why it has been gaining acceptance in recent years – and it suggests a societal harmony that is absent in Latin America.[30]

This point can be further clarified by another implication: the 'third sector' is determined by 'voluntary association' as opposed to market interaction and exercise of authority in other sectors.[31] Key characteristics of these associations are (i) the collective purpose of their members to pursue common interests, and (ii) that leaders are formally accountable to their membership. A wide range of social organisations respond to these criteria, from women's organisations to employers' associations, from churches to cooperatives. According to their goals and memberships each could be classified in several categories.[32] Throughout this book these membership (or popular) organisations will *not* be considered as NGOs, to stress that they serve different purposes in civil society.[33] Still, the question could be raised how to categorise NGOs that very much resemble popular organisations, or NGOs that have developed into a coordinating body of these organisations? In other words, how to distinguish among the variety of NGOs, and how to consider NGOs that are *informally* accountable to the clients they serve? For this purpose Carroll (1992) introduced the distinction between membership-support organisations (MSOs) and grassroots-support organisations (GSOs), the first being a service organisation (for example research or policy advocacy) that is part of – or a product of – a membership organisation. The distinction is useful, as the grey area between NGOs and popular (or membership) organisations has proven to be very diverse.[34] However, I would prefer to use a more explicit indicator for mapping differences between NGOs and popular organisations, such as *ownership*. A popular organisation is 'owned' by its constituency through the existence of 'membership' and the 'accountability' of leaders to these members, whereas a development NGO is *not* owned by a membership.[35]

In the rapidly expanding 'NGO literature' it is often assumed that NGOs have been the key players of civil society in bringing about democratic transition.[36] But this is a risky assumption, as it depends on the definition of NGO that is applied.

If NGOs are equated with the broad spectrum of non-state organisations serving as intermediaries for foreign aid, a definition still popular with many donor agencies, virtually all organisations in civil society could be labelled as NGOs. Obviously, this does not add to a better understanding of the constituent parts of civil society. The definition of NGOs used in this book – independent non-profit organisations, not owned by their members, delivering development services to the poor – implies that NGOs are probably less decisive in building up civil society than is sometimes suggested. What are often referred to as 'NGOs' either are not independent (from political parties or from the state), are actually 'owned by their members', or are national or international networks of popular organisations with low levels of internal accountability.[37]

– *Key sectors in civil society*

Distinguishing between categories such as 'NGOs' and 'popular (or grassroots) organisations' does not say very much about the power relations between the various organisations of civil society, about the internal strength of organisations, or about the relationship between civil society and the state. Typologies of associational life and the pluralist approach of the 'third sector' only refer to the organisational dimension of civil society and tend to hide potential conflictual interests that are related to the material and ideological dimensions of civil society. Civil society is not only strong because it is 'dense', but also because it is relatively 'equitable' and 'inclusive'; 'density' and 'vibrancy' of civil society do not automatically imply 'consensus'. As some organisations in civil society generally are more powerful than others, they have the potential to impose decisions favourable to their interests on others. The point is that not all organised interests share a common view about the desirability of deepening democracy (Chazan 1992). Rueschemeyer *et al.* (1992: 57) correctly argue that 'those who have only to gain from democracy will be its most reliable promoters and defenders, those who have the most to lose will resist it and will be most tempted to roll it back when the occasion presents itself.' Apparently, particular sectors tend to play a key role in strengthening civil society, whereas other sectors tend to frustrate these efforts because they are contrary to their interests. When the former manage to strengthen their legitimacy, both within civil society and towards the state, this considerably enhances the chances for a shift in the balance between the state and civil society towards democratic transition. Who are these key sectors in civil society, how are they organised and what are the sources of their 'social power'?

Only particular sets of organisations in civil society manage to play an active role in mediating and articulating demands from subordinate sectors at the level of political society during democratic transitions. Moreover, the various stages of these transitions should be carefully analysed, as different groups appear to take the lead in subsequent stages. O'Donnell and Schmitter (1986: 50) suggest that the middle classes, due to their 'superior capacity for action' and their 'lesser exposure to the risk of repression' play a 'crucial role in the earliest stages of transition', even when they are 'among the regime's earliest supporters'. Although the middle classes have been the main protagonists in the emergence of civil society, and often take the lead in founding and leading civic organisations, they are not necessarily the main protagonists in civil society during democratic transitions.

In Latin America, urban-based associations have been critical in early stages of political transitions, particularly those run by artists and intellectuals. O'Donnell and Schmitter (1986) point at the crucial role of urban-based middle-class individuals who voiced their critique of authoritarian regimes in South America by using their position in journals, universities, research centres and professional associations. But intellectuals also played a major role in later stages, as was shown in the Chilean transition where party-related intellectuals determined the opposition strategy leading to the defeat of Pinochet in the 1988 plebiscite (Puryear 1994). Human rights organisations and sections of the Catholic Church certainly also have been important channels for voicing popular protest, particularly when popular organising was still repressed. But as soon as (mostly urban-based) 'social movements'[38] began to emerge from the underground and acquired more room to manoeuvre in networks or popular fora, this small initial group of civil associations was broadened. The role of churches and NGOs in this process generally was important in providing financial resources and some kind of political protection, which was based on an externally derived legitimacy. Rural organisations generally did not take the lead in mobilising popular pressure to democratise the system, as repression often was concentrated in rural areas where the principal anti-democratic forces were located (Fox 1994).

The role of political parties deserves special attention. During authoritarian regimes in the Southern Cone, political parties were banned (or restricted) and their leaders continued their activities underground, often protected by the Church, or by setting up legal institutions with foreign support. As most social organisations were in some way or another linked to political parties, this lack of autonomy weakened the social sectors as soon as parties regained legal political space in later stages of the transition. The Chilean transition is a good example of mobilisation followed by effective demobilisation of social movements by political parties. In his study on neighbourhood associations during the military regime, Oxhorn (1995: 282) concludes: 'Whereas narrow partisan interests led political parties to try to capture the incipient movement in 1986, as the possibility of an actual transition to democracy became increasingly imminent in 1987 and 1988, political parties joined together to dismantle the movement as part of their collective efforts to secure the transition.'

Several lessons could be drawn from this brief overview of key societal actors in democratic transition. First, it underlines that one has to be careful in generalising about the identity of 'lead institutions' of civil society during political transitions. Bratton's idea (1994) of one leading actor might be true for some African experiences, but can be questioned for most transitions in Latin America. Another lesson is that the use of the concept 'non-governmental organisation' to identify key actors in civil society can create confusion and misunderstanding. Throughout this book, an effort is made to avoid this concept or at least to be specific about the type of NGO under consideration.[39] A further reason for being careful about generalisations is that the role of key players in civil society is contingent upon local political and economic conditions. This is one of the most important – and probably unintended – lessons of the transition literature. It means that the role of societal actors during democratic transitions can never be disconnected from their national context. Before analysing several key actors in the Central American transitions, Chapter 4 will therefore provide an analysis of the various dimensions in the formation of state-society relations. Finally, an historical dimension should be added to this picture, for during various stages of democratic transition new sets of actors seem to play a key role, either in civil or in political society.[40] This implies that strengthening civil society appears differently in the various stages of democratic transition and consolidation. It is therefore time to have a look at what these key organisations possibly can do to shift the balance between the state and civil society.

– *Five means for civil society building*
Relations between the state and civil society are mediated by, and organised within, political society. Figure 1.2 schematically illustrates the balance of power between the state, civil society and political society.

Within civil society, broadly speaking, organisations are located in a spectrum between full autonomy from the state (B) and co-opted by the state (A). Autonomous association is, as was argued earlier, a precondition for a strong civil society.

Figure 1.2   *The balance between the state and civil society*

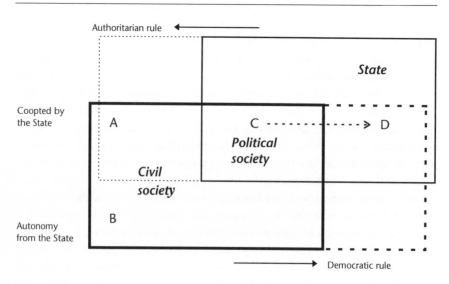

So if organisations are mostly located in area (A), civil society is generally weak, and if the emphasis is on (B), civil society is usually strong *vis-à-vis* the state. This has consequences for the interaction between the state and civil society, and thus for the strength of political society. Associations in civil society performing an intermediary role during certain transition stages become active in (and part of) political society. These associations could be political parties, but also (coalitions of) social organisations of various kinds. If these mediating actors are mostly active in area (D), political society potentially has a strong position in regard to the state, generally manifested by efforts for political and social reform. However, in most of Latin America political parties are either weak or co-opted by the state, which implies that they usually strive for short-term changes and longer term preservation of the status quo. Civil society ideally pushes mediating organisations to move from area (C) to (D), so as to increase the leverage towards the state. Any analysis of the power balance between the state and civil society should consider the composition and the strength of political society, in order to assess the potential for political change towards democratic government.

Strengthening civil society is only one part of democratic transition; the other is to strengthen the state by making it transparent and more accountable (and more efficient as is nowadays the dictum). Strengthening civil society thus is a matter of combining widening participation with increasing accountability. Shifting the balance between the state and civil society is a complementary process: civil society should become more inclusive, and the state has to become more accountable to its citizens (Fowler 1993b). Ideally, these two processes go hand in hand, where civil society and the state each have their responsibilities. This is the assumption of the 'governance' approach of the World Bank, in which the 'bottom-up' approach is combined with a governmental 'top-down' approach. In the recent history of Latin America, authoritarian regimes have proven to be rather weak in their ability and their willingness to truly reform themselves (Nunnenkamp 1995). The organisation of popular pressure from civil society to push for political inclusiveness and state accountability therefore seems to be essential, particularly in the early stages of democratic transition. In Latin America this potential political role of civil society has been identified as a way to 'open up political spaces of contestation', which comes down to rebuilding (in the Southern Cone) or constructing (in Central America) *political society* from below. This generates the question: by what means can organisations in civil society strengthen political society, and what exactly are they strengthening? A variety of complementary mechanisms have been identified for this purpose, which I group into five categories: (a) building the foundations of civil society, (b) building alliances in civil society, (c) developing intermediary channels between the state and civil society, (d) opening up transnational political space and (e) building citizenship.[41] The first two categories are central to building a strong civil society and to providing conditions for the establishment of political society, whereas the remaining three categories are central to consolidating civil society and to constructing political society.

(a) building the foundations of civil society

A condition for civil society to play a political role at all is that citizens are not excluded from participation in *collective* decision-making, either as individuals or by way of some form of interest organisation. This 'foundation' of civil society could be strengthened both by the formation of autonomous new interest organisations, but also by increasing the 'diversity' of organisations so that no particular interest is excluded from civil society. But there is also a qualitative aspect to this civic action which is often underplayed by pluralist analysts: it is important that these organisations themselves uphold democratic values and methods so that they really contribute to strengthening the democratic orientation of civil society. This applies not only to other actors in civil society, but also to internal accountability structures and transparent decision-making. Another qualitative element is to provide and enhance the capacity for key organisations in civil society to support their activities – direct or indirect via political parties – in the realm of political society. Access to information sources and communication channels is one of the capacities that is often weakly developed. Another is the ability to develop coherent proposals and longer term visions. VeneKlasen (1996) points at particular skills of organisations that need to be improved in order to effectively interact with the state: analysis and research, organisational and management skills, as well as the ability to negotiate with institutions and bureaucracies.

(b) building alliances

A further way to build a strong civil society is to develop the 'social fabric', by forging mutually beneficial relationships at various levels among constituent parts of civil society. One obvious way to build these linkages is to coordinate activities within a particular sector. This could be done at the level of communities or municipalities (Reilly 1995), but is often also applied to national and international levels. In Latin America, trade unions, cooperatives and peasant organisations have a rich tradition in forming coordinating associations to represent sectoral interests in negotiations with employers' associations, national ministries or international agencies. In addition, to bring forward demands that go beyond sectoral boundaries, often networks or alliances of representative bodies from several sectors are formed. These multisectoral alliances generally are built around one particular issue. Examples from Latin America include the Brazilian alliance of social forces campaigning for direct elections, the Honduran *Plataforma de lucha* against the adoption of new legislation turning back the land reform process, or the Civil Initiative for Central American Integration (ICIC) which includes all major organisations of subordinate societal actors in Central America. Alliances could even include political parties, especially if these parties are excluded from (or only weakly present in) political society. An example is the *Asamblea de la Sociedad Civil* (ASC) in Guatemala, where a broad spectrum of parties and social organisations monitored agreements during the recent peace negotiations.

(c) building intermediary channels

The key to a strong *political* society is the existence of democratic political parties whose leaders can be held accountable, both by a diverse membership and by the electorate. But it has already been mentioned that most Latin American countries have a weak system of political parties, and thus a badly functioning system of *formal* mediation between the state and civil society (Torres Rivas 1995). This is where the intermediary function of organisations in civil society has become extremely important, particularly for the most vulnerable sectors in civil society whose interests are not or only weakly represented. In situations of a restricted civil society, where efforts to build alliances between sectoral groups are repressed by force, *informal* intermediary channels generally are also closed. The function of articulating concerns in these situations is performed by those groups that still enjoy a certain legitimacy with the regime, such as Church leaders or journalists. This takes the form of a moral representation and is not guided by any mechanism of formal consultation. During later stages of democratic transition, when more freedom is given to articulate sectoral demands, political space is widened and increases the potential to build up new channels of communication, dialogue or negotiation with the state. This is in fact the moment in which political society is being constructed and when the 'political role' of civil society is practised.

(d) opening up transnational political space

In addition to the mechanism of building intermediary channels, there often also is an international dimension. When civil society is restricted by force, societal actors sometimes have to reach across their national boundaries to make alliances with (external) actors that could enhance their legitimacy, both within civil society and *vis-à-vis* the state. This externally derived legitimacy of course only works temporarily, but it can boost the growth of an opposition movement towards an authoritarian regime. An example of this mechanism is the impact of international awards (such as the Nobel Peace Prize) to opposition leaders that are either imprisoned, banned or ignored by the regime. Many of these laureates in South Africa, Argentina, Guatemala, Burma and East Timor generated substantial international attention for their national struggles, which could no longer be dismissed by authoritarian regimes. It often resulted in state recognition of opposition forces in civil society, forging 'political space' for these organisations. Another example of strengthening civil society via external linkages is the use of lobbying campaigns directed at international organisations to put forward particular national issues on which the regime is unwilling to negotiate. These international bodies could be governmental – such as the UN Human Rights Commission, the European Commission or the World Bank – as well as non-governmental, such as private international organisations promoting human rights or environmental issues. By enlarging their access to this 'transnational political space', societal actors of the opposition often manage to strengthen their leverage upon the national regime.[42]

(e) building citizenship

Complementary to these four means for developing political society is keeping the newly conquered political space open and institutionalising democratised relations between the state and civil society. In other words, guaranteeing that the state can be held accountable for its actions and that it will do so in the longer run. A condition for reproducing a democratic political system is to increase its legitimacy. Low voter participation in elections could be an indicator of weak legitimacy. Civic education campaigns are often mounted to increase the confidence of citizens in the new system. But this is not enough if formal citizenship is only applied to elections and not to other areas of civic action. Another condition for maintaining a viable political society is to guarantee that citizens can participate in public debates and that they can trust their elected representatives. Building and main-

Table 1.3   *Changing relations between the state and civil society during stages of democratic transition*

	Authoritarian period	Early Transition	Mid-Transition	Late Transition	Early Consolidation
Civil Society					
• building density and diversity	▬▬	▬▬	▬▬	▬▬	▬▬
• building (sectoral) alliances		▬▬	▬▬	▬▬	▬▬
• building (multisectoral) intermediary channels		▬▬	▬▬	▬▬	▬▬
• building international coalitions		▬▬	▬▬	▬▬	▬▬
• building citizenship				▬▬	▬▬
Political Society					
• disciplinary role	▬▬	▬▬			
• intermediary role		▬▬	▬▬	▬▬	
• legalise opposition parties				▬▬	▬▬
• legitimate party system					▬▬
State					
• political repression	▬▬				
• open to informal negotiations		▬▬	▬▬		
• convene free elections			▬▬	▬▬	
• civilian rule over military				▬▬	▬▬
• public accountability					▬▬

taining a strong political society thus implies that citizen participation beyond elections is highly valued and that new generations of political leadership are trained and formed (Robinson 1995a). The ultimate goal of building a strong realm of intermediation between the state and civil society is the constructive interplay between civil society and democratic political parties, whose members after all are recruited from civil society. These efforts to 'deepen' democracy are contingent upon what is called 'creating an enabling environment'. This has a national and an international dimension, to which I will return in Chapter 3 when options for international donor agencies during democratic transitions are discussed.

– *Civil and political society during stages of democratic transition*

An historical element is still missing in this examination of the construction of civil society and political society. Democratic transition is, after all, a slow process which is far from linear and in which *stages* of progress and retreat can be identified.[43] To monitor shifts in the power balance between civil society and the state, and especially to monitor the expanding space for opposition forces in political society, four stages of democratic transition have been identified: 'early transition', 'mid-transition', 'late transition' and 'early consolidation'.[44] Following the authoritarian period, in which political society is repressed by the authoritarian regime, civil society only has restricted freedom to organise. The stage of *early transition* is the phase of 'political opening', in which the authoritarian regime concedes restricted opportunities for formal channels of mediation between civil society and the state. Usually, this mediation is restricted to those political parties that are not too rigidly opposed to the regime, whereas opposition parties are still banned. However, when this 'early transition' of political openings is in motion, it often provides new opportunities for popular organisations in civil society to pronounce themselves and to conquer some space in political society. This is a key stage for democratic transition, as it entails negotiations between the elites of civil and political society and the regime that are often characterised by mutual distrust. A climate which initially seems to be favourable for dialogue can easily be reversed if one of the parties withdraws. An example is El Salvador after the violent elections of 1984, in which negotiations between the insurgents and the government ended in a deadlock due to a veto by the armed forces, prolonging civil war another seven years.

As soon as polarisation in civil society eases, and the key forces opposing each other reach a basic consensus on the need for entering negotiations in order to move democratic transition forward, the second phase of *mid-transition* starts. The main issue in this phase is to determine who are the legitimate forces to articulate the interests and demands of civil society, especially of those (subordinate) sectors in civil society that previously were excluded. In other words, mid-transition is characterised by a political struggle between civil society alliances and (old and new) political parties for a legitimate role in political society. Typical of this stage is the coexistence of popular mobilisation and elite negotiations, and a substantial role of external actors pressuring for democratic rule. As soon as an agreement (between elites) is reached about the constitutional framework for future democratic rule, civil society has to endorse this agreement to confirm the existence of a national consensus to finalise authoritarian rule. This is often the moment in which political parties of the opposition are legalised and formally admitted to political society.

The stage of *late transition* starts as soon as these political parties successfully have participated in unrestricted elections and enter legislatures at national and municipal levels. The mediation between the state and civil society during the stage of 'late transition' is now formalised into political society, the legitimacy of which gradually increases. Sometimes former (banned) opposition parties become part of the new regime, which happened for example in the recent South African transition to the African National Congress. However, practically in all Latin American transitions opposition parties have continued their oppositional role, although qualitatively improving their leverage as they have become part of national legislatures. 'Late transition' is generally considered to be a phase in which civic education programmes play a decisive role in educating the electorate about the rules of formal democracy, to ensure that democratic rule is broadly accepted and rooted in civic responsibilities (G. Hansen 1996; Fowler 1996b).

As was argued earlier, democratic transition is rarely concluded (or consolidated) when the stage of late transition is completed. Especially in countries where democracy had been absent in the past (such as in Central America) the construction of democracy requires a long process of consolidation. I would therefore prefer to identify various stages of consolidation, instead of only considering one 'end stage' which is popular with transitologists (Linz and Stepan 1996). The reason is that during *early consolidation* only initial steps are taken to end restricted citizenship. This could mean, for example, that the armed forces are put effectively under the control of a civilian government. Only in later stages of consolidation can it be ensured that democratic rule is institutionalised and that mechanisms for political participation are effectively in place, to guarantee that the state can be made fully accountable to civil society. The final stage of democratic transition could be regarded as the stage in which all other (informal) restrictions to citizenship have been tackled, such as severe socio-economic inequality or external dependencies. For that reason, it is more realistic to limit the present analysis to the stage of early consolidation.

With these stages in mind, various strands from the previous analysis are pulled together to construct an analytical framework that is depicted in Table 1.3. It points to the essential functions of civil society, political society and the state during the various stages of democratic transition. There is one important element however which is missing in this framework and needs further examination: the role of the international context.

1.3 Democratisation and the international context

The previous sections focused on democratisation as a process in which power relations are shifting both within and between the realms of civil society, political society and the state. But the role of international actors (and developments) also should be examined, as these constitute a further dimension of power relations determining democratic transitions. The international context proves to be 'a notoriously difficult variable to pin down' (Schmitter 1996: 28). Although its presence and impact are not disputed, the way in which it affects domestic political processes is dependent upon many local variables. Not long ago a broad consensus existed among scholars that external actors played only a rather marginal role, either in forging or obstructing national processes of democratisation. For example, O'Donnell and Schmitter (1986: 19) concluded in their study on political transitions in Southern Europe and Latin America that 'domestic factors play a predominant role in the transition'. Diamond *et al.* (1989) also did not pay very much attention to international actors, but admitted that they were important. After the rapid political transitions in Eastern Europe, followed by the collapse of the Soviet Union, the notion that the international context was perhaps decisive started to take root. Schmitter (1996: 27) for example, was impressed by the rapid political changes in countries such as East Germany and Albania and admitted that these would have been unlikely without the previous dramatic changes in the Soviet Union: 'perhaps it is time to reconsider the impact of the international context upon regime change'.

Although Schmitter and others assert that regime change tends to be a domestic affair, the international context can influence the balance between the state and civil society, as it can strengthen or weaken either one of them.[45] Schematically, Figure 1.4 illustrates the interdependent relationships between the 'trinity' of forces that shape or obstruct democratisation. International forces can directly or indirectly influence the strength of civil society, by either reinforcing or weakening its diversity, density or inclusiveness. These interactions between international actors and organisations operating in civil society are located in a distinct realm, which is sometimes called 'global civil society'. However, as will be analysed below, the distinction between 'global' and 'domestic' civil society cannot always be clearly drawn; international actors often are 'operational' in the South by creating 'proxies' that insert themselves inside a foreign (domestic) civil society.

Simultaneously, the state can be affected in many ways by international actors: by reinforcing its repressive function, by limiting its economic function, or by increasing its national or international legitimacy. Interactions between international actors and the state are mediated within the realm of the interstate community that I would label the 'global state system'. These interactions could develop between two (bilateral) or between various (multilateral) states, either within or outside the multilateral sphere of international organisations. By doing so, the international context ultimately influences the balance between the state and civil society. For example, if governments are forced by international actors to increase their accountability and transparency towards citizens and improve their governance, this could positively influence the strength of civil society. On the other hand, if dominant sectors in civil society are supported by external anti-democratic forces, this could negatively influence democratisation.

The scope of this international dimension of democratisation is highly diverse. International actors include governments and multilateral agencies such as the World Bank, but also non-state organisations such as (transnational) corporations, churches, labour unions or private aid agencies. The method of external interven-tion might be predominantly economic, but often also has been military, political or cultural. External influences could be direct or indirect, intended or unintended, and so forth. Whitehead (1996a: 6) identifies three categories of international factors that could affect domestic democratisation: 'contagion', 'control' and 'consent'. Contagion is in his view democratisation 'by infection', and the result of 'neutral transmission mechanisms that might induce countries bordering on democracies to replicate the political institutions of their neighbours'. Actions of third powers to impose democracy by open intervention could be categorised under the notion of 'control'. Whitehead asserts that two-thirds of democracies existing before 1990 owe their origins to these acts of external imposition. As 'contagion' and 'control' have proven to be insufficient explanations for many post-1990 processes, Whitehead suggests a third relevant factor in the international context: 'the generation of consent upon which new democracies must be based', in which the emphasis is laid on the interplay between (often non-governmental) international and domestic actors over a considerable period of time. One of the

Figure 1.4   International actors and democratisation

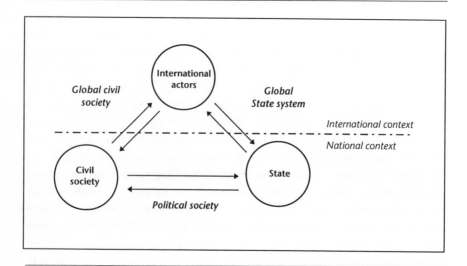

central questions guiding this study is to assess how important external (aid) interventions have been for democratic transitions. It is this 'enabling environment' that makes a distinction between the sphere of global civil society and the global state system useful for the analysis; both spheres will be examined in terms of main actors, motives and methods to enhance or 'promote' democracy.

— 'Third governments' promoting democracy

Foreign policies of governments aimed at the promotion of democracy should be analysed with caution, especially because many authoritarian regimes in the past have been supported 'in the name of democracy' (Carothers 1991). This paradox has been particularly visible in US foreign policies since the turn of this century (Drake 1991).[46] Whitehead (1986) remarks that official declarations in favour of democracy in the abstract correlated poorly with observable behaviour affecting specific real interests and international relationships. He gives two illustrations. First, there is a particular model of democracy that has been favoured by international actors, which was closely tied to Western political ideology during the Cold War: liberal democracy. With its emphasis on civil liberties, private ownership and electoral competition, liberal (or capitalist) democracy was pitted against communism.[47] This anti-communism was particularly strong in the United States, whereas European (usually Social Democratic) actors also considered socioeconomic equality intrinsic to democracy. The second point is that international actions promoting democracy predominantly have come from the Western industrialised world, and were directed at poorer countries with less political stability. Whitehead points at this 'centre-periphery aspect', in which 'catching up' in economic terms for these nations often implied the introduction of authoritarian measures to pursue national unity and internal order. This partly explains the paradox sketched earlier, in which the promotion of democracy sometimes resulted in support for authoritarian regimes.

What has driven (Western) governments to intervene in foreign political processes under the banner of 'democracy promotion'? An important factor has already been mentioned: the rhetoric of the promotion of democracy derived its legitimacy from the establishment of political democracy in the Western industrialised world. As such, it proved to be a useful tool for conquering unfriendly regimes during decolonisation and the Cold War. An attitude of supremacy about the domestic political and economic model was central to the powerful position of the United States as the principal international 'exporter' of democracy in the twentieth century. But it was the *imposition* of formal democracy abroad that contributed to establishing US international supremacy. The repeated use of armed force, which is sometimes explained as a by-product of its domestic process of nation-building, distinguishes US policies from those of European governments. US governments derived their legitimacy for democracy promotion primarily from domestic support for their foreign policy, and less from its actual implications abroad. As Lowenthal (1991: 260) puts it: 'Specific US efforts to promote democracy in Latin America are motivated more often by domestic US or broader international considerations than by particular trends within the affected country.'

European governments (individually or in a coordinated fashion through the European Community) also have actively supported democracy abroad, although with a substantially different approach than that of the United States. European governments were more inclined to use instruments of diplomacy and negotiation, instead of force. Whitehead (1986) explains this by pointing at the need for European governments to concentrate on their own region, where they also lacked adequate means to promote democracy, for example in authoritarian Spain and Portugal, or in Eastern Europe. European governments acted more cautiously and with far more patience than the United States. In part, this also was influenced by developments in (former) colonies where the extension of democracy implied a loss of privileges to European interests. The decision to support democratic forces in post-colonial states on the other hand often guaranteed a continuation of European influence. Still, the international 'police role' of the United States in the South was often welcomed and tacitly supported by European governments, although often domestically criticised. Particularly during the 1970s and early 1980s, when European (Social Democratic) governments were more critical of US foreign policy, Europe was not unhappy to perform a so-called 'third party' role in Cold War conflict areas. In this period, the role of non-governmental actors proved to be quite useful for European governments, as will be shown later.

Military intervention probably has been the most visible and vigorous instrument of third governments to influence foreign political processes. Imposing democratic rule by external military force has occurred to various degrees. The United States, for example, went from open military invasions (Grenada 1983, Panama 1989, Haiti 1994), or the threat of invasion (Dominican Republic 1978) to covert military operations (Afghanistan, Angola, Nicaragua, Cambodia) in order to establish democratic rule abroad.[48] The lasting effects of these interventions on democratic politics usually proved to be marginal; a general lesson appears to be that the more interventionist the policies of external states have been in imposing democracy, the less effect they have had in the long run.[49] Other instruments, such as economic sanctions, diplomatic action, aid packages or public statements on human rights are often considered more effective for promoting democratisation. Despite the rhetoric and the wide variety of instruments being used, a major study on US efforts to promote democracy abroad concluded that the results, with few exceptions, had been disappointing (Lowenthal 1991). The enduring effects of external interventions appear to depend largely on the local power structure and on favourable conditions at the moment of intervention (Rueschemeyer et al. 1992). Governments, and external actors in general, can back locally controlled processes and institutions, but hardly seem able to influence them directly. Even Huntington (1991: 86) concludes that foreign actors can best be thought of as 'hastening or retarding the effects of economic and social development on democratisation', instead of having the potential to determine these processes.

Schmitter (1996) makes a useful distinction between 'coercion' and 'voluntary action' in the promotion of democracy by external actors. Coercion (either by control or by conditionality) refers to actions available to governments. The control aspect is exercised by military force or economic policies, and conditionality, for example, by linking aid packages to human rights concerns. Non-state actors are unable to promote democratisation by coercion and have used other means which proved to be more effective in practice. This could possibly explain why interventions by governments are usually of secondary importance in determining local democratisation processes. Governments, and international actors in general, apparently only can perform a primary role under exceptional finely balanced circumstances, when foreign influence contributes to 'tip the scale'. The assumption of Lowenthal (1991) and Rueschemeyer *et al.* (1992) that this potential is particularly present in regions which have been highly penetrated and are most vulnerable to external influences (such as Central America or the Caribbean) is in a sense ironical. Especially in those smaller nations of Latin America where US influence was greatest, democratisation advanced least (Karl 1990).[50] In the post-Cold War period it seems to be less disputed that the promotion of democracy has functioned as 'a component in a world-wide system of alliance control' (Whitehead 1996: 14).

– *Non-governmental actors strengthening civil society*
If the relevance of governments in promoting democratisation abroad is relatively marginal, what about non-governmental actors, such as churches, labour unions, private aid agencies or human rights groups? Lowenthal (1991: 261) concludes in his study that these actors could be of greater significance: 'The US government can probably do more to promote democracy in Latin America by encouraging non-governmental policies and processes to support the region's democratisation than by direct governmental pressures.' Schmitter (1996: 39) makes the same point even more sharply by suggesting the following hypothesis: 'The international context surrounding democratisation has shifted from a primary reliance upon public, inter-governmental channels of influence towards an increased involvement of private, non-governmental organisations.'

Whitehead and Schmitter call these non-governmental organisations the *agents of consent* that have learned from earlier democratic transitions and react interactively with key domestic actors to further democratisation. Their actions can 'augment, undermine and even countermand those of the states they belong to', and 'there is reason to suspect that this world beneath and beyond the nation state has played an especially significant role in the international promotion of democracy' (Schmitter 1996: 29). Whitehead and Schmitter basically explain the increased relevance of non-governmental actors for democratisation as a result of the end of the Cold War. Dominant powers have become less concerned that uncertain processes of democratic transition will be exploited by the external interventions of competing superpowers which might destabilise international security. This has given domestic actors more freedom to determine their internal politics and choose their international allies, and it has provided new political space for international actors to intervene in domestic political processes. What is not very clear, though, is why this would particularly benefit the actions of non-governmental international actors. But assuming that this is the case, how to explain the relevant actions of non-state actors *before* the end of the Cold War?[51] The explanation seems not to be very solid, as many non-governmental actors flourished in the international arena thanks to the dynamics of the Cold War. Governments secretly made use of 'informal diplomatic channels', either through party internationals, private aid agencies, human rights organisations or churches, to intervene in those societies with which bilateral relations were politically sensitive. Well-known examples are the support from the National Democratic Institution (the private foundation of the US Democratic party) to the Chilean opposition in the mid-1980s, the support of the Socialist International to the Spanish Socialist Party in exile, and the support of European private aid agencies to opposition forces in El Salvador and Guatemala. The end of the Cold War as a (single) variable to explain the increased relevance of international non-governmental actors is therefore not very satisfactory.

Another explanation provided by Schmitter (1996: 32) is the increase in international interdependence, 'especially forms of "complex interdependence" involving a wide range of types of exchange', that has contributed to democratisation of national political institutions. He points not only at the impact of increased exchange of goods and services, but also of information. The ongoing revolution in information technology (faxes, satellite television, internet) and the resulting growth of information flows have increasingly connected societies without the approval and mediation of governments. The impact of (live) broadcast images of open resistance, such as the siege of the West German embassy in Prague by East German refugees and their illegal crossing of the Hungarian-Austrian border, definitely influenced the sequence of events in Eastern Europe.[52] Without disregarding the impact of the spectacular development of 'complex communicate interdependence' on democratisation, it seems to be insufficient to explain the increased relevance of non-governmental actors or the primacy of 'global civil society' over the 'global state system'. It could be helpful to explore the properties of this global civil society and how it is related to domestic civil societies.

– Global civil society versus domestic civil society

The meaning of 'global civil society' needs to be clarified, because it has been a controversial concept among international relations theorists. Broadly speaking two arguments are made against the existence of a global civil society. The first is that it is non-existent for the simple reason that there is no 'global state' it can relate to, as civil society and the state by definition are national entities. The second argument is that the power of transnational societal actors has been marginal compared to the power of nation states (Sullivan 1982). In recent years the idea of a global civil society seems to have gained more acceptance since both arguments have been countered. On the first point, the non-existence of a global state, Shaw (1994: 25) argues that (an 'embryonic') global civil society is a product of global interdependence, 'coming into existence in an interdependent relationship with the state system, and especially with the developing international state institutions.' The *interdependent* dynamic of the development of global civil society is the key, as it reflects its fundamental linkage with the global state system. Along the same lines, Waterman (1996: 54-55) argues that 'the development of a global civil society depends on and stimulates the democratisation, deconcentration, and decentralisation of interstate organisations and of global capitalist companies and institutions'. Although it is inevitable that global civil society interacts with states and the state system, actors in global civil society simultaneously deny that the primacy of sovereignty lies with states.[53]

The other objection to global civil society, that it is politically irrelevant, has been countered by pointing at the perceived threat of several Southern governments that transnational societal actors are challenging their national sovereignty. This was the case with international environmental actors such as Greenpeace and World Wildlife Fund,[54] but also with transnational advocacy networks on security or human rights issues, and with international relief agencies.[55] Sousa Santos (1995: 268) argues that the contestation of these actors shows successful attempts to create 'a transnational agency alternative to the TNCs and their supporting institutions. Without pushing risky symmetries too far, there is some evidence that transnational NGOs represent for the agendas of cosmopolitanism and common heritage of humankind what the TNCs represent for the agendas of localised globalism or globalised localism.' The political relevance of these transnational actors, and the global civil society they operate in, is thus not limited to the fact that they interact with or try to influence state policies. On the contrary, their political relevance lies in the ability to put into effect various forms of 'global governance' that go beyond the instrumentalist forms used by states (Wapner 1995). By combining 'vertical deepening' of domestic democracy with 'horizontal expansion' of democracy beyond state-society relations, Falk (1995a: 86-7) argues that these transnational societal actors facilitate the growth of global civil society: 'this countervision presupposes the possibility of globalization from below to establish new entities and communities, reclaiming the instrumentalities of law and global institutions to promote the goals of nonviolence, social justice, and ecological balance'.[56]

Parallel to what was suggested in the earlier discussion on domestic civil society, it could be helpful to 'map' these transnational (societal) actors that shape global civil society, especially those that have contributed to domestic democratisation.[57] A brief look at the variety of transnational actors that have intervened in domestic political transitions over the past decades shows that the Catholic Church probably has been one of the most influential transnational networks supporting opposition to authoritarianism. The changes in the social doctrine of the Catholic Church that were a product of the Second Vatican Council (1962-65) and the Latin American Episcopal Conferences in Medellín (1968) and Puebla (1979) contributed to Catholic Church leaders taking an active role in promoting domestic democratisation in Latin America (notably Brazil, Chile and El Salvador) but also in several Asian countries (Philippines, South Korea) and Eastern Europe (especially Poland). Changes within the Catholic hierarchy occurred at two distinct levels, which often contradicted each other. At the level of parishes in many Latin American countries, a new progressive (often Marxist-inspired) ideology of 'liberation-theology' politicised grassroots activities of the Catholic Church. In Brazil, for example, popular ecclesiastical base communities were central to the mobilisation of popular opposition to the Brazilian military dictatorship.[58] On the other hand, at the level of the National Episcopal Conferences, where traditional and conservative ideologies remained dominant, Catholic bishops became crucial mediating players between opposition groups and authoritarian regimes during the 1980s. The Catholic Church often was the only channel to voice critical opposition to military rulers, although in the 1970s it had welcomed most of the military coups in Latin America. International support from the Vatican, and particularly from Pope John Paul II with his frequent travels to military-dominated societies, converted the Catholic Church into one of the major opponents to authoritarianism during the last period of the Cold War.[59] It could be argued that this is only valid for countries with a strong Catholic community, though Huntington (1991) convincingly shows that out of all democratic transitions between 1974 and 1989 three-quarters occurred in Catholic societies. One of the key explanations for the successful role of the Catholic Church was its open anti-communist discourse – which coincided with (and was warmly supported by) foreign policies of the Reagan administration in the United States – combined with a more implicit (and generally grassroots-based) anti-imperialism. The Vatican, not surprisingly, opposed the latter tendency and gave priority to legitimising the intermediary role of the national clergy in pursuing a peaceful transition to democratic rule.

The example of the Catholic Church suggests that transnational support can legitimise the oppositional role of national forces confronting authoritarianism. The mechanism of deriving national legitimacy from transnational actors operating in global civil society also seems to be central to actions in other sectors. International human rights organisations, for example, have been crucial in denouncing human rights violations at an international level, but simultaneously provided security and legitimacy to national human rights committees (Sikkink 1993). Transnational networks of women's, indigenous and environmental organisations have been influential in shaping international treaties, adopted by the United Nations, which then provide opportunities to domestic movements to pressure for their ratification by national parliaments. Transnational networks of political parties, such as the Socialist International or the Christian Democratic International, have provided national legitimacy to persecuted national sister-parties.[60] Party internationals derived their political weight predominantly from some of their member parties occupying governmental offices in the North. In other words, transnational party networks often were used by Northern (European) governments as a transnational instrument to intervene abroad without risking bilateral diplomatic damage (Grabendorff 1996).[61]

Another key sector operating in global civil society is the variety of non-governmental development aid agencies, which combine support to local opposition groups in civil society with international advocacy initiatives. These 'private aid agencies' seldom are mentioned in the literature on international dimensions of democratisation.[62] This is remarkable, because these private aid agencies share some characteristics that make them potentially powerful compared to other transnational actors intervening in processes of democratic transition. Like other transnational actors they are relatively autonomous from the state, have the ability to build transnational alliances, and pursue the earlier mentioned goals of non-violence, social equality and ecological balance. However, what makes them different from many other transnational actors is their source of power: they are able to provide substantial financial resources to local organisations in civil societies in the countries where they intervene, often without the limitations of diplomatic barriers, bureaucratic procedures or ideological submission.[63] The following chapters will examine the history and strategies of these private aid agencies, of which it is assumed that they have been particularly influential in strengthening Southern civil societies.

1.4 The magic of civil society

Since the 1980s 'transitologists' have dominated theoretical discourse on democratisation by analysing the wave of political transformations in Latin America, Eastern Europe, and other regions. Discussions on the conditions for democratic transition and consolidation, or on the various types of regime change, certainly have added to understanding the (short-term) dynamics of these complex political processes. But in recent years several transitologists have admitted that their analytical framework lacks the predictive power that was suggested initially. One of the limitations of the transition literature is that many assumptions are based on a concept of 'formal democracy', a 'procedural minimum', which is certainly desirable but overlooks a number of informal restrictions to the effective exercise of citizenship which are particularly visible in the Latin American context. The use of transition stages implicitly suggests that the 'end stage' of democratisation is reached when 'democracy has become the only game in town'; presumably, here is where the pendulum between authoritarian and democratic rule stops in favour of the latter. This approach has been questioned in this chapter, although it was also argued that the identification of 'transition stages' still can be a valuable tool to monitor qualitative shifts between the state and civil society during processes of democratisation. This could be particularly useful for monitoring democratic transition in those countries where democracy still has to be *constructed*.

A key concept in analysing the dynamics of democratic transition is the sphere of *civil society*, which has become a 'magic' concept since the political transformations in Latin America and Eastern Europe, and which has been used with a variety of meanings. Although often understood as an essentially 'good thing' and often a synonym for 'freedom', it should be carefully defined as it is a complex and ambiguous concept. Civil society is understood as an intermediate associational (public) realm between the state and its citizens, populated by organisations which are separate from the state, enjoy autonomy in relation to the state and are formed voluntarily by members of society to protect or extend their interests and values. Whereas the organisational dimension of civil society is very important (and certainly the most visible property), it is often seen by pluralist analysts as the *only* dimension. However, civil society also has material and ideological dimensions. A 'strong' civil society is therefore not only 'dense' and 'vibrant', but also strong because it is 'equitable' and 'diverse'; in other words 'inclusive'. The changing balance between the state and civil society in stages of democratic transition could be monitored in *political society*, an intermediate realm of actors (political parties, but in early stages also multisectoral coalitions) and institutions (elections, legislatures) mediating, articulating and institutionalising relations between the state and civil society. The quality of democracy is determined by the combined strength of the state and civil society, which becomes explicit in the legitimacy of political society.

In the process of constructing democracy, civil society is strengthened by making it more inclusive and by making the state more accountable to its citizens. Several mechanisms have been identified to strengthen civil and political society 'from below', in which the international context appears to be a key variable. 'Third governments' seem to have been less successful in promoting democracy, especially during the Cold War, while the role of transnational societal actors is believed to have been more important. From the variety of transnational actors that have contributed to democratic transition, the role of 'private aid agencies' has received little or no attention in the transition literature, even though it is often assumed that they have played an important role in providing financial and political resources to subordinate sectors in Southern civil societies. Before looking at the results of these interventions (Chapter 3), a historical and analytical framework of these private aid agencies is required for a better understanding of their relevance during democratic transition.

2 BETWEEN COMPASSION AND SURVIVAL

The Relevance of Private Aid Agencies

Private aid agencies are currently experiencing a peculiar crisis. After a spectacular growth in income and public recognition over many years, by the early 1990s they were faced with stagnating income and growing criticism from academics and development practitioners. Instead of being a solution, they were gradually considered 'part of the problem' (Burnell 1991: 11). Even from within their own ranks, private aid agencies have been subject to a variety of critical analyses about their activities and presumed capacities. The circulation of critical reports increased to such an extent that one of the critics desperately concluded that 'it is a safe guess that more books appeared on NGOs during the first half of the 1990s than was the case over the previous two decades combined' (Smillie 1995a: 4). The peculiar nature of the current crisis among private aid agencies is that their Northern supporters, such as citizens who generously provide private donations, are generally not aware that these agencies (to which they entrust their annual contributions) are in trouble. Although they hear echoes of a fierce debate about aid effectiveness, many citizens seem to be convinced by the images of poor children from the South (either crying or laughing) central to private aid advertising and televised charity campaigns that the 'real crisis' is still 'out there', and not yet resolved. Given their success in the 'charity market', the generous public apparently is convinced that aid delivery mechanisms such as the 'NOVIB method' really are something innovative and effective, instead of a method copied from the early 1960s that was criticised early on as paternalistic. With private aid in crisis, the 'general public' in the North seems to have lost the necessary 'consciousness' that was promoted by Paulo Freire, together with an interest in the prospects for global social change. Or to use a more dramatic expression by Hulme and Edwards (1997: 279): 'NGO constituencies in the North seem no more willing now to make the personal sacrifices and changes in behaviour on which the future of the world depends.'

This chapter examines these two realities of private foreign aid: the reality of good intentions and glossy advertising, versus the reality of decreasing legitimacy and stagnating income. The analysis starts with a short overview of who these 'private aid agencies' actually are and where their resources come from. To understand the private aid crisis of the 1990s, it is necessary to examine the way in which private aid agencies emerged and how they became relevant players in international development. Was it a result of international political developments, or rather increasing income from official funding agencies? The current crisis probably has deeper causes than just a changing international political climate and

stagnating income, as will be shown. Chapter 3 analyses current policies of private
aid agencies that contribute to civil society building, but first those factors need to
be examined that have influenced the strategic choices of private aid agencies and
how these have affected the evolution of their 'mission statements'. An overview
is made of private aid intervention strategies, of which 'civil society building' has
become a central focus in the 1990s. The chapter is rounded off by analysing the
prospects for bridging the gap between the two realities of private foreign aid, or
better, between rhetoric and reality.

2.1 The growth of private foreign aid

Private aid agencies are often referred to as 'international NGOs' or 'Northern
NGOs'. In the previous chapter the point was made that the term 'NGO' is a container concept and therefore often confusing, since to some it means all organisations with a non-governmental character, while others might think of only a
specific subset of these non-state actors. The term 'private voluntary organisation'(PVO), generally used in the United States, also is avoided because the
'voluntary' nature of many of the large multi-million dollar aid agencies could be
questioned. Private aid agencies are 'private' in the sense that they are autonomous
from the state, but 'public' in the sense that they are primarily driven by humanitarian values instead of profits. This distinguishes private aid agencies from 'official'
(governmental) aid agencies and from private business organisations.[1] Private aid
agencies thus could be described as organisations autonomous from the state and
primarily founded to collect funds in the North for development aid delivery in
Southern countries on the basis of a set of humanitarian values originating in
'compassion' and 'altruism'. Secondary tasks of private aid agencies often include
development education, policy research and advocacy in their home societies. This
study focuses especially on the major private aid agencies based in Europe, which
are listed in Table 2.1.
    Private aid agencies gradually have become significant players in the world of
international development aid, particularly over the past three decades. Although
generally not very reliable, one of the few quantitative indicators to illustrate their
relevance is reflected by the amount of aid they spend. This was in the first half of
the 1990s on average US\$ 6.5 billion annually, which is almost ten percent of total
official development assistance (ODA) (OECD 1995a).[2] Aid flows originating from
private agencies have grown faster than bilateral aid disbursements, in particular
since the mid-1980s. Between 1990 and 1994, when ODA increased only by 4 percent, private aid showed an increase of 24 percent. Although official grants have
become an important source of income for many private aid agencies (particularly
in Northern Europe), most private aid still comes from gifts by Northern citizens.
Another indicator for the growing relevance of private foreign aid is the growing
number of organisations that receive grants from Northern governments or from

Table 2.1   *Overview of the largest European private aid agencies*

Private aid agency	Country	Founded	1993 budget in million us$	Dependency on official aid in %
Misereor	Germany	1958	214.5	46
Save the Children	United Kingdom	1919	130.6	49
Secours Catholique	France	1946	126.8	5
OXFAM-UK/I	United Kingdom	1942	118.5	17
EZE	Germany	1962	117.8	90
Danish Refugee Council	Denmark	1956	105.6	98
Brot für die Welt	Germany	1959	99.2	0
CEBEMO	Netherlands	1969	88.3	90
Caritas Switzerland	Switzerland	1901	84.9	51
NOVIB	Netherlands	1956	84.2	71
ICCO	Netherlands	1964	80.0	98
Médecins sans Frontières	Belgium	1980	73.7	71
Deutscher Caritasverband	Germany	1897	73.1[c]	25
Christian Aid	United Kingdom	1942	71.9	30
Welthungerhilfe	Germany	1962	71.1	43
Foster Parents Plan	Netherlands	1975	69.0[b]	0
Danchurchaid	Denmark	1922	62.9	82
Médecins sans Frontières	France	1971	56.2[a]	43
Médecins du Monde	France	1980	53.0	43
Redd Barna	Norway	1946	52.6	41
Red Barnet	Denmark	1945	49.4	91
Concern Worldwide	Ireland	1968	48.6	58
Norwegian People's Aid	Norway	1939	48.5	85
Artsen zonder Grenzen	Netherlands	1984	48.1	56
Action Aid	United Kingdom	1972	47.5	25
Norwegian Church Aid	Norway	1947	46.1[a]	75
Kindernothilfe	Germany	1961	44.6	1
Manos Unidas	Spain	1960	43.8	14
Secours Populaire Francais	France	1946	38.8	34
Médicos sin Fronteras	Spain	1986	36.1	48
Rädda Barnen	Sweden	1919	36.0	39
SOH	Netherlands	1952	35.0	67
Memisa Belgique	Belgium	1988	34.7	40
Mensen in Nood	Netherlands	1914	33.9	34
CCFD	France	1961	33.5[a]	10
Church of Sweden Aid	Sweden	1947	33.4	30
CARE Britain	United Kingdom	1985	33.0	89
HIVOS	Netherlands	1968	31.9	96
CAFOD	United Kingdom	1962	30.0	30
Tear Fund	United Kingdom	1968	30.0	5
Caritas Italiana	Italy	1971	27.5	4
Norwegian Refugee Council	Norway	1952	27.3	84
Diakonia	Sweden	1967	27.0	90
Intermón	Spain	1956	26.7	41
Ibis	Denmark	1966	26.2	99
Memisa	Netherlands	1925	26.1	45
Intercoopération	Switzerland	1982	24.9	100

[a] 1991 budget; [b] 1992 budget; [c] 1994 budget

(NB: Excluded are national ICRC committees, national UNICEF committees, volunteer-sending organisations, endowed foundations, party-related foundations, mission societies and international networks or federations)

Sources: OECD (1990, 1993, 1994, 1996); Sparre (1992); Smillie and Helmich (1993); Freres (1998); and annual reports of agencies.

private donors (citizens) for development purposes: private aid agencies have multi-plied over the past two decades and now over 2,500 agencies exist. The growth of Southern development NGOs has rocketed in the same period from a few hundred in the early 1970s to somewhere between 10,000 and 20,000 in the mid-1990s (Theunis 1992; Riddell and Robinson 1995).

An important reason for the growth in resources managed by private aid agen-cies is the enormous increase in government subsidies available for financing their activities. In nominal terms, official grants to private aid agencies increased from US$ 37 million in 1971 to US$ 2.2 billion in 1992. In the meantime, the share of official assistance to private aid agencies as part of total private aid resources rose from 2 percent to 27 percent (Thérien 1991: 268). This growth continued in the post-Cold War period, mainly because of the sharp rise in (official) emergency assistance that was channelled through private aid agencies in the 1990s. In fact, large private aid agencies that are not dependent upon official aid have become the exception rather than the rule, as Table 2.1 shows. Another reason that private aid resources grew rapidly in the 1980s was the public campaigns to collect private donations for massive relief operations to address emergencies from famines and civil wars, especially in Africa and Eastern Europe. Private fund-raising is still a very important way for private agencies to guarantee a constant flow of income and thus retain a level of autonomy from official donors. Although the levels of dona-tions by private donors appears to have remained stable in real terms, with a ten-dency to diminish, public campaigns have certainly contributed to increasing the profile of private aid agencies. This would have been unthinkable without the revolution in mass communications, especially television, in the last three decades (Salamon 1994). Dramatic images of poverty and deprivation in remote areas are presented instantaneously to the Northern public with strong impact, facilitating agency appeals for private donations.

The rapid growth of grants from official development aid sources reflected the recognition by official donors that private aid agencies had the potential to reach the lowest level income groups in developing countries more effectively and effi-ciently than official aid agencies (Cernea 1988; Fowler 1990). This was praised in the 1980s and often considered a 'comparative advantage' over governmental and multilateral agencies. The advantage stems primarily from the quality of relation-ships that private aid agencies and their partners can establish with poor people, and not so much from the quantity of aid they can handle, as Fowler (1990) and others have pointed out. This underscores the point that the relevance of private aid should actually not be expressed in quantitative terms, even though this value often has been underestimated.[3] It is generally assumed that private aid agencies and their Southern partners have promoted innovative and participatory develop-ment initiatives and have contributed to strengthening civil societies. The Com-mission on Global Governance (1995: 33) recognised that NGOs in North and South 'can offer knowledge, skills, enthusiasm, a non-bureaucratic approach, and grassroots perspectives: attributes that complement the resources of official agencies'. Similar praise has been voiced by Northern governments, the European Union, the United Nations and even by the business sector.

This recognition of private aid agencies has been matched in recent years by a number of independent studies that question the supposed impact of private foreign aid. The overall judgement of these impact studies is that private aid agencies have not always managed to reach the poorest and that their comparative advantages over official aid often has been overstated. However, taking into account their limited impact, it also has been suggested that their work 'is most likely to have an impact when it directly addresses the social relationships that underlie poverty, such as land holding relationships, territorial conflicts, or having greater power to influence the distribution of profits, and which increases the capacities of the poor to tackle these relationships for themselves' (Riddell *et al.* 1995: 79). Even if it was often unintended, as Smillie (1995b) suggests, private aid probably has had its most sustainable impact through supporting changes in these social relationships that, over the long run, have strengthened civil societies in the South. Official donors also acknowledge that private aid agencies and Southern NGOs can only play a marginal and complementary role in eradicating poverty and providing social services to the poorest. Their significance lies in 'their ability to demonstrate participatory models that governments might follow, and to keep pressure on governments (both in North and South) encouraging them to focus more on the human development of the world's poorest people' (UNDP 1993: 89). In other words, 'their importance lies more in making the point that poverty can be tackled rather than tackling it to any large extent'.

2.2 The emergence of private aid agencies

The growth in official subsidies for private aid agencies raises two questions: how has this affected their independence, and to what extent have these agencies been co-opted by the foreign policy objectives of their own governments? Although agendas often were different and sometimes conflicting, Smith (1990) argues that there have been no fundamental ideological or political contradictions between the policies of private aid agencies and their governments. He admits that the object-ives of donors (private or official aid agencies) and recipients of aid (local NGOs, social organisations or Southern governments) often were different, but that enough overlap of interests predominated 'to permit the system to function in a way not threatening to the basic nation state interests of either rich or poor coun-tries' (Smith 1990: 35). He makes a distinction between the agendas of European (and Canadian) private aid agencies that have generally been oriented towards social change, and US private aid agencies, which have worked more closely within the limits of official foreign policy objectives. These differences became visible during the Cold War in politically polarised regions, such as Central America, Southern Africa and East Asia. How to explain this difference in policy orientation between European (and Canadian) and US private aid agencies? Smith argues that these variations in agency policies could be understood as a product of the Cold War. However, this explanation seems too simple, as it does not hold for the 1990s: currently, the convergence between agendas of private and official aid agencies is probably far greater than during the Cold War, whereas contrasts between European and US agencies have remained substantial. How to understand the great variety of private aid agencies and their strategies over time? With the unavoidable danger of generalisations, it could be worthwhile to briefly examine the national and international roots which have made them into key transnational actors of the late twentieth century.

– *The roots of private aid agencies*

Three organisational peaks can be identified in the establishment of private aid agencies: one after each World War, and one in the early 1960s (Lissner 1977). The first two peaks can be explained by the increase in relief activities for victims of these wars, whereas the third was a response to the process of decolonisation. Private aid agencies established prior to the First World War all were part of what Curti (1963: 620) called 'a major philanthropic as well as a religious enterprise', coinciding with colonial expansion and often narrowly cooperating with and partly financed by (colonial) governments. A well-known example is the Swiss *International Committee of the Red Cross* (ICRC), the first major secular relief agency that was formed to help victims of the European wars of the late nineteenth century. National Red Cross societies soon were established in other countries, often with substantial subsidies from their home governments.[4] Another international network emerging in this period in Germany and Switzerland was the *Caritas* group, coordinating relief work of the Catholic Churches.

The outbreak of the First World War was followed by a wave of private initiatives in the United States to send relief aid to the victims in war-torn Europe. Major contributions came from European immigrants in the United States, which remained neutral until 1917. Small committees like the *Commission on Belgian Relief*, headed by (later US President) Herbert Hoover, soon developed into major private relief agencies funnelling millions of dollars to Belgian victims of the war.[5] The US government used these private relief organisations to channel aid to the allies without violating the Geneva conventions on international neutrality. This 'co-funding' of private aid agencies provided practical lessons for future relief programmes in the post-war period, although most of these *ad hoc* committees established during the war by US trade unions, churches or citizens' groups soon disappeared when peace was signed (Bolling 1982). In contrast, private relief agencies emerging in the aftermath of the First World War were generally more durable. Programmes were started to confront post-war famines in Germany and Russia and to contribute to Europe's reconstruction, often in close cooperation with the Red Cross. The *American Friends Service Committee* of the Quakers, for example, was initially attached to the Red Cross and in 1919 started its first independent programme by distributing food to undernourished children in Germany. The British *Save the Children Fund* was set up as a product of a similar programme and this initiative was followed by a chain of sister-organisations in a few dozen countries. Relief activities also focused on post-revolutionary reconstruction in the new Soviet Union, especially by committees of Russian-Jewish immigrants in the United States and by trade unions.[6]

Private donations to US private aid organisations and church groups experienced impressive growth during the inter-war period, mainly directed at disaster relief – such as famines in China – and relief to refugees and orphans in Europe and the Near East. *Foster Parents Plan* was set up in the United Kingdom and the United States to help refugee children in Spain and France. Corporate foundations such as the *Rockefeller Foundation* also became engaged in overseas activities, with huge public health programmes in China. While the US government kept an isolationist position on foreign assistance, US private aid agencies with explicit political agendas were able to play a key role abroad. This happened in Palestine, where Jewish organisations supported Zionist settlers, and in Spain, where activist agencies provided civil and military support to Republican forces in the Spanish Civil War. This situation changed in 1941 when the United States entered the Second World War and all private fund-raising for war relief was integrated into overall US defence policies (Bolling 1982).

In Europe, several private aid agencies emerged right before or during the Second World War. Agencies such as *Norwegian People's Aid* and the Swiss *Arbeitershilfswerk* had their roots in the trade union movement, which had been particularly active during the Spanish Civil War. Others were set up by Protestant churches to help refugees fleeing from Nazi terror (such as the French Ecumenical Aid Service CIMADE) or to provide war relief (the British *Christian Aid*). The British OXFAM started as a 'famine relief committee', an initiative by students and teachers at Oxford University to raise private donations for food and medicines to be sent to the victims of German occupation in Greece (Black 1992). After the war, European private aid agencies were founded particularly in those countries least affected by the war – such as Switzerland, Sweden and Norway – to respond to emergencies similar to those that had occurred during the inter-war period.[7] However, the geographical direction soon shifted away from post-war Europe. Decolonisation and the outbreak of the Cold War rapidly influenced the orientation of private foreign aid. It was at this point that European and US private aid strategies started to develop in different directions.

Soon after the Second World War, European relief agencies started to focus on emergencies outside Europe, especially in (former) colonial areas. Two institutions accelerated the growth of European private aid agencies in the 1950s: the United Nations and the churches. Several UN agencies involved private agencies in their relief operations and many European agencies emerged (indirectly) out of UN programmes.[8] The other incentive to create new European aid agencies came from the churches. The process of decolonisation had changed the character of traditional missionary work, and European churches had to reshape their activities in former colonies. With the emergence of national churches in the newly independent states, a distinction developed between ecclesiastical support to sister-churches and support to church-related development activities. In the Catholic Church this inter-church support was coordinated by *Caritas International*, whereas separate Catholic agencies – such as the German *Misereor* and the Swiss *Fastenopfer* – became responsible for development-oriented assistance. A similar division of tasks was implemented in the early 1960s within the World Council of Churches, the international body of the Protestant churches, in which new agencies such as *Brot für die Welt* (Germany) and *Diakonia* (Sweden) would play an innovating role in rethinking the purpose and methods of development aid (OECD 1988).

A key difference with US private aid agencies was that the vast majority of European private aid agencies emerged during the era of decolonisation, while most US agencies had been established earlier. Founded as war relief agencies, they traditionally worked closely with the US government and often became instruments of US Cold War policies. Food aid became an important part of US private aid as a result of the Korean War. US food surplus reserves had to be exported to prevent a drop in domestic food prices, and a special law was enacted to distribute this surplus abroad through US private aid agencies. As a result, food aid still is the major function of large US agencies such as CARE and *Catholic Relief Services*. Another difference between European and US private agencies was the role of official aid contributions. US private aid agencies in the 1950s were already receiving small official grants for technical assistance and relief activities, whereas European governments started these 'co-financing programmes' only a decade later, but with more substantial amounts and less tied to official foreign policy objectives. The third 'peak' of newly emerging private aid agencies in the 1960s was very much determined by these official aid programmes.

The independence of poor 'Third World' nations stimulated new theorising on development and foreign aid, in which traditional short-term relief assistance was criticised for not tackling the causes of poverty. Decolonisation in Africa and Asia was reaching a peak with more than eighty new independent nations trying to survive economically amidst fierce competition between the superpowers.[9] Economic 'modernisation' became a dominant paradigm in the Western world, assuming that 'development' would occur as a result of rapid economic growth, leading to benefits that would eventually 'trickle down' to the poor. Moreover, promoting development and alleviating poverty with aid programmes was considered to be the most promising way to stop the spread of communism in the newly independent nations (Bolling 1982). In the 1960s, private agencies were gradually shifting their orientation from a relief and charity approach towards promoting longer term benefits for the 'poor overseas', especially visible in the FAO-sponsored *Freedom from Hunger Campaign* (FFHC) that started in 1960. Over five years, national committees raised private donations for 'structural' development projects, making use of the well-known Chinese proverb 'Give a man a fish, and you feed him for a day; teach him to fish, and you feed him for life'. The campaign was a turning point for many private aid agencies. It introduced the use of educational materials at schools and shifted the orientation from short-term relief in emergency situations towards attacking the root causes of hunger and poverty. Out of the national fund-raising committees several new private aid agencies were created such as the French CCFD, the Spanish *Manos Unidas* and the British CAFOD.

The United Nations and the churches thus played a catalysing role in the emergence of European private aid agencies. However, a third and crucial catalyst was the creation of special ministries for development cooperation, which as part of their official aid programmes also provided small subsidies to private aid agencies.[10] Initially, the focus was on technical assistance and volunteer-sending programmes, following the example of the *Peace Corps* created by the Kennedy administration. But private aid agencies soon also received 'matching grants' for basic human needs programmes (food, health and education), which were considered complementary to official aid programmes. With their expertise in grassroots development and their broad networks of useful contacts in developing countries, private aid agencies had something to offer to the new ministries of development aid. Moreover, governments considered private agencies also as important instruments on the domestic front to broaden national constituencies and expand support for development aid. In Germany and the Netherlands, subsidies to private aid agencies were distributed according to the main religious and ideological currents of the society. The German churches created special agencies (the Catholic KZE and the Protestant EZE) to administer these government grants. Political parties also were authorised to receive matching grants for support to Third World trade unions and cooperatives via party-related foundations such as the Social Democratic *Friedrich Ebert Stiftung* and the Christian Democratic *Konrad Adenauer Stiftung*. The Dutch 'co-financing programme' distributed matching grants for development assistance among special private aid agencies established by the Catholic (CEBEMO) and Protestant (ICCO) churches, while smaller shares were allocated to the secular aid agencies NOVIB and HIVOS. These German and Dutch agencies that were founded in response to official co-financing programmes would later become the largest private aid agencies in Europe.

By the late 1960s, several private aid agencies emerged with a more political (often anti-imperialist) development discourse, such as the British *Action Aid* and the Danish WUS (later *Ibis*),[11] often rooted in the radicalising student movement or progressive currents within the churches. These agencies challenged the prevailing optimism regarding development aid as a tool to combat poverty, since UN targets for economic growth and development aid had not been met in the decade. On the contrary, poverty had increased substantially and reports on famines, civil wars and political exclusion dominated the news from the South.[12] The optimistic vision of development as a linear process of economic growth (following the Western model) that could be enhanced by development assistance, was increasingly challenged by the *Group of 77* (developing countries) and their supporters in the North.[13] Third World intellectuals such as Iván Illich and Paulo Freire criticised top-down approaches of Western development bureaucrats; they introduced the notion of 'self-help' and pointed at the need to raise consciousness among the poor. These ideas were 'trickling down' in Northern aid agencies, and stimulated the search for alternative development models. Although the growth of newly founded private aid agencies had slowed down by the early 1970s, a 'golden era' would start for private foreign aid.

– *The golden era of private foreign aid*

Up to the 1970s private foreign aid had been rather irrelevant in terms of financial turnover. Private aid flows accounted only for about one percent of total aid flows to developing countries. Also in terms of influencing policy debates and creating a public image in their home societies, private aid agencies had been marginal players. This was to change substantially in the next two decades. By the end of the 1980s, private aid was generally recognised as an indispensable part of development assistance initiatives. Together with Southern development NGOs, private aid agencies were even considered to be 'significant, if not major, actors in the broader efforts to reduce poverty' (Riddell and Robinson 1995: 1). How to explain this rapid increase in relevance and recognition? Four sets of related developments will be examined below: (i) a substantial increase in private aid income, (ii) a stronger domestic profile of private aid, (iii) the rise of a Southern NGO sector, and (iv) a stronger political engagement of European private aid agencies, generated by a polarising Cold War environment in the South.

The growing relevance of private aid agencies since the mid-1970s has above all been a result of the impressive growth of their financial resources in a relatively short period of time. Total income for private aid agencies increased from US$ 860 million in 1970 to US$ 4 billion in 1989, which equalled 12 percent of total development aid flows to the South. With income from private donations by the general public constant, and even temporarily dropping in real terms in the mid-1970s, the increase came entirely from governmental contributions to private aid agencies. In 1970, official aid only contributed a marginal 1.5 percent to private agency budgets, increasing gradually to 7 percent in 1974, and rapidly climbing to over 40 percent in 1980.[14] A decade later, major private aid agencies in Canada, Belgium, Germany, Norway, Denmark, Sweden, Italy and the Netherlands derived more than 70 percent of their total income from official aid sources (ODI 1995). Why did governments decide to give so much credit to private aid agencies, at a time when private aid income from public fund-raising was stagnating? One reason was related to an emerging crisis of legitimacy of official aid agencies in the 1970s. In Europe, economic growth was stagnating and the oil shocks diverted attention for international cooperation towards national concerns. In the United States, the Nixon administration faced mounting opposition from Congress, which was unwilling to approve new military assistance packages for the war in Vietnam. Furthermore, official development aid programmes were increasingly criticised for being unable to tackle the root causes of poverty, and surely (as Vietnam had shown) unable to stop communism. Official aid programmes had been directed too much at capital-intensive or infrastructural works, with little 'trickling down' impact on the poor. This growing pessimism (nowadays it would be called 'compassion fatigue') was reflected in the adjustment of the aid growth target of the First Development Decade from 1 percent to 0.7 percent of GNP (Smith 1990).

Apparently, critique of official aid performance provided private aid agencies with the benefit of the doubt; they were considered an attractive channel for foreign aid in a period when foreign aid was losing credibility (Bolling 1982). A central concern was how to improve the effectiveness of development projects, for example by more active participation of beneficiaries in the design and imple-mentation of projects. 'Self-help promotion' became one of the buzzwords of the Basic Human Needs (BHN) strategy, formulated by the ILO in the mid-1970s to improve poverty alleviation policies of official donors. However, the BHN-strategy often was imposed upon communities without serious consultation, and it was considered to be more effective if it was implemented by private aid agencies and Southern development NGOs. The assumption was that these possessed two important comparative advantages over official aid: they were better able to reach the poorest sectors at a grassroots level with a higher degree of participation by beneficiaries. Moreover, this appeared to be a cheaper way to harvest some success in the poor performance record of official aid. An additional reason for the increase in official grants to European private aid agencies was the success of their lobbying efforts towards governments to increase official aid budgets and to expand existing (and create new) co-funding schemes.[15] This all was facilitated by a recovering world economy in the late 1970s. Even stagnating income from private donations started to recover by 1979 with large fund-raising campaigns for Cambodia and East Africa.

A second development that could explain the growing relevance of private aid agencies was their more pronounced domestic profile after the mid-1970s. Activ-ities in home societies were upgraded in three areas: development education, public fund-raising campaigns, and policy oriented research and lobbying. Awareness raising among the public on the causes of world poverty had been an activity ever since the *Freedom from Hunger Campaign* of the early 1960s. But new theories on development also pointed at the need for structural changes in the industrialised world in order to combat poverty. It was argued that the problem was neither solved with economic growth, nor with sending increased aid resources overseas. Development education to influence public thinking on development issues, often combined with public appeals, became an integrated focus of private aid pro-grammes. Agencies created special departments for development education to produce magazines, films and other educational materials for schools, churches and community groups. This work was often financed by special budget lines from development aid ministries, particularly in Northern Europe and Canada. Development education on this larger scale soon became a controversial enterprise, as the messages that were transmitted often contained explicit critique of capitalism and Western life styles. This combination of development education and political campaigns contributed to politicising the profile of private foreign aid (Burnell 1991).

Large public fund-raising campaigns, in which television broadcasting played a substantial role, were another new element contributing to a stronger profile for private aid agencies. The revolution in communications delivered the reality of Third World poverty directly to a growing number of Northern living rooms (Salamon 1994). These campaigns generally focused on emergency situations, as these provided broad press coverage and dramatic images that appealed to a general public and generated massive inflows of private donations. The most successful experience with this type of fund-raising actually was developed by new *ad hoc* aid organisations. During and after the Africa campaigns of 1984-85, *Live Aid* and *Band Aid* introduced worldwide broadcasted television shows as a modern and very effective method to collect private donations for emergency relief.[16] It particularly mobilised young people and had a long-term impact on private giving to private aid agencies and on their collaboration with media and private business (Zivetz *et al.* 1991). However, these campaigns also were criticised for reinforcing a simplistic image about the causes of hunger and human deprivation and their possible solutions. Ironically, it demonstrated that decades of development aid had in fact failed to prevent these human disasters and that relief was often used as a political weapon by governments and parties involved in disasters and conflicts. As a result of the Africa campaign, official allocations to disaster relief increased and became a permanent and substantial source of income for private aid agencies.

Beside raising funds and awareness, private aid agencies also became more politically involved in their home societies by pressuring their governments on a variety of aid-related issues. The most important obviously was the level of official development aid budgets, and particularly the share channelled to private aid agencies. Development aid ministries actually welcomed this watchdog role as it created a constituency helpful in maintaining or increasing budgets for development aid (Clark 1991). Effective lobbying also contributed to the establishment of special official funds for development education activities by organisations in Northern civil societies. The first coordinated international lobbying activities of private aid agencies tried to influence agendas and decision-making at international meetings, such as Stockholm (1972) and Rome (1974), although with limited results (Van Rooy 1997). Later lobbying campaigns tried to push governments to adopt sharper positions on international issues, such as the boycott of South African Apartheid or the rescheduling of international debt.

A third development that increased the relevance of private aid agencies was the explosive growth of Southern NGOs beginning in the mid-1970s. Thousands of new development NGOs were founded in Latin America and Asia, and to a lesser extent in Africa, although reliable figures are difficult to find. Smillie (1995a) points out that Southern NGOs came up so quickly and suddenly in the late 1970s that two groundbreaking studies in this period on private aid – Lissner (1977) and Sommer (1977) – did not even mention the existence of Southern NGOs.[17] The emergence of a Southern NGO-community initially was a product of post-colonial civil society building, but was increasingly boosted by growing Northern private aid resources combined with changing perceptions on the role of local organisations.[18] Private aid agencies from Europe and Canada started to scale down their local field offices and 'operational programmes' to provide a larger role for Southern intermediaries. It was believed that local beneficiaries had to participate more directly in the implementation of aid programmes, in which new concepts such as 'self-reliance' and 'empowerment' were surfacing. This changing perspective required that private aid agencies stimulate the formation of independent local (intermediary) organisations that were able to plan and implement development projects at the grassroots with external aid resources (Brodhead *et al.* 1988). In other words, the emergence of Southern NGOs suddenly provided additional legitimacy to the existence of Northern private aid agencies.

A final element that could explain the new opportunities for private aid agencies was the polarised global political climate of the 1970s and early 1980s. Conflicts in the South, as a product of either internal political instability or post-colonial nation building, often escalated into ideological confrontations between the superpowers as part of Cold War rivalry. After the war in Vietnam, this occurred for example in Chile (1973), Israel (1973), Angola (1975), Cambodia (1979) and Nicaragua (1981). European governments in this period were reluctant to become directly involved in these conflicts and usually tried to play a mediating role. Particularly from the mid-1970s, when Social Democratic governments came to power in many European countries, foreign policies started to divert from the traditional Atlantic alliance agenda. European governments opted for a more independent position and tried to counterbalance US hegemony, particularly in Latin America (Evers 1982). Increased European attention for development issues was echoed at international fora, often within the framework of the Socialist International. An example was the 'Brandt Commission', which (despite its considerable rhetoric) called for structural transformations in the international economic system to overcome poverty in the South. These ideas were more easily accepted in Europe than in the United States, where the Vietnam trauma had fuelled the fear of communist threats. The different political environments widened the gap among the policy orientations of private aid agencies: US agencies depoliticised, whereas European and Canadian agencies implicitly assumed more political roles (Smith 1990).

In the aftermath of the Vietnam war, US private aid agencies generally continued with their intervention policies biased toward relief. While agency incomes were growing due to increased official funding, over half of this official support was granted in the form of food or food-related aid. US private aid agencies tended to avoid controversial issues in public education and lobbying activities, as it negatively affected their income from private donations.[19] US citizens, it was believed, were more willing to give donations to be used for immediate relief, than for social or political change abroad. The US Congress issued new legislation to increase co-funding opportunities for private aid agencies, while urging the agencies to stick to humanitarian assistance. European and Canadian private aid agencies evolved in an opposite direction. Growing income from official funding was allocated to longer term development objectives with more explicit political components, such as empowerment strategies for the poor and support for organisations linked to democratic opposition movements, often under the banner of 'solidarity aid'. European private aid agencies were generally critical of US foreign policy towards the South, and actively supported domestic campaigns against US interventionism in Central America, Southern Africa and Southeast Asia.

How to explain this 'politicisation' of European private aid in the late 1970s? One possible set of explanations is related to the differences in political culture between Europe and the United States, as Sommer (1977) and others have pointed out. European agencies were more closely connected to domestic networks of activist movements, and agency staff often were personally involved in solidarity committees or in the peace movement. US agencies avoided close links with advocacy groups challenging US foreign policy. Smith (1990) also points at a broader awareness of Europeans and Canadians of the root causes of poverty. But these arguments do not explain why this politicisation occurred in the late 1970s, and not earlier. A second set of explanations should therefore take two elements into account: the particular position of Europe in that period of the Cold War and the conditions for official grants to private aid agencies. Public opinion in Europe was preoccupied with the offensive character of US foreign policy, in which Europe figured as the battleground in the preparations for the next World War. Active US involvement in 'low intensity' conflicts in several areas of the South, it was perceived, could very well spark off a nuclear confrontation with the Soviet Union on European soil. European governments tacitly supported opposition movements in these conflicts, often using private aid agencies as a temporary and alternative aid channel to bypass authoritarian or incompetent governments. This happened with opposition movements against Marcos in the Philippines, Pinochet in Chile, the Apartheid-regime in South Africa, and with the authoritarian governments in Central America. Private aid agencies thus acted as informal diplomatic channels for European governments during the last decade of the Cold War.[20]

In sum, the growing international relevance of private aid agencies since the late 1970s was primarily caused by the rapid growth of income from official funding sources. Three additional elements contributed to make the 1980s the 'golden era' of European private aid agencies. The first was a more highly articulated domestic presence due to development education programmes and large public fund-raising campaigns in a period when doubts were rising about the effectiveness of official aid. This political leverage was used to pressure national governments to increase aid budgets and to shift foreign policies from an East-West to a North-South orientation. A second element was the rapid growth of Southern NGOs, offering private aid agencies a new set of 'natural' intermediaries in Southern civil societies. These local development NGOs were considered ideal channels for participatory and people-centred development interventions, with many comparative advantages over traditional official aid channels. A third element enhancing the role of (European and Canadian) private aid agencies was the polarised climate during the last decade of the Cold War, which gave them a unique function in contributing to civil society building in polarised domestic settings. As a result of foreign policy constraints by US allies, private aid agencies were performing a key role in a transnational 'informal diplomacy', especially in societies ruled by authoritarian regimes. By the late 1980s, private aid agencies and their Southern allies were considered to be a potential 'countervailing power' (Thérien 1991), performing a major role as agents for social change in the South as part of 'chains of solidarity' (Padrón 1988). The end of the Cold War and the new hegemony of market-oriented aid strategies would rapidly reverse these prospects in the 1990s.

— *The post-Cold War identity crisis*

By the early 1990s the tide was turning for private aid agencies. An indication that the flourishing period of the 1980s had come to an end was the stagnating growth of agency income. The turning point was 1993, when total official development aid (ODA) dropped to 0.3 percent of GNP, reaching its lowest level in twenty years (Randel and German 1995). The downward tendency of ODA in subsequent years suggested that 'compassion fatigue' had now become a serious issue. With many private aid agencies depending largely on official aid contributions, this was alarming news. But something more fundamental was happening to private aid agencies, something which had not really occurred in previous years: serious doubts were surfacing about their legitimacy. Within a few years, a considerable flow of critical reports on private foreign aid was circulating, followed by public denouncements by insiders and agency staff about the poor performance and lack of efficiency of private aid agencies.[21] A sudden increase in internal discussions and special workshops with project partners, often followed by profound reorganisations, suggested that private aid agencies were entering a serious 'mid-life crisis' (Bossuyt 1993).[22] One observer wrote: 'Northern NGOs have a growing identity crisis in relation to their increasingly effective Southern counterparts, most of whom want money rather than interference' (Smillie 1993: 14). Others pointed at 'the dangers involved in the processes of NGO growth and scaling up, the increasing dependence of many NGOs on official funds and the consequences of becoming the "favoured child" of donor agencies' (Edwards and Hulme 1994: 1). What had happened to private aid agencies after the collapse of communism? And what had so suddenly caused this identity crisis?

Although initially assumed so, the end of the Cold War probably was not the real cause of this crisis. But it did play a catalysing role in exposing some problematic tendencies for private aid agencies that had been covered up by the boom of the 1980s. One tendency enhanced by the collapse of communism was that the state-centred development model was discredited. In the early 1990s, a broad consensus was reached among the major development institutions about post-Cold War development policies. This so-called 'Washington consensus' promoted neo-liberal economic policies in combination with liberal democracy and 'good govern-ment' as the new orthodoxy for development interventions in the South and in Eastern Europe. The 'new policy agenda' by Northern donors prioritised market-led growth, a reduced and more efficient role for the state and a prominent role for 'civil society' in the implementation of this agenda (Robinson 1994). The implica-tions for private aid agencies were substantial. One was the discovery of the virtues of civil society by major Northern official donors, such as the World Bank, who were searching for ways to reduce state interference in the market. Southern NGOs were considered to be ideal channels for implementing this new policy agenda due to their assumed ability to reach the poor more cheaply and more effectively than governments. 'Direct funding' from official aid agencies to Southern development NGOs had been increasing already in the late 1980s, but the rapid rise in the early 1990s started to become a serious concern to Northern private aid agencies (Riddell and Bebbington 1995). Aside from the problematic interpretation of 'civil society' by these official donors and the risk of co-optation (topics that will be discussed later), the implication for private aid agencies was that they had lost their privileges as principal donors of organisations in Southern civil societies. At best, they were confined to play a role as intermediaries with little autonomy from official donors, who basically supported Southern NGOs in maintaining political stability in poorer parts of the world, as 'ladles in the global soup kitchen' as Fowler (1994) remarked.[23]

The other implication of the market-based approach as part of the neoliberal 'counter-revolution' was the pressure on private aid agencies to 'produce' better results of their development interventions at lower costs.[24] With their increased dependency on official aid resources, most private aid agencies had no other choice than to obey this directive for more efficiency, and more visible and quantifiable output. While the arguments about assumed comparative advantages of private aid agencies had been questioned already a decade earlier quite sharply by Tendler (1982) as 'articles of faith', it was now a matter of institutional survival to behave as 'for-profits' in a non-profit environment. As a result, many agencies entered a period of thorough reorganisation, supported by external management consultants who introduced modern assessment and marketing methods developed in the private sector (Sogge and Zadek 1996). However, these strategic planning and project management tools to steer and control short-term processes with measur-able outputs often created internal tensions, as they ran contrary to the longer term participatory approaches that private aid agencies had been promoting in the past.[25] A survey among British private aid agencies concluded that 'these tools may well meet the needs of donors for the efficient disbursement of funds better than the needs of partners-beneficiaries for taking control, participating and setting their own agendas for tackling social change' (Wallace 1997: 45).

The explosive growth of humanitarian emergencies since the mid-1980s (particularly since the 1984-85 Ethiopian famine) actually reinforced this tendency to produce short-term measurable outputs. Governments spectacularly increased their official aid allocations for emergency relief by over 500 percent in ten years time, of which large amounts were channelled to private aid agencies for humanitarian relief in Africa and Eastern Europe.[26] As official resources for structural development interventions were decreasing or stagnating, the relative share that private aid agencies received for channelling emergency relief thus was becoming more important. This qualitative shift away from development activities appeared to be an attractive way to respond to pressures from official donors for showing more immediate results of private aid interventions. The chain of emergency situations of the early 1990s not only provided opportunities for quick results with relief aid delivery, but also facilitated a new boom in private fund-raising appeals, as 'fund-raising around highly visible humanitarian crises raises more money at lower cost than any other form of advertising or publicity' (Natsios 1996: 71). Although emergency fund-raising was indeed lucrative, the results of relief interventions often were counter-productive: 'relief operations have often contributed to the conflict dynamic, and supported the growth of war economies', according to Duffield *et al.* (1994: 227). They add: 'the sharp moral dilemmas raised by such situations are often lost in the high-profile media attention given to food deliveries. These images in turn are often used to sustain support for such interventions among Northern constituencies'.[27] In other words, despite a growth in income of 'easy money', short-term emergency relief generally was a step backwards for private aid agencies: it increased competition (instead of enhancing coordination) and shifted attention away from less visible but more durable and participatory longer term development interventions (Smillie 1993). Moreover, as the boom of emergency situations came to an end in the mid-1990s, fund-raising from private donations through emergency appeals became less frequent and proved to be only a temporary way to solve the problem of declining income of private aid agencies.

The crisis of stagnating income of the early 1990s was accompanied by another, and more fundamental, crisis: the assumed comparative strengths of private aid agencies to combat poverty were questioned from several sides. This 'crisis of legitimacy' was already visible during emergency situations, which made clear that 'attempts by international NGOs to support the weak have generally failed' (Duffield 1993: 148). This negative assessment was fuelled by a number of (relatively independent) impact studies, reaching rather critical conclusions about private aid performance. For example, a Swedish study concluded that private aid agencies seldom reached the very poorest, and that 'they should not claim to have the degree of poverty impact that they often claim to have – in most cases, they simply do not have this impact' (Riddell *et al.* 1995: 79). Similar doubts were raised about the cost-effectiveness of private aid agencies, about their capacity to innovate development practices, about effectively addressing gender balances, and about the prospects for financial sustainability of their interventions.[28] Although some of these critical findings were echoed in the mass media, most studies only circulated in restricted policy circles and did not really damage the positive public image of private aid agencies. However, as the majority had been commissioned by official aid donors, the general message for private aid agencies was clear: project planning, evaluation methods, organisational efficiency, accountability and overall performance had to be improved to prevent future cuts from official aid donors.

It was in fact the first serious challenge to private aid legitimacy since the start of the 'golden era', underlining that they no longer enjoyed the 'security of obscurity' as marginal actors in the development business (Fowler and Biekart 1996). By the late 1990s private aid agencies were under fire from various sides: from official donors (demanding measurable results and efficiency), from Southern partner organisations (demanding less paternalism and more 'direct funding' from official donors), from (some) Northern private donors (demanding transparency), and from their own staff which was squeezed between the demands of institutional growth and efficiency (more turnover with less costs at shorter terms) and developmental impact (which had proven to be expensive and rather slow). The resulting identity crisis that struck private aid agencies in the early 1990s thus appeared to be a crisis of legitimacy concerning the assumed comparative advantages of private aid over official aid, visible in declining income. How was this crisis affecting the future prospects for private aid agencies?

The optimistic view, generally represented by agency managers, maintains that it is a matter of improving organisational efficiency, introducing systematic evaluation and monitoring systems, and engaging in more sophisticated fund-raising. In this view, private aid agencies, although under pressure to show this, continue to hold many comparative advantages over official aid agencies. Despite temporary setbacks in levels of fund-raising income, they will even become more important as official aid is diminishing and increasingly privatised. Critics are overly emphasising failures of private aid interventions, while successes generally only receive marginal media attention. The optimists point at the persistence of poverty and emergencies and presume that private aid agencies will acquire new tasks in transnational civil society building and in counterbalancing the social effects of market-led development.[29]

The pessimistic view, on the other hand, argues that private aid agencies (after their flourishing period of the 1980s) are now getting their backlash and have to accept that stronger Southern civil society sectors have taken over their main functions. This view, held by several 'aid watchers' and development practitioners, considers the fall in agency income as a structural problem of decreasing legitimacy in the post-Cold War era which is not going to be solved by improved management and fund-raising.[30] The pessimists consider the ongoing dependence of private aid agencies on official aid as a dead-end strategy, as it will further diminish their autonomy and increase the risk of being co-opted by market-led development strategies. The alternative, accepting the reality of smaller budgets but more freedom to operate as transnational actors in dynamic solidarity networks, requires a transformation process that few agencies are likely to choose: it is a risky trajectory and will possibly affect their institutional growth.

Although the future will be the judge of these scenarios, by the late 1990s only a minority of private aid agencies seems to have accepted that they are approaching the end of their life cycle and that cosmetic adaptations are not enough to overcome the crisis. This crisis was caused by a number of developments, both internal and external to these agencies, such as the crisis of state-centred development models and the rise of a neoliberal donor agenda, stagnating income from official donors and a qualitative shift of emphasis from development to relief, also as a result of a temporary rise in private fund-raising for emergency aid. On top of these issues, doubts about performance and comparative advantages underlined the end of the golden era for private foreign aid. The outcome of the current identity crisis of private aid agencies will probably depend on their capacity to face the new reality of declining income and legitimacy. This means that they have to accept that several fundamental choices have to be made, which may possibly have serious implications for current missions, organisational cultures, strategies and alliances.

2.3 A balance of private aid intervention strategies

The identity crisis of private aid agencies in the 1990s is probably not sufficiently explained by only pointing at lower income from fund-raising and declining legitimacy. These are merely symptoms of a deeper problem that was described by Edwards (1996a: 4) as 'an increasing tension between *institutional imperatives* and *developmental imperatives* – between what the agency *thinks* it has to do to survive in an increasingly difficult environment, and what it *should* be doing to fulfil its mission statement'.[31] Developmental imperatives of private aid agencies are, for example, to contribute to an empowerment of (and coordination between) excluded sectors in civil society and guarantee that interventions are financially sustainable in the long run in order to avoid external dependencies and loss of autonomy. Institutional imperatives of private aid agencies are essentially to survive as an institution, to guarantee a constant growth of income through fund-raising and visibility in the 'charity market', or by intensifying policy advocacy to secure a growing share of income from official aid resources. Institutional imperatives emphasise competition, short-term results, hierarchy, secrecy and a Northern bias, whereas developmental imperatives generally demand the opposite: coordination, longer term results, partnership, transparency and a Southern (or at least a North-South) bias.

Private aid agency policies are guided by both imperatives, although developmental imperatives are generally stressed to the outside world. Initial goals of private aid agencies were not based on maximising power or profits, but on humanitarian values, often summarised in the term 'altruism'.[32] Some agencies even had more explicit humanitarian missions from the beginning, such as social reform, or more explicit political missions such as 'international solidarity'. But for most agencies the principle of altruism has been central to mobilising Northern resources to support the Southern poor. Lissner (1977) observed that altruistic intentions, when put into practice, imply that agencies have to make choices. One of the central dilemmas for private aid agencies is to find a balance between maximising their income without compromising their ideological or altruistic principles: how can they find a balance between institutional and developmental imperatives? This section will examine those elements that shape or determine this central choice for private aid agencies, and how choices are translated into a workable strategy to pursue the goals that agencies have set themselves.

– Tension in the 'aid chain'

The balance between institutional and developmental imperatives tends to shift towards institutional imperatives in periods of financial pressure, which is generally a sign that the legitimacy of private aid agencies is under question. This is probably what happened in the 1990s. Not surprisingly, (private) aid agencies prefer institutional survival over keeping with their mission, and often downplay the negative consequences this might have for their ideological principles and their 'partners' in the South. One example is the contradictory message implicit in fund-raising campaigns. Institutional imperatives urge agencies to compete among themselves with simplified messages emphasising chaos and disaster, and promising quick results.[33] However, developmental imperatives require coordination and clarity about the complexity of development interventions that only generate (often invisible) results in the long run. Another example is the institutional imperative of maximising turnover, keeping control over budgets and centralising decision-making, whereas developmental imperatives state that project partners should become financially self-reliant and decision-making transparent and based on 'partnership'.

   This permanent tension between institutional and developmental imperatives is one of the key mechanisms to understanding the policy choices of private aid agencies. It explains why there is generally a considerable gap between rhetoric and reality. To understand the strategic choices of private aid agencies, and to analyse their struggle in order to find a balance between institutional survival and developmental impact, it could be helpful to examine those factors that determine strategies in the field. To illustrate the complex dynamics that determine their choices, a simplified diagram of the so-called 'private aid chain' is provided in Figure 2.2. It schematically shows how private aid agencies and their Northern constituencies are connected to their Southern 'partners' in a downward directed chain, in which aid resources are delivered through a number of intermediaries to the ultimate beneficiaries (which could be broadly labelled the 'Southern poor').[34] Each actor in this 'private aid chain' is part of a system of mutual dependencies: the system does not function when one of the actors in the chain fails to deliver.

As every single aid intervention is unique, private aid chains will take many forms and have different strengths and variable outputs, all of which are contingent upon local circumstances. However, aid chains have in common that interventions (and the resulting outputs) are determined by strategic choices at the top of the aid chain. These choices are influenced by a number of variables, such as for example the ideological orientations of private aid agencies. Protestant private aid agencies such as ICCO and *Diakonia* generally prefer to work with local church-related organisations, who in turn aim to deliver benefits to a particular sector of civil society with objectives matching their particular confessional principles. Secular

Figure 2.2 *Actors and aid flows in a simplified private aid chain*

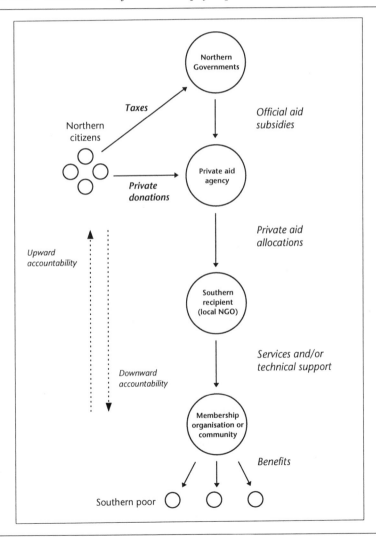

private aid agencies with roots in the labour movement, such as *Norwegian People's Aid*, are more inclined to support Southern counterparts rooted in popular movements struggling for radical social change. Not only have ideological or religious roots shaped aid agency strategies, but also organisational cultures in donor countries. Private aid agencies in the United States emerged out of a culture of private responsibility and rejection of government control, whereas Northern European private aid agencies are rooted in a culture of corporatism working closely in a consensual relation with the state (Smillie 1993). These elements – which are indicative for the identity of private aid agencies and for a particular Northern constituency or culture from which they emerged – say little however about the strategy choices in the field which are generally determined by a number of other key variables that can affect the balance between institutional and developmental imperatives. Two variables are further explored below, as they appear to be of crucial importance: the origin of private aid resources and accountability systems. A third variable, outputs of private aid agencies and the way their performance is assessed, is examined in Chapter 3.

A first variable to explain choices made by private aid agencies is the origin of their financial resources.[35] Private agencies may get their income from three different sources: gifts made by the general public, state grants financed by general taxation, or self-financing through investment or private enterprise. To each of these sources a set of conditions and expectations is attached, which in turn can determine agency strategies. Fowler (1992: 11) observes that 'each source also has a different dynamics in terms of growth or shrinkage in volume', which in turn shapes the nature of an agency, how it operates and what it achieves. The oldest source of income for private agencies is philanthropic giving, a form of moral support (often Christian inspired) from the upper classes to help the unprivileged in the colonies. Most agencies initially started with collecting this type of charitable donation from the richer segments of the general public. When official aid programmes started in the 1960s and 1970s, agency incomes from private donations were complemented by grants from governments. The proportion of income from official sources has increased steadily over the last two decades, as was shown earlier. In the 1980s, several German and Dutch agencies even became entirely dependent upon official grants. Private aid income also can be derived from the market economy. In the United States several agencies were specially created by corporate business as endowed foundations, such as the Ford and Rockefeller foundations. In contrast, funding in Europe provided by market-generated profits generally came from 'fair trading' of imported products from the South, or from charity shops. A new area of commercial fund-raising that emerged in the 1990s is public gambling, in which revenues of national lotteries are automatically transferred to private aid agencies. Only a minority of agencies depend on just one of these three income categories. In Europe, most common is 'co-funding', a combination of private donations matched by official funding, while market-based funding is still rather insignificant.

The proportional dependency on either private donations or state subsidies determines the operational manoeuvring space of private agencies. Private agencies with a high dependency ratio on state funding (say more than fifty percent) are vulnerable to official policy changes and therefore more likely to be actively involved in policy dialogue with governments and parliaments. Examples are the major private aid agencies in Germany, the Netherlands, Canada, Belgium, Denmark, Sweden, Norway, and to a lesser extent the United Kingdom. For the same reason they are also more supportive of maintaining high budgets for official development aid through public campaigns and development education. Smillie (1993: 29) is probably right when he says that 'official development assistance owes at least part of its existence in many countries to the public support base created by NGOs'. The other side of the coin is that dependency on state subsidies adds to the pressures on private aid agencies to accept policy priorities of official agencies which might run contrary to their own priorities (Elliot 1987a). In short, agencies with a high dependency ratio on state funding are better able to engage in longer term planning, and thus can make longer term commitments to Southern partners. But the price that has to be paid for this financial security can be a loss of autonomy in policy planning and priority setting.

Private aid agencies that derive their income from the general public are constrained by conditions imposed upon them by the fierce competition of the 'charity market'. One condition is the need to 'shorten the perceptual difference between giver and beneficiary' (Fowler 1992: 14), which explains why child sponsorship agencies often belong to the most successful fund-raisers. Another related condition is that they must invest a considerable amount of money in campaigning and publicity, which implies large overheads, sometimes up to thirty percent of total income. This is three to four times the average overhead of agencies dependent on state funding. An additional point was already mentioned: agencies collecting private donations have a tendency to over-simplify the problems of development to the public. Making use of images of starving babies, sometimes referred to as 'aid-pornography', often goes against actual development strategies of agencies in the field. This is still a rather painful and unresolved dilemma for many agencies that need to increase income from private donations. It shows that the reach of development education is still limited: 'many of the world's best NGOs have moved away from concepts of philanthropy, welfare and social care, towards ideas of sustainable development and community participation. But they have not taken their donors and the broader public with them' (Smillie 1995b: 255). However, private aid agencies operating in the 'charity market' have two important comparative advantages over state-funded agencies. One is their considerable flexibility in allocating aid resources in ways that they consider to be most cost-effective and developmentally sound, plus that they are more directly rooted in Northern societies due to their broad constituencies of private donors. But what influence can these individual private donors exert over strategies of private aid agencies?

This brings me to a second variable that influences private aid strategies, which is directly related to the issue of donor-base: to whom are private aid agencies accountable? Accountability is the way in which individuals and organisations report to a recognised authority and are held responsible for their actions (Edwards and Hulme 1994). Private aid agencies derive their legitimacy in the North often from an implicit (and poorly defined) representational role of the Southern poor. Controlling bodies, mechanisms or performance indicators to account for this role to donors and beneficiaries generally do not exist. This weak system of account-ability was one of the main issues fuelling the debate in the 1990s on legitimacy and 'ownership' of private aid agencies (cf. Edwards and Hulme 1995). Saxby (1996) classified agencies according to the publics or institutions they are accountable to, which gives an extra dimension to the previous discussion of agency dependency on official donors. He identified several types of private aid agencies that all have different mechanisms of accountability according to the 'clients' they have to respond to. These clients could be the state, the donating public, members or constituencies, endowment managers, or intended beneficiaries. As the majority of agencies are accountable to the state, becoming an 'owner' rather than a 'donor', he concludes that the state often displaces the voluntary character of agencies and aligns them to the requirements of official agendas. But many (especially smaller) agencies also depend on income from the general public and have to convince their private donors that donations were spent according to an unwritten contract, based on a set of values. This is sometimes achieved by direct (albeit superficial) reporting to private donors, but more so by sustaining a public image of credibility and loyalty to these values. This puts pressure on private aid agencies to prevent bad publicity (or at least any uncontrolled publicity) about their performance. The sanction of private donors, withdrawal of financial gifts, is an accountability meas-ure far more difficult to control than sanctions from the state or from a board of trustees. Moreover, agencies that are to some degree accountable to the state also potentially can be better controlled by democratic institutions than agencies only depending on the charity market.

Accountability is more than just accounting for the correct use of donated resources: it is also about accounting for the effectiveness of agency activities. This longer term accountability – or 'strategic accountability'[36] – poses problems for private agencies because accurate indicators to measure their performance are often difficult to find and results are contingent upon contextual factors. In the next chapter these problems of attributing causes to effects will be further analysed, as it is clear that this is one of the key challenges for private aid agencies in resolving their legitimacy crisis. It could even be argued that, due to the problems of meas-uring performance and attributing success to their interventions, accountability of private aid agencies will always remain weak, as Edwards (1996a) argues. Weakness in strategic accountability has become problematic for private aid agencies as it is likely to increase ineffectiveness or illegitimate interventions (Edwards and Hulme 1995). An additional dilemma for private aid agencies is that they have to respond to a variety of 'stakeholders' in the aid chain in two directions: an 'upward' accountability to agency boards and development ministry officials, and a 'downward' accountability to private donors, overseas partners and Southern beneficiaries. These 'multiple accountabilities' make it very difficult to serve all 'clients' equally. Not surprisingly, private aid agencies (and Southern partners) prioritise 'upward' accountability as they depend on donors for economic survival, and often neglect 'downward' accountability to Southern partners and beneficiaries, because it is time-consuming and might generate organisational instability. One of the dangers is that the current pressure from donors to show quick and measurable results not only drives accountability mechanisms further upwards, but also tends to replace accountability by 'accountancy'. Evaluations thus tend to be concerned mostly with controlling the proper use of donor resources and barely function as mechanisms for learning from previous experiences and mistakes (Smillie 1995a).

The current weakness in strategic accountability by private aid agencies is not likely to improve very soon. Although the need for improving performance measurement, transparency and accountability has been generally accepted by private aid agencies, most of these good intentions appear to be rhetorical: only very few are actually taking steps in shifting the balance *back* from institutional to developmental imperatives. As Edwards and Hulme (1995: 227) note: 'most give the impression that only a financial crisis will be enough to enforce more fundamental changes in this direction'. But other effective pressure on private aid agencies to redefine their current role is not really increasing, as this pressure mainly comes from academics and development practitioners and not from within the aid chain: from donors and recipients of private foreign aid.[37] Official donor agencies in the North are questioning the added value of private aid agencies in their role as intermediaries channelling official aid resources to Southern partner organisations, but have not drastically reduced co-financing programmes.[38] They realise that private aid agencies are necessary allies and effective advocates in maintaining the levels of their aid budgets, and official donors seem to be satisfied with the new emphasis of private aid agencies on 'upward accountability' towards them. Nor has the 'general public' increased pressure on private aid agencies, for example, by re-allocating their private donations to those agencies that have taken demands for transparency and informed public debate seriously. On the contrary, it seems that increasing budgets for advertising and public relations and better coordination for fund-raising (at least in the short term) is paying off, which is illustrated by the successful campaigns of 'transnational private aid agencies' such as *Plan International* and *Save the Children*.[39] By emphasising the dimensions of the problems that have to be tackled, combined with a vague notion of optimism about the virtues of quick and visible aid delivery, the Northern public has been effectively targeted with well-dosed cocktails appealing to altruism, guilt and shame, but only in exceptional cases to 'solidarity'.

If donors are barely putting pressure on private aid agencies to increase their strategic accountability, what about the pressure from *recipients* in the aid chain? Southern partners, after all, seem to have successfully pushed Northern private aid agencies to increase policy advocacy aimed at influencing policies of Northern governments, although the result of this advocacy work has been rather limited (Edwards 1993). At the same time, Southern partner organisations also have questioned the legitimacy of Northern private aid agencies to speak 'in their name' without actually establishing formal procedures to consult them. Despite regular consultations with representatives from Southern partners, the latter generally play an advisory role but seldom have a direct say in private aid policies. Fowler (1996a: 3) points at 'a fundamental Northern NGO anxiety about loss of control and reduced role which a truly empowered partner would bring'. The general absence of downward accountability procedures of private aid donors towards their beneficiaries makes sense considering the one-way financial dependency relationship and the existence of a one-way ('upward') accountability system between recipients and donors. However, this is generally not the way private aid agencies portray their relationships with organisations in the South, which are perceived as 'partners', suggesting an equitable relationship, and, more important, the existence of trust, mutual accountability and transparency.[40]

An implicit problem in developing 'partnership' (based on mutual trust, equality, transparency and reciprocal accountability) is that donor-recipient relations by definition imply unequal power relations. The core of relationships between private aid agencies and Southern partners is based on a downwards transfer of financial resources in the aid chain, and an upwards transfer of information and reporting, resulting in one-way accountabilities that automatically affect mutual trust and transparency. A growing literature on possible new avenues for mutually reinforcing North-South partnerships points at the need for private aid agencies to increase information sharing and genuine consultation with Southern recipients, to create a special independent 'ombudsman' to arbitrate in conflicts, institute a division of labour and responsibilities in policy advocacy alliances, issue joint impact assessments and 'reverse evaluations', or enlarge possibilities for Southern organisations to start public fund-raising in the North. Although not yet visible, pressure for increased strategic accountability of private aid agencies ultimately has to come from Southern partners, according to Fowler (1996a: 9), 'as they hold the key to the legitimacy of Northern aid agencies'.

– *Intervention strategies of private aid agencies*
The previous analysis shows that differences among private aid agencies can be understood by examining past and current constituencies that have determined their size and organisational structure, and by analysing the relationships they pursue with publics and partners in North and South. Private aid agencies continuously shift back and forth in an effort to find an optimal balance between money-driven (income) and value-driven (principles) determinants, between institutional and developmental imperatives, although gaps between the rhetoric of

mission statements and actual output in the field remain considerable. But private aid agencies do make strategic choices and the previous section outlined some key factors that shape or influence these. Before looking at the *performance* of agency interventions (Chapter 3), it could be helpful to look at the evolution of strategic choices that private aid agencies have made to bring their value-driven principles into practice. Based on some commonly used classifications for Southern development NGOs, an attempt will be made to construct a typology for private aid 'intervention strategies', as a necessary prelude to the analysis of private aid strategies to contribute to civil society building.

The most popular typology to map changes in private aid 'programming strategies' is Korten's generational framework. Korten (1986, 1987) identified three distinctive orientations in programming strategies: relief and welfare, local self-reliance and sustainable systems development, which he considered to be 'evolutionary stages' or 'generations' of programming strategies. Korten acknowledged that these categories were actually developed to identify strategies of individual programmes rather than of private aid agencies as a whole, implying that several generations could coexist within the same organisation. First generation strategies (relief and welfare) focus on short-term alleviation of immediate needs as a result of floods, wars or famine: provision of shelter and clothing to refugees, distribution of food or emergency health care. Relief aid is generally implemented and fully controlled by 'operational' Northern aid agencies. Many of the older private aid agencies originally started with this type of relief aid, also beyond situations of direct emergencies. Although this strategy is still widely used in emergency situations (such as in Africa in the 1990s), relief aid by definition only temporarily alleviates the symptoms of poverty. Second generation strategies are oriented to local self-reliance. They are based on the acknowledgement of the limitations of relief operations and address problems generated by poverty and exclusion with longer term projects, often community-based. The approach is oriented toward sustainability in the long run, aiming at self-reliance of local communities after external assistance has been withdrawn. Involvement of Southern NGOs (which implement projects together with organisations in the community) and a micro-orientation are other features that distinguish second generation strategies from the first. A wide variety of activities belong to this category, from delivery of health and education services to projects for agricultural applied technology transfer. The majority of private aid supported projects probably fit into this second generation category. Korten's third cluster of programming strategies (sustainable systems development) is guided by the conviction that local self-reliant community development is not sustainable in the absence of regional or national supportive environments. Third generation strategies are geared at pursuing policy changes at governmental levels and increasing coordination between organisations involved at the micro- and macro-level. The function of private aid agencies evolves from an operational to a facilitating and catalyst role. Emphasis switches from a project approach to a more integrated programme approach, in which local partners acquire considerable autonomy in policy implementation. The scope of activities could vary from programmes assisting official service-delivery systems to large scale integrated rural credit programmes. Also non-financial interventions, such as attempts by sectoral coalitions to reform public policies, could be included in Korten's third generation strategies.

Korten's generational framework of what he later called 'voluntary development action' (1990) has remained surprisingly unchallenged over the last decade.[41] The popularity of his generational framework is probably that it suggests paradigm shifts within (Northern and Southern) NGOs, although these paradigms are not necessarily endorsed institutionally (Nerfin 1992). This means that any private aid agency will likely recognise itself somewhere along this generational spectrum, combining a 'healthy' combination of generational characteristics. However, if several strategies can coexist within one private aid agency, apparently no institutional strategy adaptation is made towards a new paradigm. Korten's framework is certainly helpful in understanding changes of strategy over time, but is at the same time too general and contradictory for explaining paradigm shifts. The first two generations generally follow the modernisation paradigm of development, but the paradigm of 'alternative development' with 'empowerment' as a central concept is located somewhere halfway between the second and third generation. Korten (1990: 123-128) added to the confusion by suggesting a 'fourth generation' – in fact addressing this alternative development paradigm – in which social movements are considered as the central actors for global change. The private aid agency only plays a marginal role in this strategy and is supposed to 'coalesce and energise self-managing networks over which it has no control whatever. This must be achieved primarily through the power of ideas, values and communication links.' As these movements 'move on social energy more than on money' this approach actually contributes to making private aid in the long term superfluous.

A more useful approach to classify agency strategies was suggested by Elliot (1987a), although his scheme never achieved the popularity of Korten's generations. Instead of looking at programming strategies, Elliot distinguished between rhetoric and practice and took *activities* of private agencies as an indicator to distinguish among agency strategies. He analysed changes in behaviour of private aid agencies and identified three different 'approaches' in this process: 'welfare', 'development' and 'empowerment'. Although his approaches apparently overlap with Korten's generations, there are important differences. The welfare approach, according to Elliot, is generally adopted by missionary organisations, child-sponsorship organisations and agencies emphasising 'starving baby imagery' in their fund-raising campaigns. In practice, it is meant to deliver services (like food provision or health care) to specific groups to respond to immediate needs as a result of emergencies. The welfare approach is concerned more with quick results and a high fund-raising appeal than solving real problems of poor communities, and it covers more or less Korten's first generation. The developmental approach has as its central goal to improve the capacity of local communities in providing their own basic needs and to become self-reliant in the long run. Activities in this direction still cover the majority of projects financed by private aid agencies.

Elliot (1987a: 58) makes an important distinction between rhetoric and practice: 'although the background paradigm is often that of the modernisation school of development theory, the rhetoric is often one of self-reliance and interdependency'. He points at the frictions that emerged as soon as the development approach was implemented in the field, where it was discovered that development is not about allocating resources but about changing power relations. This is where Elliot locates a paradigm shift, towards his third approach of 'empowerment' inspired by the 'conscientisation' school of Alinksy and Freire. Within the paradigm of 'social change', 'alternative development', or whatever one wants to call it, the role for Northern private agencies is in fact rather marginal. Elliot (1987a: 59) observes that 'empowerment is something that cannot be delivered', as it is a process of change that depends on people rather than resources. The role of private aid agencies is therefore limited to offering some indirect assistance, either financial or technical, to what he calls 'loose and unstable coalitions of groups working in the village, many of which would see their own integrity threatened by too close a relationship with Northern NGOs'.

The idea of identifying evolutionary stages in strategies or activities of non-profit agencies was already suggested in the 1930s by Alva Myrdal, when she described three stages of social reform policies. The first stage was the period of curative social policy through private charity and public poor relief, which she called the 'paternalistic conservative era'. The second stage was the 'liberal era': the period of social insurance broad in scope but merely symptomatic. The third, 'Social Democratic era', was the stage where preventing the ills was attempted through protective and cooperative social policies.[42] Private aid agencies have gone through similar stages on the spectrum from paternalism to cooperation, and from altruism to solidarity. This evolution reflects a gradual change about how development is perceived and what the role could be of development aid and donor agencies. It also makes clear that the paradigm of modernisation, predominating until the mid-1970s, evolved in two different directions: one towards neoliberalism and the other towards an alternative approach that is often called 'social development' (Howes 1992). This social development paradigm is centred around concepts such as 'participation', 'partnership', 'process' and 'empowerment', and often directly linked to strategies and activities of private aid agencies and Southern NGOs (Malena 1995). However, in the late 1980s it also became clear that activities of private aid agencies and Southern NGOs had not automatically followed the alternative approach to traditional development theory: many were in fact working within the parameters of neoliberalism. Evolutionary approaches to explain private aid strategies should therefore be treated with caution.

There is an additional reason to be careful about analysing programming strategies according to evolutionary stages: many approaches or strategies are often applied simultaneously within the same private aid agency. In fact, the 1990s have shown an increase in emergency relief activities from agencies that claim to work within the paradigm of social development. If it is assumed that this coexistence of strategies is a result of cumulative evolutionary stages, why are first generation strategies (relief aid) not gradually abandoned over time by private aid agencies that also use second and third generation strategies? Therefore, despite their popularity, evolutionary stages often generate confusion rather than add to an understanding of strategic choices of private aid agencies. At best, evolutionary sequences could map gradual changes and adaptations of general mission statements of private aid agencies and Southern NGOs. However, in that case it would be more helpful to distinguish explicitly between rhetoric and practice by identifying 'intervention strategies', instead of stages, to analyse how mission statements are converted into applied policies. Many private agencies simultaneously use a variety of intervention strategies, depending on local needs and conditions, sometimes contrary to their mission statements. By mapping these intervention strategies based on their 'practice in the field', the search by private aid agencies to strike a balance between institutional and developmental imperatives also could become more explicit. In

Table 2.3   *Four types of private aid intervention strategies*

	Relief	**Service delivery**	**Empowerment**	**Civil society building**
Time frame	Immediate	Project cycle (2-3 years)	Programme (5-10 years)	Generation (>10 years)
Scope	Family Community	Community National	Community National	National International
Main actors	Northern (private) donor	Southern NGO	Grassroots organisation; supported by SNGO	Coalition of SNGOs and GROs; lobbying in the North
Fund-raising appeals	Starving children	Basic needs; safety-net	Self-help	Solidarity
Performance indicator	Stop starvation and immediate suffering	# of schools, wells, or rate of literacy	Increase of democratic and autonomous membership organisations	Density, diversity, equitability of civil society; political transformation
Accountability	Upwards within agency; weak downwards	Functional upwards: SNGO to PAA; weak downwards	Functional and strategic upwards: GRO-SNGO-PAA	Functional and strategic upwards and downwards
Partnership	Operational private aid agencies; hierarchy	Accompaniment; relative autonomy of SNGO	Accompaniment; mutual respect	Mutual autonomy; S-N division of responsibilities

SNGO = Southern development NGO
GRO = Southern membership ('grassroots') organisation
PAA = Northern private aid agency

order to map these strategies, by identifying what agencies actually do in practice, four types of intervention strategies are schematically identified in Table 2.3: relief, service delivery, participation and empowerment, and civil society building.[43] The focus of the next chapter will be to further analyse the intention and performance of private aid agencies in their strategies to contribute to civil society building.

Some final remarks should be made to avoid misunderstanding this typology of intervention strategies. Obviously, one should be careful about generalisations when putting the great diversity of intervention strategies of private aid agencies into a simple matrix. The practice is far more complex and distinctions between the four categories of intervention strategies are generally blurry instead of sharp. Many other classifications could be made and the current scheme certainly could be more elaborated. But the point is that agency strategies do have particular underlying assumptions which have fundamental consequences for agency behaviour, relations with partners and the impact of their interventions. By mapping these variables, it is possible to look beyond the rhetoric of mission statements and to identify commonalties among intervention strategies that are actually applied in the field. The typology serves as a guide, and it should be possible to determine for any private agency which (combination of) intervention strategies are being used in a particular country or sector. After all, it is not exceptional that several intervention strategies coexist at the same time in one private agency, and even in one particular project or programme. It is often preferable to combine a variety of intervention strategies to increase the likelihood of success of one of the strategies. For example, if activities are oriented towards social transformation (using empowerment or civil society building strategies), they are often 'camouflaged' by relief and service-delivery activities that are generally not perceived by an authoritarian regime as 'subversive' activities. Fowler (1992: 11) calls this the 'onion-skin strategy': 'an outer layer of welfarism that protects inner layers of service delivery around a core dedicated to transformation'. This could explain why agencies find it difficult to map their activities according to intervention strategies, as these are often serving multiple purposes.[44]

The foregoing analysis also indicates that the schematic 'aid chain' presented earlier in Figure 2.2 needs more elaboration. Private aid interventions generally coincide with official aid interventions, involving a number of other actors that were absent in the initial diagram. Figure 2.4 tries to illustrate the more complex setting in which private aid agencies are actually operating, although the situation in practice involves of course many more actors. The grey arrows represent the main directions of aid flows. Private aid income from donations (1) and from official sources (2) is diminishing,[45] implying that private aid transfers to Southern development NGOs (3) also have decreased. But at the same time, direct funding from Northern governments (a) and from multilateral donors (c) to Southern organisations in civil society has increased, despite the downward tendency of overall official development assistance (a + b + c) in the mid-1990s. It is this 'direct funding' mechanism that is mostly threatening the future existence of private aid

Figure 2.4 *Stakeholders and aid flows in multiple aid chains*

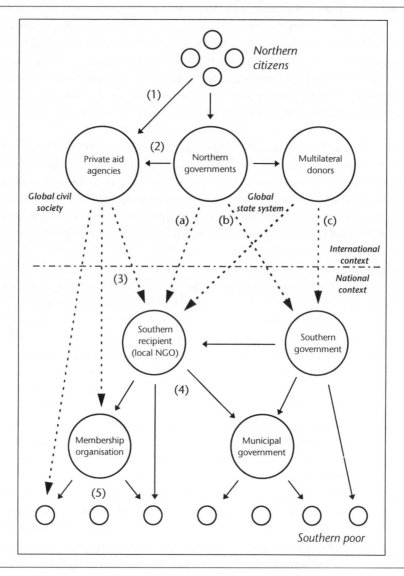

(1) private aid income from citizens' donations
(2) private aid income from official subsidies
(3) private aid allocations to Southern recipients in civil society (generally NGOs)
(4) provision of services to membership organisations or direct beneficiaries
(5) provision of benefits to members and/or other beneficiaries

(a) official (direct) funding to Southern organisations in civil society
(b) official development assistance to Southern governments
(c) multilateral development assistance to Southern governments
······▶ = (primary) aid flows

agencies as the pivotal actor in the aid chain. It is also one of the key elements to understanding the politics of civil society building. By directly funding local organisations in civil society, official aid agencies have started to enter a terrain that had largely been dominated by private aid agencies, even though considerable differences exist among their strategic orientations, as the following chapter will demonstrate.

2.4 Bridging the gap between rhetoric and reality

Private aid agencies emerged in Northern civil societies as expressions of post-colonial compassion with the Third World poor. During the Cold War, differences between European and US private aid agencies increased, as the latter predominantly continued their shorter term relief assistance in line with foreign policy objectives, whereas many European and Canadian private aid agencies became channels for 'solidarity aid', often with a considerable share of official funding. During the 'golden era' of private foreign aid, from the mid-1970s to the late 1980s, these agencies became important actors in international development assistance. Perhaps not so much in terms of quantity, as private aid never represented more than 12 percent of total aid flows to the South, but certainly in terms of innovating development thinking and strengthening civil societies abroad with people-centred strategies.

In the early 1990s, the comparative advantages attributed to private aid agencies were increasingly questioned. Income stagnated and a wave of critique challenged the legitimacy of private aid agencies, while many of their traditional partners overseas started to receive large amounts of other resources, particularly through 'direct funding' from governments and multilateral institutions. The resulting crisis of identity facing private aid agencies in the late 1990s could be characterised as a search for a new balance between their developmental goals and their survival as institutions. Some European agencies think that the crisis is a matter of improved management and marketing, and they might follow the pragmatic survivalist mode that US private aid agencies have chosen since the Cold War. Others acknowledge that longer term survival of private aid agencies will require more, such as the need to 'reinvent' solidarity by forging new national and international alliances and by mobilising Northern constituencies on the basis of arguments, instead of emotions (TNI 1996).

Part of the current crisis could be attributed to the weak accountability systems of private aid agencies, which in turn could be explained by the ambiguous character of intervention strategies: good intentions and public messages often differ from activities that exist in practice. There appears to be a time lag between innovations in development theory and innovations in agency strategies. For example, much of the rhetoric on empowerment, which had already been proposed in the early 1970s, only became part of actual agency strategies in the 1980s.[46] But there is also a gap between what agencies pretend they are doing and what is actually implemented. Fowler's 'onion-skin approach' could also be applied to describe the ambiguities of many private agencies: an outer layer of good intentions and ideal-istic principles about empowering the poor, and an inner layer of market-driven values aimed at institutional reproduction. This inner layer became more visible in the 1990s, when the growth of agency income was stagnating and institutional imperatives started to dominate private aid strategies. One of the innovations of private aid agencies has been to extend the empowerment approach towards a macro-level, by contributing to longer term civil society building. Although often generating results that were not intended initially, one of the conclusions of the previous analysis is that it is more useful to focus on what private agencies actually do in practice, than to examine their intentions which are laid down in mission statements or the promises of their fund-raising campaigns. It is therefore time to look at the output of private aid agencies, at what they actually achieve in practice, especially in terms of their contribution to strengthening civil societies.

3 LEARNING FROM FAILURE

Civil Society Building and Impact Assessment

The contribution of private aid agencies to democratic transition in the South could be enhanced if they managed to fully exploit their favourable position in 'global civil society', as was argued in Chapter 1. They are relatively autonomous from Northern governments and political parties, and have the capacity to directly provide substantial financial resources to Southern actors in civil society and to incorporate them into transnational networks for advocacy purposes. As a result, private aid agencies possess a comparative advantage over other transnational actors (that are generally unable to make use of these opportunities concurrently) in strengthening Southern civil societies. Are private aid agencies actually using this potential? And how are these civil society building policies put into practice?

After separating the rhetoric about civil society building from what is actually occurring in practice, I will look at the results of these efforts. This assumes however that it is possible to verify what private aid agencies have achieved with their interventions, which is a difficult undertaking because assessing impact encounters many obstacles and pitfalls. 'Performance' of private aid agencies is not something that can be easily 'measured', and the question is addressed whether it is possible to attribute particular achievements of Southern actors to the interventions of private aid agencies. This theme will be explored prior to looking at the results of a series of recent independent studies assessing the impact of multiple private aid interventions in the South. The findings of these studies were rather critical about the effectiveness of private aid agencies. Several methodological lessons can be learned from them, which were incorporated into the methodological framework of the present study in order to analyse private aid interventions contributing to civil society building in Central America.

3.1 Private aid chains and civil society building

The previous chapter demonstrated that the intervention strategies of many private aid agencies slowly evolved from addressing the symptoms of poverty to tackling its root causes: the unequal power relations in civil society. The conviction that 'poverty is more than the absence of material means; it is also the lack of access to power'[1] led agencies to gradually consider development as a process of change in which (poor) people identify common goals and work together to empower themselves and acquire more equal access to resources. To achieve this, human rights should be guaranteed and space and capacity have to be created for the poor to organise themselves. Private aid agencies could potentially enhance this process of social change by defending people's rights and by enhancing the level of participation and organisation of the poor. Ultimately, with these interventions donor agencies could effectively contribute to civil society building. Until recently, most private aid agencies did not include civil society building as an explicit objective in their mission statements, although some components of this strategy had been practised already for several years, especially in Latin America (Frantz 1987). But this was often included among other objectives, such as 'support to democratisation', 'defending human rights' or 'building up organisational capacity'.

Interestingly, only since the late 1980s, and particularly in the 1990s, has civil society building started to enter donor discourse as an explicit strategy. Official donors such as USAID by the early 1990s started to classify 'civil society building' or 'strengthening civil society' as a separate category (Robinson 1996b). Probably as a product of 'diffusion' of development discourse, stimulated by dependence on official aid contributions, most private aid agencies soon also incorporated the civil society discourse into their mission statements. After all, they effectively had been supporting organisations in Southern civil societies for several decades. But why did 'civil society' become a buzzword in official donor intervention strategies in the 1990s, and why was it also adopted by private aid agencies? Are civil society building strategies by private aid agencies different from those of official aid agencies? These questions are not easily answered and the analysis is further complicated by the concurrent use of different meanings of 'civil society'. Moreover, private aid agencies initially had other reasons to support civil society building than official aid agencies, although in the 1990s these differences became less distinct. Two reasons can be identified to explain why official aid agencies adopted the civil society discourse, while there is a third reason that particularly influenced private aid agencies in this direction.

The first reason for official aid agencies to focus on civil society building was their growing conviction that a strong civil society probably was a prerequisite for an efficient market economy. USAID, for example, believed that support for civil society would be an effective way to consolidate the transition from statist to market-based economies (G. Hansen 1996). This economic reason for civil society building was also influenced by the disappointing performance of official aid programmes and the perceived success of small-scale participatory programs of Southern NGOs, which were apparently better able to reach the poor. The use of participatory methods turned out to be helpful for the design and implementation of social compensation programmes a few years later to alleviate the impoverishing impact of structural adjustment programmes. Influential policy documents of official donors, notably from the World Bank, started advocating the need for participatory approaches and praised the potential of Southern NGOs (Cernea 1988). Support for civil society building in this, essentially neoliberal, approach thus appears to be synonymous with guaranteeing free markets, privatising public services and meeting immediate needs of the poor to prevent social unrest.

Another reason for official donors to 'reinvent' civil society was closely related to these economic reasons, as part of newly emerging policies oriented at democratisation and 'good governance'.[2] The political demise of communism and the chain of political transformations in Eastern Europe, Central Asia and Sub-Saharan Africa required adaptations of donor policies towards the new post-Cold War political climate. Traditional policies of democracy promotion (as outlined in Chapter 1) were rephrased and shifted their emphasis from security to development objectives. This 'new policy agenda' of official donors aimed at improving governance in two broad ways: enhancing the efficiency of Southern governments, and making the state more accountable to civil society (Robinson 1994). In practice, these policies promoted reform of civil services, decentralisation, and (often simultaneously) reform of judicial and constitutional systems, electoral assistance and the strengthening of political parties. These policies initially had a top-down approach and tended to strengthen 'the institutions of government and political society as opposed to building constituencies from within civil society' (Robinson 1996a: 202). In later documents the need to build a 'pluralist' civil society as a counterweight to government and as a means to further democratisation also was mentioned explicitly (OECD 1995b).[3] However, this pluralist approach of supporting civil society – often using the pleonasm 'civil society organisations' (CSOs) – was criticised for being superficial and ignoring unequal power relations in civil society. Critics pointed at a potential risk that the status quo could be strengthened when donors were not explicit about *which* organisations in civil society they were supporting, not to mention the risk of strengthening undemocratic forces in civil society.[4]

These economic and political reasons for supporting civil society, closely interrelated as part of the 'new policy agenda' of official aid donor agencies, also influenced the agendas of private aid agencies. But an additional reason especially spurred the latter to phrase their strategies more in terms of civil society building: the growing critique from outsiders about the poor performance of micro-projects and the lack of impact at the macro-level (Edwards and Hulme 1992). This debate about the quality of development interventions and the search for new ways to increase effectiveness pushed some agencies to gradually incorporate wider issues into their empowerment strategies. Enhancing organisational capacity at the grassroots level would not lead to structural changes in power relations if it was not combined with measures that addressed the national and international structures that cause poverty and disempowerment. Private aid agencies therefore increasingly decided to pursue interventions that had the potential to impact more widely, indirectly promoting changes in power structures and policy reform from below. These efforts to increase citizens' participation, counter the exclusion of marginalised sectors and pressure governments to become more accountable, turned civil society building into one of the key topics of private aid policy discussions in the 1990s.

Civil society building strategies thus were triggered by three different motivations: to promote market-led development, to promote democracy and to enhance impact. Although separated for analytical reasons, these three purposes in practice are often combined in the variety of civil society building strategies pursued by private and official donors, despite containing development objectives that are sometimes incompatible.[5] Not surprisingly, this has generated confusion about the precise meaning and purpose of civil society in these intervention strategies, as was demonstrated earlier. 'Strengthening civil society' as an intervention strategy can be better understood when it is explicitly attached to certain development objectives that explain why civil society should be 'strong', and which organisations in civil society are prioritised for support. The 'neoliberal' approach supports civil society because it is instrumental for privatising state functions. It therefore supports organisations in the area of service provision to substitute for these functions, in addition to strengthening private enterprise. The 'pluralist' approach to supporting civil society aims to strengthen the efficiency and accountability of the state and the participation of societal actors in order to strengthen political society. It generally applies values from the Western political tradition and pays little attention to inequalities within civil society that reproduce the causes of poverty. Just as neoliberals, pluralists tend to artificially separate state and civil society, instead of analysing them in relation to each other (Macdonald 1997). Not surprisingly, these approaches to civil society building are sometimes perceived by Southern organisations as imposed upon them and as an expression of 'cultural imperialism' (Clayton 1996).

The 'inclusive' approach of civil society building on the other hand points at these unequal power relations and contributes to forging democratisation by incorporating the most vulnerable sectors into civil society.[6] This approach recognises the existence of conflicting interests within civil society, and tries to identify strategic alliances to promote social and political change (Trivedi and Acharya 1996). Although most official (and many private) aid agencies generally work with a pluralist civil society concept, it is not always easy to separate the various development objectives. It is not uncommon that several of these three approaches are applied simultaneously by the same (private) aid agency, despite their incompatibility in terms of furthering democratisation (Edwards and Hulme 1996). But again, the key test to identifying these strategies is to determine which organisations have been selected for support, and for what purpose. A shift from agency rhetoric to the actual intervention practices of civil society building illustrates this point.

– *Options for civil society building*
Private aid agencies often have multiple objectives, and use a variety of intervention strategies to achieve their goals. Acknowledging this complexity, for analytical reasons it could be helpful to disaggregate the variety of actors and strategies that are part of private aid interventions that aim to contribute to civil society building.

In Chapter 2 the dynamics of aid intervention were schematically represented in the 'aid chain' (Figure 2.2). This figure will now be connected to another schematic diagram, introduced in Chapter 1, which illustrates the dynamic balance between the state and civil society (Figure 1.2). By combining these two figures, the variety of choices of private aid intervention strategies related to civil society building can be shown. The resulting diagram (Figure 3.1) provides a schematic overview of relationships and dynamics that develop during aid interventions aiming at civil society building. Interventions (and aid flows) from official aid agencies and private aid agencies both are placed in the same figure to underline that these aid chains cannot be entirely separated. On the contrary, in many cases they might even be complementary, as will be argued later on.[7]

'Inclusive' civil society building strategies of private aid agencies aim to actively incorporate marginalised sectors into civil society and try to further democratisation by increasing the leverage of civil society *vis-à-vis* the state. As was explained in Chapter 1, this type of civil society building essentially aims to strengthen *political society*. Five interrelated mechanisms were identified concerned with how societal actors could enhance conditions for strengthening political society. I distinguished between building (a) organisational capacity, (b) alliances among organisations in civil society, (c) intermediary channels, (d) transnational political space and (e) citizenship. It was also argued that these mechanisms had different functions in subsequent democratic transition stages. In a variety of ways, private aid agencies have contributed to these five mechanisms of civil society building by providing technical and financial support, either directly to beneficiaries or through intermediary organisations. Figure 3.1 schematically shows how this private aid support is channelled through a variety of aid chains.[8] The choices that private aid agencies make in these various intervention strategies will be more closely examined below.

Strengthening the organisational capacities of societal actors representing sectoral interests is the basis of civil society building (a). It is the 'foundation' of civil society and could be explained as a process of increasing 'social energy' (Hirschmann 1984) or 'social capital' (Putnam 1993) in addition to countering fragmentation and disaggregation to achieve 'social cohesion' (Lechner 1995). It is not limited to strengthening existing societal actors, but also includes the formation of new autonomous organisations that represent interests from those sectors that were previously excluded from civil society. Private (and official) aid agencies make choices regarding *which* organisations they select for external support.[9] Do these organisations represent vulnerable and marginalised sectors of civil society, or do they represent dominant interests? In other words, do aid interventions contribute to the inclusion of vulnerable (and excluded) sectors of civil society or do they maintain the customary exclusion? This is generally a useful tool for identifying which concept of civil society (common or conflicting interests) is being applied by donor agencies. Many private aid agencies often explicitly choose to support organisations that represent weak or vulnerable sectors, such as for example

Figure 3.1   *Private aid chains and civil society building*

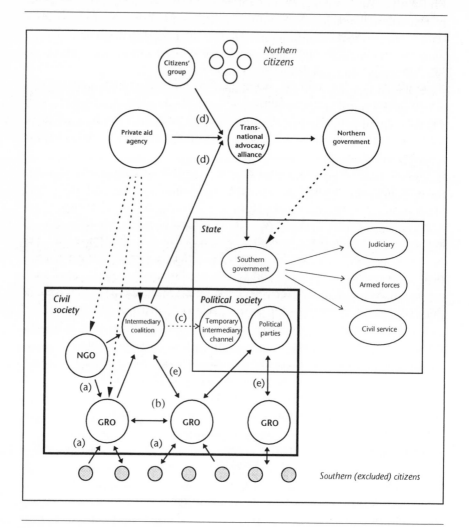

(a) building organisational capacity
(b) building alliances and coalitions
(c) building intermediary channels in political society
(d) building transnational alliances for policy advocacy
(e) building citizenship

NGO = Non-governmental development organisation
GRO = Grassroots or 'popular' (membership) organisation
······▶ = aid flows

indigenous groups, women's organisations or gay groups. Other donors prefer to work with urban-based organisations of professionals (journalists, lawyers, entrepreneurs) or well-established institutions such as trade unions, churches or research centres. Support to these organisations has become an explicit target of democracy promotion programmes instituted by official donors, usually with private aid agencies acting as intermediaries (Robinson 1996b).

Private aid agencies often combine support for building organisational capacity with activities aimed at service delivery. The advantage is that these projects have a lower political profile and that it is generally more effective to organise citizens on 'bread and butter' issues. Moreover, organisations providing services often are expected to have a better chance of becoming sustainable over the long run (Carothers 1995). This is considered to be crucial as dependency on external funding can negatively affect the internal accountability and democratic procedures of an organisation (Esman and Uphoff 1984). Aid agencies can tackle the danger of donor dependency and low internal accountability by enhancing the capacity of organisations to collect beneficiary contributions or to raise funds from more diverse sources. Strengthening civil society in a sustainable way can for example lead to only financing the 'transaction costs' of organising, in order to safeguard organisational autonomy and internal vitality (Hadenius and Uggla 1996). Support to autonomous organising in civil society can be obstructed during the period prior to democratic transition, when all forms of independent civil activity are repressed by the state. However, at that stage it is probably the only option for donors to contribute to civil society building, aside from putting external pressure on the state.

The second option for donors to contribute to civil society building is to encourage and enable the establishment of vertical and horizontal linkages between autonomous societal actors (b). These relationships are fundamental to creating what the Latin Americans call *el tejido social*, the 'social fabric' of civil society, even if the threads have different strengths and the fabric shows many holes. Linkages do not necessarily have to be formalised (such as federations), since loosely articulated networks of societal actors have proven to be very effective by acting in the manifold arenas where power is exercised and reproduced. The hidden strength of these horizontal alliances lies in the 'fragmentation of collective action', in which each organisation fulfils (as part of a network) a particular and mutually complementary role (Escobar and Alvarez 1992: 324). Horizontal linkages are important, but it is also commonly agreed that societal actors are even more effective when they operate at multiple levels. Esman and Uphoff (1984) have called these 'multi-tiered' organisations, in which the lower tier performs a 'solidarity' function at the local level and the macro-tier is responsible for policy-making and securing access to resources. Alliances between organisations in civil society are the key to civil society building. They enable societal actors to join forces for mobilisation on common claims, but alliances also can contribute to forging a new democratic political culture – inside and between individual organisations – within a 'parallel

public sphere' (Hadenius and Uggla 1996). Donor agencies have stimulated networking between societal actors by financing meetings and national coordination
offices, although large-scale financial support also can destroy these alliances as will
be demonstrated in Chapter 6. When downward accountability is weak, these
coordinating bodies can become institutionalised and basically function as aid
recipients independent from their constituencies. Accountability under these circumstances is mainly directed 'upwards' to report to donor agencies, and eventually
damages the social fabric of civil society.

    Democratically and autonomously organised civil associations, operating in a
diversified social fabric at multiple levels in civil society, is one condition for political society to be able to function. The other condition is the availability of transparent and legitimate channels of interaction between the state and civil society,
a function generally performed by political parties. But when these parties are
weak, repressed or co-opted by the state, this generates a vacuum in political society
(Fox 1994). Formal, legitimate and democratic intermediary channels of interaction
in political society are typically absent during authoritarian rule and during early
stages of democratic transition. Informal intermediaries from civil society sometimes fill this vacuum, albeit temporarily (c). When civil activity is repressed, this
function is often performed by the churches or by human rights organisations. The
latter, although without a formal constituency, potentially play an (informal)
intermediary role in political society, or more precisely, a 'disciplinary role' vis-à-vis
the state (White 1994). When civil society has acquired some space for civil action,
alliances and coalitions of societal actors can perform this role with more legitimacy.[10] To be effective, these alliances of societal actors generally should meet
several conditions. They should represent more than one civil society sector,
operate at a national level, voice concerns from a majority (or a large minority) of
civil society, and operate autonomously from the state and from existing political
parties (even if these belong to the opposition). Particularly this last condition is
seldom met and can lead to internal tensions, making intermediary coalitions less
effective in political society (Craig and Mayo 1995). An additional reason for these
coalitions to be cautious in engaging directly with political parties is the reluctance
of private aid agencies to support political parties, especially if these are involved
in armed struggle against the regime.[11] Private aid agencies have supported activities
of many of these intermediary coalitions in highly polarised societies, such as Chile,
El Salvador, the Philippines, South Africa and Guatemala. To prevent political
repercussions in their home country, support was often funnelled through church
institutions, also because these alliances seldom acquired a legal status. Generally,
they had to accept a (gradual) retreat from political society as soon as legitimate intermediary actors (such as political parties) were elected to take over their
function in the period of late transition. This was often not easy for these coalitions, as they lost their protagonist role and often disintegrated after democratic
transition was completed, despite having played a decisive role in pushing the
momentum in favour of democratisation.

Putting pressure on the state from below during democratic transitions often has proven to be insufficient to provoke political reforms and to tilt the balance in favour of civil society, as authoritarian regimes generally reject the legitimacy of informal intermediary coalitions as representatives of civil society. In these cases, support from the international community could enhance the position of these coalitions (d). Requesting foreign governments or transnational actors to put pressure on an authoritarian regime is another measure that could be complementary to the pressure exerted from below. In addition to supporting intermediary coalitions with aid, private aid agencies can play a role in these advocacy efforts by actively supporting these coalitions and their lobbying campaigns directed at Northern and (indirectly) Southern governments. In recent years, special training courses on advocacy methods have been organised for Southern coalitions to improve their access to multilateral institutions and to enhance access to global civil society (Everts *et al.* 1996). Figure 3.1 illustrates how policy advocacy of civil society coalitions from below, combined with indirect pressure by transnational actors on the national government, potentially reinforces the role of these (temporary) coalitions in political society.

In later stages of democratic transition private aid interventions also can contribute to civil society building by supporting activities aimed at strengthening citizenship, in order to increase the legitimacy of a new (democratic) political power balance (e). Two types of civic education activities were identified in Chapter 1: those that enhance passive citizenship (such as electoral participation) and those activities in which citizens are encouraged to participate in public debates and are trained in democratic leadership for their community or organisation, stimulating more active forms of citizenship. This type of private aid intervention is generally implemented by specialised NGOs, often formerly engaged in popular education or in defending human rights. Especially in stages of late democratic transition, official agencies also become directly involved in supporting activities which aim at civic education. Financial support is either channelled directly to these specialised NGOs, or through semi-governmental bodies such as ombudsmen. This again brings up the question what are the comparative advantages of private aid agencies over official agencies concerning civil society building interventions in later stages of democratic transition. In other words, are official aid agencies taking over the role of private aid agencies in the area of civil society building?

– *Compatibility between official and private aid programmes*
To examine this question, the new official aid programmes supporting democratisation, human rights and 'good governance' need some closer examination. Basically, they are post-Cold War products, although several of these programmes advocating a 'new conditionality' have their roots in the late 1980s (Crawford 1995; De Feyter *et al.* 1995). The discourse on civil society building was an important part of these new official donor policies, although it can be questioned whether this

was really a break with previous policies. Robinson (1996a: 214) observed that these policies often are poorly defined and that 'there has been a tendency among some donors to reclassify reliable projects originally classified as developmental as being oriented at strengthening civil society'. For many official donors, support to Southern service-delivery NGOs or business associations had been common practice during the Cold War, and this support was often reclassified in the 1990s as part of civil society building programmes. The German government for several decades co-financed programmes of the party-affiliated *Stiftungen*, aimed at strengthening trade unions and (indirectly) sister-parties in the South, changing their stated function from 'supporting democracy' to 'strengthening civil society'. The US government (learning from the German experience) initiated similar programmes in the 1980s through the quasi-governmental *National Endowment for Democracy* (NED). These programmes generally pursued counter-insurgency objectives during the Cold War and were also rephrased in civil society terms by USAID, particularly to strengthen the private sector (W. Robinson 1996).

Therefore, these new post-Cold War programmes of official donors should be viewed with some scepticism. They implicitly advocate a market-led type of civil society building under the banner of pluralism, replacing the traditional anti-communist rhetoric.[12] Some authors even argue that the new policy agenda of official donors is part of a Western offensive 'to crush once and for all the ideology of socialism and replace it unambiguously with the ideology of free enterprise world-wide' (Bayra 1993: 16). Although Crawford (1995) and others criticise this view for being too conspiratorial, most of the new donor agenda on democratisation and strengthening civil society should be critically examined; practice has yet to prove that it represents a paradigm shift in official development strategies as some argue (Williams 1995). Most official donors tend to understand civil society building as part of the neoliberal approach of strengthening the private sector. Nevertheless, as Pearce (1997a: 65-6) has argued, it makes no sense for official aid donors to use the concept civil society when it actually *only* refers to associations, NGOs, human rights committees or other pressure groups: 'it reflects an aspiration [...] that somehow traditional elites, corrupt state officials, old-style party bosses and conservative economic forces will wither if "civil society" is stronger'. Or is increased attention from official donors for supporting civil society building a way to control similar activities of private aid agencies oriented at social change?

In the post-Cold War period the traditional difference between official and private aid agencies, where the first predominantly supported governmental institutions, and the latter societal actors, seems to have vanished. This division of labour was present in aid policies directed towards countries under authoritarian rule, when official agencies were reluctant to work with governments and preferred to contribute indirectly to democratisation by channelling their support through non-governmental aid chains. This division of tasks also was visible in top-down approaches of official donors to strengthen the rule of law and monitor elections, and bottom-up approaches of private aid agencies to support civil society building. However, it could be questioned whether this division of labour really changed in the 1990s. Crawford (1995) and Van Rooy (1998) show that civil society building programmes of official donors did not exceed ten percent of total official budgets dedicated to 'democracy promotion' between 1991 and 1995. Moreover, from this relatively small share available for civil society building, more than half was channelled through private aid agencies.[13]

The strategic orientation of civil society building programmes of official aid agencies also differs from those of many private aid agencies. USAID, the largest official donor involved in civil society building, has taken the lead in designing programmes oriented at 'building pluralism' in civil society as a motor for democratic policy reform (G. Hansen 1996). The purpose of USAID is to increase 'competition' between organisations in civil society and at the same time, as Blair (1997: 28) argues, to 'moderate the potentially destabilising effects of single memberships in exclusive groups (such as those based on ethnic, religious, territorial or economic cleavages)'. In other words, as long as aid recipients in civil society do not oppose their governments, they are eligible for official donor support.[14] It illustrates how official donors, and USAID in particular, use democracy promotion as a tool to achieve economic and political stability, which could conflict with civil society building strategies of private aid agencies that aim to make civil society more inclusive at the cost of (temporary) instability.

Despite losing several of their comparative advantages to official aid agencies in the post-Cold War period, particularly in terms of directly funding organisations in Southern civil societies, private aid agencies do not seem to have lost their *potential* to contribute to social change. For example, by operating autonomously from Northern governments and corporate interests, and their ability to enable and develop linkages within global civil society between transnational social actors in North and South.[15] An assumption of the present study is that private aid agencies actively contributed to civil society building in the South long before the end of the Cold War, and that they were particularly successful in pursuing this strategy throughout the 1980s. Even if this function is apparently dwindling in the post-Cold War period, and is partly being taken over by official aid agencies, it is important to consider these achievements in more detail. After all, results, or the absence of results, are too often assumed instead of carefully examined.

3.2 Pitfalls of assessing (private) aid impact

Private aid agencies (and those who finance them) obviously want to know what happens to their resources that are transferred annually to Southern recipients. Not only do they want to be sure that their money is spent according to the rules that were attached to it, but they also want to know the results of their interventions. Increasing effectiveness and improving 'performance' has become one of the top priorities of private aid agencies in the 1990s, as was explained in the previous chapter, for it largely determines their public credibility. More than just *proving* that results are positive, agencies have to *convince* the public that aid is working, as negative public attention is damaging to donor agency interests (Cassen *et al.* 1986). Another reason for assessing aid performance is to learn from the past, and especially to learn from failures. Incorporating lessons from previous interventions into future policies and implementation strategies may also increase effectiveness.

A common way to assess the performance of individual aid interventions is to evaluate results in relation to their initial objectives. The main purpose of evaluations is to identify strengths and weaknesses of a particular project, and to incorporate these into new programming strategies. However, the practice was different in past decades. Project evaluations by donor agencies were generally executed either to *control* recipients or to *reassure* donors, or both. They were rarely primarily meant for *learning*. Larger donors, such as the World Bank, have been particularly interested in the way their money was spent, and they often limited their evaluations to a simple cost-benefit exercise. Private aid agencies always criticised this (non-participatory) approach, but were not doing any better in practice as their evaluations generally focused on short-term trends, inputs and outputs. In her influential study of USAID-financed private aid programmes Tendler (1982: 129) questioned the gap between the rhetoric of process-oriented aid interventions and the persistent practice of output-oriented evaluation: 'That participation leads to improvements in poor people's lives is an article of faith for PVOs [Private Voluntary Organizations], not a hypothesis that one is interested in testing.' Despite assurances from the private aid sector that evaluation would be taken more seriously, little has changed since Tendler's observation. Riddell and Robinson (1995: 44) confirm this by adding: 'For most European NGOs working in the development field, evaluation is still very new and, if used at all, tends to be more of a one-off affair, most often embarked upon either because things have gone very wrong – the fire-brigade approach – or when a particular project has been completed but there is a request for further funding, or when a second or third phase of a particular project is to be launched.'

– *The evaluation paradox*
What explains this wide gap between the rhetoric and the reality of private aid evaluations? Why do agencies continue to remain sensitive to criticism from outsiders about an instrument (evaluation) that could potentially strengthen their work? Part of the explanation was given in the previous chapter, when the tension between institutional and development objectives was sketched. While the quality of private aid interventions (and maybe even their existence as institutions) depends on sound evaluations, simultaneously there is an apparent internal resistance to prioritise evaluations and to innovate assessment methods. Although there are signs that this tendency is changing now, it is important to examine this contradiction. Three interrelated factors could possibly explain this 'evaluation

paradox'. The first has to do with what Smillie (1995b: 158) calls 'the failure to learn from failure'. Private aid agencies have difficulty remembering what went wrong in the past and what can be learned from that: 'there are few reasons to disseminate the positive lessons of development, and many more powerful reasons to conceal and forget the negative ones'. This learning disability is integral to the propagandistic public image that is projected by private aid agencies in fund-raising campaigns, in which it is promised that small aid donations have direct effects as if they were 'magic bullets' able to kill poverty (Vivian 1994). To maintain this image (and the level of income) positive achievements and negative circumstances often are exaggerated and simplified. Serious evaluations that unmask problematic sides of this image are therefore not usually encouraged. But 'learning disability' is not sufficient as an explanation, as any institution probably prefers to project positive images about their activities, even though they know that the reality often is more complex.

Therefore, another explanation for the poor evaluation record of private aid agencies is the *absence of outside pressures* to seriously assess the effectiveness of their interventions. The persistence of upward accountability over many decades has made private aid agencies immune to outside pressures to examine the results of their activities. Southern counterparts obviously were least interested in systematic evaluations, as they would be most affected by this, due to their dependent position in the private aid chain. Nor did agency boards consider it necessary to dedicate more time and resources to evaluations, as long as aid disbursements seemed to be spent according to the rules, and income growth was not affected. The donating public, where the real pressure for evaluation should come from, was neutralised by effective private aid propaganda of isolated success stories in a world of misery. In fact, most effective has been the pressure from official donors, who started to demand more efficiency and better monitoring and evaluation by private agencies when official donations to private aid agencies skyrocketed in the 1980s. The trend of increased official funding for private and non-profit organisations was accompanied by a growing demand for accountability within government bureaucracies. Indirect pressure for evaluation also came from independent consultants, whose recommendations to use evaluation as an instrument for institutional learning found fertile ground in private aid agencies in the 1990s, when a wave of reorganisations accompanied the introduction of for-profit private sector management techniques in the non-profit sector. Evaluation as a learning tool was no longer concerned with improving the effectiveness of aid interventions, but also with institutional survival (Edwards 1997).

While outside pressures for systematic evaluations possibly contribute to tackling learning disabilities, private aid expenditures on evaluation still are only a tiny fraction of what is spent on fund-raising. This has to do with the problem that *evaluation is a complex affair*. Although it is not a valid reason to give it a low priority – as fund-raising also appears to be far from simple – evaluating results indeed involves a number of obstacles. One of the main arguments of private aid agencies to illustrate the complexities of evaluating their performance is to point at the difference between traditional development projects of official agencies (improving infrastructure or balance of payments) and support for social development. The construction of schools and roads is more easily visible and measurable than the empowerment of a community. Social development is considered to be a slow and long-term process, affected by many different variables and with diffuse and not very quantifiable results (Marsden and Oakley 1990). In theory, enormous advances have been made over the last decade in developing new methods for evaluating social development. Oakley (1996: 2) speaks of 'a number of key conceptual break-throughs' in the search for 'a more process-orientated, qualitatively sensitive and "learning form" of evaluation'. But whereas the theory prescribes programme strategies and process-orientation, the bulk of aid interventions in practice still operate in the 'project mode'.[16] Despite the cautious emergence of a new 'evaluation paradigm', the rhetoric is still running ahead of the practice (Marsden *et al.* 1994). After all, given the complexity of evaluating social development, the overwhelming current attention to evaluation suggests that private aid agencies simply have not tried hard enough in the past.

The three factors – learning disabilities, lack of outside pressure and complexity – to some extent explain the gap between the theoretical acceptance and the practical resistance towards evaluations. But there is an additional element that could explain the *persistence* of the evaluation paradox, which is hidden in the answer to the question: why is it necessary to evaluate at all? In the 1990s a consensus emerged among aid agencies that the evaluation of aid performance is not a goal in itself: it is a tool for periodic assessment of the relevance, performance, efficiency and impact of aid interventions in the context of previously stated objectives (Couderé 1994). In theory, there is probably also a consensus about the two main purposes of aid evaluation: *learning* and *control*. In other words, evaluation can be helpful in learning from the past, and adapting strategies in such a way that aid interventions will be more effective in the future, and on the other hand in increasing the accountability of aid agencies, so that their actions can be controlled by all parties involved. The evaluation paradox lies in the difficulty of finding a *balance* between these two purposes. Private aid agencies, as well as official agencies, have been interested primarily in the question whether aid has been 'working', since they have been pressured to show results of their activities. Only recently have they asked themselves the necessary additional question: why has aid worked at all, or why has it failed? (Smillie 1995a: 21). This question addresses issues that go beyond an exercise to measure quantifiable outputs, as it looks at the wider context in which these interventions take place and at the dynamics of the aid chain. Therefore, while it is important to assess the results of aid interventions, the way these results were achieved is probably of greater importance. Before elaborating on this argument, it should be clear what is understood by *impact* of aid interventions.

– *Difficulties involved in impact assessment*

According to Fowler (1997), results of aid interventions can be classified into three different categories: outputs, outcome and impact (see Table 3.2), as part of the sequence goals-objectives-activities-outputs-outcome-impact. Output is understood as the result of implemented activities, which is a measure of the invested *effort*. Outcome gives an indication of the *effectiveness* of a particular activity, a result that depends on more variables than the invested effort. Output and outcome are generally laid down in (project) objectives. Goals refer to the final (desired) result, the impact, of an intervention. Impact refers to sustained effectiveness over a longer period of time. Impact of private aid thus can be defined as *sustainable change* in the long term as a result of one or more development interventions. Impact can be negative or positive, intended or unintended, depending upon the initial development goals of interventions.

Table 3.2   *Points for assessing achievement of development initiatives*

Point of measurement	What is measured	Indicators
Outputs	Effort	Implementation of activities
Outcomes	Effectiveness	Use of outputs and sustained production of benefits
Impact	Change	Difference from the original problem situation

Source: Fowler (1997)

It is useful to consider this output-outcome-impact sequence as interlinked stages over a longer period of time, for it shows that results become more complex down the sequence, and thus will be more difficult to assess. Output generally can be rather precisely identified; outcome might take on a variety of appearances; and impact is never a single phenomenon: a wide variety of processes, people or institutions can have changed over time. This is caused by the fact that 'downwards' in the aid chain the number of actors involved increases, with each actor having their own perspective and vested interests. But impact also is complex to assess because the role of *external influences* increasingly affects results of aid interventions further down the aid chain, and over time. For example, it is relatively easy to control the construction of a road (output) to make a remote area in the countryside accessible, but whether the road really will be used (outcome) depends on variables outside the control of those that initiated its construction, whereas the changes that the construction of the road might have on the development of a remote area (impact) is contingent upon many other variables at the local and national levels. Finding out how, and to what extent, this aid intervention to construct a road caused (or ed to) a sustainable change in the development of a remote area, is referred to as *impact assessment*.[17]

relationships between activities, output, outcome and impact usually are) establish, as many new variables influence the results of aid intervention :. Linear cause-effect relationships are exceptional in development processes, which makes reliable assessments of outcome or impact of aid interventions very problematic. The example of the road was given to illustrate that, despite all the difficulties involved, impact assessment is not an impossible undertaking. However, in cases where output is more fluid and less visible, outcomes and impact automatically will become more diffuse and thus far more difficult to assess. This is generally the case with the desired results of interventions aimed at social development, such as 'empowerment' and 'civil society building'. Although impact assessment is without any doubt a complex affair, it would be too easy to conclude that it is *impossible* for private aid agencies to determine their impact; it probably has not been tried enough, and the current practice suggests that much can be learned from recent experiences.[18] Problems implicit to impact assessment can be grouped into three categories: complexities of the development process, methodological difficulties and organisational constraints.[19]

The first set of problems has to do with the fact that (social) development and aid interventions seldom are linear processes. Although it is now generally agreed that supporting social change is different from constructing a road, the input-output model in which effects are linked (in a linear mode) to causes still persists. The bulk of development aid is still predominantly based on projects, in which the underlying assumption (communicated in fund-raising campaigns) is that aid interventions will produce predictable results. However, logical frameworks to analyse and plan these interventions are unable to predict the complex process of social development which is contingent upon human behaviour, timescale and many other variables beyond donor agency control. That many private aid agencies raise false expectations with their simplified messages of attributing cause to effects is uncovered by examining the difficulties related to impact assessment. A look at the position of private agencies in the aid chain illustrates this. The majority of private aid agencies is dependent upon 'proxies' in the South, as was laid out in Chapter 2. These partner organisations (usually Southern development NGOs) often also perform a role as intermediaries by delegating the implementation of development activities to local membership organisations or community groups. As a result of their 'high' position in the aid chain, private aid agencies can hardly value their own performance because they are dependent upon other organisations further 'down' the chain for the realisation of their objectives. In terms of impact, the most private agencies can try to determine is how the relationship with the primary counterpart possibly affects the ultimate achievement of a particular activity.[20] In such a linear situation, which is highly theoretical as was noted earlier, the output of a private aid agency (information or resources) becomes the input for the intermediary organisation, whose outputs (resources or training) are the inputs for the implementing organisation. However, during every stage in this sequence the Northern agency loses more control, while external influences increasingly dominate. This makes the attribution of final output (let alone outcome or impact) to donor interventions rather difficult.

The same difficulty of attributing causes to effects applies to 'operational' agencies (such as *Save the Children* or *Plan International*) even if they fully control all intermediary organisations involved in an intervention and if they manage to 'minimise' the role of external influences. However, by doing so they probably will not be very successful in obtaining sustainable changes, because sustainability occurs when the impact of external interventions can be maintained within the society after a donor agency's withdrawal. In other words, if donors want to contribute to the sustainability of their interventions, they have to integrate the benefits of their interventions into the wider social, economic and political context. The implication is that results directly attributed to aid agency interventions cannot be 'measured' separately from this wider context. This explains the primary need for making a thorough analysis of the local (and sometimes international) context in which aid interventions take place before assessing their results (Couderé 1994).[21]

The difficulty of establishing linear relationships between aid interventions and impact also implies that caution is required in generalising about the results of individual (private) aid interventions in relation to overall agency performance. The overall objectives of donor agencies usually are laid down in 'mission statements' which guide strategic choices for combined aid interventions. But to assess the overall performance of aid agencies it is essential to examine results of individual projects as these still form the basic units of their output. The problem is that, on the one hand, mission statements are rather general and vague and often difficult to operationalise in concrete objectives that could be assessed against their results. On the other hand, aggregated performance of aid agencies is more than just the sum of individual project results, as many other factors beyond the project environment also determine final impact. To use the metaphor of projects as building blocks for development: you cannot define the characteristics of a wall just by looking at one brick, neither can the bricks be ignored in assessing the quality of the wall. In other words, there is no alternative for assessing performance of private aid agencies than by looking at individual projects, although these only give a partial picture of overall agency performance.

Another set of problems is generated by the choice of appropriate instruments and methods to determine the results of aid interventions. These problems also are related to the earlier mentioned difficulty of separating achievements of individual interventions from the complex context in which they take place. Therefore, the key to evaluating social change is to acknowledge the existence of non-linear relationships and recognise that, in the best case, only a 'relative causality' can be attributed to aid interventions.[22] However, rejecting linear and deterministic models to understand development processes does not imply that it is impossible to systematically survey the achievements of aid interventions. Assessing 'relative causality' requires a clear picture of the initial situation prior to intervention, against which results are to be measured. These so-called 'baseline data' often are not available, which means that they have to be reconstructed. A variety of quantitative and qualitative methods can be used to collect information about the situation prior to intervention. Direct involvement of beneficiaries to judge these data is an essential condition, for which several participatory techniques have been developed over the past decade (Chambers 1993, 1997).[23] In order to determine the level of relative causality, it is important to distinguish between baseline data directly linked to a project and data about variables outside the direct project environment.

Several obstacles are encountered in collecting baseline data. One is that a (private) aid agency has to be clear about the final development goals that are pursued and the means to achieve those. If an agency does not have an explicit 'theory of cause and change', symptoms and causes of the problems that are being tackled can be confused (Fowler and Biekart 1996). This has repercussions for the type of baseline that is constructed, as each cause requires a different solution and thus a different baseline. This obstacle can become more complicated when development goals are adjusted during the period of intervention, which is not exceptional, because it implies that multiple achievements have to be assessed (Blankenberg 1995).[24] Another obstacle is that generally too much information is collected to construct a baseline, or that the information available is not adequate to assess outcome or impact (Oakley 1996). This is a recurrent problem of evaluations, which can be avoided by maintaining an attitude of what Chambers (1993: 19) calls 'optimal ignorance': 'It requires experience to know what it is not worth knowing, and self-discipline and courage to abstain from trying to find it out.'

After reconstructing a baseline, giving a picture of the situation prior to intervention, choices have to be made about how to 'measure' the achievements during and after intervention. The challenge is to find suitable *indicators* to assess social change, which depends on: the assessment of tangible or intangible achievements; whether short- and medium-term objectives (output, outcome), or longer term development goals (impact) are to be assessed; the level on which change occurs (family, organisation, society); whose change is mapped; when these indicators are used; and who determines the choice of these indicators.[25] Qualitative indicators are appropriate if they comply with some general standards: they should be consistent, unambiguous, specific, easy to collect and sensitive; in other words, they should be reliable (Casley and Kumar 1987). One of the pitfalls in developing indicators is that they tend to measure those results that are either expected or desired. But social change is generally not very predictable and the role of external (not expected or controlled) variables also should be part of the assessment. As unintended or unexpected results of aid interventions often emerge during impact assessments, indicators often have to be adjusted during the process. This can affect the assumptions on which an impact assessment has been built and can frustrate the whole effort as new baselines have to be constructed.[26] The previous overview also suggests that there is seldom a single indicator for assessing impact. Usually a combination of variables is selected to map social change for which several appropriate indicators have to be chosen, with the implicit danger that an overload of qualitative indicators can make the interpretation of achievements a rather complex exercise. The choice of indicators is probably less problematic than the challenge to translate these qualitative indicators into verifiable and recognisable actions that can be monitored (Oakley 1996).[27]

A third set of problems that agencies encounter in their efforts to assess the impact of their interventions is related to organisational constraints. Serious impact evaluation is costly, time-consuming and requires specially trained staff. Most (smaller) agencies cannot afford this, also because overheads have to remain low for fund-raising purposes. If aid agencies would prioritise learning as a means towards institutional survival, rather than prioritising public fund-raising, impact assessments could become an integrated part of the 'project cycle'. In the past, organisational performance assessments of donor agencies were often delinked from assessing performance of projects 'in the field'. But growing pressures on agencies to improve performance *and* accountability accelerated the need for integrating organisational performance into their impact assessments (Edwards and Hulme 1995). The key problem for assessing organisational performance of private aid agencies (and of non-profit organisations in general) is the absence of a tangible *bottom line*, that is, a set of criteria that serves the same purpose as profit for the performance of business enterprises.

A bottom line for private aid performance could be constructed by those organisations and groups that directly or indirectly affect (or are affected by) the activities of an agency (Fowler 1997). These so-called 'stakeholders' are more than just direct beneficiaries or target groups of an aid agency ('primary stakeholders'), they also include other groups to which it has formal obligations: intermediary organisations, governments, official donors, individual private donors, agency boards and the agency staff itself ('secondary stakeholders').[28] Fowler (1997: 173) defines a non-profit bottom line as 'the effective satisfaction of the rights and interests of legitimate stakeholders in keeping with its mission'. Aid agency performance is thus determined by the extent to which it manages to serve multiple stakeholders. It implies that agencies cannot just set their own standards of performance (or bottom lines), but that these are determined by negotiation among (legitimate) stakeholders. By implementing these structured stakeholder performance assessments, private aid agencies also can solve the earlier mentioned problems of improving their (functional and strategic) accountability.[29] In other words, only when performance standards and bottom lines are negotiated among multiple constituencies, are private aid agencies potentially able to strengthen their multiple accountabilities (Edwards and Hulme 1995).

But again, theory regarding these matters seems to have made more progress than the reality in the field. Not surprisingly, negotiation among stakeholders is often frustrated by differences in power and vested interests. Private aid agencies tend to be more responsive to those groups that have the most leverage over their decision-making, such as donors or governments, than to their primary stake-holders in the South. Moreover, despite good intentions, most private aid evaluations still only examine direct outputs and immediate results and seldom try to engage in more time-consuming and complex assessments of outcomes or longer term impacts of aid interventions.[30] But if their legitimacy continues to be challenged, as was the case in the first half of the 1990s, private aid agencies will be forced – for the sake of institutional survival – to take performance assessments more seriously. It could serve as a tool to learn from past failures and it could potentially improve their strategic accountability.

3.3 Impact assessment in practice

The early 1990s generated a substantial number of empirical studies assessing the impact of private aid interventions. Although often called 'impact studies', most of these actually focused on immediate results, rather than longer term impact. They could be classified in three different groups. The first group of studies focused on the impact of aid interventions of one particular private aid agency, often in several Southern countries. Generally, they were sponsored by the agencies themselves, sometimes as part of programme or country reviews co-financed by official donors. These impact assessments usually examined the results of one particular programme or project, but a multi-project approach has become popular to compare results from projects in different national contexts. Examples are studies by the *Inter-American Foundation*[31] (Carroll 1992), ICCO (Hardeman *et al.* 1995), NOVIB-OXFAM UK/I (Blankenberg 1995) and *Save the Children* (Edwards 1996b). A second set of impact studies focused on the impact of multiple private aid agencies with a high dependency ratio on official funding, generally initiated and financed by official aid agencies. Examples are impact studies by USAID (Tendler 1982; Blair *et al.* 1995), the Danish impact evaluation (Bering *et al.* 1989), the British ODI study (Riddell 1990; Riddell and Robinson 1992, 1995), the Dutch impact study (Stuurgroep 1991), the Finnish impact study (Riddell *et al.* 1994), the British ODA study (Surr 1995), the Swedish SIDA study (Riddell *et al.* 1995) and the Australian NGO Programs Effectiveness Review (AIDAB 1995).[32] A third group of impact studies was designed and implemented by independent researchers and often financed with academic resources. Many studies in this category actually did not focus on private donor agencies but on Southern recipients. Examples are Smith's study of Colombian NGOs (1990), Farrington and Bebbington (1993), Fowler's study on Kenyan NGOs (1993b), Van Niekerk's research on rural NGOs in the Andes (1994), Macdonald (1997) on Nicaraguan and Costa Rican NGOs, and Put (1998) on Indian NGOs. What can be learned from these studies, and what do they conclude about the impact of (European) private aid interventions?

All these studies apparently share the same objective: to assess the development impact of private aid interventions. But a closer look indicates that they serve different purposes. Carroll (1992) only examined local intermediary organisations, because the *Inter-American Foundation* was primarily interested in seeing what thirty 'well-performing' partners had achieved in terms of organisation and development strategies. The British ODI study also only examined Southern NGOs, and focused particularly on the effectiveness, impact and sustainability of sixteen poverty-alleviating projects in Bangladesh, India, Uganda and Zimbabwe (Riddell 1990). The Danish NGO evaluation examined the comparative advantages of private aid agencies over official agencies, and the changing relationships between private agencies and the official Danish aid agency DANIDA (Bering *et al.* 1989). Although the Dutch, Finnish and Swedish impact studies explicitly aimed at assessing the effectiveness and efficiency of private aid agencies, the emphasis was primarily on immediate outputs of recipient Southern NGOs and not so much on the longer term impact of private aid interventions. The four Dutch private aid agencies, which initiated and financed the Dutch impact study, were mainly interested in direct results to counter growing public doubts about the quality of their projects in the South.[33] The Finnish and Swedish impact studies, coordinated by an independent evaluation team, were financed by official aid agencies (FIN-NIDA and SIDA), which also determined the focus and design of the studies. Officially, they were meant to map the strengths and weaknesses of private aid agencies, but in practice the studies were biased towards assessing the performance of Southern partners. SIDA wanted to have a better picture of the activities of Swedish private aid agencies, and especially about the use of official aid funds and their effects (Riddell *et al.* 1995: 18).[34] This suggests that the major purpose of these impact studies was to reassure donors (and to a lesser extent to control recipients), and not primarily to learn from failures in the past.

What can be learned from the methodology of these multi-agency impact studies, and how were all the pitfalls intrinsic to impact assessment confronted? Although they used different methodologies, a similar approach can be identified within these studies. Aid resources and the immediate objectives of private aid agencies (approved by official donors) were considered as inputs for development interventions, generating certain outputs along the aid chain, either at the level of project executing agencies or at the level of beneficiaries. Depending upon the time-frame that was used, outputs or outcomes were assessed and analysed within a broader context of developments and trends in a particular country. The Dutch study acknowledged that it was impossible to measure impact, due to a lack of reliable baseline data and explicit project objectives (Stuurgroep 1991). The Swedish study tackled this last point by identifying general criteria, based on SIDA policy documents, against which the performance of the case studies was judged in addition to evaluating immediate project objectives.[35] These broad development criteria were proposed as indicators for development impact. But given the short time framework of projects (three years) and impact study (six months) it would have been more reasonable to state that what was at most 'measured' was project outcome, rather than impact.

The project-oriented approach of the case studies revealed a secondary concern for development processes and dynamics inside aid chains. As many Nordic and Dutch private aid agencies often depend on official aid resources for over eighty percent of their budgets, they in effect perform a role as intermediaries of official aid, which makes aid chains even more complex. The Swedish impact study observed that between SIDA and the final beneficiaries sometimes five 'administrative layers' were involved, all serving as intermediaries of aid resources.[36] This is an important observation, because it triggers the question: *whose* impact is being assessed? And as was explained earlier, it is virtually impossible to disaggregate the aid chain into parts that are linked with one another in a linear fashion.[37] A common element in these impact studies was to portray the role of official donors as passive outsiders. In fact, the complex interdependent relationships within aid chains received little attention, and all the impact studies primarily focused on local recipient organisations as project executors. However, local aid recipients often receive funding from several private aid agencies, which means that multiple objectives have to be assessed.[38] Although the complexities involved in 'isolating' project executors from the aid chain were acknowledged by the evaluators, the impact studies rather looked at linearity than at relative causality. This resulted in two issues of *methodological* concern: the selection of appropriate case studies and the analysis of aid impact within the broader local context.

Impact studies generally work with a case study approach. Despite the difficulty of generalising about results for an agency as a whole, it is inevitable that a limited number of projects are selected for more detailed evaluation.[39] The point is which criteria are used to select case studies, and who determines these criteria. Selection criteria generally are donor-driven and are seldom defined in a participatory process with beneficiaries. Selection of case studies in large impact studies proved to be a two-step exercise. First, a number of countries were selected in order to get a balanced view from several continents. Taken together, the selected countries generally represented the priority areas of the private aid donors.[40] Second, from these countries a sample of projects was selected, representing the variety of sectors and intervention strategies of the entire programme. Although seldom stated explicitly – such as in Carroll (1992) and Macdonald (1997) – most studies usually selected the more 'successful' projects for evaluation.[41] The reason for not making this known was probably to avoid comments that these impact studies wanted to provide only a positive picture of impact. But also from a learning perspective it is often best to select well-performing projects, as the extent of the impact will be more clear and easier to detect than with frustrated project interventions.

In all the impact studies under review it was recognised that evaluations of selected case studies had to be analysed within a wider national context, as it is not unusual that 'any positive changes in the lives of the poor are primarily attributed to the development projects initiated by NGOs, even though they might result from factors external to the project' (Riddell and Robinson 1992: 31). The relevant data needed to analyse this wider environment varies considerably among impact studies. The British study focused on poverty alleviation projects and was therefore interested in two particular issues: the policies, achievements and failures of government and official aid agencies in alleviating poverty, and the role and impact of local NGOs in this wider picture. The Dutch study focused on different types of private aid interventions and made an inventory of local NGO practices in the selected countries, combined with an analysis of the relations of these NGOs with government policies, political parties and churches, target groups and donor organisations.[42] These country studies served as a framework for the case studies, but since results of the latter were never published, the relation between case studies and context analyses remains unclear. The Finnish and Swedish studies integrated context and case studies analyses into separate country case studies. Social and economic context analysis was combined with an analysis of governmental and official aid agency activities in relation to the projects that were evaluated. The Swedish study also analysed Swedish private aid interventions in relation to the strengths and weaknesses of the totality of local NGO development efforts. This integrated approach, although quickly and superficially executed, certainly was a step forwards. It emphasised the challenge for impact studies to link micro- and macro-analysis, and to integrate project evaluations and country context analyses in order to judge the role of external factors as part of impact assessments.

Impact studies ultimately are meant to judge the impact of development interventions, in this case of European private aid agencies. Before looking at the conclusions of these studies, a comment should be made about the *validity* of their findings. The samples of selected case studies on which these conclusions were based were relatively small and biased towards more successful projects. If this is added to the variety of project interventions and project objectives, national contexts that cannot be compared, and the fact that most projects were still ongoing, obviously any generalisation about these findings should be treated with caution. Difficulties intrinsic to impact evaluations – such as a lack of baseline data, unambiguous initial objectives and undisputed qualitative indicators – led the Dutch study to conclude that evaluating under these conditions meant at best 'judging'. This confirms an earlier assumption: instead of 'measuring' impact it is more appropriate to speak of 'judging' or 'assessing' impact. Two areas of private aid impact addressed in these studies will be summarised below: poverty alleviation and civil society building.

– *Findings of impact studies*
For several decades, the broad overall objective of private aid interventions has been to contribute to tackling poverty. The British ODI study, exclusively designed to assess the performance of poverty alleviation projects, was rather doubtful about

impact in this area. Although three-quarters of private aid-financed projects evaluated broadly met their immediate objectives and produced expected outputs, findings of outcome and impact were less favourable.[43] Three issues repeatedly were mentioned as crucial elements in assessing the impact of projects aimed at reducing poverty: *poverty reach* (reaching the poorest), *poverty impact* (improving the economic situation of the poor) and *project sustainability*. One of the major findings of the British study was that private aid interventions failed to reach the poorest: 'almost without exception, the poor benefited to a greater extent than the poorest, and men to a greater degree than women' (Riddell and Robinson 1992: 15). Although the study suggests that this might have been caused by the absence of specific objectives to target the poorest, the Dutch study found that income-generating programmes were indeed directed at the very poorest, but that it was not proven that they had actually benefited from those activities.

Carroll's study found that the 'middle poor' generally tended to benefit more from private aid interventions, and even the 'best performing' projects counted relatively few direct beneficiaries among the poorest rural households (Carroll 1992: 67). Along the same lines, the Finnish study concluded that private aid had been targeted at poorer sections of society, but that it was hard to discern whether these were really the poorest: 'Indeed, a few projects which claimed to be for the poorest were in fact not' (Riddell *et al.* 1994: 133). The Swedish study, reaching the same conclusions, explains this by pointing at the lack of initial baseline studies to identify and target the poor. As a result, Swedish private aid agencies too often assumed that they were targeting the very poorest, instead of verifying that this was the case. The studies concluded that it is not always easy to identify the poorest layers of a society as the poorest are generally unorganised. Even when it was possible to identify them, it proved to be difficult to find a way of working with them. The Swedish study also pointed at circumstances in which it might be preferable to work with the less poor segments of society, for instance in experiments with ecological farming techniques. But this leaves the conclusion in these impact studies in tact that private aid agencies have been unable to reach the poorest sectors of society.

Disappointing poverty *reach* does not automatically mean that poverty *impact* was also limited. Did private aid interventions have an impact on *reducing* poverty? Evidence from the impact studies is not very encouraging. The British ODI study evaluated income-generating projects and found that in only a quarter of the projects was the income of the poorest raised significantly. The British ODA study (Surr 1995) concluded that these projects rarely resulted in benefits for the poor which could be regarded as significant enough to challenge the existing social or economic status quo in their local areas. The Dutch impact study also concluded that it was not clear whether the poorest really benefited from income-generating programmes, while the non-poor in some cases did. Credit programmes potentially could improve the income and employment opportunities of the poor, but their impact also was found to be limited (Riddell *et al.* 1995). A concern was that these programmes were very dependent upon external resources and thus not very sustainable (Stuurgroep 1991).

Project interventions aimed at the delivery of social services (health care, education or drinking water) generally performed better and often had a significant impact on the living conditions of the poor, according to the Dutch study. But results appeared to be rather short-term and biased towards outcome instead of impact. The Swedish study pointed at the negative impact of social service delivery, in which private aid resources substituted for decreasing government expenditures for basic social services. Not only did these projects have a limited impact and lack sustainability, but they also 'only very indirectly attempt to address poverty' (Riddell *et al.* 1995: 77). Limited resources of individual projects were often not sufficient to make the necessary investments that could enhance income and employment, according to the evaluators.[44] Another explanation that was suggested was that these private aid interventions were not based on an adequate conceptualisation of what poverty is, how it is caused or how it is to be addressed. An appropriate 'theory of poverty' would emphasise the political dimension of poverty: the need to build organisational and political capacity among the poor, which could address dominant power relationships. The Swedish case studies suggested that private aid 'is most likely to have an impact when it directly addresses the social relationships that underlie poverty – such as land holding relationships, territorial conflicts, or having greater power to influence the distribution of profits – and which increases the organisational, political and entrepreneurial capacities of the poor to tackle these relationships for themselves' (Riddell *et al.* 1995: 79). In other words, strengthening civil society is probably a key tool for enhancing the poverty impact of private aid interventions.

This was confirmed by an additional element that negatively affected the lasting impact of private aid interventions aimed at poverty alleviation: the lack of (financial) *sustainability* of projects. 'Virtually none of the NGOs evaluated in this study would be able to survive without foreign aid resources', observed the Dutch study (Stuurgroep 1991: 41), largely confirming the earlier findings of the British ODI study. The inability of local project partners to become self-sufficient after private aid interventions had been completed, was mentioned as a general concern. The problem of sustainability appeared to be particularly acute in projects delivering social services to the poor, who are obviously unable to pay for these services. Ideally the state, with adequate tax revenues, should take responsibility to finance and organise delivery of social services to the poor, but in an era of structural adjustment and downsizing of government budgets this is unlikely to happen;[45] where governments are inefficient and weak, aid interventions aiming at service delivery often tend to contribute to 'gap-filling'.

What causes the lack of financial sustainability? The British ODA study argued that the inability of (Southern) governments to take over project financing and the lack of local resources to replace foreign assistance is the main cause of low sustainability (Surr 1995). But the Finnish study also blamed private aid agencies

who had not seriously anticipated how to sustain processes they had been supporting until only the end of projects, when shifting to sustainability obviously was
difficult. The Swedish study found that the likelihood of financial sustainability is
greater when project executors consider sustainability a priority issue, when
beneficiaries are not among the poorest (and are able to make their own contributions) and primary stakeholders have a firm commitment to a project. Most studies
arrive at similar conclusions: stimulating self-financing mechanisms should be part
of integrated efforts to strengthen the capacity of overseas counterparts.

The Finnish and Swedish studies go even further and point at the need to view
sustainability as a broader objective, beyond thinking of self-sustainability only in
terms of resources. These studies point at sustainability as a *process*, that is, the way
in which a project enables primary stakeholders to survive without external
inputs.[46] Strengthening the capacity of these primary stakeholders – through
training, learning and organisation – can generate an impact that lasts well beyond
the completion of aid interventions, given that these interventions 'aim to enhance
the capacity of the poor to respond to political and economic processes' (Bebbington and Kopp 1995: 68). Similarly, Carroll (1992: 178-9) concludes that 'the only
way service-provision can become a sustainable and cumulative process is if the
recipients learn to manage their resources, deal more effectively with the government and the market, and develop community-based institutions of their own'.
This seems to be the case also for income-generating projects. Van Niekerk (1994)
in his impact study of rural development NGOs in Peru and Bolivia, found that
their limited economic impact could only be improved if the organisational
capacity of Andean peasants was increased with empowerment strategies that
would enable them to exert the pressure that could lead to better political and
economic conditions.

What is suggested here is that private aid interventions aimed at poverty
alleviation are more likely to increase sustainability (and consequently, their
impact) when they simultaneously manage to empower primary stakeholders. This
appears to be a crucial point as it implies that civil society building, of which
organisational capacity building is only one element, possibly could enhance the
impact of private aid interventions. Although none of the studies assessed the
impact of civil society building interventions as a separate strategy, most of them
did examine one or more of the elements that were mentioned earlier. Five types
of private aid interventions contributing to civil society building were identified
earlier: building organisational capacity, building sectoral alliances, building
intermediary channels, building international alliances, and building citizenship.
Several impact studies addressed the issue of organisational capacity, although
framed in concepts such as 'empowerment', 'participation' or 'consciousness
raising'. Building organisational capacity (the most basic form of civil society
building) was disaggregated by the Dutch study into four steps: mobilising
unorganised people, building cohesion within a group, developing capacity and
'consciousness' with training programmes, leading to collective action. The case

studies found that mobilisation was generally successful, but that no evidence was provided that cohesion was sustainable. The achievements of training and collective action were difficult to assess due to a lack of adequate instruments and clear objectives. Although some examples indicated that organisations could be successful in achieving results with collective action, the overall picture was not convincing: 'there are no examples of fundamental changes in power relations, nor of an essentially changed way of decision-making. Regarding gender relations there have been hardly any changes at all' (Stuurgroep 1991: 35). Other impact studies also found that the impact of private aid interventions questioning gender relationships and enhancing the capacity of women had been limited or absent.

Carroll's study (1992) found that 'well-performing' partners of the *Inter-American Foundation* scored low on building organisational capacity, but relatively higher on service delivery and poverty reach. He concluded therefore that access to resources and services did not necessarily enhance the capacity of grassroots organisations. He distinguished between an internal dimension of group capacity building (learning how to manage resources collectively) and an external dimension in which groups learn how to make claims on power holders. It turned out to be more difficult to mobilise for group management, requiring more sustained activity and dealing with individual and group dynamics, than to mobilise for claim-making. But when groups managed to accomplish concrete joint tasks this often led to more demanding and complex endeavours, creating a positive dynamic fuelled by Hirschmann's 'social energy'. While the effectiveness of poverty alleviation interventions demanded group capacity, Carroll suggested that the effectiveness of social change and claim-making also depended upon a solid core of tangible benefits around which community participation could take place. He recognised the paradox implicit to top-down planning with external resources in order to enable the poor to participate from the bottom up, a process that Uphoff (1992) calls 'assisted self-reliance'.

The key to success, according to Carroll, is that aid interventions manage to teach networks of individuals and informal groups how to deal effectively with the wider environment. As local organisations are generally not fixed or stable, 'capacity building at this level often implies sustaining and reinforcing networks of individuals and informal groups of people. [...] These multiple, fluid, often overlapping networks form the organizational base within which specific forms of aggregations appear, disappear, and reappear' (Carroll 1992: 104). These groups should therefore attempt to internalise and reproduce this collective experience so that it can have an effect even after a particular organisation has ceased to exist. Carroll also admitted that it is very difficult to assess the impact of capacity building interventions on such a fluid and mutating organisational network. He made an interesting point by suggesting that the conversion of 'social energy' to a network of organisational capacities can best be accomplished with 'outside independent and sympathetic assistance' and with a support structure that provides both vertical power linkages and horizontal networks of civil engagement (1992:

181). However, the success of this external assistance is assumed since its actual achievements were unfortunately not assessed.[47]

Two elements thus appear to be critical in the evaluation of case studies oriented at building organisational capacity: *participation* and *sustainability*. Participation can be defined as the direct involvement of citizens in decisions that affect their livelihoods. It has two dimensions in relation to aid interventions: input (participation of primary stakeholders in intervention processes) and output (participation of primary stakeholders in political processes). The first aspect has become highly valued in development discourse and can be considered an indicator for the quality of partnership and internal accountability. It is assumed that aid interventions are more effective when beneficiaries are actively involved at all stages (project design, planning, implementation, monitoring and evaluation). Despite the rhetoric, stakeholder participation generally has proven to be weak as Carroll (1992) and Riddell *et al.* (1995) have shown. Even if tangible benefits are provided in the short term, stakeholder participation seldom has led to long-term growth in participation (Carroll 1992: 92). Unintended effects of organisational capacity building also have occurred, for example when organisations were strengthened primarily to adapt themselves to the requirements of funders. This is risky, because the purpose of organising can become depoliticised in the process of organisation building when 'organisation' is limited to a simple way of getting access to external resources. Complacency and dependency have in some cases even resulted in 'disempowerment', as was argued elsewhere (Fowler and Biekart 1996).

A recurrent dilemma of organisation building is the predominance of successful charismatic leadership which many organisations are dependent on for their effectiveness. Although this appears to be less damaging for the level of participation, it often contributes to a loss of dynamism in later stages of organisational development, as it affects the sustainability of aid interventions (Carroll 1992; Fisher 1994). As part of building organisational capacity, the Swedish study warned that private aid agencies should encourage partners to broaden authority, experience and skills in their organisation, and prevent it from becoming too dependent upon one individual. This has proven to be problematic, because personal relationships between funders and recipients often are crucial for maintaining fluid communications about the progress of programmes. The Swedish study found that private aid agencies sometimes (unconsciously) have contributed to a concentration of power and authority in one (charismatic) leader. Despite this, it was also suggested that investments in human and organisational capacity, in the long run, are likely to have more sustainable impact than any other aid intervention (Riddell *et al.* 1995: 85).

Particularly relevant for building organisational capacity is the second dimension of participation, in which members of an organisation are committed to changing their livelihoods. Riddell *et al.* (1994: 140) somewhat ambiguously stated in the Finnish study that 'in some cases the beneficiaries have quite genuinely been empowered; in others any empowerment remains nebulous both in concept and practice'. They pointed at the difficulty of building capacity simultaneously on many fronts: 'if management skills are in place but financial support is not, then there is insufficient "capacity" built to ensure sustainability'. Due to unfavourable environments in which private aid agencies (and their partners) operate, the report added that it is unreasonable to expect organisations to build capacity on all fronts in the short term. The Swedish study argued that building grassroots capacity is the most crucial dimension of participation, although the authors concluded that (with some exceptions) little evidence was provided in the case studies that private aid agencies have attempted to address these issues seriously.

Only in the 1990s did civil society building become an explicit objective of private aid interventions, as was outlined earlier. Although several elements of this strategy already figured in earlier mission statements of private aid agencies – such as building organisational capacity or building alliances – it was seldom stated as a primary objective. Not surprisingly, most impact studies discussed here included cases that were primarily oriented at either service delivery or income-generating projects, often with a component of capacity building. None of them studied organisations that, for example, had as their primary objective to influence government policies or to serve as intermediaries between civil society and the state. The emphasis of most impact studies was on local organisations dedicated to poverty alleviation, with little attention for advocacy-oriented and policy-reforming local organisations. However, most multiple agency impact studies mentioned the *potential* of private aid agencies and their partners to mobilise groups to oppose authoritarian governments, albeit without really assessing the impact of these interventions.[48] Some evidence on private aid impact in relation to civil society building programmes was provided by the earlier mentioned 'third category' of 'independent' impact studies.

Fowler, for example, assessed the potentials and constraints of Kenyan NGOs in shaping political processes. He found that aid interventions often contribute to regime stability, and even 'undermine people's ability to assert themselves towards the state in their own interest' (Fowler 1993b: 209). He suggested that through their micro-development work – improving the conditions of the poorest, enabling the formation of new civic groups, mediating with government agencies at local level – Kenyan NGOs had a passive effect on civil society building, thereby confirming what was said earlier about building organisational capacity. But he also found that they had been unable to create inclusive coalitions at the macro-level between sub-national groupings that could strengthen political society, 'which suggests an over-optimism on the part of donors who articulate such an optimism' (Fowler 1993b: 209). He identified two obstacles for Kenyan NGOs to increase the inclusiveness of civil society and accountability of the state. An internal obstacle was their fragmentation and lack of cohesion as a result of competitiveness, which prevented the creation of a representative structure to influence state policies. Externally, the government managed to diminish the autonomy of NGOs by incorporating them into the development administration, partly as a result of conditions from official donors, and partly because the government decided to prioritise support to ethnic groups with whom NGOs traditionally had been working. The consequence was that increased official aid reduced the ability of Kenyan NGOs to function as what Fowler (1993b: 300) calls 'genuine expressions of Kenya's civil society'.[49] The increase of official aid to Kenya, and the lack of local financial resources to sustain NGO activities, also had an unintended impact: increased dependence on foreign aid threatened these NGOs with becoming 'local agents in a system of global service delivery' (Fowler 1993b: 301).

The evidence from Latin America is more pronounced, as private aid interventions generally had a stronger political dimension, particularly during the 1980s in countries with repressed oppositions under authoritarian regimes. In the case of Colombia, Smith (1990) assessed the political impact of thirty-six Colombian NGOs, all financed by North American and European private aid agencies. Some of these private aid agencies stated that their primary objective was to pursue social and economic change through political empowerment of the poor. A vast majority of his sample of Colombian NGOs indicated that they had tried to act as mediators between grassroots organisations and local governments, or national authorities, in order to improve public services for the poor. Half of them admitted that they had been successful in persuading government officials, particularly in improving public services for the poor. Smith concludes that the function of Colombian NGOs as brokers between local communities and government agencies thus was successful, even if it did not produce any fundamental reordering of power in society. Interestingly, he found that the objectives of private aid agencies (pursuing social and economic change) generally were not shared by Colombian partner NGOs. On the contrary, Colombian NGOs 'not only seldom attempt to mobilize the poor to confront political and economic elites, they also enhance social stability by meeting some of the basic needs of those who do not benefit significantly from the system' (Smith 1990: 263). In other words, in line with what Fowler argues, he concludes that private aid interventions contributed to enhancing the political and economic status quo in Colombia, and that NGOs generally served as 'gap-fillers' in the provision of public social services.

Smith's findings and his far-reaching conclusions need some closer examination, particularly since his study is one of the few independent efforts trying to assess the political impact of private aid interventions in Latin America. However, his methodology (semi-structured interviews) and time-frame (three months) indicate that his evaluation of Colombian NGOs could at best detect short-term results. Evaluation of longer term impact of private aid interventions would probably generate other outcomes. He actually admits this by suggesting that in the long run these interventions could be quite significant: 'quiet but steady growth in self-confidence and autonomy among beneficiaries might spill over into more overt political opposition – especially if there is greater cooperation between the non-profit sector and if non-profits eventually forge alliances with partisan political movements' (Smith 1990: 277). Unfortunately, he does not assess this longer term impact and only points, similarly to studies mentioned earlier, at the *potential* impact of private aid interventions. Smith's findings about the short-term stabilising and 'gap-filling' effect of private aid interventions are important to take into consideration for impact evaluations in other regions. Although his hypothesis was tested in the Cold War context of the 1980s, it possibly still holds true for the 1990s, but this needs to be assessed carefully. The weak part of his conclusions is that he makes assumptions about presumed long-term political impact of private aid interventions (which he finally considered to be irrelevant), without seriously monitoring or evaluating these trends. Smith's overall conclusion (1990: 282) that the international private aid network 'performs a system-maintenance function, both at the international level among nations and within rich and poor countries themselves' is therefore not convincingly sustained by evidence.

A more recent independent impact study of private aid interventions in Latin America is Macdonald's study on Costa Rica and Nicaragua. She evaluated six private aid interventions of North American and European private aid agencies, primarily aimed at civil society building. Macdonald criticises Smith's generalisations about private aid impact for creating a false dichotomy between interventions providing short-term benefits (reform) versus those contributing to structural transformations (revolution). Instead, Macdonald (1997: 147) proposes an intermediate position, in which 'NGOs as agents of civil society' are considered to be 'potential contributors to democratisation and greater social equality, as neither completely irrelevant nor the prime movers of social change'. Despite selecting relatively successful local NGOs, for the most part working with combined poverty alleviation and empowerment objectives, she found that these NGOs contributed little or nothing to the material well-being of the poor.[50] This confirms her initial assumption that the political impact of NGO activities was potentially of greater importance than short-term poverty alleviation, despite the difficulty of mechanically separating the economic and political dimensions of interventions: 'NGOs must thus address the question of how to create economic alternatives for the poor in such a way that also contributes to their levels of organization, democratic participation, and ability to challenge entrenched structures of power' (Macdonald 1997: 146).

It also confirms the assumption of the Swedish impact study about the need for civil society building as a condition for enhancing the impact of private aid interventions aimed at poverty alleviation. But what does it prove? In Costa Rica, Macdonald found that NGOs were not very successful in trying to mobilise organisations promoting social change, due to co-optive measures by the state and clientelistic social structures. In Nicaragua during the Sandinista revolution, NGOs were better able to mobilise for social change although often strengthening the Sandinista state instead of civil society. Macdonald's findings are rather ambiguous, possibly because she pays little attention to the dynamics inside the aid chain. Her conclusion that NGOs (despite the limited autonomy of civil society from the state) are contributing to a long-term process of constructing civil society in these countries actually is an assumption. But, unfortunately, it does not *prove* the potential of private aid agencies to contribute to civil society building.

In sum, little concrete evidence so far has been provided by impact studies about the contribution of private aid agencies to building alliances in civil society and strengthening intermediary roles of civil society coalitions *vis-à-vis* the state. This point is confirmed by a recent synthesis of virtually all multi-agency impact studies, which concludes (concerning private aid contributions to civil society building) 'that the impact is modest, but that there is little hard evidence and no indicators with which to judge progress or performance' (Kruse *et al.* 1997: B-29). More evidence has recently been appearing on the impact of international advocacy, and in particular on the role of transnational alliances operating in 'global civil society' aimed at influencing multilateral organisations and other international actors.[51] Private aid agencies can contribute to providing access for local civil society organisations to these transnational alliances, as another important element of civil society building strategies. For example, by targeting policies of the World Bank with transnational advocacy efforts, national alliances could potentially democratise development policies of their home countries (Fox 1996). Yet the variety of these alliances, and the diversity of their purposes and working methods makes it difficult to generalise about their achievements, let alone about the effectiveness of private aid involvement in these alliances. Without any doubt significant gains have been made by transnational advocacy alliances, especially in mobilising international media and Northern public opinion (Krut 1997). But this is also a potential danger, as unequal power relations between private aid agencies and Southern coalitions could be further enhanced, making aid chain dynamics even more complicated (Edwards 1993). Jordan and Van Tuijl (1997) argue that it is extremely difficult for Southern organisations to operate effectively outside their own political arena without the risk of compromising their local political responsibilities. Consequently, assessing the impact of advocacy campaigns via aid chains that oscillate between global and local levels appears to be even more difficult (Keck and Sikkink 1998).

The previous overview has shown that evaluating the impact of (private) aid interventions aimed at civil society building is still in a pioneering phase. There is a consensus in the literature that private aid agencies have the potential to contribute to civil society building. But there also is a consensus that there is still a lack of firm and reliable evidence on the impact of private aid interventions, especially when it concerns civil society building: 'most impact assessments rely on qualitative data and judgements and most are undertaken very rapidly. The majority have been content to report on and record outputs achieved and not outcomes achieved, or broader impact' (Kruse *et al.* 1997: vii). Another obstacle is the learning disability of private aid agencies, resulting in a low priority for innovating monitoring and evaluation systems. A former OXFAM-UK/I staff-member commented that 'few funding NGOs will have any knowledge of projects where funding stopped five or ten years ago. They probably will not even know whether the project survives, nor whether there have been any lasting benefits and if so to whom' (Clark 1991: 71).

Although this situation has improved in the mid-1990s, other obstacles remain, such as the reluctance of Southern partners to be involved in (external) evaluations, which often are considered as a means of control. Howes (1992: 393) remarks that the empowerment approach apparently made little contribution to the advancement of evaluation methods: 'Some exponents are openly hostile to evaluation in particular, arguing that it only appears to be a way of promoting greater efficiency, when its real function is to provide an additional means by which powerful external forces may exert political control over the poor.' A further set of obstacles has already been mentioned several times: impact evaluation is time-consuming, methodologically difficult and the results are often not something to be proud of. Brown and Tandon (1994: 10) warn against spending too much time and energy reinventing the wheel that has been created by others: 'many agencies are so overwhelmed with the challenges of responding to difficult problems with inadequate resources that they have little time or energy to reflect on past experience, little skill in conceptualizing issues, and restricted access to others' solutions'. Fortunately, the present study has benefited enormously from previous pioneering private aid impact research, and the main lessons of this will be drawn in the following pages.

3.4 Impact assessment methodologies

Despite limited practical experience in assessing the impact of private aid interventions aimed at civil society building, the growing number of private aid impact studies provides some valuable lessons. A first major lesson from previous impact assessments is that expectations about potential findings are often *too ambitious*. Methodological and practical difficulties make it virtually impossible to assess the impact of private aid interventions. Due to unclear objectives or the absence of baseline data, it is sometimes not even possible to assess direct outputs of these interventions. Fowler's distinction between outputs, outcomes and impact is helpful in distinguishing evaluation goals. Recent impact studies suggest that the 'output' of aid interventions can be generally determined rather easily, whereas the 'outcome' (effectiveness) is more difficult to assess. But it appears to be unrealistic to suggest that the 'impact' (sustained social change over a longer period) can be attributed to (private) aid interventions given the complexity of actors in the aid chain and the diffusing effects of external factors.

A second lesson is that the outcome (not to mention the impact) can only be assessed *if interventions are monitored over a longer period of time*. This is a crucial condition for impact analysis, as the context variables become more relevant over time. But also because the objectives of interventions often are adapted to internal and external circumstances. All impact studies that were reviewed were either *ex post* evaluations, or (more commonly) snapshots of ongoing projects. Monitoring not only is important from the very beginning of an intervention (project design), but particularly after external interventions have ended. Development impact of private aid interventions possibly can only be judged seriously at least several years after interventions have been completed (Bebbington 1997a). This suggests that impact evaluation perhaps only generates satisfactory results when it is used as a tool for learning, implying that it becomes an integrated part of project cycles (Blankenberg 1995). This requires more sophisticated monitoring systems that continue to supply information after projects are completed. Unfortunately, this method is still rarely applied by private aid agencies, despite its enormous potential to improve impact evaluations.

A third lesson is that impact evaluations generate better results when they are *participatory* and try to maximise the collaboration of stakeholders in the evaluation process. This is not only useful in transforming evaluations into learning experiences, which has been argued repeatedly, but active participation of stakeholders also can considerably improve the quality of impact evaluations. Assuming that primary stakeholders are the experts in determining which changes interventions have caused in their lives, they also are best placed to determine the indicators for impact evaluation and even to choose evaluation methods. Generally, this will reveal that aid interventions often have multiple impacts, instead of the single impact view with which many evaluation methodologies are working. When beneficiaries have no 'ownership' over their evaluation procedures, it is likely that they are not getting any benefits other than simply fulfilling donor obligations (Oakley et al. 1998). However, Howes (1992: 388) also points at a problematic side of participatory approaches, in which differences between monitoring and evaluation could become blurry: 'Evaluation has ceased to be a means of yielding insights for application in other places and at other times, and has been transformed into a device for adapting existing practice more closely to beneficiary needs in the light of evolving experience. [...] Such developments are clearly in the interest of project beneficiaries, but often do not produce data of sufficiently uniform character to facilitate comparisons with what has been achieved elsewhere.' This is generally the main reason for donor agencies to limit participatory evaluation methods to informing or consulting beneficiaries, rather than delegating responsibilities to them.

A fourth lesson from the impact studies is that only *an integrated approach* of private aid interventions potentially generates useful data. If aid interventions are not analysed in the context of an interdependent chain of actors that become more sensitive to external influences as they are 'lower' in the chain, agencies tend to apply a simple 'blueprint' assumption of attributing cause to effect. The current practice of 'isolating' project executors and assessing their impact against donor-driven objectives will lead either to erroneous conclusions, or to obvious observations that external influences have negatively influenced project performance. Whereas Robinson (1996b: 3) is right to point out that 'the primary unit of analysis is the recipient organisation, rather than the aid donor', the key lesson of previous impact studies is that the internal dynamics of the aid chain as a system need to be analysed in the context of dynamics external to the aid chain. This certainly is not easy, and this approach will seldom yield undisputed impact data. However, it moves the analysis away from quickly measurable results towards assessing aid chain dynamics within a wider context. This is less ambitious, but it could help to understand the 'relative causality' of aid interventions, and how aid-related and non-aid related variables affect the outcome of private aid intervention strategies.[52]

A fifth lesson that can be drawn from multi-project evaluations (although not undisputed) is to preferably select case studies from project interventions which have been *relatively successful*, so that effects are more pronounced and thus more easy to detect. At the current pioneering stage of impact assessments, the ambiguity of aid-related variables should be minimised, which is certainly not easy. To prevent additional complications, a pragmatic approach is probably justified by which case studies are selected whose objectives have been fairly constant and are the least complex. It is, as was argued earlier, very difficult (if not impossible) to mechanically separate poverty alleviating objectives from 'empowerment' object-ives. For the present study it is therefore important to select project interventions that in practice were explicit in their civil society building objectives, even if donor agencies preferred to use other terms in their project documents. Furthermore, it is helpful to select those interventions in which obstacles to impact assessments are as limited as possible. For example, it is important to select case studies in which all actors are willing to cooperate, and where sufficient previous evaluation data exist. Consequently, selected case studies meeting these criteria will not be repre-sentative, making generalisations rather difficult. But as was concluded earlier in this chapter, every project intervention deals with a unique set of variables, both internal and external, inhibiting broad generalisations about its performance anyway.

A final lesson to learn from the above is the necessity to keep searching for *new and innovative methods* to improve the prospects for successfully assessing private aid performance. Even if it is concluded that impact assessment is virtually impossible, this does not imply that any effort is doomed to fail. New methods and techniques have to be developed continuously, and the current priority for performance assessment amongst private aid agencies will likely accelerate this search. Impact assessment, particularly if applied as a participatory and learning exercise, in the years ahead will be one of the crucial methods for private aid agencies and their stakeholders to confront growing criticism about legitimacy, transparency and accountability. It will be the only way to learn from failures in the past, and more importantly, to prevent these failures from being reproduced unconsciously. Current practice indicates that innovations of impact assessment methodologies predominantly come from circles external to private aid agencies, particularly from academics and independent consultants. It underlines Clark's (1991: 73) famous, and still valid, advice that 'Northern NGOs would probably benefit from more rigorous, constructive scrutiny and perhaps they should invite this by making more strenuous efforts to describe to academics, development specialists and the general public exactly what it is that they do and why.'

— *An assessment framework*

By pulling together the strands of earlier experiences, a framework has been developed to assess the effectiveness and the dynamics of civil society building in private aid chains during democratic transitions in Central America. The assessment has to focus on the impact of private aid interventions on the organisational capacity of key recipients in civil society, and on their achievements in terms of articulating and mediating demands from civil society, within the sphere of political society, in order to further democratic transition. The focus is on those elements of civil society building that have contributed to *strengthening political society*: building national and international alliances, and building intermediary coalitions in civil society. Slightly adapting Couderé's (1994) inter-project evaluation approach, achievements are considered to be contingent upon the national context, aid chain dynamics and organisational capacities. Context variables are determined by the historical development of the balance between the state and civil society, but also by international influences. These context variables are explored for the Central American situation in Chapter 4 by identifying various stages of democratic transition that can provide valuable baseline data.

As all stakeholders of aid interventions are linked interdependently in the aid chain, a solid aid chain analysis is needed for each intervention. This will indicate the main actors, their mutual relationships and possibly the range of objectives that were handled during the process. It should be clear *what* is actually being assessed (output, outcome or impact) by making explicit what the specific objectives were of private aid interventions, *how* these objectives were formulated and implemented downwards in the aid chain, and *whose* output, outcome or impact was actually evaluated. Despite dealing with multiple actors who define multiple objectives that influence final results, I have followed Robinson's (1996b) suggestion to define the recipient of private aid as the primary unit of analysis, and not the private aid donor. After all, impact assessments always contain two key questions: what has been the impact of local societal actors on changing state-civil society relations, and to what extent could the achievements of these actors be attributed to one or multiple aid interventions of external donors? In order to address these questions, it is important to monitor how private aid intervention policies changed during the subsequent transition stages that were identified in the context analysis. Chapter 5 analyses the history of private aid interventions in Central America and examines the roles and objectives of European private aid agencies' contributions to democratic transitions in this region. This will provide the main framework for analysing aid chain dynamics.

Another important component for analysing aid chain dynamics is the relationship between donor and recipient, which is generally reflected in the quality of 'partnership'. This can for example be assessed by looking at the level of

Table 3.3   *A framework for assessing civil society building performance*

	Focus	Variable	Parameter
Context analysis	Dynamics of democratic transition	Balance between the state and civil society	Strength of civil society (density, diversity, equitability) Legitimacy of political society State accountability
		External interventions	'Top-down' democracy promotion 'Bottom-up' civil society building
Aid chain analysis	Relationships between donors, recipients and beneficiaries of aid	Private aid intervention policies	Orientations Priorities and limitations Instruments
		'Upward' and 'downward' relationships of recipients in civil society	Partnership Autonomy (from political parties or the government) Self-sufficiency
		Position of beneficiaries or beneficiary organisations	Level of exclusion Participation of members
Performance assessment	Results of civil society building interventions (output, outcome, impact)	Organisational capacity	Participation and leadership Accountability Sustainability
		Role in civil society building	Articulation Mediation Representation Policy impact

recipient participation in the design of projects and in the preparation and implementation of evaluations. Aid chain dynamics also are influenced by the extent of autonomy recipients have from political parties or from membership organisations, even though this often changes in the course of democratic transition. The position of beneficiaries in the aid chain also has to be carefully analysed: who is actually targeted by the aid intervention, how are these intended beneficiaries participating and to what extent is the intervention responding to particular local demands or to externally imposed priorities? This analysis can make clear, for example, whether local beneficiaries have become better organised in order to improve their own situation, or whether the aid chain merely has created a new system of relationships to administer and spend external funding. These themes will come back in Chapter 6, in which four Central American aid chains are more closely examined.

'Civil society building performance' is assessed in Chapter 6 at two different levels. The achievements of the recipient organisation in contributing to civil society building are evaluated at the macro-level, by looking at changes in the balance between the state and civil society. Two variables are used: the capacity of these organisations to articulate and mediate demands between civil society and the state, and their capacity to contribute to strengthening political society. The role of external aid in these achievements is assessed at the micro-level of the recipient organisation and its beneficiaries in the aid chain. Important variables that could affect this organisational impact are the dynamics of internal participation, the level of internal accountability, and the sustainability of organisations as a result of private aid interventions. An overview of this framework is provided in Table 3.3.

3.5 The potential of civil society building

Although only in exceptional cases phrased as a coherent strategy, 'strengthening civil society' has become an important new ingredient of donor policies in the 1990s. Implicitly, private aid agencies had already contributed to civil society building prior to the 1990s with policies aimed at strengthening the organisational capacity of their partners and by forging their sectoral alliances. Other elements of civil society building, such as enhancing the policy advocacy capacity of multisectoral coalitions or providing access to transnational political space also were part of private aid policies during the Cold War. The new element is that civil society building became an explicit policy of official donors in the early 1990s, when they discovered that civil society was a useful concept to stimulate market-led development strategies, downsize the role of the state and make governments more efficient. Although some private aid agencies have played a (minor) role in the implementation of the new governance agenda of official donors, they generally work with a more 'inclusive' concept of civil society building compared to the official donor concept which tends to reinforce existing power relations. Private aid agencies run the danger of being co-opted by the new official agenda, and performing what Smith (1990) calls a 'system maintaining function'. However, they also have the potential to contribute to social and political change if they manage to address the power relationships that underlie poverty and authoritarianism. In fact, this is probably where their potential impact is believed to be larger than that of any other development intervention, as several impact studies have suggested.

It is not only an obligation (to paraphrase Clark), but also a challenge for private aid agencies to be more explicit about what they are actually strengthening in civil society, and why. This could demystify the current rhetoric on civil society building of official donors, which is generally not geared towards transforming existing power relations. By showing what they have achieved in practice, this could also increase the legitimacy of private aid agencies and overcome their weak accountability. But the previous analysis also made clear that it is very difficult, and sometimes impossible, to identify the longer term achievements of private aid interventions aimed at civil society building. This is further complicated by a lack of methods to assess the results of interventions that are often phrased in vague and general terms. More than a coherent strategy, civil society building presently is rather a *category* of various (old and new) intervention strategies, whose purposes often only become visible when their achievements are carefully examined. Evidence from a number of recent studies suggest that private aid agencies indeed possess the potential to contribute to civil society building, but that possible achievements are diffused by external influences and internal dynamics of the aid chain. One of the major lessons from these studies is that much can still be learned by examining *why* and *how* private aid agencies contribute to civil society building, rather than only trying to find out *how much* they have contributed to this process. More evidence is needed from the practical experiences of private aid agencies involved in civil society building, which eventually could contribute to further developing instruments for assessing their impact. The second part of this book examines some of these key experiences in a (former) priority region of the international donor community: Central America.

PART II

CENTRAL AMERICA

4 THE ABSENCE OF A THIRD OPTION

Democratic Transitions in Central America

The theoretical framework of the previous chapters provides an analytical basis for examining the role of private aid agencies during democratic transitions in Central America. This traditional 'backyard' of the United States attracted international attention in the early 1980s, when civil wars in three of the five small countries affected regional stability during the last phase of the Cold War. Although fuelled by external forces, in particular by the Reagan administrations, these conflicts were the eruption of profound *internal* tensions in civil society rooted in a history of social and political exclusion of the impoverished majority. They were signs of a deep crisis of sustained authoritarian rule, eventually triggering processes of democratic transition all over the region. To avoid abstract 'transitology', the meaning of 'democratic transition' in the Central American context needs to be considered more carefully. For that purpose, four premises are examined in this chapter.

A first premise is that the dynamics of current democratic transitions have to be understood within a wider historical context, in which the stubborn permanency of the authoritarian state has obstructed the development of political society. Following Moore's argument discussed in Chapter 1, a historical examination of the key obstacles to democratic transition is a necessary exercise, as past conflicts and institutional structures have long-term effects and are of critical importance for later developments. What were these key obstacles in the Central American context, and what were the driving forces shifting the balance between the authoritarian states and exclusionary civil societies? A second premise highlights the relationship between democratic transition and peace. Frustrated efforts to democratise the system fuelled a violent climate of political repression and civil wars. But in the process of searching for peace, all parties finally realised that democratisation was an essential condition for peace, and vice versa. In other words, the civil conflicts during early transition stages obstructed democratic transition in the short term, but enhanced it in the longer run, which was most clearly illustrated by the Salvadorean civil war (1980-91). A third premise states that democratic transitions in Central America are not yet completed. Various observers have grappled with this problem, either by labelling the incomplete process 'pacification' (Dunkerly 1994: 3) or by calling the new regimes 'hybrids' of previous authoritarianism and newly emerging democratic politics (Karl 1995: 73). This confusion about the nature of democracy in Central America can be cleared up by carefully analysing the transition stages that were proposed in the theoretical framework. A fourth premise is about the role of external actors: it is assumed these have played an important role in stimulating democratic transitions, in particular by contributing to depolarisation of civil society and peaceful settlements and by (re)building the political centre.

Each of these premises will be examined separately, providing the following structure to this chapter on Central America's democratic transitions. The first section examines the long period of authoritarian rule and early efforts at civil society building, while trying to explain the causes of postponed democratic transitions. The second identifies the key actors in civil and political society that opposed the authoritarian state, and analyses how the latter entered into a serious crisis in the 1970s. Section three examines shifting power balances in three selected countries during the early, mid and late transition stages. The fourth section looks at the role of external actors and distinguishes between governmental and non-governmental actors intervening in the region. Based on this analysis, the premises are reconsidered in the final section, where they are discussed in the light of future prospects for democratic consolidation in Central America.

4.1 Causes of postponed democratic transitions

Democratic transitions in Central America have differed essentially from most transitions in South America, as argued earlier. They were not concerned with re-establishing a form of democracy that had existed previously, but were rather transitions in a process of *constructing* democracy. The origins of South American democratisation can be traced back to the depression of the 1930s, when populist regimes came to power and contributed to the growth and diversification of civil societies. In Central America, democratic rule simply had been non-existent up to the late 1940s, when it emerged in Costa Rica and (only temporarily) in Guatemala. Since the emergence of independent nation states in the post-colonial period of the early nineteenth century, the dominant classes in Central America considered the state to be an instrument for prolonging authoritarian rule and seldom a product of political legitimacy. The continuity of authoritarian rule in Central America (and the recurrent failures of democratisation) can be understood by looking at the permanency of family networks, commerce, forms of political interaction, cultures and the mentality of the dominant classes (Acuña 1995). The history of Central American authoritarianism is marked by three more or less distinct stages, before its demise in the violent crisis of the late 1970s and early 1980s.

The first period of authoritarianism was characterised by *caudillo* regimes, ruling the whole of Central America in the first half of the nineteenth century. The term 'ruling' is probably overstated, for it was actually a period of civil wars between Conservative and Liberal elites reflecting frustrated efforts to construct nation states on the remnants of the Spanish colonial administration. The Conservatives generally represented traditional large landowners who had acquired special licenses from the Spanish crown for land titles and export monopolies. They advocated authoritarian rule, centralised government and special privileges for the Catholic Church. Liberals represented large landholders and tradesmen without privileges derived from the colonial period, and therefore promoted decentralised government, (limited) representative democracy, less economic regulation and a separation between the Church and the state. Liberals advocated a modernisation of the economy by an export-led growth model, facilitated by the state (Booth and Walker 1993). Conservatives and Liberals were the core political currents in the nineteenth century, although differences gradually disappeared. Rivalry and open warfare between these two factions of the dominant classes contributed to the dissolution of the Central American Federal Republic (1824-1838) into five separate nations: Guatemala, El Salvador, Honduras, Nicaragua and Costa Rica.[1]

This period of anarchy gradually ended in the 1870s with the introduction of moderate Liberal reforms to facilitate landownership for coffee production. The second stage of authoritarian rule was marked by the start of massive coffee cultivation as a primary export crop for the world market, with profound social and political consequences for the entire region. A new coffee oligarchy emerged as a hegemonic force in civil society, backing legislation to guarantee private property and the availability of cheap labour necessary to institute a competitive agro-export development model. Communal lands of indigenous communities and Church-owned lands were expropriated. Under the slogan 'order and progress' the new Liberal regimes used the armed forces to repress *campesino* revolts and protests from oppositional elites.[2] It was in this period that the basis was laid for a firm interdependent alliance between the military and the coffee oligarchy that would last until the 1980s. The 'progress' promised by the Liberal rulers (such as education and universal suffrage) was not realised in practice, which illustrated the two golden rules of the new elite: 'The rich do not pay taxes, nor concede any concessions to the poor.'[3] Progress had a different meaning for the Liberal rulers, such as the construction of ports and railways to encourage foreign investment and European immigration. As Paige (1997: 14) remarks in his detailed account of the Central American coffee elite: 'They built new wealth and created vast poverty.' Indirectly, the agro-export model provided the basis for consolidating the process of constructing nation states, although built on social exclusion. The third stage of authoritarian rule would run from the 1930s to the 1980s, and will be analysed in more detail below. A key characteristic of this period was the prominent role of the armed forces, who not only acquired political power but gradually also substantial economic power. Their investments in banking, industry and agriculture converted the armed forces into a powerful and autonomous institution, whose officers developed from the guardians to full members of the political and economic elite (Rouquié 1987; Cerdas 1992).

Although continuity of authoritarian rule was a general pattern all over Central America, differences in political systems have existed among the five countries ever since the colonial period. Guatemala and Costa Rica, for example, inherited opposite colonial arrangements. In Guatemala, the cultivation of *indigo* contributed to a feudal structure in which the indigenous population was exploited via involuntary servitude, determining social relations up to the late twentieth century. The large landowners together with merchant elites formed a powerful oligarchy, directly controlling the state or indirectly ruling via the armed forces. In Costa Rica, the indigenous population was smaller and had been largely eliminated during the conquest. Costa Rica's rather marginal role in colonial trade permitted a more balanced development based on subsistence farming. Due to a relatively weak oligarchy and a growing rural middle class, social relations were more egalitarian; authoritarian rule in Costa Rica was therefore short-lived. El Salvador's development resembled that of Guatemala, but was less extreme as a result of a smaller indigenous population. In the Liberal period, Guatemala, El Salvador and Costa Rica managed to achieve relative political stability, whereas the absence of a hegemonic social power in Honduras and Nicaragua led to disorder and civil wars, eventually leading to US interventions in the early twentieth century.

Furthermore, due to differences in social relations and levels of institutionalised repression, coffee cultivation had remarkably diverse effects: in Costa Rica it contributed to democratisation, whereas in Guatemala and El Salvador it actually reinforced authoritarian trends (Cerdas 1992). In Honduras and Nicaragua, with their absence of a strong oligarchy, the state was generally controlled by military officers, often part of an economic-military dynasty such as the Somoza clan in Nicaragua.[4] In Honduras, the development of the political system was very much determined by US investments in the banana enclaves on the northern coast, where US companies ruled autonomously from the Honduran state. While the dominant presence of the United States in Honduras and Nicaragua certainly reinforced existing authoritarian practice, I tend to agree with Acuña (1995) who argues that authoritarian rule in Central America had its roots long before the United States became the hegemonic external power in the early twentieth century. Continuing patterns of colonial dominance and the impact of the agro-export model, visible in an unequal system of land tenure combined with coerced labour, were probably more decisive for the permanency of the ruling classes than external intervention.[5]

– *The first period of civil society building (1919-32)*
What about the balance between the state and civil society prior to the late 1920s, the first period in which authoritarian rule was questioned? After a few decades of nation building, the Liberal governments had not really managed to build strong state institutions. Permanent debt and a lack of public resources hampered the consolidation of nation states. As there were no domestic markets with a taxable wealth base, the major source of income for the state was provided by introducing fiscal policies directly linked to the export economy (Torres Rivas 1971). Increasing import and export taxes thus made the customs authority one of the earliest stable state institutions. But the armed forces certainly were the strongest institution of the state. They were professionalised under the Liberal governments and gradually

increased their power during the third period of authoritarian rule. The development of other state institutions in most of the countries generally started only after the Second World War (Acuña 1995).

Civil society also was quite weak until the early 1920s. Family networks of the coffee elite and their associations were the only strong actors in civil society in the Liberal period, and their power often remained unchallenged up to the 1990s.[6] In rural areas semi-servitude predominated and rural workers were unable to organise, due to their full dependence upon the hacienda system. Civil associations actually started in urban areas, where foreign investment attracted skilled workers and craftsmen (artesanos), and in the banana enclaves. Since the coming to power of Liberal regimes workers in the cities had been forming craft guilds (mutuales), which started as associations for mutual help and developed after the First World War into the first labour unions. This type of urban organising was most diverse in Costa Rica, where the first trade union (of bakers) in the region was founded in 1919, inspired by European anarcho-syndicalism. Similar small sindicatos of shoemakers, bakers, typographers and carpenters emerged in the 1920s all over Central America, followed by the formation of broader federations – such as the combative Salvadorean Regional Workers Federation (FRTS) – and several women's organisations.[7] Many of these new federations of trade unions were influenced by international political networks linked to Mexican and Russian revolutionary parties, which also stimulated the formation of Communist parties throughout the region.

These newly emerging actors in civil society were still small-scale, urban-based and rather fragile.[8] But by the late 1920s they started to question authoritarian rule by Liberal governments. It was not so much the popular overthrow of the Estrada Cabrera regime in Guatemala in 1920, following mobilisations organised by the Liga Obrera, that alarmed the Liberal rulers. Neither was it the wave of strikes and the Labour Day marches in 1925, leading to formal approval of an eight-hour working day. What worried the Liberal governments was the risk that the spark of social mobilisation could leap from the cities to the coffee plantations in the countryside. This concern was aggravated by the impact of the worldwide Depression, leading to a dramatic fall in coffee prices on the world market after 1929. In addition, Central America lost important export markets to other coffee-producing countries, such as Brazil. The resulting wage cuts and growing rural unemployment fuelled strikes and other social protest in the countryside. Prospects for change, such as the short-lived reformist attempt by Araujo in El Salvador, were soon eliminated by the armed forces who took power under the leadership of General Hernández Martínez in 1931. An armed rebellion by (largely Indian) peasants in the key coffee zone of western El Salvador, triggered by the Communist Party of Farabundo Martí, ended in a massacre.[9] This so-called la matanza symbolised the violent way in which military regimes disrupted the first period of civil society building in Central America.

It can be argued that the newly emerging political parties in Central America lacked the maturity to really provide an alternative to the prevailing two-party system. Indeed, the *Partido Unionista* in Guatemala (which briefly took over in 1920), the *Partido Reformista* in Costa Rica and the *Partido Laborista* in El Salvador (in power for ten months in 1931) were overwhelmed by their success and unable to provide a serious alternative, comparable to the populist regimes emerging in South America in the 1930s.[10] But it was also clear to the Liberal oligarchies that the economic recession provided little space for social and political reforms, which made them decide to hand over political power to military *caudillos*. The chain of military take-overs in the early 1930s started with General Jorge Ubico in Guatemala (1931-44), who came to power in elections after the US had condemned an earlier coup. This was followed by General Maximiliano Hernández Martínez (1931-44) in El Salvador and General Tiburcio Carías Andino (1932-48) in Honduras. Nicaragua was somewhat different, as the rise to power of General Anastasio Somoza García (1936-56) was more a consequence of a popular guerrilla struggle led by dissident General Augusto César Sandino, opposing the invasion of US marines that wanted to end a civil war between Liberals and Conservatives. After Sandino's army successfully expelled US troops, he was assassinated and Somoza took power as commander of the US-trained National Guard. Costa Rica again was the exception, in the sense that the rule by 'civilian *caudillo*' Léon Cortés Castro (1936-40) was short-lived. The Liberal oligarchy resisted armed take-overs and even introduced several reforms, such as a minimum wage for rural workers. The Communist Party entered parliament after staging a successful strike in the banana enclaves against the United Fruit Company in 1934. As will be shown later, the early enlargement of Costa Rica's political society sharply contrasted with the repression of the political opposition in neighbouring countries, generating diverging patterns of democratisation in the region after the 1930s.

– Attempts towards democratisation (1944-54)

Towards the end of the Second World War the military dictatorships entered a serious political crisis. In 1944, multisectoral alliances managed to overthrow the military regimes of Guatemala and El Salvador. In Honduras and Nicaragua similar alliances emerged, but with less national impact. These coalitions were formed by students, middle-class professionals, merchants and young military officers, and mobilised a popular urban class that had rapidly grown since the Depression of the 1930s.[11] It was, as Torres Rivas (1971: 117-8) points out, an 'extremely heterogeneous, initially weak and inexperienced social group'. But their demands for social and political reform, postponed by the *caudillos* for over a decade, certainly had a powerful resonance. Particularly their demand for democracy stimulated the formation of new (mostly reformist) political parties challenging the traditional two-party systems. However, political society remained closed for these challengers, with the exceptions of Costa Rica and Guatemala. The Cold War environment and the reactivation of the export-based economies, with an emphasis on cotton and meat in addition to coffee, would prolong authoritarian rule for another three decades.

The regional political crisis started in April 1944 in El Salvador, when an aborted coup attempt by young officers (who wanted to prevent a prolongation of General Martínez's regime) unleashed a wave of repression, followed by a general strike. Martínez had to resign under US pressure (the US government was afraid that social protest would lead to radicalisation) and was temporarily replaced by General Menéndez who called for elections. But the reformist movement was gaining such strength (led by Romero's National Democratic Union) that a bloody pre-emptive military coup was staged to prevent their electoral participation. Subsequent military coups gave power to a young and modern military elite that would rule El Salvador for the next three decades. Events in El Salvador contributed to an increase of popular mobilisations in Honduras and Nicaragua against the military regimes of Carías and Somoza, but were crushed without generating organised opposition in the form of new political parties (Bulmer-Thomas 1987). Costa Rica also was affected by the wave of political protests in the region, but the end of authoritarian rule would only come four years later. The first successful challenge to *caudillismo* occurred in Guatemala, where a general strike in June 1944 forced General Ubico to resign. Despite attempts by the parliament to appoint a successor who could prolong authoritarian rule, the opposition forged an alliance with young military officers that staged a successful coup in October 1944.[12] A few months later, opposition leader Juan José Arévalo won the presidential election and launched one of the most remarkable episodes in Guatemalan history.

Pérez-Brignoli (1989: 128) observes that the wave of reforms in the 1940s 'was more important for the social forces it unleashed than for its legacy of success fulfillment'. This certainly applies to Guatemala, where the 'revolution' only lasted until 1954 when it was violently aborted by a CIA-supported coup. Although some important reforms were introduced under Arévalo – such as social security programmes, improved health and education, abolishment of forced labour and municipal elections – they were seldom more radical than those of neighbouring countries where authoritarian rule continued. The key difference, according to Dunkerly (1988: 135), was 'that this developmentalist project was undertaken in conditions of unprecedented political democracy'. Important was the Labour Code of 1947, contributing to rapidly increased rural unionisation and a growing influence of the Communist Party in the large labour unions and federations.[13] The large landowners and the United Fruit Company were concerned about the growth of social mobilisation, even more after new measures were introduced concerning the forced rental of uncultivated estates. Opposition also came from the military that staged a few dozen coup attempts against Arévalo, but none of these were successful. This was largely thanks to his defence minister Jacobo Arbenz, who would succeed Arévalo after winning the 1951 presidential elections. Reform policies radicalised under Arbenz, who derived his support from the popular sectors, particularly from the labour unions that were dominated by the (relatively small) Communist Party.[14] Bilateral relations with the United States deteriorated, especially after Arbenz launched a land reform programme largely affecting fallow lands of the United Fruit Company. After this North American company pressured its home government in Washington, the Arbenz regime was depicted as a 'communist threat' and overthrown in July 1954 following a covert US-led invasion. The armed forces took power under the leadership of Colonel Castillo Armas, reversed the reform programme and effectively destroyed unions and political parties previously supporting Arbenz.

Therefore, the only successful democratic transition as a result of the reformist winds blowing throughout Central America in the 1940s took place in Costa Rica. As was already pointed out, Costa Rica experienced a different political development than its northern neighbours due to the absence of profound political and social polarisation. A gradual but cautious process of 'early' democratic transition had been occurring since the 1930s with social reforms and a broadening of political society. However, political polarisation increased during the populist government of Rafael Calderón who came to power in the 1940 elections, defeating the weak Communist-led opposition with a large majority. Surprisingly, Calderón introduced a number of social reforms, such as a social security system and a Labour Code, thereby losing support from his original allies, among them the larger coffee growers. Calderón could only survive after forging an alliance with the Communist Party – renamed the Popular Vanguard Party (PVP) – and the Catholic Church. This alliance stayed in power after winning the 1944 elections, although they were accused by the opposition of committing electoral fraud. Increased competition among labour confederations was fuelled by Cold War rhetoric and seriously challenged Costa Rica's traditional social equilibrium.[15] Political polarisation erupted into civil war after the opposition won the 1948 elections, although the victory was nullified by the ruling coalition which obtained a parliamentary majority. In response, a group of armed insurgents led by José Figueres and supported by President Arévalo of Guatemala managed to overthrow the government in little more than a month.[16] The communist PVP and its unions were outlawed, a new constitution was drawn up endorsing the social reforms of the previous years, and most remarkably, the armed forces were abolished.

Social stability in Costa Rica was restored in the early 1950s and democratic transition was consolidated under Figueres's presidency (1953-58) with his National Liberation Party (PLN), taking full advantage of the economic boom. Ever since, political society has been dominated by two political parties (PLN and the conservative Party of Social Christian Unity, PUSC) operating in the political centre and alternating power in regular elections. The Costa Rican model of gradual reformism would become a paradigmatic example of political stability for Latin America (Diamond et al. 1989). It functioned thanks to the existence of a diverse and autonomous middle class and a Liberal oligarchy that was not defeated but became dispersed over various political projects. However, the Costa Rican democratic transition also sacrificed the Communist movement, which had been a key actor in the struggle for reforms in the 1940s. With the abolishment of the armed forces, a stable balance between civil society and the state was achieved in the 1950s in such a way that the 'subsequent negotiation of political power was situated within the domain of civil society and that of economic mediation within the orbit of the state much more emphatically than elsewhere' (Dunkerly 1988: 133). This balance would only become distorted during the regional crisis of the 1980s.

By the mid-1950s, in a flourishing Cold War, all other Central American governments were run by the armed forces. These had been modernised with US support and severely restricted labour unionisation. Only in Honduras did labour unions experience a boom after workers of the Tela Railroad Company went on strike in April 1954, shortly before the invasion in Guatemala to topple Arbenz. They demanded better social conditions and the right to unionise. The strike spread to other US banana estates along the Honduran coast and was finally (after the successful removal of Arbenz in Guatemala) resolved with promises for a Labour Code and social legislation. These measures were effectively introduced in the late 1950s by President Ramón Villeda Morales of the Liberal Party, who later also supported agrarian reform until he was removed by a coup in 1963. As a result of these modest reforms, social polarisation in Honduras would never acquire levels comparable to those in Nicaragua, El Salvador or Guatemala.

– Seeds of a social and political crisis

For Central America, the 1944-54 period symbolises a lost opportunity for early democratic transition, which would have bitter consequences a few decades later. The violent crisis of the late 1970s and early 1980s was rooted in the persistence of authoritarian rule by the dominant classes (with an increasingly military component) over a long period of time, combined with the failure to introduce reforms to tackle the problems of social and political exclusion. Only Costa Rica, and to a certain extent Honduras, managed to escape the wave of political escalation starting in the late 1970s. What these 'postponed democratic transitions' in Guatemala, El Salvador and Nicaragua had in common was a 'double denial' of the dominant classes. On the one hand, they refused to introduce a series of social reforms necessary to confront growing social inequalities. On the other hand, they were unwilling to open up political society for new reformist political parties led by the urban middle sectors. The result was that social discontent and political exclusion in the twenty-five years between the violent end of the 'Guatemalan revolution' and the start of the Sandinista revolution had to be contained by state-led repression. Three additional factors that facilitated the postponement of democratic transitions and gradually aggravated its consequences became visible in the late 1970s: economic expansion, ambiguous policies of US governments and anti-communism fuelled by the Cold War.[17]

The first element was the recovery of the Central American economies in the 1950s, which suggests that the export-led growth model was not yet exhausted. Rising coffee prices and a diversification of export crops (cotton, beef and sugar) contributed to a sharp increase in exports. This economic expansion facilitated a transformation in the export sector and contributed to an expanding and modernising state apparatus. The traditional member of the oligarchy also underwent a gradual transformation from a 'landlord-capitalist into a capitalist-landlord' who could prosper thanks to the over exploitation of rural labour (Torres Rivas 1989: 49-50).[18] That is, the expanding modern export-economy also contributed to a semi-proletarisation of *campesinos*, the small agricultural producers of basic grains for local consumption. Rapid population growth (one hundred percent increase in twenty years) and uneven land distribution dramatically increased rural unemployment and contributed both to rural and urban impoverishment. This in turn would create a breeding ground for radical protest and social mobilisation in the 1970s.

A second factor influencing the outcome of these postponed transitions was the ambiguity of US foreign policy. Although US governments were aware of the need to introduce social reforms and to contribute to political liberalisation in Central America, these 'good intentions' (as President Kennedy called them) were overshadowed by Cold War imperatives. Two examples illustrate this ambiguity. One was the active US role in removing the reformist Arbenz government in Guatemala, which had been labelled as a communist threat to the hemisphere. But most reforms introduced during the Guatemalan revolution were quite moderate and would have been perfectly in line with the reform policies promoted by the United States in the early 1960s (Dunkerly 1988). Another example was Kennedy's *Alliance for Progress*, a US aid programme intended to stimulate social reforms in Latin America in reaction to the 1959 Cuban revolution. However, this programme soon became a tool for counter-insurgency operations in which Central American armed forces received modern weapons and training to combat emerging guerrilla activity. Even if it is argued that US policy was only ambiguous on paper and that in practice it deliberately supported authoritarian regimes in their efforts to resist popular pressures, the outcome is the same: the United States was a key factor in postponing democratic transitions in Central America up to the 1980s.

A third factor that furthered the practice of social and political exclusion was ideological: a primitive and belligerent anti-communist culture that had been flourishing in the region since the 1930s. It was not simply Cold War anti-communism, stimulated by the United States and cultivated by the Catholic hierarchy and the armed forces that had taken root in Central America; especially after the removal of Arbenz (1954) and the Cuban revolution (1959), anti-communism became the leading ideology of Central America's dominant sectors against the advocates of social and political change. Torres Rivas (1996a: 26) observes that it was more than just a political ideology, 'as it also contained religious values, affirming the family, private property, tradition, a sense of obedience, authority, hierarchy, and therefore did not identify opponents but enemies, political enemies'. In the name of this right-wing nationalist ideology, the worst crimes against human rights were justified against leaders of popular organisations, progressive intellectuals and any other opponent of the authoritarian system. The following section will take a closer look at the composition of this political opposition.

4.2 Polarisation prior to the crisis

The paradox of democratisation, according to Falk (1995a: 126-7), is that 'it cannot be realized unless it overcomes hegemonic distortion, yet the non-violent means to control hegemony are themselves controlled hegemonically'. By obstructing democratic transitions and artificially closing off political society for several decades, a price had to be paid by Central America's dominant sectors. That price was a radicalisation of the political opposition from a reformist to a revolutionary orientation. The revolutionary popular movements that gained strength in the 1970s transformed the struggle for democracy of the middle classes into an armed revolutionary struggle by those most marginalised by authoritarian rule. This happened in Nicaragua, El Salvador, Guatemala and Honduras, although in Honduras the process went somewhat differently. How to explain the role of these revolutionary movements during democratic transitions? This question will be examined by looking at the changes occurring in the composition of civil society, the exhausted options in political society, the reaction of the 'counter-insurgency state' and finally, by determining the key factors contributing to the crisis of the late 1970s.

– *Expansion and polarisation of civil society*
The growth of civil society in the 1960s and its polarisation in the 1970s partly explains the problematic start of Central America's democratic transitions in the 1980s. Five social sectors particularly contributed to the expansion of civil society in this period: student and teachers' unions, the Catholic Church, development NGOs, labour and peasant unions and political-military organisations. The emerging strength of these sectors had different origins. With the gradual growth of the education system and the autonomy claimed by universities in the 1940s, student and teachers' unions represented a new generation of intellectuals that also would play a key role in other popular organisations, especially in the revolutionary movements of the 1970s. These intellectuals had been influenced by the reformist Guatemalan and Costa Rican experiences and by the Cuban revolution of 1959, and were able to stage sectoral protests that contributed to the growth of (urban) popular organising. Examples are the long and successful strike of the Salvadorean teachers' union ANDES in 1968, and the Revolutionary Student Front (FER) in Nicaragua that became a driving force of the FSLN in the mid-1960s.

Changes in the Catholic Church also contributed to civil society growth. Influential was the change of doctrine proposed at the Second Vatican Council in 1962, which asserted that the Church had a social role to play in addition to its spiritual role. The traditional conservative position of the Church in Latin America of allying with the armed forces and the dominant classes was challenged and gradually became politicised after the Second Latin American Episcopal Conference in Medellín in 1968. Here it was explicitly decided to take the position of a 'preferential option for the poor' and to 'defend the rights of the oppressed'. The formation of Christian Base Communities (CEBs) to organise the poor and the active contribution of local priests to the formation of peasant unions had an enormous impact on civil society growth all over Central America. Writing on El Salvador, where Church activism was strongest, Montgomery (1995: 87) observes that CEBs had an impact on civil society in four ways: they offered an opportunity for organising people, they stimulated leadership, they offered an experience in participatory democracy and they were an important medium for liberation theology. As will be shown later in the case studies in Chapter 6, differences existed between the upper hierarchy of the Church and the (generally more progressive) priests at the local level, some of whom joined the armed struggle in the late 1970s.

Civil society growth also was boosted by a sustained increase in labour unionisation since the introduction of labour legislation in the 1950s, combined with the growth in the 1960s of the public sector and the manufacturing industry during the period of the Central American Common Market. Most of these labour federations were dominated by ORIT, a Latin American federation financed by the US labour organisation AFL-CIO, to neutralise communist influence in the labour movement. Not surprisingly, most of these federations were supported by the ruling parties, except in Honduras and Costa Rica. Here, labour federations were more autonomous and also proved to be more successful, largely because of the lower levels of repression (Bulmer-Thomas 1987). Although relatively weak and organising only a small share of the labour force in the 1960s, labour federations became more influential after the economic recession of the mid-1970s. The same happened with rural workers, which by the early 1960s were barely organised, except in Honduras.[19] With support from the Catholic Church (and the new Christian Democratic parties), rural workers' unions were set up all over the region in the 1960s to confront the proletarianisation of the peasantry. As a result of the economic crisis of the 1970s, these rural unions also radicalised and their leaders soon joined the ranks of revolutionary movements.[20]

A fourth group of new actors in civil society that started to emerge in the late 1960s was a wide variety of development NGOs. They were either promoted by US aid programmes, or founded under the umbrella of the Catholic Church, as will be explained in Chapter 5. The church-related NGOs started their work at the grassroots level in rural and urban communities and were involved in training popular leaders, setting up research programmes or in the promotion of agricultural cooperatives. Financial support for these NGOs generally came from abroad, either from USAID (as part of the *Alliance for Progress*) or from North American and European Catholic organisations, such as CARE and the German *Misereor*. Although still small in number, in the 1970s most development NGOs started to work closely with the growing popular movement and their activities became more politicised. The emphasis shifted towards popular education, communication training, setting up radio stations and directly supporting peasant organisations. Also involved in relief operations after several natural disasters in the mid-1970s (earthquakes and hurricanes), these NGOs gradually became the legal shield for a persecuted opposition. Their number would rapidly expand after foreign aid flows started to increase in the 1980s.

A fifth group that emerged (clandestinely) in civil society in the early 1960s would play an important role in the democratic transitions of the following decades: political-military organisations. The evolution of these revolutionary movements comprised two periods, or better, two generations. The first actually consisted of tiny political parties, inspired by the Cuban revolution, trying to set up *focos* of resistance in rural areas. In Guatemala these groups were initially formed by progressive military officers, who rebelled against government corruption and the absence of democratic liberties.[21] Throughout the 1960s, the Guatemalan revolutionaries effectively managed to stage protracted guerrilla warfare, which was not paralleled in neighbouring countries. Not even in Nicaragua, where the Sandinista National Liberation Front (FSLN) undertook several aborted attempts to start an armed struggle against the Somoza regime. However, well-organised counter-insurgency operations by the US-trained security forces managed to defeat all these revolutionary guerrilla groups by the late 1960s, thereby unleashing a widespread campaign of terror that would continue for another decade.[22] The second generation of political-military organisations – emerging in the early 1970s in Guatemala, Nicaragua and El Salvador – learned their lessons from the earlier defeats and therefore improved their organisational structures and acquired popular support in both rural and urban areas. In Guatemala, new guerrilla organisations (EGP and ORPA) started to build up popular support in the Indian highlands. The FSLN in Nicaragua, after going through a serious internal crisis, was slow in building up popular support and only expanded after 1977.[23] The five small revolutionary groups in El Salvador, all emerging in the 1970s, would gain strength after exposure of extensive electoral fraud, also in 1977.[24] It was something all these small political-military organisations had in common: only in the late 1970s would they transform into broader revolutionary movements.

– *Exhausted options for political society*
Several reformist opposition parties were founded throughout Central America in the early 1960s, responding to the resistance by ruling political parties and the armed forces to structural social and political reforms. The authoritarian governments were however pressured by the Kennedy administration to allow some political opposition, spurring the emergence of (mostly) Christian Democratic and Social Democratic parties with programmes for moderate social and political reforms as a 'third option' between right-wing military dictatorship and left-wing revolution. Although initially small, some of these parties managed to play an

important role in political society, such as the Christian Democratic Party in El Salvador; the Social Christian Party and the Independent Liberal Party in Nicaragua; and the Christian Democratic Party and the Revolutionary Party in Guatemala.[25] Some of them even managed to get substantial electoral support from the middle class and the urban working class. But electoral victories by reformist opposition coalitions were systematically obstructed by the use of electoral fraud or pre-emptive military coups. Moreover, the militarisation of rural areas often made it impossible for these opposition parties to extend electoral campaigns into the countryside.

A good example of these new political parties that was initially successful in opening up the political centre was the Christian Democratic PDC in El Salvador. After achieving some success in the 1964 elections, the PDC gradually expanded until it became one of the strongest parties in parliament in the late 1960s. Led by José Napoleón Duarte, the PDC headed the National Opposition Union (UNO), a broad coalition of opposition parties that was formed to participate in the 1972 presidential elections. On election day, the government and the armed forces had to engage in widespread electoral fraud in order to thwart Duarte's victory. In Nicaragua and Guatemala similar broad opposition coalitions emerging in the late 1960s were intimidated by repression or became the victim of fraudulent elections.[26] In Honduras, political opposition beyond the two traditional political parties had been absent since the moderate reformist Liberal government of Villeda Morales (1957-63). The Honduran armed forces would rule the country until 1981. In other words, political society in Central America (outside Costa Rica) remained restricted or closed to opposition parties in the decades of economic prosperity. The frequency of elections had nothing to do with democratic openings, for they never resulted in handing over power to the opposition.

It would be incorrect to attribute the failure of these reformist opposition parties (to consolidate a democratic alternative in political society) only to repression and fraud by authoritarian regimes. Even though this was an important element, there were other problems in the 1970s that prevented them from acting as a political channel for their growing constituency in civil society; in fact, they ceased to be a solid alternative to US-backed authoritarianism. The reason, as Torres Rivas (1989: 78) points out, is that they were paralysed more by the fear of revolution than by the reality of authoritarianism: 'In the long run these moderate forces perceived the popular sectors as little more than an auxiliary force for their own struggles. They always feared, for example, the autonomous and radical behaviour of the working class. When push came to shove, they repeatedly chose to make deals with the most reactionary sectors of the bourgeoisie, with the military, and with imperialism.' This incapacity, or unwillingness, to incorporate new (popular and more radical) sectors into their ranks, would contribute to the political escalation of the late 1970s. It would also eliminate the prospects for a viable 'third option' between authoritarian rule and revolution.

– *The emergence of the counter-insurgency state*

Having briefly examined developments in civil society and political society since the 1960s, the broad picture can now be made more complete by looking at developments at the level of the state. The post-war decades were a period of substantial growth of state institutions, parallel to the rapid growth and diversification of the export sector, combined with policies to promote import-substituting industrialisation. Government policies were determined by a commitment to prevent a repetition of the Cuban revolution in the region by stimulating economic development (and allowing minor social reforms) and strengthening the counter-revolutionary capacity of the state apparatus. Both policies were supported by the *Alliance for Progress*, the US aid programme that started in 1961. The economic component of this programme aimed at strengthening and modernising the state apparatus by creating state banks and planning institutions to promote production and to channel credits to new business activities and agricultural research institutes (Vilas 1995). Development funds were also supposed to establish programmes for agrarian reform, but a redistribution of land was either not implemented at all (El Salvador) or only in a very mild form (such as in Honduras).[27] Economic aid largely benefited US-owned firms and banks, and enterprises of the Central American oligarchies (LaFeber 1993).

The military component of the *Alliance for Progress* had a deeper impact on the development of the state apparatus, particularly after the economic component was reduced by the Johnson administration in 1963. The goal of US military assistance was to enhance the quality of the Central American military and security bodies by providing training courses in modern methods of control of political and social unrest. A key element of this programme was to set up new military intelligence units, whose officers were trained in the tactics of counter-insurgency operations at special US academies (such as the School of the Americas in the Panama Canal zone). Since it was believed that the 'communist threat' would primarily mobilise in rural areas, a new system of rural intelligence with paramilitary groups was developed in which *campesinos* themselves became key actors in espionage and repression.[28] Torres Rivas (1987) observes that this so-called 'counter-insurgency state' had a pro-active character, as it was established prior to the emergence of revolutionary movements in the region. The exception was Guatemala, where the counter-insurgency state was established as part of the counter-revolutionary offensive of the late 1960s and perfected in the following two decades. In El Salvador and Nicaragua the counter-insurgency state gradually developed from the institutionalisation of military dictatorships in which the armed forces were to become the executives of state power.[29]

In her analysis of military dictatorship in Guatemala, Jonas (1991) mentions four key characteristics of the US-sponsored counter-insurgency state that emerged in the 1960s. First, it was a class-based corporate state consisting of the oligarchy and the armed forces, in which the latter protected the interests of the former. Second, the counter-insurgency state did not merely aim to defeat the enemy, but its mission was to annihilate revolutionary movements *and* their social support base – a form of 'state terrorism' most radically employed in the Indian highlands of Guatemala. A third characteristic of the counter-insurgency state was discussed already: it precluded the possibility of pluralistic politics, as it ruled by coercion and denied the exercise of civil and political rights. It reflected also what Torres Rivas (1989: 97) calls 'a profound vacuum of legitimacy of the dominant sectors', underlining that 'the state was well armoured, but weak'. Political society was closed, and subordinated sectors in civil society were repressed. A fourth characteristic mentioned by Jonas is somewhat controversial. She maintains that military rule (after successful counter-insurgency offensives) was sometimes replaced by restricted civilian rule, as long as military hegemony was not challenged. This is what apparently happened in the 1980s in El Salvador and Guatemala. But later in this chapter I will argue that this return to civilian rule, rather than an extension of the past, indeed announced the start of democratic transition.

– *The crisis of authoritarian rule in the late 1970s*
Spurred by the worldwide economic recession of the mid-1970s, the authoritarian political systems of Central America entered into a serious political crisis with international repercussions. The crisis became visible in the second half of the 1970s and would lead in Nicaragua to the breakdown of the system of domination. In El Salvador and Guatemala the crisis would fuel violent civil wars, whereas in Honduras it would lead to a deepening of the militarisation of the state. Even Costa Rica was affected, as the regional crisis contributed to a US-induced militarisation of the police. However, in all countries the region-wide political crisis eventually developed into (fragile) processes of democratic transition, which had been postponed or interrupted a few decades earlier. Although different in rhythm and outcome in each of the Central American countries, four common factors contributed to unleashing the crisis of authoritarian rule. These can be interpreted as important shifts taking place in the late 1970s in civil society, political society, the state and within the international context.[30]

A first shift occurred in civil society, where political-military organisations rapidly expanded their popular base by incorporating radicalising urban and rural popular sectors, leading to the formation of well-organised unified revolutionary movements: URNG in Guatemala, FMLN in El Salvador and FSLN in Nicaragua. The Guatemalan revolutionary organisations drew their popular support mainly from the rural (Indian) population who had been the victims of an intensive campaign of state terror by the military regime of Lucas García, which came to power in 1978. The new rural and urban organisation structure of the Guerrilla Army of the Poor (EGP) coincided with the emergence of the CUC, a new radical peasant organisation founded by Indian *campesinos* from the highlands. While military repression had seriously weakened the urban labour movement, the CUC managed to organise large demonstrations and a successful strike in the southern sugar and cotton plantations in early 1980, in which also migrant workers and poor

Ladinos took part. Continued repression on a large scale contributed to the unification of the revolutionary movement within the URNG in 1982.[31]

In El Salvador, popular support for guerrilla organisations increased both in rural and urban areas. Broad popular fronts of mass organisations emerged, such as the United Popular Action Front (FAPU) and the Revolutionary Popular Bloc (BPR). Their incorporation of strong labour unions such as ANDES and FECCAS typified a radicalisation of the Salvadorean popular movement. These popular fronts were either set up (BPR) or taken over (FAPU) by political-military organisations, among which five different political tendencies existed by 1979.[32] Although primarily starting in urban areas, increased repression after the assassination of Archbishop Romero in 1980 forced these popular fronts to go underground and to shift their emphasis towards rural areas, where the FMLN was formed in 1981 to coordinate armed struggle.

The incorporation of popular organisations into a combined rural and urban revolutionary struggle started later (but advanced most rapidly) in Nicaragua, leading to the popular insurrection of 1979. The level of popular mobilisation was still low in late 1977 and only accelerated after the assassination of opposition leader Pedro Joaquín Chamorro in January 1978. By that time the FSLN was becoming united and had moral support from a group of prominent middle-class individuals (Los Doce), which later merged into a broader opposition coalition. The FSLN increased its popularity after demonstrations during Chamorro's funeral were called off by the moderate opposition to prevent escalation, and after successful attacks at army barracks and a spectacular raid on the National Palace in August 1979. Within a year, the FSLN managed to control the rural and urban unions and formed the United Popular Movement (MPU), demanding a series of social and political reforms. This programme was effectively implemented by the new Sandinista government after the FSLN defeated the National Guard in the large-scale offensive of 1979. More than in any other Central American country, the Nicaraguan state was directly challenged by civil society and finally taken over by force, which was facilitated by divisions among the dominant sectors.[33]

A second shift was visible in political society in the early 1970s. Despite growing support, reformist political parties were unable to take power, mainly as a result of manipulated electoral outcomes. The constituencies of these parties started to realise the limits of electoral politics, and mistrust arose about the viability of a 'third option' between authoritarianism and revolution. In 1972, electoral fraud in El Salvador prevented the victory of Christian Democratic presidential candidate Duarte. The same happened five years later, although the Christian Democrats presented even more moderate candidates.[34] This time the exposure of electoral fraud produced a wave of popular protest, which led to many people becoming radicalised and, ultimately, civil war. Dunkerly (1988: 175) argues that the electoral fraud of 1977 'was the most decisive in modern Central American history'. It ushered in a period of repression against progressive forces, causing the Christian Democrats and other moderate forces to openly conclude that the legal path had been exhausted. In Guatemala this turning point came in 1974, when the electoral victory of a broad opposition coalition led by the Christian Democrats was nullified by the military regime, unleashing a wave of popular protest. Voter turnout had already been low and would further drop to thirty percent in 1978, indicating a total loss of confidence by the electorate in the fraudulent and crumbling political system.[35] After two prominent opposition leaders were assassinated by the military in 1979, any hope for moderate political reforms went up in smoke. The impossibility of opening up political society in Nicaragua was confirmed in the elections of 1974, leading to the formation of a moderate anti-Somoza front, the Democratic Union of Liberation (UDEL) headed by Pedro Joaquín Chamorro. The formation of UDEL was a sign that even conservative sectors of the business elite no longer believed in political changes through electoral politics. However, after Chamorro's assassination UDEL merged with the larger, FSLN-dominated FAO alliance, and in the process lost control over a radicalising opposition and was condemned to play a secondary role after Somoza's defeat.

A third shift occurred at the level of the state, where divisions within the dominant sectors contributed to undermining the system even further. Here the parallel between Guatemala and El Salvador is remarkable, as these divisions appeared inside the armed forces. Young military officers in both countries wanted to bring an end to military dictatorship and were (in the Salvadorean case) even advocates of social and political reforms. Their rebellion initially was effective, but short-lived. The military coup in El Salvador of October 1979, for example, was welcomed by popular organisations and the entire opposition, whose leaders accepted several cabinet posts in the new *junta*. However, conservative army officers refused to be placed under civilian control and sabotaged the progressive programme presented by the new *junta*. Accelerated repression brought about *de facto* an end to the reformist *junta* a few months later. The 1982 coup by young officers in Guatemala was led by former presidential candidate General Ríos Montt, as a protest against electoral fraud by the Lucas García regime and because of discontent inside the army over the failure to defeat the guerrilla movement. The new *junta* only ruled for a little over a year, in which the bloodiest counter-insurgency campaign of modern Central American history was waged before it was replaced by the old military hierarchy.[36] In Nicaragua on the other hand divisions did not occur in the National Guard, the stronghold of Somoza's dynasty. The cracks in Nicaragua's authoritarian regime appeared when private business leaders started to distance themselves from Somoza's virtual monopoly, especially when international relief operations after the 1972 earthquake mostly benefited his family companies. While the business sectors in Guatemala and El Salvador remained united in resisting reforms, divisions within Nicaragua's dominant sectors decisively contributed to the erosion of the Somoza dynasty.

A fourth and last shift affecting the outcome of the crisis in the late 1970s concerned the role of international forces, and in particular the ambiguous new policies of the United States government. The Carter administration that came to power in 1977 was dedicated to using human rights enforcement as a diplomatic tool in Central America. President Carter believed that the United States had to take the lead in 'protecting the individual from the arbitrary power of the state'.[37] But the military governments in El Salvador and Guatemala, aware that the new US administration would cut off military aid as a result of human rights abuses, decided to search for military aid outside the United States; the diplomatic tool thus did not work. In Nicaragua, on the other hand, despite proposals by the US Congress to cut military aid to Somoza's government, Carter refused to do so. By supporting Somoza until shortly before his fall, the US government actually contributed to strengthening international support for the FSLN, as few governments were still willing to support the Somoza regime. The contradiction in Carter's Central America policy was, according to LaFeber (1993), that he wanted political and social reforms without risking revolution. This policy in fact echoed the central goal of Kennedy's *Alliance for Progress*, which eventually also converted into a military counter-insurgency aid programme under Johnson in the mid-1960s. President Carter and his aides misjudged the explosive potential of the Central American political crisis: by 1979 it was already too late to go for the reformist option. The only way to prevent further erosion of US hegemony, it was believed, was to stop aid to the Sandinista government and to actively support the counter-revolution throughout the region.[38]

— *The outbreak of civil wars*

All these shifts affected Central America concurrently between 1977 and 1979, although the impact in each country was quite different. By 1980, the Nicaraguan authoritarian regime had been eliminated and the entire National Guard was expelled to neighbouring countries, where some of them would later start the US-financed counter-revolution. The new Sandinista government enjoyed international support for its basic principles (political pluralism, a mixed economy and non-alignment) and introduced fundamental political and social reforms, among them a land redistribution programme. In El Salvador, the reformist programme of the new military *junta* – including agrarian reform and the nationalisation of banks and foreign trade – was sabotaged by the oligarchy and only contributed to further escalation towards civil war, after Archbishop Romero and the entire leadership of the moderate left-wing opposition were assassinated in 1980. In Guatemala, the political crisis was responded to by increased military repression followed by genocide among the indigenous population and the (virtual) defeat of revolutionary movements.

Although affected by developments in neighbouring countries, only Costa Rica and Honduras managed to avoid the escalation of political polarisation into civil wars. The shifts in these countries were less dramatic thanks to an earlier opening of political society (Costa Rica), or the introduction of social reforms that prevented radicalisation of the urban and rural unions (Honduras). As a result, state-civil society relations became far less polarised and were mediated by more or less

functioning political societies. In Costa Rica, power was transferred to the opposition after the 1978 elections and in Honduras the Liberal Party came to power
with a large victory in the 1980 elections. However, increased US military aid to
destabilise the Sandinista government and to support the counter-revolutionary
offensive in El Salvador did affect the internal politics of Costa Rica and Honduras,
particularly after the *contras* started operations from their territories. Due to its
favourable geo-military position (bordering Nicaragua, El Salvador *and* Guatemala), Honduras was selected by the Pentagon to become the centre for military
bases and joint military manoeuvres. This externally induced militarisation would
seriously affect the pace of democratic transition in Honduras and prolong civil
war at its borders.

4.3 Stages and dynamics of democratic transitions

Due to the crisis of authoritarian rule, the traditional 'triple alliance' between the
landed oligarchy, the armed forces and the interventionist role of the US embassy
was shown to be falling apart. This alliance had been the nucleus of prolonged
'reactionary despotism' since the nineteenth century (Gorostiaga 1993). The crisis
of authoritarian rule triggered democratic transitions throughout Central America.
In each country these transitions had different dynamics, which is understandable
given the unique national power balances between the state and civil society. They
certainly influenced each other however. The 1979 triumph of the FSLN in
Nicaragua, for example, had enormous influence on the entire region and was not
restricted to the obvious impact it had on revolutionary movements in El Salvador
and Guatemala.[39] The following section will examine these democratic transitions
in more detail at the national levels, focusing on Honduras, El Salvador and
Guatemala.[40] The early transition stages in these countries were essentially what
Torres Rivas (1989) has called 'authoritarian transitions', in which political society
was opened up by the armed forces, while they simultaneously repressed civil
society and refused subordination to civilian rule.

Although the early stages of these three democratic transitions appeared to have
many similarities, they had different internal dynamics. The transition framework
presented in Chapter 1 will serve as a framework to analyse these differences. Four
stages were identified which followed the period of authoritarian rule: early
transition, mid-transition, late transition and (early and late) consolidation. Sharp
dividing lines between these stages are drawn for analytical purposes, but were of
course far more gradual in practice. By dividing up the process of 'constructing
democracy' into clearly marked 'stages', it can be overlooked that actually several
transitions occurred simultaneously. Therefore, the analysis is based on treating
democratic transitions as processes taking place simultaneously in the realms of the
state, civil society and political society, albeit with different intensities.[41] As is
demonstrated below, early transition stages were often controlled 'from above' and

triggered by the dominating powers in their attempt to prevent a radicalisation of civil society. During mid-transition, democratisation dynamics 'from below' by subordinated sectors in civil society started to gain momentum. It was a process particularly advocated by revolutionary movements and aimed to transform the political and social structures of domination, to achieve democracy with social justice. In the stage of late transition the emphasis shifted towards political society, which incorporated previously excluded parties of the left-wing opposition.

In Honduras and El Salvador the first two stages of democratic transition had been completed at the time of this writing, meaning that the stage of 'late transition' still prevails. As will be demonstrated, Guatemala's democratisation process is still in the stage of 'mid-transition', pending the outcome of the implementation of the peace agreement. This is important to mention, as it indicates that democratic transitions have not yet been completed and could still be reversed. Still, it is a great advantage to analyse these processes with hindsight in the late 1990s, at a time in which academic and political attention for Central America has practically vanished compared to a decade ago. It is now possible to recognise that

amidst the 'Central American crisis' (as it was called ten years ago) gradual democratic transitions were actually taking place.[42] In other words, underlying the political crisis that lasted throughout the 1980s and until the early 1990s several transitions were taking place simultaneously at national levels (Cerdas 1996). Most urgent and violent were the transitions from civil wars (affecting the entire region) to peace, which obviously attracted most (international) attention. The crisis was fuelled by economic transitions from state-led development to a market-led development model, a process of structural adjustment that started to take shape in the mid-1980s.[43] In addition to this, political transitions from authoritarian to democratic rule were in motion, transitions that will be more closely examined for Honduras, El Salvador and Guatemala.

– Honduras: challenging military impunity

The Honduran democratic transition was gradual, by far not as spectacular as in Guatemala or El Salvador, and only similar to Costa Rica in the way labour reforms were introduced starting in the 1950s. After Somoza's fall in Nicaragua, the US government pressured the Honduran military leaders to hand over power to a civilian government. Honduras was regarded by the Pentagon as an ideal territory from which to implement its counter-revolutionary offensive, but as a key military ally it needed a democratic image. The Honduran armed forces had been in power since 1963 and were professionalised and equipped with US assistance. They even promoted several social reforms such as land redistribution, but they had low esteem for the weak traditional political parties, the Liberals and the Nationalists.[44] In return for increased military aid, the United States convinced the Honduran armed forces to convene elections and install a civilian government.[45] The armed forces conditioned their retreat upon full autonomy regarding military affairs. The price that the Hondurans were to pay was twofold: a loss of national sovereignty – US troops were deployed on Honduran territory, along with a training centre for Salvadorean officers and bases for anti-Sandinista *contras* with Argentinean and Israeli military advisors – and a legitimised increase of power for the armed forces. The poorest Central American country with the weakest state institutions was suddenly trapped in a process of externally-led militarisation. How did civil society react and how did this affect democratic transition?

Although it is difficult to determine a precise moment for the start of early democratic transition in Honduras, the 1980 parliamentary elections and the 1981 presidential elections marked the beginning of a gradual (albeit formal) transfer from military to civilian power.[46] Presidential candidate Roberto Suazo Córdova, a conservative in the Liberal Party, received the confidence of the electorate to lead this transition from military rule. But instead of demilitarising the regime, the opposite happened. The power of the Honduran military substantially increased, particularly as a result of increased US military aid and the appointment of army commander General Alvarez Martínez. Backed by the new US ambassador John Negroponte, Alvarez launched a violent counter-insurgency programme against

Table 4.1   Stages of democratic transition in Honduras

Honduran transition stages	Political context
Authoritarian period until 1980	1963 Coup by General López Arellano prevents election of Liberal (and reformist) government of Rodas Alvarado. Start of military 'arbitration'. 1969 Defeat in four-day 'soccer war' with El Salvador 1971 Government of national unity under president Cruz 1972 General López Arellano re-installed as president; new period of agrarian reforms 1974 Hurricane Fifi strikes northern coast: 12,000 casualties 1975 López removed after charges of bribery, General Melgar installed (March); Massacre of peasants in Olancho (May) 1978 Melgar replaced by Policarpo Paz after drugs scandal (July) 1979 US pressure to re-install civilian government
Early transition 1980-1990	1980 Liberals win parliamentary elections (April); Massacre of 600 Salvadoran peasants at the Sumpul border river (May) 1981 Human rights group CODEH founded (May); John Negroponte new US ambassador to Honduras; First joint US-Honduran military manoeuvres (Oct); Suazo Córdova wins presidential elections (Nov); 1982 General Alvarez Martínez appointed chief of staff; start dirty war against opposition leaders (Jan); US military aid increased by 50 percent (March); US troops deployed at Palmerola Air Base 1984 Alvarez removed and replaced by Walter López Reyes (March) 1985 Large US-Honduran military manoeuvres Big Pine III, Universal Track (May); Azcona de Hoyo wins presidential elections (Nov) 1986 Start of Iran-*contra* scandal (Nov) 1987 Esquipulas II agreement (Aug) 1988 Assassination of vice president human rights committee CODEH (Jan); Escalation of right-wing protest at US embassy (April); Government sentenced by Inter-American Court for Human Rights (July) 1989 Retired General Alvarez Martínez assassinated (Jan); Bush takes over from Reagan (Jan); Callejas wins presidential elections (Nov)
Mid-transition 1990-1993	1990 Callejas inaugurated (Jan); Contras leave Honduras (April); Frente Morazanista renounces armed struggle (April); Military chief Arnulfo Cantarero removed (Dec) 1991 Congress approves general amnesty (July); Violated and dead body of young student Riccy Mabel found (July) 1992 Neoliberal Agricultural Modernisation Law ends agrarian reform (March); Human Rights Ombudsman appointed (Sept) 1993 *Ad hoc* Commission appointed for military and judicial reforms (March); First military officer sentenced by civilian court (July); Carlos Alberto Reina wins presidential elections (Nov); Report on forced disappearances published (Dec)
Late transition 1994-	1994 President Reina inaugurated (Jan); Forced military recruitment abandoned (May); Secret service DNI dissolved (June) 1995 Armed assault against President Reina's residence (March); Exhumations identify bodies of the disappeared 1996 Judicial order to arrest a dozen former army officers responsible for forced disppearances (June)

Sources: Lapper and Painter (1985); Dunkerly (1988, 1994); Norsworthy and Barry (1994); Schulz and Sundloff Schulz (1994); Funes (1995); Méndez and Salomón (1995); Inforpress Centroamericana; CODEH (1996).

(potential) Honduran supporters of the Sandinista revolution and the Salvadorean rebels. Activities by small revolutionary organisations opposing the US counter-revolution on Honduran soil were a pretext for Alvarez to repress opposition leaders in civil society and to violate human rights.[47] Using 'Argentinean methods' (torture, disappearances and extrajudicial killings by death squads), the dirty war initiated by General Alvarez made clear that democratic transition was subordinate to regional US 'low intensity warfare'. In this scenario, the Honduran armed forces performed a (covert) role by giving logistical support to the Nicaraguan *contras*. It was apparent that President Suazo was a puppet of the armed forces who were basically receiving orders from the United States in return for sophisticated arms and *carte blanche* for a dirty war against the opposition.

But Alvarez's enthusiasm to 'combat communism' (and the Sandinista government in particular) – in addition to his efforts to create a neo-fascist constituency backed by the Moon sect, and moves to increase his personal power – led to his fall in March 1984 when he was removed in a coup led by air force commander General Walter López. Only by endorsing this coup did President Suazo prevent his own ouster as well. Meanwhile, large demonstrations against the presence of US military troops and the *contras* (who had contributed to criminal violence, drugs and arms trafficking) indicated that civil society demanded an end to the servile role of Honduras in the anti-communist crusade of the Reagan administration. As the US Congress had decided to cut direct aid to the *contras*, US aid now had to be channelled secretly via the Honduran armed forces. But growing mobilisation by unions and human rights groups also was a sign of growing political opposition against the Suazo-López regime. In the previous four years, President Suazo had done little to introduce urgent electoral and judicial reforms or to combat corruption, let alone to curb military power. The problem was that a political party in the centre to incorporate these demands was absent; the two traditional parties were only engaged in factional struggles between candidates for the November 1985 elections.[48] Liberal candidate José Azcona de Hoyo finally emerged as the new president, although his victory was achieved under dubious circumstances.[49]

The real power in Honduras still resided with the armed forces, and this would not change under the weak presidency of Azcona (1986-90). But the armed forces also lacked internal unity, which was caused by personal rivalries and corruption, and fuelled by dissatisfaction of young reformist officers over Honduran support to the US *contra* war. After a rebellion was prevented in December 1985, General López was purged by conservative officers right before Azcona was inaugurated, which illustrated the full autonomy of the military from civilian authorities.[50] While massive US military aid was pouring into Honduras, the armed forces were able to dictate the political process. But this tendency was about to change: the Iran-*contra* scandal erupting in the United States would be the beginning of the end for the *contras*. The Esquipulas peace process (consistently sabotaged by Azcona upon US request) and the end of the Cold War contributed to a gradual return to peace in the region, with direct consequences for the Honduran armed forces. A decline in US military aid by the end of the 1980s and waning popularity of the armed forces suggested that demilitarisation of the Honduran political system was indeed beginning. A sign of this declining influence was a growing movement in civil society against military 'impunity' for human rights abuses in the recent past, illustrating that controlled democratic transition from above was being challenged from below.[51]

It is this declining power of the armed forces that marks the shift from early to mid-transition, which can be situated around the inauguration in early 1990 of newly-elected President Rafael Callejas. This young neoliberal technocrat represented a Nationalist Party that had been modernised during its opposition against the Liberal governments of Suazo and Azcona. Between Callejas's election victory of late 1989 and his first months in office the regional power balance had completely changed. The Cold War was over, peace negotiations were about to start in El Salvador, the Sandinistas were out of power and the *contras* were demobilised. Moreover, US military aid to Honduras had dropped to the lowest level of the (previous) decade and revolutionary opposition groups announced an end to armed struggle.[52] The new political climate facilitated measures to tackle one of the key obstacles to democratic transition in Honduras: the uneven civil-military balance. Mounting pressure from civil society (notably from human rights organisations) and from the new US ambassador urged the Callejas government to curb military power. A special commission was created to propose reform of the military and judicial system, eventually leading (in 1994) to the dismantling of the secret service DNI, which was replaced by a civilian-controlled body in addition to a new Prosecution Counsel. Callejas also appointed a special human rights ombudsman whose first task was to investigate the disappearances of the 1980s. In December 1993, a detailed report was presented by the ombudsman, documenting over 150 cases of forced disappearances and concluding that military-led death squad activity was still going on.[53] It very much resembled the Salvadorean Truth Commission report (presented earlier that year) with one major difference: the names of the responsible officers were made public. With the recommendation of legal action against these top military officers, military impunity finally had become a key political issue.

Meanwhile, neoliberal structural adjustment policies of the Callejas administration contributed to rising protest from trade unions and peasant organisations against worsening socio-economic conditions, although coordinated opposition from civil society (such as the *Plataforma de lucha*) was short-lived. The declining popularity of the Nationalist Party and its decision to present a former ally of General Alvarez as a candidate for the presidential elections added to growing support for the Social Democratic faction in the Liberal Party led by the Reina brothers. With the electoral campaign dominated by the issue of military impunity, Carlos Alberto Reina easily won the presidency with a large victory, although voter abstention had increased compared to the 1980s. Under President Reina (1994-98) proposals contributing to demilitarisation were effectively implemented: forced military recruitment was abolished, judicial reforms restricted military impunity, steps were taken to bring the police under civilian control and the military budget was gradually reduced. These important measures suggested that the Honduran democratic transition during the Reina administration moved into a stage of late transition. But caution is required, as the influence of the armed forces was also determined by their economic power accumulated over the previous decade in banking, construction and several state institutions that had been privatised in the early 1990s. Added to the active involvement of the military in the drugs trade since the presence of the *contras*, it is still too early to conclude that civilian authorities have shifted the civil-military balance in their own favour.[54] Clientelism and patronage continue to obstruct the growth of an autonomous civil society in Honduras. Moreover, political society remains weak with the absence of a serious challenger to the traditional two-party system (Sieder 1996b).

– *El Salvador: democratic transition during civil war*

The Salvadorean democratic transition is a clear example of a 'transition from above' guided by reformist principles to prevent a revolutionary take-over. It provoked fierce reactions from extreme-right opposition groups and (fuelled by US military aid) initiated a decade of civil war and deadlock. Democratic transition was disrupted until the end of the Cold War, when the revolutionary perspective was fading and democratic rule had been accepted by the dominant forces. Early transition started with the October 1979 coup by young military officers against the Romero regime, which had been criticised by the Carter administration for its human rights violations. The purpose of the coup was to start demilitarising Salvadorean society and introduce social and economic reforms. Power was handed over by the military rebels to a *junta* composed of key reformist opposition leaders of the Popular Forum, a broad opposition coalition led by Social and Christian Democrats such as Guillermo Ungo and Rubén Zamora.[55] The new *junta*, regarded as the most progressive government in Salvadorean history, would only last for three months as conservative elements in the armed forces started a counter-revolutionary offensive against popular organisations. Being unable to stop this repression, the *junta* collapsed and the reformist leaders knew that civil war had become inevitable.[56] The short period of democratic transition from above thus came to an end with the restoration of authoritarianism.

The following twelve months of 1980 witnessed a complex process of rapid social and political polarisation in which the political centre virtually disappeared. A dissident section of the Christian Democrats together with the Social Democratic parties MNR and PSD (forming the FDR) forged an alliance with the revolutionary left, which soon decided to move from mass mobilisation to armed struggle under the umbrella of the FMLN. The old *junta* was replaced by conservative Christian Democrats and led by José Napoléon Duarte, who enjoyed US support for his moderate reformist programme. Meanwhile, conservative elements in the army

Table 4.2   *Stages of democratic transition in El Salvador*

Salvadoran transition stages	Political context
Authoritarian period until 1979	1960 Coup by young reformist military officers
	1961 ORDEN and Christian Democratic Party (PDC) founded
	1964 PDC wins parliamentary elections; Duarte elected mayor of the capital
	1969 'Soccer war' with Honduras; Formation of UNO
	1972 UNO election victory (Duarte and Ungo) denied by military
	1977 Duarte's victory again dismissed in fraudulent elections; General Romero inaugurated as new president; Death squad activity starts
Early transition 1979-1990	1979 Military coup by young officers against Romero (Oct)
	1980 Ungo and Zamora resign from *junta* (Jan); Assassination Archbishop Romero (March); Duarte enters *junta* and announces agrarian reform (March); FDR founded (April); General strike (Aug); FMLN founded (Oct); Leadership FDR assassinated (Nov)
	1981 'Final offensive' FMLN (Jan); President Reagan inaugurated in US (Jan); Formation of ARENA (Sept); FMLN recognised by Mexico-France (Aug); Massacre of 600 peasants at El Mozote (Nov)
	1982 Extreme-right wins parliamentary majority; PDC largest party (March)
	1984 Duarte beats D'Aubuisson in presidential elections (May); First attempt towards peace talks with the FMLN
	1985 Christian democratic majority in parliament
	1986 UNTS founded; Military sabotage peace talks; Earthquake in capital kills 1,500 people and displaces over 10,000 persons (Oct)
	1987 Esquipulas regional peace agreement (Aug); Ungo and Zamora withdraw from FDR and form CD (Nov)
	1988 ARENA wins parliamentary elections (Mar); Split in PDC
	1989 FMLN offers to participate in elections (Jan); Alfredo Cristiani wins presidential elections (Mar); Cristiani installed (June); Peace talks Mexico (Sept) and Costa Rica (Oct); Offensive by FMLN; Aerial bombings of capital; Assassination of UCA Jesuits (Nov)
	1990 Cristiani and FMLN request UN to moderate peace talks (Jan); Electoral defeat of Sandinistas in Nicaragua (Feb)
Mid-transition 1990-1994	1990 Peace negotiations start (May); Human rights agreement (June); US Congress cuts military aid by 50 percent (Oct)
	1991 US helicopter downed by FMLN, Bush administration releases frozen military aid (Jan); Left-wing CD voted into parliament (March); Agreement on constitutional reforms: breakthrough in negotiations (April); ONUSAL mission established (June); Agreement on military issues in New York (Sept); Final agreement (Dec)
	1992 Signing of Peace Accords in Chapúltepec (Jan); Cease fire implemented (Feb); FMLN demobilised and becomes legal party (Dec)
	1993 Truth Commission report published; Parliament approves amnesty law (March); Assassination of former FMLN commander López (Dec)
	1994 FMLN becomes second party in parliamentary elections (March); ARENA candidate Calderon Sol beats CD-FMLN candidate Rubén Zamora in presidential elections (April)
Late transition 1994-	1994 FMLN enters legislature (May); ERP and RN withdraw from FMLN (Dec)
	1995 Former soldiers occupy legislature to demand severance (Jan); ONUSAL mandate ends (March); Former FMLN commander Villalobos and his new Democratic Party sign pact with government (May); Government proposes new law to control development NGOS
	1996 Legislature approves electoral reforms (Nov)

Sources: Dunkerly (1988, 1994); Lungo (1990); Montgomery (1995); Murray (1995); Spence *et al.* (1997).

continued their repression campaign with support from extreme right-wing death squads financed by the oligarchy, opposing the agrarian reform programme proposed by Duarte.[57] A key moment in this polarisation process was the assassination in March 1980 of Archbishop Romero, one of the few mediators who might have been able to prevent civil war and who unsuccessfully urged the Carter government to suspend military aid. Romero's funeral turned into a massive demonstration against repression and against the Duarte *junta*, but ended in bloodshed when security forces opened gunfire on the crowd. A widespread campaign of terror by death squads (such as the liquidation of the entire FDR leadership in November 1980) eroded the possibility of a popular insurrection and probably also contributed to the failure of the FMLN military offensive in January 1981 (Byrne 1996).

By that time, President Reagan had been inaugurated in the United States and a civil war had started between two clearly defined alliances: the armed forces and the extreme right with the Christian Democrats in government and held together by US military aid, versus the FMLN and its political allies of the FDR with moral support from the Latin American left and European Social Democracy.[58] The alliance led by the armed forces was determined to defeat the FMLN, but there were different views about how to achieve this. The armed forces considered the war and US military aid as a way to restore power, the oligarchy was determined to weaken the popular base of the FMLN, while the PDC used the alliance to regain popular support with a US-sponsored programme of reforms. The other alliance, led by the FMLN, was more coherent and aimed to seize power by political and military means followed by the installation of a revolutionary government (Byrne 1996). Despite successful military offensives in 1982 and 1983, in which it established control over considerable rural areas, the FMLN was unable to defeat the US-backed armed forces.

International pressure to resolve the conflict through direct peace negotiations was responded to by President Duarte's call for legislative (1982, 1985) and presidential (1984) elections to legitimise his government and to assure the continuation of US support. The Reagan administration was actually opposed to a negotiated solution, although vulnerable to international criticism for its support to an unconstitutional regime. The US government considered elections part of a counter-insurgency strategy to weaken popular support for the FMLN. Amidst civil war and without the participation of reformist opposition parties (that had gone into exile), these elections basically were a contest between Duarte's PDC and the right-wing ARENA led by Major Roberto D'Aubuisson, considered to be the intellectual perpetrator of Archbishop Romero's assassination. Although the 1982 elections resulted in a right-wing majority in parliament, Duarte managed to win the presidency in 1984 and secured a parliamentary majority in 1985. The election strategy had proven to be a useful tool to politically isolate the FMLN, regain support from the US Congress and reinstate economic aid from several European countries (notably West Germany). By the time Duarte was elected president, the war had caused 60,000 deaths (mostly civilians) and created over a million refugees and internally displaced persons, representing a quarter of the entire population.

The Duarte government (1984-89) marked the start of a new phase in the war, with the FMLN and the armed forces entering a military stalemate despite the use of more sophisticated weaponry and strategies such as aerial bombing. Duarte and the FMLN were meanwhile each trying to enlarge their popular base. Several rounds of peace talks were convened between the two parties, but without any result; both sides still believed that a military victory was the only solution to end the war.[59] Willingness to negotiate was in fact equated with surrender. With human rights violations diminishing and political space widening after the elections, civil society started to regain strength. Strikes and demonstrations against the Duarte government targeted his structural adjustment policies (which had decreased real wages) and his failure to bring an end to the war. One of the largest and most militant coalitions emerging in this period was the National Union of Salvadorean Workers (UNTS), a federation of rural and urban unions with strong FMLN influence. The foundation of UNTS reflected a shift in strategy of the guerrilla movement towards increasing its urban popular support base to prepare for an insurrection. The former FDR parties meanwhile decided to re-enter the electoral path with the Democratic Convergence (CD), led by prominent members of the 1979 *junta* such as Guillermo Ungo and Rubén Zamora.[60]

The Christian Democrats were gradually weakened by internal divisions, charges of corruption and growing popular opposition against the austerity measures. With the FMLN still aiming for a military victory and the CD still poorly organised, it was the right-wing ARENA that managed to gain electoral confidence. It won the 1988 parliamentary elections and in 1989 the presidency with Alfredo Cristiani. As a representative of the urban business sector who enjoyed support from moderate factions within the armed forces, Cristiani announced his willingness to open peace talks with the FMLN to achieve political stability and economic recovery. However, by late 1989 peace talks stagnated as both parties refused to make concessions. A wave of right-wing political violence from opponents to negotiations triggered a nationwide military offensive in November by the FMLN that would turn the tide. Although not leading to a popular insurrection, the FMLN demonstrated that it had not yet been militarily defeated. But more important, the offensive convinced the United States that the war could not be won militarily by either one of the parties. The US Congress had already been reluctant to continue military aid and, given the changing Cold War balance, the FMLN and the government realised they both had to win by negotiations, which finally started in May 1990 under UN auspices.[61]

The shift from early to mid-transition occurred in these five months between the November 1989 offensive and the start of negotiations in Geneva in May 1990. The breakthrough was the acceptance by both parties (opposing each other for a decade) that negotiations and the search for compromise was the only way to end the war. They both realised that only a national peace agreement would move democratic transition forwards. This mutual acceptance of the need to negotiate an end to the conflict had been triggered by international as well as national factors. The international factors (demise of communist ideology, changes in US policy and declining regional support for the FMLN after the removal of Noriega in Panama and the Sandinistas in Nicaragua) have been mentioned already, and will be analysed later in more detail. At a national level, the FMLN realised that armed insurrection was no longer an option. ARENA and moderate factions within the armed forces realised that (right-wing) power also could be secured via legal means, which was confirmed by Violeta Chamorro's victory in Nicaragua. An additional element at the national level was the new unity achieved among previously divided popular organisations in civil society, who demanded an end to the war through negotiated compromise.

Under UN mediation, and supported by a group of *países amigos*, peace negotiations would be concluded within less than two years.[62] An agreement was soon reached about the agenda, in which military reforms, human rights, social and economic reforms, judicial and electoral reforms, constitutional reforms and verification figured as central issues. It was the beginning of a complex diplomatic process in which demilitarisation obviously was one of the key obstacles. The negotiations started with the issue of reform and reduction of the armed forces, in which military power would be subordinated to the executive, and with the demilitarisation of the police. Initially, the FMLN wanted to abolish the army. But when this appeared to be unrealistic, it called for incorporation into a sanitised army. The issue was resolved by US pressure to cut military aid and by allowing FMLN participation in a new national civilian police force. The March 1991 parliamentary elections, in which the CD received twelve percent of the votes and no party achieved a majority, also contributed to spur an agreement.[63] Other issues provoking antagonism were the clean-up of the armed forces (resolved by appointing an *ad hoc* commission under UN supervision), guarantees for the physical survival of FMLN-members' families (land distribution) and formal incorporation of the FMLN as a new political party in political society. A special peace commission (COPAZ) composed of all political parties would oversee the implementation of the agreement. COPAZ in fact would act as a parallel (non-elected) government of national unity, which also symbolised the key instrument to overcome previous polarisation: the search for compromise and concerted action *(concertación)*.[64] The final details were resolved under pressure on New Year's Eve 1991, when Pérez de Cuellar's term as UN Secretary General would end. Although not all issues had been thoroughly addressed, a final peace agreement was signed in January 1992, followed by a ceasefire that would hold.

The implementation of the agreement was not without conflict and indicates that the intermediate transition stage (mid-transition) continued until the 1994 general elections. The scheme for FMLN demobilisation was seriously delayed by charges made by the armed forces that weapons had been withheld and by death squad attacks against former FMLN combatants. The purge of the armed forces also was a difficult process and was only resolved after the US government put pressure on the army hierarchy, prolonging demobilisation until late 1992 when the FMLN formally became a political party. The peace agreement essentially was an elite compromise, requiring a depolarisation and even a demobilisation of civil society (Dada 1995). However, the agreement was successful in dealing with two problems underlying El Salvador's authoritarian past: it succeeded in demilitarising Salvadorean society and bringing the armed forces under executive (and therefore not necessarily civilian) control, and it opened the door for democratising the political system. The absence of military coup attempts since the agreement and the clean general elections of March 1994, in which the FMLN became the second largest political party, confirms that these achievements were consolidated into practice. However, the electoral victory by the right-wing ARENA party in 1994, the internal FMLN split and deficient government policies for tackling socio-economic inequality also suggest that the stage of late democratic transition still was fragile.

— *Guatemala: the search for consensus after the genocide*

Early democratic transition in Guatemala started in January 1986, with the inauguration of civilian president Vinicio Cerezo of the Christian Democratic Party. Compared to El Salvador, the Guatemalan transition was even more a 'transition from above' and entirely controlled by the armed forces. Jonas (1991) even argues that the Cerezo government was not really a rupture with past military rule (as was the case with the 1979 coup in El Salvador), but rather an adaptation of the counter-insurgency state by giving it a civilian appearance. The basis for this transition from above was laid in March 1982 by General Ríos Montt, who brought an end to the Lucas García regime with support from junior army officers. In their opinion, Lucas García had not been serious about opening up the political system for civilian rule, which was considered to be a necessary condition to stop the insurgency led by the URNG.[65] Ríos Montt was a Christian fundamentalist who had been denied the presidency as a Christian Democratic candidate in the 1974 elections. He promised to restore constitutional government after the insurgents were defeated. Indeed, the coup was followed by the bloodiest counter-insurgency campaign in Guatemalan history, with a death toll of an estimated 100,000 (mostly Indian) civilians. Although successful in containing the insurgency, Ríos Montt rapidly lost support from the military hierarchy for his populist behaviour and was replaced in August 1993 in a new coup by General Mejía Víctores, who continued the gradual process of return to constitutional rule. This process was warmly supported by the Reagan administration, although the armed forces refused to accept US military aid.[66] Similar to the Honduran and Salvadorean military retreats, elections for a Constituent Assembly were convened (in June 1984) followed by presidential elections (in November 1985) that were dominated by political parties from centre-right to extreme-right. The Christian Democratic DCG, which had moved to the centre-right in previous years, emerged as the largest party in these elections.[67]

The high level of abstentionism in these elections (56 percent, despite compul-

Table 4.3   Stages of democratic transition in Guatemala

Guatemalan transition stages	Political context
Authoritarian period *1954-1985*	1954 Military coup against Arbenz 1962 Start of guerrilla warfare 1972 Defeat of FAR, formation of EGP 1976 Earthquake in the highlands and the capital kills 22,000 people and leaves over a million homeless; Formation of CRN 1978 Lucas García president (March); Foundation of CUC (April); Panzós massacre (May) 1979 Formation of ORPA 1980 Massacre Spanish embassy (Jan); Guerrilla groups form alliance 1981 Intensified counter-insurgency campaign in highlands (June) 1982 Formation of URNG (Feb); General Guevara wins fraudulent elections (March); Coup by Ríos Montt and start *Victoria 82* campaign (March) 1983 Ríos Montt announces elections for Constituent Assembly (June); Coup by General Mejía Víctores (Aug) 1984 Elections for Constituent Assembly, majority won by Christian Democrats (June); Foundation of GAM (June) 1985 General elections, Christian Democrats win 51 percent of Congress seats (Nov); Christian Democrat Vinicio Cerezo wins presidential elections by beating Jorge Carpio in second round (Dec)
Early transition *1986-1993*	1986 Installation civilian government of Cerezo (Jan) 1987 Esquipulas agreement (Aug); First talks government and URNG (Oct) 1988 Abortive coup attempt (May); Foundation CONAVIGUA (Sept) 1989 Abortive coup attempt (May) 1990 Peace talks reopened in Oslo (March); Foundation COMG (June); Foundation *Majawil Q'ij* (Oct); Serrano wins first round of presidential elections (Nov); Massacre of Santiago Atitlán (Dec) 1991 Serrano new president (Jan); 'Mexico Agreement' on agenda for negotiations (April); Encounter '500 years of resistance' (Oct) 1992 Formation *Mesa Maya* (Oct); Nobel Peace Prize for Menchú (Oct) 1993 'Triple alliance' between MAS, UCN, and DCG falls apart (April); *Autogolpe* Serrano (May); De León Carpio appointed as interim president (June); Purge of corrupt Congress and Supreme Court (Aug); Agreement for referendum in Jan. 1994 to change constitution (Nov)
Mid-transition *1994-*	1994 Peace talks reopened (Jan); Human rights agreement (March); Foundation COPMAGUA (May); Installation ASC (May); Consensus on Indian rights in ASC (May); Agreement on displaced and on Truth commission (June); PAN and FRG largest parties in parliamentary elections, with 80 percent abstentionism (Aug); UN mission MINUGUA formally installed (Nov) 1995 Bishop Quezada leaves ASC (Jan); Refugee repatriation starts (Jan); Indian rights agreement (March); Massacre of returned refugees in Xamán (Oct); FDNG wins six deputies in general elections, and Alvaro Arzú (PAN) wins presidential elections (Nov) 1996 Arzú inaugurated as new president (Jan); Socio-economic agreement (May); Final peace accord signed (Dec) 1997 International donor conference to support implementation of peace agreement (Jan)

Sources: Dunkerly (1988, 1994); Jonas (1981); Barry (1992); *Inforpress* (1995, 1996); Palencia and Holiday (1996); Aguilera *et al.* (1996); Torres Rivas (1996b).

sory voting) and ongoing repression by security forces suggests that a period of 'electoral authoritarianism' had started, similar to that in El Salvador. But the Cerezo government (1986-90) was quite different from the Christian Democratic government in El Salvador. The Guatemalan armed forces actually wanted to restore civilian rule to limit social protest and not so much (as in the Salvadorean case) to please the US Congress, although they were conscious that the new civilian government could improve Guatemala's international image. The re-emergence of trade unions, human rights groups and 'Maya' organisations, especially in the second half of Cerezo's term, illustrates that popular sectors in civil society were starting to gain force after the dark years of military massacres. The emergence of these social actors indeed suggests that a democratic transition had started. However, the Cerezo government had little control over the armed forces, who continued their counter-insurgency war. Cerezo acted cautiously, afraid to lose support from the military and the business sectors who continuously attacked him for his indecisiveness and his inabiliy to combat corruption. Popular organisations criticised Cerezo's economic austerity programme and his failure to curb military power and to improve human rights conditions. In fact, it was only for his role in the regional Esquipulas peace process that Cerezo enjoyed some popularity. But when he announced his willingness to explore the possibility of peace talks with the URNG (a commitment resulting from the Esquipulas agreement) the armed forces reacted furiously and staged several coup attempts in 1988 and 1989. When he took office, Cerezo estimated that he exercised only thirty percent of executive power in comparison to the armed forces, and predicted that the figure would be seventy percent when he was to leave in 1990 (Painter 1989). But instead of strengthening civilian power by limiting right-wing leverage over his government, Cerezo actually lost most of his credibility and contributed to a worsening of the civil-military balance.

Important steps to confront polarisation in civil society were taken by the Catholic Church, and in particular by Bishop Rodolfo Quezada. He urged the government in 1988 to formally start a National Dialogue between social sectors, as had been stipulated in the Esquipulas regional peace agreement. Chaired by Quezada, it started in early 1989 with participation from a broad spectrum of nearly fifty organisations from civil society, although openly boycotted by the two major business associations, the right-wing opposition and the government.[68] A wide range of social and political issues were discussed in separate commissions and it was in fact the first time that representatives from such a variety of civil society sectors sat together to jointly search for solutions to Guatemala's major problems. Meanwhile, the URNG successfully canvassed international support for peace negotiations and expanded its political agenda to include issues such as Indian rights and socio-economic reforms in an effort to present itself as a true representative of the politically excluded and socially marginalised sectors in civil society (Palencia 1996). The changing international political climate at the end of 1989 and regional advances in the peace process (in Nicaragua and El Salvador) in addition to the upcoming presidential elections gradually created an environment in Guatemala in which peace talks became a serious option. In February 1990 President Cerezo announced that he was willing to explore possibilities for a direct dialogue with the URNG without prior conditions and appointed Bishop Quezada to chair a first meeting, which was held one month later in Oslo. Similar to El Salvador, where peace talks were to start in May, it appeared to be a major breakthrough towards ending the war.

The Guatemalan process, however, was much more slow and complex. The Oslo talks resulted in a series of bilateral meetings between the URNG and key sectors of civil society: churches, popular organisations, business associations, educational institutions and political parties. Building on the framework of the National Dialogue, they laid a foundation for peace talks by exploring points of consensus that would have to be tackled in a future peace agreement. A clear division in civil society between the business sector and most other associations surfaced in these meetings. Conflicting views existed about the need for socio-economic reforms and about the legitimacy of the URNG to negotiate issues beyond a mere solution to the military conflict. These different viewpoints were openly discussed and not only stimulated public debate but also contributed to civil society growth, in particular of a group that had been excluded up to that point: the Indian population.[69] Unlike in the Salvadorean peace process, where polarisation within civil society was replaced earlier by social consensus, in Guatemala it was more deeply rooted due to the social and political exclusion of the Indian population. The polarisation was also far more difficult to overcome as a result of the relative strength of the armed forces, and of the military and political weakness of the URNG compared to the FMLN. By distinguishing between 'substantive issues' (such as socio-economic and judicial reforms) and 'operative issues' (related to ceasefire and demobilisation), the URNG further complicated the start of direct peace talks.

Although minor differences existed among presidential candidates, the 1990 election campaign was characterised by promises for peace talks and by the absence of left-wing opposition candidates and parties. Jorge Serrano Elías, a Christian fundamentalist and a cabinet member under Ríos Montt, was elected president on a programme advocating peace talks and civilian control over the armed forces. Direct talks mediated by the UN were started in April 1991, resulting in agreement on an agenda which was even broader than the agenda agreed one year earlier in the Salvadorean talks.[70] But negotiations on the first issue of this agenda, democracy and human rights, immediately provoked fierce reactions from the armed forces and from the business sector. They argued that democracy would only be achieved by demobilising the URNG, instead of changing the constitution and subordinating the armed forces to civilian rule (Inforpress 1995). International pressure to accelerate talks increased after the Salvadorean peace agreement of late 1991. But only minor advances were made, such as an agreement to dissolve the Civil Defence Patrols (PAC's)and to appoint a human rights ombudsman. President Serrano was pressured by the 'tough sector' (*sector duro*) of the armed forces (threatening to stage a new coup if negotiations on military issues continued), but also by a variety of civil society organisations arguing that peace and social justice could not be separately discussed.

This atmosphere of polarisation was aggravated by the absence of a legitimate political society.[71] In May 1993, Serrano made a desperate move in order to regain political control: he suspended the constitution, closed down Congress and the judicial system and announced new elections. This so-called *autogolpe* failed as it was unanimously rejected by all components of civil society, and eventually also by the armed forces. Serrano had to flee the country and human rights ombudsman Ramiro de León Carpio was appointed by Congress to serve as interim-president until the 1995 elections. The shock of the Serrano coup actually had a positive impact on the peace process. All civil society sectors (despite their opposing views) suddenly realised the value of democratic institutions and that peace and democratic transition would come about by bilateral negotiation rather than unilateral imposition. De León Carpio proposed to negotiate the 'operative' and the 'substantive' issues separately, in which the latter would be based on prior consultation with a forum composed from civil society. He also managed to convince the armed forces and the business associations that they had much to gain by the establishment of civilian rule, particularly when negotiations would take place within a constitutional framework.[72]

Peace talks were finally resumed in early 1994 in a depolarised atmosphere. The two sides agreed on a set of basic conditions and commitments, suggesting that democratic transition was shifting to the stage of mid-transition.[73] An innovation (compared to the Salvadorean talks) was the installation of a special Assembly for Civil Society (ASC) chaired by Bishop Quezada, which would prepare consensus documents for the negotiation table on five substantive themes: human rights, refugees and the displaced, Indian rights, socio-economic reforms and strengthening civilian rule over the military. Although boycotted by the business sector, the ASC stimulated the involvement of previously excluded groupings with particularly women's organisations and coalitions of Indian organisations taking advantage (see Chapter 6). Under UN supervision three agreements were quickly reached between the government and the URNG in the first half of 1994: on human rights supervision, on the reintegration of refugees and the displaced, and on the installation of a Truth Commission. The last item was strongly rejected by human rights organisations, however, because human rights violators would not be mentioned by name or legally prosecuted. As a result, the URNG slowed down the speed of negotiations in mid-1994 and only resumed talks after the UN human rights verification mission MINUGUA became operational. The most important agreement was the one on Indian rights, as it tried to address the deeply rooted colonial (and racist) attitudes against the Indian majority. With active public pressure from Indian organisations the agreement was signed in March 1995, guaranteeing Guatemala's multi-ethnic and multi-cultural character. It was an agreement welcomed by the national Indian coalition COPMAGUA as an important first step in ending the marginalisation of the Mayan people.

Negotiations again entered an impasse in 1995 over the issue of socio-economic reforms. The business sector rallied against a land distribution programme and wanted to downsize the role of the state. It would take another year before an agreement was reached, also because the upcoming elections of November 1995 were expected by both sides to be instrumental in strengthening their negotiation power. The URNG had not yet been transformed into a political party and therefore was unable to participate in the elections. But much of the URNG agenda was taken up by the new left-wing Democratic Front for a New Guatemala (FDNG), a party formed by popular organisations a few months before the elections.[74] FDNG performed rather well, given its short preparation time, and managed to win six seats (7.5 percent) in Congress and several mayoralties in Indian municipalities in the highlands. Still, the business sector won the overall elections with their centre-right presidential candidate Alvaro Arzú, an urban businessman in many respects similar to Alfredo Cristiani in El Salvador.[75]

President Arzú realised that once the socio-economic agreement was signed, all other issues would be a matter of time. The signing took place in May 1996, but only weakly reflected the URNG demands of earlier years.[76] Despite heavy criticism by peasant organisations and trade unions, it was clear that a rejection of the socio-economic agreement would have reversed the whole peace process, putting the URNG in a weaker position than ever before. President Arzú apparently made a secret pact with the URNG leadership about the final stage of the negotiations. Fundamental issues, such as limiting the power of the agro-export sector and civilian control over the armed forces, had been tacitly arranged to achieve a final peace accord by late December 1996.[77] The power of the armed forces was restricted by dissolving the counter-insurgency system of Civil Defence Patrols (PAC's) and military commissioners. Furthermore, a civilian police force was created and it was agreed to clean up the ranks of the armed forces by purging officers accused of corruption and human rights abuses.

With the endorsement of the December 1996 peace agreement, the process of demilitarisation was initiated. The shift of Guatemala's democratic transition to a stage of 'late transition' will very much depend upon successful implementation of the peace accords (with an important role for the UN) and on the incorporation of the URNG into political society, which is expected to happen after the general elections of the year 2000. Until that time, Ríos Montt's FRG remains the major opposition party in the Guatemalan Congress and will use any opportunity to undermine the implementation of the peace agreement. Two additional problems make the prospects for democratic transition in Guatemala rather bleak. One is that the URNG, despite growing popular support, by far does not have the institutional strength nor the political legitimacy comparable to the Salvadorean FMLN to act as a strong left-wing opposition party. A second problem is that the peace agreement did not seriously challenge the (economic) power of the Guatemalan armed forces, which could become the main obstacle for transforming the peace agreement into a tool for democratic transition.

— *Peace agreements and 'hybrid' democratic transitions*

The previous analysis confirms the assumption contained in the premise that democratic transitions in Central America have been profoundly linked with transitions from civil war to negotiated peace. It could be concluded that the political process in Central America essentially has been a process of 'pacification', rather than a transition from authoritarian to democratic rule as Dunkerly (1994) argues. However, the term 'pacification' can be confusing, as it seems to equate two processes with different dynamics and outcomes. Too much focus on the evolution of regional conflict to national peace process seems to have overshadowed the long-term process of authoritarianism in Central America in which the growth of civil society was obstructed but not entirely repressed by military regimes. The seeds of democratic transition, in the form of organised opposition in civil society, started to germinate in the 1920s. These were developed enough in the 1940s to create broader democratic movements, which were denied access to political society except in Costa Rica and Guatemala. When these opposition movements re-appeared even stronger in the 1970s they were faced with military counter-insur-gency, which unleashed the regional crisis of the 1980s. By using the term 'pacifica-tion', the pressure from broad opposition movements in civil society (whether armed or peaceful) can be underestimated. This pressure was a key factor in promoting judicial and constitutional reforms, opening up political society for opposition parties and (slowly) forging a new political culture based on consensus rather than coercion.

This is not to say that democratic transitions in Central America have been completed. On the contrary, democratic transitions are still in mid or late stages and it will probably take several generations to erase the heritage of an authoritar-ian past. The notion of 'hybrid regimes', suggested by Torres Rivas (1989) and Karl (1995), more precisely explains that the newly emerging regimes in Central America have both authoritarian and democratic characteristics. The term 'hybrid regime' makes clear that, although a rupture was made with the old order of the traditional 'triple alliance', authoritarian tendencies such as the culture of violence and military impunity still persist, suggesting a continuity of 'reactionary despotism' (Rojas 1995). The remnants of authoritarianism limit civilian control over the state and obstruct efforts to confront social exclusion, thereby slowing down the speed of democratic transition. To analyse the hybrid character of democratic transitions it can be useful to highlight the interplay of dynamics between civil society, the state and political society in successive transition stages. In the three countries described, early transition stages started when established rulers took steps to initiate democratic transition from above. During the second half of early transi-tion, prior to a shift towards mid-transition, civil society sectors started pushing democratic transition from below. This was often followed by a demobilisation of civil society and a new role for an enlarged political society, with active participa-tion of (formerly excluded) opposition parties. It was the increased strength of political society that shifted democratic transition from a mid to a late stage.

However, a healthy balance between the state and civil society that can sustain democratic rule is still absent. At the most, it is present in a hybrid form and thus vulnerable to political instability and to external influences.

4.4 External actors and democratic transitions

Roughly between 1978 and 1981, the political crisis in Central America escalated from a number of local conflicts into a regional crisis with international dimensions, particularly after the Reagan administration decided to make the rollback of revolution in Central America a top priority of US foreign policy. After the Sandinista victory in Nicaragua, a further loss of US hegemony in its traditional sphere of influence was perceived by the hardliners in Washington as a potential threat to US security. By substantially increasing military aid to Central America, the United States converted the Central American region into a major battleground of the Cold War.[78] Outside the United States, opposition to this belligerent US policy particularly came from Latin America and a number of countries in Europe, where governments, political parties, peace movements and solidarity groups were alarmed by the escalating crisis and feared a threat to global stability. Since the early 1980s a broad array of these external actors gradually acquired a presence in the Central American region, basically in response to US intervention. Latin American and European governments, especially after the 1982 Malvinas war, tried to prevent open US military intervention in Nicaragua and simultaneously to contain revolutionary struggle in El Salvador (Smith 1995).

The previous pages have demonstrated that early democratic transitions in Central America were very much determined (and delayed) by civil wars and foreign intervention, whereas mid-transition stages were determined by the search for negotiated peace agreements. In other words, democratic transitions accelerated as part of the regional peace process. External actors played a role both in the escalation of the crisis and in the negotiations for peace, but how important were they for accelerating democratic transitions? How did these external actors contribute to the shift from early to mid-transitions? Which elements in civil society were supported from abroad and what were the policy objectives of these external actors? To examine these questions it is necessary to unravel the complex relationship between external support for the regional peace process and the (often simultaneous) support for democratic transitions.

– *Peace process and external actors*
Although external actors have influenced the outcome of the peace process, the basis for durable peace settlements was laid by the Central American governments themselves. The Reagan administration intervened militarily and politically with low intensity warfare strategies with the purpose of bringing down the Sandinista government and to defeat other revolutionary movements in the region 'in the

name of democracy'. It could be argued that this was achieved in the long run –
although this view often tends to ignore decisive local factors – but this goal was
not achieved during Reagan's term in office. Nor did Latin American countries,
such as those organised in the Contadora group (an initiative backed by the
European Community), manage to solve the regional crisis by peaceful means. The
failure of US policy and diplomatic initiatives by the Contadora group gave room
to the Esquipulas peace agreement, a regional peace plan developed in 1986 by
Costa Rican president Oscar Arias and signed by the five Central American
presidents in August 1987 in the Guatemalan town Esquipulas. It paved the way
for peace negotiations and national reconciliation, and ultimately moved democratic transition forwards all over the region. The Esquipulas peace agreement was
an explicit rejection of foreign influence in domestic political processes and is
sometimes regarded as 'Central America's second declaration of independence'
(Moreno 1994: 135).

Despite this appealing rhetoric, it was the Reagan administration that effectively
delayed the implementation of the Esquipulas agreement, although it was forced
(due to the Iran-*contra* scandal) to formally accept its contents. The US government
continued its support to the Nicaraguan *contra* war and successfully pressured
other Central American governments up to the Fall of 1988 not to comply with the
agreement as long as the Sandinistas were unwilling to make concessions. This
policy changed under President Bush, who stopped military aid to the *contras* and
embarked upon a more diplomatic approach towards the Sandinistas, more in line
with Esquipulas. In return, the Soviet Union ended its military aid to the Sandinistas in April 1989, which was an early sign that the Cold War confrontation in
the region was about to end. Implementation of the key elements of the Esquipulas
agreement (the start of peace negotiations and a national dialogue with opposition
forces) effectively began in 1989, first in Nicaragua (where it was agreed to hold
general elections in February 1990) and later in other countries. The combination
of a waning Cold War and the electoral defeat of the Sandinistas was an important
element in removing the option of revolutionary victories in El Salvador and
Guatemala, where peace negotiations eventually succeeded with UN mediation and
broad support from the international community.[79] The end of the Cold War
without doubt facilitated the Central American peace process, but it would be
wrong to simply *explain* the transition from civil war to peace as a product of a
global power struggle. This would downplay the importance of regional dynamics
and local actors. Even if all these external actors in different degrees contributed to
peaceful settlements in the region, it does not necessarily follow that they *determined* the acceleration of democratic transitions.[80]

– *Foreign aid and democratic transitions*
The United States and the majority of European governments had different views
about how to rebuild the 'political centre' that was destroyed by authoritarian
regimes in the late 1970s, and about how to strengthen civil society. US assistance

had a clear 'top-down' approach, by channelling economic and military aid to quasi-democratic regimes and by supporting specific groups in civil society to counterbalance revolutionary movements. Until the mid-1980s, European and Canadian governments kept a low profile in the region, with the exception of Nicaragua. Assistance was channelled mainly through multilateral agencies for emergency relief and, to a lesser extent, via private aid agencies to support opposition groups in civil society.

us military and economic aid packages to Central America were substantially increased in the early 1980s. Unlike traditional counter-insurgency assistance, this aid became part of an integrated political-military strategy to combat the 'communist threat', symbolised by the revolutionary movements, under the umbrella of 'low intensity conflict' (LIC). The formula was a product of post-Vietnam evaluations of us foreign policies and emphasised the need to combine military, economic, diplomatic, political and psychological approaches. It was meant to target not only the military enemy but also the civilian population, to adapt campaigns to local political and cultural circumstances and to stimulate the creation of new factors within civil society responsive to us interests that could provide an acceptable alternative to revolutionary movements (El Salvador, Guatemala) or revolutionary governments (Nicaragua).[81] One new element was the emphasis on incorporating 'institution building' into economic assistance programmes, creating institutions to promote and implement the neoliberal model in the region. Another new element, compared to traditional counter-insurgency, was the upgrading of the political component in the LIC strategy, which would become a central foreign policy objective under the heading 'democracy promotion' (W. Robinson, 1996). Both elements will be further examined.

Economic assistance to Central America (over US$ 5.8 billion in the 1980s) was mainly channelled through the US Agency for International Development (AID) and had four main components: relieving balances of payments with capital injections, private sector investment (particularly promoting non-traditional agricultural exports), support to structural adjustment packages required by multilateral financial agencies, and support to community development programmes, cooperatives and housing projects aimed at the rural and urban poor to support larger counter-insurgency programmes (Sanahuja 1992). Community development support was handled by existing or newly established development NGOs, which were often linked to us right-wing foundations or fundamentalist churches as part of Reagan's regional anti-communist crusade. To promote the private sector, AID stimulated the formation of new business associations and policy think-tanks in civil society that would be instrumental in the transformation of the economy towards a neoliberal model. The new business associations were meant to strengthen modernising elements among the business elite, and back those who were willing to support neoliberal measures including tax reforms and social stability packages in the form of social investment funds. The creation of neoliberal think-tanks and business foundations was particularly successful in El

Salvador, where FUSADES played a key role in restructuring the private sector and pushing the modern business elite inside ARENA, the right-wing party that came to power in the late 1980s.[82] By privatising state institutions and creating a 'parallel state' – a process begun in Costa Rica in 1982 – AID laid the groundwork for a profound transformation of the Central American economies which later was carried out by the World Bank, the IMF and the Inter-American Development Bank (IDB).[83]

Democracy promotion was the other new component of US assistance as part of its LIC strategy in the 1980s. The idea was that new institutions had to be constructed in political and civil society responsive to US political and economic interests that would be capable of absorbing tensions and maintaining social stability. In the past, this political aid had been covertly supplied by the CIA. But the agency had proven to be better at destabilisation than at creating stability, and often even had weakened domestic support for US foreign policy operations. Therefore, in 1983 a new quasi-private agency was founded, the National Endowment for Democracy (NED) entirely funded by the State Department through AID and the US Information Agency (USIA).[84] NED would provide private US organisations with funding for direct support to political parties, trade unions, journalists, business associations and other civil society sectors in the South, with Central America as a primary target.[85] Massive NED funding went to the Nicaraguan opposition in the late 1980s. In Guatemala, NED supported think-tanks related to Jorge Serrano's political party MAS, and in El Salvador it actively supported Cristiani's ARENA party. Substantial AID funding for democracy assistance was allocated to election monitoring, voter participation campaigns and reforms of legislative and judicial institutions. Particularly the extensive financial support to all major elections in Central America in the 1980s illustrated a 'top-down' and US-biased approach to democratic transition (Carothers 1995).

The large US economic and political assistance programmes of the 1980s considerably influenced the composition of civil society. Financial and technical assistance from AID and other US agencies contributed to the emergence of 'modern' and strong business associations, (conservative) labour and peasant unions, policy research centres, the mass media and other institutions that were instrumental to US foreign policy interests. AID's emphasis on supporting an entrepreneurial NGO sector in Central America created a vast boom in new development NGOs as part of neoliberal stabilisation programmes. Many Central American NGOs at some stage became dependent on funding from AID. Obviously, progressive development NGOs, peasant organisations or human rights groups linked to the opposition in Guatemala, Honduras and El Salvador as well as left or centre-left political parties were excluded from US assistance up to the early 1990s.[86] These segments of civil and political society started to receive support from the Canadian and several European governments, often indirectly channelled through private aid agencies.[87]

European aid flows to Central America generally ran contrary to those of the

United States, at least until the mid-1980s. European development assistance to the Sandinista revolution started in 1979, after a call by the Socialist International was responded to positively by several Social Democratic governments (among them Spain, Sweden, West Germany and France).[88] Towards El Salvador, Europe took a position opposite to the United States: the European Community gave humanitarian aid to Salvadorean refugees in Honduras, the French government legitimised the role of the FMLN (with the Franco-Mexican declaration of August 1981), while the European Parliament condemned the undemocratic nature of the Salvadorean elections. After 1982, European policies towards Central America would become more cautious. The German Social Democrats lost the elections and the new Christian Democratic government moved closer to a US position which included reduced aid to Nicaragua and support for the Salvadorean Christian Democratic government. The Malvinas war and the US invasion of Grenada contributed to a lower European profile in Central America, as it was feared that open US intervention in the region could escalate the crisis. EC documents started to emphasise the economic and social roots of the crisis and advocated a regional solution to the conflicts. Open European support for the Sandinista government became less clear-cut and shifted towards more 'neutral' statements calling for the establishment of democratic principles and strict observance of human rights. In 1984, the EC initiated the *San José Dialogue*, an annual European-Central American conference, laying the basis for a long-term cooperation agreement for political and economic aid and support for the regional peace process together with Contadora. As a result, European bilateral and multilateral aid would gradually increase. Ten years later, Europe would become the largest provider of development aid to Central America.[89]

In contrast to the 1990s, official European development aid during the 1980s seldom was aimed at influencing democratic transitions (Sanahuja 1994). The massive support to the Sandinista government in Nicaragua was, however, a clear sign that European governments rejected US policy and that they were reluctant to support the LIC strategy. Only West Germany provided substantial aid to the Christian Democratic governments in El Salvador and Guatemala, although this aid was symbolic compared to US assistance. Support to opposition groups in these countries was channelled mostly through non-governmental agencies, such as party-related foundations, churches, solidarity groups and private aid agencies. The four German party *Stiftungen*, directly financed by the German government, indirectly supplied funding to their sister-parties and related organisations throughout the region. The two Christian Democratic German party foundations, *Konrad Adenauer Stiftung* and *Hanns Seidel Stiftung*, acted most in line with US LIC strategy by supporting the Nicaraguan opposition and the governing parties in El Salvador and Guatemala. The *Friedrich Ebert Stiftung* concentrated more on Costa Rica, supporting Social Democratic labour unions and research institutes, next to the small centre-left parties elsewhere in the region. Despite opening up new contacts for these parties to international networks and funding training programmes, the activities of the German foundations actually had little impact on the composition of political society (Grabendorff 1996).[90]

The activities of solidarity groups, churches and (the more progressive) private aid agencies from Europe, Canada and the United States were more important for the Central American opposition movements outside Nicaragua. It was not so much their financial support to the Sandinista revolution and to popular movements in other countries that characterised their influence on democratic transitions, although this became significant in the late 1980s. Rather it was the flow of information on human rights abuses, refugees and increasing poverty that especially had an impact on public opinion in their home countries. A region that had been known only for earthquakes and bananas had become front-page news in the early 1980s and would continue to be a major foreign policy issue until the early 1990s. The international attention boosted the Central America budgets of private aid agencies, especially when they were directly dependent on official funding, such as the German, Dutch, Swedish, Danish, Norwegian and later also the Spanish private aid agencies. Until the early 1990s these agencies supported opposition groups by providing financial resources to popular organisations, development NGOs and human rights groups. How and to what extent this assistance contributed to accelerating democratic transitions will be analysed in the next two chapters.

4.5 Constructing democracy: prospects and barriers

By way of conclusion, the premises stipulated at the start of this chapter will be examined more closely. The first maintained that the dynamics of democratic transitions in Central America could not be explained without understanding the long history of authoritarianism, in which subordinated sectors in civil society were repressed and access of opposition parties to political society was blocked. This point has been largely confirmed, but can be posed even more sharply. The history of prolonged authoritarian rule exerts an influence that appears to persist during democratic transitions and delays (or even undermines) the process of constructing democracy. This is illustrated by the slow process of demilitarisation, the continuation of military impunity, ongoing human rights abuses and resistance to social and political reforms. It all points at the persistence of a political culture based on domination and political exclusion penetrating all layers of society. The traditional economic and political elite, represented by solid family networks, was able to preserve or even to recover its influence thanks to what Vilas (1996: 33) calls 'the negotiated character of the post-revolutionary peace process'. It is true that the private sector was modernised in the 1980s and embraced democratic principles (and eventually rejected US counter-insurgency) to pursue its neoliberal economic strategy. But this 'new right' – which was represented by the presidents Cristiani, Calderon Sol, Serrano, Arzú and Callejas – knew it could hardly be challenged by a young and inexperienced political opposition in electoral contests. To paraphrase

Barrington Moore, the absence of a revolutionary break with the past apparently further delays the construction of democracy, which can be seen in the hybrid character of Central America's post-authoritarian regimes.[91]

The second premise, about the combined search for peace and efforts to open up the political system, also needs some further elaboration. During early transition stages in El Salvador and Guatemala political society was only partially opened up, that is, only to those political parties willing to accept military domination and to facilitate US counter-insurgency. Consequently, initiatives to start peace talks with those forces excluded from political society (such as the URNG and the FMLN) were undermined by authoritarian elements. The Esquipulas peace agreement of 1987 provided a framework in which the search for peaceful settlements was linked to measures that would liberalise the authoritarian system. This had a profound impact on subordinated sectors in civil society, which became better organised and diversified throughout the region; they were a key force rallying for peace negotiations in El Salvador and Guatemala, and for curbing military dominance in Honduras. These negotiations coincided with the stage of mid-transition in which an elite compromise was reached between the 'new right' (the right-wing political parties supported by a modernised private sector) and the former revolutionary movements about their integration into political society, moving the conflict from a military to a political terrain. During the stage of mid-transition it was also evident that social mobilisation was decreasing. The reasons for this are further examined in the following chapter. The premise could be extended by pointing at the tight intertwining of the economic and political interests of the ruling elite, making a transformation of the (labour intensive and externally vulnerable) Central American economies a key condition for the construction of democracy (Karl 1995).

This brings me to the third premise, stating that democratic transitions have not yet been completed. Two sets of obstacles make the prospects for a shift from late transition to democratic consolidation highly problematic and even threaten to undermine political stability (which could reverse democratic transition altogether). The first set of obstacles is related to the economic model of export-promotion of tropical products based on the supply of cheap labour, which has accentuated unequal income distribution and widespread poverty. Poverty figures further deteriorated during the 1980s: by 1990 three-quarters of the population of Honduras, El Salvador, Guatemala and Nicaragua lived below the poverty line. In absolute figures, this represents an increase of over fifty percent in less than ten years. Even more alarming is the increase in income polarisation, particularly in Honduras and Guatemala. Socio-economic inequality is not conducive to democratic transition, or as Castañeda argues at the start of this book, poverty and democracy do not easily mix.[92] On the contrary, poverty undermines confidence in the political system, as it leads to fragmentation of civil society and threatens political stability. Structural adjustment programmes implemented after the mid-1980s have worsened the outlook for change in this panorama since austerity measures and a reduced role for the state are obstructing the implementation of necessary social reforms and negatively influencing what Morales (1995b: 31) calls 'a transition economy'.

The other set of obstacles to democratic consolidation has to do with building democratic institutions and creating a political culture of tolerance and compromise which together are a very slow process. Looking more closely at the three realms in which this process should be rooted does not add to optimism. At the level of the state, structural reforms (necessary to establish the rule of law and to guarantee civil and political rights) continue to be undermined by the traditionally dominant sectors. Although civilian control over the military has been formally established, the armed forces retain considerable autonomy from the executive branch due to their economic power and their active involvement in drugs trafficking. Despite truth commissions, the impunity of high level security officers remains unchallenged and demilitarised police forces continue to apply traditional repressive methods against popular organisations of the opposition. Added to the slow process of judicial reform, necessary to confront corruption and establish a clear separation of powers, it appears that Central American societies continue to be politically insecure and lack the guarantees to exercise full citizenship (Rojas 1995). In the realm of political society, the main obstacle is the weak system of political parties and their incapacity to play an intermediary role between civil society and the state (Torres Rivas 1995). Despite the increased diversity of political society with the emergence of new (formerly revolutionary) parties, political culture continues to be dominated by traditional clientelism, institutional opportunism and what Cerdas (1996: 48) labels 'inter-party cannibalism' during election campaigns. The enormous gap between politicians and the electorate – Cerdas (1993) calls this *el desencanto democrático* (the 'democratic disenchantment') – probably is one of the key explanations for the high rates of voter abstentionism.

In the realm of civil society a variety of previously excluded actors (particularly Indian and women's organisations) have emerged with a new democratic discourse, claiming autonomy from political parties. These organisations certainly have contributed to democratic transition by strengthening civil society from within (building capacity and forging alliances) and from below (opening up political society). However, as will be shown in Chapter 6, these organisations often also have been hampered by hierarchy, paternalism and weak internal accountability, which are all signs of a persisting political culture of authoritarianism and exclusion. The problem seems to be, as Vilas (1996: 56) remarks, that 'Central American authoritarian cultural patterns are nurtured both by socio-economic structures and by ruling class political practices, which inevitably tend to be reproduced and adapted way down the social ladder by subaltern actors with a relative autonomy of ideological definitions or party affiliations.'

The last premise pointed at the role of external influences. It was assumed that some external actors had played an important role in moving democratic transitions forward by advocating peaceful solutions and by supporting reformist political parties. International pressure was indeed important in advancing the peace negotiations in Nicaragua, El Salvador and Guatemala at key moments. European support for the Contadora group, for example, eventually contributed to the success of the Esquipulas peace plan. At a later stage, cuts in US military aid indirectly speeded up democratic transition in Honduras and El Salvador, and the prospects for a substantial increase of foreign aid certainly contributed to break the deadlock in Guatemala's peace negotiations. The role of the United Nations also was crucial for mediating negotiations and implementing the peace agreements. But the role of external actors should not be overstated. A variety of international efforts to support a 'third option' between authoritarianism and revolution largely failed. The Christian Democratic parties in El Salvador and Guatemala were unable to fulfil this function and were even severely criticised for their internal corrupt practices (Vilas 1996). Other smaller reformist parties, such as the Social Democrats in Guatemala and El Salvador, only received marginal electoral support, despite their substantial political and financial aid from abroad. It is not yet clear what the massive international aid flows of the 1980s contributed to Central America's democratic transitions, other than economically stabilising the war-torn economies. After all, only a small portion of this so-called 'reconstruction aid' was intended to finance (necessary) social and political reforms, or to contribute to strengthening civil society. The next two chapters will therefore examine more closely how private aid agencies have contributed to Central America's democratic transitions.

5 A TACIT CONSENSUS

Private Aid Intervention Strategies in Central America

Research and analysis of private aid policies in Central America is surprisingly scarce. The few studies produced so far either concentrate on humanitarian aid (Eguizábal *et al.* 1993), on private aid agency profiles (Sparre 1992; Ortega Carpio 1994) or on individual project interventions, usually meant for internal evaluation purposes. The study by Macdonald (1997) of private aid interventions in Nicaragua and Costa Rica is the only comparative analysis of private aid policies in Central America, although unfortunately it does not include shifts that have occurred in the 1990s. The importance of European private aid agencies in Central America's democratic transitions is sometimes mentioned (Vilas 1996; Foley 1996), but often also completely ignored even when one would have expected it to be discussed (such as in Dunkerly 1988, 1994; Roy 1992; Tangermann 1995; Sieder 1996a). Even Whitehead (1996b: 242) in his generally excellent analyses of the international components of Central America's peace process ignores private aid agencies: '[But] the reconstitution of an effective political centre should not be viewed solely in terms of inter-governmental relations. This potentiality was powerfully reinforced by the interplay of a series of prominent non-governmental agencies and institutions operating throughout the region – notably the Catholic Church, but also the party internationals, networks of human rights and social activists, the media and the professions.' Why is the role of private aid agencies a black hole in the literature?

An explanation can be that private aid agencies themselves generally have maintained a low profile in Central America. Their interventions often have had a political character which made them vulnerable to repression by local authorities, but also to repercussions in their home societies and from the governments which provide their income. Another explanation may be that the private aid sector is difficult to analyse: it is a rather diverse sector, including small solidarity groups as well as large professional enterprises handling multi-million dollar budgets. Moreover, many of them do not have offices in Central America which make them often invisible for those who are doing local field research. There is also a methodological problem involved because documents of private aid agencies are not easily available as a result of dispersed archives and a general culture of confidentiality and secrecy. This is justified by arguing that interests of project partners have to be protected, which certainly makes sense. But this argument also often has been used as an excuse to mask the absence of transparency and a culture of external accountability.

One of the premises of this study is that private foreign aid, in particular from

Europe, played a key role in maintaining and supporting the political opposition to authoritarian rule in Central America during the 1980s. That this role was more important than the literature suggests is illustrated by the amount of aid that was channelled to popular organisations, churches, human rights groups and local NGOs that were linked to oppositional forces. Although exact figures are difficult to acquire, in 1987 the forty largest European private aid agencies channelled approximately US$ 130 million to Central America, a figure that increased to almost US$ 200 million in 1992.[1] In relative terms this was about ten percent of total bilateral and multilateral aid flows to the region and more than forty percent of total bilateral aid flows to Central America of all the European governments combined (see Table 5.1). In other words, in quantitative terms these agencies were major international players in the Central American region.

However, as was argued earlier, the quantity of private aid flows does not say very much about the quality of private aid interventions. The central concern of this chapter is to examine the role of European private aid agencies during successive democratic transition stages since the early 1980s in Central America. The analysis will focus on private aid policies aimed at contributing to democratisation 'from below', and how these policies affected the diversity and density of civil society, particularly in Honduras, El Salvador and Guatemala. To facilitate the analysis, the chapter is divided into four periods: the arrival of private aid agencies in the region in the early 1980s, activities of private aid agencies during the US-sponsored low intensity war, policies in periods of early transition after the 1987 Esquipulas agreement, and private aid interventions following the political watershed of 1989-90.

5.1 Growth of European private aid in the early 1980s

Prior to the 1980s, only a dozen (mostly confessional) European private aid agencies were active in Central America, providing support to local development projects of the Catholic and Protestant churches. Their number gradually increased in the 1970s in response to a number of natural disasters, such as the Managua earthquake of 1972, hurricane Fifi in Honduras (1974) and the Guatemala earthquake of 1976. The latter, for example, prompted the activities of a number of Norwegian private aid agencies in Guatemala,[2] but also the entrance of various North American fundamentalist Protestant sects to the highlands. Starting with emergency aid, some of these agencies soon discovered the polarised social and political climate in the region and decided to continue their presence by providing structural aid oriented at poverty alleviation. But the vast majority of European private aid agencies started to operate in Central America in the early 1980s and thereafter: from only a dozen prior to 1980, they numbered over a hundred organisations by the late 1980s.[3] How to explain this substantial increase of European private aid interventions in Central America?

A key element for understanding the growth of private aid initiatives in the region was the victory of the Sandinista National Liberation Front (FSLN) in Nicaragua. The Sandinista revolution fuelled hope in progressive circles worldwide about the viability of a socialist alternative in the South. It was the first successful revolutionary struggle in Latin America since the Cuban overthrow of Batista in 1959. Moreover, it occurred at the time that the Latin American left had been defeated by military regimes and their leaders driven into exile, many of them to Europe. The Sandinista revolution generally was viewed with sympathy by progressive private aid agencies, churches and solidarity groups in the North, also thanks to wide media coverage during the last year of the popular struggle against Somoza's National Guard.[4] Writing about the British OXFAM, Black (1992: 202) observes: 'Not surprisingly, many of those voluntary agencies committed to solidarity with the poor became stalwart allies of the Sandinista regime, some of the more idealistic among them heralding a socialistic utopia. As in Tanzania, OXFAM found itself able not only to support small-scale local projects, but to add its modest contribution to the general thrust of social action nationwide.' This illustrates the influence of solidarity groups (and the public opinion that was supporting them) on the priorities of private aid agencies. A NOVIB project officer points at the general euphoria of the early period of the revolution 'in which anything was possible', and in which 'NOVIB in its zeal for Nicaragua knew that it was supported by the sympathy and admiration of broad ranks of Dutch society' (Lambregts 1996: 7).[5]

A second element to explain the increased presence of European private aid agencies in Central America was the tension in the Atlantic Alliance due to the interventionist policy of the Reagan administration after 1981. Underlying this tension, as was explained in the previous chapter, was Europe's more active presence in Latin America after the late 1970s, and its rejection of the 'Reagan doctrine' in Central America.[6] European governments considered the socio-economic inequalities in the region as the main source of civil conflict, and not so much the external role of Cuba and the Soviet Union. Moreover, Europe advocated support to moderate currents within revolutionary movements to avoid further radicalisation, and therefore rejected the militarist US approach to the conflict which was not only threatening the Alliance consensus but also fuelling a growing peace movement back home against deployment of US cruise missiles. The escalation of the Salvadorean civil war as a result of increased US military aid limited prospects for a rapid negotiated solution to the conflict, which was advocated by European Social Democrats. In addition, growing concern about postponed elections in Nicaragua defused European criticism of US interventionism. As was demonstrated earlier, European diplomacy became more cautious, especially after the 1983 Grenada invasion (which was not officially condemned by any European government). The electoral defeat of the German Social Democrats in October 1982 marked a retreat of European diplomacy, which would only regain strength with its support to the Arias peace plan in 1986.[7] This lower profile on the part of European governments gave more prominence to the activities of non-governmental European actors in the region, especially private aid agencies depending on official aid contributions. Support to these private aid agencies was a way for European governments to indirectly express 'opposition to US policies without having to pay the price that direct action on their part would entail' (Smith 1990: 202).

This changing emphasis from official towards private aid channels in the early 1980s coincided with a third development stimulating the activities of European and Canadian private aid agencies in Central America: their increased relevance within the international aid sector, particularly after the late 1970s as was demonstrated in Chapter 2. Growing doubts about the efficiency of official aid policies and their inability to tackle poverty effectively gave more prominence to private aid channels. Official aid contributions to private aid agencies increased considerably as a result of new co-financing systems established in the second half of the 1970s. Private aid agencies gradually became stronger transnational actors due to improved domestic profiles as a result of lobbying activities, public education campaigns and televised fund-raising appeals. This financially stronger and politically more prominent role was particularly visible in Latin America, where opposition to authoritarian regimes was supported with a combination of funding and political campaigns. The Sandinista revolution actually occurred at one of the most favourable moments in the history of private aid agencies, due to their improved infrastructure in Latin America and growing financial resources. Moreover, Nicaragua was a challenging target as 'anything was possible' to put methods and ideas about alternative development strategies into practice.

A fourth element markedly influencing policy choices of European private aid agencies in Central America was the growth and politicisation of the Central American NGO sector after the early 1970s, eventually leading to its polarisation in the 1980s. The root causes of this polarisation should be situated in the early 1960s, when local development NGOs emerged as a result of two external factors.[8] One was the AID-financed aid programme *Alliance for Progress*, creating and funding a new generation of local development organisations to implement social and economic reforms at the grassroots level. The other factor was the new social doctrine of the Catholic Church resulting from 'Vatican II' and 'Medellín' (with its 'preferential option for the poor') giving birth to a number of local NGOs, cooperatives and peasant organisations with the purpose of combating poverty and organising the poor. In the early 1970s, the latter started to receive financial support from Catholic and Protestant private aid agencies in Europe and Canada (such as *Misereor*, CEBEMO and *Caritas*), whereas the former entirely depended on AID funding, often in the form of food aid supplied through Catholic Church agencies.[9] The main difference between the two NGO currents was that the AID-funded NGOs were more integrated into top-down governmental development planning, whereas the so-called 'historic' NGOs operated autonomously from the state and, as a result, often stood closer to subordinated sectors in civil society. Due

to the growing polarisation of the political climate in Central America the two
NGO tendencies started to politicise. AID-financed NGOs soon became part of state-
induced counter-insurgency and economic stabilisation programmes, operating
under fairly centralised national umbrellas.[10] The NGOs of Social Christian origin
evolved in the opposite direction, emphasising popular education, 'conscientisation' and popular organising as a tool for social change (Holt 1988). This
historic (or popular) NGO tendency was strongest in Guatemala, where local NGOs
mushroomed after the 1976 earthquake, although they also experienced a serious
setback after repression increased a few years later. In Honduras and El Salvador
the majority of the historic NGOs were established after 1980, performing a key
supportive role for opposition groups in civil society.[11]

The increased presence of European private aid agencies in Central America
cannot be understood without examining how the confluence of these four
elements in the early 1980s occurred in a period of rapid social and political
polarisation. It was the 'revolutionary project' of the Sandinista government and
its political allies in neighbouring countries versus the counter-revolutionary
project of the military regimes supported by the United States. In this polarised
climate a 'third option', advocated by moderate European and Canadian external
actors (and deliberately frustrated by the US government), was completely absent
until the mid-1980s. This polarisation also was reflected in the way private aid
interventions in civil society were perceived by the United States: private aid
agencies either supported the counter-revolution, or were allies of revolutionary
movements. As a result, humanitarian aid (for example to refugees and displaced
persons) would inevitably acquire a political character, as it was impossible to
support both sides in the conflict simultaneously.

5.2 European private emergency versus US counter-insurgency aid

A review of private aid policies in Central America inevitably starts with Nicaragua,
simply because the majority of European and Canadian private aid to Central
America in the early 1980s was concentrated here. For many private aid agencies,
Nicaragua had been the 'port of disembarkation' for the region. The destruction
caused by the civil war demanded fresh external resources and the new revolutionary *junta* welcomed international aid for reconstruction. Large bilateral aid
programmes were initiated, particularly by Germany (until 1982), Sweden, Spain,
Italy, France, the Netherlands and Canada, allocating half of their total official
development assistance for Central America between 1980-85 to Nicaragua (IRELA
1994b). After 1980, the United States – which had been the largest single aid
provider to the Somoza regime – would drastically scale down its support to
Nicaragua and successfully blocked new loans from the World Bank and the Inter-
American Development Bank (IDB). However, US pressure on the Atlantic allies
to boycott Nicaragua was only responded to by the conservative British govern-

ment and some oil-exporting Latin American countries. Nicaragua would become the (new) 'darling' of the Canadian and several European official aid agencies.[12]

In the slipstream of these new bilateral donors, a large number of private aid agencies, churches, solidarity groups and 'twinned cities' entered Nicaragua in the early 1980s. Their financial contribution was less spectacular compared to official aid: US$ 30 million annually, an estimated five percent of total aid flows (Barraclough *et al.* 1988). But their presence was crucial to prevent international isolation of the Nicaraguan revolution and to support its survival after the 1985 US trade embargo. The relevance of private aid agencies for Nicaragua was twofold. First, in the early years it was a channel for financial and technical support to large national campaigns (literacy crusade, health, education), and later for channelling support to regional and municipal governments for community development, training of agricultural cooperatives and strengthening mass organisations. Private aid also was a tool for new development experiments (such as alternative energy provision or sustainable agriculture) although these priorities were not always shared by state institutions.[13] After 1982, when attacks by the *contras* started to obstruct development projects, the emphasis of private aid gradually shifted back to the provision of emergency aid to refugees and the internally displaced.[14] With large US private aid agencies such as CARE and CRS pulling out of Nicaragua, and official aid agencies cautious to provide humanitarian aid, about 75 percent of this aid was provided by European and Canadian private aid agencies (Eguizábal *et al.* 1993).[15] The largest private aid providers were German (*Brot für die Welt, Terre des Hommes*), Canadian (CUSO, CARE, CANSAVE, OXFAM-Canada), Dutch (ICCO, CEBEMO, HIVOS, NOVIB) and Belgian (OXFAM), followed by smaller funding from Sweden (such as the Swedish Cooperative Centre and *Diakonia*), Norway (*Norwegian People's Aid*), France (*Frères des Hommes*), Switzerland (*Fastenopfer, Helvetas*) and Great Britain (OXFAM-UK/I, *Christian Aid, War on Want*) (Barraclough *et al.* 1988; Sparre 1992).

The other significant role, next to being providers of 'solidarity aid', was that private aid agencies and solidarity committees were instrumental in shaping public opinion in their home countries about the achievements of the Nicaraguan revolution and human rights violations in neighbouring countries. Governments and parliamentarians were lobbied to condemn US intervention and to maintain official aid programmes to Nicaragua, despite US pressure for a boycott. Regular visits by official delegations and coffee brigades to Nicaragua produced updated reports by eyewitnesses. This diverse international advocacy work, organised by hundreds of solidarity committees and supported by most of the larger private aid agencies, had a high profile in Europe and Canada. It would contribute to keeping Nicaragua and other Central American countries on the political agenda and in the news headlines throughout the 1980s. This advocacy work served as an important counter-weight to the international misinformation campaign of the Reagan administration, trying to portray the US-financed *contras* as 'freedom fighters' and Nicaragua as a satellite of the Soviet Union. A positive side-effect was that private aid agencies acquired a new and activist constituency (partly from the peace movement) successfully pushing for increased support to the Sandinista revolution and to revolutionary movements in other Central American countries. German private aid, for example, was considerably increased after the German Christian Democratic government decided to stop its official aid programme to Nicaragua in late 1982. It also had an impact on private aid agency budgets for El Salvador and Guatemala, which would grow at a steady rate after the mid-1980s.

— *Emergency aid to refugees and the internally displaced*
Private aid support to other Central American countries also was directly determined by US intervention in the region. From their offices in Nicaragua, Mexico and Costa Rica, agency representatives were confronted with a deteriorating political climate in El Salvador and Guatemala (and to a lesser extent Honduras). This was visible in rapidly growing flows of refugees from these countries and internally displaced persons – up to nearly three million civilians in 1982, that is, 14 percent of the Central American population[16] – moving in various directions (Stein 1997). The first large group of refugees came from northern rural zones in El Salvador and crossed the border in 1981 to Honduras, or fled to Nicaragua and Costa Rica to escape carpet bombings by the Salvadorean air force as part of search and destroy operations against the FMLN. In addition, thousands of displaced *campesino* families poured into the cities. The second flow consisted of a few hundred thousand Guatemalan refugees from indigenous communities of the highlands, crossing the Mexican border between 1981 and 1983 to escape from the scorched earth operations of the Guatemalan armed forces. One group decided to flee to the forests of northern Guatemala where they created the Popular Resistance Communities (CPR's). A third major flow of refugees came from Nicaragua, although from two distinct groups. The first was part of the indigenous Miskito and Sumu population of the Atlantic coast, which had been forced by the Sandinista government to relocate their communities at the border river with Honduras to new inland settlements. A few thousand decided to cross the river to refugee camps in Honduras. The other group was composed of rural families fleeing the *contra* war, often because their relatives were accused of belonging to the *contras*, escaping to refugee camps in Honduras and Costa Rica. These Nicaraguan refugees soon received humanitarian support from US-backed initiatives as part of the low intensity war against Nicaragua. But the Guatemalan and Salvadorean refugees and internally displaced were not adequately serviced by humanitarian aid agencies, despite initial support from UNHCR and the *International Committee of the Red Cross* (ICRC). These 'uprooted populations' would become a primary target group of European (and some Canadian and US) private aid agencies, some of which decided to coordinate their assistance within the *Project Counselling Service* (PCS).[17]

The Salvadorean refugees in Honduran camps (set up by the UNHCR) were better off than the displaced populations in El Salvador who were distrusted by the authorities as potential supporters of the guerrillas. The internally displaced were more difficult to reach, as some of them had fled to provisional camps in the cities, while others were still in the middle of conflict zones where even the ICRC was often unable to give food aid and medical care. With the state of siege prevailing, the Salvadorean Catholic Church was one of the few actors in civil society to give legal protection and humanitarian assistance to the displaced.[18] Together with Protestant churches and some local NGOs a special coordinating agency was set up by the new Social Secretariat of the Archdiocese of San Salvador for this purpose: DIACONIA. This ecumenical NGO in the early years of the war became the major (and often the only) channel for international (confessional) private aid agencies to provide emergency aid in the form of food, shelter and medical care to the dispersed groups of displaced people.[19] Consequently, the national network of the churches, supported by rural organisations that had gone underground, provided the only infrastructure still available for legal humanitarian assistance.[20]

In Guatemala, this infrastructure was less developed. The Guatemalan Catholic Church was unable to set up a coordinating body similar to the Salvadorean DIACONIA, also because civil society had become more disarticulated (Eguizábal et al. 1993). The terror of military search and destroy operations in the highlands had generated fear and distrust among the internally displaced; it would only be after ten years of hiding that the thousands of Indians of the northern CPR communities would make their existence public. The magnitude of the problem was even greater than in El Salvador, as the number of Guatemalans internally displaced in the northern departments had risen to about 1.5 million by 1982 (Sollis 1996). Due to the militarisation of the country, up until 1985 it was virtually impossible for private aid agencies to find counterparts in rural areas beyond the official channels. Displaced people searching for shelter in the cities were more easily accessible, and support was often channelled through church-related organisations such as the Guatemalan Religious Conference (CONFREGUA) and the Conference of Evangelical Churches (CIEDEG). An additional problem was the distrust of Indian communities towards Guatemalan Ladino-dominated NGOs. Most of the attention of European private aid agencies in this period therefore was directed at the Guatemalan refugees in Mexico which were supported through Mexico-based organisations, although restricted by the UNHCR and the Mexican government (Burge 1995).

Private aid agencies were confronted with a difficult problem in the provision of humanitarian assistance to refugees and the uprooted: it was impossible to take a neutral position in the midst of the conflict. Most of the internally displaced and refugees were elderly, women and children, and often supportive of the guerrilla movements. They were therefore reluctant to accept support from governmental aid programmes such as the National Commission for the Displaced (CONADES) and the National Commission for the Restoration of Areas (CONARA) in El Salvador and the Committee for National Reconstruction (CRN) in Guatemala. These bodies were controlled by the armed forces and financed by AID as part of counter-insurgency campaigns, and their programmes were often implemented by right-wing US private aid agencies such as *Project Hope* or *World Relief*. On the other hand, the (more progressive) European aid agencies were careful not to be identified with direct support to the insurgents, as it could harm their work and also potentially scare off their constituencies in Europe. The 'accompaniment' approach advocated by European private aid agencies required not only that their counterparts be trusted by the displaced populations, but also that these counterparts have a low political (if not 'neutral') profile.[21] The well-connected infrastructure of DIACONIA therefore provided, next to a handful of church-based NGOs such as FUNDASAL and CREFAC, just about the only channel for private aid agencies to give support to those most affected by the war in El Salvador. That many leaders and staff members of these NGOs (including DIACONIA) were members or sympathisers of the FMLN was an inevitable consequence of the polarised political climate.[22] As an OXFAM-UK/I representative commented: 'In El Salvador, the key was to carry out legitimate humanitarian work *within* a politicised reality, rather than seeking a (non-existent) "non-political" space' (Thompson 1996: 331).

By intervening in a highly polarised political setting, emergency assistance to persecuted sectors in civil society provided by European private aid agencies automatically politicised their interventions. By choosing not to work with governmental programmes, private aid flows to refugees and the displaced functioned as a protective international shield for clandestine work of the opposition. Initially, humanitarian aid was used for the uprooted in conflict zones to survive physically. But there was a 'tacit consensus' between agency representatives and their counterparts that this assistance was instrumental in rebuilding the opposition against authoritarian rule.[23] As Thompson (1996: 330) noted for the Salvadorean situation: 'They were not just surviving: they were breaking the cycle of violence. For some this meant a commitment to the FMLN; to others it meant opposition to the government.' Newly emerging organisations of the displaced (CRIPDES in El Salvador and CONDEG in Guatemala) and of refugees (such as the Permanent Committees, CCPP, of Guatemalan refugees in Mexico) would lay the basis for repopulation and repatriation efforts after the mid-1980s. By supporting initiatives of those sectors most affected by counter-insurgency programmes, private foreign aid effectively contributed to rebuilding highly fragmented civil societies. However, the discourse of civil society building was not yet used, as private aid policies in this period were generally defined in terms of 'support for refugees' or 'support for human rights'.

– *Political polarisation of the Central American NGO sector*
The increase of European and Canadian bilateral aid to Nicaragua coincided with a huge increase of US economic and military aid to all the other Central American countries. The United States channelled over US$ 5.8 billion in bilateral economic aid to Central America between 1980 and 1989 (Sanahuja 1992). Official military aid in this period was much smaller – almost US$ 1.7 billion, excluding an esti-

mated US$ 500 million in military and humanitarian aid to the Nicaraguan *contras* – provoking Burbach and Núñez (1987: 96) to observe that 'in Central America, the banana republics have now been replaced by the "AID republics"'. In the previous chapter it was already mentioned that a considerable share of US economic assistance was channelled by AID to a number of US private aid agencies in Central America or directly to (often newly established) local NGOs linked to the business sector who had started to perform a key role in US-supported LIC strategies. This would lead to profound antagonism within the Central American NGO sector, generating two clearly distinct tendencies by the mid-1980s: AID-supported local NGOs loyal to the government and historic (or 'popular') NGOs closely working with the political opposition and supported by European and Canadian private aid agencies.

The rapid increase of both AID funding and European private aid to Central America strengthened this antagonism and created a politically polarised NGO sector (Kaimowitz 1993). However, this polarisation only became visible in the mid-1980s whereas polarisation in civil society had been deepening already since the late 1970s. Moreover, as was mentioned at the start of this chapter, several European and Canadian private aid agencies had been supporting the historic NGO sector already since the 1960s. So why did this polarisation not occur in the early 1980s? The main explanation for this time gap is the profound militarisation of civil society in that period, which seriously limited the access of European private aid agencies to persecuted sectors in civil society. Only the churches could guarantee this access, especially in El Salvador. As a result, AID in the early 1980s controlled foreign aid flows to civil society, due to its close relationships with governments and the armed forces. But soon after the installation of elected civilian governments in the mid-1980s, opportunities for European private aid broadened. This was illustrated by the coordinated action of historic NGOs rejecting offers of AID funding because these were associated with US-backed counter-insurgency. It was also visible in the rapid growth of new popular organisations and development NGOs, of which a majority would receive support from European and Canadian private aid agencies.

In El Salvador, this polarisation between the two NGO tendencies was hidden until 1985. Initially, in 1980, AID focused its support on agrarian reform, which was considered to be instrumental for generating support among the rural population for Duarte's Christian Democratic Party, the PDC. The agrarian reform programme benefited the AIFLD-created peasant organisation UCS and excluded the independent cooperative movement supported by the Catholic Church (Rosa 1993). When reformist policies were abandoned and replaced by LIC strategies under the Reagan administration, AID changed its civil society focus to a three-pronged strategy: political demobilisation and control of the population, political and economic stabilisation, and private sector support (Barry 1990). Support for pacification in rural areas was channelled through governmental agencies such as CONARA and CONADES for the civic action programmes of the armed forces.

Political stabilisation aimed to provide the Duarte government with a democratic image, whereas private sector support contributed to the creation of new business associations to promote non-traditional export policies and to privatise state services. The neoliberal think-tank FUSADES, founded in 1983, would become the main channel for AID support aimed at creating a range of local private sector NGOs in the 1980s.[24] Meanwhile, AID approached a number of US private aid agencies to open up new development programmes in El Salvador, although several refused to be part of US counter-insurgency programmes.[25] In 1985, the historic NGOs in El Salvador created the Coordinating Council of Private Institutes for Human Promotion (CIPHES), which would become the main coordinating body of Salvadorean NGOs rejecting AID funding.

In Guatemala, the same type of temporary AID monopoly predominated in rural areas during the early 1980s, especially during the scorched earth operations in the highlands under the military governments of Lucas García and Ríos Montt. The main channel for AID was the Committee for National Reconstruction (CRN), a governmental institution created after the 1976 earthquake which was controlled by the armed forces. In the first half of the 1980s, AID provided funding for counter-insurgency activities in the so-called *polos de desarrollo*, where internally displaced peoples were organised in model villages under military supervision.[26] US food assistance programmes to these settlements were coordinated by US private aid agencies such as *Catholic Relief Services* (CRS), CARE and *Project Hope*. Also funded by AID, through CRN, were activities of a growing number of Guatemalan and US right-wing evangelical churches operating in conflict zones. Especially under Ríos Montt – member of *El Verbo* church, a branch of the US neo-Pentecostal organisation *World Gospel Outreach* – these evangelical sects expanded their influence among indigenous communities.[27] Similar to El Salvador, AID in Guatemala also supported 'modernising' tendencies within the business sector and financed the creation of several new private sector development foundations to pave the way for neoliberal alternatives to traditional agro-export policies.[28] The covert role that AID was playing in supporting counter-insurgency programmes through CRN led a group of a dozen historic Guatemalan NGOs to decide in 1985 to leave the NGO umbrella ASINDES. A new NGO coordinating body was formed, the Council of Development Institutes (COINDE), whose members would become the main beneficiaries of European and Canadian private aid agencies.[29]

In Honduras, AID policies were not essentially different, although the country was not afflicted by open civil war. But the presence of the *contras* and the deployment of US troops certainly contributed to militarising Honduran society. Starting in 1980, a vast number of US private aid agencies and evangelical churches entered Honduras to start development programmes or to provide humanitarian assistance to the *contras* (or 'Nicaraguan refugees' as they were euphemistically called by the US embassy). The number of Honduran NGOs tripled between 1980 and 1987, and this rapid boom was entirely due to the increase of AID funding; it was difficult to find Honduran NGOs *not* financed by AID.[30] Political pacification, economic stabilisation and private sector support also in Honduras figured as the primary goals of AID's top-down policies to strengthen civil society. Local NGOs were either directly created by AID (such as the private sector NGOS AVANCE and CADERH) or indirectly through US private aid agencies such as *Private Agencies Collaborating Together* (PACT), the *Inter-American Foundation* (IAF) and the *Pan American Development Foundation* (PADF). AID funding for social services and small business development was channelled through a new Honduran NGO umbrella created in 1982, the Federation of Private Development Organisations (FOPRIDEH), of which several members also depended on European private aid support.[31] The more progressive peasant, worker and community organisations and development NGOS were excluded from AID funding and were entirely supported by European private aid agencies. Only in the late 1980s, when US aid to Honduras was declining, did FOPRIDEH take a more critical approach towards AID.

The previous analysis demonstrates that European private aid to Central America until the mid-1980s was concentrated in Nicaragua, and that its role in early transitions in the rest of the region was limited until 1985. Emergency assistance to displaced populations and refugees characterised European and Canadian private aid support to El Salvador, Guatemala and Honduras, often channelled through local organisations related to the churches. Militarisation of society and large US aid flows limited the opportunities of European private aid agencies who refused to work with the governments of these countries and instead preferred to support a minimal infrastructure for the (often clandestine) organisations of the opposition. As many European governments also were reluctant to start bilateral aid programmes to the authoritarian governments of El Salvador and Guatemala, private aid channels were increasingly used to counter-balance US-supported counter-insurgency programmes. After the installation of civilian governments in the mid-1980s these private aid flows not only increased, but also contributed to highlighting the hidden polarisation in civil society.

Two competing views on civil society building would prevail in this second phase of early transitions: the top-down 'market-oriented' approach by AID and the bottom-up 'inclusive' approach by European and Canadian private aid agencies. The AID approach aimed to set up new business associations and private sector foundations with the primary goal of 'modernising' the business sector, stimulating a non-traditional export model, and facilitating privatisation of state services. Development and service NGOS set up or supported by these AID programmes implemented market-oriented training and media programmes, generally aimed at the small and medium-size business sectors, whose umbrellas (such as ASINDES and FOPRIDEH) also served as an aid channel. The vertical focus meant that local organisations were not actively involved in the design and implementation of these projects, often leading to weak institutionalisation and aid dependency (Reuben 1991). The European approach to civil society building was to stimulate existing or emerging organisational structures and to work directly with these groups and their development NGOS on the basis of 'accompaniment' and perceived needs. This bottom-up approach often also included non-monetary forms such as training and advocacy (Macdonald 1997). The primary goal was to enhance the participation of marginalised sectors, strengthen their local organisations, and stimulate critical thinking about the way to confront their immediate and medium-term political and social needs. The polarised character of these two approaches could be termed 'political pacification versus political transformation'. In the next section the implementation of the inclusive European approach on civil society building will be examined more closely.

5.3 Civil society building during early democratic transitions

After 1983 the character of the Central American conflict gradually changed from open warfare to more subtle counter-insurgency campaigns as part of a sophisticated LIC strategy in which humanitarian aid would become a key ingredient. In Guatemala popular militias – Civil Defence Patrols (PAC's) – and development committees were formed under supervision of the armed forces, while President Ríos Montt launched his *frijoles y tortilla* ('bread and beans') campaign to win the hearts and minds of the indigenous population. It was a highly politicised form of humanitarian aid, implemented with support from US fundamentalist evangelical churches and their related private aid agencies. As a US general in the region frankly commented on the methods used in counter-insurgency tactics: 'In a guerrilla war, the most important piece of territory is the six inches between a peasant's ear.'[32] In El Salvador these governmental aid programmes as part of counter-insurgency campaigns started in 1983 with the provision of (US-sponsored) humanitarian aid to civilians in conflict zones, combined with psychological warfare designed to separate the FMLN from its support base. In addition, the installation of elected civilian regimes (Duarte in El Salvador and Cerezo in Guatemala) was recommended by the US bipartisan commission led by Henry Kissinger to give a democratic image to its LIC strategy (Byrne 1996). Despite military domination of these new civilian governments, civil society would take advantage of the new political space opening up after 1984 in El Salvador and after 1986 in Guatemala. The same happened in Honduras, after the forced removal of General Alvarez in 1984. During this second phase of early transitions, the policies of European private aid agencies shifted from providing emergency aid to war victims to more structural support for new organisation building in civil society. The regional Esquipulas peace agreement of 1987 further increased the opportunities for private aid agencies to focus on civil society building policies, which will be examined in more detail for each country.

– *Honduras: forging unity within the popular movement (1985-89)*
European private aid support to strengthen Honduran civil society was quite different compared to Nicaragua, El Salvador and Guatemala. The level of aid was

more constant throughout the 1980s, but on average also smaller as fewer agencies had programmes in Honduras. A key 'handicap' was, as a member of the opposition frankly stated, that despite being the poorest country in the region, Honduras lacked the perspective of a revolutionary transformation; private aid to Honduras therefore always was in some way related to the processes in El Salvador and Nicaragua.[33] The Honduran political-revolutionary movements that emerged in the late 1970s (particularly after the Sandinista victory) were marginal compared to the movements in neighbouring countries, although they had a function in providing logistical support to those external movements and in stimulating the formation of several domestic popular organisations. However, the strong presence of US troops, AID and Nicaraguan *contras* had converted Honduras into a US stronghold for regional low intensity warfare, and the resulting militarisation of the country seriously limited popular organising until the mid-1980s.

Despite these limitations, over twenty European private aid agencies were active in Honduras. Catholic agencies (such as *Misereor*, CEBEMO, CAFOD, CIIR, *Fastenopfer* and *Trocaire*) had been supporting social activities of the Church since the 1970s, although this work also was restricted by state repression.[34] Several Protestant agencies (such as EZE, DCA, ICCO, HEKS, *Christian Aid*, *Diakonia*, LWF, *Brot für die Welt*) and a number of secular private aid agencies (HIVOS, NOVIB, *Norwegian People's Aid*, OXFAM-UK/I, OXFAM-Belgium, *Ibis*) and party-related foundations (*Friedrich Ebert Stiftung*, *Friedrich Naumann Stiftung*) increased their support to Honduras, especially in the second half of the 1980s. These agencies had in common that they rejected US intervention (both military and economic) and preferred to support those organisations of the opposition that were not funded by AID. In the early 1980s support was given to Salvadorean refugees, the churches, to a handful of new local NGOs working with peasant and community organisations and to human rights organisations that were just about the only public voices for the opposition. Development NGOs founded with European private aid support had programmes on literacy, popular education, agricultural training, cooperatives and primary health care, and were generally closely linked to the left-wing opposition and rejected AID funding.[35] Some of them, such as the Christian Development Commission (CCD), that was supported by Protestant agencies, also worked in remote areas at the Salvadorean border where the army tried to control and intimidate the rural (often indigenous) communities by setting up civil defence committees to prevent contact with the FMLN (Barry *et al.* 1989). The main focus of these 'independent' development NGOs was to strengthen the leadership and institutional capacity of popular organisations, which had been weakened by repression in rural areas. Unlike in El Salvador and Guatemala, this type of civil society building had not been disrupted by civil war and represented a more gradual follow-up to the traditional social work of the Catholic Church.

After militarisation eased with the removal of General Alvarez in 1984, mobilisation of civil society sectors increased (especially against the presence of *contras* and US troops) and several new organisations emerged. This was also a time in which European private aid flows increased considerably, and it was preferred to support popular (membership) organisations directly rather than indirectly through development NGOs.[36] A major focus was the peasant movement, traditionally strong in mobilising the rural population for land occupations and demands for governmental subsidies, and the trade unions. However, the peasant movement was weakened by internal competition among peasant leaders, provoking internal divisions and co-optation efforts by the government.[37] In the early 1980s the militant (Social Christian) National Peasant Union (UNC) was, for example, successfully 'neutralised' by the Honduran government (Norsworthy and Barry 1994). Therefore, the formation in 1985 of a new independent peasant confederation, the National Central of Rural Workers (CNTC), was welcomed as a promising initiative to unite the divided Honduran peasant movement. To avoid dependence on AID or governmental funding, CNTC turned to European private aid agencies for support. The response was amazing: within two years CNTC received funding from seventeen different private aid agencies (for literacy, credit and training programmes), making it the largest counterpart of these agencies in Honduras with an annual budget of more than a million dollars.[38] However, CNTC lacked the capacity to administer these large aid resources. Internal tensions and charges of corruption followed and within a few years serious internal divisions existed. Most agencies admitted that in their enthusiasm to strengthen independent popular organisations they had 'overfunded' the CNTC and actually indirectly contributed to weakening civil society in Honduras. Probably, this also was due to poor coordination among the donor agencies.[39]

The CNTC experience made private aid agencies more cautious in supporting Honduran popular organisations and their national coordinating bodies.[40] Lack of coordination among popular organisations and competition between their leaders appeared to be structural obstacles to breaking the hegemony of the bipartisan political system. Several newly emerging civil society coalitions were supported by European private aid agencies, but lacked the capacity (or the unity) to serve as temporary actors in political society. Examples are the Coordinating Committee of Popular Organisations (CCOP) and later in 1988 the Coordinating Council of Peasant Organisations (COCOCH) and the *Plataforma de lucha*, a broad civil society coalition against the neoliberal adjustment programme of President Callejas.[41] His government tried to break the unity of these coalitions by provoking divisions or by setting up parallel alliances, such as the National Development Coalition of Honduran Peasants (CONACADH) which incorporated several COCOCH unions (Posas 1992). The difficulty of uniting forces was also visible in failed efforts to establish an NGO coordinating organ separate from the AID-funded FOPRIDEH.[42] The lack of unity among opposition forces, recurrent divisions within popular organisations and rivalry between leaders represented serious limitations for European private aid agencies in pursuing policies that could contribute to strengthening civil society. Particularly the lack of autonomy of popular organisations from the small left-wing parties and the dominant influence of AID-sponsored organisations limited their possibilities in Honduras.

Faced with these adverse circumstances, many European private aid agencies gave a lower priority to their work in Honduras, shifting their emphasis more to newly arising opportunities in El Salvador and Guatemala, especially after the repatriation of Salvadorean refugees from the Honduran camps. This gradual retreat, becoming visible in the early 1990s, fuelled suspicions by Honduran counterparts that European agencies only considered their presence in Honduras as instrumental to their activities in the surrounding countries. Nevertheless, political conditions for civil society building in Honduras had improved with the end of the *contra* war, making room for new domestic priorities such as organising women, indigenous people, workers in the *maquila* and workers in the informal urban sector. The defeat of the Sandinistas also defused sectarian struggles by left-wing revolutionary parties within the unions, indirectly contributing to the emergence of more autonomous social organisations with support from private foreign aid. An outstanding example of this shift was the increased role of women's organisations (together with human rights groups) in mobilising civil society in the early 1990s to accelerate demilitarisation and prosecution of human rights abuses.[43] This mobilisation of civil society eventually helped to shift the neoliberal programme of President Callejas to more progressive and less polarising policies under President Reina, which would move democratic transition into a new stage.

– El Salvador: support to repopulation and rebuilding the popular sector (1984-89)
European private aid agencies were able to operate more openly in El Salvador after the installation of President Duarte in 1984. Activities initially were aimed at supporting human rights groups and displaced populations, who founded their own membership organisation: the Christian Committee of Displaced Persons (CRIPDES). The churches wanted to close down the special camps in urban areas for displaced people and relocate them to the countryside, among other things because they feared that their inhabitants were starting to become passive and too dependent upon external assistance. This was an incentive for the displaced to set up CRIPDES, which would organise the repopulated communities, facilitate basic needs and help them in finding humanitarian assistance from churches and foreign private aid agencies (Thompson 1995). The government opposed the initiatives by CRIPDES, which it considered to be an FMLN-controlled organisation. The Duarte government wanted to place the displaced people in civic action programmes and require them to take part in civil defence patrols that could serve as a guard against the guerrilla forces. Meanwhile in 1985-86 the army started to depopulate entire areas in order to isolate the FMLN, which generated a record number of around half a million displaced persons.[44] Efforts to find a structural non-militarist solution for the displaced led to a proposal by DIACONIA and FUNDASAL (a local NGO specialised in housing projects)[45] for a pilot-project to relocate displaced people to a formerly destroyed town: Tenancingo. Almost entirely funded by European private aid agencies, the reconstruction of Tenancingo was meant to create a

'neutral area', respected by the FMLN and the government, and symbolising the start of structural repopulations. Although the project failed because of its top-down design, Tenancingo did become the start of reconstructing civil society for the victims of the war (Edwards and Siebentritt 1991).[46]

During the second half of Duarte's term the internally displaced started to return to their destroyed communities, some quietly in small numbers (mainly to northern Morazán), others openly and in large groups (Burge 1995). In 1986 the repopulation movement increased its organisational capacity by forming the National Coalition for Repopulation (CNR) to promote and organise the repopulation of the internally displaced. This provided new opportunities for European private aid agencies to increase their funding to El Salvador as CNR and CRIPDES would become more open channels to support repopulated communities in rural conflict zones. More important, the focus of support now shifted from emergency assistance to more structural development aid with which the new communities were able to set up durable solutions such as agricultural cooperatives and small enterprises, and to improve the local infrastructure with drinking water, health care and education projects. Not surprisingly, the government opposed these repopulations to areas that had been deliberately depopulated by the armed forces to create free-fire zones against FMLN guerrilla forces; in fact, the government often denied the existence of these repopulated communities. But good internal organisation of the communities and advocacy through international networks of churches (the *World Council of Churches*), private aid agencies (such as ICVA) and solidarity groups provided effective protection against armed forces and governmental interference. Through these connections, organisations of the uprooted had access to what Pritchard (1996: 125) calls a 'transnational political space', from which they appropriated universal human rights demands into their struggle such as the right to return to their place of origin.

The Esquipulas peace agreement of August 1987 spurred the first of a series of repatriations of Salvadorean refugees from their camps in Honduras, a movement of people that was also stimulated and facilitated by the earlier repopulation efforts. By financing the repopulations and repatriations to conflict zones, European and Canadian private aid agencies were aware that they were frustrating governmental plans to control the displaced through civic action programmes and that depopulation of these areas as a military strategy would become impossible. Support to the new communities in the FMLN-controlled zones of Morazán, San Miguel, Chalate-nango, Cabañas, Cuscatlán, Usulután and La Libertad actually implied that private aid agencies actively supported the FMLN,[47] but this was not made explicit for security reasons.[48] Initially, DIACONIA and the new community organisations served as intermediaries for foreign aid, but after Esquipulas this function was gradually taken over by newly created intermediary NGOs, all closely linked to the FMLN. These new NGOs operated as coordinating bodies, each servicing a particular geographical area controlled by one of the five FMLN member parties, and actively searching for new external private aid resources.[49] In addition, dozens of new development NGOs had emerged in the capital since the mid-1980s, of which the ones linked to the opposition (and thus who rejected AID funding) often were part of the NGO umbrella group CIPHES.[50] This boom in new development NGOs was further stimulated by the growing availability of aid resources provided by private aid agencies, the European Community and after 1989 by the UN-sponsored CIREFCA programme, all channelling substantial aid resources through these local NGOs.[51] A certain level of competition for foreign aid resources also became apparent among the five parties and their affiliated NGOs, although the FPL (the largest FMLN tendency) attracted the greatest share of private foreign aid.[52]

Between 1988 and 1994 private aid agencies would channel over a hundred million dollars to these new Salvadorean NGOs for developing a few dozen settlements such as San Antonio los Ranchos and Guarjíla (Chalatenango), Copapayo (Cuscatlán), Santa Marta (Cabañas), Nueva Gualcho (Usulután) and Segundo Montes (Morazán). These new settlements were strategically important for the FMLN, but also politically significant as they represented opportunities to construct a new type of society which served as an alternative model for El Salvador's unequal social and economic structure (Macdonald and Gatehouse 1995). Due to the absence of governmental authorities, all infrastructure, health, education and production systems had to be constructed by the communities themselves, for which foreign aid agencies provided the resources. The population in the settlements was very well organised, with a high level of participation by women and priority given to collective methods of production. Community councils formed regional organisations, providing an organisational framework through which aid assistance was negotiated with foreign-funded local NGOs.[53] The shift from emergency assistance to the provision of structural aid for social services, agricultural cooperatives and small enterprises also contributed to the rapid expansion of foreign aid flows to these communities after 1990.[54] However, the alternative development model promoted by the repopulation movement had serious limitations. As these communities were located in conflict zones, community participation often was subordinated to FMLN interests, creating vertical organisation structures (Foley 1996). Another limitation was that it was difficult to replicate the social and economic model of the communities in other rural areas, and to make the communities economically sustainable due to their total dependence on foreign aid flows (Thompson 1995). Both limitations would become major concerns for private aid agencies after the signing of the peace accords in 1992.

Next to repopulated and repatriated communities in rural El Salvador, the other key focus of private aid agencies after the mid-1980s was to support new popular organisations in urban areas. Between 1981 and 1983 existing popular organisations were forced to go underground, often using the Catholic Church or human rights groups as a legal shield for protection.[55] The 1984 election campaign provided new political space for the popular movement, first visible in the formation of the Salvadorean United Labour and Association Movement (MUSYGES, 1983). Under Duarte's presidency new unions emerged, some of them AID-sponsored to create a constituency for the Christian Democrats, but most of these organisations were linked to the opposition such as the State and Municipal Workers Coordinating Council (CCTEM, 1985) and the National Coalition of Agricultural Cooperatives (COACES, 1985). New national alliances were created, coordinating a broad array of rural and urban associations such as the Worker's Solidarity Coalition (CST, 1985), a follow-up to MUSYGES which later merged into the National Union of Salvadorean Workers (UNTS, 1986). All these organisations received substantial support from European private aid agencies, either directly or through their member organisations.[56] The government soon responded by creating a similar coalition, the National Worker and Peasant Union (UNOC, 1986) which was loyal to the government and composed of AIFLD-sponsored unions (Lungo 1995). UNTS and UNOC would sharply oppose each other until the late 1980s, when they decided to join efforts against the new ARENA government in the Democratic Peasant Alliance (ADC, 1989).

Similar polarisation in civil society occurred after the October 1986 earthquake, with the arrival of emergency relief from US agencies and evangelical churches, but also from European private aid agencies. The latter channelled their support through UNTS-affiliated organisations and development NGOs and spurred the formation of new marginalised urban community organisations, creating a diverse and radical urban popular movement.[57] Most of these organisations would become active participants in the National Debate for Peace (CPDN), a forum initiated by the Catholic Church in 1988 to demand a negotiated solution to the war.[58] Apart from financial aid, private aid agencies also played an important role in removing obstacles for humanitarian assistance, particularly prior to and during the November 1989 FMLN offensive. By setting up a coordinated information service, they actively mobilised international support for peace negotiations.[59]

Private aid flows to El Salvador were highest in 1990-91, after regional attention moved from the defeated Sandinistas in Nicaragua to the Salvadorean peace talks, although official foreign aid flows would achieve their peak after the peace negotiations were successfully concluded in late 1991. However, the basis for rebuilding civil society was laid between 1984 and 1989, when a few hundred new popular organisations emerged, organising traditional sectors (such as workers, peasants and teachers) as well as new social sectors such as displaced populations and marginalised urban communities. Many of these organisations – and in particular their national umbrellas such as COACES, UNTS and CPDN – had been financed by European private aid agencies. These organisations, in addition to the network of new local NGOs linked to the opposition, provided a key infrastructure for the FMLN to survive politically during the war years. European private aid support thus was a vital element in implementing the strategy of the FMLN leadership. Many believe that without this private aid support, organised pressure from civil society for peace negotiations would not have acquired the level that became visible after the election of President Cristiani in 1989, which eventually moved the political process into the stage of mid-transition.[60] Probably more than anywhere else in the region the international advocacy work of private aid agencies was an important factor in mobilising the international community to move democratic transition forward.

– *Guatemala: contributing to national consensus (1988-93)*
The way private aid agencies supported repatriation of Guatemalan refugees in Mexico to their places of origin resembled the Salvadorean experience, although with two important differences. For one thing, these refugees belonged to Guatemala's Indian majority and distrusted non-Indian interference; for another, the repatriation occurred almost five years later in a completely new regional political setting as was shown in the previous chapter. The Guatemalan democratic transition process not only started later, it also had a slower pace compared to El Salvador and Honduras. Hence, European private aid support to the process of rebuilding civil society in Guatemala started about five years later, in 1988-89, during the final years of the Cerezo administration. Prior to these years, aid agencies unwilling to work with military-controlled emergency assistance and repopulation programmes sponsored by AID encountered difficulties working in rural areas affected by military operations. Emergency assistance to displaced communities and other war victims was channelled through the rural network of the churches, and often coordinated by church-related agencies such as CONFREGUA and CIEDEG. But this support was marginal compared to the large flow of aid from US evangelical churches and AID-supported NGOs. Only in non-conflict areas had private aid agencies been able to continue supporting rural communities with social services and building organisational capacity: programmes implemented by the historic NGOs assembled in COINDE.[61]

During the Cerezo government political space was rather limited for the handful of popular organisations in civil society, most of them having come into existence in 1988 or later when repression against popular leaders became more selective (Gutiérrez 1997). Human rights groups were established to assist war victims (such as GAM, CIEPRODH, CONAVIGUA, CERJ), or to organise the displaced populations (CONDEG), in addition to a number of unions (such as UNSITRAGUA, CUSG and CGTC) most of which merged into the Labour and Popular Action Unity (UASP). All these organisations started to receive support from European private agencies, although their capacity to mobilise civil society was by far less strong than in El Salvador, where the revolutionary movement was more united and relations between leaders and constituency firmer. Moreover, radical strikes and marches of UASP in 1988-89 reinforced sectarianism and contributed to political polarisation, while new forms of social mobilisation were required to break the cycle of violence (Castañeda Sandoval 1993). Faced with the violent and polarised political climate in Guatemala many private aid agencies searched for ways to support the reconstruction of marginalised Indian communities in rural areas that had been the site of conflict. National reconciliation between the Indian and Ladino population was considered to be a key condition for a successful peace process, and hence for contributing to democratic transition. Therefore, next to supporting human rights groups and an emerging (urban) popular movement, the priorities of European private aid agencies in Guatemala in the late 1980s were to support displaced rural populations, strengthen Indian organisations and prepare the return of Indian refugees from Mexico.

Conditions to support the displaced in Guatemala were adverse compared to El Salvador, where the FMLN had been successful in undermining the government's repopulation and pacification programmes. In Guatemala the URNG was smaller, weaker and unable to provide protection to the scattered displaced populations, with the exception of the thousands that fled to the North to form the CPR's.[62] Independent community organising had been destroyed by military operations; the high death toll of men had fundamentally changed the composition of Indian communities, and fear resulting from this terror had made civil defence patrols and military commissions the only remaining forms of social organising in rural areas affected by the conflict (Alecio 1995). Access of international aid agencies to these communities was risky if collaboration with the armed forces was to be avoided. Only the displaced that had fled to the capital and other cities could be reached through local NGOs, although this assistance was hampered by their low level of organisation. During the second half of the Cerezo government conditions slowly improved for rebuilding organisations of the victims of the war. Apart from the earlier mentioned church-related organisations and networks, private aid support was increasingly channelled through a number of secular NGOs which managed to open offices in former conflict areas.[63] Gradually (and covertly), organisational capacity of the communities improved also thanks to close coordination with popular organisations such as GAM, CERJ and CONAVIGUA and, after 1990, with the National Council of Displaced People (CONDEG). But even in 1990 community organising was considered by the armed forces as a form of subversive action: the army continued its selective repression against popular leaders or responded to community mobilisations with gunfire resulting in massacres such as in Santiago Atitlán in December 1990 (Perera 1993).

In addition to the Ladino-dominated NGOs, in the late 1980s a new category of local development NGOs emerged in Guatemala which were entirely managed by staff of Indian descent and advocated *desarrollo indígena*, a development strategy in which the traditional Maya culture was respected and promoted. These Indian NGOs established direct links with Indian communities which often became part of their organisational structure in the form of 'community associations' or 'development councils'. Their leaders generally had been trained in the 1970s in programmes offered by the historic NGOs, spoke one or more Maya languages and had grown up in the Maya culture. This was of course an enormous asset in the Indian highlands.[64] Some of their NGOs, such as the Caqchikel Coordinating Agency for Integral Development (COCADI), initially started as a grassroots organisation in the early 1980s, although due to repression it had to shift its focus to social assistance. Other Indian NGOs emerged in the mid-1980s, often as initiatives by local Indian leaders to improve the bad living conditions in the communities and increase local participation and community organising with an integrated approach which is typical of the so-called 'Maya cosmovision'. Examples are the Western Rural Development Agency (CDRO, 1984) in Totonicapán, the Foundation of the Educational, Social and Economic Development Association (FUNDADESE, 1985) in El Quiché and the Association of Indigenous Cooperation for Integrated Development (COINDI, 1986) in Sololá. After 1988 various European private aid agencies started to support these Indian NGOs and their community development programmes, particularly because they aimed to strengthen civil society at a local level.[65] As a result of increasing external aid, many of these new NGOs expanded the scope of their activities in the 1990s and started to work in those communities in which the Civil Defence Patrols (PAC's) had been the only form of local organisation. (The case of FUNDADESE will be further examined in Chapter 6).

Private aid agencies also started to support newly emerging Indian membership organisations. Following the establishment in the 1980s of Indian NGOs, a coalition of organisations was founded in 1990 in which several of these NGOs actively participated: the Guatemalan Council of Maya Organisations (COMG). The foundation of COMG symbolised the start of a 'rebirth' of popular organising among the Indian population of Guatemala which had been absent since the CUC went underground in the late 1970s. The growth of Indian organisations was spurred by an international revival of movements promoting the defence of indigenous rights. Their demands were supported by international treaties (such as Convention 169 of the ILO) and received broad attention in 1991 throughout Guatemala, where the continental counter-celebration of the 500 years commemoration of the 'discovery' of the Americas was organised. The awarding of the 1992 Nobel Peace Prize to CUC leader and human rights activist Rigoberta Menchú and the growing importance of the 'identity and rights of indigenous people' – which was a central issue during the peace negotiations between the URNG and the government – further stimulated the formation of Indian organisations, a few hundred of which would emerge in the early 1990s (Bastos and Camus 1995). Many of these organisations, in particular the national coalitions assembled in the Coordinating Council of Organisations of the Mayan People in Guatemala (COPMAGUA), would become primary beneficiaries of European private aid in the 1990s.

One of the priorities of private aid agencies was to support the return of Guatemalan refugees and the repopulation of the displaced in the CPR's to their places of origin. Refugees and the internally displaced were those most affected by the war who feared that resettlement in Guatemala would imply renewed subordination to the armed forces.[66] The government organised individual repatriations in 1987, but the returned families faced threats from the armed forces and civil defence patrols and received virtually no social support for their resettlement (Garst 1993). In response, refugees in Mexican camps demanded collective repatriation, guarantees for their security and better social conditions prior to their repatriation. In 1988 they organised themselves into the Permanent Committees (CCPP) and started negotiations with the Guatemalan government on the conditions for their return, receiving international support from a group of private aid agencies, churches and solidarity committees.[67] This international advocacy was crucial as the zones of resettlement were heavily militarised: combat and aerial bombing in the northern Ixcán area (where CPR's were hiding) would continue until April 1993, and the local population was firmly controlled by civil defence patrols. The absence of an organised civilian population sympathetic to the returnees made the Guatemalan repatriation far more complicated than it had been in El Salvador. This was aggravated by the scarcity of cultivable land, generating serious tensions between local communities and the returning refugees (Burge 1995; Pritchard 1996). Furthermore, stagnating peace talks and disagreements between the URNG and popular organisations did not contribute to a smooth and coordinated resettlement process. Only after an agreement was reached between the CCPP and the government in 1992 did the first of a series of successful repatriations start in January 1993 with the return of a few thousand refugees to the Ixcán municipality in El Quiché.

European private aid agencies were key players in supporting the reintegration of the uprooted population back into Guatemalan civil society. While the operational costs of repatriation were covered by multilateral funds (UNHCR, CIREFCA, PRODERE and EU) private aid was instrumental in building up the organisational capacity of the refugees (CCPP and ARDIGUA)[68] and of the displaced, who since 1989 had been organised in the National Council of Guatemalan Displaced (CONDEG). Moreover, international lobbying by European private aid agencies successfully guaranteed a major role for local NGOs in channelling large flows of multilateral funding (from CIREFCA and PRODERE) to the repatriation and repopulation process. The impact of this international pressure was illustrated by the source of these funds: over ninety percent was provided by European governments.[69] On the Guatemalan side this advocacy was organised by CONGCOOP, in which over a dozen Guatemalan NGOs working with the uprooted were brought together, including most historic NGOs.[70] CONGCOOP and its members received support from all major European private aid agencies and played a role similar to that of the Salvadorean NGOs facilitating the reintegration process in Salvadorean former conflict zones. However, the Guatemalan process was complicated by cultural differences (Ladino-dominated NGOs versus Indian popular organisations), the slow pace of the peace process and by internal divisions within the CCPP.[71] In addition, the CCPP accused Indian organisations in the resettlement areas of being manipulated by the URNG, although competition for control over large external resources appeared to play a role in these accusations (Krznaric 1997). This generated concern among European agency representatives, who complained about the weakness of Guatemalan popular organisations and the lack of professionalism of local NGOs, but also about the poor coordination among foreign aid agencies.[72]

Another serious limitation was that Central America in the early 1990s was losing its priority for (European) donor governments, just at the start of the Guatemalan process of reconciliation and when it most needed international support. In addition, funding regulations were becoming stricter in the early 1990s as will be seen later in this chapter, leading to a lower 'peace dividend' than in El Salvador. Despite these limitations, support from European private aid agencies to strengthen new independent organisations in civil society during the last stage of early transition was substantial: the vast majority of social organisations and NGOs of the opposition received support from these agencies, which had shifted their emphasis after 1992 from El Salvador to Guatemala.[73] As the level of AID funding had dropped and lost its counter-insurgency focus, European private aid support would become even more important for rebuilding Guatemalan civil society, where a slow process had started to forge a national consensus about a peaceful solution to the civil war.

– *Regional Central America strategies of private aid agencies*
In addition to the national policies described above, several European (and Canadian) private aid agencies meanwhile had started to support regional networks of civil society associations. Notably the four Dutch private aid agencies, the German *Brot für die Welt*, the Danish *Ibis*, the *Norwegian People's Aid*, the Swedish *Diakonia* and the British OXFAM-UK/I started to finance the formation and the operational costs of these regional networks. They were primarily formed to exchange national experiences, but later also to link micro-level action with national and international advocacy campaigns. The networks were a typical product of the regional crisis, and soon became, as one agency policy document formulates it, 'part of a strategy to break the US-imposed isolation of Nicaragua in the 1980s, to develop a scheme of popular regional integration [...] as an alternative to the government-based regional collaboration' (Bye *et al.* 1995: 31). These regional civil society networks emerged in three 'generations'.

The first group of regional networks was founded at the start of the Central American crisis and in the early years of the Nicaraguan revolution, roughly between 1978 and 1981. Responding to increased political repression by militarised security forces, in 1978 a human rights commission was formed in Costa Rica to denounce these acts of violence: CODEHUCA. Initially established as a committee, CODEHUCA soon functioned as a network of national human rights committees throughout the region. Other networks emerged in the early years of the Sandinista revolution in Nicaragua, such as *Alforja* (a network of institutes developing methods for popular education) which played a key role in the Nicaraguan literacy campaign, and CRIES, a regional network of research institutes, founded in 1981. Continuing the intellectual work of CSUCA (the older academic network) CRIES contracted international researchers to analyse the regional crisis and to develop alternative socio-economic policies for the region. These networks seldom organised a membership base and were all actually coalitions of specialised service-delivery NGOs. The exception was CCC-CA, a continental network of cooperatives, whose

Central American section was chaired by the Nicaraguan small farmers' association UNAG.[74]

The second group of regional networks was founded in the period 1988-89, in the aftermath of the 1987 Esquipulas peace agreement. As was explained earlier, this agreement marked the formal start of the regional peace process, generating new political space for a variety of national and regional civil society associations. The need for better coordination was reflected in the formation of national networks of development NGOs rejecting AID interference, such as CIPHES in El Salvador and COINDE in Guatemala. Their activities often coincided with coordination efforts at a regional level between NGO networks such as CODEHUCA, *Alforja* and the Latin American NGO network ALOP. This increased coordination between national and regional NGO networks spurred the formation of the Central American Coalition of Development Organisations (CCOD, 1988, also known as *Concertación*) in which national NGO coalitions participated, as well as most of the earlier established NGO networks (CRIES, CODEHUCA, *Alforja*, CELADEC, ALOP). This new regional NGO coordinating body started lobbying bilateral and multilateral donors to get them to support democratic transitions and initiate programmes to combat social inequality.[75] In the years following 'Esquipulas' also a number of regional coalitions of membership organisations were formed such as CTCA (social democratic trade unions), COCENTRA (radical trade unions), UPROCAFE (small coffee growers), CONCAPE (small and medium business associations) and FCOC (slum dwellers' associations). In 1989, after development NGOs became involved in the CIREFCA process, a start was made to create ARMIF, a regional coalition of NGOs involved in the resettlement of refugees and the displaced (Pacheco and Sarti 1991; García *et al.* 1994).

The third cluster of regional networks emerged after 1990, when the Nicaraguan elections and the Salvadorean peace negotiations contributed to a climate of depolarisation. A symbolic moment was the presidential summit in Antigua (June 1990) in which political discussions for the first time were dominated by economic issues. The presidents agreed to revive the regional integration process with the formation of the System of Central American Integration (SICA), which would start in 1993. Despite presidential rhetoric, civil society sectors had not been involved in the conception of SICA with the exception of FEDEPRICAP, the regional network of (large) business associations. This was one of the reasons for small farmers' associations in 1991 to found ASOCODE, the Central American Association of Small and Medium Agricultural Producers. ASOCODE would become one of the most dynamic regional civil society coalitions and was a driving force for the formation of an umbrella organisation of most of the regional networks previously mentioned, the Civil Initiative for Central American Integration (ICIC), which is further examined in Chapter 6.

European private aid agencies had several reasons for supporting these three 'generations' of regional civil society networks. A key reason was that their partners in Central America, it was thought, would benefit from closer coordination at a regional level. That European agencies themselves had demonstrated a lack of inter-coordination was of course ironic. But from a funder's perspective it was under-standable to want to enhance the quality of their partners' performance by stimulat-ing regular communication and exchange of experiences with similar organisations in other countries. Another reason for private aid agencies to support regional networks was to strengthen civil society at the national and regional levels, particu-larly in the 1990s. Better coordination between civil society sectors, it was hoped, would foster the democratic process.[76] In addition, these networks were instrumen-tal as counterparts in advocacy work: CCOD, ASOCODE, CODEHUCA and ICIC all served as Central American counterparts to lobbying initiatives of the European network of private aid agencies, the Copenhagen Initiative for Central America (CIFCA). It was also hoped that increased regional coordination could articulate the problems associated with political and economic restrictions (experienced at local project levels) to national and regional policy levels. As will be shown later, this micro-macro linkage was often absent and was one of the greatest weaknesses of the regional civil society networks.

– *Civil society building policies of private aid agencies: deliberate or accidental?*
The previous overview underscores that in the last phase of early democratic transitions European and Canadian private aid agencies were key providers of aid resources for organisations in civil society linked to the opposition. They provided valuable 'transnational political space' to those groups that had been locally isolated and marginalised by their governments. This was particularly important for the large number of refugees and internally displaced, whose improved level of organisation was essential for reintegration into civil society. Based on a review of reintegration policies by CIREFCA and PRODERE, Stein (1997: 173) remarks that 'international assistance, which was primarily sought and defined in economic terms, had mostly a positive political impact by increasing political space and expanding civil society. [...] These beneficial impacts were not the primary goal of international assistance, but instead resulted from implementation practices of consensus building and impartiality that encouraged reconciliation.' Basically the same argument could be used for private aid agency policies: support to the uprooted and persecuted was primarily seen as a form of emergency assistance, which would later shift to more structural development aid after the installation of civilian governments and the signing of the regional Esquipulas peace agreement. Support to oppositional forces essentially was a way for private aid agencies to counterbalance US counter-insurgency programmes, which obstructed peace negotiations and democratic transitions. That civil society was strengthened was merely a by-product of this support, and in the 1980s was nowhere phrased as a deliberate policy, but only referred to in terms of 'survival' and 'empowerment'. Only after 1990, when El Salvador and Honduras had entered mid-transition stages, would private aid agencies pursue civil society building as explicit policy. But by that time they would no longer be the exclusive owners of this discourse.

5.4 The political watershed of 1989-90 and the end of solidarity aid

The end of the Cold War, as it was unfolding in the last quarter of 1989, accelerated the speed of democratic transitions in Central America as was shown in the previous chapter. However, a closer look at developments in the region indicates that between October 1989 (when peace talks between the FMLN and the government stalled) and April 1990 (when these talks were restarted) a 'political watershed' occurred which cannot be completely explained by the end of the Cold War. Suddenly, the political climate in Central America shifted in these seven months from civil war to peace negotiations, from revolutionary armed struggle to institutional political participation, and from US foreign policy priority to low key international attention. Several developments were responsible for this shift: the November FMLN offensive in El Salvador (showing that none of the parties could win the war with military force), the assassination of the Jesuits (making the US government reluctant to continue supporting the Salvadorean armed forces), the US invasion in Panama (reaffirming US supremacy in the region) and the electoral defeat of the FSLN in February 1990 (marking the definitive end of revolutionary strategies in Central America). By April 1990 peace negotiations had been started by the FMLN and the URNG, and the *contras* in Honduras had been demobilised.

This political watershed marked the start of a new stage in the democratic transitions of El Salvador and Honduras (from early to mid-transition) while in Guatemala the start of mid-transition was delayed until peace talks would gain momentum in 1994. These fundamental changes in the region also affected the policies of European private aid agencies towards Central America, although this only became visible after 1992. The following section examines these (gradual) policy shifts in three steps. The first part analyses what was really new in private aid policies in the 1990s, and to what extent these policies changed as a result of developments in Central America or as a result of 'external influences'. The second part looks at the implementation of these policies in the three countries under review. Here the key question is if (and how) policies aimed at civil society building underwent (fundamental) changes. In the last part, an assessment is made of the relevance of European private aid agencies in Central America's post-Cold War and post-civil war political setting, particularly during 'mid-transitions'.

– *From political survival to economic development*
Except for sudden emergency situations, aid agencies tend to react rather slowly to new circumstances: only a few years after the political watershed in the region, adaptations in private aid policies towards Central America were becoming visible.[77] Although the level of private foreign aid to the region remained stable until the mid-1990s, private aid flows to Honduras began to decrease after 1990 and to El Salvador after 1991, while the funding to Guatemala started to increase in 1992. Looking at the democratic transition stages of these countries (see Tables 4.1, 4.2 and 4.3) reveals that private aid flows tended to be largest during the last phase

of early transitions. In terms of policy priorities a gradual shift occurred in the early 1990s from what an agency representative called 'criteria of political relevance towards criteria of economic relevance'.[78] Consequently, counterparts of private aid agencies in the region were now confronted with tighter criteria regarding reporting, internal management and evaluation methods, in addition to demands for transparency, more quantifiable results and methods to decrease aid dependency. Although it was obvious that the region was evolving from a high priority area for 'emergency aid' towards a low priority region for 'development aid', counterparts were surprised by these new criteria, even in Guatemala where private aid increased after 1992.[79] It generated confusion about the new 'political agenda' of private aid agencies and fuelled the concern that the 'era of solidarity aid' had ended with the electoral defeat of the Sandinista government and the (approaching) end of the Salvadorean civil war. This concern was reinforced by signs in the early 1990s that the Central American solidarity movement in the North was losing its momentum.

Although variations existed among European private aid agencies concerning the new policy criteria towards the region, the general tendency of their revisions were remarkably common. New criteria for supporting local projects focused on gender and environmental sustainability and prioritised support for activities that were aimed at generating income. These so-called 'productive projects', often with a substantial component of credits in combination with technical training, had become more important in the late 1980s and gradually replaced support for activities aimed at political survival. Instead of popular education and institutional support as methods for strengthening organisations in civil society, support shifted to management training and methods to strengthen the productive capacity of organisations in order to increase their likelihood of economic sustainability. Most private aid agencies recognised that the gradual end to civil warfare and the slow start of demilitarising rural areas demanded a shift from the short-term provision of (politically biased) emergency assistance to structural development aid which would generate prospects for diminishing aid dependency in the long run. A stronger local presence of agency representatives and the use of technical consultants in the field was considered to be a logical consequence of this shift, which was particularly visible in El Salvador and (after 1993) in Guatemala where private aid agencies had been confronted with hostility by the authorities throughout the 1980s.

This change of emphasis was further accompanied by stricter requirements for internal management and financial administration in order to increase the level of professionalism of local partner organisations. Staff often perceived this as increased control by private aid agencies over their work.[80] In the 1980s it was not exceptional when a share of foreign donations was transferred to revolutionary organisations; the agencies usually tolerated this as long as the funds were not used for purchasing arms.[81] This acceptance of semi-legal practices was inevitable during the war, but in the early 1990s funders required legalisation of organisations, transparent procedures and external audits. In addition to efficiency and professionalism, private aid agencies also demanded more (and more visible) results of their aid interventions. To increase their effectiveness and generate tangible impact, local organisations in Central America were trained in the systematic application of new methods for project planning, monitoring and evaluation. Although these new criteria and procedures were not rejected, many organisations were reluctant to accommodate to this new culture of efficiency and effectiveness which was seen as 'externally imposed'.[82]

Another change in private aid policies was increased concern for internal democracy and downward accountability of organisations in civil society, basically requiring a revision of the relations between service-delivery NGOs and grassroots organisations. The issue centred around a redefinition of the role of development NGOs, which were increasingly pressured by neoliberal policies to substitute for (privatised) governmental services, while on the other hand their legitimacy as representatives of the poor was being questioned by newly emerging membership organisations in civil society. In the post-war climate of broadening political space many Central American development NGOs that had served during the 1980s as legal shields for the opposition were entering an existential crisis. They were forced to make a shift from supplying services to popular organisations to a situation in which these popular organisations were actively involved in defining their own needs.[83] This required according to some private aid agencies more transparency in policy-making, better coordination among NGOs and a more professional attitude, conducive to becoming an actor in the market instead of being an autonomous actor in civil society.[84] Other agencies preferred a more participatory role of development NGOs in civil society, in which relationships with popular organisations would become more interwoven, for example by demanding membership contributions to pay for the delivery of services. Most agencies agreed that the traditional clientelistic relationships between NGOs and political parties had been undesirable and required revision, as they impeded the construction of autonomous organisations in civil society.

The shift from political criteria that were concerned with supporting organisations of subordinate sectors in civil society in the 1980s to an emphasis on economic criteria in the 1990s can be explained by a combination of factors. First of all, the end of the 'revolutionary option' in Central America had unleashed a crisis of perspective, for the Central American partners as well as for the European private aid agencies who had supported them. This process had started in 1987, when recognising the legality of elected governments was designated as the core of the Esquipulas agreement, automatically delegitimising armed revolutionary (and counter-revolutionary) struggles (Sarti 1991a). Consequently, implicit ideological criteria were losing their meaning and the 'tacit consensus' seemed to vanish, also because these criteria often had been applied by individual agency representatives on the basis of personal friendship. But the changing political context in Central America also spurred changes in the composition of private aid agency staff, as many who had been active in these agencies since the early 1980s returned to

Europe or were transferred to other regions.[85] It also implied that private aid agencies had to discuss new strategic priorities for the region, leading to adaptations of previous policies, if they existed at all. Surprisingly, three quarters of the agencies visited for this research admitted that they had no written policy documents for Central America throughout the 1980s. Aid allocations were often a reaction to short-term needs and based on personal judgements. Whereas one of the main policies in the 1980s had been to empower 'popular movements' – an all-purpose concept to identify the combined opposition forces to social exclusion and political repression – the policy documents of the 1990s would prioritise support for 'strengthening civil society'.[86]

If the actual practice of the 1980s had become part of 'new' strategies in the 1990s, were these shifts in agency criteria after all only rhetorical? This can be doubted, for the new private aid policies also were influenced by the global trend toward market-oriented strategies that had entered the discourse of official donors in the late 1980s. Requirements for more efficiency and output-oriented method-ologies were the product of a new wind blowing through the (private) aid sector, as was demonstrated in Chapter 2. A greater role for the market and a reduced but more efficient state apparatus offered new (and less politicised) opportunities for local development NGOs.[87] This was further stimulated by the growth of multilat-eral aid flows to Central America of which the share directed toward social compen-sation funds – to counter impoverishment generated by structural adjustment programmes – was increasingly handled by local development NGOs. The World Bank, for example, increasingly involved local NGOs in the implementation of their programmes.[88] Initially, only the AID-funded NGOs participated in these social compensation funds, but soon also the historic NGOs supported by European private aid agencies were accepting this type of funding. This trend of 'direct funding' also was employed by bilateral official donors who no longer needed to rely on private aid channels to support organisations in civil society. Several private aid agencies therefore became concerned about their function as traditional supporters of 'inclusive' civil society building in the post-war setting.[89] This was further exacerbated by the drastic reduction of AID funding to Central America and increased funding by the European Union to sectors that had been traditionally supported by private aid agencies, who in turn also faced stricter requirements regarding efficiency and effectiveness by their own governments on which they financially depended.

The result was that private aid agencies entered a period of uncertainty about their future strategies in Central America, especially apparent after the 1992 peace accords in El Salvador, which generated serious internal discussion and reflection on their work in previous years. A conclusion reached through these discussions was that better coordination among private aid agencies in the region would increase the prospects for improving their results.[90] Lack of agency coordination in the past often negatively impacted on the performance of Central American partners, who were also urged to coordinate better among themselves. Coordination also was required for effective lobbying activities in the North, particularly towards European governments and the European Union, to maintain funding levels to the region and to influence their agenda setting.[91] Another result of this internal reflection was that private aid agencies became conscious of the need to rethink their comparative advantages *vis-à-vis* bilateral and multilateral agencies promoting neoliberal economic strategies. The problem was, however, that many of them also were directly dependent upon these official aid resources and were feeling the pressure to increase agency efficiency by giving more aid to fewer counterparts. This would have problematic consequences for the sustainability and the accountability of Central American counterparts, to which I will return in the next chapter.

— *European private aid policies during mid-transitions*
Despite this newly emerging policy agenda, the 'old priorities' still prevailed in the early 1990s. Private aid flows to El Salvador would reach a peak with support to repopulated communities, the social reintegration of ex-guerrillas, and capacity building of membership organisations and coalitions such as UNTS and CPDN. Since the late 1980s, however, the boom in multilateral funding has gradually come to interfere with private aid policies. Large multilateral aid programmes such as CIREFCA and PRODERE, aimed at the uprooted population, became a more important source of income for local development NGOs working with refugees and the displaced than private aid funding. In addition to that, (bilateral and multilateral) funding from the European Union grew steadily in the early 1990s so that Europe became the largest provider of development aid to Central America in 1993, also because AID funding was drastically reduced in the same year (see Table 5.1); Central America would become the largest *per capita* recipient of official development aid from the EU in the world (F. Hansen 1996).

But more important was the qualitative difference between AID and EU funding, as the latter channelled substantial support to subordinate sectors in civil society and to governmental human rights programmes. AID and the Inter-American Development Bank (IDB) also attempted to strengthen civil society by providing support to service-delivery NGOs, although accompanied by a neoliberal discourse about strengthening the business sector and privatising state services.[92] As a result, official (particularly EU) aid resources started to become a significant source of (additional) income for organisations traditionally supported by European private aid agencies, whose relevance as aid providers thus would considerably diminish in the 1990s.[93] The consequences for the three countries under review are examined below.

In Honduras this tendency was visible for example in the role played by the new official Human Rights Ombudsman – largely financed by the EU – who in 1993 pushed the sensitive issue of the forced disappearances onto the political agenda. As will be demonstrated in the next chapter, this governmental human rights office gradually took over some of the tasks of the non-governmental human rights committee CODEH. Another recipient of European multilateral funding was the

Table 5.1   Official development assistance to Central America[a] (1985-95)
(in US$ million committed)

	1985	1990	1991	1992	1993	1994	1995	1990-95
Austria	6	8	21	5	17	20	21	92
Belgium	1	5	6	7	6	7	11	42
Denmark	1	15	27	26	28	26	27	149
Finland	3	13	26	14	8	5	7	73
France	13	14	14	36	26	21	39	150
Germany	32	107	124	133	100	123	266	853
Italy	30	65	60	46	36	127	24	358
Netherlands	34	69	29	63	68	63	110	402
Spain	-	33	50	33	52	59	82	309
Sweden	13	41	72	80	56	46	52	347
United Kingdom	2	5	5	7	8	11	8	44
Japan	22	142	154	241	164	200	216	1,117
United States	735	837	905	716	437	300	215	3,410
Others[b]	35	82	104	92	77	85	100	540
Total bilateral[c]	927	1,436	1,597	1,499	1,083	1,093	1,178	7,886
Total multilateral[d]	188	229	316	426	385	465	487	2,308
Total	1,115	1,665	1,913	1,925	1,468	1,558	1,665	10,194

[a] Includes Guatemala, El Salvador, Honduras, Nicaragua, Costa Rica and Panama
[b] Includes Norway, Portugal, Ireland, Luxemburg, Switzerland, Australia, New Zealand and Canada
[c] Total Official Development Assistance from DAC member countries of the OECD
[d] Includes funding from all multilateral organisations (including the EU) and the Arab countries

Sources: IRELA (1994b); Hansen (1997)

social compensation fund FHIS, for which the Callejas government tried to set up a liaison committee for local development NGOs. However, the organisations feared that this committee would be used as a tool to control European private aid flows, and rejected the proposal (Mangelschots and Ventura 1994). In general, the historic Honduran NGO sector remained weak and divided and was unable to develop a collective identity (Caballero and Salomón 1996). Added to the serious internal struggles in the peasant movement (leading to a split between CNC and COCOCH in 1990) and a prevailing culture of corruption, co-optation and clientelism by leaders of popular organisations, several European private aid agencies seriously considered in the mid-1990s closing down their Honduran programmes.[94]

Despite the reduction of private aid to Honduras, two civil society sectors supported by European private aid agencies blossomed in the period of mid-transition: women's groups and organisations of indigenous people, who often worked together with human rights groups. Due to their autonomy from political parties and the government, these organisations often managed to combine social mobilisation in civil society with constructive dialogue with the government. Although they needed to increase membership participation to improve internal accountability, European private aid agencies appeared to be willing to continue their support to these new organisations, next to their traditional support for community development in rural areas (Wils *et al.* 1992; Sparre 1996). But the problem that Honduran organisations were least active in regional civil society networks persisted, with the exception of the trade unions (COCENTRA) and the peasant organisations (ASOCODE). Therefore, they were often disconnected from relevant development policy discussions in the region, such as on the issue of collaboration with state institutions or on the search for alternative sources of income. This relative isolation was further exacerbated by the low presence of European aid agency representatives in Honduras and by the absence of new actors in political society that were able to challenge the bipartisan and corrupt political system. Despite extreme poverty figures, the gloomy outlook for social change further marginalised Honduras on European private aid priority lists.[95]

El Salvador was the main recipient of European private aid in Central America, particularly during the peace negotiations of 1990-91. Several agencies moved their offices from Managua to San Salvador to monitor growing aid flows, especially those that were aimed at the resettlements in former conflict zones. Large amounts of multilateral funding from the CIREFCA programme complemented the booming budgets of local development NGOs working with the uprooted population. Due to the enlarged presence of private aid staff in El Salvador and improved access to rural areas, private aid agencies also started to realise that the work of many beneficiary organisations needed critical assessment. Salvadorean development NGOs appeared to be weakened by competition for funding, lacked good planning and evaluation systems, and their relations with intended beneficiaries were often not very transparent or democratic (Alvarez and Martin 1992). During the war, donor-recipient relationships had been based largely on mutual trust, but with the peace accords approaching this was changing. It became clear to many agencies that historic NGO agendas often had been donor-driven and had been determined by a limited group of individuals on the basis of personal relationships. The rapid growth of budgets had not automatically contributed to strengthening the institutional capacity of local organisations (Jäger 1996). Due to the competition for funding, Salvadorean development NGOs linked to the opposition apparently had responded more to Northern donor agendas than to local demands (Alvarez and Martin 1992).[96]

Meanwhile, private aid agencies wanted to prevent Salvadorean counterparts from being excluded from the implementation of the post-war National Reconstruction Plan (PRN), for which bilateral and multilateral donors provided over US$ 1.6 billion (Boyce 1995). The problem was twofold. On the one hand the government was reluctant to channel this funding through the historic NGOs, which they considered politically dependent upon the FMLN and which lacked the administrative capacity to implement large development programmes.[97] The historic NGOs on the other hand were unwilling to work directly with the Salvadorean government, as the implementation of the PRN was controlled by organisations responsible for rural counter-insurgency operations during the war (O'Brien and Catenacci 1996). This problem had already surfaced during the peace negotiations, when the historic NGOs in CIPHES refused to work with the Salvadorean Social Compensation Fund (FIS), a governmental fund mainly aimed at improving infrastructure at the municipal level which was not responding to local needs (Van der Borgh 1997).[98] Due to international pressure the government promised that development NGOs would have a larger role in the implementation of the National Reconstruction Plan, starting in 1992, for which over thirty percent of funding was to be channelled through non-governmental agencies. However, the historic NGOs only received a minor share of these resources as the government preferred to work with private sector NGOs and operational US private aid agencies who were loyal to the government (Murray *et al.* 1994). Indirectly, through UNDP and *Catholic Relief Services,* the (historic) NGOs linked to the opposition – including the *Fundación 16 de enero* which was created by the FMLN to accompany the reintegration of ex-combatants – still managed to channel some reconstruction funding to former conflict zones. European private aid agencies were not directly involved in PRN, but provided important complementary support to the historic NGOs and popular organisations working in these zones.

With European private aid flows reaching record levels, the level of funding probably should have been the lowest concern for the historic NGOs, but it was not. In addition, major weaknesses were their inability to engage in constructive partnerships with public sector institutions, their poor institutional and administrative capacity and the absence of participatory planning and decision-making towards local communities. In fact, the historic NGOs financed by European private aid agencies took little advantage of the post-war environment of reconciliation and reconstruction, although they were best placed to contribute to participatory development at the municipal level with public reconstruction funds. According to Sollis (1995: 537) this can be explained by their dependence on external resources, which 'acted as a disincentive to NGOs that seek access to national public resources',[99] and a lack of clear development objectives in the new political setting. Several European agencies recognised this dependency on (private) foreign aid and encouraged a process of 'conversion' of historic NGOs to better serve the needs of local communities, although this turned out to be a 'complex and painful process of change' (Murray *et al.* 1994). A survey among eighty Salvadorean development NGOs in 1994 found that only five of them had managed to achieve a high degree of participation by beneficiaries of their projects (Foley *et al.* 1995). This low figure possibly was spurred by scepticism on the part of beneficiaries, who had become apathetic due to 'assistantialist' development projects. But it was, according to Foley (1996: 93), certainly also political rivalry and manipulation that were reinforcing polarisation in civil society rather than contributing to national conciliation. It underscored that, despite 'accompaniment', 'bottom-up' approaches of civil

society building under certain conditions turned out to have 'top-down' characteristics, such as low levels of participation, the absence of downward accountability
and little prospect for sustainability.[100]

To stimulate conversion of the Salvadorean historic NGOs, European private aid
agencies urged them during the stage of mid-transition to actively engage in policy
advocacy directed at national and local governments.[101] Some agencies provided
special training programmes in advocacy methods, which were a radical break with
the confrontational methods of the war years. All factions of the FMLN also
established policy research institutes in order to develop policy proposals in the
wake of the 1994 elections (although this was also in response to new private foreign
aid agendas). In addition, special NGOs were established to initiate programmes for
civic education to mobilise voter turnout at these elections, in which the FMLN
would participate for the first time.[102] Instrumental links between many historic
NGOs and the FMLN became more controversial after the elections, when the party
split up into two factions. The tendency led by ERP leader Villalobos founded the
Democratic Party (PD) and forged a temporary pact with ARENA. In 1995 it even
supported a governmental plan to regulate private foreign aid flows with the
purpose of controlling the NGO sector. The plan evoked criticism from both
historic and private sector NGOs and showed that Salvadorean development NGOs
during the stage of late transition indeed were becoming more autonomous from
the political parties that had used them as key instruments until the elections
(Murray 1995; Spence *et al.* 1997). Sharp criticism from many civil society sectors
(both from the left and the right) about the elitist character of political parties and
their corrupted leaders was also an indication that democratic transition was
advancing slowly. Guido Béjar (1995) even suggests that increased popular
mobilisation can become a new threat to the system if political society fails to
perform its intermediary role between the state and civil society.

Private aid flows during Guatemala's stage of mid-transition showed many
similarities to El Salvador, although occurring several years later. The failed coup
attempt by President Serrano in May 1993 was a decisive moment for democratic
transition in Guatemala, comparable to the November 1989 offensive in El
Salvador. Shortly after the coup attempt, broad coalitions in civil society joined
forces in the National Consensus Body (INC) to call for a negotiated end to the civil
war. The INC laid the basis for the creation in 1994 of the Civil Society Assembly
(ASC). As was shown in the previous chapter, the coup altered the political balance
in Guatemala in favour of civil society and created conditions for the final round
of peace negotiations in early 1994, marking the start of mid-transition. European
private aid agencies played an important role in this period by lobbying the
international community together with Guatemalan human rights organisations to
advocate a return to constitutional rule and to resume the peace negotiations. Most
organisations active in the ASC received direct support from European private aid
agencies, although these Guatemalan counterparts (like in El Salvador) also were
confronted with stricter criteria by private aid agencies. The difference was that

Guatemalan organisations experienced these adaptations *prior* to the peace negoti-ations. After all, when Guatemala's mid-transition was initiated in 1994, Honduras and El Salvador were already moving into the stage of late democratic transition.

After 1993, strengthening civil society – in particular the most vulnerable sectors such as women's organisations and indigenous communities – became a priority issue for private aid agencies in Guatemala, even if this had been a *de facto* policy already since the late 1980s. The difference was that the role of intermediary development NGOs in civil society building was increasingly questioned in the mid-1990s. Large flows of private aid had been channelled with few conditions through these historic NGOs to rural communities, in which support was based on personal relationships and mutual confidence. There had been little control over the use of these funds, nor was it possible to evaluate their results. Although even more 'tacitly' than in El Salvador, part of this aid had been channelled to the armed opposition, which was facilitated by the absence of transparent bookkeeping and a lack of internal accountability (Umaña *et al.* 1996). But verticalist structures and undemocratic practices, in addition to a lack of professional capacity inside development NGOs, started to be an issue of concern for private aid agencies. It forced Guatemala's historic NGOs (as the main recipients of European private aid) to review past practices and to improve working methods and internal organisation structures. They gradually became convinced of the need for (sometimes radical) changes 'to realise more impact with fewer resources' (Garoz *et al.* 1996: 195).

One of these necessary changes for the historic NGOs was to develop a closer relationship with Guatemalan state institutions, especially at the level of munici-palities, although considerable mutual distrust had to be overcome. Since 1989 the AID-funded NGO network ASINDES had been involved in governmental plans, stimulated by the World Bank, to create a Guatemalan Social Investment Fund (FIS).[103] However, the fund was only formally established in 1993 due to political discussions about its focus and critique by ASINDES over the lack of NGO influence on the policy-making process (Garst 1993). Meanwhile, a special National Peace Fund (FONAPAZ) had been created by the Serrano government in 1991 in anticipa-tion of external aid flows aimed at post-war reconstruction. FONAPAZ was particu-larly meant to coordinate social programmes for the uprooted population in (former) conflict zones, implemented either by municipal and national government institutions or by NGOs, and to exercise greater governmental control over external aid flows to these areas.[104] Apparently, the historic NGOs working with the uprooted considered FONAPAZ as a governmental instrument for political propaganda and refused to collaborate in order not to be identified with the government and the armed forces. This attitude was changing in 1993, when ASINDES, COINDE and three other NGO coalitions decided to set up the Forum of NGO Coalitions to work out joint proposals for NGO-government collaboration, particularly in the frame-work of the more autonomous FIS. This shift towards increased policy advocacy also was visible in the active role this NGO forum took in the ASC during the peace negotiations.

Another development that forced Guatemalan NGOs to adapt their strategies was the growth of independent popular organisations in civil society, particularly among the Indian population. As will be seen in Chapter 6, the new political space after 1993 was efficiently used by several coalitions of Maya organisations who during the peace talks advocated a long-term solution to the political, cultural and socio-economic marginalisation of the Indian majority. The historic NGOs thus had to change their role as intermediaries for foreign aid and the moral representatives of marginalised groups towards becoming professional service-delivery organisations responding to the criteria and priorities of organised sectors in civil society. It implied a shift of emphasis from upward accountability to donors towards downward accountability to beneficiaries. Simultaneously, donor agencies wanted to prevent the conversion of popular organisations into institutions essentially performing an intermediary role as service providers; the quality criteria for civil society building strategies (diversity, internal democracy, mutual coordination) apparently became more important than simply increasing the number and size of organisations (Umaña *et al.* 1996).

Consequently, during the peace negotiations, several European private aid agencies decided to phase out their support to the 'traditional' opposition-related organisations, such as GAM, CONAVIGUA and CONFREGUA. The focus shifted towards supporting newly emerging popular organisations and to the local *comités cívicos* which put up (Indian) candidates for the 1995 municipal elections. Indirect support also was given to the new progressive opposition party FDNG, which would gain several seats in parliament, most of them going to popular leaders of organisations such as GAM and CONAVIGUA that had been supported by European private aid agencies since the mid 1980s. Still, the major part of private foreign aid during the stage of mid-transition was allocated to human rights organisations, resettlement of refugees and the displaced, rural community development programmes and (more generally) to activities related to the peace process. The increased role of multilateral funding agencies (IDB, UNDP, EU, World Bank) and the allocation of bilateral funding to activities traditionally supported by private aid agencies, forced the latter to rethink their aid policies for the post-war setting in Guatemala.[105] Based on the Salvadorean experience, it was expected that the final peace agreement of 1996 would generate huge flows of external (official) aid for reconstruction programmes. But the post-war donations for reconstruction aid turned out to be far less than had been hoped (Spence *et al.* 1998). With the last civil war in Central America concluded, the region definitely had lost the preferential status of the international donor community.

– *Compatibility between official and private aid*
The prominent role of European private aid agencies during Central America's early transitions of the late 1980s thus appeared to be seriously limited during mid-transitions by the overwhelming bilateral and multilateral aid flows that accompanied post-war reconstruction programmes. But private aid agencies also were

constrained by their own shifts in policy priorities and project implementation requirements emerging in the 1990s. Their role in mounting international diplomatic pressure to reach successful peace agreements certainly was and continues to be important. But in terms of building organisational capacity in civil society, new multilateral programmes such as PRODERE have proven to be equally effective and demonstrate that this is no longer an exclusive role for private aid agencies (O'Brien and Catenacci 1996). The levels of European private aid funding remained considerable, especially on the eve of the 1994 Salvadorean elections (to contribute to a strong positioning of the FMLN in political society) and in the last phase of the Guatemalan peace negotiations. But given the difficult 'conversion' of Central America's historic NGOs to the post-war setting, which was also due to considerable dependency on private aid, the question arises whether private aid agencies still have a role to play in Central America's (incomplete) democratic transitions, or whether they have lost their comparative advantages to official aid agencies.

The practice of the late 1990s suggests that opposing visions exist concerning strategies to contribute to civil society building. The general view of multilateral agencies such as the World Bank and IDB is to give a prominent role to the market to combat poverty, to increase citizens' participation at local levels and to scale down the role of central governments while also trying to make them more efficient. The key actors that are supported in civil society are the private sector NGOs, which respond to market demands and are controlled by a small business elite which has a long tradition of exclusion. As Foley (1996) and others have pointed out, this is probably not leading to a healthy civil society and might even reawaken polarisation in a society based on social inequality. Despite the tendency towards depolarisation in civil society during the mid and late transition stages, in which it was no longer unusual for the historic NGOs to accept funding from AID, a top-down market-led development model could turn out to be incompatible with a more inclusive approach of civil society building in which the state plays a regulating role to guarantee more equal income distribution. This view is shared by a minority of official European donors, which have shown the willingness and the potential for counterbalancing the market-oriented approach. European private aid agencies thus could either choose to compete with these official donors, or to complement them by trying to guarantee that their governments pursue strategies aimed at supporting inclusive civil societies. Although private aid agencies in practice try to find a balance between these two options, it is unlikely that they will regain their prominent role in contributing to civil society building in Central America unless the situation deteriorates similar to what happened during the 1980s.

5.5 Agents of an informal diplomacy

It would be unfair to ignore the distinctions among European private aid agencies and the diversity of intervention strategies they have pursued during Central America's democratic transitions. The next chapter will highlight some of these dissimilarities in more detail on the basis of individual interventions. But as a category, European private aid agencies certainly have exhibited many commonalties. When they first arrived in Central America in the late 1970s, their emphasis was on emergency aid to provide relief for victims of natural disasters. It was essentially 'assistantialist' and did not directly contribute to longer term solutions to poverty and political repression. But having witnessed the magnitude of the social and political emergencies because of their presence in the disaster zones, many agencies decided to stay in the region and to work with local churches and church-related organisations. It was in this work that private aid agencies were confronted with the dominating presence of organisations linked to US counter-insurgency programmes. In this period several agencies established contacts with revolutionary organisations. After the Sandinista victory in 1979, a large number of private aid agencies and solidarity groups poured into Nicaragua to support the reconstruction of a war-torn society and to contribute to the ideals of an alternative development model that was socialist-inspired but economically independent from the Soviet bloc. Nicaragua became a laboratory for new participatory and human-centred development methodologies in a period of increasing private aid flows. The role for private aid agencies in these years, in which 'anything was possible', was to bear the 'solidarity banner' of a progressive constituency in Europe and Canada (and partly also in the United States), acting as a vanguard of a generation that had been politicised during the Vietnam War and consciously supported the anti-imperialist discourse of the Sandinistas with 'solidarity aid'. Due to the attention for Nicaragua, the political struggles in El Salvador and Guatemala soon also would receive international attention and direct support from a broad array of progressive constituencies.

Particularly during the first half of the 1980s, European private aid agencies provided a shield of protection to the persecuted opposition forces in Honduras, El Salvador and Guatemala. By supporting organisations in civil society (such as churches and human rights groups) that were able and willing to serve as legal shelters for groups that needed to hide from political repression, private aid agencies contributed to the temporary survival of the progressive opposition during the years of authoritarian rule and US low intensity warfare. When repression eased after the installation of civilian governments, newly emerging coalitions of popular organisations would broaden this shield-function to include organisations that had re-emerged from the underground. Tacitly, support for these alliances also implied (indirect) support for the struggles of revolutionary movements. After the Esqui-pulas peace agreement broadened political space for the opposition, the first groups of refugees (and part of the internally displaced populations) would return to the zones of conflict in which new settlements had been constructed. These zones were generally controlled by revolutionary movements, which used a network of local development NGOs to acquire international resources for their struggle. In the new settlements the seeds for a new society were cultivated with active support from European private aid agencies. They actively contributed to incorporating marginalised sectors into civil society, particularly during the last years of early transitions: in El Salvador between 1984 and 1989, and in Guatemala between 1988 and 1993.

Throughout the Central American crisis many private aid agencies acted as agents of an 'informal diplomacy' by providing transnational political space for local organisations of the opposition in international fora such as the United Nations and the European Union. Although often operating with a 'megaphone' and seldom achieving legal status as observers or representatives, this international advocacy role was crucial in protecting the lives of local opposition leaders and returning refugees in areas dominated by the armed forces. This informal diplomacy also served to stimulate peace negotiations at an early stage and, in the early 1990s, to keep Central America on the agenda of the international donor community. European private aid agencies also were important as aid channels for those official donor agencies that were reluctant to directly support military-controlled regimes in the region. Private aid agencies often acted as 'scouts' for these official agencies and influenced their policy priorities after the region had become *salon-fähig* for bilateral and multilateral interventions in the late 1980s. Due to European pressure, funds of CIREFCA (the special UN programme for refugees) were partly channelled through the historic NGOs. The downside of the scouting role was an unintended consequence: many traditional partners of European private aid agencies in the 1990s gradually started to receive bilateral and multilateral funding, seriously reducing the prominent role that private aid agencies had performed throughout the Central American crisis. What they effectively have achieved with their civil society building interventions will be examined in the next chapter.

6 FOUR AID CHAINS IN CENTRAL AMERICA

Assessing Civil Society Building Performance

The dynamics of civil society building with private foreign aid resources will now be analysed in more detail by examining several aid chains in Central America. The analysis of individual aid chains is an essential (but given their singular character certainly not ideal) method for drawing broader conclusions about the achievements of private aid interventions aimed at speeding up democratic transitions. There are many risks involved, some of which were already mentioned in Chapter 3. Two appear to be critical. One is the risk of downplaying the importance of unique local context variables; aid chains primarily dealing with civil society building therefore should be carefully analysed within the specific socio-political context of national democratic transitions. The other risk is the temptation to generalise findings of individual (and unique) aid chains towards overall agency impact. Too often, aid performance assessments have been based on anecdotical evidence which in the end appeared to be either poorly researched or even underpinned the opposite of what had actually been intended to be proven. A careful selection and analysis of case studies in which the unique nature of each intervention is preserved but which simultaneously offers opportunities for broader generalisations is therefore a key challenge.

Four criteria were used to select a number of case studies for assessing the role of private aid agencies during democratic transitions in Central America: the character of intervention, the level of perceived success, geographical distribution and the length of intervention. By discussing these criteria it will become clear why they have been used. Five intervention strategies that contribute to civil society building were identified in previous chapters: strengthening organisational capacity, fostering alliances between societal actors, strengthening intermediary channels in civil society, providing access to transnational political space and contributing to building citizenship. It was argued that some intervention strategies might be applied simultaneously, often in combination with poverty alleviation strategies. The central criterion for selecting the Central American case studies was that the aid chains contain a primary component of any of these five civil society building strategies. As the stages of early and mid-transition were central to the analysis, it was obvious that the focus should be on those intervention strategies that are most appropriate to these two stages. Consequently, organisations were selected when they emphasised either fostering alliances or strengthening intermediary channels, preferably with a component of international advocacy.

A second selection criterion was that organisations be perceived by donors (and also by local experts) as 'outstanding performers'. At first sight, this might seem a controversial point as it would automatically bias the assessment towards 'success stories'. But as was explained in Chapter 3, by selecting relatively successful organisations outcome and impact can be expected to be more clear and easier to determine. An additional advantage is that well-performing organisations usually have clearer objectives which are not continuously changing over time. The problem is, however, how to define 'success'. Private aid agencies were therefore requested to list those Central American counterparts that in their perception, based on recent and qualified external evaluations, had been 'fairly successful' in meeting their immediate objectives. An advantage of this method was that the use of evaluation reports provided valuable reference material for the impact analysis, as they often contained key baseline data.

Since the entire Central American region is the geographical focus of the research, choices had to be made about which countries to select for case study analysis. As was explained earlier, I decided to take more than one country in order to facilitate comparative analysis and increase the validity of the final conclusions. This was also logical from a (European) donor perspective, in which Central America is commonly categorised as a regional entity. However, choosing five or even seven countries (if Panama and Belize are included) would have been too ambitious. Three countries were therefore selected in which private aid interventions have been primarily concerned with civil society building and contributing to democratic transition: Honduras, El Salvador and Guatemala. It was also decided to include 'regional civil society networks' in the analysis, as these important counterparts of private aid agencies have performed a key role in linking up national civil society coalitions at the Central American level.

A final selection criterion was that the organisations had depended for the majority of their income on financial support from European private aid agencies for a substantial period of time, preferably starting in the 1980s and embracing at least two transition stages. The reason for choosing this long time frame was in order to get a better understanding of the relation between aid interventions and democratic transitions, but also because impact was defined earlier as 'sustainable social change over a longer period of time'. An additional advantage of trying to find aid interventions that had started in the 1980s was that this could contribute to understanding the impact of the 'political watershed' in Central America of 1989-90 on the dynamics of private aid interventions.

These four criteria were discussed with fifteen major private aid agencies in Europe. On the basis of this survey, a shortlist was made of eight organisations, all well known in the Central American region.[1] During preliminary fieldwork, all the organisations were visited and consulted about their ability and willingness to participate in the present study. Several major private aid donors of each organisation also were requested to contribute to the study by providing documents and other key background information. Finally, the shortlist was reduced to four organisations, based on a number of practical criteria: the availability of sources, the willingness to collaborate, the diversity of private aid agencies involved, the diversity of aid intervention strategies, and the feasibility of realising fieldwork. As a result, the following four case studies are presented in this chapter: the Honduran human rights organisation CODEH, the Salvadorean peace alliance CPDN, the Guatemalan indigenous development NGO FUNDADESE and the regional network of peasant organisations ASOCODE.[2]

6.1 Defending human rights in Honduras: CODEH

During the 1980s, the Honduran human rights committee CODEH was the public face of the excluded opposition in Honduras. Or as one observer asserted, CODEH not only symbolised the opposition to military rule and occupation by foreign troops, it *was* in fact the only opposition.[3] CODEH often is mentioned in one breath with the name of one of its founders who has served as president ever since: Ramón Custodio. A medical doctor, Custodio, together with four other intellectuals, was alarmed by the increased militarisation of Honduras starting in 1981, a by-product of the US response to civil wars in neighbouring countries.[4] Their concern about the sudden rise in human rights violations eventually led in 1983 to the foundation of the Committee for the Defence of Human Rights in Honduras (CODEH).

The newly-elected Reagan administration decided in 1981 to convert Honduras into a buffer zone for US-led counter-insurgency operations to support the Salvadorean army in their struggle against the FMLN and to destabilise the Sandinista government in Nicaragua by arming and training counter-revolutionary forces. The US embassy in Tegucigalpa was upgraded under the leadership of Ambassador Negroponte, a diplomat with long-standing experience in counter-insurgency warfare. Deployment of several hundred US military advisers was combined with huge increases in military aid, making Honduras the second highest recipient of US military assistance in Latin America by 1982. Critics ironically spoke of the 'Pentagon republic' (Lapper and Painter 1985). In 1980, General Gustavo Alvarez Martínez was appointed commander of the national police forces FUSEP, automatically becoming the chief of the intelligence branch DNI. General Alvarez was an anti-communist hardliner, known for his admiration of the Argentinian military rulers and a firm supporter of the National Security military doctrine. The Reagan administration considered him to be a reliable partner in its plan to reshape Honduras into a military stronghold for low intensity warfare in Central America. Alvarez developed a close relationship with Roberto Suazo Córdova, Liberal Party candidate for the 1981 presidential elections. After Suazo was elected, Alvarez Martínez not only became the new commander-in-chief of the armed forces, but also managed to marginalise his main military rivals.

The trinity Negroponte-Alvarez-Suazo (in that order)[5] virtually ruled Honduras over the next two years, a period in which human rights violations rapidly increased. As chief of the national intelligence service DNI Alvarez had been responsible for persecuting Salvadorean refugees allegedly linked to the FMLN. His philosophy (inspired by his training in Argentina) was based on 'decapitation': destroying 'subversive movements' by eliminating their (potential) leaders. The first clandestine cemetery was discovered in September 1981, with bodies that had been previously tortured. Reports on selective disappearances, systematic torture and political assassinations by death squads and military officers suggested that the (Argentinian-style) National Security Doctrine had been officially adopted. Selective repression of Honduran political activists was combined with collective repression against militant popular organisations (Funes 1995). It seemed paradoxical: the start of a democratically-elected government was paralleled by a sudden increase in human rights violations.

– Activities of CODEH

In this atmosphere of US-led militarisation of Honduran society, combined with counter-insurgency operations against political and popular organisations, two human rights organisations were founded: CODEH and COFADEH, the committee of families of the detained-disappeared. Both organisations denounced human rights violations committed by the national security forces FUSEP, the national intelligence agency DNI and the death squad *Batallon 3-16*. This battalion was set up by Alvarez in the late 1970s as a special department of investigations and was converted in 1981 into an instrument for kidnapping political opponents who were interrogated in clandestine prisons and often 'disappeared'. A special section of *Batallon 3-16* was recruited from former members of Somoza's National Guard and trained by Argentinian military advisers with CIA support. The worst human rights abuses of the 1980s in Honduras were attributed to this death squad, which could flourish with impunity in a militarised society with tacit US approval.[6]

CODEH documented and denounced these violations to the security forces, to the US embassy and to the judiciary, but they generally refused to take appropriate action. Therefore, international organisations were informed and with press conferences and street protests CODEH tried to speak out in public against these human rights abuses. In its early years, CODEH operated as a small and informal committee publishing a weekly bulletin and putting advertisements in local newspapers. In this period, Custodio was the only publicly visible member of CODEH in order to reduce the risk of retaliation. The worst abuses occurred between 1981 and 1984, the period in which General Alvarez was commander-in-chief.[7] In late 1983 CODEH was formally founded as a committee, although the government refused to accept its legal status until the mid-1990s. The idea of a permanent national committee was earlier launched by the Jesuit priest Padre Guadalupe, who had founded several local human rights groups linked to the Church.[8] This network of local human rights groups would form the basis of the institutionalised CODEH, which opened a small office in the Honduran capital Tegucigalpa.

After 1984, the activities of CODEH were extended from documenting and denouncing human rights violations to providing legal assistance and developing educational activities on human rights. An assembly elected a national directorate for two years, of which for security reasons only the president (Custodio) and the vice-president would be publicly known. In 1985 a lawyer was employed to provide legal assistance. With support from private foreign aid additional staff-members were appointed to manage CODEH's main activities: documentation, press conferences, legal assistance, human rights education and publications (including audio-visual productions). The number of local committees rapidly increased from a few dozen in the early 1980s to over 150 groups nationwide in the mid-1990s. However, the total number of employed staff remained relatively limited: from a handful in the 1980s to 24 in 1996. Regional offices were opened in several departments in the early 1990s to service these local groups. Many local committees were run by priests, nuns and lay-priests, although the hierarchy of the Catholic Church refused to work with CODEH. The bishops generally took sides with the armed forces and Custodio was considered to be a communist radical who abused CODEH for his 'subversive political purposes'. Although Custodio never concealed that he was an advocate of progressive change in Honduras, his strongest tactical weapon was probably that he carefully prevented CODEH from losing its independence by refusing to link it to any political party.

The existence of local human rights committees in virtually all major municipalities in the country, linked to the national office in Tegucigalpa, meant that CODEH was better organised than any other organisation of the opposition. These committees often consisted of a combination of local community leaders and local lay-priests, so-called *celebradores de la palabra.*[9] As they were elected by the community, these committees had a certain legitimacy but (for security reasons) still kept a low public profile. The Honduran bishops, aware of local collaboration by priests with CODEH, at some point in the mid-1980s tried to establish parallel Church human rights groups at parish level. But they soon discovered that this initiative would only further legitimise CODEH, as local parishes were the building blocks of the committee. A separate Church organisation for defending human rights as emerged in neighbouring countries therefore remained absent in Honduras.

Local human rights groups performed several functions for CODEH. They served as an antenna for detecting local human rights violations, which were reported to the main office or denounced to local authorities. For this purpose CODEH trained members to become *procuradores populares*. Another function was to improve the knowledge of local communities about their political and civil rights. Additionally, those communities most affected by the abuses of local security forces started to become better organised. There existed, however, a considerable gap between the national committee and these local groups, who were barely represented at the national level and complained about the lack of feedback, information and resources. The strict hierarchy of CODEH resulted in a serious crisis in 1989 when a majority of the staff members left the organisation after disagreements with Custodio about his centralised way of leading the organisation. In response, CODEH was reorganised: six regional assemblies were founded in the early 1990s, each with their own office, to bridge the gap between the national and the local committees. More volunteers joined the organisation and the main office gradually came to be staffed by professionals.

— *Private foreign aid to CODEH*

Since its foundation in 1981 CODEH has depended on financial support from private aid agencies, mostly from Europe. The *World Council of Churches* was the first to support CODEH. After the office was opened in 1984 the *Ford Foundation* financed the development of a documentation centre and later the Central American human rights work of CODEHUCA (of which Custodio also was a president in the 1980s). Due to CODEH's close relationship with the Catholic Church at local levels, several European church-related private aid agencies decided to support CODEH's activities after the mid-1980s. Among them were *Christian Aid, Brot für die Welt,* CEBEMO, *Danchurchaid,* HEKS and *Diakonia.* The only non-church organisations supporting CODEH were the *Ford Foundation* and OXFAM-UK/I.[10] In the 1990s support also was received from official agencies, such as the European Union and the Dutch ministry for development cooperation. The Dutch agency CEBEMO (renamed *Bilance* in 1996) has been one of CODEH's major funders since 1985 and therefore has been selected for closer examination.[11]

CEBEMO started supporting CODEH because of recommendations from Jesuits working with local human rights groups.[12] They claimed that CODEH was a vital national channel for coordinating the denunciations of human rights violations and making these public to national and international bodies. Initially, CEBEMO only financed selected activities of CODEH (audio-visual department, press and publication department), but decided after some years to also provide institutional support. Respect throughout the country for his integrity and the international fame of Custodio (who had received various human rights awards) gave CEBEMO a 'low-risk warranty', even though CODEH's lack of administrative capacity was, given the large number of foreign funders and the diversity of their activities, admitted to be one of its weaknesses. But CEBEMO argued that CODEH played a crucial role in Honduras, not only by denouncing human rights violations, but also by organising workshops and training courses to make people aware of their basic political and civil rights. CEBEMO considered CODEH to be the most important opponent to military impunity by effectively documenting human rights abuses at the local level (churches, peasant unions, women's organisations) and channelling this material to the national level.[13]

CEBEMO's role as external funder was perceived as positive by CODEH. Contrary to some other agencies that had put conditions upon them, such as more participation of women in leading positions or more transparency in financial reports, CEBEMO generally did not want to interfere in internal policy discussions.[14] By accepting the broad framework of CODEH's structure and policies, CEBEMO was a passive provider of financial resources. Only because of policy restrictions by the

Dutch government did the agency have to turn down requests to finance second and third generation human rights activities, which were started by CODEH in the early 1990s. *Diakonia*, the other major funder of CODEH, took a more active position by searching for ways to improve the organisational structure and the financial sustainability of the committee. But this was a difficult task, as will be shown later.

— *Achievements of CODEH*

The major achievement of CODEH was that it managed to break the silence in Honduras about disappearances, political assassinations, torture, abuse of power by security forces and the absence of justice. More generally, it managed to reveal the shortcomings of the political and judicial system. To use White's (1994) terms, CODEH performed civil society's 'disciplinary role' *vis-à-vis* the Honduran state. It proved with numerous cases that an elected government tolerated impunity and that democratic elections had not automatically contributed to democratising the political system. CODEH served as the unofficial opposition during the 1980s and it offered legal and moral protection to those popular sectors that were persecuted by the armed forces, intelligence services, foreign military advisers and *contras*. As journalist Manuel Torres observes: 'CODEH has been an independent pressure group, a voice looking beyond current events and guiding us towards what should be the great objectives of consolidating civil society in our country.'[15]

CODEH's central goals throughout its existence have been to educate the Honduran people in defending and promoting human rights,[16] to promote the defence of these rights without distinguishing between race, political ideas, social conditions or engaging in other forms of discrimination, and to work against impunity of human rights violators. There is no doubt that CODEH has been quite successful in all three areas. Numerous examples can be given of CODEH's achievements: disappeared persons that reappeared due to CODEH's pressure, military officers who were successfully charged and convicted in trials, and thousands of Hondurans that were trained in human rights workshops, to name a few. But what was accomplished with these activities? Did they contribute to strengthening (or as Torres argues, to 'consolidating') civil society? Did the 'watchdog' role of CODEH influence the balance between the state and civil society? And did CODEH eventually surpass its disciplinary role by simultaneously playing a (temporary) intermediary role in political society by mobilising the Honduran opposition? Before addressing these questions, it can be helpful to look at two key examples in which CODEH managed to discipline the Honduran state, especially the armed forces.

The first example is a legal case of the 1980s against the Honduran state to determine its responsibility for the disappeared, which was presented by CODEH to the Inter-American Commission of Human Rights.[17] The victims were Manfredo Velásquez and Saúl Godínez, two Honduran trade union activists who disappeared in the early 1980s after having been arrested by security forces.[18] As their relatives had been unsuccessful in getting legal confirmation of their arrests, they turned to

CODEH who filed petitions to the Inter-American Commission of Human Rights to investigate these cases. Requests from the Commission to the Honduran government to provide information and to investigate the cases were not satisfactorily handled. Therefore, in 1986 the Commission submitted the cases to the Inter-American Court of Human Rights. The trial that followed was unique, as it was the first time that a government was brought before a court on charges of death squad activity. The Court heard a large number of witnesses in relation to disappearances between 1981 and 1984. One witness was a former interrogator of the *Batallon 3-16* death squad, who confirmed the existence of clandestine prisons to interrogate and torture suspects of subversive activity.[19] Kidnappings had been selectively and well prepared, using civilian vehicles with tinted glass and false license plates. The testimonies made clear that the government systematically had denied detentions and that no formal arrest warrants had been issued (Hydén 1996). During the hearings in late 1987, CODEH members received several death threats and posters with their photographs appeared in the streets with the text 'promoters of subversion'. Custodio, who was also heard as a witness, publicly denounced the existence of a plan to kill him. Ten days later, the vice-president of CODEH, Miguel Angel Pavón (who also testified before the Court) was assassinated by a death squad.[20]

In July 1988 the Inter-American Court of Human Rights ruled that the government of Honduras had been responsible for the disappearance of Velásquez. The same conclusion was reached in the Godínez case, six months later.[21] The Court found that enough evidence was presented to conclude that between 100 and 150 persons had disappeared in Honduras in 1981-84, and that this had been a deliberate and systematic policy carried out by the Honduran security forces.[22] The government of Honduras was sentenced to compensate the relatives of the disappeared, to investigate all other forced disappearances of the 1980s and to identify and punish those responsible. The sentence of the Court was a precedent in international law for it was the first time ever that a government was convicted for deliberately 'disappearing' its citizens. In January 1989, a few days after the Court ruled in the Godínez case, retired General Alvarez Martínez (responsible for the systemic disappearances in the early 1980s) was assassinated in Tegucigalpa. Although the government blamed the murder on the left-wing opposition, the professional way in which the execution was carried out suggested a revenge by his former colleagues.[23]

The unprecedented sentences handed down by the Inter-American Court were a major success for CODEH. The Azcona government, the armed forces and the US embassy were of course very unhappy with this outcome, and Custodio continued to be threatened as he was held responsible for the wave of violence and killings that followed the Court ruling. Presidential candidate Callejas promised an amnesty for military officers who had been involved in human rights violations, which was effectively decreed in 1991 after his election. Nevertheless, gradual changes became visible during the early 1990s in the Honduran judicial system. A national Commissioner for the Protection of Human Rights was appointed by the government in

1992 to monitor human rights violations. Similar ombudsmen had been installed in neighbouring countries as part of the Esquipulas peace plan. The Honduran Commissioner Leo Valladares published a report in which 179 disappearances since 1980 were documented (Comisonado 1994). It was the first time the government officially admitted its responsibility for the disappearances. A special prosecutor for human rights was appointed in 1995 to investigate these cases, followed by 'exhumations' of the disappeared. Although the new political context was conducive for these achievements, they could be largely attributed to CODEH's active campaign against impunity which was not paralleled in any other Central American country.[24]

The second example in which CODEH (together with several other organisations) played a prominent role in defending human rights is the 'Riccy Mabel case'. It started in July 1991 when an anonymous phone call led to the discovery of the dead body of a 17-year old girl, with signs of torture and rape. The victim was identified as Riccy Mabel Martínez, a student who had visited a military base two days earlier to request the release of her boyfriend from military service. Up to that point, Riccy seemed to be just another (female) victim of a cruel homicide by common criminals that had been shocking Honduran society for over a decade.[25] However, fellow-students were convinced that army base commander Colonel Castillo, and possibly other senior officers at the military base, had been involved in Riccy's violation and execution.[26] A witness declared that he had seen her leaving the base, where she received a ride from an non-military vehicle.

The next day, two thousand students demanding justice marched to the Supreme Court building, where CODEH's president Custodio addressed the crowd and urged military and judicial authorities to conduct a transparent investigation and to bring the assassins to trial. Meanwhile, a military spokesman quickly rejected the possibility of military involvement in the cruel homicide, and denounced press reports (which did suggest this involvement) as part of a campaign to discredit the armed forces. Similar declarations by the chief of the armed forces, General Discua, only added to the suspicion that top military officers were responsible.[27] Five days after the murder, Sergeant Ilovares 'voluntarily' presented himself to the investigating judge and confessed that he alone had committed the homicide. But Ilovares's declarations were full of contradictions and he soon admitted that he had been pressured by his superiors to plead guilty, in order to protect others. Even so, a spokesman for the investigating police forces FUSEP declared that he considered the case to be resolved, and that it was proven that no superior army officer had been involved. Gradually it became clear that military officers were indeed involved and that the armed forces had tried to cover up the case, just as they had done in previous murders over many years.

Relatives of Mabel turned to CODEH for legal support and requested that the military officers under suspicion be subjected to DNA tests. A civilian judge ordered the arrests of Colonel Castillo and Captain Andino, two high-ranking officers at the military base, but the National Police Commander refused to effectuate this warrant. He asserted that a civilian judge had no jurisdiction over active military officers and that they would be tried by a military tribunal.[28] CODEH proclaimed publicly that the Supreme Court of Justice was now confronted with a historical decision that would show where the real power resided in Honduras: with the military or with the civilian authorities. After mediation by the US ambassador, civilian and military judicial authorities agreed to initiate a combined investigation, in which the FBI would examine DNA samples of the suspects and the victim. Six weeks after the crime Colonel Castillo and Captain Andino 'voluntarily' retired from military service and were sent to prison, finally opening the way for a civilian trial.

The court case that followed was exceptional. It was the first time ever that senior military officers were tried by a civilian judge in Honduras. It was also the first time the US embassy fully endorsed a trial against military officers, which illustrated that the tide was turning in Honduras.[29] The combination of an innocent female student from a poor family who was brutally raped and killed by military officers, and the awkward efforts by the armed forces to frustrate a transparent trial, turned the Riccy Mabel case into a symbol of the struggle against military impunity. Street protests in various cities by student, women's and human rights organisations to rally against impunity showed that the silent majority of civil society had lost its fear of the armed forces. The Honduran mass media were instrumental in the construction of a combative public opinion against military impunity by sustaining a constant stream of information on the trial and publishing every detail of new evidence provided by CODEH and the lawyer during press conferences. An editorial in the daily newspaper *El Tiempo* welcomed the 'valuable and critical participation of different sectors of civil society [...] as the only way to safeguard the confidence of the people in our judicial system'.[30]

In July 1993, Colonel Castillo was sentenced to sixteen-and-a-half years imprisonment for the rape and murder of Riccy Mabel, while Sergeant Ilovares was condemned to ten-and-a-half years for murder.[31] The DNA tests had served as the main evidence against both officers. All the national newspapers published what they called 'the historical sentence' against top military officials. The *fuero militar*, in which the armed forces managed their own system of justice, was falling apart.[32] Shortly before the judgement, Congress restricted military jurisdiction only to crimes committed by military officers in active service, thus enabling civilian jurisdiction over common crimes committed by the military. The military-led intelligence service DNI was abolished and replaced by a civilian-controlled body for criminal investigations. A year later, Congress amended the constitution to abolish forced military recruitment after strong pressure by popular organisations. In 1995 it was decided to bring the military-led security forces FUSEP under civilian control. What remained unresolved, however, was the prosecution of those responsible for disappearances and other human rights violations in the 1980s.

CODEH's role in breaking the silence on disappearances in Honduras and overcoming the widespread fear in civil society of the armed forces is well illustrated by the previous two examples. During early transition, CODEH performed a disciplinary role within civil society *vis-à-vis* the state, a 'watchdog' role, as it was the main voice of opposition to the armed forces and US military presence during the 1980s. By systematically denouncing human rights violations, CODEH managed to break the silence about the internal situation in Honduras in a period in which international attention focused overwhelmingly on Nicaragua and El Salvador. CODEH was not liked by the US State Department as it transmitted denunciations via international human rights groups and private aid agencies to the international media, thereby accusing the Reagan administration of tolerating military impunity.[33] The successful outcome of the Inter-American Court cases increased CODEH's international recognition, but more important, it also boosted its national profile. The armed forces, the government and the US embassy could no longer ignore the existence of human rights violations in Honduras.

When the tide was turning in Central America in late 1989, and US policy gradually changed to post-Cold War rhetoric, civil society in Honduras started to 'open up'. Peasant organisations and trade unions rallied against the neoliberal austerity measures of the new Callejas government with an alliance established in the *Plataforma de lucha*. Although it virtually paralysed the country with national strikes in June 1990, the *Plataforma* never managed to consolidate itself as an intermediary alliance in political society. Despite temporary unification of the marginal left-wing parties, ideological and personal differences soon dominated this promising initiative that presented an alternative programme to the neoliberal policies pursued by the two traditional political parties. CODEH kept its distance from the *Plataforma de lucha* as Custodio considered it to be a 'limited project'.[34] The fact that other initiatives to forge concerted action between popular sectors – such as the Coalition of Popular Organisations (CCOP) – had been marginal or unstable, gave more prominence to CODEH's actions on human rights issues.

Despite the existence of a nationwide network of local committees and broadly supported demands to stop military impunity, during the stage of mid-transition CODEH did not really play a pronounced intermediary role in political society on this issue, not even in the Riccy Mabel case which had generated the broadest public rejection of military impunity since the 1980s. One of the obstacles was that Custodio was reluctant to share the coordination of the movement against impunity with other organisations in civil society, such as student and women's associations who took the lead in street protests and public mobilisations.[35] While civil society was opening up and had lost its fear in the trials against the top military officers, CODEH was unable to change its function after the leading role it had played in the 1980s. From a voice of the opposition, it was not prepared to transform itself into a broader alliance of societal actors. CODEH even feared losing its traditional watchdog function, given Custodio's negative reactions upon the installation of the governmental Commissioner for Human Rights (the ombudsman) in late 1992.[36]

In 1993 the Honduran democratic transition was about to enter the stage of late transition. It was the year of presidential elections, in which disappearances and military impunity became key electoral issues.[37] A consensus emerged on the need to reform judicial and police institutions, and shortly after the elections the official report on disappearances was published. The election of President Reina (a personal friend of Custodio) in late 1993 marked the beginning of a period in which a range of key reforms were effectuated. CODEH was granted legal status, which had been repeatedly rejected by previous governments.[38] CODEH's working style had gradually changed from public protest and legal action to policy reform and quiet diplomacy. Custodio envisaged transforming CODEH into a 'civic movement' acting as a 'moral pressure group' on a range of human rights issues.[39] He considered CODEH to no longer be part of the opposition. Instead, he preferred to work more closely with the government, although this transformation from a persecuted watchdog in the 1980s to a legalised advisory group in the 1990s proved to be a difficult process. One problem was that Custodio refused to democratise the internal structure of CODEH. Another was that the government's Human Rights Commissioner was gradually taking over many tasks previously handled by CODEH.

In sum, CODEH played a major role until 1989, and to a lesser extent up to 1993. Its systematic denunciations undoubtedly contributed to restricting the power of the military and brought the issues of disappearances, extrajudicial killings and impunity to the top of the national political agenda of the 1990s. CODEH's active role in the first Ad Hoc Commission, which made recommendations to the government on police and judiciary reforms, was a logical and successful follow-up to these denunciations. By effectively limiting the autonomous powers of the armed forces, new space was indirectly created for civil society. However, CODEH was reluctant to take the lead in translating these new opportunities into the forging of alliances of societal actors to open up space in political society. CODEH's crucial political role clearly diminished during the period of late transition, which was partly due to internal frictions, as will be analysed below.

– CODEH in the aid chain

CODEH's success in restricting military power can be attributed for a considerable part to the charismatic leadership of Ramón Custodio. He personified the struggle for the defence of human rights in Honduras, and it was no coincidence that the armed forces declared him as their number one enemy. Despite numerous death threats and attempts to eliminate Custodio, he continued his verbal attacks on the military hierarchy when the rest of civil society observed a fearful silence. By combining political instinct, courage and stubbornness, Custodio built CODEH into the key organisation of the Honduran opposition in the 1980s, achieving national and international recognition and admiration. Custodio could never have gained that reputation without the nationwide network of local committees that was channelling information on human rights abuses to the central office. Due to the voluntary nature of this network, the level of bureaucracy was relatively low, and communications were rapid and efficient. A further strength of CODEH was the reliability of information it provided on human rights violations, which made it a credible source for the national media which often incorporated CODEH's declarations in its reporting. Custodio's international contacts with human rights organisations and aid agencies guaranteed him and other CODEH activists a certain level of protection. This reputation was reinforced by Custodio's efforts to prevent any direct relationship developing between CODEH and political parties. The government tried several times to link CODEH to the radical left-wing party *Cinchoneros*, to the point of accusing Custodio of being the intellectual leader behind the assassination of his colleague Pavón in 1988. However, among opposition leaders it was accepted that CODEH wanted to keep its autonomy from political parties and prevent its independent profile from being damaged.[40]

If the secret to CODEH's success was Custodio's charismatic leadership, his stubborn and authoritarian management style also gradually weakened CODEH. For security reasons, during the 1980s it was essential that only the president and the vice-president be known in public. But the negative consequence of this was that Custodio acquired absolute power over decision-making inside CODEH, tolerating no internal opposition. CODEH members who questioned his authoritarian style were dismissed, leading to a crisis in 1989 when more than half of the central office staff left the committee.[41] The centralised structure of decision-making was formally changed with the installation of regional assemblies in the 1990s, but local committee members kept complaining that it was difficult to directly contact Custodio. This might explain why CODEH was unable to transform itself into a 'movement' of the opposition during mid-transition, when civil society was acquiring more 'political space'. CODEH in fact continued in its role as an intermediary NGO between local committees and the public by focusing on the optimal use of the mass media, rather than broadening its role as a movement of societal actors. Custodio's refusal to coordinate activities with other organisations, such as groups struggling for the defence of women's rights, was due to his perception that they lacked leadership capacity. Others argued that Custodio wanted to take all the credit for the successful campaign against impunity, to the point that he refused to share information with the other allies in this struggle.[42] Custodio's inflexible attitude weakened CODEH's position and obstructed its adaptation to the new political circumstances. But CODEH was very dependent upon his decisions, as Custodio was the only one negotiating external funds with private aid agencies.

To the question whether CODEH's achievements were affected by funding from European private aid agencies, Custodio responded unambiguously that European aid had been crucial to the work of CODEH; the organisation probably could not have existed without this external aid as it would have been unable to finance the office and pay for the travel costs and meals of the voluntary members. Along the same lines, he argued that human rights work would always depend on external funding for it could not easily generate its own resources. In terms of partnership with private aid agencies, Custodio distinguished between agencies that put conditions on their funding, and agencies that provided unconditional aid. The first category had proven to be 'not useful', as it tended to force an agenda upon CODEH that the organisation was not prepared to adopt. Custodio mentioned that some agencies, for example, felt the need to suggest that CODEH should pay more attention to women's rights, while he considered aid for transport, expenses to run the regional offices or an emergency fund to protect witnesses from persecution as higher priorities. This had created tension in the past and various agencies decided to cut their funding relations with CODEH after its refusal to meet certain conditions.[43]

CEBEMO and *Diakonia* were mentioned by Custodio as private aid agencies that had not posed any conditions upon CODEH's agenda. CEBEMO only warned CODEH not to put too much emphasis on socio-economic and cultural human rights, as it envisaged problems in then getting these activities approved for co-funding by the Dutch government. Both agencies also pressured CODEH to improve its financial administration, as decent reporting had become a top priority for the aid agencies in the 1990s. The question remains however how CEBEMO, as CODEH's major funder, perceived its role in the successes of the committee. Would the achievements as described earlier have been possible without its financial support? According to CEBEMO external support was crucial in order to maintain CODEH's structure, as it had no local resources to finance its activities. But CEBEMO also admitted that a number of funders contributed to maintaining CODEH's structure; if one funder would have stepped out, certainly others would have replaced CEBEMO. CODEH's achievements were therefore not directly attributable to CEBEMO's financial support, but it certainly made a difference. Moreover, CODEH was considered to be one of their most successful partners in the region.[44] CEBEMO and other agencies emphasised that, besides financial aid, active moral support to CODEH and political support to international campaigns also had been part of their relationship with CODEH. Given the passive attitude of CEBEMO, and the dominant nature of CODEH's leadership, the impact of private aid was above all indirect. Both *Diakonia* and CEBEMO refused to directly question the authoritarian way in which Custodio ran the committee, although they were among the few that had the power to do so. *Diakonia* did implement a participatory external evaluation procedure which tried to address several key internal obstacles that CODEH faced, but it had mixed results. CEBEMO kept its distance from these internal problems and actually preferred to continue performing a role as resource provider rather than become involved in 'accompaniment'.

– *Assessing CODEH's civil society building performance*
In Chapter 3 two variables were proposed for assessing the performance of private aid aimed at strengthening civil society: the organisational capacity and the intermediary role of these key counterpart organisations in civil society. The first variable is considered by examining the level of internal participation, the accountability of leadership and the sustainability of the organisation as a result of private aid interventions. The intermediary role is assessed by focusing on the

capacity of an organisation to articulate and mediate (conflicting) interests and demands from civil society, and by examining the extent to which the balance between the state and civil society has been shifted towards democratic transition by the strengthening of political society. If these variables are applied to CODEH, the following conclusions are reached.

In terms of internal participation and accountability, necessary preconditions for establishing a viable membership organisation, CODEH scored remarkably low. Up to the early 1990s an internal structure for consultation and democratic decision-making was absent, which was understandable given the fierce repression in Honduras. But even after the installation of an assembly with an elected executive board *de facto* decision-making power was concentrated in one person. Although Custodio enjoyed a high level of credibility, he did not tolerate any internal opposition. This situation deteriorated when possible candidates to succeed him (which he also trusted enough to hand over some of his tasks) suddenly died.[45] Participation of women at decision-making levels was low and Custodio refused to accept criticism on this issue. The network of local committees, important for articulating demands from the micro- to macro-level, generally performed well thanks to the active participation of local Church representatives. But as a membership structure it was weak and people participating in these committees often considered themselves above all to be part of a religious community.[46] The meso-level structure of regional assemblies identified more with CODEH as an organisation, not only because they had shorter communication lines with the central office, but also because they coordinated educational activities and thus benefited more from CODEH's financial resources. Custodio's monopoly over contacts with funding agencies was not challenged by the agencies, although these contacts represented a considerable source of power. By questioning neither the structure of CODEH nor the absolute power of Custodio, private aid agencies complicated the start of a much needed internal reorganisation.

This problem-ridden internal hierarchy also negatively affected the prospects for CODEH's sustainability in the long run. In terms of activities, key functions of CODEH were gradually taken over by the Human Rights Commissioner (the ombudsman), the Prosecution Counsel and, for example, women's organisations, although human rights education and legal support were two areas in which CODEH continued to perform an important role in the 1990s. With several private aid agencies wanting to reduce their support to CODEH, the question arises whether it will manage to survive in the longer term with less external support.[47] Self-sufficiency was to be increased, according to funders, by creating a demand-oriented human rights service for those who needed legal assistance. However, CODEH's technical capacities were too limited to transform the committee into a supplier of such income-generating activities, even apart from the question whether poor people would at all be able to pay for these services. An additional problem was that private aid agencies failed to offer technical assistance to CODEH for expanding its institutional capacity. As beneficiary contributions do not exist as an alternative source of income, it is realistic to predict that CODEH will remain highly dependent on foreign assistance in the future. But this has become scarce since Honduras has dropped out of many of the Central American funding schemes of foreign aid agencies. If this is added to the difficult internal transition to a more accountable organisation, it must be concluded that the future for CODEH is very insecure. Pessimistic observers even foresee a rapid disintegration if no successor is found to the all-time president Custodio.

On the intermediary function, CODEH performed far better, at least during the 1980s, by articulating demands from civil society to end impunity for members of the security forces. Due to repression of opposition groups in civil society during the 1980s, CODEH was one of the few organisations capable of transmitting these demands to the media and to the international community. Its major success in that period was getting the Honduran government condemned by the Inter-American Court of Human Rights for being responsible for forced disappearances. But when military domination eased in the early 1990s, CODEH did not expand its function by forming coalitions with other societal actors to forge an intermediary alliance in political society. CODEH rather aimed to transform itself from a human rights committee into a civil rights movement, although in practice its structure barely changed. Aid agencies did not push CODEH into reviewing its function as a key actor in civil society in the early 1990s, after Honduras began moving into a stage of mid-transition. It is likely that continued (and passive) private aid support, which was barely adapted to the new political circumstances, impeded CODEH from actively searching for new alliances with other societal actors and adjusting its internal structure, which could have improved its performance and prospects for future sustainability.

CODEH's most tangible achievement probably has been its impact on public policy, which became visible during the stage of late transition. The continuous campaign against impunity for human rights violators resulted in 1993 in the creation of an advisory committee to recommend reforms leading to a demilitarisation of the police forces. This *Comité Ad Hoc de Alto Nivel* was established after security forces had been found responsible for several murders in early 1993. CODEH, as one of the committee members, organised a seminar in March 1993, together with academic experts and the Lutheran Church, to discuss proposals to demilitarise Honduran society (CODEH 1993). Many of CODEH's recommendations were taken over by the Ad Hoc Committee, such as the demilitarisation of the police, the replacement of the intelligence service by a department for criminal investigations and the creation of a Prosecution Counsel. Subsequent advisory commissions, also with CODEH's participation, further elaborated proposals for reform of the judiciary and the penitentiary system. In addition, CODEH played a major role in getting the government to prosecute those military officers responsible for disappearances in the 1980s, as one of the obligations following the Court ruling in 1988.[48] Private aid support had been crucial in making these achievements possible, although they contributed little to improving CODEH's organisational structure or to enhancing its leading role in civil society due to the fact that Custodio did not tolerate any interference in internal affairs. The main funders, CEBEMO and *Diakonia*, realised that (even constructive) criticism would risk an end to their partnership with CODEH – one of their most successful partners in the region – and that other donors would be keen to replace them. Moreover, the absence of any coordination between the funders further weakened their leverage over Custodio, which actually made them indirectly responsible for weakening CODEH's potential to contribute to strengthening political society in Honduras. After all, CODEH was at certain times during the period of mid-transition probably the only actor in Honduran civil society that was capable of forging a broad alliance of the opposition that could have challenged the deeply entrenched bipartisan political system.

6.2 El Salvador's national peace debate: the CPDN

The peace agreement signed in January 1992 between the FMLN and the Salvadorean government formally ended one of the bloodiest civil wars in recent Central American history. The agreement started a process of demilitarisation of Salvadorean society, a society which had been deeply polarised by two major positions, either in support of or against a revolutionary solution to the Salvadorean crisis. Nowhere in Central America had political positions been so antagonistic and apparently clearly defined as in El Salvador during the 1980s: oligarchy *versus* peasants, counter-insurgency *versus* revolution and foreign intervention *versus* anti-imperialism. The importance of the peace agreement was that it reconciled these extremes by combining demilitarisation with guarantees for democratic participation of excluded sectors. This shifted the battleground from the rural areas of Chalatenango and Morazán to the political arena of the capital. The US-financed armed forces were 'purified' and drastically reduced; former guerrilla fighters were incorporated into civilian life and the FMLN was transformed into a political party, becoming the second largest political force after the 1994 elections. Polarisation did not vanish, but certainly was diminished and 'pacified'.

The process of depolarisation and reaching consensus on a peace agreement will be examined by focusing on a key actor in Salvadorean civil society during the early 1990s: the Permanent Committee for the National Peace Debate (CPDN). This broad national alliance of civil society sectors, set up by the Catholic and Lutheran Churches, was a forum for discussion and public action to contribute to a peaceful solution to the war. The CPDN represented a diverse 'popular' opposition to the government and gave a voice to those organisations not present at the negotiation table. The CPDN demanded to be present at these negotiations as a 'third force' representing civil society. Although direct participation was denied, the CPDN emerged as an important reconciling actor in El Salvador's democratic transition. Its activities were financed by two major European private aid agencies which had actively supported popular organisations in El Salvador throughout the war. The case study examines in what way these agencies indirectly contributed to peace and democratic transition in El Salvador.

– *Emergence and activities of the CPDN*

The early Salvadorean democratic transition was slow and lasted more than a decade, as was shown in Chapter 4. It started with the coup of young military officers in October 1979, which marked an end to the repressive Romero regime that had been confronted with an upsurge of mass demonstrations, labour strikes and left-wing kidnappings. The growing strength of revolutionary movements and the Sandinista victory in July 1979 convinced the new government of the need to introduce several socio-economic reforms such as agrarian reform and the nationalisation of banks. However, the new *junta* was unable to control the armed forces and curb their repression of popular unrest or to stop death squad activity organised by right-wing opponents. Because of this the progressive civilian members of the *junta* decided to resign after a few months. The failure of the October *junta* to stop political violence and to acquire legitimacy within a polarised civil society, exacerbated by the assassination of Archbishop Romero in March 1980, further complicated the start of early transition. Death squad violence and massacres by armed forces in the countryside intensified social polarisation and led to the left opposition uniting its forces in the FDR-FMLN and deciding to opt for revolutionary armed struggle.

The failure of the FMLN to bring down the regime in January 1981 with a military offensive was followed by an increase in military aid from the new Reagan administration which would unleash a decade of civil war. The civilian government of Christian Democrat Napoleón Duarte, elected in 1984, was unable to get the peace process started and to speed up democratic transition. Beginning in 1987, three positive elements contributed to breaking the deadlock of stagnating negotiations. The first was the regional Esquipulas peace plan, which created a conducive climate for peace negotiations. A second positive development was the return from exile of the two opposition parties MPSC and MNR in 1987 (forming the Democratic Convergence with the Social Democratic PSD) and the re-emergence of popular movements in the mid-1980s with more autonomy from the FMLN than before. Notably the formation of the National Union of Salvadorean Workers (UNTS) in 1986, a broad coalition of rural and urban associations, underscored the rebirth of a strong popular movement in civil society (Lungo 1995). A third positive element was the active role of the Catholic Church in promoting a renewal of peace negotiations, particularly after the right-wing parties had won a majority in the National Assembly in the elections of March 1988. The Catholic bishops were aware that the growing popular movement was excluded from any discussion about peace, which also had contributed to its radicalisation.[49] The bishops therefore decided to initiate a national debate among social sectors with the purpose of achieving consensus on a peaceful solution to the civil war. Such a debate was considered to be complementary to the dialogue between the government and the FDR-FMLN (Acevedo 1988).

In June 1988 Archbishop Rivera invited over a hundred organisations from all civil society sectors, except political parties, to present and discuss their viewpoints on the prospects for peace and to forge a consensus concerning the future development of the country.[50] Although organisations related to the (right-wing) ARENA party initially welcomed the initiative, pressure from extreme right-wing groupings made them and several business associations decide to reject the invitation. They argued that the search for national consensus was an exclusive task of the political parties; an understandable position given the new ARENA-majority in parliament. About sixty organisations accepted the invitation and participated in a survey to give their opinions about a list of propositions related to the causes of the war and possible solutions for peace. At a plenary session in September 1988 participants voted on these issues and reached a remarkable consensus about the fundamental obstacles and opportunities of the peace process. Although most political tendencies, except for ARENA, were (indirectly) present at the meeting, a large number of organisations (if not the majority) seemed to be sympathetic to the FMLN.[51] At the end of the meeting, Bishop Rosa Chávez proposed a final declaration that urged all political parties to incorporate the consensus issues in their programmes for the upcoming 1989 presidential elections, called upon the FMLN and the government to deal in a responsible way with the resolutions and invited absent social organisations to actively participate in the national peace debate. This final declaration was approved unanimously and was, as Acevedo (1988: 779) notes, 'spontaneously followed by a standing ovation of several minutes'. The leading Jesuit Ignacio Ellacuría of the Central American University (UCA) welcomed the debate as one of the most promising events in 1988, and criticised the government and the right for not having the courage to involve civil society directly in the search for a solution to a problem that mostly affected the people they supposedly represented (Ellacuría 1988).

At the same public assembly it was agreed to create a committee to continue the national peace debate and provide follow-up to the adopted resolutions. This *Comité Permanente del Debate Nacional* (CPDN) was made up of representatives of sectoral organisations that had participated in the meeting, such as trade unions, churches, universities, peasants, women, communities, development NGOs, human rights committees, small business associations and professional associations. Initially, the Catholic Church also participated in the committee, but decided in November 1988 to leave the CPDN as it preferred to keep a low public profile in its efforts to demand negotiations.[52] As a result, other churches (notably the Lutheran and Baptist Churches) together with the UNTS (the broad alliance of peasant and trade unions) would become the driving forces behind the CPDN. At a forum organised by the UCA a few weeks later, presidential candidate Alfredo Cristiani acknowledged that he agreed with 85 percent of the conclusions of the national debate. He also promised that a future ARENA government would initiate a permanent dialogue with the FMLN (Whitfield 1994).

The first public CPDN activity was a large peace march, organised by thirty member organisations in November 1988. Its aim was to influence the Organisation of American States (OAS), meeting at that moment in San Salvador. The 30,000 participants demanded a political solution to the war, possibly with OAS mediation. Contrary to earlier public street protests, the march was peaceful and did not unleash riots and confrontations with security forces. A second peace march was organised just before the presidential elections of March 1989, in which Ellacuría assured the crowd that 'peace was closer than ever'.[53] Two months earlier, the FMLN had unexpectedly proposed to participate in the elections on the condition that these would be postponed for six months. Although the Duarte government eventually rejected the proposal, it did create an atmosphere of dialogue and prospects for a political settlement. However, the right-wing ARENA was convinced it would win the elections; initial talks in Mexico between the FMLN and several political parties therefore soon stagnated. ARENA's candidate Alfredo Cristiani indeed won the presidency easily in the first round, also because the Christian Democrats were seriously divided. Democratic Convergence (CD), the small left-wing alliance of former FDR-parties led by Guillermo Ungo, only received a handful of votes.[54]

Shortly after his installation in June 1989, the new president called for direct peace talks with the FMLN. But opposition from the extreme right wing of his party and ongoing political violence delayed the reopening of talks until September. Meanwhile, the CPDN tried to speed up the process of dialogue by organising several national 'peace encounters'.[55] The CPDN started using three different methods to advocate a negotiated solution to the Salvadorean civil war: (i) public promotion of a political settlement via peace marches, newspaper and television advertisements and public meetings, (ii) organising bilateral meetings with CPDN members and the armed forces, the government, political parties and the FMLN, to convince them of the need to restart negotiations and (iii) putting pressure on the US Congress and international bodies such as the OAS, UN, EC and international networks of churches and aid agencies. As a representative of social sectors, the CPDN also demanded to become a direct observer during the negotiations. At the first two rounds of the peace talks – in September 1989 in Mexico and October in Costa Rica – representatives of the Episcopal Conference were invited alongside OAS and UN officials, meeting separately with the two parties. Among the Church representatives was Baptist pastor Edgar Palacios, the coordinator of the CPDN. However, little progress was made during the talks, apart from a fragile agreement about implementing a ceasefire in November prior to a next meeting; the armed forces and the FMLN still thought they would be able to defeat each other. According to Ellacuría, the FMLN wrongly believed that it had built up enough popular support to provoke a general insurrection against the regime. Increased mobilisation of social forces and popular discontent was erroneously perceived by the FMLN as support for their insurrectional strategy. What the majority of the population wanted, argued Ellacuría on the basis of opinion polls, was a negotiated and peaceful solution to the war (Byrne 1996).

The immediate reason for the start of the November 1989 FMLN offensive was the bombing of the FENASTRAS office, killing ten trade union leaders, and bombings of the Lutheran Church and Rubén Zamora's residence. With this political violence targeted at people and organisations promoting a peaceful settlement, the FMLN concluded that the government was not serious about negotiations. A plan for a national guerrilla offensive was put in motion, and thousands of FMLN fighters invaded the capital, leading to aerial bombings by the air force of slum neighbourhoods and heavy fighting in all fourteen departments. The purpose of the offensive was ambiguous. On the one hand, the FMLN had been planning a national military campaign for several years, aimed at provoking a popular insurrection and the fall of the ARENA government. On the other hand, the FMLN knew it could not win the war as long as US military aid continued. Comments by the Cristiani government and US officials during the October talks that the FMLN had been militarily defeated further convinced some commanders that they had to strengthen their position at the negotiation table.[56] In response to the offensive, the armed forces decided to liquidate the entire leadership of the Central American University (UCA), the intellectual leaders behind the promotion of a peaceful solution. By trying to cover up the killings and putting the blame on the insurgents, the army accidentally provided a turning point in the Salvadorean war. The brutal assassination of Ellacuría and five other leading Jesuits had direct impact on the US Congress, which eventually decided to curb military aid to El Salvador.[57] Gradually the United States started to accept that the war had entered a deadlock, as neither of the two parties was able to achieve a military victory. The rapid changes in Eastern Europe, added to the growing conviction by the FMLN that peace would be more beneficial than continuing the war, contributed to renewed steps for peace negotiations.

In the midst of the offensive, CPDN leaders were forced to flee the country. With support from North American churches and solidarity groups an office was opened in Washington (led by Pastor Edgar Palacios) to lobby the US Congress and the United Nations. Meanwhile, the mobilisation of social forces in El Salvador was entirely directed by FMLN leaders.[58] It was not until January 1990 that the CPDN was able to regroup itself, this time in a political climate more open to dialogue than ever before. A new leadership was elected, presided over by Palacios, with a stronger presence of FMLN members.[59] Secret bilateral meetings organised by UN top official Alvaro de Soto in December 1989 revealed that the FMLN and the Salvadorean government were willing to resume talks under UN mediation. Strong pressure on both parties to negotiate also came from the Central American presidents.[60] After intensive diplomacy, a new meeting between the two parties was held in April 1990, marking the start of an active negotiation process that ended with the peace agreement of Chapúltepec, signed in January 1992.[61]

Although the CPDN was not accepted as a third party nor as an observer to the negotiations, it played a key role in mobilising national and international support for the peace process. After implementation of the agreement, the CPDN continued operating as a civil society alliance, but shifted its focus toward socio-economic issues. To understand the evolution of the CPDN, three periods can be identified. The first runs from its foundation in 1988 to the demobilisation of the FMLN in late 1992. In this period the CPDN tried to build a consensus within civil society for a peaceful settlement, and critically followed the negotiation and implementation of the accords with massive street rallies, public debates and civil diplomacy. The second phase of the CPDN covers the period from early 1993 until the elections of March 1994, leading to the formal incorporation of the FMLN into political society. With the peace process concluded, the CPDN had to redefine its role and decided to prioritise the search for a consensus among social forces on post-war reconstruction, for which a widely discussed document gave a number of recommendations regarding future government policies.[62] In a third phase, since the 1994 elections, the CPDN has remained active as a public forum for discussion mainly focusing on socio-economic issues. As will be demonstrated, the most influential period of the CPDN was the first phase until 1992.

– *Private foreign aid to the CPDN*
Direct support from private aid agencies to the CPDN started during and after the November 1989 offensive. Until that period, activities were financed with funds from member organisations, in particular from churches and large trade unions such as the UNTS and FENASTRAS. Fundraising became necessary because the CPDN wanted to prevent dependence on its larger (and FMLN-controlled) members. Additional funding was required to finance transport and meals for participants from rural areas in the peace marches and to pay for the expensive spots on radio and television. Under the umbrella of the church-related NGO DIACONIA,[63] fundraising started in September 1989 when prospects for renewed negotiations were increasing. The Lutheran Church – one of the key participants in DIACONIA and a leading member of the CPDN in the person of Bishop Medardo Gómez – provided contacts to external funders through its international networks of the *Lutheran World Federation* and the *World Council of Churches*. This resulted in contacts with the German *Brot für die Welt*, which decided to support the Washington office of the CPDN soon after the November offensive had started. Contacts with the Dutch private aid agency ICCO also were made prior to the offensive, but due to the emergency situation in El Salvador it took until early 1990 to materialise into concrete support. Both agencies were impressed by the broad alliance of social forces for peace that the CPDN had managed to bring together.

   The start of the (final) peace negotiations in April 1990 contributed to acquiring new foreign aid resources, although private aid agencies were relatively slow in approving funding for the CPDN in contrast to the rapid advances being made in the negotiation process. This generated liquidity problems in 1991, leading to additional appeals for funding. By the end of 1991, with the negotiations nearly concluded, the CPDN had managed to raise over US$ 300,000 from private aid agencies. This was enough to cover its expenses for marches, advertisements, press conferences and meetings throughout the negotiation process. The largest share came from the two Protestant agencies ICCO and *Brot für die Welt*, in addition to smaller grants from *Norwegian People's Aid*, CEBEMO, OXFAM-UK/I and several churches. The official endorsement of the peace accords in Chapúltepec (January 1992) gave an additional impulse to the activities of the CPDN. New projects for social mobilisation and media advertisements were planned to press for implementation of the agreements according to the agreed schedule. With its small staff and rather short-term planning, the CPDN worked out a number of new project proposals (instead of multi-annual budgets which were preferred by the agencies) and presented these to the same group of private aid agencies.

Due to the promising developments in the Salvadorean peace process, ICCO, *Brot für die Welt* and other private aid agencies responded positively to these new appeals and increased their contributions to the CPDN. Consequently, donor income more than doubled between 1992 and 1993. In response to these increased donor contributions, and given the general increase of foreign aid resources flowing into El Salvador after the peace agreement, the CPDN adjusted its budgets again. It planned expenses of around US$ 1.6 million between 1993 and the election year 1994, which was probably more than it could handle. It was certainly more than the agencies were willing to contribute, for the CPDN only had a small staff and some agencies felt the organisation also had to generate income from member contributions. Despite these concerns, private aid agencies supporting the CPDN greatly valued its role in consolidating the peace process and stimulating civil society to actively participate in the electoral process. Consequently, foreign support kept growing in these years, although it was only in late 1994 that the agencies discovered that the CPDN was unable to spend all these funds. As will be analysed later, the CPDN started to create large financial reserves that were presented to the agencies as 'member contributions', but were in fact saved up donor funds. *Brot für die Welt* decided for that reason in 1995 to stop funding the CPDN, although support was resumed the following year. Most contributions from smaller agencies had already stopped after 1993.

The largest donor of the CPDN, the Dutch ICCO, accounted for over half of its income throughout these years. The significance of this role justifies a closer examination of ICCO's motivation to support the CPDN.[64] ICCO had known the CPDN from its early beginnings in 1988, as several of the member organisations also received funding from ICCO. In late 1989, after the November offensive and with the peace process still in a deadlock, ICCO decided to support the CPDN for three reasons. First, because it positively valued the broad alliance of social organisations (from the moderate right to the radical left) that the CPDN was bringing together to rally for a negotiated settlement. Second, because it shared the concerns of coordinator Palacios, a Protestant pastor, about the dominant role of FMLN-related NGOs that wanted to convert the CPDN into an organ of support for the FMLN. Moreover, ICCO recognised the need for CPDN's financial independence from its 'richer' members such as the UCA, to improve internal unity. The CPDN was considered to be one of the few alliances in civil society where all political ten-

dencies of the opposition worked together to discuss key political issues. A third
reason was political: (indirect) funding from the Dutch government would boost
the international legitimacy of the CPDN and would add to the diplomatic weight
of the Washington lobbying office.

– Achievements of the CPDN

One of the principal goals of the CPDN was not realised: to be present as a third
party representing civil society at the peace talks. Still, in the period from mid-1989
to early 1992 the CPDN achieved several important objectives. First of all, it
succeeded in bringing together a large variety of social and political forces in El
Salvador, from the radical left to the moderate right, under the banner of the peace
negotiations. This creation of *concertación* among the majority of societal actors in
El Salvador was a remarkable achievement given the deep polarisation in the war
period; it initiated a process of depolarisation necessary to move democratic
transition forward. Due to the absence of the powerful business sector in the CPDN
it was not possible to speak of a 'general consensus' of civil society on a peaceful
solution, but the alliance was probably the broadest possible at that time. It had
taken over several functions of the dissolved opposition alliance FDR, which had
acted in the 1980s as the civilian branch of the FMLN. Although individual FMLN
members had a strong voice in the CPDN, the guerrilla movement was aware of the
need to give an autonomous role to 'the popular movement' (assembled in the
CPDN) during the peace process. The CPDN was therefore used by the FMLN as a
sounding board for discussing proposals that were prepared for the negotiations.[65]
In addition, the CPDN performed an intermediary role between the FMLN and its
constituency by 'decoding' messages coming from the negotiation table.[66]

   A further achievement of the CPDN was its success in mobilising national and
(particularly) international support for the peace process, making optimal use of a
period in which conditions for reaching an agreement were favourable. At the
national level, pressure from civil society through mass marches contributed to
breaking the deadlock at key moments during the peace negotiations. One of the
biggest marches was held in December 1991, a few weeks before the negotiations
were to be finalised in New York, organised to counter efforts by the army and
extreme-right forces to frustrate the upcoming agreement.[67] These social
mobilisations were recognised by newly-elected leaders of the opposition as a sign
of an expanding civil society.[68] Press conferences and jingles on the radio and
television were used by the CPDN as instruments to communicate with the government and the armed forces, but also with its constituency. At the international
level, the CPDN approached international organisations and governments of the
'Group of Friends' to put pressure on the Cristiani government for keeping the
peace process moving.[69] As an 'unauthorised third party' in the peace process, the
CPDN effectively used its international network in Canada, the United States and
Europe to especially target a key player in this process: the US Congress. The latter
was pressured to cut military aid to El Salvador, or at least to make it conditional

upon advances in the negotiations and on the prosecution of the assassins of the UCA Jesuits. This lobbying proved to be effective, as the House of Representatives in May 1990 voted in favour of cutting military aid and the Senate decided in October to make half of the military aid to El Salvador conditional upon advances in the peace talks and the Jesuit case. Civil diplomacy by the CPDN was of course not a determining factor, but certainly was important throughout the peace talks which had been criticised for their secret and elitist character.[70] Although UN mediator De Soto spoke of a 'negotiated revolution', many observers have correctly pointed out that the agreement did not fundamentally alter the existing power balance: 'the core institutions of the Salvadorean government remained untouched' comments Foley (1996: 77).

Another achievement was that the CPDN had created a national forum for political debate on key issues parallel to the National Assembly. Until the 1994 elections (and definitely until the 1991 elections) the Salvadorean parliament was unable to perform that intermediary function because opposition parties were not yet incorporated into the political arena. During the negotiations and the implementation of the agreement, sectoral representatives of the CPDN formed what they called a 'popular parliament'. Meeting weekly, this (unelected) group of representatives from various societal sectors was the central policy-making body inside the CPDN that discussed peace proposals, monitored the implementation of agreements and made preparations for the elections. An influential product of this group was the June 1993 publication of a consensus document called 'Contributions to the Project for a New Nation'. Based on broad consultations among CPDN members the document launched policy proposals for a future government prior to the electoral campaign. This proved to be rather effective as several parties incorporated these proposals into their campaigns, particularly the FMLN. But it was in a sense also undermining for the CPDN because the successful participation of the FMLN in the 1994 elections implied that its role as mediator for the 'underrepresented' in civil society had become redundant.

After the elections the CPDN continued organising street marches, press conferences, discussion seminars and elaborating proposals for post-war reconstruction. It also kept emphasising the need for compliance with the peace accords, some elements of which were deliberately delayed or frustrated by the governments of President Cristiani and his successor Calderon Sol. But the CPDN had lost its momentum as a national peace forum and as a temporary actor in a political society in transition. Gradually, many organisations left the CPDN, often because of profound internal divisions in the FMLN, but also because post-war circumstances provided new opportunities for constructing other fora to articulate social demands. One of the FMLN tendencies gradually started to dominate the CPDN, which seriously damaged its relative autonomy. After 1994 the national dialogue and policy-making on post-war reconstruction was transferred to the National Assembly, in which the FMLN had become the second largest political party. The CPDN had to reformulate its mission, transforming itself from a one-issue movement (peace) into a less attractive multi-issue forum promoting reconciliation and social justice. Despite producing proposals supported by a wide array of social organisations, the CPDN barely survived this transformation and its influence soon became marginal.

The activities of the CPDN had contributed to strengthening civil society by forging an alliance between a growing number of sectoral organisations and by playing an intermediary role between civil society and the state during the peace process. A closer examination suggests that both functions were only performed temporarily. In the first period (1988-1991) the combination of building an alliance for a political solution to the war and the transmission of this demand to national and international actors contributed to depolarising the tense climate after the November 1989 offensive. Despite its failure to get the associations of private enterprise on board, the CPDN was in a sense 'the miracle of creating unity in civil society' as Palacios called it. Unity referred to the alliance among the more radical organisations (such as the labour unions of the UNTS) opting for an active support-ive role in an armed insurrection, and the moderate organisations opting for peaceful solutions. Some tendencies inside the FMLN were well aware that they could not afford to alienate themselves from these moderate organisations (Byrne 1996: 145). Furthermore, the dissolution of the FDR, the civil branch of the FMLN between 1980 and 1987, had created a vacuum on the side of civil diplomacy. A Church-sponsored initiative to create a national peace debate therefore offered a useful instrument for the insurgents to build a broad popular constituency during the peace talks and to lobby international actors. After the 1992 peace agreement, when the FMLN transformed itself into a political party, this alliance-building role of the CPDN lost its significance as it was no longer supported by all FMLN ten-dencies.

The same happened in fact with the intermediary role of the CPDN, and perhaps even earlier. Ellacuría (1988) envisaged a role for the CPDN as a 'suprasectoral assembly', acting on social issues parallel to the political issues of the National Assembly. However, due to the absence of FDR or FMLN representatives in parlia-ment, the CPDN in fact also functioned as a channel for political demands in the early period of the peace process. This intermediary role ended with the election of eight ex-FDR opposition candidates as part of the Democratic Convergence (CD) in the National Assembly in the March 1991 elections. Especially the role of Rubén Zamora was important, as he became a vice-president of the National Assembly.[71] During the peace talks he emerged as a key informal mediator between the oppos-ition, the government and the international community. Zamora eventually was designated the presidential candidate for the FMLN-CD alliance in the 1994 elections, where he was defeated by ARENA candidate Calderon Sol in the second round.

The intermediary role of the CPDN also was weakened by the creation of two new institutions as part of the peace agreements: the National Commission for the Consolidation of Peace (COPAZ) and the Forum for Economic and Social Consult-ation (FOCES).[72] COPAZ was formed by representatives of all political parties in parliament, the government and the FMLN. It was installed to oversee the implementation of the peace accords, as a complement to the UN verification process, and to monitor the participation of civil society in this implementation process. Between the final agreement of January 1992 and the elections of March 1994, COPAZ functioned as an unofficial 'transition government' and as a body that worked to create consensus on conflicting civil society interests (Johnstone 1995). It was illustrative that it was not the CPDN that was granted consultative status to COPAZ (with ONUSAL) but the Catholic Church. The other body replacing one of the functions of the CPDN was the Forum for Economic and Social Consultation (FOCES), in which labour unions, employers' associations and the government had to reach a consensus about the implementation of socio-economic issues outlined in the peace agreement. Although some short-term advances were made on workers' rights, FOCES was not a success. The business sector simply was unwilling to discuss fundamental socio-economic issues and to 'negotiate the revolution', leading to considerable frustration in lower FMLN ranks (Byrne 1996: 189).

The contribution made by the CPDN to strengthening civil society therefore should not be overstated. It forged important alliances previous to and during the peace process – initially despite, and later thanks to the FMLN – but after 1992 lost most of its relevance to other actors. This is not surprising, for it was primarily focused on getting the negotiations started and securing the demilitarisation of society. This achievement should not be exaggerated since there already existed a rather broad national consensus about the need for peace talks right after the November 1989 offensive, and only a small minority wanted to continue the war. On issues on which it could have been strong, such as socio-economic reforms, the CPDN surprisingly had no serious proposals. Alternative development plans were only elaborated after 1992 when the momentum of the transition process had passed. The CPDN was unable to get a grip on the 'substantive issues' of the negotiations, the issues that had been conducive to the war and that had been central to the struggle of many CPDN members. This illustrates that it actually did not have the capacity to anticipate issues that exceeded the agenda of the peace negotiations. Or as Ponciano (1995: 130) suggests, the CPDN was so focused on political-military issues that it failed to recognise that the Cristiani government actively kept its neoliberal stabilisation programme from becoming part of the negotiation agenda. The inability of the CPDN to focus in an early stage of the negotiations on the issues of post-war reconstruction – which would have created friction with immediate FMLN-leadership interests – was one of the main reasons for its downfall after the final peace accords were signed.[73]

– The CPDN in the aid chain

Between 1988 and 1991, the CPDN certainly was an influential peace alliance in civil society, combining three strong assets. First, it had an explicit and unambiguous goal: a negotiated resolution to the civil war, a goal that could not be compromised and was finally reached. Second, the CPDN managed to bring a wide spectrum of popular organisations together in a loose coalition, producing and discussing constructive proposals without direct interference of the two contending parties. Despite close links between the FMLN and the larger organisations participating in the CPDN, the insurgents were reluctant to directly interfere. The FMLN leadership recognised the value of a discussion platform outside its ranks, as internal discussions often were hampered by hierarchically organised structures and military considerations. In fact, the constituency of the FMLN was more reluctant to engage in compromises with the armed forces than the leadership, and this is where the CPDN played a buffering role. A third factor contributing to its achievements was the strategic timing for launching proposals or protests. Much of this timing was directed by its charismatic leader Edgar Palacios, who was respected by the armed forces, the government and the FMLN, and knew how to handle the press. Without his combined role as a spokesperson, mediator and civil diplomat, the CPDN would probably not have been successful at all.[74]

The main weakness of the CPDN was its inability to anticipate the challenges to be faced in the post-war period, including its own role. The absence of a long-term vision on the role of civil society in post-war democratisation, other than simply demanding its participation, made it easy for the advocates of the prevailing development model to pursue their own strategy without any serious opposition. The short-lived relevance of the CPDN has to do with the fact that it was a product of the war and not of post-war democratic transition. Many member organisations of the CPDN were accustomed to performing a mobilising role in civil society, whereas their leaders were often restrained by the logic of the political-military struggle. The transition to peace forced these member organisations to transform their discourse, their organisational structure and their mission in order to address newly emerging sectoral interests. This forced transformation, in addition to the confusion created by the internal FMLN splits, generated a climate of insecurity concerning the new role of societal actors in the stage of mid-transition. The inevitable crisis that emerged in many social organisations affected internal debates in the CPDN and seriously weakened the previously existing consensus.[75] As a multi-sectoral alliance for peace, the CPDN also had to redefine its role and tried to secure a consensus in 1992 under the banner of 'constructing peace'. This effort failed as it was unable to reconcile the many conflicting interests in civil society that were emerging in a process of 'constructing democracy'. Although the formal number of member organisations increased to over eighty in 1995, in practice the 'alliance of social forces' and the 'conscience of Chapúltepec' had become a remnant of the past. Private aid agencies supporting the CPDN failed to recognise this dramatic shift.

Support from private aid agencies, in particular from ICCO and *Brot für die Welt*, was indispensable to financing the activities of the CPDN. Without these external resources the CPDN would have had a lower profile in the Salvadorean peace process, according to coordinator Palacios.[76] This private foreign aid enabled the CPDN to mobilise more (rural) participants for public marches (pay for transport and meals) and to finance media advertisements. However, a closer examination of aid flows to the CPDN reveals that these increased after 1992, in other words after the period of peace negotiations and the implementation of the agreements when it achieved its main results. Given the low level of institutional consolidation it is likely that the increase of aid flows *after* the CPDN had lost its momentum negatively affected its performance. To examine this assumption, it may be helpful to address two questions: Why did private aid agencies increase their contributions while the role of the CPDN actually was diminishing? And how did this affect its (intermediary) role in Salvadorean civil society?

A look at the figures shows that private aid support to the CPDN increased twofold between 1991 and 1992, which was a direct response to the successful conclusion of the peace agreement of Chapúltepec in January 1992. The CPDN budget for 1993-94 was on average four times the budget it had handled between 1990 and 1991, which was the period of the main achievements of the CPDN. Although only half of the requested funding was effectively received, 1993 and 1994 still were the years in which the CPDN received the largest contributions from private aid agencies. Several reasons can be given to explain this phenomenon. One is technical: there is always a certain period between funding requests and final disbursements. But in the case of ICCO, the largest funder of the CPDN, this period was rather long: usually more than one year. This was caused by ICCO's lengthy application procedure for co-funding at the Dutch ministry, but also by its slow internal process of approval and disbursements.[77] As a result, the CPDN had to raise additional funding to fill the liquidity gaps created by delayed disbursements.

Another reason for the increase of private aid flows to the CPDN after 1992 was that private aid agencies apparently did not make an accurate political analysis of what role the CPDN would play after the peace agreements. With the legalisation of the FMLN as a political party, the CPDN's intermediary role was gradually taken over by the former guerrilla organisation. Poor coordination among the private aid agencies supporting the CPDN and the absence of a proper monitoring system meant that the agencies did not realise that the CPDN was loosing its political momentum.[78] The only external evaluation of the CPDN, carried out in late 1994 at the request of ICCO, actually came two years too late. Even though this evaluation was not very critical, its recommendations were not seriously incorporated into future planning.[79] While local agency representatives were rather critical about the performance of the CPDN, desk officers of the Protestant agencies gave it the benefit of the doubt, largely because CPDN was run by a leading member of the Salvadorean churches.[80]

A further reason for the income growth of the CPDN has to do with the 'chemistry' of donor-recipient relations. Recipients often exaggerate their budgets in project proposals because they know donors tend to approve lower funding than is requested. Although ICCO was somewhat surprised by the US$ 1.6 million budget for 1993-94, it did not seriously question the implications of this considerable increase in anticipated expenditures. ICCO decided to accept this growth and increased its support for these years by almost fifty percent compared to previous years.[81] Despite the incapacity of the CPDN to spend ICCO's contribution in the period agreed, funding continued even after 1995. Another element in the chemistry was that ICCO's decision to continue support to the CPDN encouraged smaller funders to also continue their support, as they trusted that contributions to the CPDN would be carefully monitored by ICCO, which was responsible for half the CPDN's income between 1990 and 1996. This monitoring was, as argued earlier, poor if not virtually absent.

Possibly one of the key shortcomings of the donor agencies was that they did not put enough pressure on the CPDN to request contributions from member organisations in order to make the alliance more self-sufficient. Although the CPDN argued that members did contribute, in reality the CPDN was channelling funds to its members for the organisation of marches and the implementation of activities. These 'reverse aid flows' were a direct product of 'overfunding' by the agencies. Starting in 1992, with the first large increase in aid funding, the CPDN gradually created its own financial reserves as it was unable to spend all its income.[82] This might have been understandable – given the small administrative staff, rather short-term planning and the exaggerated budget – but for some reason it did not alarm the agencies. It was not until 1995, after finding contradictions in financial reports, that ICCO became more strict about proper financial reporting and eventually demanded replacement of the 'external' accountant. However, funding to the CPDN was not made conditional upon a certain level of member contributions, and this generates the second question about the impact of 'overfunding' on the performance of the CPDN.

The large amount of agency income, combined with the low level of member contributions, meant that member organisations increasingly considered the CPDN as a channel to attract foreign aid resources and less as an intermediary alliance in civil society. Starting in 1993, many members started to become 'delinked' from the CPDN for three reasons. First, because they had other channels (such as the FMLN) to voice their demands to the state. Second, because they encountered considerable problems in renewing their leadership and adapting their internal organisation and discourse from confrontation to constructive dialogue and concertación. Third, because the policy of the CPDN to secure consensus among societal sectors was effective on the issue of peace, but did not work for (the more complex and often contradictory) socio-economic demands. Due to the continuous inpouring of foreign aid, the policies of the CPDN became scattered as it kept offering a variety of fora and seminars with poor outcomes.[83] To avoid bureaucracy, the implementation of these activities was generally delegated to member organisations. This is not to say that the CPDN was not a useful forum for discussion (which it certainly was for young cadre) but it lacked the coherent strategy that had been followed in the late 1980s. Continued and increased private aid support and the absence of member contributions thus transformed the CPDN into a donor-driven alliance in civil society.[84]

— *Assessing the civil society building performance of the* CPDN

One of the striking lessons from the CPDN aid chain is the apparent difficulty private aid agencies experience adjusting their intervention policies to rapidly changing political processes. Essentially, support from private aid agencies increased *after* the CPDN had lost the political momentum. What was the impact of this on the organisational capacity of the CPDN? Let me first examine the level of participation by members and the character of internal accountability. It was shown that the CPDN started as a membership organisation with a rather flat structure, with active participation of members and a high level of downward accountability. Members that were closely linked to the FMLN (which had vertical and centralised organisational structures) indeed became influential in the CPDN during and after the 1989 offensive. But they did not convert the CPDN into a *fachada* (a puppet) of the FMLN, although right-wing opponents claimed that this was the case. Policy-making and implementation were coordinated by a *directorio sectorial*, a weekly meeting of representatives from all sectors active in the CPDN. Daily coordination and decision-making was performed by a revolving small committee (in which FMLN members were a minority), which also maintained contacts with funders. The 'sectoral directorate' served as an intermediary between the coordination committee and the national assembly in which all member organisations had two seats. Because of the active participation of many sectors during the peace negotiations, the assembly decided to change the image of the CPDN from that of a 'permanent committee' into a 'social movement'. However, this movement character had *de facto* ended with the end of the war, when (a striking coincidence) a separate CPDN office was opened in late 1991. After 1992, and certainly during the electoral campaign, the sectoral directorate started to disintegrate with fewer members participating, followed by its eventual dissolution in 1994. As a result, direct feedback to member organisations diminished and communication to the constituency of the CPDN went mainly via the mass media.[85] The decline of the CPDN therefore could be seen in its transformation from a membership organisation into a pressure group and a debating forum. Due to the absence of member contributions (and the availability of increasing private aid funds) this weakening of the institutional structure was not recognised as a problem by CPDN's leaders or by the donor agencies.

Consequently, the financial sustainability of the CPDN was entirely dependent upon foreign aid resources and the prospects for long-term survival were therefore not very encouraging. This negative outlook can be largely attributed to the changed political circumstances after the peace agreement was implemented, which led to demobilisation and ideological confusion for many popular organisations. Without fully realising this, the CPDN gradually became transformed from a membership organisation into a sort of 'socio-economic human rights NGO'. But it continued to call itself 'an expression of the Salvadorean social movement', although it was never financially sustained by this movement. On the contrary, as was argued earlier, the CPDN became a donor-driven committee paying organisations for particular activities that they might have done anyway. Private aid agencies (in particular the two largest funders ICCO and *Brot für die Welt*) therefore made four mistakes in increasing their support to the CPDN in 1993: (i) they did not make an assessment of the political changes after the implementation of the peace agreement and how these affected popular organisations and the position of the CPDN, (ii) they did not press enough for the need to collect member contributions, (iii) they did not invest in improving the weak institutional structure of the CPDN and (iv) they did a poor job coordinating between each other, and only started to do so (after 1994) when it was in fact too late.

Regarding its role in civil society building the CPDN combined several elements. It boosted the formation of a peace alliance and performed an intermediary role in civil society *vis-à-vis* the state and the international community. The alliance between radical FMLN-controlled mass organisations and moderate societal actors was realised in 1988, before private aid started to flow to the CPDN. It is therefore likely that private aid agencies did not play a significant role in forging this alliance. It is even doubtful if the performance of this alliance would have been different if private aid had been absent in the period until the final peace agreement was signed in early 1992, as the FMLN had a vested interest in keeping a solid unity of oppositional forces in civil society during the negotiations. Nevertheless, by performing an intermediary role in civil society the CPDN was an effective alliance pushing for a negotiated solution, particularly in the year prior to the November 1989 offensive. After the offensive the FMLN increased its influence in the CPDN, which was the same period in which it started to receive private aid support. The activities of the lobbying office in Washington and the street marches which took place during the negotiations (and were partly financed by private foreign aid) were important contributions to the peace process. Without private aid support the activities of the CPDN to pressure the government and international actors would probably have taken place on a smaller scale, and the lobbying work might even have been absent. But it would be unreasonable to conclude that the outcome of the negotiations would have been any different without this support. The (negative) influence of private foreign aid was particularly visible after 1992, when the intermediary function of the CPDN declined despite increased aid contributions.

The strongest policy impact of the CPDN was achieved prior to the start of negotiations and during the peace talks. In September 1988, a few months before the presidential elections, the CPDN managed to get ARENA's presidential candidate Cristiani to endorse important elements of the consensus document. One year later, organised pressure from the CPDN was one of the factors that pushed President Cristiani to open the dialogue with the FMLN. This was all in the period prior to private aid support for the CPDN. As the peace process had a strong dynamic of its own, it is hard to tell to what extent the CPDN directly influenced the texts of the peace agreements. According to Palacios the initial agreement on demilitarisation (May 1991) was drafted on the basis of a proposal from the CPDN, but David Escobar Galindo, a key negotiator for the government, denies this.[86] The CPDN probably contributed to influencing Democratic Senators in the US Congress, although they were lobbied from many sides. Still, private aid funding to the Washington office of the CPDN was important for lobbying and networking with churches and solidarity groups in the United States and for keeping European and Canadian partners informed. Policy impact after 1992 was marginal, except maybe for the 'Project for a New Nation' of June 1993 of which some elements were adopted by the FMLN-CD coalition (with which direct linkages already existed). Policy impact of the CPDN thus was minimally related to the inflow of private aid support, with the exception of the Washington lobbying office.

In sum, it might be concluded that the needs of temporary alliances in civil society do not always coincide with the logic of private aid agencies, which are often not geared toward providing instant and adequate support to these alliances. Private aid donors prefer to build up longer term partnerships, which often contradicts the temporary nature of civil society coalitions. Institutionalisation of the CPDN, although required by the agencies, generated internal resistance and rejection of bureaucracy but not a rejection of foreign aid. The private aid agencies ICCO and *Brot für die Welt*, for their part, have become reluctant to continue their support to the CPDN, as it no longer performs the functions it did when partnerships were established in 1989. It is possible that the CPDN will survive the late 1990s, for example as a 'social coalition against poverty'. But it will have to sustain itself through contributions of actively participating members. In other words, just like when it started out at the very beginning.

6.3 Incorporating *indígenas* in Guatemalan civil society: FUNDADESE

While the previous two case studies focused on human rights and on peace negotiations, the Guatemalan case study combines these two issues, albeit in a special way. Despite many political and historical commonalties between Central American countries, only Guatemala has an indigenous majority. Among the Guatemalan *indígenas* (Indians) five major ethno-linguistic groups and more than twenty different native languages have been identified, the majority descending from the Mayas.[87] Another characteristic of private aid funding to Guatemala that is relevant for this study is that the amount of aid increased when it was stagnating in other Central American countries, as was demonstrated in the previous chapter. The reason for this increase was the resumption of peace talks between the armed opposition and the government and the emergence of a number of new associations in civil society. Particularly 'Indian' organisations, which had been most affected by military counter-insurgency operations, demonstrated remarkable growth in the early 1990s. It is therefore plausible to focus the Guatemalan case study on an Indian organisation that received substantial European private aid support.

Various organisations working with indigenous communities were suggested by European agencies for the present research.[88] The problem was that none of these organisations explicitly performed an intermediary role for Indian organisations in civil society, although one of them did have an impressive record in this area: FUNDADESE. This local development NGO was chosen because its leaders played a key role in Indian organisations that participated in national civil society alliances. But also because it was considered by many private aid agencies as one of the most successful Indian NGOS in Guatemala. FUNDADESE's local development activities were praised, as well as its active role in opening up new political space for indigenous people during the Guatemalan democratic transition of the 1990s.[89]

The case of FUNDADESE is however rather complex as it deals with a large number of Indian organisations that were either created or supported by its own leaders since the late 1980s. As all these organisations are in some way interconnected, an outsider could quickly get lost in the forest of abbreviations. The first part of this case study will therefore sketch a necessary overview of the recent revival of Indian organisations and coalitions. Furthermore, the case is far from transparent as FUNDADESE's leaders often played a key role in several other Indian organisations, as representatives of FUNDADESE or personally. Another difficulty is that the Guatemalan peace process (and the democratic transition it spurred) is not yet complete. Although the peace agreement was signed in December 1996, by the time of this writing many agreements still have to be implemented and the outcome of the peace process is therefore inconclusive. However, the complexity of this case study probably also underscores that an analysis of private aid funding aimed at civil society building seldom is linear, transparent or simple.

– *Participation of Indian organisations in the Guatemalan peace process*
The current revival of Indian organisations in Guatemala has its origins in the 1960s, when social and economic developments contributed to a transformation of the impoverished and marginalised indigenous communities.[90] The Catholic Church gradually introduced fundamental reforms with its influential rural programme *Acción Católica*, challenging the traditional authority of the priest-shamans and the religious brotherhoods (*cofradías*). Schools were built, cooperatives were set up and political parties (in particular the Christian Democratic Party) entered the communities to participate in municipal elections.[91] Gradually, a consciousness developed among *indígenas* that this new space offered by external actors could be used to demand better social and political conditions. A new generation of Indian leaders (often catechists trained by *Acción Católica*) was replacing the traditional elderly community leaders and started to mobilise indigenous communities, eventually leading to the formation of a national Indian peasant organisation: the Committee for Peasant Unity (CUC).[92] This new organisation emerged in the northern department El Quiché, a few years after the disappointing 1974 election results of the Christian Democrats. The CUC would increase its support in the highlands after the 1976 earthquake created a political vacuum in rural areas. This vacuum also was filled by right-wing US fundamentalist and Pentecostal sects that massively invaded indigenous communities after the earthquake (Perera 1993).

By the late 1970s, CUC had taken the lead in a broad, popular and predominantly Indian social movement which was quickly radicalising. Many CUC affiliates opted for revolutionary armed struggle, especially after the armed forces systematically started to kill Indian peasant leaders in the Alta Verapaz and in the Ixil and Ixcán areas (Carmack 1988).[93] The massacre of 140 Indian peasants in Panzós (1978) generally is considered to be the start of the indigenous rebellion in the highlands.[94] The army justified the killings by saying they believed the Indian peasants were part of the guerrilla movement, although this was not (yet) the case.[95] The selective military repression was in fact counter-productive: whilst death squads tried to eliminate radical indigenous leaders, revolutionary groups started to grow and incorporated new members from persecuted indigenous communities. A key moment in this process was the massacre of a CUC-led delegation of nearly forty Indian peasants in the Spanish embassy in January 1980, who were protesting against the mounting repression in the Quiché department. The massacre made many indigenous communities decide to join with the guerrillas, creating a strong Indian-Ladino popular movement (Jonas 1991).

Ongoing popular protest, a large strike of sugar cane workers and rapid growth of guerrilla-controlled areas was responded to by the military regime of Lucas García with a counter-insurgency offensive in mid-1981 in order to defeat the revolutionary movement, which meanwhile had achieved unity in the URNG.[96] Falla (1994: 183) describes how the army seeded terror in the indigenous communities: 'a growing degree of violence was used in the abductions, killings, and selective massacres: disfigured corpses were dumped and bodies were hung from trees in an attempt to instil terror'. Although causing thousands of casualties, the campaign did not deter guerrilla resistance. General Ríos Montt, who had replaced Lucas García in the March 1982 coup, therefore decided to apply scorched earth tactics by physically eliminating indigenous communities in guerrilla-controlled areas. The purpose was to destroy the popular basis of the guerrilla movement and regain control over these areas. Jonas (1991: 149) even argues that the war was 'an assault by the Ladino state against the Indian population', as the military intended to destroy ethnic unity and Indian identity. Between 50,000 and 75,000 civilians were killed or disappeared in this genocide, which left 440 villages destroyed and nearly one million *indígenas* displaced, of which around 200,000 sought refuge in Mexico.[97] In an effort to consolidate its control over the conflict zones, the army established 'model villages' in which special committees implemented development projects under military supervision. In these model villages, but also in hundreds of villages in the highlands, 'Civil Defence Patrols' (PAC's) were established. These paramilitary organisations, in which during the mid-1980s up to one million civilians would participate, became a key instrument of the military for keeping control over rural indigenous communities and to counter guerrilla activity.

Indian organisational structures appeared to be effectively destroyed by the large-scale counter-insurgency campaign of the early 1980s. The URNG had not been eliminated, but was politically defeated and was pushed back to remote areas from where it continued attacks on military targets.[98] What was left of the CUC leadership was either underground or in exile, and CUC was not re-established until 1986. Although the process took more than a decade, Indian organisations were slowly rebuilt and would even become stronger and more diverse actors in civil society than before. This process of indigenous organisation building can be divided into three periods: (i) from 1984 to 1990, when human rights violations were emphasised, (ii) from 1990 to 1993, when the emphasis was on Indian rights, and (iii) from 1993 to 1996, when Indian organisations were actively incorporated into the peace process.

The first period of rebuilding Indian organisations runs (almost) parallel to the new civilian government of President Cerezo (1986-1990). However, the first organisation serving as a national channel publicly denouncing disappearances and atrocities committed in indigenous communities had already emerged in 1984: the Mutual Support Group (GAM). This human rights organisation was formed by a group of relatives of disappeared, led by Nineth Montenegro, and would become one of the most active opposition groups in civil society during the 1980s. Although initially founded by Ladinos, it soon also incorporated Indian members. Other human rights organisations more dominated by *indígenas* were set up after the Esquipulas agreement. The international attention generated by this Central American peace plan, and the call for a National Dialogue, provided new political openings for the Guatemalan opposition. Human rights organisations run by *indígenas*, such as CONAVIGUA (the organisation of Indian widows and orphans), CERJ (that rallied against civil patrols in the highlands) and CONDEG (which tried to organise the internally displaced) made the international community aware of the genocide that had struck the Indian communities.[99] And more important, that paramilitary violence was continuing under the Cerezo administration. Within the framework of the National Dialogue, these organisations started to coordinate their activities.[100] Until that time coordination around specific Indian issues had not existed publicly.

The second phase of rebuilding Indian organisations started in 1990, when the first round of peace talks began in Oslo between the URNG and the government. It was an election year and the presidency was won in the second round by conservative candidate Jorge Serrano.[101] Two new coalitions of Indian organisations were founded in this election year: *Majawil Q'ij* and COMG. The first was an alliance formed during preparations for the Latin American counter-celebration of the fifth centennial of the 'discovery' (a campaign called '500 years of popular and Indian resistance') organised with several other Indian organisations from Latin America. A large international gathering of these groups was convened in Guatemala in October 1991 by the new coalition *Majawil Q'ij*, a joint effort of several Indian organisations including CUC, GAM, CONAVIGUA, CONDEG, CERJ and the CPR's.[102] The gradual shift of emphasis of these organisations from socio-economic demands and human rights issues in the 1980s to an ethnic discourse in the 1990s illustrated a fundamental shift to prioritise Indian demands. This was an obvious move to prepare for input on Indian issues from civil society at the peace talks in Oslo. According to Bastos and Camus (1995) the 'popular Indian' organisations also were influenced by another current of Indian organisations emphasising and reaffirming their 'Maya identity'. This diverse set of organisations – including the Guatemalan Maya Language Academy (ALMG), the Maya education centre and publisher *Cholsamaj*, and several development NGOs, among them FUNDADESE – in 1990 formed the other new Indian coalition: the Guatemalan Council of Maya Organisations (COMG).[103] These two coordinating bodies of Indian organisations, representing a 'popular Indian' current and one dedicated to Maya self-determination, were the first signs of a dynamic process in which Indian organisations would become active players in Guatemalan civil society.

COMG and its 'Mayanist' institutions stayed away from the October 1991 gathering of Latin American Indian organisations in Quetzaltenango (which was hosted by *Majawil Q'ij*) as COMG considered the event too dominated by Ladino organisations.[104] However, progress in the peace talks forced the two coalitions to work together: point three of the negotiation agenda mentioned 'Indian rights and identity'. The organisations of COMG feared that this issue would be decided by Ladino-composed delegations of the URNG and the government. Together with *Majawil Q'ij* and others, COMG stated publicly that Indian organisations had the right to directly participate in the debates about this issue. In October 1992 they created a special section in the Coalition of Civil Sectors (CSC), the so-called *Mesa Maya*, to work out proposals on Indian issues and discuss them with the negotiating parties.[105] The *Mesa Maya* thus became the first united civil society alliance of Indian organisations, in which the basis was laid for a unified proposal on the issue of 'Indian rights and identity'.[106] An additional impulse for concerted action by Indian organisations came in October 1992, when Rigoberta Menchú was granted the Nobel Peace Prize. By that time, however, the peace process had stagnated and even come to a deadlock, meaning that Indian organisations would be unable to discuss their proposals with the negotiating parties until after the talks resumed in 1994.

The incorporation of Indian organisations into the peace process characterises the third period of Indian organisation building, and starts in the aftermath of Serrano's *autogolpe* (self-staged coup) of 25 May 1993. With Serrano's forced resignation, the system of 'controlled democracy' that had reigned in Guatemala since Cerezo's election in 1985 was exhausted. A combination of economic crisis, widespread corruption and the inability to push the peace process further led to a temporary political crisis that would become a turning point in Guatemala's democratic transition. In the confusing days after the coup, in which Ramiro de León Carpio was elected by Congress to serve as a provisional president, Indian organisations convened a large meeting. The purpose of this Assembly of the Maya People, in which 86 Indian organisations were represented, was to guarantee their participation in the political process following the coup. They demanded a Maya representative in a new provisional government, and announced the formation of

a Permanent Maya Assembly (APM) to guarantee and monitor the effective incorporation of Indian organisations in the post-coup process. However, this effort to
form a united coalition of Indian organisations failed as the 'popular Indian'
organisations that were left over from the *Mesa Maya* took part in another alliance
formed by civil society actors, the National Consensus Body (INC). Within the
INC, the 'popular Indian' organisations constituted a new alliance: the Maya Unity
and Consensus Body (IUCM). The reason for not achieving a united coalition of
Indian organisations apparently had to more do with frictions among leaders than
with the content of the proposals (Bastos and Camus 1995). Others believed that
the lack of unity was the result of an internal struggle between various tendencies
of the URNG and those organisations (especially ALMG and COMG) that refused to
follow URNG tactics at that time.[107] But all Indian organisations were conscious of
the need to coordinate efforts in order to exploit the new political circumstances in
favour of indigenous incorporation into the peace process and the process of
democratic transition.

   It took another year before one united coalition of Indian organisations would
be established that would directly influence the peace negotiations. This delay was
caused by efforts of newly-appointed President De León Carpio to change the
framework for negotiations.[108] But in January 1994 the two parties finally reached
an agreement in Mexico on a framework for peace talks, in which the UN would
serve as moderator.[109] It was also agreed that representatives of Guatemalan civil
society would not be admitted to participate directly in the talks (despite demands
by various societal sectors) but that a newly created Civil Society Assembly (ASC)
would perform a consultative role, with two important functions. On the one hand,
the ASC was invited to present its own proposals on six 'substantive' issues.[110] On
the other hand, the ASC was assigned the task of endorsing the agreements made by
the government and the URNG. Chaired by Catholic Bishop Quezada, the ASC was
composed of all major civil society sectors that had been active in previous talks,
except for the representatives of the business sector (CACIF).[111]

   Indian organisations realised that they had to close their ranks in order to achieve
the best possible outcome on the issues that most affected them: the refugees and
the displaced, and most of all the agreement on 'Indian rights and identity'. With
this in mind, all the existing alliances of Indian organisations met in early 1994 to
prepare their proposals on these important issues. Present were the ALMG (which
was actually more an academic institution than an alliance) and COMG, plus the
two new alliances that had arisen after the political crisis of 1993, APM and IUCM.
Although differences existed over the priority of demands they should put forward,
particularly on the issue of Indian autonomy, an agreement was reached. The four
alliances also decided to form a new organisation to coordinate their work in the
'Maya sector' of the ASC: the Coalition of Organisations of the Maya People of
Guatemala (COPMAGUA), established in May 1994, one week before the ASC was
officially installed by Bishop Quezada. COPMAGUA would become one of the most
important players in the ASC during 1994 and 1995 because it managed to get the

best possible agreement on Indian rights approved by the two parties. COPMAGUA's composition changed in late 1994, when the APM stepped out and two new alliances (*Tukum Amam* and UPMAG) entered the new coalition of Indian alliances.[112] All these alliances together represented over a hundred (national, local, sectoral and multisectoral) Indian organisations. Within five years not only had the number of Indian organisations reached a record but also the level of unity had never been as advanced as with the formation of COPMAGUA. One of the key actors in bringing about this level of coordination among Indian organisations was FUNDADESE.

— *Emergence and activities of FUNDADESE*

In the slowly depolarising political climate after the installation of the Cerezo government, several small relief organisations were formed in the highlands to give assistance to indigenous communities affected by the counter-insurgency war. Some of these organisations were related to North American evangelical churches, others were development NGOs set up by Indian leaders. One of them was FUNDADESE, founded in 1985 in Chichicastenango, in the southern part of the Quiché department. In the 1970s a dense network of organisations, committees and cooperatives existed in this area (mainly stimulated by the activities of *Acción Católica*) which developed into a broad opposition movement against the authoritarian regimes and the armed forces. Many Indian communities joined the ranks of the guerrilla movement in the early 1980s. As a result, repression was brutal and counter-insurgency activities destroyed most of the existing organisational structures. It was an area in which the Civil Defence Patrols (PAC's) were combative and actively frustrated the work of human rights organisations. FUNDADESE's goal was to counter the influence of these PAC's by contributing to a revival of community organisation structures.

Initially, FUNDADESE organised relief projects for orphans, widows and other victims of the counter-insurgency campaign.[113] With primary health care it tried to gain the confidence of communities 'in which repression had left an illness called fear' (Carrera 1994: 39). Only after community councils began to trust their work did FUNDADESE start up new projects on collective enterprises, cultural promotion and organisation building. The idea was to rebuild the social fabric in the communities by strengthening new civil structures and pushing back the influence of the PAC's. FUNDADESE wanted to revalue Indian identity and revive cultural values as a means of counterpoising the military domination in these communities. It stimulated the formation of sectoral and community councils, in order to integrate these into intercommunal councils that in turn served as consultative entities for FUNDADESE's policies. A longer term purpose was that this association of community councils would present their development needs to the local municipality for financial support. In other words, in the long run the municipality would take over FUNDADESE's role as a supplier of funding.

Due to private foreign aid support, FUNDADESE grew quickly and expanded its activities in the late 1980s from southern Quiché to the Sololá and Totonicapán areas. New activities were started on infrastructure, education and agriculture. In 1989 FUNDADESE inaugurated *Pop Wuj* in Chimaltenango, a Maya education centre for technicians in integrated community development. The foundation gradually decentralised its activities and opened a third office in 1993 in Quetzaltenango to assist the displaced and returning refugees in the departments of Quetzaltenango, San Marcos and Retalhuleu. The executive board of FUNDADESE was formed by three of its founders: Israel Sequén (director of *Pop Wuj* in Chimaltenango), Alberto Mazariegos (director of the Quetzaltenango office) and María Riquiac (director of the central office in Chichicastenango). These three founders and their three offices would form the core of FUNDADESE.

This decentralisation was partly the result of different priorities held by the three directors concerning the activities that FUNDADESE should pursue at a national level. Since the late 1980s the foundation was active in two national networks: the Council of Maya Organisations, COMG, and the national NGO coalition COINDE. This dual membership reflected the identity that FUNDADESE had developed from the beginning: being a 'Mayan' development NGO while simultaneously acting as an association of indigenous communities that through FUNDADESE became (founding) members of COMG. Alberto Mazariegos soon became one of the leading figures in COMG, where he advocated closer collaboration with the 'popular Indian' organisations of *Majawil Q'ij* in which FUNDADESE indirectly participated as part of COINDE. Mazariegos also actively participated in the *Mesa Maya* in 1992, when the document on 'Indian rights and identity' was edited. He soon became publicly known as one of the national Maya leaders advocating a pluri-ethnic solution to the controversy over the position of the Indian population. In early 1994, Bishop Quezada invited Mazariegos – together with Rosalina Tuyuc and Juan León[114] – to form the 'Maya sector' in the ASC in which COPMAGUA would draft the position paper on Indian rights and identity as input for the peace talks. Shortly before COPMAGUA was formed, Mazariegos left COMG because he was increasingly criticised for advocating positions too closely associated with the URNG.[115] As most members of COMG wanted to stay politically independent, Mazariegos formed *Tukum Amam*, a new alliance of Indian organisations active in the south-western part of the highlands (where FUNDADESE had set up a new office in 1993). Although a formal member of COPMAGUA only in early 1995, *Tukum Amam* would serve as Mazariegos's constituency, legitimising his leading role in COPMAGUA and in the ASC.[116]

On account of its other two directors, FUNDADESE also was present in other national alliances. María Riquiac initially participated as a delegate of COMG in the Maya sector of the ASC and later in 1994 in the NGO sector through COINDE.[117] Israel Sequén was active since the early 1990s in several human rights groups, and founded the Mayan human rights commission *Wuqub' Noj*, which was a member of COMG but also part of the human rights sector of the ASC.[118] FUNDADESE's education centre *Pop Wuj* (directed by Sequén) was represented in the ASC as one of the research centres and as part of ALMG. In addition to that, Mazariegos was a

Figure 6.1   *The three FUNDADESE offices (1994-96): Aid chains and linkages with the Civil Society Assembly (ASC)*

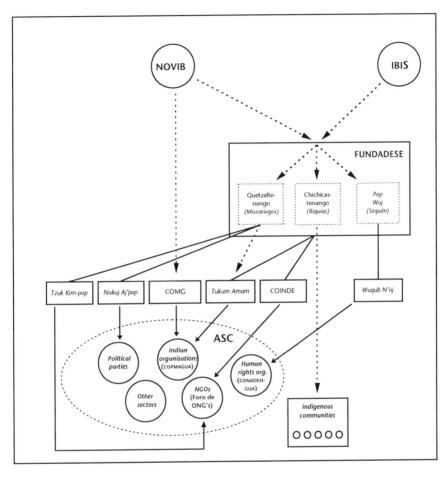

· · · · ·▶ = aid flows

member of the organisational committee of the ASC. As a result, due to the presence of its leaders, FUNDADESE gradually became one of the most active players inside the ASC as it had representatives in a variety of societal sectors. The complexity of this network of relationships is illustrated in Figure 6.1.

The active participation of FUNDADESE and other Indian organisations in various sectors of the ASC was obviously meant to get COPMAGUA's position paper approved on 'Indian rights and identity'. After a lively and emotional debate, and intensive lobbying by Indian leaders, the ASC finally reached consensus on the key points proposed by COPMAGUA: recognition of Guatemala as a pluri-ethnic and pluri-lingual nation, the need to restructure the state and guarantee equitable relations in a new political system and the recognition of a number of Indian rights.[119] Rejected were more radical points on the restitution of expropriated communal lands and the demand for political autonomy. The conciliatory role of Bishop Quezada as a chair of the ASC and the efforts by Indian leaders such as Mazariegos to reach a consensus were fundamental to getting one of the most critical issues in the peace process approved by the ASC.[120] The next step was to get the agreement endorsed by the URNG and the government. However, the peace talks were stagnating as a result of strong negative reactions from within civil society against the agreement on the Truth Commission.[121] The fear was that the Indian rights agreement also would be compromised at the negotiation table, leading to a vague and superficial document. COPMAGUA kept insisting that it wanted to participate at the negotiation table and that Indian organisations were to verify the agreement. To put pressure on the two parties, a number of massive public marches were organised in October and November 1994 by COPMAGUA members, including the FUNDADESE-led *Tukum Amam* in Quetzaltenango. The URNG commanders, disturbed by the negative reactions from civil society, announced in December that from now on they would accept the consensus documents of the ASC without modifications. In reaction, the Catholic Church decided to withdraw Bishop Quezada as chair of the ASC, afraid that it would be identified with URNG positions.[122] The prominent role of the ASC was seriously reduced by Quezada's departure, but the Indian organisations knew that 'their document' had been saved.

After strong international pressure, by the UN and the *países amigos*, peace talks were resumed in March 1995, although the government refused COPMAGUA's participation at the negotiation table.[123] The process had to be speeded up as campaigns were gradually starting for the November 1995 presidential elections. Finally, at the end of March the two parties reached an agreement on the Indian rights issue, in which the basic proposals of the ASC consensus document were included. Alberto Mazariegos and Rosalina Tuyuc were invited as representatives of COPMAGUA to witness the formal signing of the agreement. In a special assembly, COPMAGUA discussed the outcome with its members and finally endorsed it as 'a first important step that opened the door' (Bastos and Camus 1995: 84). Many issues still had to be worked out in detail, for which the agreement proposed to establish special commissions *(comisiones paritarias)* in which Indian organisations would actively participate under UN supervision. In this follow-up stage FUNDADESE also performed an active role, as *Tukum Amam* was elected to take part in six of the eight working groups preparing positions for these commissions.[124] With the agreement on Indian rights approved, Mazariegos used his position in the ASC to prepare for the upcoming elections of November 1995. In the framework of the new progressive political alliance organised to take part in these elections, the Democratic Front for a New Guatemala (FDNG), various Indian alliances participated as part of the Maya front *N'ukuj Ajpop*.[125] Mazariegos was one of the founders of this front and a member of the political council of the FDNG, which nominated Indian leader Juan León as a candidate for vice-president. The FDNG successfully attracted voters from the Indian communities and managed to get six deputies elected to Congress, among them Indian leaders Rosalina Tuyuc (CONAVIGUA) and Manuela Alvarado from Quetzaltenango, a member of *Tukum Amam* and trained by FUNDADESE's education centre *Pop Wuj.*

In 1996, after the presidential elections, FUNDADESE's activities in the ASC were scaled down. The Indian rights issue had been resolved and the new government of President Alvaro Arzú promised that the final peace agreement was only a matter of time. María Riquiac had already concluded her activities in the ASC in early 1995 as the office in Chichicastenango required her presence to continue coordinating the programme, which (after the successful elections) now also included building and maintaining municipal power structures. Sequén and Mazariegos both left the ASC in 1996, although they remained active in the preparatory work for the *comisiones paritarias.* Mazariegos's priority had shifted from creating national political space for Indian organisations to assuring financial support for a new regional coalition of NGOs working in the south-western part of the highlands: the *Movimiento Tzuk Kim-pop.*[126] Directed by Mazariegos, this coalition counted eighteen local NGOs, among them FUNDADESE. Its purpose was to contribute to strengthening civil society by supporting and coordinating local and regional development projects aimed at building up local Indian organisations. As a leader of *Tukum Amam,* Mazariegos participated in several follow-up commissions for the implementation of the Indian rights agreement. He also continued to advocate for the active participation of Indian organisations in the political arena as part of his activities in *N'ukuj Ajpop.* Gradually he handed over his responsibilities for FUNDADESE's Quetzaltenango office to others, although he stayed on as a member of the foundation's executive board.

— *Private foreign aid to FUNDADESE*

The initial activities of FUNDADESE were financed with resources from the health ministry and with support from other NGOs such as CAPS and IDESAC. Contacts with several international agencies in 1987 resulted in small donations from the Spanish IEPALA, the *Inter-American Foundation* and OXFAM-America (who financed the community development programme until 1990). Meanwhile, three European aid agencies decided in 1989 to support the new education centre *Pop Wuj* in Chimaltenango: NOVIB, *Brot für die Welt* and OXFAM-Belgium. In the same year, the Danish *Ibis* and the Spanish CIPIE expressed interest in financing the Chichicastenango programme. Particularly the support from *Ibis,* starting in 1990, meant a considerable enlargement in the community development programmes.[127] Two years later, NOVIB decided to finance a similar programme, which would triple the amount of communities serviced by the foundation. *Ibis* and NOVIB would become FUNDADESE's main funders by contributing to a rapid expansion of its community development programme in the 1990s.[128] Both agencies highly valued FUNDADESE's strategy of strengthening the process of community organisation by supporting locally identified development needs. *Ibis* originally would have preferred to support a local Indian membership organisation, but these were still hard to find in 1989. Moreover, it considered FUNDADESE's hybrid structure (between a service-delivery NGO and a community-based organisation) an attractive alternative.[129] FUNDADESE's active participation in several Indian networks, such as COMG, confirmed perceptions by *Ibis* and NOVIB that it was linked to key national efforts to strengthen Indian participation in civil society.[130] However, surprisingly little coordination existed between the two main donors of FUNDADESE.

NOVIB, also a funder of COMG, was approached by FUNDADESE director Mazariegos in early 1994 to see whether it would be willing to support his activities in the ASC. Mazariegos by that time had left COMG and was building up his new Indian alliance *Tukum Amam*. A few months earlier he also had started 'his' new office in Quetzaltenango, although funds were still channelled through the central office in Chichicastenango. Mazariegos asked NOVIB to finance the consolidation of COPMAGUA in the ASC, and in particular to facilitate the incorporation of *Tukum Amam* into COPMAGUA. The request was approved, as Mazariegos represented an important NOVIB partner and had proven to be a key person in contributing to unity among the Indian alliances within the ASC. By supporting Mazariegos's activities in the ASC, NOVIB also hoped to get a better understanding of discussions and alliances within the complex and rapidly changing network of Indian organisations.[131] An additional reason for supporting the request was that NOVIB considered active participation of NGOs and popular organisations in the ASC crucial for the peace process.[132] Although NOVIB was aware that Mazariegos's activities in the ASC were not directly related to FUNDADESE's local work, the legal structure of the foundation was used to channel support for his work to *Tukum Amam* for two years.[133] These financial resources enabled Mazariegos to operate independently from COMG, but also from the other FUNDADESE directors.

– *Achievements of FUNDADESE*
The previous analysis suggests that FUNDADESE's achievements should be examined at the two levels on which it contributed to incorporating *indígenas* into civil society. At a local level the central office in Chichicastenango focused on supporting Indian communities by rebuilding Indian organisational structures. These activities, which have been running for over a decade, are rather well documented and have been examined by several external evaluations.[134] The other level is FUNDADESE's active role in national civil society coalitions, in particular its role in COPMAGUA which participated in the ASC. These efforts spurred the approval of the Indian Rights and Identity Agreement as part of the peace process. Because this work has not yet been evaluated, most attention of the fieldwork was concentrated on these macro activities. Although both areas of activities are narrowly linked from a political perspective, they were funded separately by private aid agencies and I therefore would prefer to examine them one by one.

The main goal of FUNDADESE's community work in Chichicastenango was to rebuild local organisational structures and 'community consensus', all destroyed during the early 1980s. The method used was the implementation of health and socio-economic projects to tackle the extreme poverty in the area, actively steered by local community groups. FUNDADESE had to walk on eggs, as local communities were reluctant to become involved in any organisational activity of a political nature: this had in the recent past been synonymous with guerrilla activity (Højrup Jensen 1995: 8). This is not to say these indigenous communities had no organisational structure, on the contrary,[135] but existing organisations often had fractured the communities and made villagers reluctant to get involved in joint community activities.[136] Many had even turned away from the Catholic Church (which had been associated with the guerrilla movement since the late 1970s) and become members of evangelical sects as a means of physical protection. FUNDA-DESE's strategy was to work initially with existing *comité's pro-mejoramiento*, identifying members willing to set up new committees around particular projects.[137] In this way it tried to neutralise the interference of sects and PAC's in community development. These new committees were coordinated by a community council which would form the new organisational basis of the community; linkages between several communities were based on similar project activities (intercommunity councils). Their leaders were trained by FUNDADESE to solicit their project funding in the long run directly from the municipality. In short, the programme aimed to improve the capacity of communities for self-management and planning, and to increase their negotiation capacity *vis-à-vis* the municipality.

What did FUNDADESE achieve with this local empowerment model? The statistical outputs were impressive: working over a decade in more than twenty communities (in three different municipalities) resulted in the formation of about fifty local project committees, six community councils and five intercommunity councils (on health, culture, trade, agriculture and infrastructural improvement).[138] Local project committees, which presented their development priorities to FUNDA-DESE, generally most valued support in the area of infrastructural improvements (water and electricity), small credits for agriculture and support to improve trade conditions. Organisational and cultural projects scored rather low, which is understandable given the widespread poverty in these communities. However, the project outcome was not that community councils were strengthening cohesion in the communities. Participation of project beneficiaries decreased soon after projects had been approved, as most beneficiaries considered participation in community councils as a *condition* to get funding (Cabrera and Camposeco 1996). Consequently, new community organisation structures were not very sustainable as they depended entirely on financial input from and institutional decisions by FUNDADESE. The long-term purpose, to make the communities self-sufficient by increasing their negotiation capacity with municipalities, thus was far too ambitious.

Evaluation missions identified several problems inherent in FUNDADESE's approach. One was poor integration of projects and educational activities, which were not only badly attended but also of low quality. Another problem was that FUNDADESE often imposed a new organisational model in communities without respecting traditional organisation structures or cultural patterns. A lack of involvement of target groups in the design phase of projects and a priority for working with young leaders (and disregarding the traditional importance of the elderly in Maya communities) generated various conflicts. Furthermore, FUNDADESE's policy of increasing women's participation in community organisations had not been very successful: men dominated all newly established organisations and projects were reproducing traditional roles for women, rather than challenging their subordinated position. Despite this fundamental critique, an *Ibis* evaluation pointed at the positive outcomes: communities slowly were getting reorganised, were starting to recuperate their ethnic identity, and new leadership was emerging. However, it was not clear to what extent external aid had contributed to these achievements, or whether this would have happened anyway. Given the severe conditions, spectacular results could not be expected in the short run, according to *Ibis*. But in the longer run the model was expected to contribute to integrated collaboration among popular organisations, NGOs and local governments, which was considered to be an important basis for future reconciliation (Bye *et al.* 1995: 35).

While FUNDADESE's achievements at the local level were not (yet) very tangible, at the national level it managed to achieve at least three visible results. First of all, FUNDADESE (and more particularly Mazariegos and Sequén) from the late 1980s stimulated the formation of new Indian organisations. It started of course with FUNDADESE itself, followed by the foundation (together with other 'Mayanist' organisations) of the national Maya coalition COMG. Meanwhile, although only visible after 1992, FUNDADESE actively contributed to the formation of new Indian organisations in the south-western highlands, such as the human rights organisation *Wuqub'Noj* and the Indian peasant organisation *Consejo Campesino Kabawil*. Both became members of *Tukum Amam*, where FUNDADESE played an active role as provider of technical and financial support, but also as a channel for access to foreign aid agencies. This facilitating role as intermediary between local Indian organisations and international aid agencies could be played thanks to FUNDADESE's reputation derived from its community development work in the Chichicastenango area.[139]

A second achievement of FUNDADESE at the national level was its contribution to the unity among Indian organisations. Mazariegos had been a strong advocate for unity among Indian organisations and NGOs, blaming its lack on the mentality of divisiveness within Ladino culture.[140] Mazariegos played an active role in trying to establish a temporary alliance between the 'popular Indian' organisations of *Majawil Q'ij* (later IUCM) and the 'Mayanist' coalitions COMG and ALMG. As a leader of COMG, he managed to get the two currents united in 1992 within the *Mesa Maya*, a forum in which for the first time a broad spectrum of Indian organisations discussed the key issues of a future peace agreement on Indian rights and identity. The *Mesa Maya* lost its momentum when the 'Mayanist' organisations felt too little attention was given by the popular Indian organisations of *Majawil Q'ij* to three fundamental issues: the explicit recognition of a Maya people, the right to education in Maya languages and the issue of autonomy. After Serrano's coup of May 1993 (the so-called *serranazo*), Mazariegos again tried to get the two groups united into a temporary alliance in order to maximise the influence of Indian organisations on the peace process. Although he initially failed in this effort (and was forced to leave COMG in late 1993) he did play a key role in founding COPMAGUA, in which all major Indian alliances finally worked together. This temporary unity was crucial in achieving the best possible result during the discussions about the Indian rights agreement in the ASC.

The third achievement of FUNDADESE at a national level was the active role it played in the preparation and approval of the peace agreement on Indian rights and identity. Even if it can be argued that FUNDADESE as a development NGO did not have a high profile in the ASC, its influence was illustrated by the active participation of Mazariegos, Sequén and Riquiac in several sectors of the ASC. Mazariegos was, beyond doubt, the most prominent of the three, as he was the leading representative of COPMAGUA in the ASC. His attitude was important, as he took an intermediate position between the two extremes within COPMAGUA. Most sectors active in the ASC confirmed that Mazariegos had been one of the key persons in the adoption of the consensus document on the issue of Indian rights, which was probably the most controversial issue of the entire peace process.[141] That the final peace agreement on Indian rights was not essentially different from the ASC position paper was a clear political victory for COPMAGUA and its constituent organisations. Of course, a favourable political context and national and international pressure also contributed to the approval of the agreement on Indian rights, which had been the most difficult and complex step during Guatemala's democratic transition. Moreover, the agreement generated the sense that the peace process was entering its last stage (Aguilera *et al.* 1996).

An additional achievement was the incorporation of several representatives of Indian organisations into the political arena after the 1995 elections. However, it could hardly be characterised as an achievement of FUNDADESE itself: rather it was a personal accomplishment of Mazariegos, who actively supported the participation of Indian organisations in the electoral alliance of the FDNG as part of *N'ukuj Ajpop* in June 1995. Other members of COPMAGUA (COMG and ALMG) rejected this political alliance and feared that it would affect the independent position of COPMAGUA in the follow-up to the Indian rights agreement. But Mazariegos and his colleagues in *N'ukuj Ajpop* believed that the opportunity for Indian organisations to participate in political decisions had to be utilised, especially because they lacked any experience in this area (Bastos and Camus 1995). The effort was successful: the FDNG won six deputy seats and was broadly supported by Indian communities of the highlands, despite low voter participation.[142] After the elections, it was clear that Mazariegos gradually had withdrawn from FUNDADESE, which in fact had been a stepping stone for him to get involved in the national Indian alliances and to direct a new NGO coalition in Quetzaltenango.

What did all these achievements of FUNDADESE and its leaders contribute to the strength of Guatemalan civil society? At the local level, with the community organisation programme in Chichicastenango, it is still too early to determine whether one can speak of a process of sustainable change regarding demilitarisation of civil society. The influence of the PAC's certainly decreased, but this was also the case in other parts of the country. Neither did the organisational model that was promoted function as it was intended: instead of empowering the communities by supporting the formation of community councils, evidence suggests that the communities were in fact disempowered and that the *locus* of empowerment was with FUNDADESE. This could not have been the intention of the donor agencies. But at the regional and the national levels, FUNDADESE's activities (which served to stimulate Indian organising and coordination) no doubt contributed to the increased participation of *indígenas* in civil society.

An important characteristic of FUNDADESE, and in particular of Alberto Mazariegos, has been the commitment to a long-term vision of recovering 'Maya identity'. On the basis of that vision, FUNDADESE's leaders carefully analysed the various stages in which Guatemalan civil society provided new political openings for Indian organising. FUNDADESE reacted adequately in order to occupy these new political spaces, or perhaps more accurately: to occupy *every possible* space. Consequently, the evolution of FUNDADESE's activities runs virtually parallel to the periods of Indian organisation building mentioned above. In the first period of the 1980s FUNDADESE focused exclusively on rebuilding Indian organisations at the local level in an area deeply affected by counter-insurgency warfare. As soon as the political climate eased in the early 1990s, when the second period started with the emergence of national Indian alliances, FUNDADESE was one of the active founders of COMG. This organisation strongly influenced the discussion on 'Indian rights and identity' within the *Mesa Maya*. In the third period, after Serrano's coup and the resumption of peace talks, FUNDADESE's leaders were active at several levels and in different sectors of the ASC to achieve the best possible agreement on Indian rights, followed by efforts to incorporate Indian organisations into the political arena.

Together with other 'Mayan' NGOs, working closely but tacitly with opposition-related popular organisations, FUNDADESE contributed to strengthening civil society, but also to opening up political society for the excluded indigenous majority of Guatemala. This process lasted a little over a decade and was of course also influenced by the favourable political climate in Central America after 1990. The peace process was carefully exploited to guarantee that this newly conquered space would lead to constitutional reforms and the acceptance of a series of Indian rights that were to prevent marginalisation of *indígenas* in the future. As the agreement states: 'every issue directly concerning indigenous peoples requires their active involvement, and the current agreement wants to create, broaden and strengthen structures, conditions, opportunities and guarantees for participation by indigenous peoples, fully respecting their identity and the exercise of their rights' (COPMAGUA 1995: 1). This affirmed that Indian organisations would be actively incorporated in decision-making, thus ensuring that the proposed changes could not be reversed. The Guatemalan agreement on Indian rights and identity therefore was, as a top UN official commented, 'of transcendental importance and unique in the world'.[143]

— *FUNDADESE in the aid chain*

The 'secret' of FUNDADESE's success at the national level was in the first place based on the way it used its status as a local development NGO to legitimise its national role as an Indian membership organisation. FUNDADESE was a 'launching pad' for Indian leaders such as Mazariegos to acquire key positions in Indian organisations operating at a national level. From the moment Mazariegos became active in COMG, he began to co-found an amazing number of new Indian organisations. In all of them, he occupied a central position, which made him a spider in the rapidly expanding social web of Indian organisations. In addition to that, he (together with the other two FUNDADESE leaders Sequén and Riquiac) was well aware that unity was a precondition for achieving results for Indian organisations in the peace process. Thus, working towards consensus on polarised positions in the 'Maya sector' without compromising an explicit Maya focus was critical to his successful work in the ASC.

The question could be raised why Mazariegos needed FUNDADESE at all after he had acquired his leading position in COPMAGUA. The answer is that he was well aware that the conquest of political space for Indian organisations had to be combined with concrete actions to improve the well-being of indigenous communities (Bastos and Camus 1993: 192). This had been the method in Chichicastenango, and it was later applied to the communities attended by the Quetzaltenango office. But Mazariegos had learned from the Chichicastenango experience, in which competition with other local Indian NGOs (such as COINDI) had weakened FUNDADESE's performance. This competition was not only a result of political rivalry, but also an attempt to get access to foreign aid resources. This is why he established *Tzuk Kim-pop*, the NGO coalition in the south-western highlands. In this area political rivalry was minimal and various local development NGOs worked together in a complementary way, presenting integrated proposals to private aid agencies. Popular organisations that were formed or strengthened with *Tzuk Kim-pop*'s community development projects were in turn linked to the national level through the network of *Tukum Amam*. In this fashion, Mazariegos used his political prestige to increase private aid flows to indigenous communities, and his contacts with donors to stimulate the formation of new Indian organisations that would in turn strengthen his own political platform.

Although this 'stepping stone' tactic created a vast number of Indian organisations in a short period, it also had negative sides. Linkages between national alliances and local Indian organisations, for example, were not very well developed.

Communication between the national and local levels during the negotiations over the Indian rights agreement generally had a one-way and top-down character. The communities supported by the Chichicastenango office were informed about the ongoing negotiations, but provided no input. Although most member organisations of *Tukum Amam* in Quetzaltenango had discussed the ASC consensus documents (gatherings for which FUNDADESE had provided the funding) feedback on the final peace agreement sometimes took considerable time.[144] All the Indian organisations forming *Tukum Amam* still were very young and lacked strong internal structures to keep their leaders accountable. Consequently, discussions at the level of the ASC between national alliances about the peace process took place in a relatively small and elitist environment, in which little time or priority existed for consultations with the local organisations that these networks represented. This point can be refuted, however, by arguing that it is unfair to expect such consultations considering the short time frame of the negotiations and the embryonic stage of Indian organising.

The key weakness of FUNDADESE was in fact its organisational structure. In the Chichicastenango area it maintained an ambiguous image as a hybrid between a local development NGO and a membership organisation. This was apparent in the existence of two assemblies functioning parallel to each other. One assembly was basically formed by executive board members, who decided on FUNDADESE's priorities and policies. The other was composed of members of the intercommunity councils, who were elected by the communities. The second assembly had no legal basis, and only functioned as an advisory board to FUNDADESE's directors. Although the intention was that members of the 'community' assembly would become part of the executive board of the foundation, this did not happen in practice. One reason was that these council members often did not represent the communities, but only the *projects* supported by FUNDADESE. Another reason was that the gradual 'decentralisation' of FUNDADESE into three autonomously functioning offices with different development goals made the formation of a membership organisation highly problematic (Cabrera and Camposeco 1996). The biggest problem was that the three directors were unable to agree on common priorities while maintaining an (unworkable) organisational structure that was only kept up to please funders. Mazariegos's preference to work at the national level and Riquiac's priority to continue the community development activities were in fact no longer compatible. This explains Mazariegos's gradual retreat to other organisations (such as *Tzuk Kim-pop*). The fracturing of FUNDADESE into three separate organisations would only be a matter of time.

NOVIB and *Ibis* both proposed FUNDADESE as a case study for the present research as it was considered to be one of their most successful partners in Guatemala. However, independent studies and evaluations suggested that the community development programme in Chichicastenango suffered from several deficiencies:[145] low beneficiary participation in project design, too many activities for the communities, overworked (and often unqualified) staff, absence of a gender focus, lack of educational activities, poor administrative systems for the revolving funds and worst of all: a method of organisation building that contributed to the disempowerment of the communities. Given this rather negative assessment of the community development programme, the question could be raised why NOVIB and *Ibis* were so positive about FUNDADESE. Part of the answer is that the local consultants, who were supposed to monitor the programme and give advice, hardly visited the communities, so that desk officers of the agencies had to rely on the (overly positive) biannual reports submitted by FUNDADESE.[146] But this explanation is not completely satisfactory, as these desk officers should have known the critical content of the independent evaluation studies. More likely, the agencies gave FUNDADESE the benefit of the doubt, as it had to work under difficult political conditions (Bye *et al.* 1995: 35). In addition, their assessment of the community development programme might have been put off track by FUNDADESE's successful activities at the national level.[147] Only in 1996 did both agencies realise that FUNDADESE had been unable to handle the rapid increase of external funding.[148]

The erroneous perception by both agencies of the quality of FUNDADESE's community organisation programme illustrates that NOVIB and *Ibis* performed a rather passive donor role in their aid chains. This should be taken into account when the contribution of NOVIB to FUNDADESE's national work is assessed. Although allocated to FUNDADESE as an institution, it was clear that NOVIB's support for the ASC activities was handled personally by Mazariegos. NOVIB was aware that this was caused by the gradual decentralisation of FUNDADESE from one to three separate and autonomously operating offices, of which only the oldest in Chichicastenango had legal status. Mazariegos's 'chameleonic behaviour' due to his responsibility for several organisations at the same time, often added to the confusion.[149] Notwithstanding his multiple hats, Mazariegos enjoyed confidence among funders, and NOVIB knew that they were actually financing the formation of the new Maya alliance *Tukum Amam*, albeit formulated as a FUNDADESE project. But this was not contrary to NOVIB's objectives, one of which was to strengthen Indian participation and unity in the ASC. From that perspective NOVIB directly or indirectly had supported all the tendencies that were present in COPMAGUA, the national coalition of Indian alliances.[150]

The ASC played a temporary role in political society during the peace negotiations as it actually functioned as a parallel parliament.[151] Virtually all organisations participating in the ASC were dependent on support from private aid agencies. The same was true for Indian organisations, who would not have been able to participate at the national level without private foreign aid.[152] Without this support many alliances in the ASC would not have been able to meet, to travel and to elaborate proposals. It is therefore likely that NOVIB's support to Mazariegos added to the unity of COPMAGUA, and thus indirectly contributed to the successful adoption of the Indian rights agreement. However, NOVIB also contributed to the formation of umbrella organisations with poor organisational capacity below the level of their national leaders. Another downside to NOVIB's support for Mazariegos's work in *Tukum Amam* was that it accelerated the internal fracturing of FUNDADESE, as the need to achieve consensus over priorities was inhibited by the availability of foreign funding. Closer monitoring by NOVIB would have revealed that the national activities of FUNDADESE were virtually delinked from their local activities. By not actively promoting the incorporation of the FUNDADESE-supported indigenous communities into the macro-activities of COPMAGUA, a chance was missed to reverse the disempowering impact of the community development work which was also funded by NOVIB. It is surprising, given their priority for linking micro-level community development with macro-level policy advocacy, that both NOVIB and *Ibis* paid so little attention to making use of this unique opportunity in the case of FUNDADESE.[153]

– Assessing FUNDADESE's civil society building performance

Not only for funders but also for me the case of FUNDADESE turned out to be rather complex. It actually deserves even more detailed treatment than what is possible in the framework of the present study, as FUNDADESE represents a good example of a newly emerging type of Indian development NGO in Latin America. In contrast to the other case studies, I will first make an assessment of the role of FUNDADESE in civil society building, before examining its organisational capacities.

The Guatemalan peace negotiations that started in 1990 stimulated the process of democratisation, which had entered a stage of early transition with the inauguration of a civilian government in 1986. The gradual incorporation of Guatemalan *indígenas* into civil society and the formation of multisectoral alliances (such as the CSC in 1992) suggested a step towards mid-transition. However, the return to military campaigns in the countryside in 1993, followed by Serrano's *autogolpe* represented a temporary setback in this promising process. With the resumption of peace talks in January 1994 and the installation of the ASC as a forum for discussion among civil society sectors, the mid-transition phase started, leading to the final peace agreement in December 1996. It was in this period that FUNDADESE, together with other Indian organisations, gave a decisive push to the peace process by demanding recognition of Indian rights and formal incorporation of the indigenous majority into Guatemalan civil society.

The main goal of private aid agencies supporting FUNDADESE was to contribute to this process of incorporating marginalised indigenous communities and groups into civil society, in particular those groups and communities in the highlands that were disarticulated by the counter-insurgency campaigns of the early 1980s. Two intervention strategies were used to achieve this goal: rebuilding the organisational capacity of indigenous communities by supporting self-identified development needs, and strengthening unity among national alliances of Indian organisations in order to guarantee their participation in the discussions about the agreement on Indian rights. The complexity of the FUNDADESE case is that these intervention strategies were delinked from one another, both by funders and by FUNDADESE itself, and thus have to be examined separately. The outcome of the community organisation programme, which received most of the private aid funding, generally was disappointing. Recent evaluations have even suggested negative consequences of FUNDADESE's intervention model, which contributed to disarticulating communal structures. The impact of private aid on strengthening civil society at the local level thus turned out to be rather negative.[154]

The policy impact of the activities by individual FUNDADESE leaders at the national level, through a variety of national coalitions – initially COMG and COINDE, later CONADEHGUA and *Tukum Amam* – was more successful. Particularly Mazariegos and Sequén tried to achieve unity among the variety of Indian alliances assembled in COPMAGUA, which served as an intermediary coalition for Indian organisations in the peace process. However, the adoption of the Indian rights agreement was only an indirect achievement of FUNDADESE. Thanks to his position as director of FUNDADESE, Mazariegos was able to enter the leadership of COMG and participate in the *Mesa Maya*, which provided him with the credits to apply for external funding that would enable him to set up *Tukum Amam* in 1994 after his political conflict in COMG. Besides strengthening the 'sectoral' alliance of Indian organisations (in COPMAGUA), Mazariegos also managed to open up intermediary channels in political society by promoting the participation of Indian candidates (as part of the Maya front *N'ukuj Ajpop*) in the FDNG. This progressive political party acted as a new alliance of societal sectors in political society and will possibly become one of the key pillars of a future political alliance of the left-wing opposition together with the URNG. In other words, indirectly FUNDADESE and their funders contributed to opening up space in political society that had been blocked for four decades.

The participation of local members in the activities of the national alliances was low or absent: negotiations took place in the capital and, at best, final results were reported to member organisations. However, the legitimacy of COPMAGUA was never publicly questioned by any of the parties, nor by the organisations active in the ASC. Although representatives from the organisations composing COPMAGUA were elected by their constituent members, below the level of national leaders little capacity and structure existed to make them accountable to the local communities that they represented. Of course, most Indian organisations had emerged only a few years earlier and were still in a process of building this capacity. But FUNDADESE seldom managed to integrate these local and national initiatives, which could have been an opportunity to bridge that gap. Mazariegos and other Indian leaders spoke on behalf of communities that were barely organised, and represented Indian organisations with a handful of members. Furthermore, the low participation of women in the leadership of Indian organisations was remarkable given the active participation of women's organisations inside the ASC. Private aid flows after 1993 stimulated the formation of new Indian organisations, including *Tukum Amam*, but their top-heavy structure revealed a lack of downward accountability.[155]

The sustainability of FUNDADESE and its community organisation programme, considered as an outcome of private aid interventions, turned out to be rather weak. The empowerment of the communities actually followed the pattern of the aid chain: private aid flows were channelled by FUNDADESE to the communities on the condition that they organised community councils. This pattern strengthened FUNDADESE's influence in the communities, without strengthening the communities *vis-à-vis* the municipalities. As long as aid flows continued, communities had no reason to actively search for funding from local governments. A reduction of aid flows to the communities would probably have destroyed the community councils, which left funders with no other choice than to continue funding the programmes and demand better integration of these councils with existing power structures in the communities. Only if the councils in the future were truly assimilated by the communities, would prospects be generated for getting municipal funding. The sustainability of national activities was better, not only because of the temporary character of the peace talks, but also because the amount of aid involved was relatively low. A new organisation, *Tukum Amam*, was set up with this temporary funding and would continue to acquire resources from Mazariegos's multiple activities in other Indian organisations. The case of FUNDADESE seems to confirm what was found in other case studies as well: modest and temporary funding based on detailed (political) analysis by funders generally generates better results in strengthening civil society than large amounts of funding, especially if serious monitoring is neglected.

6.4 Strengthening civil society from a regional level: ASOCODE

The fourth case study is not limited to one country, but covers the entire Central American region. It focuses on one of the strongest regional civil society networks that appeared in the early 1990s: the Central American Association of Small and Medium Agricultural Producers, ASOCODE. Founded in 1991, this regional coalition of national peasant organisations quickly impressed Central American governments and international organisations with its direct and innovative approach to pursuing alternative economic strategies for the Central American region. ASOCODE proposed to restructure the agricultural sector in post-war Central America, arguing that peace would not be sustainable as long as widespread poverty persisted in rural areas. ASOCODE's leaders soon managed to negotiate directly with the ministers of agriculture, and were even invited to the summits of the Central American presidents. ASOCODE's performance stimulated the formation of other regional civil society networks, eventually leading to a regional coalition of Central American civil society networks in 1994, the Civil Initiative for Central American Integration (ICIC). Private foreign aid played a key role in this development, as will be shown in the following case study.

— *Roots of regional coordination among peasant organisations*

The timing of the establishment of ASOCODE (the early 1990s) needs some explanation: why was this Central American network of peasant organisations not established earlier, for example in the aftermath of the Esquipulas agreement?[156] After all, it was in 1988 that similar regional coalitions were set up for labour unions (COCENTRA) and development NGOs (CCOD). One reason is that *campesinos* constitute a very heterogeneous sector: they include landless peasants as well as landholding agricultural entrepreneurs producing export crops.[157] Another reason is that some organisations had tried since 1988 to establish a regional coalition, but were faced with several obstacles.[158] By the early 1990s, a concurrence of at least five developments created new opportunities for regional coordination among peasant organisations: the end of the civil wars, re-emergence of a regional integration perspective, a new generation of peasant leaders, the end of the Sandinista revolution and new priorities of private foreign aid agencies.

As the rural population had been seriously affected by the civil wars of the 1980s, the regional peace process created new opportunities for peasant unity. Military repression had been strongest in rural areas and Central American *campesinos* often had confronted one another, for example during the Nicaraguan *contra* war (Bendaña 1991; Van Heijningen 1994). Many peasant organisations had been organically linked to guerrilla movements, which made them dependent upon the priorities of (often vertically organised) political parties. This changed with the regional peace process unfolding in the early 1990s. Still, peasants were facing serious problems of economic survival generated by stagnating economies and structural adjustment programmes. Rural areas were afflicted by poverty rates often exceeding seventy percent: unemployment was widespread and there were few prospects for improvement in a sector that employed half of the Central American population. Liberalisation of markets had increased cheap agricultural imports and facilitated a rise in transnational agro-export capital. This tendency threatened the existence of small farmers, especially while cheap credit programmes and price subsidies were being cut by governments. Peasant leaders from various Central American countries increasingly realised that they were confronted with similar problems, and that better coordination was a precondition for survival of the *campesino* sector (Arias and Rodríguez 1994).

The emergence of ASOCODE also was a response to a new regional governmental policy agenda that became visible after the 'political watershed' in Central America of 1989-90. At the Antigua summit in June 1990, with the Chamorro government installed in Nicaragua and peace talks underway in El Salvador and Guatemala, it was clear that the emphasis of the agenda had shifted from political to economic issues. But even more important, the presidents were no longer divided on political issues and agreed to renew Central American regional integration, creating new regional institutions as was explained in Chapter 4. The presidents announced a 'broad process of consultation between governments and societal sectors' to enable them to take a leading role in regional decision-making. Peasant organisations realised that they had been absent at these regional fora and reacted suspiciously to this shift in attitude. As one representative remarked: 'the appeal for *concertación* [...] is no more than a tactical concession to enable them to continue with structural adjustment and trade liberalisation' (Campos 1994: 28-29).

The rise of a new generation of peasant leaders was another element that spurred the foundation of ASOCODE. Contrary to older generations, these young leaders had been to school or were trained in numerous 'popular education' courses offered by churches and NGOs. Some of them even had academic degrees.[159] Furthermore, this generation was politically formed amidst the Central American crisis. They witnessed how peasant organisations had been abused by political parties and by the *contras* and how clientelistic relationships had weakened their organisations. The new generation also was better informed about the political situation in the rest of Central America, due to better communication and regular international travel. These leaders were accustomed to an urban culture with its negative perceptions of the traditional peasantry: they wanted to turn that image around, and considered *campesinos* as 'small agricultural producers'.[160] Edelman (1995) labelled them 'peasant intellectuals', although it is probably more correct to speak of a new generation of 'modern peasant leaders', supported by a new generation of young intellectuals committed to working closely together with peasant organisations.

The new generation of peasant leaders and their technical advisers were in the majority composed of Nicaraguans and Costa Ricans. The latter already had struggled for several years against structural adjustment programmes, which only recently had been started in neighbouring countries.[161] The Nicaraguans took the lead as they had the strongest peasant union (UNAG) of the region. With its international network of contacts, UNAG often served as a meeting point for other Central American peasant organisations. In 1989 UNAG became president of the regional association of agrarian cooperatives CCC-CA, among other things to prevent political isolation of the Sandinista government (Blokland 1992). However, soon after the electoral defeat of the Sandinistas, UNAG loosened its ties with the FSLN. The greater autonomy from political parties that the Costa Rican and Nicaraguan peasant organisations had was a key element in the formation of ASOCODE.[162] The end of the Sandinista revolution, in which internationalism was subordinated to the party, thus gave room for new forms of regional cooperation between peasant organisations.

A final factor stimulating the foundation of ASOCODE was the availability of funding from private foreign aid agencies. Two issues are important here. One was a growing reluctance within peasant organisations to depend financially on local NGOs and their international contacts.[163] Related to this was the success of the Central American Coalition of Development Organisations (CCOD) in getting access to private foreign aid, while acting simultaneously as a representative of Central American civil society sectors at international fora. Some European agencies offered financial support for initiatives aimed at better regional coordination of national sectoral associations, as was analysed in Chapter 5, and were particularly interested in directly funding 'popular movements', instead of going indirectly through intermediary NGOs.

ASOCODE's gradual birth started in the margin of a seminar on food security in November 1990, in which peasant leaders participated from Panama, Nicaragua, Costa Rica, Honduras and El Salvador. The seminars were part of a European Community-sponsored programme on food security, organised by the Panamanian research institute CADESCA.[164] The timing was significant, as the Central American governments were preparing their future agricultural policies for the region. A commission was formed to prepare a regional peasant conference in July 1991 and, in the meantime, to search for foreign aid to finance the founding process (ASOCODE 1991b).[165] The commission was coordinated by leaders from the Costa Rican farmers' association *Justicia y Desarrollo*. In April 1991 a document was produced to highlight priority issues of the future regional association: production, trade, credit, agro-industry and agrarian reform. This so-called 'productive strategy' urged the presidents to 'democratise the Central American economies' as a fundamental condition for peace and equitable socio-economic development. The document warned in a sharp and dramatic tone that if current policies were not fundamentally adapted, the *campesino* sector as a key producer of basic grains was going to disappear.[166] The document was sent to the Council of Central American Ministers of Agriculture (CORECA) and to the seven Central American presidents. The latter, in their summit of July 1991, surprisingly adopted a resolution which welcomed the new initiative and promised to study its proposals. Even before it was formally founded, ASOCODE had been recognised by the Central American governments as the legitimate representative of the *campesino* sector.

Although the establishment of a regional coalition had been a slow and gradual process, developments accelerated in 1991: in December ASOCODE was formally launched.[167] For the first time in Central America's history, a regional *concertación* of peasant organisations was established after an agreement was reached about the key issues of the 'productive strategy'. All major peasant organisations from Central America, including Belize, were present at the founding congress in Managua.[168] However, the Guatemalan delegation was divided about its membership in ASOCODE, and only started to participate actively in 1993.[169] A Regional Commission was elected, consisting of two peasant leaders from each Central American country. This commission would function as a coordinating body for the national associations, which each kept their own national autonomy, thereby making clear that ASOCODE was formally not a federation. The Regional Commission acted as a meeting space *(mesa de encuentro)* on a two-year mandate of the congress. The commission was chaired by Wilson Campos, a young and charismatic peasant leader from Costa Rica, and supported by a small team of technical advisors for policy-making and lobbying activities. The six (later seven) national peasant associations were considered to be the 'building blocks' of the new coalition where final decisions were taken by consensus. This organisational structure reflected the fear of national member organisations that ASOCODE would convert itself into a powerful bureaucracy, speaking on behalf of five million *campesinos*.[170]

ASOCODE's central goal was to 'democratise the Central American economies' by improving the economic and political conditions for small and medium-size agricultural producers. According to the statutes this was a fundamental condition to securing peace in the region and to facilitate a just socio-economic development (ASOCODE 1991b). For this purpose, specific proposals on credit, access to land, commercialisation and sustainable land use were elaborated to lobby national and international decision-making bodies. The driving idea behind this emphasis on proposals was the slogan *no hay protesta sin propuesta*: it is useless to protest at political levels without offering alternative proposals. A natural target for these proposals was the ministries of agriculture and their regional council (CORECA), with whom ASOCODE managed to convene regular meetings. Another target was the biannual summit of Central American presidents, in which political and economic integration was one of the central topics of discussion. But ASOCODE also wanted to confront the international community with the devastating impact of neoliberal economic policies on the vulnerable position of the Central American rural population. For that purpose ASOCODE delegations lobbied the European Union, European governments, the Inter-American Development Bank (IDB), the World Bank and a wide variety of non-governmental development agencies and farmers' unions outside Central America.[171] Apart from political support for ASOCODE's 'productive strategy', these delegations also requested financial support to develop training and research activities and to convene regular meetings of affiliated organisations.

– *Private foreign aid to ASOCODE*

Close relationships were developed with private aid agencies from the very beginning. Although the national member associations would have been able to finance the foundation of ASOCODE, it was decided in early 1991 first to search for 'fresh' foreign funding.[172] The provisional regional commission, led by Wilson Campos, approached various private aid agencies to request financial support for the foundation of the new regional body. Most agencies reacted positively and were enthusiastic that the initiative for more coordination was taken by peasant organisations themselves, and not by intermediary NGOs.[173] They were also charmed by ASOCODE's priority for sustainable agricultural land use and its determination to request participation in the 1992 Earth Summit in Rio de Janeiro. Within a few months the necessary US$ 110,000 for the first year was covered by half a dozen agencies, of which the largest part was granted by the Dutch agencies HIVOS and ICCO.[174] Most of this budget was meant to finance travel and organisation costs for national and regional meetings, and to cover the expenses for a small secretariat in Costa Rica.

At the founding congress the newly-elected regional coordinator, Wilson Campos, straightforwardly criticised foreign aid agencies for funding peasant organisations indirectly through intermediary NGOs. This support in many cases had not benefited peasants, 'but only the great number of NGOs who used our name' (ASOCODE 1991b: 22). He called for a restructuring of foreign aid flows directly to the popular sectors of Central America.[175] With (private) foreign aid to Nicaragua and Costa Rica declining, this was a risky move. However, more private aid agencies did show interest in funding the regional coalition and even the EC promised to consider financial support.[176] This positive response to ASOCODE's foundation demonstrated that private aid agencies had high expectations of the new coalition even though ASOCODE's only achievement up to that point had been to bring all the major Central American peasant organisations together into one alliance. Nevertheless, several agencies had doubts about the creation of a supranational coordinating body of peasant organisations, which they feared could lead to more verticalist structures and less attention for coordination at the micro level.[177]

The generous support from private aid agencies overwhelmed ASOCODE. The Regional Commission was pleased with the positive reactions from what they called *la cooperación internacional solidaria*, but they also realised that an uncontrolled influx of resources could eventually damage the fragile peasant unity. To prevent this, ASOCODE decided to convene a meeting with private aid agencies, delegations from national associations and their technical advisors to discuss a general framework in which foreign aid would be more adequately attuned to the process of regional coordination (ASOCODE 1993a). This was in fact a unique initiative, as the scarce efforts towards donor coordination always had been initiated by donors and not by recipients. The meeting was postponed several times as ASOCODE first had to draft its own long-term policy programme, for which consultations with all the national associations took considerable time. Two problems arose during these consultations. The first was that the national associations wanted to utilise the new contacts with private aid agencies to secure funding for their own organisations. They were reluctant to delegate this task to the Regional Commission, as it would then acquire enormous power by monopolising relationships with the agencies. It was decided that the Regional Commission would first secure funding for the regional process, and that national delegations in addition could raise funding to strengthen their national associations. The other problem was that the increasing influx of aid resources (nearly US$ 200,000 in 1992) could no longer be handled by the Regional Commission. Financial administration and reporting to funders were neglected, creating organisational chaos and frustrations with donor agencies.[178] To improve this problematic situation, an executive director was appointed with a small staff to coordinate financial administration at a new office in Nicaragua.[179]

Private aid agencies present at ASOCODE's first conference on development aid in 1993 expressed concerns about the future development of the association.[180] Was ASOCODE really a *mesa de concertación* or was it transforming itself into a new supranational organisation with separate projects, a luxury office and a steadily growing budget? The fear was expressed that aid resources were directed too much at strengthening an 'elitist leadership', instead of strengthening local member organisations.[181] The general message from the agencies was that ASOCODE was to actively make its coordination structure self-financing in the long run. Moreover, they preferred to support local organisations directly instead of supporting the national coordinating bodies, which eventually could lead to a more democratic structure. Although most of these critical comments were formally accepted, the practice turned out to be different. The problem was that the *instancias nacionales* wanted to receive a share of ASOCODE's expanding aid resources: they considered themselves as the building blocks of the regional coalition.[182] Contrary to what the agencies had requested, it was decided that sixty percent of ASOCODE's income would be divided over the national associations (ASOCODE 1993d: 88). In other words, the initial agreement to finance the regional coordination structure with payments from the member associations was completely turned around: ASOCODE had become a chicken with golden eggs.[183]

The Dutch private aid agency HIVOS, which was ASOCODE's main funder, obviously was concerned about this development. The absence of self-financing measures made ASOCODE highly dependent on foreign aid resources. With aid flows to Central America declining in the mid-1990s, cuts in ASOCODE's high level of aid income could possibly affect its longer term existence.[184] HIVOS considered the lack of internal accountability and transparency of the Regional Commission to be a direct result of these 'inverted' aid flows to the national associations, as this had provoked a lack of ownership: ASOCODE was not 'owned' by its members. This problem was however not seriously taken on as ASOCODE's income was growing steadily and its convincing public image attracted new agencies that were eager to give support. Trips to Europe and North America by members of the Regional Commission generated new contacts and additional cooperation agreements with private and governmental aid agencies.[185] The budget would rise to US$ 1.5 million in 1996 to finance large regional training programmes which lacked (according to several funders) clear strategic priorities. HIVOS was worried about this enormous increase and feared that it obstructed the search for self-financing measures. HIVOS also realised that it had become useless to demand this, or even to threaten cutting support, as it would have been quickly replaced by other new donors who were all eager to support the successful regional peasant coalition.

– Achievements of ASOCODE

In its short period of existence, ASOCODE was quite successful in consolidating a united regional alliance for the *campesino* sector. Its formation had been hampered by a variety of adverse political conditions and by the diversity of the *campesino* sector itself. A key condition for establishing a regional coalition was the existence of well-functioning coordinating bodies at the national levels. Except for Honduras (COCOCH) and El Salvador (ADC) this national unity had been absent in most Central American countries, generally as a result of political differences or due to fragmentation of civil society. The need for coordinated negotiation with the government encouraged the development in Costa Rica of a unified national association (CNA), which was formed in May 1991. As a direct result of ASOCODE's foundation, new national alliances emerged in Panama (APEMEP) and in 1992 in Guatemala (CONAMPRO). The latter was not based on a genuine nationwide representation of small farmers' organisations, which became clear when two major organisations left CONAMPRO as a result of internal political friction within the Guatemalan opposition. In Nicaragua and Belize, where unity was absent, national coordinating bodies were represented by major farmers' organisations.[186] ASOCODE considered the national associations to be essential pillars of the regional coalition, although it also was believed that better regional coordination would actually reinforce these *instancias nacionales*. The process of building unity thus was a top-down exercise, from regional to national level, with several problematic implications as will be seen later.

Apart from political differences, peasant unity also was hampered by the enormous diversity within the *campesino* sector. ASOCODE unified a variety of social segments (from landless peasants and small cooperative workers to medium-sized agricultural producers) but also organisations with different historical and cultural backgrounds. The founders of ASOCODE realised that the key to its success would be the search for commonalties, as the articulation of dissimilarities had been the main source of fragmentation in the past. A key condition for unity therefore was to work together on the basis of *concertación* and to develop joint alternatives, rather than creating unity from confrontation with a common enemy. The other key condition was to establish an inclusive and transparent regional coordinating body, in which the traditional gap between leaders and grassroots would be seriously tackled (Román 1994). Although ASOCODE did not represent the entire organised *campesino* sector, it certainly incorporated the vast majority of peasant organisations in Central America. It was therefore understandable that the Central American presidents recognised the legitimate role of ASOCODE as an intermediary alliance for organised small agricultural producers in the region. But what was actually achieved by ASOCODE during these top-level contacts with governments?

ASOCODE targeted the Central American governments at three levels: the Regional Council of Agricultural Ministers (CORECA); the biannual summits of Central American presidents; and the consultative group of the Central American Integration System (SICA). Initially, lobbying efforts were aimed at influencing the agricultural ministers who were preparing new regional agricultural policies. These plans reflected the overall shift toward neoliberal policies with an emphasis on modernising agro-exports and with little attention for agricultural production oriented at the internal market. In meetings with the ministers ASOCODE strongly criticised free trade agreements that were affecting regional food security, as this had stimulated extraregional imports of cheap basic grains. The ministers were surprised by ASOCODE's well-prepared arguments and diplomatically responded that they would carefully analyse their proposals. However, in practice the regular meetings with the ministers did not lead to any change in agricultural policies. Only at national levels, particularly in Nicaragua and Costa Rica, did regional pressure speed up negotiations between the national associations and the ministries of agriculture. But at a regional level it was clear that the ministers were not willing to negotiate: meetings were cancelled or delegated to less influential vice-ministers. As coordinator Wilson Campos remarked: 'it turned out to be easier to meet with the presidents than with their ministers of agriculture' (ASOCODE 1995b: 21).

An explicit result was achieved at the 12th Presidential Summit in Panama (December 1992) at which Wilson Campos was invited to address the presidents. The invitation was the result of several months of lobbying to influence the new agricultural policy framework that was on the agenda of the summit. Together with the associations of coffee producers UPROCAFE and the cooperative movement CCC-CA, ASOCODE and its technical advisors had prepared a joint package of proposals to improve the conditions of small agricultural producers.[187] After detailed review of governmental policies and consultations with lower ranking officials, ASOCODE decided to request the establishment of a special regional credit fund to improve conditions for agro-industrial development and the internal trade of small agricultural producers. The proposal was accepted and almost thoroughly integrated into the final declaration of the presidential summit. Although the fund was never established, the example illustrates that ASOCODE's policy advocacy methods were rather sophisticated.[188] They were based on presenting well-prepared proposals in the name of a broad constituency to meetings where rhetoric generally predominated. By opening up political channels for negotiation and dialogue that had been closed in the past, ASOCODE also generated jealousy and adverse reactions. For example, the conservative Honduran President Callejas in early 1993 tried to set up a counter force to ASOCODE by founding a similar regional network of peasant organisations, albeit smaller and more friendly to neoliberal policies. The obvious intention was to frustrate the recent unity of peasant organisations at the regional level. But soon after its foundation, COCICA (as it was called) and the handful of right-wing peasant groups that it had organised appeared to be no threat to ASOCODE's unity.

Another level on which ASOCODE tried to gain influence was the new framework for regional integration. This Central American Integration System (SICA) was created by six Central American countries to revive the Central American common market that had fallen apart during the crisis of the late 1970s.[189] SICA was modelled according to the European Community and had created a Consultative Committee for civil society sectors operating at a regional level.[190] It was in this committee that ASOCODE confronted its major opponent: FEDEPRICAP, the powerful regional association for private enterprise and considered to be the most important ally of the Central American presidents for the implementation of structural adjustment policies. Although discussions in the Consultative Committee were merely on procedures, ASOCODE considered its membership as a 'strategic political space' for involving civil society in decision-making on regional integration. Together with several other regional networks a coordinating body was created in late 1993 composed of regional associations of various sectors. This Civil Initiative for

Central American Integration (ICIC) was considered to be a 'voice of the voiceless' in Central America, and was invited to several international fora. The coordination of ICIC was soon delegated to ASOCODE, with mixed results as will be analysed later on. But the fact that it managed to get a wide variety of civil society sectors united to demand participation in the process of regional integration certainly was a major achievement of ASOCODE.

Another achievement of ASOCODE was its recognition by crucial international players in the region: the European Union, UNDP, FAO, the Organisation of American States (OAS), AID, IDB, the World Bank and several national governments. Contacts with some of these actors were established during several international trips of ASOCODE delegations.[191] Frequent meetings with ambassadors in the region and Wilson Campos' appearance at a UNDP-sponsored international conference in Tegucigalpa (October 1994) further boosted ASOCODE's international profile.[192] Efforts by ASOCODE-ICIC, supported by European private aid agencies, to demand participation of civil society sectors in the annual ministerial conference between Europe and Central America (the San José Dialogue) were seriously discussed. To improve relations with these important international actors ASOCODE organised another conference on development aid in February 1995. On this occasion Campos urged the international financial agencies to increase direct participation of excluded civil society sectors in the preparation and implementation of development aid policies. The EU ambassador even openly criticised neoliberal policies and their devastating impact on small agricultural producers (ASOCODE 1995a). The participants generally supported ASOCODE's demand to increase consultations and dialogue with popular sectors about foreign aid policies towards the region. Within five years, ASOCODE managed to open doors that only had been open for a privileged sector in the region. The obvious challenge was to use this newly conquered space.

The positive spirit that characterised ASOCODE's approach of looking for constructive dialogue instead of confrontation, combined with the presentation of concrete proposals, facilitated access to the holders of power. Mass media, ministers, presidents, ambassadors, international organisations and others were impressed by ASOCODE and particularly by the convincing performance of Wilson Campos. One of ASOCODE's central demands was to request participation of politically excluded and impoverished rural workers in decision-making about economic development policies, aid allocation and regional integration projects. As a result, ASOCODE's leaders were invited to speak at high-level summits, negotiated with ministers and participated in consultations. What was the impact of ASOCODE's activities on the strength of civil society, and did they really manage to influence or change policies?

There is no doubt that ASOCODE strengthened civil society by creating new intermediary channels at the national and regional level, and by encouraging excluded sectors to effectively use these channels for defining the socio-economic and political framework of post-war Central America. ASOCODE's dynamic conquest of 'political space' for dialogue and negotiation has not been equalled by any other (regional) organisation in Central America's recent past except maybe by the federation of private enterprise FEDEPRICAP.[193] Other regional networks that had been established earlier than ASOCODE – such as the regional network of development NGOS (CCOD) or the trade union network COCENTRA – had not achieved a tiny fraction of what ASOCODE was able to realise in a relatively short period of time. It is therefore not exaggerated to assume that ASOCODE was one of the most important intermediary alliances of civil society to have emerged in Central America since the early 1990s. It created previously non-existing channels to transmit widespread concerns about the undemocratic character of the existing political system (and the destructive economic policies it pursued) without completely rejecting that system. In other words, it performed a temporary intermediary role in political societies that were not functioning properly either at the regional level (the Central American parliament), or at the various national levels.

A closer examination of ASOCODE's achievements shows that political pressure and lobbying were targeted one level higher than where it eventually had to be effective. By addressing the presidents at their regional summits, they harvested results in their national negotiations with agricultural ministers. To pressure their presidents to adapt economic policies, they turned to international organisations such as the European Union or UNDP. This 'roundabout-policy' was not deliberate, but a result of ASOCODE's policy of maximising the employment of external contacts. It was in fact similar to the way in which some of the national associations of ASOCODE had been formed, that is, in a top-down direction. The existence of a regional coalition thus gave an impulse to the creation of national coordinating bodies. ASOCODE functioned both as a shield for protection and as a supranational pressure group.[194] For example, in its contacts with foreign governments ASOCODE made a plea for more pressure on the Guatemalan government to respect human rights and initiate peace negotiations.[195] Meanwhile, Guatemala's President Ramiro de León Carpio was invited to inaugurate ASOCODE's second Congress in December 1993 in order to increase the legitimacy of Guatemalan peasant organisations associated with ASOCODE. The latter, however, were not allowed to openly criticise their president for his clumsy human rights record.[196]

The political space conquered by ASOCODE thus was carefully handled and used to 'reshape official rhetoric' as Edelman (1995: 31) calls it. The strategy of constructive lobbying was effective enough to prevent marginalisation, and it proved to be contagious as the establishment of ICIC showed. The formation of ICIC had been a follow-up to collaborative lobbying work between ASOCODE and several regional networks of labour unions to influence decision-making at presidential summits.[197] They realised that a broader forum for regional civil society networks would have more impact on the presidents and their discussions on regional integration than the lobbying work of individual sectoral associations. In 1994 eight regionally organised sectoral associations founded ICIC; it included labour unions, peasant organisations, federations of small and medium enterprise, development NGOS and federations of community organisations.[198] ASOCODE became the coordinating entity of ICIC, as it had built up experience in this area and provided the largest constituency, plus it contributed most of ICIC's resources for the first year.[199]

The creation of ICIC was an ambitious and unique step taken to confront the neoliberal agenda of the Central American governments, which had been heavily pushed by the federation of private enterprise (organised in FEDEPRICAP) and which was reluctant to admit ICIC into the committees of SICA where the future regional integration system was discussed. FEDEPRICAP therefore formed its own network of regional civil society associations (CACI) as it was afraid of losing control of SICA's Consultative Committee.[200] ICIC on the other hand maintained that 'popular' civil society sectors had been excluded in the regional integration process and deserved to have a voice since political parties had lost their legitimacy.[201] In practice, the complex composition of ICIC meant that it needed time to consolidate as a regional coalition representing 'popular' civil society sectors. This was however, as one document admits, a 'slow and difficult process' (ICIC 1996a). A major problem was that ICIC did not have national associations (the key to ASOCODE's regional structure) making the feedback to member organisations rather complex. At its second assembly in August 1996, ICIC slowly started to consolidate, and ASOCODE was re-elected to lead the coordinating committee.

Despite opening up new intermediary channels between state and civil society and opening doors that had been closed in the past, at least in the short run ASOCODE did not really manage to change governmental policies. Although it was unrealistic to expect quick results, concerns were raised in early 1994 within ASOCODE's ranks about the viability of the strategy of constructive dialogue.[202] Some leaders feared that ASOCODE was being co-opted by the Central American presidents. They rather wanted to organise street marches and land occupations to put pressure on their governments. This was effectively done in October 1994, when peasant organisations simultaneously mobilised their members during a one-day protest throughout the region. But it was rather a manifestation of strength than a return to confrontational strategies, although a minority did advocate for the activist approach.[203] It was also evident that the process of internal consolidation of ASOCODE had been neglected due to its emphasis on lobbying and building up external contacts; ASOCODE had become a huge head with a tiny body. From mid-1994 onwards, ASOCODE therefore paid more attention to its internal structure, which also affected ICIC in which it played a leading role. ASOCODE's leaders realised that policy changes would take time and that building internal capacity and strengthening the national associations was needed to prevent the young coalition from falling apart. ASOCODE had shown that *campesinos* had lost their fear to talk to those in power. However, Campos warned that success would depend on the capacity to strengthen both the organisation and its proposals, for 'those who are in power do not respect us if we do not show our strength' (ASOCODE 1994b: 7).

– ASOCODE in the aid chain

The emergence of ASOCODE as one of the most important regional civil society networks of the 1990s was in the first place a result of favourable political conditions. The end of civil wars, the shift from a political to an economic agenda, the emphasis on regional integration policies and the (albeit rhetorical) call from governments to increase participation of societal actors all were fertile ground for ASOCODE's encouraging performance. At least three other factors distinguished ASOCODE from other regional networks. The first was its capacity to develop a fresh and sharp discourse based on minimal consensus (*concertación*) among the varied peasant organisations in the region. It was a discourse distinct from the politicised discourse of the 1980s, for it was critical of existing (progressive) political parties and their instrumentalist NGOs. But also because it was constructive and innovative. A second factor was the capacity of ASOCODE to occupy the new political space that it was offered by prioritising networking and lobbying work as part of a so-called *estrategia de incidencia*.[204] A third key factor that undoubtedly boosted ASOCODE's profile was the charismatic and sometimes brilliant leadership of Wilson Campos. This young and energetic Costa Rican peasant leader possessed the skills to unite and motivate ASOCODE's rank and file, and at the same time to speak the diplomatic language of governmental officials. As one peasant leader commented, 'probably seventy percent of ASOCODE's success is the product of Wilson Campos, the rest was done by others'.[205]

As other case studies show, dependence on charismatic leaders is risky. After his re-election for a second term as a regional coordinator in December 1993, Campos was increasingly criticised by some colleagues for monopolising external contacts and not properly informing other members of the Regional Commission. Eventually this would generate a serious internal crisis and in 1995 Campos was accused of misusing ASOCODE's funds for personal ends.[206] The crisis articulated two serious weaknesses of ASOCODE's internal structure: the lack of 'strategic accountability' (see Chapter 2), and a declining ability to respond to the high expectations raised in the first few years. Not only was the head bigger than the body (the constituency), the head was also in disorder. Although the structure of the national associations *(mesas nacionales)* as building blocks of the regional coalition certainly was innovative, it only worked when these national pillars were really controlled by their member organisations. Some national associations did not work properly and lacked active participation and feedback from their members; their representatives in the Regional Commission were, as a result, not kept accountable by the members they represented.[207] But this was also a product of the regional diversity that was intrinsic to a regional coalition containing several national thrusts.

Due to its emphasis on external relations and its top-down development, ASOCODE was often equated with the regional part of its organisational structure, and less with its national components (Candanedo and Madrigal 1994). Moreover, lack of harmony and capacity inside the Regional Commission put too much weight on the role of coordinator Campos, who became overwhelmed by his international agenda. Campos admitted that the emphasis on external relations had slowed down the internal process of building a strong and transparent regional coalition. Others argued that ASOCODE simply took up too many issues without setting priorities.[208] This was also one of the main concerns of the aid agencies financing ASOCODE.

Private aid agencies were crucial in the early phase of ASOCODE's development. Although ASOCODE initially feared that agencies would prefer to finance a regional peasant coalition by going through the channels of Central American NGOs, they soon learned that many European private aid agencies in fact shared ASOCODE's concerns about the problems associated with this route. Another fear, that agencies would impose their priorities upon ASOCODE, also turned out to be a non-issue. Over the years, an open dialogue appeared to be possible with agency representatives, which was highly valued on both sides.[209] Although most funders took on a passive role as providers of aid, agencies such as *Ibis* and HIVOS were fairly active. HIVOS stressed the need to actively increase the participation of women in ASOCODE, to improve its administrative operations and to strengthen the national associations. The 1994 evaluation, also sponsored by HIVOS, served as a learning experience rather than a tool for control: most recommendations were incorporated in the following years. *Ibis* performed a different role, but also was one of the most active funders. *Ibis* contributed to improving the lobbying capacity of ASOCODE by offering technical support and actively linking up several Central American regional coalitions with European lobbying networks. Although *Ibis* was cautious about providing large-scale funding to ASOCODE, it could not prevent expectations being raised about getting access to foreign resources. This was often at the expense of viable and self-sufficient networks being built up.[210] An evaluation even concluded that weaknesses in the regional structures were very much a reflection of *Ibis*'s way of working; in other words, these weaknesses appeared to be donor-driven (Morales and Cranshaw 1997).

Looking at its diversified funding base, it is reasonable to conclude that ASOCODE became the Central American 'darling' of international private aid agencies in the early 1990s. Some even argued that ASOCODE *was* a product of international aid.[211] Wilson Campos rejected this suggestion, as he was convinced that both ASOCODE and ICIC would have been established anyway. But he admitted that ASOCODE became very dependent upon private aid, which in turn generated the impression (also internally) that the process of regional peasant unity would have been impossible without foreign aid resources.[212] Of all the case studies presented in this study, ASOCODE therefore is probably the clearest example of the 'private aid paradox': private foreign aid facilitated the emergence of influential intermediary actors in civil society, but simultaneously created new problems that obstructed their organisational development.

One element of this private aid paradox is the outright rejection of local intermediary NGOs by ASOCODE, while actually becoming an intermediary NGO itself.

In the first year after its foundation, Wilson Campos on several occasions criticised the role played by Central American NGOs in the 1980s.[213] His critique contained three elements: (i) NGOs had acted as 'representatives' of the *campesino* sector, without properly consulting it, (ii) NGOs had monopolised relations with private foreign aid agencies (preventing direct funding to peasant organisations) and (iii) NGOs with their dispersed projects lacked a coherent and common strategy. Implicitly, Campos criticised the regional *Concertación* of NGOs (CCOD) which was heavily financed by (predominantly Dutch) private aid agencies. Ironically, CCOD assisted ASOCODE in establishing contacts with these agencies, which soon decided positively about their support. Private aid agencies increasingly preferred to work directly with membership organisations, as was analysed in Chapter 5, as long as they had enough capacity to administer (large-scale) funding. Although it was soon clear that ASOCODE did not have this capacity (the regional office only started to work well after mid-1993), foreign aid increased rapidly. As a result, ASOCODE quickly managed to isolate local NGOs from aid resources directed at peasant organisations, while creating its own bureaucracy that was barely controlled by the member organisations. ASOCODE's critique of NGOs (bureaucracy, inefficiency, lack of internal democracy, monopolising relations with funders) eventually came back like a boomerang, this time from its own members (Candanedo and Madrigal 1994).

Although ASOCODE's establishment apparently was not donor-driven, some of its priorities definitely were. Another element of the private aid paradox is that these priorities were assumed, while in reality they were actually generating considerable internal tension. HIVOS, for example, prioritised two issues: active incorporation of women and a focus on sustainable agriculture. The last issue figured in early ASOCODE documents, but was soon relegated to the backseat.[214] Others funders, especially after the celebrations surrounding the fifth centennial of the 'discovery', requested more clarity about the participation of Indian peasants in ASOCODE's ranks. But this issue also did not reach the stage of critical internal debate, possibly as a result of existing cultural prejudices.[215] The main donor-driven issue therefore was the gender balance within ASOCODE. Various private agencies funding ASOCODE were concerned about the absence of serious efforts to incorporate women into the regional coordination process.[216] Despite the establishment of a women's commission and several meetings of peasant women within ASOCODE, it was clear that a majority of members maintained a *machista* position. Proposals to incorporate women into the national and regional coordinating bodies provoked strong resistance, except from Nicaragua, Costa Rica and Honduras who were already accustomed to this practice. The agencies felt that gender balance was too much seen as a 'problem' *(la problemática de la mujer)*, and therefore artificially dealt with. Wilson Campos very much welcomed this 'critical dialogue' with private aid agencies, particularly on gender, as long as these issues were not imposed upon ASOCODE.[217] The position of women active in ASOCODE's member organisations was eventually strengthened, partly as a result of pressure from the agencies.[218] An indication was that in 1996 five national associations elected a female representative to the 14-person Regional Commission, which had been exclusively dominated by men between 1991 and 1994.[219]

A further element of the paradox is that private foreign aid to ASOCODE increased rapidly at a time that it was actually least needed, creating a situation of 'overfunding' with all its negative consequences. In several documents ASOCODE acknowledged that one of its major achievements had been to secure financial support from international aid agencies.[220] Foreign funding to ASOCODE quickly increased from 1993 onwards, when its international profile skyrocketed and successes were achieved in opening up new political space for dialogue. Budgets were adapted and new activities were proposed to respond to the offers from private aid agencies.[221] In other words, financial support created new needs that had been absent prior to these offers. ASOCODE initially aimed at financing only the establishment of a regional structure, but due to foreign aid income it soon was able to also finance the national associations.[222] As was shown earlier, this redistribution of funds became increasingly more important and strengthened the top-down structure of ASOCODE. This had repercussions for the participation of lower-level member associations, who saw no need to contribute fees to ASOCODE and increasingly felt that it was not 'their project' (Candanedo and Madrigal 1994: 148). This had, in turn, a negative effect on the accountability of the Regional Commission and of the national associations. Or to put it differently: the large influx of foreign aid negatively affected ASOCODE's 'ownership' and its accountability to its members.

A last element of the paradox is closely related to the issue of overfunding, that is, the demand on ASOCODE to search for alternative methods of income generation, eventually leading to self-sufficiency. The paradoxical point is that agencies which threatened to withdraw if self-sufficiency was not considered seriously never did so, as they knew that other funders would simply replace them. To put it more bluntly: private aid agencies would be acting against their own interests if they stopped funding a project that was achieving results and generating international recognition.[223] Within ASOCODE's ranks dependency on foreign aid was a concern from the very beginning, although not equally shared by all national associations. Particularly the Costa Ricans, who had more experience with collective farming aimed at generating income for an entire group, made the point that ASOCODE had to decrease its dependence on external aid and that more effort had to be made to incorporate self-financing measures.[224] But with steady external aid support, the majority of ASOCODE's leaders did not consider this to be a high priority (Candanedo and Madrigal 1994). ASOCODE's main funder HIVOS hoped that the regional coalition would invest more time in looking for alternative sources of income as long as resources were still abundant. But HIVOS also admitted that only a decrease in international aid to the region, expected for the late 1990s, would force ASOCODE to scale down its ambitions and to increase its self-sufficiency.[225]

– Assessing ASOCODE's civil society building performance

Although ASOCODE's case might be exceptional compared to other regional civil society networks, it clearly illustrates how private foreign aid can affect an organisation's internal dynamics. Although differences exist among the Central American regional networks, in general there has been poor linkage between regional networks and their local member associations. Morales and Cranshaw (1997) argue that the regional networks were seldom a product of local needs, as they pursued an (additional) agenda which was often not the agenda of their member organisations. The participation and accountability of national members within ASOCODE's regional structure was poor and it was clear that improvements in this area would take time. ASOCODE was formed as a leadership of leaders (*la cúpula de cúpulas*) and was often not known to the *campesinos* at the grassroots that it was supposedly representing. ICIC was even one level higher, as it was a regional coalition of regional coalitions. Not surprisingly, ASOCODE's legitimacy was sometimes questioned. Not by the Central American presidents – who were accustomed to the absence of genuine consultations with their citizens – but by local farmers' organisations in countries where national coordination among *campesinos* was weakest, and by several private aid agencies. Starting in 1994, ASOCODE therefore prioritised strengthening the national associations and increasing their accountability. A positive indication of improved participation was the election of female representatives to ASOCODE's Regional Commission in 1996. But despite this (for Central American standards remarkable) improvement, it was clear that it would take a long-term effort for ASOCODE to really be owned by its members. A transition from dependence on external aid to dependence on contributions from member associations could be a way to confront this problem.

Financial sustainability of ASOCODE had been an issue in its early years, but was deprioritised when access to external aid appeared to be more than easy. A minority position considered this dependence on foreign aid to be rather risky and it seems that this position has grown, in part as a result of donor pressure to look for alternative financial resources. According to ASOCODE, alternative financing could come from three different sources: self-run productive enterprises, official aid agencies or Central American governments. The second option is not a real alternative to current private aid flows, as official aid from bilateral agencies or from multilateral agencies such as the IDB and the EU would not solve ASOCODE's dependency on foreign aid. On the contrary, the larger amounts of resources involved and their closer affiliation with the dominant development model that ASOCODE has been criticising hardly could be considered an alternative. Neither is support to be expected from Central American governments, despite their promises at presidential summits. This implies that ASOCODE's only realistic alternative lies with production-related income-generation, possibly combined with the introduction of member contributions. This transition will take time to evolve, as it implies, as Campos observed, a 'change of mentality from receiving to generating funds'.[226] As long as private aid flows to ASOCODE continue to grow at the rate of the last few years, such a transition will become more difficult. This is even more so because the recent past has demonstrated that private aid agencies (despite arguing the opposite) are intrinsically unable to push for alternative income-generation methods. Therefore, initiatives to improve self-sufficiency have to come from ASOCODE itself, in order to eliminate aid dependency and to survive as a crucial societal actor beyond the 1990s.

As for its intermediary function, ASOCODE probably performed better than any of the organisations described in the other case studies presented in this chapter. It managed to play intermediary roles for several constituencies at several levels. First of all, ASOCODE opened a channel for dialogue with the Central American governments in the name of organised (1.5 million), but also non-organised (an estimated 4 million) *campesinos*, a channel that was also recognised by the governments and by the international community. The diversity within the *campesino* sector and the internal divisions generated by civil wars make the achievements of ASOCODE especially relevant. Second, it contributed to either establishing or strengthening the intermediary roles of national associations *vis-à-vis* their governments, many of which had been reluctant to negotiate previously with peasant organisations.[227] And third, ASOCODE was the major force behind the establishment of ICIC, the first regional coalition of societal actors that ever existed in Central America.[228] In all these alliances, ASOCODE stressed the need to maintain autonomy from political parties, local development NGOs, governments and international organisations. The new channels also were used by ASOCODE to target international organisations, either in alliance with extraregional farmers' organisations or with other Central American civil society networks. ASOCODE thus also opened political space within 'global civil society', although it is still premature to assess the impact of these activities.

Improving the policy impact of ASOCODE will be a key test for its future existence. Although the organisation has received official recognition from the presidents (as well as several unfulfilled promises) ASOCODE has not yet managed to force fundamental policy changes upon the Central American governments. Again, it would not be fair to expect this from a coalition that is still in its early childhood. But concrete results will be needed to prevent ASOCODE being questioned by its members, possibly resulting in internal cleavages as were sometimes visible in the 1994-95 period. One lesson to be drawn from the early years is that it is necessary to elaborate more on specific peasant-related proposals and to develop alternative market-oriented methods. Previous demands too much echoed rhetoric and calls for participation, without being specific about its implementation. It could even be argued that calls for participation were merely ways to get access to foreign aid resources. The newly-elected Regional Commission in 1996 therefore decided to prioritise economic issues: access to land and credit, and improving production and trade conditions. This implied that the political agenda would become less prominent, which will probably decrease ASOCODE's profile as an intermediary alliance in the years ahead. But given ASOCODE's central role in ICIC, its large constituency in the region and its wide international network of contacts, there is no doubt that it will continue to be the leading regional actor representing popular demands from civil society in Central America.

6.5 Learning from private aid chain dynamics

The civil society building performance of four Central American organisations was assessed according to the methodological framework developed in the first part of this book. By taking into account specific context variables and analysing the achievements of these organisations as a product of particular aid chain dynamics, it was hoped to get a better understanding of the ways in which private aid agencies have contributed to civil society building in Central America. The case studies highlight the rich variety of methods aimed at strengthening civil society and fostering alliances that have eventually contributed to opening up political society. For instance, all organisations proved to be rather effective in challenging traditional authoritarian rule by giving a voice to the excluded, and demonstrated the capacity to play an intermediary role by articulating demands from civil society at crucial moments during democratic transition. This role was generally performed temporarily and was particularly effective during early stages of democratic transition when space in political society still had to be opened up. The organisations in Guatemala and El Salvador also spurred (indirectly) the entrance of new opposition parties into political society during mid-transition, although they sometimes paid a price by compromising their autonomy *vis-à-vis* these parties (CPDN). The Honduran CODEH remained strictly autonomous and decided not to compromise its position, but because of this it lost the political momentum needed to open up the bipartisan political system. The case of ASOCODE underlined how membership organisations managed to take over the lead from development NGOs in the process of opening up negotiation space with the Central American presidents at the regional level. But upon closer examination a number of weaknesses of these organisations become apparent, especially regarding internal organisation, downward accountability and longer term sustainability.

Private aid support was crucial for all four organisations to finance their organisational expenses and to expand the scale of their activities. Several organisations even argued that their success would have been negatively affected if this support had been absent. However, a closer examination shows that private aid support often increased after success was achieved. Moreover, weak internal accountability measures and prospects for financial sustainability were generally made worse by the absence of membership contributions, for which private aid actually functioned as a substitute. But it would be incorrect to simply attribute the weaknesses of these organisations to the influx of private foreign aid, because organisational capacities, adverse political circumstances or the quality of leadership are factors beyond the control of donors. Along the same lines, it would be a harsh simplification to explain the achievements of these organisations as a product of private aid interventions. The case studies actually show that it is imprecise to speak of the 'performance of aid recipients' or to focus on the 'performance of (private) aid agencies'. If achievements of local organisations are judged in relation to foreign aid contributions it is probably more accurate to focus on 'aid chain performance', in which all actors involved in a particular aid chain contribute collectively to the outcome or the impact of an aid intervention. This has enormous methodological implications, as it would become inaccurate to evaluate only selected actors in the aid chain, which is the current practice. It implies that the 'upper actors' in the aid chain (official donors and private aid agencies, which are generally excluded in aid performance assessments) also will become subject to evaluation. New assessment criteria have to be developed for these multiple units of analysis, in addition to new planning and monitoring systems at all levels of the aid chain. This certainly is a complex and costly undertaking, but it can open new avenues for aid evaluation: it can encourage participatory evaluation methods among all actors in the aid chain aimed at learning from past experience, which eventually will be beneficial for improving the quality of aid interventions.

THE PARADOX OF PRIVATE FOREIGN AID

Conclusions

With hindsight it should be admitted that the central goal of this study was rather ambitious: to find out how and to what extent European private aid agencies have contributed to democratisation in Central America. A series of conceptual and methodological obstacles had to be overcome before being able to address the central research question. One obstacle was to define the character of democratic transition in countries where democracy still had to be constructed. It proved to be helpful to identify successive transition stages in which the changing balance between the state and civil society was analysed, particularly by looking at the legitimacy of 'political society' as an indicator for the quality of democracy. Another obstacle was how to incorporate the international context – in Schmitter's words 'a notoriously difficult variable to pin down' – into the analysis. From the vantage point of a global civil society in which transnational actors operate with the purpose of contributing to domestic civil society building, private aid agencies were identified as key transnational players with the capacity to foster democratic transition in the South. By channelling (often governmental) funding via intermediaries to grassroots organisations, complex 'aid chains' were created; in this way private aid agencies had the potential to contribute to domestic civil society building 'from below'. The problem was, however, how to assess the results of these interventions. This methodological obstacle was confronted by proposing a framework in which the assessment of private aid performance was made contingent upon context and aid chain variables.

The second part of this book examined how private aid agencies contributed to democratic transitions in Central America and how effective this was, given the variety of constraints put upon them by context and aid chain variables. Democratic transitions in Honduras, El Salvador and Guatemala were examined as key settings in which European private aid agencies actively intervened with policies promoting civil society building. The case studies illustrated how difficult it is to attribute the achievements of local intermediary alliances to particular private aid interventions. Although the analytical framework presented in the first part of this book proved to be a useful tool, the practice of civil society building appears to be far more diverse and complex than was initially suggested. Moreover, Central America's democratic transitions took place under circumstances that cannot easily be found in other countries or regions that have recently experienced similar transitions with strong external interference such as South Africa, Haiti or Palestine. This makes general conclusions about private aid performance premature. Nevertheless, external interventions in, for example, El Salvador and

Guatemala generated important lessons that have been widely applied to other regions, particularly regarding the peacekeeping role of the United Nations. Some important achievements (and failures) of private aid-supported processes of civil society building in Central America can probably also have a wider application. These final pages will try to assemble these findings into several key points that have shaped private aid agencies' performance in their attempts to contribute to civil society building.

Beginning in the late 1980s, private aid agencies gradually acknowledged the weakness of micro approaches aimed at empowering marginalised sectors, which often turned out to have little impact on a wider national context. By ignoring the highly significant role of political society in the process of social change, private aid agencies in the past often were unable to address the power balance between the state and civil society. Although not explicitly focusing on the role of political society, intervention strategies in the 1990s have indeed devoted more attention to the need of forging alliances in civil society, increasing the coordination among local counterparts and giving more priority to policy advocacy initiatives. In that sense, a step forward has been made in private aid strategies' contribution to furthering democratisation beyond just supporting individual organisations in civil society. However, the main components of a coherent civil society building strategy – such as aiming at macro impact, alliance building, autonomy, downward accountability and sustainability – are only incidentally applied by private aid agencies. These elements are sometimes incorporated into short-term poverty alleviation strategies, despite growing evidence that these strategies only generate limited results. The potential of civil society building interventions has been underutilised due to the use of a pluralist approach which emphasises the organisational dimension of civil society. Civil society building is therefore often reduced to merely trying to increase the 'density' of civil society, and in many cases even limited to supporting local development NGOs. A key problem has been the absence of a clear definition of civil society which embraces its 'diversity' and 'equitability' and incorporates these into a theory of social change.

'Strengthening civil society' as an intervention strategy started to enter donor discourse in the early 1990s, spurred by the political transformations in Eastern Europe and the end of the Cold War. It was in particular the 'organisational dimension' of civil society building that became a popular tool for market-oriented development strategies. However, civil society building had been practised long before the end of the Cold War, not only by private but also by official aid agencies, as the experience of Central America has demonstrated. The US government combined counter-insurgency programmes with initiatives to transform local civil societies by supporting newly created private sector NGOs to facilitate the privatisation of state functions, and by efforts to make governments more efficient.

Most (progressive) European private aid agencies, on the other hand, pursued policies that were aimed at improving the organisational capacity of marginalised sectors with the purpose of strengthening the opposition against authoritarian regimes and US-led militarisation. Support to these 'popular sectors' took many forms – emergency assistance, defending human rights or improving policy advocacy – and was generally based on an 'inclusive' concept of civil society, although rarely phrased in these terms. The return to peace and the acceleration of democratic transitions in Central America contributed to a shift of private agency priorities, away from unconditional support to these popular sectors, thereby terminating what some Central Americans had perceived as 'solidarity aid'.

The case studies demonstrate how national contexts overwhelmingly have determined the outcome of aid interventions. They also suggest however that private aid agencies can contribute to tipping the balance between the state and civil society at critical moments. Private aid support can make a difference, particularly in early transition stages, by supporting broad alliances in civil society that are capable of performing an intermediary role in political society, especially when political parties are weak or delegitimised. Flexible and adequate support from private aid agencies can stimulate these alliances at a time when democratic transitions are stagnating, as was shown by the Salvadorean CPDN and members of the Guatemalan Civil Society Assembly (ASC). By giving them access to trans-national political space where their national demands were boosted by the addition of an international dimension, private aid agencies furthermore showed that they had the capacity to contribute to building transnational alliances. Even at a Central American level several regional networks (such as ASOCODE and ICIC) emerged in this 'global civil society' which had been actively stimulated by European private aid support.

The case studies also reveal that the choice of the moment of intervention for 'tipping the balance' toward democratic transition often was accidental, rather than a deliberate strategy. Few private aid agencies systematically analysed the local political and economic context prior to intervention, as their 'intelligence' efforts generally focused on analysing the reliability and the quality of potential project partners. The vast majority of European private agencies worked with 'proxies' rather than having their own local infrastructure to monitor the use of aid resources in the aid chain. Several agencies even preferred not to have a local field office in the region, in order to keep distance and to avoid interference with policies of their partners in the aid chain. Other private aid agencies that did maintain this presence were sometimes criticised by their recipients for not giving enough technical support or paying too little attention to their needs. This passive attitude of private aid agencies often contrasted with their constant concern for the submission of financial reports and their demands for showing tangible results. Systematic monitoring was however exceptional and the majority of evaluations reviewed for the present case studies were of a poor quality, executed to control recipient organisations and certainly not meant for 'learning'. In the cases of CODEH and

FUNDADESE, for example, donor agencies were not familiar with each others' evaluation reports. This lack of coordination among private aid agencies created friction between donors and recipients and negatively affected the performance of private aid interventions, as was shown in several cases.

Better coordination among agencies – even if this is organised by recipients, as ASOCODE demonstrated – and more careful monitoring of aid chain dynamics and national contexts can contribute to improving private aid performance. Poor timing in particular can have a detrimental impact on the effectiveness of private aid interventions. The case studies show that funding often was increased *after* counterparts achieved particular results, in a period in which they actually least needed this increase in income. This is probably the product of a certain logic inherent to aid allocation policies, generally prioritising well-performing partner organisations over weak performers. The consequences of this can be devastating for longer term organisational sustainability if internal accountability systems are weak. Due to 'overfunding' of organisations in civil society whose leadership was not held accountable by its members, private aid sometimes contributed to further weakening this internal accountability. Consequently, rather than building stronger organisations, private aid agencies have also unconsciously contributed to weakening organisations that played a key role in civil society building. This happened for example in the case of ASOCODE, where 'inverted' aid flows contributed to weakening the accountability of the Regional Commission, leading to serious internal tensions that negatively affected the driving power of this regional alliance of peasant organisations at the regional level. Therefore, collecting member contributions and encouraging partner organisations to secure alternative sources of local income can be a way to improve downward accountability, although this is not what donor agencies generally advance.

The tensions described here are caused by several contradictions that seem to be fundamental to private aid interventions aimed at civil society building, which illustrates what I have called the 'paradox of private foreign aid'. One contradiction is that under conditions of surplus and competition 'successful' grantees cannot become autonomous. Many private aid agencies require that their partners become self-supporting and financially sustainable in the long run, which is considered to be the key to the autonomy and empowerment of civil society actors. However, the more successfully a partner organisation achieves its goals, the more a donor agency is inclined to continue (or even to increase) its support, as 'successful partners' are the exception rather than the rule. Stopping or scaling down support to these well-performing organisations can be risky, as tough conditions generally create serious frictions between donors and recipients. Moreover, other private aid agencies can possibly take advantage of this situation by enjoying the benefits of long-term investments by the departing private aid agency. As a result, efforts to make organisations in civil society self-supporting and financially independent are often contrary to private aid agency interests.

Another contradiction is that private aid aimed at civil society building is intended to make (membership) organisations strong and accountable, while dependency on foreign aid flows often reinforces hierarchy and weakens internal accountability. A common element in the four Central American case studies is the presence of charismatic leaders who played a pivotal role in the successful achievements of these organisations. In some cases these leaders displayed an authoritarian management style, which seems a paradox in itself for organisations that aim to increase the inclusiveness of civil society. But this is (at least in Latin America) in fact rather common for (successful) organisations without members to which they are accountable, such as many development NGOs. The provision of (private) aid tends to reinforce centralised and elitist leadership ('*caudillismo*'), as contacts between donor and recipient are often based on mutual confidence and seldom made transparent to other primary stakeholders. Moreover, a lack of well-functioning internal accountability procedures could also lead to a (gradual) transmission of Northern values and priorities by donor agencies to these leaders. These donor-driven values are then artificially incorporated into the strategies of recipient organisations without being assimilated by its rank and file. Although not intended by donors, this could harm the legitimacy of leadership *vis-à-vis* their constituency, but also further damage their downward accountability. In this sense, it can be doubted whether private aid is an adequate instrument for improving the internal democracy of organisations and for contributing to civil society building 'from below'.

A further contradiction is related to the discussion in Chapter 2 about the shifting balance from developmental toward institutional imperatives in periods of financial pressure, often creating considerable tension in the aid chain. Coordination among private aid agencies is necessary to improve the results of aid interventions (and to improve agency legitimacy), but competition with other private aid agencies (for 'successful partners' or private donations) is in periods of financial pressure even more necessary to guarantee institutional survival. This attitude generates short-term thinking, secrecy, bureaucracy, top-down planning, pressures for quantifiable outputs; in short, a whole range of mechanisms running contrary to how agencies actually claim they are working in practice. But even worse, this attitude also is reproduced downwards in the aid chain: these dynamics are reinforced in the process of civil society building, because local organisations do not have a choice to resist these, for they are dependent on resources and requirements coming 'from above'. The paradoxical point is that these types of aid chain relationships can contribute to reinforcing inequality in civil society and are not really conducive to civil society building as long as aid resources are the (only) basis for these relationships.

Meanwhile, private aid agencies feel the pressure to show tangible results of their interventions, as they either 'perform or perish' in the charity market. But measuring the impact of private aid interventions has proven to be difficult, if not impossible. Attempts can be made to assess how aid is handled throughout the aid chain and under which circumstances it is likely to produce successes, failures or unintended effects. Moreover, as it is already highly problematic to assess the impact of short-term private aid interventions, it is virtually impossible to attribute the outcome of civil society building to the efforts of private aid agencies. Outcome and impact of these longer term aid interventions are almost entirely diffused by the dynamics of the aid chain and by external influences. Organisational capacities, qualities of leadership, accountability systems and the complexity of aid chains are factors that cannot be controlled by private aid agencies, let alone the local and the international contexts that affect the outcome of these interventions. Private aid agencies therefore can only claim to contribute marginally to the longer term impact of civil society building interventions, as this is predominantly determined by context, organisational and aid chain factors.

Therefore, the question to what extent have private aid agencies contributed to democratic transitions in Central America can only be answered speculatively. But this conclusion should not at all be alarming: from a learning perspective it is generally more productive to examine how and why private aid agencies intervened and under which particular circumstances. This can also generate lessons about the circumstances in which it may be wiser not to intervene, or even in which it may be better to stop external aid support. Consequently, it is generally more useful to assess the quality of interventions than trying to measure the quantity of aid agency impact, which rarely generates reliable or satisfactory data. A combination of methods could be used to assess the quality of civil society building interventions, by making a detailed historical analysis of the balance between the state and civil society, by mapping key actors in civil society and their roles at critical moments during democratic transitions, by carefully examining aid chain dynamics from donor to final recipient (and vice versa) and by analysing the quality of partnership between donor and recipient. If these methods are part of a monitoring system with active participation of key stakeholders, it would be possible to use them as a learning tool and not simply as a method for donors to control the proper use of aid resources.

The present study has shown that the traditional list of comparative advantages of private aid agencies over official aid agencies needs to be updated in the post-Cold War period. Private aid agencies no longer have an edge because of their poverty reach, participatory approaches or their effectiveness, as official agencies appear to perform similarly or even better in these areas. Private aid agencies still have their strengths in using their capacity to react *quickly* to Southern demands, providing *modest amounts* of financial aid adapted to carefully identified needs at *critical moments* with a *minimum of conditions* attached to it, in *close coordination* with other agencies and local actors, and combined with *non-financial support* such as technical assistance and the incorporation of partners into transnational policy advocacy networks. Official aid agencies are unable to provide this type of support: their bureaucratic procedures prevent them from reacting to sudden needs, they generally only provide large amounts of (financial) aid and they are rarely capable of (or willing to) coordinate their interventions with other donors. However, the tendency among the major (European) private aid agencies is generally not to utilise these comparative advantages. They increasingly prefer to channel larger sums of aid rather than smaller amounts, as the latter put constraints upon the goals of cost-effectiveness. As a result, they have become slower in responding to sudden needs (except for emergency operations) and feel no need to better coordinate their interventions with other donors, unless it provides opportunities for lowering overhead costs. Although understandable from a short-term perspective, this tendency implies that private aid agencies could be crowded out in the longer run by official aid agencies, with whom they have to compete for successful partners, as demonstrated in the Central American analysis.

Looking back at the experiences of the past decade in Central America, private aid agencies have exhibited two particular assets that made them into influential external actors during the regional crisis. One was their attitude of providing unconditional support to oppositional movements in their struggle against authoritarianism. This 'solidarity aid' was of critical importance, even if it only symbolically counterbalanced the massive flows of US military aid for counter-insurgency purposes. The key strength of this solidarity aid was its unconditional character, provided on a basis of 'tacit consensus', giving revolutionary movements the opportunity to strengthen their position at the negotiation table in the early 1990s. But the absence of accountability requirements also was a weakness of these aid flows, which came to an end in the post-Cold War period, coinciding with the emergence of a culture of tighter requirements and depoliticised criteria. The other asset of private foreign support was that it provided channels for policy advocacy at a transnational level, linking up national civil societies with global civil society. Private aid agencies have the potential and the resources to sustain the 'material dimension' of this global civil society, provided that they are an expression of those sectors in the 'global North' that are willing to contribute to social change in the 'global South'. It would mean that they have to make closer alliances with legitimate transnational networks that lack these resources, but who could become an important counterweight to the current 'globalisation from above'.

The majority of private aid agencies are no longer seen as one of the solutions to global poverty reduction, but are increasingly considered part of the problem itself. Their legitimacy was questioned during the 1990s, generating signs of an identity crisis about their new role and mission in the post-Cold War period. Their steady income growth stagnated and many agencies experienced considerable budget cuts, despite a temporary increase in income from public fund-raising for post-Cold War emergency relief. In addition, governmental co-funding schemes have come under pressure as a result of shrinking official aid budgets. However, it could be questioned whether the level of agency income is the real problem. If it is true, as various impact studies have maintained, that the struggle against global poverty is only effective if its underlying causes are targeted by making civil society denser, more diverse and more equitable, then private aid agencies can only improve their performance record by maximising their impact in contributing to (inclusive) civil society building. The present study has shown examples of this being possible with modest aid resources combined with initiatives aimed at strengthening transnational alliances. The tendency of private aid agencies to maximise their income in order to secure their institutional survival therefore seems to be conflictive with achieving their developmental objectives.

It can be questioned whether the current tendency of decreasing income for private aid agencies really is so detrimental from the perspective of agency effectiveness. Or to put it more sharply, private aid agencies could even benefit from lower income levels, for it would force them to tackle a number of problems related to the 'private aid paradox' that remain unsolved as a result of choosing to maximise income and the fixation on short-term results: the problem of weak accountability toward their constituencies, sustainability of their interventions, poor coordination among donors, the lack of autonomy (for example from governments) and general poor performance. The future prospects for private aid agencies striving for social change possibly will depend on their capacity to reposition themselves within the donor aid community by focusing more on their political roles, rather than becoming mere providers of aid resources to sustain a global welfare system. In Central America, but also in other regions, they have acquired rich experience by providing key support that has indirectly contributed to important political transformations. In the years ahead, progressive private aid agencies will have to choose whether or not to use this experience in order to 'reinvent' solidarity, for example by performing an active role in forging transnational alliances and bridging the gap between Northern and Southern civil societies, a function that is currently being performed, unchallenged, by the transnational corporate sector.

Notes

Chapter 1

1. For a more detailed overview of contemporary discussions on democracy I refer to Sørensen (1993), Beetham (1994), Luckham and White (1996); and for the Central American context to Torres Rivas (1987, 1989, 1992), Booth (1989), Rojas (1995), Vilas (1995, 1996).

2. Others argue that minimal as the Schumpeterian conception might be, if one starts with civil war or authoritarian regimes and the complete absence of any democratic process, a model that requires the circulation of elites through competitive elections is better than nothing (Shapiro 1993).

3. The analytic coherence suggested by the term South America is of course problematic, as huge differences exist in political-historical patterns throughout South America. However, the difference between South and Central America could be justified on these grounds, as long as it is clear that Mexico (although geographically located in Central America) is understood to be part of 'South America'. For a discussion of this analytical pitfall see Slater (1991).

4. The wave of democratic 'transitions from authoritarianism' – starting in Southern Europe in the 1970s, followed by South America in the 1980s and Eastern Europe in the 1990s – generated a lively academic debate on the dynamics of democratic transition (Drake and Silva 1986; O'Donnell *et al.* 1986; Baylora 1987a; Stepan 1988; Diamond, Linz and Lipset 1989; Munck 1989) and of democratic consolidation (Fukuyama 1989; Huntington 1991; Przeworski 1991; Higley and Gunther 1992; Rueschemeyer *et al.* 1992; Diamond 1992, 1993; Linz and Stepan 1996; Domínguez and Lowenthal 1996).

5. Exceptions include Drake and Silva (1986), Huntington (1991) and Rueschemeyer *et al.* (1992).

6. In the middle classes of Latin America they include 'urban professionals, state employees, employees in the private sector, artisans and craftsmen, and small entrepreneurs, sometimes joined by small and medium farmers' (Rueschemeyer *et al.* 1992: 185).

7. In a recent article, they elaborate on the term 'full democracy' by distinguishing between 'participatory democracy' and 'social democracy', and replace 'restricted democracy' by 'formal democracy' (Huber *et al.* 1997).

8. Exceptions are Costa Rica after 1948 and Guatemala between 1944 and 1954, as will be argued in Chapter 4.

9. See for example Linz and Stepan (1996), who in their broad empirical study on democratic transition and consolidation only refer to Nicaragua, Guatemala, El Salvador and Honduras in a tiny footnote.

10. See Beetham (1994). However, this implies that the term 'transition' would become useless, as the 'end stage' would be a utopian situation. Despite this caveat, I believe the concept 'democratic transition' should not be dismissed, as it provides a valuable tool for comparative analysis.

11. These sequences were partly inspired by Gary Hansen (1996), and are further specified in 1.2 and in Chapter 4.

12. Although superficially elaborated in O'Donnell and Schmitter's chapter 'Resurrecting civil society (and restructuring public space)' (1986: 48-56), the idea of 'resurrecting civil society' apparently triggered the imagination of many scholars, as it is still commonly used. However,

both the concept and the chapter are rather descriptive, and no definition of civil society is provided.

13 The concept 'societal public sphere' was introduced by Habermas to distinguish it from the 'public authority of the state', and to avoid that civil society is understood only as the 'private (economic) sphere'.

14 The definition is taken from Rueschemeyer *et al.* (1992), who say 'production-related', instead of 'economic', to stress that entities that produce goods or services are excluded from civil society, whereas employers' associations and labour unions do belong to civil society. However, this definition could be criticised for its 'class' and 'male' bias, by excluding gender balances in the private domestic sphere.

15 Pearce (1997a: 79) concludes that the current Chilean political elite, among them many ex-socialists, believe that 'a depoliticized, disarticulated population is more likely to guarantee democracy than the highly mobilized population of the pre-Pinochet period.'

16 Fine (1997: 9) therefore makes a useful distinction between the *concept* 'civil society' (as a product of the Enlightenment) and 'civil society theory'. The latter is a combination of approaches that emerged during the anti-authoritarian struggles of the 1980s in Latin America and Eastern Europe which 'privileges civil society over all other moments or spheres of social life, on the ground that civil society furnishes the fundamental conditions of liberty in the modern world', in other words 'civil society theory justifies *the primacy of civil society* over the political and economic spheres.' For variations on this argument, see Foley and Edwards (1996).

17 Wood (1990: 79) even argues that these 'loose conceptions of "civil society" represent a *surrender* to capitalism and its ideological mystifications'.

18 Based on his research in Africa, Bayart (1986: 112) writes: 'civil society is not necessarily embodied in a single, identifiable structure. It is by its very nature plural [...] covers all sorts of different practices [...] is not merely the expression of dominated social groups.'

19 Such as Bobbio (1988), Keane (1988), Cohen and Arato (1992).

20 See Fowler (1993b), who elaborates on Bratton's three dimensions.

21 Gramsci (1971: 262-3) writes: 'the general notion of the State includes elements which need to be referred back to the notion of civil society, in the sense that one might say that State = political society + civil society, in other words hegemony protected by the armour of coercion.' Various analysts have pointed at inconsistencies in Gramsci's definition of political society (which was for him in fact synonymous with the state); I therefore will not use Gramsci's equation. Instead, throughout this book I prefer to use the equation in which the nation is composed of state and society, and in which political society is the realm that organises relations between the state and civil society.

22 Linz and Stepan (1996: 8) define political society as the 'arena in which the polity specifically arranges itself to contest the legitimate right to exercise control over public power and the state apparatus.' A 'democratised political society' is composed of political parties, elections, electoral rules, political leadership, inter-party alliances and legislatures.

23 Schmitter (1996) makes the same point; I will come back to this in 1.3.

24 Notwithstanding this limitation, Robinson (1995a: 75-76) correctly points out that most donor agencies prefer to use this 'pluralist notion' of civil society, in which civil society organisations work towards a common goal of strengthening democracy without conflicting interests.

25 Cohen and Arato (1992: 53-8) point at the implicit tension between civil and political society during democratic transition by discussing the potential impact of pacts and elections on the strength of civil society: 'the turn to political society has potentially demobilizing consequences with respect to civil society.'

26 Pearce (1997a: 70) argues that much of the transition and consolidation literature is dominated by the pluralist-elitist view which assumes no contradictions between economic liberalisation, a

stronger civil society and the goals of political and social equality: 'The concerns are with the stability, sustainability, and legitimacy of the political order. The associations of "civil society" can positively contribute to these as long as they accept the limits of their role as well as the fact that the health of the entire order demands the aggregation and channelling of their interests by political parties. Associational life, by implication, will disrupt rather than deepen democracy if it retains the over politicized role which helped it bring down non-democratic governments.'

27 Fowler (1993b) refers to 'informal expressions of civic associations', particularly in Africa, where civic systems existing prior to colonialism were overruled by Western norms and behaviour.

28 This sectoral analysis, an approach popular among pluralists, identifies three sectors with complementary functional characteristics. The first function is to protect the rights of citizens and the sovereignty of the nation by maintaining the rule of law and applying the monopoly of coercive power. This function has been assigned to the government and is in the liberal tradition labelled as the 'first sector'. The second function is to ensure livelihoods by creating and accumulating wealth, assigned to the business sector, in which both for-profit and non-profit organisations serve their customers. The 'third sector' comprises organisations in society that serve personal and social interests based on shared values, commonly referred to as 'voluntary organisations'. All three sectors have distinct but complementary functions with a common objective to serve others. For an elaboration of the three-sector approach related to NGOs see Korten (1990), Nerfin (1992), Brown and Tandon (1994), Fowler (1996b).

29 Tandon (1996: 120) notes that many NGOs in India, or 'voluntary development organisations' as he calls them, have been exclusively dependent upon state funding. Because of their increasing tendency to function as governmental organisations, a point could be made to include them in the first sector.

30 Writing for USAID, Gary Hansen (1996) and others introduced a 'subset' of civil society organisations, which they call *civil advocacy organisations* (CAOs), referring to 'non-state groups that engage in or have potential for championing adoption and consolidation of democratic governance reforms.'

31 The term 'voluntary' is often misleading, as it refers to income from voluntary donations (which is rarely the case in the South) and unsalaried work (while most staff is actually employed by these voluntary organisations).

32 Diamond (1994) identifies seven categories: (1) economic, (2) cultural (including religious), (3) research and education, (4) interest-based, (5) developmental (including NGOs), (6) issue-oriented and (7) civic associations. Diamond also includes media as part of civil society.

33 Synonyms that will be used in this book for membership organisations include *popular organisations*, and *grassroots organisations*. The latter actually refers to the level of activity, but is commonly used to refer also to membership organisations operating at macro-level.

34 Farrington *et al.* (1993: 4) propose a useful method to differentiate among NGOs, using the following criteria: *location* (North or South), *scale* (community or supra-community), *ownership* (MSOs or non-MSOs), *orientation* (profit or value-driven), *approach* (top-down, 'functional' participatory or 'empowering' participatory) and *operational dimensions* (research and innovation or action and implementation).

35 Accountability is understood as the degree to which members (or citizens) can hold their leaders (or politicians and bureaucrats) responsible for their actions. For a discussion of measures of accountability see Fowler (1993b: 26-28).

36 Recent examples include the essays in Clayton (1996), Cleary (1997) and Fisher (1998). This point will be further discussed in Chapter 3.

37 Many urban-based NGOs – such as research centres or human rights organisations – during democratic transitions often have operated as a legal voice for underground popular organisations or political parties, although officially they had no members. These 'pseudo NGOs' were formally

independent, but in practice directly accountable to their underground constituency. These NGOS thus served four purposes: (a) they gave a shield of legal protection for their members to operate above ground; (b) they served as policy think-tanks and as institutions for political training of leaders; (c) they provided banned parties and popular organisations with an infrastructure to maintain and develop their constituencies, both in rural and urban areas; (d) they were an important channel for deriving income from external aid agencies to finance political campaigns, and sometimes also to finance armed struggles. Many of these party-controlled 'pseudo NGOS' vanished or entered a crisis soon after political parties were legalised in the course of democratic transitions. See Brunner and Barrios (1987) for Chile, Argentina, Brazil and Uruguay; and Levy (1996) for Latin America in general.

38 The concept 'social movements', to point at certain 'collective actions' by organisations of civil society, will be avoided in this book. It is preferred to use the term 'popular' or 'social' organisations and to be specific about the purpose of this 'collective action'. For discussions about the pitfalls of defining (new) 'social movements' see Escobar and Alvarez (1992: 1-8) and Foweraker (1995: 38-9).

39 The term *societal actor*, to label a member of civil society, is preferred over the use of *non-governmental organisation* or *non-state actor* with their state-centred bias.

40 For example, the role of NGOS in Latin America changed dramatically after democratic transitions of the 1980s in the Southern Cone; their role was also seriously altered by the consequences of structural adjustment programmes (Wils 1995). I will return to this theme in the next chapter.

41 This classification is an elaboration of categories developed by Renshaw (1994), Diamond (1994), Robinson (1995a), VeneKlasen (1996) and Fowler (1993a, 1996b). It also incorporates some of the ideas of White (1994) that were mentioned earlier in this chapter. Although these categories apparently resemble White's four roles, they do not totally overlap. The first two functions (establishing the foundations of civil society and building alliances) are necessary conditions for civil society to perform all four political roles that White mentions. Building intermediary channels is a condition to perform the 'disciplinary role', but also the intermediary role, which can be oriented at the state but also beyond the state towards transnational societal actors or foreign governments. Building citizenship is a condition for sustaining and consolidating democracy, and is the only category that overlaps with the 'constitutive role' that White identifies.

42 The term 'transnational political space' is borrowed from Pritchard (1996). It is a broader formulation of what could be called 'global civil society', a concept that will be examined later in this chapter.

43 The 'transitologists' have also started to recognise this in recent years, and are now reviewing their earlier transition stages of 'liberalisation' and 'democratisation' (see O'Donnell 1993; Linz and Stepan 1996). For example, a USAID-sponsored study on the role of civil society in democratic transition and consolidation identified four phases of democratic transition: pre-transition, early transition, late transition and (democratic) consolidation (G. Hansen 1996). These categories were further elaborated for the present analysis in the way that was earlier mentioned in this chapter.

44 The stages of 'mid' and 'late' *consolidation* are not discussed here, as they refer to degrees of 'participatory democracy' or 'social democracy' that are still utopian in the present Central American context.

45 Schmitter (1996: 27) remarks: 'Regime change tends to be a domestic affair, and democratisation is a domestic affair *par excellence*', whereas Whitehead (1996a: 24) concludes that 'in the contemporary world there is no such thing as democratisation in one country, and perhaps there never was.'

46 US administrations from President Wilson to President Hoover implemented policies promoting democracy (or better: electoralism) in Latin America, using the tool of direct military intervention

in small countries such as Haiti, Nicaragua and the Dominican Republic to impose proxy regimes. The primary goals of US intervention in the inter-war period were to guarantee regional security and economic expansion, for which the promotion of democracy was a useful tool, but certainly a subordinate objective. In the period after World War II the United States used indirect instruments for promoting democracy abroad, but the covert overthrow of democratic governments (such as in Guatemala 1954) and simultaneous support for authoritarian regimes in Europe (Greece) and Latin America suggested that the level of rhetoric of this policy remained unchanged. Although the Kennedy administration initially intended to foster democracy with its 'Alliance for Progress', it soon favoured military regimes in Latin America. This policy became less strident under President Carter (with his active human rights policy), but President Reagan's support to authoritarian regimes again illustrated the paradoxical undertone of promoting democracy abroad (see Lowenthal 1991; Carothers 1991; W. Robinson 1996).

47 The US blockade against 'communist' Cuba, and the extension of sanctions toward those nations that continue trade relations with Cuba (Helms-Burton act) suggests that this characterisation is still valid in the post-Cold War period.

48 Whitehead (1991, 1996a) elaborates on the variety of these efforts of imposing democracy by distinguishing between 'incorporation', 'invasion' and 'intimidation'.

49 One exception where US imposition of democratic rule might have had a lasting effect is Puerto Rico, which was 'democratised by incorporation' (Whitehead 1991).

50 It is important to recognise that the international context for democratisation is probably more relevant at a regional level than at a global level. By pointing at the influence of the 'contagion' factor during democratic transitions in the Southern Cone and in Eastern Europe, Schmitter (1996: 40) suggests that the really effective international context 'has increasingly become regional, and not binational or global'.

51 A related question is: What is the point at which the international context is most influential? In other words, in which stage of democratisation are external actors most effective? Schmitter (1996: 40-41) suggests that 'regardless of the form that it takes, external intervention will have a greater and more lasting effect upon the *consolidation* of democracy than upon the *transition* to it' (emphasis added). His hypothesis seems to be inspired by the transitions in Southern Europe of the 1970s. And even then, this might be valid for governmental actors in other regions, where a change from covert operations to more open and longer term interventions proved to increase the likelihood of success. But does it also apply to transnational actors? I would challenge this proposition and suggest that transnational actors are probably most influential during stages of democratic *transition* and that they become more marginal, as political players, in the stage of *early consolidation*. This assumption will be further examined in following chapters.

52 'With one's neighbours and the world watching, the cost of repression has gone up and, most of all, the benefit of increased resistance has greatly increased' (Schmitter 1996: 34).

53 Lipschutz (1992: 398-399) refers to a 'global consciousness' of actors in global civil society, challenging not only the cultural shape of international relations but also the logic governing them.

54 Wapner (1995: 315) illustrated the magnitude of these transnational environmental actors by pointing at their combined budgets (US\$ 200 million in 1992), being four times the budget of the UN Environmental Programme (UNEP).

55 New terminology has not yet been agreed upon. For example, Wapner (1995) speaks of TEAGS (Transnational Environmental Activist Groups), and Sousa Santos (1995) uses the term TANGOS (Transnational Advocacy NGOS).

56 Due to the absence of a 'global state', I do believe it would be wrong to speak of a 'global *political* society'. The earlier mentioned 'transnational political space' refers to the sphere in which transnational societal and political actors operate, and is therefore part of global civil society.

57 I prefer to avoid the term 'international NGOs', as it is used by Willets (1996) and others, basically

because it disguises the crucial power difference between donor and recipient NGOs.

58 Lehmann (1990: 139) analyses the origins of these CEBs, and talks of 'an informal Church, loosely related to the Church hierarchy, and organised principally to communicate the message of liberation'.

59 Pope John Paul II visited most of the authoritarian regimes of the 1970s and 1980s at critical moments: Poland 1979, 1983, 1987; Brazil 1980; Philippines 1981; Argentina 1982; Guatemala, El Salvador, Haiti 1983; Korea 1984; Chile 1987; Paraguay 1988 (Huntington 1991: 83).

60 Although informal access to key political leaders in the North via these transnational party organisations was probably more relevant for Southern members than the impact of political activities undertaken by these organisations. (Author's interview with Jaime Castillo Velásco, former president of ODCA, the Latin American section of the Christian Democratic International, Santiago de Chile, 18 December 1988). For a detailed analysis of transnational party networks see Kopsch (1987) and Biekart (1989).

61 An additional advantage for (mostly Latin American) party leaders to participate in transnational party networks was their access to political funding from (mainly German) party foundations. International financial aid to party-related training and research centres was crucial in maintaining the infrastructure of domestic political parties in periods of repression and financing election campaigns in periods of democratic transition. This 'political aid' proved to be very effective at particular moments, such as the support to the election campaign of Napoleón Duarte, the Salvadorean Christian Democratic presidential candidate in 1984, or to the Chilean moderate opposition in 1987-88. It is often argued that the political foundations were a useful non-governmental instrument of governments during the Cold War, but their impact is often overstated. Pinto-Duschinsky (1996: 248) argues, for example, that the *Konrad Adenauer Foundation* 'has not been very successful in Latin America'.

62 Private aid agencies are absent actors in the transition literature, but also in subsequent comparative studies on democratisation. Short references to private aid agencies are sometimes made in enumerations of transnational societal actors, such as Schmitter (1996: 39) who mentions 'foundations' among many other non-governmental actors, or Shaw (1994: 23) who refers to 'humanitarian aid agencies'.

63 Analogous to the discussion on domestic civil society, a point could be made about the material, organisational and ideological dimensions that have shaped the emergence of global civil society. It is likely that private aid agencies particularly possess a comparative advantage over other transnational actors in strengthening the 'material dimension' of global civil society with the provision of private aid resources.

Chapter 2

1 This distinguishes private aid agencies also from 'public service contractors', who are market-oriented 'non-profits' selling their services to official aid agencies and governments. For a discussion of this category, see Korten (1990: 102-4) and Robinson (1997).

2 Unlike figures of official development assistance, it is difficult to get reliable statistics on private aid transfers, as Smillie and Helmich (1993: 40-41) point out. Official OECD statistics give figures on private aid spending that do not include contributions in kind (food aid). OECD figures also are incomplete as figures from some major official donors are not available.

3 Sommer (1977: 8) and Lissner (1977: 46-51) point at the inaccuracy of quantitative figures concerning private development aid because they do not take into account the value of the 'voluntary' component. They argue that the 'actual benefit' of private aid for the South is up to fifty percent higher than that of official aid, although this seems highly speculative.

4 The Red Cross in the United States was an exception, as the US government was unwilling to get involved in aid overseas prior to the Spanish-American War of 1898. The main reason was that the US constitution did not authorise Congress to use public funds for foreign relief (Lissner 1977).

5 Hoover's committee received substantial contributions from the French, British and American governments and enjoyed diplomatic privileges, and could actually be considered as a quasi-governmental organisation (Curti 1963: 231-7).

6 Although the new Soviet leaders considered foreign relief as a potential instrument that could undermine the revolution, a great variety of private aid agencies was allowed to enter the Soviet Union, including the counter-revolutionary and semi-governmental *American Relief Adminis-tration* of Herbert Hoover. The Russian famine relief programme was the largest private multi-agency relief operation up to that period (Curti 1963: 279-293; Smith 1990: 33-35).

7 Most of the early Canadian private relief agencies were also created immediately after the Second World War, often as branches of foreign aid agencies; see Brodhead *et al.* (1988).

8 These UN campaigns were the Children's Emergency Fund UNICEF (1948), World Refugee Year (1959) and the Freedom from Hunger Campaign of the FAO (1960). European private aid agencies founded in this atmosphere of the 1950s include the Swiss *World Vision* and *Helvetas*, the Dutch NOVIB, the *Danish Refugee Council*, and the German *Kindernothilfe* (Smith 1990).

9 The new 'Third World' nation states became members of the United Nations and urged the General Assembly to adopt a resolution to designate the 1960s as the UN Development Decade. The target was to achieve minimal annual growth rates of five percent by the end of the decade in the developing world. The resolution asked the industrialised countries to dedicate one percent of their GNP to developing countries in the form of development aid and technical assistance (OECD 1988).

10 Special ministries to administer development aid were created in France, Germany and Switzer-land in 1961; Belgium, Denmark and Sweden in 1962; the Netherlands in 1963; Great Britain in 1964; and Canada in 1968. An active role was played by the Development Assistance Committee (DAC) of the OECD (created in 1960) through which the United States urged European govern-ments to become more involved in development aid (Smith 1990).

11 WUS-Denmark was founded in 1966 as a branch of the *World University Service* (a Geneva-based cultural exchange network) and changed its name to *Ibis* in 1992.

12 Major fund-raising campaigns were launched after emergencies in the South, such as the famine in India (1969), the civil war in Nigeria and the famine in Biafra (1967-70), the famine in Bangladesh (1971), the drought in the Sahel-zone and Ethiopia (1973-74), and the earthquake in Guatemala (1976). Agencies specialised in emergency aid such as *Médecins sans Frontières* (MSF) were set up as a response to these disasters. With branches in several European countries, MSF is currently among the largest private aid agencies in Europe (see Table 2.1).

13 Early critics of development aid already pointed at the false assumption that an increase in foreign aid would accelerate economic growth (cf. Jepma 1995).

14 The figures are from OECD (1988). Hellinger *et al.* (1988) and Clark (1991) remark that part of the increase in official funding to private aid agencies is sometimes 'tied', and that it is not always clear from the figures how much of the private aid share is actually free of conditions.

15 Lobbying by private aid agencies in the mid-1970s became better coordinated at a European level by the Catholic network CIDSE and the NGO-EC Liaison Committee, complementing the UN-oriented lobbying efforts by ICVA. The European Community, and the governments of the United Kingdom, Finland, Belgium, Switzerland, France and Ireland all started new co-funding programmes for private aid agencies in the late 1970s (Smith 1990).

16 In the United Kingdom alone the *Band Aid Trust* collected £35 million in private donations, and worldwide over £100 million (Burnell 1991: 203).

17 Although this point should not be overstated: in the previous chapter it was argued that 'NGOS' became a container concept in which many organisations in civil society of the 1960s and 1970s would easily fit today. In other words, it is a matter of how 'NGOS' are defined.

18 A survey among official donor agencies in 1984 showed that governments developed particular interest in supporting private aid agencies, as they were expected to 'strengthen partner NGOS in developing countries' (OECD 1988: 26).

19 Smith (1990: 126) quotes a director of *Catholic Relief Services* in the early 1980s who experienced negative public reactions in a campaign to raise awareness about the deeper structural causes of injustice in Central America: 'US people respond better to appeals to the heart than to the head'.

20 Spoerer (1987) uses the term 'informal diplomacy' to refer to non-governmental contacts between European diplomats and Latin American NGOS in the era of authoritarianism.

21 Earlier critical analysis of private foreign aid and the effectiveness of local development NGOS, notably the report by Tendler (1982), did not generate these denouncements. In the Netherlands, the debate slowly started around 1988-89 (cf. Achterhuis 1993; Lieten and Van der Velden 1997) and gained momentum after the impact study (Stuurgroep 1991) was published. In Belgium, a critical report on private aid agencies from an ex-agency staff-member (Barrez 1993) initiated the debate on private foreign aid, followed by a public response from the major Belgian private aid agencies (De Ekstermolengroep 1994) and others (Vandepitte *et al.* 1994). In the United Kingdom this debate was concentrated in (and partly fuelled by) the 'Manchester workshops' in 1992 and 1994 (cf. Edwards and Hulme 1992, 1995; Hulme and Edwards 1997).

22 A 1993 survey among European private aid agencies revealed that three out of four agencies just had completed (or were in the process of) major staff and management reorganisations (Biekart 1995). Four Protestant European aid agencies (*Christian Aid, Brot für die Welt,* ICCO and EZE) started a process of internal reflection on their role as private donor agencies (Riddell 1993), and major Catholic agencies such as CEBEMO and *Misereor* organised profound discussion rounds with overseas partners (CEBEMO 1993), to give only two examples of this internal reflection process.

23 An additional consequence of increased 'direct funding' to Southern organisations in civil society was that the latter started to be more openly critical of earlier interventions by private agencies. See for example Perera (1997) on private aid support by the Dutch NOVIB to the Sarvodaya Shramadana movement in Sri Lanka.

24 Toye (1993) points out, however, that the start of this 'counter-revolution' in development thinking had started already in the early 1980s.

25 Moreover, private aid agencies are very slowly adapting to the fashions borrowed from the corporate sector. Edwards (1997: 241) remarks that many are still using formalistic strategic planning models which were abandoned years ago by the corporate sector.

26 Emergency aid from bilateral donors increased on average from 1.6 percent in 1984 to 8.4 percent in 1994. For several official donors these figures were even more spectacular, such as the European Community (from 1.7 to 16 percent), the Netherlands (from 2.2 to 17.8 percent), and Norway (from 4.4 to 21.9 percent) (Randel and German 1996: 236).

27 Growing evidence from other studies has confirmed this point. See for example African Rights (1994), Prendergast (1997), De Waal (1997), Middleton and O'Keefe (1998).

28 These impact studies will be further examined in Chapter 3; a synthesis of these studies was published by Kruse *et al.* (1997).

29 This optimistic view can be found in De Ekstermolengroep (1994), Watkins (1995), Riddell and Robinson (1995) and Van den Berg and Ojik (1995, 1998).

30 There are several 'gradations' of pessimism; Smillie (1993, 1995b), Van der Velden (1996) and Sogge *et al.* (1996) still see 'a way out', while Tandon (1991), Barrez (1993), Vandepitte *et al.* (1994) and Maren (1997) are rather negative about this prospect.

31 In the same way, Lissner (1997) argued that the behaviour of agencies is determined by three organisational considerations: (i) the desire to maximise the influence of agency values on public opinion, (ii) the desire to maximise income and (iii) the desire to maximise agency respectability and leverage.

32 Although Smillie (1995b) remarks that other motivations to help the poor also play a role, such as 'guilt' and 'shame'.

33 Van den Berg and Ojik (1998: 119) admit that the 'disaster strategy' of private aid fund-raising is unavoidable and more beneficial in the shorter term than emphasising positive results of private aid interventions.

34 This simplified version of the aid chain is inspired by Padron (1988) and Fowler (1993b) and will be further elaborated on at the end of this chapter.

35 As the primary focus of this book is on financial transfers of private aid agencies, non-financial aid (such as volunteer sending or advocacy and development education work in the North) is not examined here. See Brodhead *et al.* (1988), Clark (1991), Burnell (1991), Edwards and Hulme (1992) and Smillie (1995b).

36 Avina (1993) and Edwards and Hulme (1995) distinguish between short-term 'functional accountability' (accounting for correct use of resources and immediate impacts) and longer term 'strategic accountability' (accounting for structural impact and effectiveness).

37 Critical external reports from independent analysts are generally internally welcomed and seriously discussed by policy departments, while publicly dismissed as 'old arguments' and 'nothing new' (cf. Achterhuis 1993).

38 Although some governments have decided to maintain (and even increase) their aid contributions to private aid agencies (such as in the Netherlands and the United Kingdom), this was likely the result of effective policy advocacy by agencies towards their (Social Democratic) governments and not so much a product of fundamental changes within these agencies. The Dutch agencies, for example, although maintaining that they had indeed structurally improved their internal management, still remain weak in strategic accountability as will be shown in Chapter 6.

39 Smillie (1995b: 212) criticises some of these transnational private aid agencies for trading 'long-term development impact for growth, short-term child sponsorship and emergency donors'.

40 There is no consensus in the literature on what 'partnership' actually means, and it is more likely referring to an ideal relationship between Northern and Southern NGOs than to a description of real existing relations (Malena 1995). The concept 'partnership' entered the development vocabulary in the late 1970s, when the rapidly expanding Southern NGO sector demanded more autonomy from Northern donors and more control and responsibility over design and implementation of development projects. In contrast to mainstream development thinking of large bilateral and multilateral donors, Southern NGOs and Northern private aid agencies emphasised the need for small-scale and decentralised development projects with active participation by beneficiaries at the grassroots level. This required the construction of local organisational capacities to sustain development initiatives in the long run and to diminish dependency on external resources. More equal and interdependent relationships between Northern donors and Southern recipients were needed to pursue these goals, as traditional top-down donor-recipient relations turned out to be inadequate to guarantee sustainability and grassroots participation. In other words, to improve longer term outputs of development interventions, private aid agencies acknowledged that their traditional 'operational' role in the South had to be reconsidered.

41 Examples of the unchallenged reproduction of Korten's framework can be found in Thérien (1991: 273-5) and Smillie (1995b: 31-34).

42 The reference to Myrdal is taken from Smith and Lipsky (1993: 15-16)

43 This typology is inspired by combining the approaches of Elliot (1987a), Korten (1990) and

Carroll (1992). Carroll developed evaluation criteria for private agency-sponsored projects along three patterns of goals: (i) development services, (ii) participation and empowerment, and (iii) wider impact.

44 That is why several agencies started to classify their activities according to the 'primary purpose' of their intervention. The Dutch agency NOVIB, for example, classifies activities into three categories of 'primary goals': direct poverty alleviation, civil society building and policy reform, and allocates resources to these areas following a 6:3:1 ratio (Interview with Theo Bouma 1995).

45 Not included here is private aid income from official contributions of *multilateral donors*, such as the European Union. For some agencies, such as OXFAM-Belgium, this contribution accounts for one-third of total agency income.

46 Korten (1990: 118-9) points at the considerable gap between the appearance of Sommer's influential book *Beyond Charity* (1977) in which a plea was made for a 'development approach' and against a 'welfare approach', and the practice of applying 'second generation' strategies: 'too many of these interventions give little more than lip service to self-reliance and, in fact, build long-term dependence on the assisting NGO'.

Chapter 3

1 According to the 1993 *Mission Statement* of OXFAM-UK/I.

2 The governance agenda was a result of both economic and political concerns of bilateral and multilateral donors. Archer (1994: 11) summarises the agenda as follows: 'The good government approach claims that sustainable prosperity is generated by an inter-dependent organic relationship between the market economy, the state, and civil society. A wealth-producing economy and a well-run government will help to sustain the vigour of civil society; a well-run government and a vigorous civil society will give impetus to economic growth; a strong efficient economy and a well-organised civil society are likely to produce efficient government.'

3 These new official donor policies for democracy assistance and supporting pluralism in civil society are analysed in Crawford (1995), De Feyter *et al.* (1995), Robinson (1996b) and Van Rooy (1998).

4 This was a major critique from Southern organisations directed at private agency representatives at the INTRAC-sponsored workshop 'NGOs, Civil Society, and the State' in Oxford in December 1995 (Clayton 1996).

5 Since a distinction can be made between economic and political purposes in strengthening civil society, Robinson (1995a) suggests the term 'foreign political aid'. Although this might be helpful in identifying democracy assistance programmes of official donors, it also suggests that donor interventions with predominantly economic objectives would *not* be political, which is questionable. Therefore, the term 'foreign political aid' is avoided.

6 Macdonald (1997) calls the 'inclusive' approach to civil society building the 'Gramscian approach'. I prefer not to use this term, as many other thinkers have contributed to the inclusive concept of civil society. However, I also agree that a more appropriate label is still needed.

7 As was pointed out earlier, donor agencies could of course contribute to democratisation in three different ways. They could either put pressure on public institutions in the South and try to make governments more accountable to their citizens, or they could strengthen civil society by making it more inclusive and increase its autonomy from the state, or they could combine these two efforts. Only in the last case are (private and official) donor interventions contributing in a sustainable way to democratisation, by building up and sustaining the functions of political society.

8 The scheme is of course simplified for analytical reasons. Not included are 'direct funding' aid

flows from official donors to Southern organisations in civil society, or, for example, direct aid flows to municipal governments.

9 A policy officer of OXFAM-USA indicated that it preferably supported 'those elements of civil society that most reflect our vision and values' (Renshaw 1994).

10 USAID and other official donor agencies sometimes use the term 'civil advocacy organisations' (CAOs) for societal organisations operating in political society. However, this term is avoided here as it suggests that the political and economic roles of societal actors can be separated, which is actually very difficult. See Gary Hansen (1996) and Robinson (1996b).

11 Support from the Dutch private aid agency ICCO to the Philippine trade union federation KMU led to a special investigation in 1991 by the Dutch ministry of development cooperation, following accusations that funds to the KMU allegedly had been channelled to the armed struggle. Although no evidence was found that private aid had been used to purchase weapons, ICCO was implicitly criticised for directly supporting revolutionary organisations of the political opposition.

12 Carothers (1995: 67) relates the current attention for 'bottom-up' approaches in US democracy assistance programmes to the arrival of the Clinton administration: 'Within the field of democracy assistance US liberals tend to favour a relatively stronger emphasis on grassroots development and bottom-up programmes, generally, than do US conservatives.'

13 Crawford (1995) analyses 'governance aid' from the European Union, Sweden, the United Kingdom and the United States. Interestingly, 25 percent of this support for civil society building (mainly to human rights activities) in 1995 was allocated to Central America and the Caribbean, whereas only 2 percent of total ODA went to this region in the same year.

14 Van Rooy (1998) interviewed Gary Hansen, one of the authors of USAID's civil society building programme, who explains that USAID had been selectively supporting organisations for over 30 years, in particular trade unions. But 'up to the end of the Cold War, we feared that supporting nongovernmental groups would destabilize friendly governments'. It still has to be proven that 'after the end of the Cold War' this policy has fundamentally changed.

15 This was one of the recommendations of the Dutch Advisory Council on Development Cooperation. Not only could this so-called 'twinning' contribute to more sustainable North-South relationships, it could also strengthen the support base for development cooperation in the North (NAR 1992: 28).

16 Smillie (1995a: 13) notes that this project orientation is reinforced by Southern governments who contract Southern NGOs to implement bilateral aid projects, and by direct funding from Northern donors to Southern NGOs: 'These arrangements are almost exclusively designed within a project framework.'

17 As 'impact' refers to longer term consequences and to ongoing change, 'impact evaluation' can rarely be retrospective. Therefore the term 'impact assessment' is more appropriate, as it emphasises that impact is analysed at certain stages in this process of social change. For a discussion see Oakley et al. (1998: 35-42).

18 Although I agree with Fowler (1997: 166) that 'in practical terms it is seldom possible for NGDOs to measure their organisational impact, especially for international NGDOs with a global vision and mission. From a performance point of view [...] vision and mission function primarily as reference points for judging coherence between impacts and strategic choices and policy decisions.'

19 A detailed elaboration of problems implicit to impact assessment can be found in Fowler (1995, 1997) and Fowler and Biekart (1996).

20 In fact only the direct output of a private aid agency (resources or training) and the impact on behaviour or capacity of recipient organisations can be assessed with some 'safety' (Charlton and May 1995).

21 An additional advantage of examining the external context of project results is that this can

contribute to assessing the prospects for replication in other regions or countries (Riddell and Robinson 1995).

22 This came up in a discussion with Chris Roche of OXFAM-UK/I, who pointed out to me that the absence of linear cause-effect relations does not automatically exclude the possibility of *correlations* between aid interventions and development achievements. In his critique of linear approaches, Uphoff (1992: 394) suggests we are dealing with 'deterministic disorder': 'Systematic knowledge and effective action are possible if we learn to "go with the flow", trying to hit moving targets and influence evolving relationships.'

23 A more traditional method to judge social change as a result of aid interventions is to use a *control group* that did not benefit from external aid, but experienced similar circumstances prior to, and during, the period of intervention. However, control groups are seldom useful in assessing impact of social development as it is impossible to find identical groups, let alone social, political and economic circumstances that are similar (Coudéré 1994).

24 This is why good *monitoring systems* are generally considered to be a key condition for successful evaluations and impact assessments (Oakley 1996).

25 This last issue is relevant if impact assessment is meant to be a learning exercise; active participation of the 'primary stakeholders' (also in the identification of indicators) is considered to be an important condition for determining impact. This is based on the conviction that only those directly affected are best able to judge how and how much their situation has changed.

26 To avoid this problem, it is sometimes suggested that 'rolling baselines' be used, in which information collected through monitoring of running projects is used to construct baselines for future projects; see Oakley *et al.* (1998: 141).

27 Although progress has been made in developing and 'translating' qualitative indicators for 'participation' and 'empowerment' (Shetty 1994), less advance has been made in the development of indicators for 'strengthening civil society'. As each process of social change is unique, new indicators need to be developed for every attempt to assess impact. I will come back to this issue when the methodology of the case studies is discussed.

28 A third group of 'tertiary stakeholders' includes those organisations that try to influence an aid agency, but to which it has no formal obligations. These are generally groups that oppose aid agencies, or obstruct their activities in the field, and are often considered to be illegitimate stakeholders.

29 A rather new method in the assessment of an agency's performance against standards negotiated among multiple stakeholders is the *social audit*. This method has been used recently by small organisations involved in alternative trade and even by transnational corporations such as *The Body Shop*, in which the entire performance of these organisations is judged by the stakeholders on a regular basis. The social audit technique was further developed by the *New Economics Foundation*, which has conducted social audits of *Tradecraft* and *Shared Earth* since 1993. See Zadek and Gatward (1995).

30 In recent years, several agencies (such as NOVIB and OXFAM-UK/I) have started to experiment with new participatory evaluation methods to involve their stakeholders more actively in policy advice and planning (Es *et al.* 1996). Results suggest that private aid agencies should acknowledge the need to change current practices despite all the problems and obstacles intrinsic to impact assessment.

31 The *Inter-American Foundation* is in the strict sense not a private aid agency. It is a semi-autonomous governmental organisation, set up to support NGOs and social organisations in Latin America, and could therefore be compared with many Nordic, Dutch and German private aid agencies that also are highly dependent upon governmental aid resources.

32 A useful synthesis of several of these studies was published in Kruse *et al.* 1997, listing major results and analysing evaluation methods. For a more detailed analysis of these impact studies see

Van Dijk (1994), Fowler and Biekart (1996) and of course the studies themselves.

33 The final report of the Dutch impact study, coordinated by an independent Steering Group, was rather critical about both the transparency and efficiency of the four Dutch private aid agencies. But the implicit goal of the study, to consolidate or increase official contributions to private aid agencies, was nevertheless secured. Van der Velden (1994b: 5) therefore classified it as a 'political rather than an empirical report'. See also Van Dijk (1992) and Hoebink (1994).

34 Riddell *et al.* (1995: 110) use the phrase 'promoting development by proxy'.

35 These criteria were: reaching the poorest; extent of people's participation; gender characteristics; environmental factors; performance of Swedish technical assistants; innovativeness; extent of pre-project appraisal, monitoring and evaluation; sustainability; inclusion of issues related to democracy and human rights. It could be questioned whether it was justified to judge project achievements against criteria that were not applied initially to projects (Riddell *et al.* 1995: 49-54).

36 In their search for the final project executor the evaluators were faced with SIDA, Swedish 'framework organisations', Swedish NGOs, local recipient organisations local executive organisations and beneficiaries (Riddell *et al.* 1995: 44).

37 Not surprisingly, the Swedish study hence found a major gap between the development objectives of funders (either SIDA or Swedish private aid agencies) and the achievements of development impact (Riddell *et al.* 1995: 109).

38 The 19 projects selected in the Dutch impact study on average received donations from six different foreign aid agencies (Stuurgroep 1991: B:30).

39 The four Dutch agencies were running 5,500 projects in 104 countries at the time of the impact study, for which 19 projects were selected (Stuurgroep 1991).

40 The Danish study selected India, Tanzania, Zimbabwe, West Africa and Central America (total 17 projects); the British study selected Bangladesh, India, Uganda and Zimbabwe (16 projects); the Dutch impact study selected Brazil, Chile, Zimbabwe, Burkina Faso, India and Indonesia (19 projects); the Finnish study selected Ethiopia, Nepal, Nicaragua and Uganda (29 projects); the Swedish study Bolivia, Kenya, Zimbabwe and India (37 projects).

41 The Dutch private aid agencies were directly involved in the selection of case studies and proposed (for obvious reasons) the better performing projects, although the 'Steering Group' recognised that those selected were 'illustrative' rather than 'representative' (Stuurgroep 1991: 6-7; Hoebink 1994: 28). The same procedure was used in the British and Swedish studies, which resulted in a selection of 'less contentious' projects (Riddell and Robinson 1995: 65), that was 'biased more in favour of better development impact' (Riddell *et al.* 1995: 48). The evaluators thus explicitly recognised that the selection was not random.

42 The evaluators identified three project types: production projects, social services, and training and awareness raising. These categories were not mutually exclusive; projects were selected on the basis of having their primary focus on either one of these categories (Stuurgroep 1991: B-14).

43 'Twelve out of sixteen projects broadly achieved their objectives, and had a positive impact in alleviating poverty, even if only one was clearly successful in achieving all the objectives set' (Riddell and Robinson 1992: 7).

44 This does not imply, however, that larger capital investments should be the key to tackling poverty. On the contrary, evaluations from large bilateral aid programmes suggest that this depends largely on an existing 'enabling environment' (Jepma 1995).

45 Riddell *et al.* (1995: 88-89) point at some exceptional cases (popular education projects or training of union leaders) in which it might be preferable to remain autonomous from governmental resources.

46 In considering sustainability as a process, Riddell *et al.* (1995: 55-59) are making a useful distinction between financial, institutional and environmental sustainability, which are all complementary elements.

47 Carroll (1992: 114) admitted this by stating: 'Evaluators lack the means to adequately measure or illustrate progress in organisational capacity. Furthermore, the interaction between 'outsiders' and 'insiders' is a protracted and subtle process that is exceedingly difficult to grasp and document.'

48 The Dutch impact study mentioned some techniques that are used by Southern NGOs for pressuring governments, but provided no data concerning results (Stuurgroep 1991: 36-7). The Finnish study did the same, and suggests: 'NGOs across many countries [...] worked with, nurtured and opposed a range of popular movements to oppose (often successfully) the excess of national security states and unrepresentative military juntas' (Riddell *et al.* 1994: 13). The British ODA study (Surr 1995: ix) concluded that NGOs can 'play an important role both in strengthening civil society and in promoting good government', providing examples from two Indian organisations supported by OXFAM-UK/I.

49 This situation apparently changed after the study was completed in 1990. In a postscript, Fowler notes that the 1992 presidential elections, and introduction of a multi-party system, improved democratic conditions and prompted more unity among Kenyan NGOs, which was necessary for them to be able to play an intermediary role in civil society.

50 As causes for low performance, Macdonald (1997: 144) mentions ill-conceived or poorly executed projects, lack of pre-project consultation with beneficiaries, and most of all an unfavourable political and economic environment, both national and international.

51 See for example Weiss and Gordenker (1996), Krut (1997), Van Rooy (1997), Fox and Brown (1998).

52 Couderé (1994), for example, distinguishes between three sets of variables that affect the outcome of project activities: context variables, project variables and project-system variables. Context variables (political and economic environment) can only be marginally influenced, whereas project variables (stakeholders, sector, region) are determined before the project starts, but once decided cannot be influenced by project activities. However the project-system variables (project design, organisation, implementation) can be influenced, as these are determined by the way the project is executed. By making this distinction between independent and dependent variables, the connection between internal and external factors that determine project outcome or impact become more explicit. This is generally the weak point of impact studies in which the country context analysis often is delinked from the case study analysis.

Chapter 4

1 Although Belize and Panama are nowadays also part of the Central American Integration System (SICA), their histories are quite distinct from the five other Central American states. Belize, the eastern zone of Guatemala, was incorporated into the British empire in the mid-nineteenth century and only became independent in 1981. Panama, which is culturally more connected to South America, was part of Colombia until its independence in 1903, and since then has been an 'unofficial US protectorate' due to the construction and exploitation of the Panama Canal.

2 It would be erroneous to consider the Liberal regimes as a dramatic break with previous Conservative rule, although secularisation and the expansion of the public sector certainly were new policies. But most of the new nation states had Liberal and Conservative characteristics (see Pérez-Brignoli 1989: 94-5).

3 Translated quotation from Acuña (1995: 71).

4 Cerdas (1992: 27) points out that Anastasio Somoza García was not simply a tyrant, but that his dictatorship was very solidly constructed. He combined military power (as head of the US-trained National Guard), political power (president of the Republic), economic power (after his marriage with Salvadora Debayle, a woman from a leading colonial family) and regional power, by

becoming the key interlocutor in the region for US governments.

5 The predominance of authoritarian rule in Central America for over one and a half centuries did not mean that it was simply rule by coercion. Since the Liberal reforms, regular elections were convened to legitimise the forces in power, although only male literates were eligible to vote. With illiteracy oscillating between eighty and ninety percent of the population, the oligarchy was easily able to restrict the electoral participation of other social or political sectors (Taraceno 1993: 170). This was justified by arguing that the people were still not mature enough to vote and had to be educated first. In a later stage, when universal suffrage was introduced and political exclusion formally was abandoned, outcomes of elections were determined by a combination of co-optation, clientelism, *compadrazgo* and electoral fraud. Even the latter was for a long period not considered to be a violation of the rules, but a legitimate measure accepted by all contenders as a necessary practice, although rhetorically rejected (Acuña 1995: 83-4).

6 Paige (1997: 26) even argues: 'the dominance of lawless military regimes has made family ties the only effective guarantee of personal safety and the only institutional route to political power'. Paige looks at the coffee oligarchy in Costa Rica, Nicaragua and El Salvador. For a similar study on Guatemala, see Casaus (1995).

7 For a detailed analyses of civil society growth in the 1920s see Acuña (1993). Among the new women's organisations was the *Sociedad Cultura Feminina*, which later became a founding member of the *Federación Sindical Hondureña*. In Costa Rica female teachers founded the *Liga Feminista Costarricense*, which (among other things) rallied for civil rights for women. Their campaign eventually succeeded with the adoption of the new constitution in 1949.

8 The new labour federations were fragile for two reasons. One, they were relatively small as they had no rural base, except for some combative unions of railway workers in the banana enclaves. Second, because they were ideologically weak and therefore often manipulated by North American and Mexican communist 'fellow travellers', especially in Guatemala and El Salvador (Dunkerly 1988: 74-76; Acuña 1993: 296).

9 Between 10,000 and 30,000 peasants were killed in the insurrection, also virtually eliminating Indian culture in El Salvador. According to Dunkerly (1988: 97) the absence of any major peasant rebellion in the coffee zones during the civil war of the 1980s could be explained as a result of this traumatic event.

10 For details on these parties see Acuña (1993) and Bulmer-Thomas (1987).

11 Urban middle-class employment had grown since the 1920s (notably in health and education, governmental institutions and services) and had increased the numerical importance of the middle classes (Bulmer-Thomas 1987).

12 The lead was taken by university students who had been demanding the replacement of faculty deans at the San Carlos University. A march, at the end of June 1944, demanding institutional autonomy of the university evolved into a larger demonstration in which full political democracy was demanded, in line with the new UN charter (Dunkerly 1988: 136).

13 Although Arévalo called himself a 'spiritual socialist', he obstructed the legal foundation of the Guatemalan Communist Party (PGT) until 1952 (Dunkerly 1988: 140-1; see also LaFeber 1993: 115-6).

14 Membership of the PGT was estimated at a few hundred, with a little over a thousand sympathisers. For a detailed analysis of the PGT see Dunkerly 1988 (145-8) and Jonas (1991: 30-8).

15 Fierce competition emerged between the Communist-led Costa Rican Workers Confederation (CTRC, founded in 1943), which also was supported by the government, and the Rerum Novarum Workers Confederation (CTRN), which was set up in 1944 with support from the Catholic Church. This competition boosted unionisation, especially after the introduction of the Labour Code (see Rojas 1993: 91-2).

16 José Figueres, a wealthy agro-industrialist, Social Democrat and above all anti-communist, often

is considered to be the intellectual founder of modern Costa Rican democracy (Dunkerly 1988; Salom 1991).

17 Paradoxically, all these factors actually contributed to democratic transition in Costa Rica. Bulmer-Thomas (1987: 151) observes that 'by the beginning of the 1960s, Costa Rica stood out as the republic best able to combine the export-led growth model with agricultural diversification, fiscal and social reform and political democracy'.

18 Paige (1997: 317) analyses how part of the old agrarian coffee oligarchy gradually transformed into an agrarian-industrial elite: 'The division between the agrarian and the agro-industrial factions of the elite is fundamental to understanding what happened in Central America in the eighties.'

19 In Honduras, the National Honduran Peasant Association (ANACH) was founded in 1962 with support from the AFL and ORIT, and was supported by the government of Villeda Morales to prevent independent organising during the introduction of agrarian reform. In the late 1960s ANACH also radicalised (Dunkerly 1988).

20 Church-sponsored peasant unions were for example FECCAS in El Salvador (1965), ACASH in Honduras (1964) and FCG in Guatemala (1967). Most of these unions radicalised in the 1970s, or were challenged by more radical peasant unions such as CUC in Guatemala, ATC in Nicaragua and FUNC in Honduras (Bulmer-Thomas 1987; Rojas 1993).

21 I am referring to the Revolutionary Movement of 13 November (MR-13), founded in 1960. In the same year, the Communist party PGT also had decided to support 'all forms of struggle'. Two years later the Rebellious Armed Forces (FAR) was formed, which (despite being defeated twice by the armed forces) later became part of the URNG (Rojas 1993).

22 Dunkerly (1988) points at the different origins and tactics of the early guerrilla struggles in Guatemala and Nicaragua. The former was rooted in the overthrow of the Arbenz government and had closer relations with the Cubans. Moreover, the FAR and MR-13 really were a challenge for the state and suffered (just as their successors after their defeat in 1971) from more sustained repression in several waves, ending in the massacres among the indigenous communities in the early 1980s. Although the early FSLN in Nicaragua also was seriously weakened by repression by Somoza's National Guard, its rural *foquismo* strategy until 1971 had been a failure due to a lack of political and military infrastructure.

23 In 1977 the FSLN had only 200 active militants, who were moreover divided on their strategy. The organisation was split into three factions: the 'proletarian faction' (emphasis on the urban workers, led by Wheelock, Carrión and Núñez), the 'protracted people's war' (prolonged rural campaign, led by Borge, Ruiz and Arce), and the '*tercerista* faction' of the Ortega brothers and Tirado, who promoted multi-class coalitions to prepare for insurrection, which became strongest (Black 1981).

24 The Communist Party, which had been established in 1930, turned to armed struggle in the 1970s even though its secretary-general Cayetano Carpio had left the party in 1970 to form the Popular Liberation Forces (FPL). Other emerging political-military organisations were the People's Revolutionary Army (ERP, founded in 1972), of which the Armed Forces for National Resistance (FARN) split off in 1975, and the Central American Revolutionary Workers Party (PRTC, founded as a regional party in 1976 and active in El Salvador after 1979) (Montgomery 1995: 101-9).

25 Christian Democratic parties were founded in Guatemala (DCG, 1957), Nicaragua (PSC, 1957), El Salvador (PDC, 1960) and Honduras (PDC, 1968), although the last remained marginal. Social Democratic parties generally have been smaller, but received some electoral support in coalitions with Christian Democrats, such as the PSD (1960) and the MNR (1964) in El Salvador. See Goodman *et al.* (1992); Rojas (1993).

26 The Independent Liberal Party (PLI) and the Social Christian Party (PSC) led a broad coalition in the 1967 elections, but due to manipulation and repression Somoza won the presidency with

seventy percent of the vote (Vilas 1995: 94). In Guatemala the United Front of the Revolution (FUR), an opposition coalition of Christian and Social Democrats, was unable to win the 1970 presidential elections, although it won the important mayoralty of the capital. This mayor was, just as many other moderate opposition leaders, assassinated in the late 1970s.

27 The limited land reforms in Honduras of the late 1950s and early 1960s were largely the result of a better organised peasant movement (Bulmer-Thomas 1987).

28 In El Salvador these paramilitary activities were carried out by the National Democratic Organisation (ORDEN). In Guatemala the *comisonado militares* already existed in rural areas, and were complemented by a large number of private anti-communist death squads. In Nicaragua this role was performed by the *jueces de mesta* (Torres Rivas 1987; LaFeber 1993).

29 This was particularly true for Nicaragua; the turning point for 'institutionalisation' in El Salvador was the coup of January 1961 (Torres Rivas 1989).

30 The first three factors are a further elaboration of key elements identified by Bulmer-Thomas (1987: 225-9) to explain the 'breakdown of the established order'.

31 The process of radicalisation among indigenous communities and the evolution of Indian organisations and their links with the guerrilla groups EGP, ORPA and FAR is further elaborated in the Guatemalan case study in Chapter 6. For details on the Guatemalan revolutionary movement, see Jonas (1991) and Le Bot (1992).

32 The political-military organisations were strongest in El Salvador, where popular fronts allied (and later merged) with military fronts. Five alliances of military and popular fronts were formed, prior to the foundation of the FMLN from previously existing organisations (dates refer to the year of foundation): FPL (1970) and BPR (1975); RN (1975) and FAPU (1974); ERP (1972) and LP-28 (1978); PCS (1930) and UDN (1967); PRTC (1976) and MLP (1979). In 1980 the popular fronts were dissolved and only the military organisations continued (Montgomery 1995).

33 Torres Rivas (1989: 93) comments that the FSLN probably came closest to the model of a popular army, as it managed to receive unconditional support from practically the entire population in the final offensive against Somoza's National Guard.

34 The presidential candidate of the PDC-led coalition UNO was retired Colonel Ernesto Claramount, with the former PDC mayor of San Salvador José Antonio Ehrlich Morales as candidate for the vice-presidency.

35 Low voter turnout in 1974 (42 percent) also reflected lack of confidence in the Christian Democratic Party (DCG). The presidential candidate of the Christian Democrats was General Ríos Montt, who had been the chief of staff during the counter-revolutionary campaign of the late 1960s, and would continue to lead the campaign of terror in the early 1980s. Between 1957 and 1985, the Guatemalan Christian Democrats never proposed civilian candidates for presidential elections (Dunkerly 1988).

36 Jonas (1991) points out that divisions within the Guatemalan military were not about the content of policies (like in El Salvador) but about the right person to lead the counter-insurgency campaign. Ríos Montt was removed by his defence minister Mejía Víctores (in August 1983) basically to polish up Guatemala's human rights record internationally and to prepare for a so-called 'authoritarian transition' to democracy.

37 President Jimmy Carter in his inaugural address in January 1977, quoted in LaFeber (1993: 210).

38 It is sometimes argued that the economic recession of the late 1970s also was a factor fuelling the Central American crisis. But it is important to note that the impact of the global recession, deteriorating terms of trade and balance of payments, affected the Central American economies only after 1979, the year in which the political crisis escalated (Bulmer-Thomas 1987).

39 In left-wing circles all over the region the popular slogan was actually reminiscent of Reagan's domino theory: *'si Nicaragua venció, El Salvador vencerá'* (Freely translated as 'a victory in Nicaragua will inevitably lead to a victory in El Salvador').

40 Costa Rica is not part of the analysis because democratic transition started there already in the late
    1940s. Equally, the Nicaraguan democratic transition will not be further analysed as it started
    essentially as a democratic transition from 'below' and was not initiated 'from above' by the
    military as happened in El Salvador in 1979, in Honduras in 1980 and in Guatemala in 1982.
    Another reason for excluding Nicaragua in the analysis is that since 1979 the political process
    there has received enormous academic (and political) attention, disproportionate to, for example,
    the Honduran democratic transition. In addition, conditions for field research in Nicaragua were
    adverse in the early 1990s, due to chaos in the NGO community after the electoral defeat of the
    FSLN.

41 I recall Schmitter's observation (mentioned in the first chapter) about the existence of 'multiple
    regime transitions', which was implicitly a warning to apply 'transitology' too strictly in the
    Central America context, particularly concerning Honduras, El Salvador and Guatemala (and
    Nicaragua after 1990).

42 There are two reasons why 'democracy' only became an 'issue' in the 1990s. First, it has been a
    postponed discussion, as it made no sense to think of the construction of democracy when state
    repression and civil wars were contributing to large numbers of victims among the civilian
    population. Second, as Torres Rivas (1989) observes, democracy in the 1980s was very much
    associated with the counter-insurgency state. The driving ideology of revolutionary movements
    therefore was to defeat the authoritarian political system entirely, and build on its ruins a genuine
    democratic political system.

43 Structural adjustment policies were first introduced in Costa Rica (1982), followed by Guatemala
    (1986), El Salvador (1987), Nicaragua (1988) and Honduras (1988). See Menjívar (1992).

44 Although in 1963 they ended a reformist period, the armed forces under López Arellano took the
    initiative in 1972 to renew the programme of land redistribution which had started in 1962. In
    fact, it had been one of the most radical agrarian reforms in Central America (Lapper and Painter
    1985).

45 US pressure on the Honduran armed forces started in late 1979 by Carter's Assistant Secretary of
    State Viron Vaky, resulting in the 1980 parliamentary elections. After the election of civilian
    president Suazo (November 1981) the US embassy was upgraded (with the arrival of Negroponte),
    and the Reagan administration increased military aid by fifty percent in early 1982 (LaFeber 1993;
    Schulz and Sundloff 1994).

46 Sieder (1996b: 22) takes December 1977 as a starting point when Melgar Castro passed legislation
    facilitating a *de jure* enlargement of political society. However, the April 1980 elections for a
    Constituent Assembly could be regarded as a *de facto* start of transition for several reasons: it
    produced a victory for the (more progressive) Liberal Party, an extremely high voter turnout (81
    percent) and the entrance of the small opposition party PINU into parliament. This indicated
    confidence and hope by the electorate for political change.

47 Several political-military groups emerged in Honduras: *Frente Morazanista, Lorenzo Zelaya,
    Cinchoneros* and PRTC. However, none of them had a broad popular base nor managed to develop
    military strength; only the *Cinchoneros* staged some spectacular actions in 1981-82, and the
    Honduran branch of the PRTC tried to establish a *foco* in southern Honduras, which was crushed
    by combined US-Honduran military action. Although severely weakened during the Alvarez
    period, all groups remained active until the early 1990s.

48 The irony of Honduran political culture was that when these struggles escalated into a constitu-
    tional crisis – President Suazo was trying to continue his mandate and the armed forces
    threatened to remove him by force – negotiations between the parties to overcome their internal
    fights were mediated in May 1984 by the armed forces at the Air Force headquarters.

49 Not only were half of the ballots misprinted, but Nationalist candidate Callejas actually received
    the largest amount of votes. However, as was agreed in the May 1985 'arbitration' to add up votes

of candidates from one party (in which the Liberals performed slightly better), Azcona was designated the victor (Dunkerly 1988).

50 The rebellion by young nationalist officers was possibly prevented with CIA support: the US was keen to get rid of dissident officers on key army posts, although it is unclear whether the purge of López was US-inspired (Schulz and Sundloff 1994). The military hierarchy apparently feared that López had made unfavourable concessions to President-elect Azcona (Rosenberg 1994).

51 This was also caused by the intransigence of new army commander General Humberto Regalado, a hardliner who reintroduced repressive measures against the opposition. Major victories by human rights groups were achieved in 1988 and 1989, when the Inter-American Court on Human Rights sentenced the Honduran government for systematic disappearances in the early 1980s (see Chapter 6).

52 The *Frente Morazanista* was the first to renounce armed struggle in April 1990. The *Lorenzo Zelaya* front conditioned this step upon guarantees for their safety and an amnesty, which was granted in July 1991. By the end of that year most of the left-wing opposition leaders had returned from exile. Several former guerrilla groups formed the Democratic Unification Party (PUD) to participate in the 1993 elections (Norsworthy and Barry 1994).

53 Military impunity had been a major issue in the 1993 electoral campaign, due to public pressure by human rights organisations and women's organisations. This point is further elaborated in Chapter 6.

54 On military involvement in drugs trafficking, see Jelsma and Celada (1997) and Maldonado (1998).

55 This Popular Forum *(Foro Popular)* was formed in September 1979 by the PDC and MNR, and supported by popular unions like FENASTRAS and LP-28 (with strong Communist Party influence). The Forum rallied for free elections, economic reforms and a clean-up of the armed forces (Dunkerly 1988: 380-1).

56 Rubén Zamora would later say that the democratic movement in late 1979 was at a dead end, that alternatives were exhausted and that it was either a question of joining the revolutionary movement (and 'reinstate democratic practices later on') or going into exile. But with hindsight he concluded that it had been an error to join the *junta*, and another error to step down in order to provoke a crisis that would spark off an insurrection: 'My decision to provoke a crisis was premature and not well analysed' (Zamora 1997: 169-70; 176).

57 The agrarian reform of the Duarte government ('the most sweeping land reform in Latin American history', according to US Ambassador White) was announced in March 1980 and would be implemented in three phases, of which only the second phase would affect the principal coffee *fincas*. However, after a number of estates as part of the first phase had been expropriated, fierce reaction by the oligarchy made the government decide (after less than two months) to stop the programme (Pearce 1986; Dunkerly 1988).

58 The Socialist International openly declared its support for the FDR-FMLN in January 1981 and in August 1981, when Mexico and France issued a joint declaration recognising the FDR-FMLN as a representative political force in El Salvador.

59 Six meetings were convened between 1984 and 1989 to negotiate a peaceful settlement: three during 1984 in La Palma, Ayagualo and Sesori (postponed), one after the 1987 Esquipulas agreement in San Salvador and two in 1989 (Mexico and San José) prior to the November offensive.

60 The CD first participated in the 1989 presidential elections (candidate Ungo), but only received 3 percent of the votes. In the 1991 parliamentary elections its support rose to over 12 percent, growing to 25 percent in the 1994 presidential elections with the Zamora candidacy on a combined FMLN-CD ticket.

61 In Chapter 6 this crucial period of late 1989 is analysed in more detail with special attention

to changes in civil society favourable to peace negotiations.

62 As this process has been analysed elsewhere in detail, only the main outcome will be discussed here. See Karl (1992), Munck (1993), Montgomery (1995), United Nations (1995) and Byrne (1996).

63 Military, judicial and electoral reforms required an amendment of the constitution to be ratified by two consecutive parliaments. The outgoing parliament would have its last session in late April 1991 and was thus under pressure to agree to reform the constitution. With hindsight, this was the key breakthrough in the negotiation process (Karl 1992: 157).

64 This *concertación* also was visible in the creation of other institutions such as the national civilian police (PNC), the Socio-economic Forum (FOCES), the *Ad hoc* Commission and the Truth Commission.

65 Gramajo (1997) and many other officers involved in the 1982 coup consider this moment as the start of democratic transition, despite the genocide against the Indian population that they were responsible for in the months following the coup.

66 US military aid was cut under Carter in 1977, after which the Guatemalan military received arms and training from US allies such as Taiwan, South Korea, Argentina and Israel. US economic aid was not interrupted, and military assistance was resumed under Cerezo (Aguilera 1989). However, the Guatemalan armed forces refused to participate in Reagan's regional counter-insurgency project and often took a 'nationalist' position, indicating sensitivity with regard to the 1954 US-supported coup (Dunkerly 1988).

67 The small Social Democratic Party (PSD) also participated in the presidential elections after pressure from General Mejía, but apparently had no substantial following in Guatemala. Most leaders had gone into exile between 1979 and 1985, and candidate Mario Solórzano only received 2 percent of the vote. The Christian Democratic DCG of Cerezo probably won the elections because it was least associated with corruption and military repression in the past. The DCG received 68 percent of the presidential vote, 51 percent of the parliamentary seats and 73 percent of the mayors (Painter 1989).

68 Despite national and international pressure to also include the URNG in this National Dialogue, Cerezo went along with Defence Minister General Gramajo who maintained that the URNG first had to lay down arms before any dialogue with the government could be a topic of discussion. And even then, Cerezo made clear, he distrusted the National Dialogue and was unwilling to accept a role for intermediaries between the government and the URNG (Delli Sante 1996: 221-3).

69 After the destruction of Indian organisations by the counter-insurgency campaigns of the late 1970s, two new coordinating bodies were formed in 1990 following the Oslo meeting: *Majawil Q'ij* and COMG. The rebuilding of Indian organisations is further analysed in Chapter 6.

70 Eleven issues figured in the 'Mexico agreement' of April 1991: democracy and human rights, strengthening civilian power over the military, Indian rights and identity, constitutional reforms, socio-economic reforms, agrarian issues, resettlement of the displaced, incorporation of the URNG in the political arena, preparations for a ceasefire, implementation schedule and verification, and the signing of the final peace agreement.

71 One of the key obstacles to accelerating Guatemala's democratic transition is the weakness of political parties, which lack clearly defined principles and are poorly rooted in civil society. As a result, political society is highly fragmented and based on fragile leadership pacts. Serrano's government, for example, was based on a political alliance between his right-wing Solidarity Action Movement (MAS), the right-wing National Centre Union (UCN) and the Christian Democrats, but collapsed shortly before the municipal elections of May 1993 (Torres Rivas 1996b).

72 A special body, the National Consensus Instance (INC), was formed after the May 1993 coup which included virtually all societal sectors and political parties. It made proposals to Congress

about the election of a new president and the implementation of several constitutional reforms to weaken the influence of the executive on the legislature, the judiciary and municipal government. These reforms were endorsed by a national referendum in January 1994, although boycotted by a group of popular organisations supporting the URNG and organised in the Multisectoral Forum (Inforpress 1995; Palencia 1996). The low voter turnout for this referendum (16 percent) and for the parliamentary elections of August 1994 (20 percent) illustrated the lack of confidence of the public in these elections.

73 These preconditions were negotiated in late 1993 and finally laid down in the Framework Agreement of January 1994. The main points were: to negotiate on the basis of the 1991 agenda; to tackle both 'operative' and 'substantive' issues under UN mediation and supported by a group of *países amigos* (Colombia, Mexico, Venezuela, Unites States, Spain and Norway); a commitment from both sides to rise above their individual military interests contributing to reconciliation; and an active involvement of civil society in the peace process.

74 Initially the plan was to set up a 'broad front' of popular organisations and various small political parties, but this effort failed due to personal rivalries. The FDNG, using the legal status of the old Revolutionary Party (PR) of Arbenz, was a political instrument of the 'popular sector' of the ASC, and tacitly supported by the URNG (Palencia and Holiday 1996).

75 Arzú had been elected mayor of the capital (1985-90), representing the National Advancement Party (PAN), with a two percent margin against Alfonso Portillo of the Guatemalan Republican Front (FRG), the party of General Ríos Montt. A victory of Ríos Montt's party would have meant a serious blow to the negotiations, as the URNG would have had to make a deal with the man responsible for the massacres of the 1980s (Rosada 1997).

76 It was above all a 'declaration of good intentions' concerning social justice, a minor land reform programme and tax reform that had already been planned anyway. For details, see Inforpress (1996: 224-39).

77 See Rosada (1997) who served as president of COPAZ under De León and criticised the URNG for making a political deal with the government to guarantee its incorporation into the political arena instead of being tough in the last negotiation phase.

78 Between 1980 and 1991, the United States officially channelled US$ 1.7 billion in military aid to Central America (of which 65 percent went to El Salvador, and 30 percent to Honduras). In practice, the amount was even higher because the figure does not include covert operations (Aguilera *et al.* 1991: 36-7; Sanahuja 1992). The domestic incentives for Reagan's Central American policy have been analysed from different perspectives by Chomsky (1985), Sharpe (1988), Arnson (1993) and Whitehead (1996b).

79 Of course, the revolutionary option in Guatemala had already been buried following the successful military offensive of the early 1980s. Whitehead (1996b: 221-2) and others convincingly argue that the two main revolutionary movements in the region, the FSLN and the FMLN, had been 'strategically defeated' by 1985, after Reagan's re-election and well before the end of the Cold War.

80 When US officials argue that the battle for peace in Central America was finally won in Washington, it should be added that the battle for a continuation of counter-insurgency war also was lost in the US: the Iran-*contra* scandal and the Jesuit killings were the key elements contributing to the demise of US low intensity warfare in Nicaragua and El Salvador respectively (Moreno 1994; Whitehead 1996b). The assassination of the Jesuits was one of the key reasons for the US Congress to cut military assistance to El Salvador in 1990 (see Chapter 6).

81 LIC strategies in Central America have been analysed in Klare and Kornbluh (1988), Barry and Preusch (1988), Vergara *et al.* (1989), W. Robinson (1996).

82 FUSADES received over US$ 150 million over a ten year period for research, implementing programmes to stimulate export-diversification and small business, and strengthening business

associations. Leaders of FUSADES in 1989 became key government executives: Cristiani (President), Murray Meza (Director Social Investment Fund, FIS) and Orellana (President Central Bank). See Rosa (1993).

83 It is beyond the scope of this analysis to elaborate on this issue and I refer to some excellent studies on AID's policies in Central America: Sojo (1991); Rosa (1993); Saldomando (1992); Escoto and Marroquín (1992). On the impact of US Food Aid on small farmers see Garst and Barry (1990); on the impact of non-traditional agricultural export promotion see Conroy *et al.* (1996); and on the impact of structural adjustment policies on the public sector see Evans *et al.* (1995).

84 The 'Project Democracy' initially proposed by Reagan's advisers was more ambitious and larger, including the creation of political foundations similar to the German *Stiftungen* and propaganda activities previously implemented by the CIA, but the US Congress turned down the proposal and only approved the creation of NED and a package of AID democracy assistance programmes; NED's budget rose from US$ 18 million in 1984 to US$ 48 million in 1993 (Carothers 1996: 127-9; W. Robinson 1996: 73-116).

85 The 'core group' of these private US foundations were the two party foundations of the Democrats (National Democratic Institute for International Affairs, NDI) and the Republicans (NRI, later IRI), the Centre for International Private Enterprise (CIPE) of the US Chambers of Commerce and the Free Trade Union Institute (FTUI) of the trade union federation AFL-CIO. In addition to these organisations, many other US foundations, think-tanks and universities (such as Freedom House, the Council on the Americas, the Center for Democracy) served as channels for support to civil society sectors in the South (Carothers 1996).

86 Since 1990 AID has scaled down its operations in Central America, although democracy assistance programmes have continued with an emphasis on civic education, judicial reform, strengthening municipal governments and civic advocacy.

87 In addition to Canadian and European (private) aid, US progressive churches and US private aid agencies and solidarity groups also were important supporters of the progressive opposition. This support will be further examined in the next chapter.

88 Hertogs (1985) argues that the role of the Socialist International in formulating EC policy often has been overstated, for example by Schori (1982). For a US critique on the role of the European Social Democrats in Central America see Mujal-León (1989).

89 European Community aid to Central America would increase from US$ 13 million in 1980 to US$ 164 million in 1993, whereas total bilateral aid from European countries in the same period grew from US$ 81 million to US$ 396 million. The five largest providers of aid in this period were Germany, the Netherlands, Italy, Sweden and Spain (in that order) (F. Hansen 1996). See also Freres *et al.* (1992), Smith (1995) and Table 5.1.

90 See also Freres and Grugel (1994), Pinto-Duschinsky (1996), Mair (1997).

91 I therefore disagree with Paige (1997) who argues that this 'revolutionary break with the past' (next to Nicaragua and Costa Rica) also was realised in El Salvador: the previous analysis has shown that continuity actually prevails.

92 This position has been extensively documented for the Central American region in Stein and Arias (1992), Rojas (1995) and Vilas (1996).

Chapter 5

1 These figures are estimates (based on data collected by the author) as it is impossible to define exactly how much aid the hundreds of European agencies and solidarity committees channelled to Central America. It is assumed that the forty largest European private aid agencies represent approximately eighty percent of private aid flows to Central America – an assumption based on

a 1991 survey of Nordic private aid flows to Central America (Sparre 1992).

2 The Norwegian agencies entered Guatemala for an odd reason: Guatemalan President General Kjell Laugerud (1974-78) was of Norwegian descent, and made a special appeal to Norway for humanitarian assistance after the 1976 earthquake. This also explains the dominant presence of Norwegian private aid agencies in Guatemala throughout the 1980s, and the key role Norway played in the peace talks of the 1990s (Interviews with Petter Skauen 1995; Hans Petter Buvollen 1995).

3 An indication of the number (and variety) of European agencies can be found in a list of the Nicaraguan Secretariat of International NGOs, which in 1989 registered 109 private aid agencies and solidarity groups with representatives residing in Nicaragua. Over eighty percent of these organisations were of European origin. The total number of European private organisations supporting projects in Nicaragua in the 1980s certainly was much higher, as many agencies had no local field office.

4 European private aid to the Nicaraguan opposition actually started only after 1978 (Interviews with Claire Dixon 1995; Sally O'Neill 1995).

5 Smith (1990: 153-7) also points at the close relationship between many progressive private aid agency staff members in Europe with solidarity groups and with the peace movement in the early 1980s.

6 Europe's 'rediscovery' of Latin America is analysed in Grabendorff (1984) and Van Klaveren (1986).

7 The increased strength of Christian Democratic governments after 1982 (notably in Germany, the Netherlands and Italy) that were more supportive of US policy towards Nicaragua and eager to give legitimacy to their political sister-parties in El Salvador and Guatemala, also influenced this changing attitude. For an analysis of the policies of the European Social Democratic parties, see Mujal-León (1987, 1989), although my impression is that he overestimates their role.

8 NGOs established as local charity organisations have a longer history, but do not correspond to the definition of 'local development NGOs' that was given in Chapter 1. González (1992) discusses a number of these 'charity NGOs' that emerged in El Salvador in the 1950s.

9 AID often used *Catholic Relief Services* (CRS), the private agency of the US Catholic Church, as an intermediary agency; CRS channelled food aid to the *Caritas* agencies of the local Churches (Garst and Barry 1990; González 1992).

10 Examples of these AID-supported NGO coordinating agencies are ASINDES in Guatemala, ACORDE and FOV in Costa Rica and FOPRIDEH in Honduras.

11 Data on the early history of Central American NGOs for El Salvador are taken from González (1992), for Guatemala from Sugranyes and Gutiérrez (1990), for Honduras from Ventura (1990) and for Nicaragua from Pinzón (1989).

12 International aid to Nicaragua after the Sandinista victory of July 1979 tripled compared to the pre-revolutionary level. Between 1980 and 1986 international assistance to Nicaragua was on average US$ 600 million annually (to a country of three million inhabitants) of which twenty percent came from Europe and Canada. The share of the Socialist bloc increased from 30 percent in 1981-83 to 65 percent in 1984-86. (Barraclough *et al.* 1988).

13 The Nicaraguan government established a special foundation for private aid contributions, the Augusto César Sandino Foundation (FACS), meant to coordinate (or to 'control', as opponents argued) the enormous variety of private aid flows. Many agencies bypassed FACS to avoid bureaucracy, causing the head of FACS to complain that 'In some cases the projects implemented reflected, first and foremost, their (private aid representatives') priorities, which were not necessarily those of the Nicaraguan government' (cited in Barraclough *et al.* 1988: 62). However, in the mid-1980s not only popular organisations, such as the small farmers organisation UNAG, but also municipal governments started to criticise FACS for wanting to control all private aid

flows, which was a reason for them to establish direct contacts with private aid agencies (Macdonald 1997: 136-9).

14 OXFAM-UK/I spent around ninety percent of its aid to Nicaragua between 1980-83 on development projects. After 1983, this dropped to less than fifty percent: the other half was dedicated to emergency relief as a result of the *contra* war (Melrose 1985: 27-38).

15 A considerable share of this private aid either went to FACS or to Sandinista state institutions such as the Nicaraguan Institute for Social Security and Welfare (INSSBI). Protestant private aid agencies generally preferred to channel support to the Evangelical Committee for Development Aid (CEPAD) (Barraclough *et al.* 1988: 87-8; see also Pearce 1997c: 446).

16 By 1982-83 Central America counted two million internally displaced persons (mostly in Guatemala) and almost one million registered refugees (Sollis 1996).

17 Project Counselling Service (PCS) was formed in 1979 by a dozen European private aid agencies (among them EZE, HEKS, ICCO and *Brot für die Welt*) with the purpose of coordinating assistance to Latin American refugees *in the region*, thus preventing a massive flow of refugees from coming to Europe (Pearce 1996a; Interview with Gordon Hutchinson 1995).

18 It should be repeated here that the Salvadorean Catholic Church, despite suffering many casualties (ten priests were assassinated between 1977 and 1980), under Archbishop Romero continued giving a voice to the opposition. By taking a clear position against increased human rights violations since the late 1970s (through the *Socorro Jurídico*) the Salvadorean Catholic Church positioned itself more explicitly on the side of dominated sectors than any other Catholic hierarchy in Central America (see Cardenal 1995).

19 DIACONIA came out of several efforts to set up an ecumenical humanitarian aid agency in El Salvador, with participation of the Catholic, Lutheran, Episcopal and Baptist Churches, and two federations of the cooperative movement: FUNPROCOOP and FEDECOOPADES. In 1981 DIACONIA worked with an annual budget of US$ 6 million; during the war it would channel in total about US$ 65 million to the uprooted population (González 1992; Eguizábal *et al.* 1993; Thompson 1995).

20 Clandestine support to the population in conflict zones in Guatemala and El Salvador was implemented by 'cross-border agencies' who worked closely with guerrilla movements. This aid was funnelled through their bank accounts and organisations in Mexico, Nicaragua and Panama (Eguizábal *et al.* 1993).

21 A key role was played by the *Lutheran World Federation* (LWF), based in Geneva, which operated through the Salvadorean Lutheran Church and in which Lutheran Bishop Medardo Gómez was the central figure. Gómez was one of the first prominent Salvadoreans to publicly endorse the repatriation of refugees in 1987 (Edwards and Siebentritt 1991). Gómez would also play a key role in the formation of CPDN (see Chapter 6).

22 Although this was for security reasons never openly admitted during the war (Interview with Víctor González 1992; González was director of DIACONIA in the 1980s).

23 As one leading NGO director commented: 'Support from some European private aid agencies was more than just humanitarian assistance: it was *solidarity aid*. With those committed agencies we had a *consenso tácito* about the focus and reach of our activities; without using many words, they knew exactly what it was about' (Interview with Salvador Orellano 1995).

24 FUSADES (Salvadorean Foundation for Economic and Social Development) created or supported with AID funding for example the following private sector development NGOs and associations: the Industrial Foundation for Labour Risks (FIPRO), the Business Foundation for Educational Development (FEPADE), the Programme for Strengthening Associations (FORTAS), the Salvadorean Anti-drug Foundation (FUNDASALVA), the Coordinating Committee for the Economic Development of Eastern El Salvador (COMCORDE) and the Centre for Support to Small Enterprises (CAM). Between 1983 and 1992 FUSADES received over US$ 150 million from AID

(Rosa 1993; Foley 1996). In addition, AID supported several other private sector programmes in El Salvador such as the Association of Young Entrepreneurs (APROSJU) and the International Executive Service Corps (IESC), and channelled support through operational US private aid agencies such as *Foster Parents Plan* and *Sister Cities* (Barry 1990: 117).

25 AID even paid the trips of US private aid agency representatives to El Salvador. US agencies working with AID support included *World Relief, Project Hope, Technoserve, International Rescue Committee,* but also the *Knights of Malta* and the *Family Foundation of America* which are known for their close relationship with the military. US private aid agencies such as *Save the Children, OEF International, Catholic Relief Services* (CRS) and *World Vision* are known to have rejected AID funding in El Salvador. CRS, for example, had worked closely with the Catholic Church and refused in 1985 to implement *Plan mil,* the large AID-funded resettlement programme for displaced persons (Smith 1990: 172-3; Barry 1990: 117-20).

26 Although the US Congress decided in 1984 that AID funding was not meant for counter-insurgency operations of the Guatemalan army, AID support for the National Security and Development Plan continued indirectly through infrastructural programmes (road construction), social programmes of CRN in conflict zones and food assistance programmes (Barry 1992: 263-4).

27 US evangelical churches and their relief organisations started to pour into Guatemala after the 1976 earthquake and their membership has grown since then by twelve percent annually; by 1987 almost one third of the Guatemalan population belonged to an evangelical church. The great majority of evangelicals preach individual salvation and strongly oppose Catholic liberation theology. Social programmes of these evangelical churches have been financed predominantly by US private aid agencies such as CARE, *700 Club* and *World Vision* (Barry 1992: 200).

28 Several new business associations were formed with AID support: in 1982 the Enterprise Chamber (CAEM) and the Guatemalan Non-traditional Export Association (GEXPORT) were founded, and in 1983 the Free Market Chamber (CLE). Under CAEM several new private sector development NGOs emerged: the Foundation for Integral Development (FUNDAP), the Guatemala Development Foundation (FUNDESA), the Technology Foundation (FUNTEC) and the Foundation for Financial Assistance to Development Institutions (FAFIDESS) (Barry 1992; Escoto and Marroquín 1992).

29 COINDE actually was a continuation of an informal umbrella of historic NGOs formed after the 1976 earthquake (Interview with Ana Sugranyes 1991a).

30 See the overview of US-financed Honduran organisations in Resource Center (1998a). As some local NGOs received funding from governmental agencies or through US private aid agencies they were often not aware that they enjoyed AID funding (Interview with Víctor Meza 1991).

31 Some FOPRIDEH members formed an informal group of NGOs critical of AID funding, including among others CCD, CEPROD, ASEPAD and EDUCSA (Resource Center 1988a).

32 Quote taken from Thompson (1996: 327).

33 According to Efraín Díaz Arrivillaga, member of parliament for the small Christian Democratic Party and president of the Centre for Human Development (CDH) (Mangelschots and Ventura 1994: 22).

34 Catholic private aid agencies had been supporting the Social Christian movement in Honduras since the late 1960s, particularly through the local NGO coordinating body CONCORDE. However, after a massacre of peasants in Olancho in 1975 the Church hierarchy withdrew its support of CONCORDE and of the popular church, leading to the disintegration of CONCORDE in 1978. After that, the organisations supported by foreign Catholic aid agencies suffered from mounting state repression (Resource Center 1988a: 4-7).

35 These European-funded Honduran development NGOs, created between 1978 and 1982, included the Honduran Institute for Rural Development (IDHER), the Christian Development Commission (CCD), the Centre for Human Development (CDH), Counsellors for Development

(ASEPADE), the Centre for Studies and Promotion of Development (CEPROD) and the Community Health Education (EDUCSA). Although not institutionally linked, most of these NGOs were connected through their leaders to one of the small revolutionary parties (Interview with Xiomara Ventura 1991).

36 A regional tendency was visible in the mid-1980s, including in Nicaragua, of European private aid agencies to prefer direct support to membership organisations (instead of indirect through intermediary NGOs) despite the limited capacity of these organisations to administer large (external) resources. With hindsight, many agency representatives consider this to have been a problematic tendency (Interviews with Stefan Declerq 1991; Alois Möller 1993; Gitte Hermansen 1996).

37 In Honduras it is not exceptional for the government to financially support particular peasant leaders when they are up for re-election, which enables them to 'buy' a majority of delegates. Accusations of corruption and fraud usually accompany these conflicts often leading to internal divisions, although in some cases ideological differences also have caused these internal splits (Posas 1992: 5).

38 The largest funder of CNTC was the Dutch private aid agency ICCO (Interviews with Rafael Alegría 1991b; John Contier 1995b).

39 CNTC also was keen to obstruct agency coordination (Interview with Oscar Avila 1991). With hindsight, most agencies conclude that CNTC lacked the administrative capacity to handle large sums of aid and that indirect support through development NGOs would have been preferable. Information on the CNTC case is based on interviews with agency staff (Interviews with Stefan Declerq 1991; Frans van Ballegooij 1993; Alois Möller 1993; John Contier 1995b; Sally O'Neill 1995; Gitte Hermansen 1996; Rolando Sierra 1996) and CNTC staff (Interviews with Erik Nijland 1991; Rafael Alegría 1991b; Doris Hernández 1991).

40 Some private aid agencies admit that their decisions in the 1990s to scale down private aid to Honduras have been influenced by the negative experience with the CNTC in the late 1980s (Interviews with John Contier 1995a; Gitte Hermansen 1996).

41 The formation of COCOCH and the *Plataforma de lucha* was financed by the *Friedrich Ebert Stiftung* (FES), especially to boost the role of ANACH and CTH. Although some believe that FES was very influential (though not successful) in Honduras in the 1980s, a FES representative voiced his disappointment about the lack of unity and the weak leadership inside Honduran popular organisations (Interviews with Aníbal Delgado 1991; Hilmar Ruminski 1993). For an analysis of the demands of the *Plataforma de lucha* see Noé Pino and Posas (1991).

42 After 1987 FOPRIDEH wanted to move away from AID dominance and decided to incorporate more European funded NGOs. However, this effort was only partially successful: in 1991 an alternative NGO network was formed, which soon fell apart due to internal divisions and personal rivalry. Coordination among NGOs has since remained weak in Honduras (Interviews with Xiomara Ventura 1991; Gilberto Ríos 1991b; Sally O'Neill 1995).

43 These women's groups were either membership organisations such as CODEMUH and CODIMCA, development NGOs such as CEM-H, or human rights groups such as *Visitación Padilla* and CDM. All these groups received support from European private aid agencies (Mangelschots and Ventura 1994; Wils *et al.* 1992. Interviews with Gilda Rivera 1996; María Elena Méndez 1996).

44 This was particularly the product of *Operation Phoenix* in 1986, a search and destroy operation by special military battalions in the Guazapa volcano area (one of the FMLN strongholds) and surrounding departments. Many displaced soon returned to their destroyed communities, initiating a broader repopulation movement (Thompson 1995: 126-9).

45 FUNDASAL, funded by the Catholic agencies CEBEMO and *Misereor*, is often considered as the 'mother' of the historic NGOs in El Salvador and as a training centre for various directors of the 'new' NGOs emerging in the late 1980s (Interviews with Rafael Villalobos 1991; Edín Martínez 1995b; Rafael Guido Béjar 1995).

46 Apart from a wide range of predominantly European (Dutch, British, Belgian and Nordic) private aid agencies, the Tenancingo project also was financed by the EC and the Swedish governmental agency SIDA. It was however not reproducible because of the large amount of investment involved (Eguizábal *et al.* 1993: 49). Despite its failure, Tenancingo definitely put the issue of the internally displaced on the national agenda. According to an OXFAM-UK/I representative, Tenancingo was the first coordinated effort by external funding agencies towards rebuilding civil society in El Salvador and an important lesson for later repopulations (Interviews with Víctor González 1992; Martha Thompson 1993; Patricia Ardon 1993; Pauline Martin 1995; René Ramos 1995).

47 The first repatriation of 4,000 refugees from Mesa Grande to Chalatenango started in October 1987, followed by massive return operations between 1988 and 1990. The FMLN was well-organised in these camps: Mesa Grande was dominated by the FPL (and partly by the RN), San Antonio by the PRTC and Colomoncagua by the ERP. Refugees in these camps were repatriated to zones of conflict controlled by these three FMLN-tendencies: Chalatenango, Cabañas and Cuscatlán (FPL and RN), Usulután (ERP and PRTC) and Morazán, San Miguel (ERP) (Interview with Víctor González 1992).

48 The dilemmas and tensions of private aid agencies resulting from the security situation in El Salvador are described in Thompson (1997a).

49 All five parties of the FMLN had their own coordinating NGOs: the FPL had CORDES (1998) and later CII (1991, in which CORDES and several NGOs such as PROCOMES, *Provida* and a number of unions worked together); the ERP established FASTRAS (1987), the Communist Party worked with FUNSALPRODESE (1988), the PRTC with ASDI (1986) and the RN with REDES (1989) (Martell 1994).

50 González (1992: 54) shows that the number of Salvadorean NGOs increased by 125 percent between 1984 and 1989, numbering 70 by 1989. In 1992, after the peace agreement was signed, the number of Salvadorean development NGOs had risen to 186 (UNDP 1992). AID-related sources claim that the number of NGOs in El Salvador was even higher (Urra 1993).

51 The International Conference on Central American Refugees (CIREFCA) was a combined effort by European donor governments and UNHCR to contribute to a lasting solution to the problems of displaced persons and refugees, and a direct response of the international community to the Esquipulas agreement of 1987. The CIREFCA programme ran from 1989 to 1994, and channelled US$ 438 million to resettlement programmes, of which an estimated forty percent was handled by NGOs and beneficiary organisations (Stein 1997: 169). The other major international programme for reintegrating the uprooted population was PRODERE, which was executed by UNDP and later integrated into CIREFCA. For a discussion of these programmes see Sollis (1995, 1996) and Stein (1997).

52 The ERP tendency and their NGO FASTRAS was the second largest recipient of private aid resources, especially after the establishment of the Segundo Montes community. FPL's dominance in securing private aid can be explained by its more developed international diplomatic network (Interview with Hans Peter Dejgaard 1996).

53 These regional councils were the Coordination of Repopulated Communities (CCR) in Chalatenango; in Cuscatlán and Cabañas (CRCC) and the Development Council of the Repatriated Communities of Morazán and San Miguel (PADECOMSM) (Thompson 1995: 136-7).

54 As was mentioned earlier, after 1990 private aid was complemented by large official aid flows, channelled through local NGOs, from the EC, the CIREFCA programme and its related Italian government sponsored programme PRODERE.

55 No less than ten human rights groups or institutions were active in El Salvador in the 1980s, some of them linked to the churches (such as *Tutela Legal* and *Socorro Jurídico*), others linked to universities or to the opposition (Torres Rivas and González-Suárez 1994: 57).

56 CST organised seven major national federations of trade unions with a total of 65 member organisations, whereas the UNTS united around 100 organisations and claimed a membership of 350,000 workers (Montgomery 1995: 193-5).

57 Organisations of marginalised communities arose in 1986 to respond to the failure of the Duarte government to attend to the needs of the earthquake victims; they formed councils which would later merge into the Salvadorean Communal Movement (MCS), representing over two hundred urban popular communities. MCS received European private aid support through local NGOs such as CREFAC and PROCOMES (Resource Center 1988b; Martell 1994).

58 CPDN's activities and its relation with European private aid agencies will be examined in Chapter 6.

59 This El Salvador Information Project (ESIP) was financed by a group of European private aid agencies and provided updated information on developments in El Salvador prior to and after the peace talks. It also served as a valuable source for journalists, for example in the investigations following the Jesuit killings.

60 This is the conclusion of a study by Martell (1994), and affirmed by perceptions of many agency staff and Salvadorean popular leaders interviewed by the author, including FMLN cadre (Interviews with Blanca Flor Bonilla 1995; Celina de Monterrosa 1995; Alberto Enríquez 1996). An additional, and not less important, achievement of European private aid was of course that many lives of Salvadorean opposition leaders were saved (Interview with Pauline Martin 1993).

61 There were actually less than a dozen historic NGOs that made up COINDE, among them IDESAC, CIF, ALIANZA, CAPS, ASECSA and CONCAD. Most of them came into existence after the 1976 earthquake, although some were older and were often linked to the social work of the Catholic Church from the 1960s.

62 These displaced populations were organised in three separate Communities of Populations in Resistance (CPR's): La Sierra, Ixcán and El Petén, and only announced their existence publicly in 1991.

63 Community development programmes were for example re-established after the mid-1980s by ALIANZA (with programmes in Huehuetenanago and El Quiché), CIF (in Baja Verapaz) and ASECSA (in Alta and Baja Verapaz). All these programmes received majority support from European private aid agencies. Moreover, these were large programmes: ASECSA's budget (mainly for public health) was higher than that of the Guatemalan health ministry (Gálvez and Klüsmann 1992).

64 Interviews with Marco Azurdia (1991) and Alberto Mazariegos (1995).

65 The Danish private aid agency *Ibis*, for example, supported these Indian NGOs in order to strengthen collaboration between popular organisations, NGOs and local governments, in the expectation that local 'anti-militaristic' candidates would eventually run for local municipal elections on the local *comité cívico* lists (Bye *et al.* 1995).

66 After all, the simple fact of having lived in a conflict area was for security forces often enough proof of sympathy for the URNG, with all its consequences: 66 leaders of the internally displaced were killed by government forces between 1987 and 1989 (*Reunión*, August-September 1994, Vol. 1, No. 4-5, p. 2).

67 Led by the International Council for Voluntary Agencies (ICVA), the International Group for the Accompaniment of the Guatemalan Returnees (GRICAR) was established in the early 1990s, which supported the CCPP in their negotiations with the UNHCR and the Guatemalan government. The *World Council of Churches* participated in GRICAR from 1993 (García *et al.* 1994: 62).

68 In addition to the refugees recognised by UNHCR, there also was a large group of dispersed refugees, not organised within the CCPP. In 1992 some of them founded the Association of Dispersed Refugees in Guatemala (ARDIGUA), which only represented about ten percent of non-recognised Guatemalan refugees (Burge 1995: 154).

69 Stein (1997) reports that for the entire Central America programme of CIREFCA and PRODERE between 1989 and 1994 US$ 438 million was raised, including the US$ 115 million provided by the Italian government for PRODERE.

70 Most of the 'old' COINDE-affiliates (such as ALIANZA, IDESAC, CONCAD, ASECSA, CIF, CAPS) and the newer members (COINDI, PRODESSA, FUNDADESE) also were part of CONGCOOP, which brought together over twenty development NGOs, two NGO coordinating agencies (COINDE and SAT) and the Federation of Agricultural Cooperatives (FEDECOAG).

71 Problems were generated by the division of the CCPP into three *vertientes* (North, North-west and South). Despite their negotiating a common deal with the government, each had their own priorities and policies for repatriation to their respective zones of return. This created considerable friction with the NGOs of CONGCOOP that assisted in the return (Burge 1995: 157-8; Krznaric 1997: 73. Interviews with Danuta Sacher 1995; Helmer Velásquez 1996).

72 Only the private aid agencies working together in the *Project Counselling Service* (PCS) – to support returning refugees and the displaced – and a group of Protestant agencies that had established a Regional Coordinating Office (OCR) achieved a workable level of mutual coordination (Interviews with Beate Thoresen 1995; Corina Straatsma 1995; Wendy Tyndale 1995; Hans Magnusson 1996).

73 A 1991 survey among 44 Guatemalan organisations found that 75 percent received external support, and 22 percent expected to receive external support in the short term. Three quarters of this external support was provided by private aid agencies. Given the growth of private aid to Guatemala after 1992, these numbers would probably have increased if the survey had been done in 1993 (COINDE 1991).

74 Several other Latin American networks started a special Central American section in the 1980s. ALOP should be mentioned here (a network of development NGOs which founded a Central American secretariat in the 1980s), FLACSO (a continental network of social sciences faculties, with members in Costa Rica and Guatemala, and after 1993 also in El Salvador) and CELADEC, an ecumenical network founded in 1962, in which Protestant educational institutes were organised.

75 A series of 'regional consultations' were organised by CCOD between 1989 and 1992 on the new directions of international development aid to the region. See CCOD (1990, 1991), Garst (1991), Campos (1992), Morales and Cranshaw (1997).

76 This has been a central goal of one of the firmest supporters of regional networking, the Danish *Ibis* (Bye *et al.* 1995).

77 The analysis of this section is based on a survey of private aid policy documents and interviews with agency representatives between 1993 and 1996. The following organisations were included: *Christian Aid*, CAFOD, OXFAM-UK/I (United Kingdom); ICCO, CEBEMO, NOVIB, HIVOS (Netherlands); DCA, *Ibis* (Denmark); *Brot für die Welt*, EZE, *Misereor, Friedrich Ebert Stiftung* (Germany); *Trocaire* (Ireland); *Diakonia, Rädda Barnen* (Sweden); *Norwegian Church Aid, Norwegian People's Aid* (Norway); OXFAM-Belgium, FOS (Belgium); *ACSUR Las Segovias*, IEPALA, *Manos Unidas, Solidaridad Internacional, Intermón* (Spain). Preliminary results were published in Biekart (1994).

78 Interview with Frans van Ballegooij (1993). A similar conclusion was reached by evaluators of the Central America programme of the Swedish private aid agency *Diakonia*, who add that the 'institutional strength' of partners as one of the key selection criteria had become more important in the 1990s than political criteria (Torres *et al.* 1996: 29).

79 The director of CONGCOOP, the Guatemalan coalition of NGOs assisting the resettlement of refugees and the displaced, remarked that the demand of European private aid agencies to shift the emphasis of their activities from 'emergency' to 'development' was too radical and could hardly be implemented given that the new requirements were made when the repatriation process

was already in motion. It surprised him that the agencies of 'solidarity aid' were suddenly so demanding compared to a few years before (Interview with Helmer Velásquez 1994).

80   These comments were for example voiced in 1991 by counterparts of the agencies ICCO, EZE and *Brot für die Welt* at *consultas nacionales* (national meetings), in which the new agency policies were presented (Interview with Rolando Sierra 1996).

81   Of course, it was impossible to really control the destiny of redirected funding to revolutionary organisations. The German *Misereor*, for example, was aware that its funding to DIACONIA was directed at FMLN-controlled conflict zones, and it therefore posed strict conditions on the purchase of food and medicines (Interview with Heinz Öhlers 1995). An urban popular organisation in El Salvador complained after the peace accords that due to stricter administrative criteria it ran into financial problems as the traditional share channelled to the party could no longer be justified to the funding agencies (Interview with Allan Martell 1993).

82   This observation was made in an independent programme evaluation of income generating projects funded by ICCO in El Salvador in the early 1990s (Hardeman *et al.* 1995).

83   See *Pensamiento Propio* 87 (January-February 1992) in which ASOCODE coordinator Wilson Campos openly criticised those NGOs which had been supporting peasant organisations in a paternalistic way in the past. It generated a heated discussion in *Pensamiento Propio* 91 (June 1992) about the relation between NGOs and popular movements. This issue is discussed further in the ASOCODE case study in Chapter 6.

84   The need to redefine the role of development NGOs in this direction was a central issue of a consultation process by CEBEMO with its key Latin American partners (CEBEMO 1993: 20-21).

85   One representative commented that after the electoral defeat of the Sandinistas many agency workers 'of the 1968 generation' searched for new prospects and were replaced by a younger (and less ideologically driven) generation (Interview with Alun Burge 1993).

86   This change of discourse in the early 1990s was confirmed in interviews with several agency representatives (Interviews with Pauline Martin 1993; Sally O'Neill 1994a; John Contier 1995b; Ulrik Sparre 1995). See also Ianni (1998).

87   Thompson (1997b: 461) points at the rapid shifts Salvadorean NGOs had to make towards funders after the peace accords: 'NGOs were supposed to move from emergency responses into comprehensive development work, almost overnight. Funders wanted complex project proposals based on economic growth and a neoliberal model, different in both conception and philosophy from the communal economic survival projects that had been developed in the conflict zones during the war.'

88   Sollis (1992) points at a considerable increase since 1990, when 25 percent of World Bank-supported projects involved local development NGOs.

89   The Central American representative of OXFAM-Belgium warned that a 'real revolution' was taking place in the Central America NGO world, with the danger that the supply of multilateral aid resources *and* the need to survive would fundamentally alter their priorities (Declerq 1994).

90   Interviews with Heinz Öhlers (1995), Cecilia Millán (1995) and John Nielsen (1996).

91   This lobbying activity was coordinated by the European networks CIDSE, APRODEV, EUROSTEP and by CIFCA, a network of European private aid agencies and solidarity groups founded in 1991 to influence the San José Dialogue (the annual ministerial summit between Europe and Central America).

92   For the Central American IDB strategies in the 1990s aimed at strengthening civil society see Ferraté (1995); Rosenberg and Stein (1995); Pearce (1998); Ianni (1998).

93   For example, several regional networks (CODEHUCA and ASOCODE) received direct support from the EU, as well as a number of development NGOs (such as those working with refugees), peasant unions, women's and indigenous organisations (Munting and Dejgaard 1994). Of course, many European private aid agencies also received part of their income from the European Commission:

OXFAM-Belgium for example covered over forty percent of its budget between 1987 and 1991 from this source.

94   Notably HIVOS (Netherlands) and *Ibis* (Denmark) felt that after a decade of support to Honduran organisations with little results, prospects for continued presence were bleak; many other agencies scaled down their allocations to Honduras (Interviews with John Nielsen 1994; Sally O'Neill 1994b; Chris Bransz 1995; Ulrik Sparre 1996). See also Sparre (1996).

95   This waning interest for Honduras can be understood by pointing at a 1992 *Christian Aid* policy document, stating that donor countries were selected on the basis of their strategic importance and on the probability of social changes which would potentially have a regional influence.

96   Burge (1995) and others have confirmed this by commenting that the Salvadorean NGOs have been the most sophisticated of all Central American counterparts in securing external private aid funding by closely monitoring and addressing Northern aid agendas.

97   This was in fact an argument used by AID to guarantee that reconstruction funds only were channelled to private sector NGOs which had been supported by AID during the war, and which were loyal to the government (Yariv and Curtis 1992).

98   FIS was created in late 1990 and was funded mainly by the IDB, UNICEF and several bilateral donors such as Japan and Germany. By 1994 it had a budget of US$ 75 million, which was considerable but not enough to address local reconstruction needs (Murray 1995: 83-4).

99   In a later version of this article he adds: 'In short, the gap between local NGOs and their national governments, accentuated by international efforts, became constraints on sustainable development and effective democratic practice' (Sollis 1996: 27).

100 It can even be argued that, given the top-down direction of aid flows, civil society building with foreign aid resources by definition cannot have a 'bottom-up' character, unless priority-setting and aid allocations are entirely controlled by recipient organisations and their beneficiaries.

101 With its Salvadorean programme Municipalities in Action (MEA, running since 1986) AID had determined the local debate on NGO-local government collaboration. After the 1994 municipal elections, in which the FMLN won several mayoralties, the historic NGOs would complement this support of municipal governments (Blair *et al.* 1995; Interview with Ulrik Sparre 1993).

102 An example is the Social Initiative for Democracy (ISD), an NGO linked to the FMLN and created in December 1992 to stimulate voter participation, train community leaders and forge consensus at municipal levels. This civic education was no luxury, as an opinion poll just before the 1994 elections showed that 83 percent of the electorate 'had no or little interest in politics' (Spence *et al.* 1997: 10).

103 A distinction should be made between Social Emergency Funds (FES) and Social Compensation Funds (FIS). The first was introduced in Bolivia, Honduras and El Salvador and aimed to set up short-term projects for local infrastructure development and employment creation. The latter was more long-term orientated and focused on social programmes (education, health, water) and productive projects. It was this type of FIS that was planned for Guatemala (Garst 1993: 10-11).

104 Initial funding for FONAPAZ was provided by UNDP, the Italian-funded PRODERE programme, BCIE, UNICEF, WHO and the government of Taiwan. After 1993 funds for FONAPAZ were also provided by the IDB, the World Bank and the European Union (Garst 1993: 32-6).

105 An example was the PRODECA programme of the Danish government, a regional programme started in 1992 which aimed to strengthen the peace process, support democratisation and enforce human rights (Macdonald *et al.* 1997).

Chapter 6

1 These organisations were: FUNDASAL, CPDN (El Salvador); CAPS, FUNDADESE (Guatemala); CNTC, CODEH (Honduras); CCOD, ASOCODE (Regional).

2 This choice reflects a mix of membership organisations and development NGOs, several strategies of civil society building, a wide variety of aid chains, and interventions by key private aid agencies from the Netherlands, Germany, Sweden, the United Kingdom and Denmark.

3 Interview with Manuel Torres (1996).

4 The outbreak of civil war in El Salvador spurred reconciliation between Honduras and El Salvador, whose relations had been tense ever since the 'soccer war' of 1969. In May 1980 six hundred Salvadorean refugees were killed by Salvadorean military forces when crossing the Sumpul River on the Honduran border, where they were forced back by Honduran troops. Similar massacres by combined Salvadorean-Honduran troops occurred in March, October and November 1981 at the Lempa River (Comisión de la Verdad 1993).

5 According to Lapper and Painter (1985: 83), the three members of this 'triumvirate' complemented each other: 'Suazo's role was to turn the Assembly into a rubber stamp for executive policy. Negroponte's relationship with Alvarez was never as crude as that of puppeteer to puppet. In fact they shared the same basic goals: a deep anti-communism and desire to bring down the Sandinista government.'

6 Officially the US refused to confirm human rights abuses by Honduran security forces. However, diplomatic officials knew very well what was going on, but often preferred to look the other way (Schulz and Sundloff 1994: 87).

7 From 1981 to 1984 CODEH documented 133 political assassinations (almost half of them Salvadoreans), 25 non-political assassinations (by abuse of power), 124 permanent and 169 temporary disappearances, and 169 cases of torture (Custodio 1986).

8 Padre Guadalupe (his real name was James Carney) was a North American Jesuit priest who had been in Honduras since 1962. Having become a follower of liberation theology in the 1970s, Padre Guadalupe started working closely with peasant organisations in northern Honduras. He promoted the conversion of local 'Justice and Peace' church commissions into human rights committees, by incorporating leaders of progressive popular organisations. These Regional Commissions for the Defence of Human Rights in Honduras (CODDERHH) were formed in early 1979 to give, according to Carney, 'the poor their own strong voice' (Carney 1983: 192-5). Given the enormous division between and within popular organisations, Carney considered the Church as the only neutral force capable of uniting the poor to defend their rights. Carney was expelled from Honduras in November 1979, but returned clandestinely in July 1983 as part of a guerrilla force led by PRTC leader Reyes Mata, which entered Olancho from Nicaragua. The offensive was sabotaged and after the group was captured by the armed forces (with US assistance), General Alvarez ordered their assassination. Nearly seventy people were killed, including Carney (Schulz and Sundloff 1994).

9 These *celebradores de la palabra* worked with the peasant and labour unions CGT and UNC and were often persecuted by the Honduran oligarchy and the armed forces, who had been responsible for the massacre in Olancho in 1975 in which twenty people were killed, among them two Jesuit priests and several lay-priests (Cardenal 1995).

10 Interviews with Jorge Irías (1995a), René Ramos (1995), Ramón Custodio (1996a), Henk Dielis (1996).

11 Between 1985 and 1994 CEBEMO channelled over one million guilders (approximately US$ 550,000) to CODEH, half of which came from the co-financing scheme of the Dutch government. CODEH's annual expenditures were on average in this period US$ 220,000. During one decade, CEBEMO therefore financed around one quarter of CODEH's annual budget (Inter-

views with Ramón Custodio 1995; Henk Dielis 1996).

12 Beside CODEH, CEBEMO also supported legal assistance activities of the parishes of El Progreso and Las Mercedes, which were both linked to local human rights groups of CODEH.

13 Interviews with Holke Wierema (1995) and Henk Dielis (1996).

14 The Danish agency *Danchurchaid*, on the other hand, decided in 1996, as a result of disagreements over these conditions, to end its relationship with CODEH (Interview with Dorte Ellehammer 1996).

15 Speech by Manuel Torres to the 9th National Assembly of CODEH, Valle de Angeles, December 1993 (author's translation).

16 Initially only civil and political rights were mentioned. Since the late 1980s, economic, social and cultural rights, as well as the rights of vulnerable groups (indigenous people, women, children and others) also are explicitly defended (CODEH 1995a).

17 This Commission was established in 1959 by the Organisation of American States (OAS). It supervises the American Convention (adopted in 1969) and one of its functions is to process and investigate petitions by individual citizens when domestic remedies have been exhausted. The Commission can refer cases to the Inter-American Court of Human Rights in Costa Rica, whose decisions are legally binding (Hydén 1996).

18 Manfredo Velásquez, a student and labour activist, was arrested by the DNI in Tegucigalpa on 12 September 1981; Saúl Godínez, a teacher and activist in the teachers' union, was arrested by military personnel in Choluteca on 22 July 1982. The Inter-American Commission combined these two cases with the disappearances of Francisco Fairén and Yolanda Solís, two Costa Rican students, who were apparently arrested in Honduras in December 1981 when travelling from Costa Rica to Mexico. The cases of Velásquez and Godínez were brought to the Court by CODEH in 1981 and 1982, the case of the Costa Rican students was handled by one of their parents.

19 This death squad member, Florencio Caballero, admitted that he and 25 others had received special training from US, Argentinian and Chilean military advisers. During his testimony, he gave names of key military officers involved. One of them was José Vilorio, who was assassinated on 7 January 1988 in Tegucigalpa, shortly before he was to testify before the Court. The government blamed his death on the *Cinchoneros*, a small revolutionary left-wing organisation, but the murder was never resolved and had all the signs of a death squad execution (Schulz and Sundloff 1994: 226).

20 Just like the assassination of José Vilorio (see note 19), the January 1988 murders of Pavón and his friend Moisés Landaverde (who was killed at the same time) were never solved. The government even suggested that Custodio was the intellectual perpetrator of the assassination, just as it linked the murder of Vilorio to CODEH (Interview with Ramón Custodio 1996b).

21 However, in the case of the two disappeared Costa Rican students (which was not handled by CODEH) the Honduran government was not found guilty.

22 See Inter-American Court of Human Rights, *Godínez Cruz Case*, Judgement of 20 January 1989, §191.

23 After General Alvarez was removed in a military coup by his colleagues in March 1984, he went into exile in the United States where he worked as a consultant for the Pentagon. While there he was converted to Pentecostalism and decided to return to Honduras in early 1988 to convert his countrymen. Although Alvarez had many enemies, he refused to accept a bodyguard as he was convinced that God was watching over him. The perpetrators of his assassination were never found, but his family is convinced that the military was responsible for his death (Schulz and Sundloff 1994: 250-1).

24 Interview with Marjet Uitdenwilligen (1996).

25 It should be mentioned that Riccy Mabel had no political background, unlike many victims of apparently 'common crimes' who indeed often were student or peasant leaders or otherwise

political activists. The assassination in May 1991 of five peasants of the cooperative *El Astillero*, presumably by military officials, definitely also influenced the storm of indignation following Riccy Mabel's murder.

26 Riccy's sister Ony confirmed this suspicion; she heard Colonel Castillo declare on television that he had never seen Riccy before, but she knew that Castillo had known Riccy for about a month (Méndez and Salomón 1995).

27 *El Tiempo* (19 July 1991). Méndez and Salomón (1995: 12) point at the amazing solidarity among top-level officers, which is totally absent in the lower ranks of the (Honduran) armed forces.

28 *El Heraldo* (27 July 1991). However, the two officers were not arrested immediately by military authorities, as the 'Military Code' proscribed that this could be done only after clear evidence was presented to prove their guilt.

29 In a desperate reaction, Colonel Castillo, the main suspect, accused the US anti-drugs agency DEA of being responsible for the murder of Riccy Mabel (*El Tiempo*, 26 February 1993).

30 *El Tiempo* (19 July 1991; author's translation). See also Méndez and Salomón (1995: 30-34).

31 Captain Andino however was absolved from any charges. The lawyer for Mabel's family, Linda Rivera, was not satisfied with the sentence because the maximum penalty for rape and murder was 28 years but, according to Rivera, Judge Maria Mendoza de Castro was pressured by the military to lessen the penalty. The staff of the judge also had been intimidated by the intelligence service DNI (Interview with Linda Rivera 1996; see also Rivera 1994). Two years later, the sentence was upheld by a court of appeal.

32 A good illustration of the drastic changes in relation to military impunity is that only five years earlier (in 1988) a low-ranking military officer killed a judge of the Supreme Court and was released shortly thereafter by a military court.

33 For example, in 1988 journalists from the *New York Times* and the *Washington Post* were expelled from Honduras after reporting on death squad activity and military involvement in extrajudicial killings. In the same year, US Ambassador Briggs labelled Custodio an 'old-fashioned, hard-line communist with terrorist proclivities' (Schulz and Sundloff, 1994: 246).

34 According to Custodio the *Plataforma de lucha* represented an artificial union between leaders of left-wing political parties and was too much a product of external funding from the German *Friedrich Ebert Stiftung* (Interview with Ramón Custodio 1996b).

35 One year after Mabel's murder a broad alliance was established within the *Comité Interinstitucional del primer Aniversario sin Justicia para Riccy Mabel Martínez* that organised a national protest in July 1992. But this alliance (in which human rights groups, churches, teachers' unions, student and women's associations worked together) did not last (Méndez and Salomón 1995). Friction also occurred when CODEH in July 1993 published a newspaper advertisement without the signatures of other organisations rallying against impunity, although they had requested to make a joint declaration. According to Custodio this was normal, as the other organisations wanted to sign the declaration but refused to share the costs (Interview with Ramón Custodio 1996b).

36 After Valladares was appointed in mid-1992, Custodio suggested that the government wanted to establish a parallel human rights committee in order to eliminate CODEH. However, after the report on disappearances was published in December 1993, the relationship between Custodio and Valladares considerably improved. In 1996 both even admitted to fulfilling complementary tasks (Interviews with Leo Valladares 1996; Ramón Custodio 1996a).

37 Dunkerly and Sieder (1995) note that the publication of the Truth Commission Report in El Salvador (March 1993) might have had a 'demonstration effect' on Honduras, where the disappearances were one of the key electoral issues. The presidential candidate for the National Party, Ramos Soto (who allegedly was involved in supporting General Alvarez in the 1980s), was severely damaged by this issue.

38 The legal status was personally presented to CODEH by President Reina on 8 November 1994, while praising CODEH for having contributed in 'a valuable and decisive way to promoting citizenship in Honduras' (CODEH 1995b: 31).

39 The *American Civil Liberties Union* in the United States served as an example for Custodio of how to remodel CODEH in the future (Interview with Ramón Custodio 1996a).

40 Interview with Xiomara Ventura (1995). However, this position was not only to protect CODEH: Custodio also affirmed that he blamed the weakness of the left-wing Honduran opposition on the poor quality of its leaders (Interview with Ramón Custodio 1996b).

41 Among them Bertha Oliva, the current President of COFADEH (Interview 1996). As a result of the internal crisis of 1989 some reorganisation led to an improvement of internal decision-making and to the recruitment of a more professional staff. However, complaints about the pyramidal structure of CODEH and bad communication between regional assemblies and central office continued, according to *Diakonia*'s evaluation of CODEH (Ramos 1996).

42 The special prosecutor for human rights asserted that certain cases against military officers were about to be lost as a result of CODEH's refusal to submit crucial information (Interview with Soña Martina Dubon de Flores 1996).

43 Interviews with Ramón Custodio (1995, 1996a, 1996b). *Brot für die Welt* decided in the early 1990s to end its support for CODEH as it refused to submit detailed financial reports (Interview with Rolando Sierra 1996). *Danchurchaid* also decided to withdraw its support after friction arose (among other issues) about CODEH's refusal to search for local funding sources in order to increase its self-sufficiency. Custodio considered *Danchurchaid*'s demands to be a lack of respect for the achievements of CODEH.

44 Interview with Henk Dielis (1996).

45 Custodio had high esteem for CODEH's vice-president Miguel Angel Pavón, who was assassinated in 1988. A second candidate that was supposed to succeed him, vice-president Jorge Sierra, suddenly died in 1993. Since then, no acceptable candidates have been proposed to Custodio for following him.

46 Interviews with Rene Ramos (1995, 1996), who reviewed a number of local CODEH committees in 1996 as part of an evaluation for the Swedish agency *Diakonia*. He found that only a few of these committees functioned properly. Some committees could not even say whether they belonged to CODEH, the Church or to the governmental Human Rights Commission.

47 CEBEMO had already been planning to phase out its support to CODEH between 1996 and 1998, at a time when CODEH was experiencing serious financial shortages (Interview with Eric Bloemkolk 1996).

48 To facilitate legal action, in 1995 CODEH started to coordinate the exhumation of bodies, with support from foreign experts. Apart from ending impunity, these legal cases were started to demand indemnification from the Honduran state.

49 Initiatives for such a national debate had been proposed by the bishops since early 1987, before the Esquipulas agreement urged the Central American governments to also go in this direction (Acevedo 1988; Ramos 1993).

50 The preparation and logistics of the meeting were coordinated by Ignacio Ellacuría, rector of the Central American University (UCA) in San Salvador (Ramos 1993). Ellacuría is generally considered to be the 'intellectual founder' of the CPDN although the bishops had a delicate relationship with him (Whitfield 1994). Moreover, he was accused by the army of being a key advisor to the FMLN (Rosa Borjas 1995).

51 Of the 164 propositions presented, 147 were approved by a majority vote in the plenary. Propositions that were rejected were for example 'The Sandinista revolution had a demonstration effect on the origins of the Salvadorean civil war', or 'Armed struggle is not a valid method to legitimise power.' This caused some participants to comment that the debate was dominated by

FMLN-directed organisations (Acevedo 1988: 779). For a discussion about whether these organisations were *fachadas* of the FMLN see Lungo (1995).

52 Archbishop Rivera wanted to prevent the Catholic Church from being identified with opposition to the Christian Democratic government of Duarte. Pressure from ARENA and the (conservative) nunciature to refrain from political activities (given the upcoming elections) also influenced the decision of Rivera to leave the CPDN (Berryman 1994: 94; Interview with Carlos Ramos 1996).

53 Quoted from *El Mundo* in Whitfield (1994: 321).

54 It was the first time the CD participated in elections and had expected to get ten percent of the votes. However, they only received 3.8 percent due to fraud and a low voter turnout caused by a transportation strike and ongoing fighting during election day between the army and the FMLN (Zamora 1991).

55 These *Encuentros Nacionales por la Paz*, convened by the CPDN in July and September 1989, were positively influenced by a declaration of support for negotiations from the Central American presidents during their summit in Tela in early August, in which Daniel Ortega mediated between Cristiani and the FMLN (*Proceso* no. 397, 23 August 1989, p. 4).

56 Inside the FMLN leadership few believed that the November offensive could lead to an armed insurrection. FPL leader Samayoa has acknowledged that some sectors in the FMLN pursued this option, but that the *comandantes* knew that it was foolish to believe the occupied areas of the capital could be militarily defended. The military purpose might have been to overthrow the government, but the political goal was to relaunch the negotiation process. See interviews with Salvador Samayoa in Ueltzen (1994: 162-4), and with Francisco Jovel in Montgomery (1995: 217-20).

57 Discussions about US military aid cuts had been going on for years and were only effectively implemented in October 1990, when the US Congress decided to cut military assistance by fifty percent and to make the other half conditional upon prosecution of the murders of the Jesuits and advances in the peace talks. However, when the FMLN launched a new offensive in late 1990, using sophisticated surface-to-air missiles and killing two US soldiers, the Bush administration restored aid (Byrne 1996).

58 Interview with Alberto Enríquez (1996), a former FMLN commander who was in charge of the 'popular sector' in the capital during the November offensive.

59 The CPDN kept a certain autonomy from the FMLN, although its influence increased after the November offensive when the FMLN urged coordinated pressure from civil society to get the negotiations started. The CPDN was not subordinated to FMLN policies, nor did all five tendencies have a seat in the national coordination committee, which was also composed of Christian Democrats and Social Democrats (Interviews with Alberto Enríquez 1996; Héctor Córdova 1996; Leonardo Hidalgo 1996).

60 The final agreement of the presidential summit in San Isidro de Coronado (10-12 December 1989) urged the FMLN to cease hostilities and requested the UN Secretary General 'to do everything within his power to take the necessary steps to ensure the resumption of dialogue between the government of El Salvador and the FMLN' (United Nations 1995: 101). The surprising element was that Nicaragua's President Daniel Ortega supported the declaration, in which 'any armed action' was explicitly condemned.

61 Between April 1990 (Geneva) and the final talks in December 1991 (New York) agreements were negotiated (under UN mediation) in five major areas: human rights abuses in the past (Truth Commission), demilitarisation (demobilising the FMLN and reducing the armed forces), police reform (installation of a new National Civilian Police), judicial reform and a land transfer programme. For a detailed account see United Nations (1995) and Byrne (1996).

62 This document was called 'Contributions for the Project of a New Nation and a Programmatic Platform for a New Government' and was publicly released by the CPDN in September 1993 with

the purpose of influencing the electoral campaign. It was based on extensive consultations with all member organisations.

63 As was shown in Chapter 5, DIACONIA coordinated large projects for resettling refugees and the displaced all over the country and was in the late 1980s one of the key channels for private foreign aid to the opposition.

64 Based on interviews with Frans van Ballegooij (1995, 1996) and Karel Roos (1996).

65 MacDonald (1998) argues that the CPDN soon became 'another support base' of the FMLN, the main reason why the Catholic Church stepped out in 1988. However, according to leaders of the CPDN who were also FMLN members, the CPDN was deliberately not transformed into an instrument of the FMLN, among other things so that less radical organisations would not leave the alliance (Interviews with Celina de Monterrosa 1995; Héctor Córdova 1996).

66 One of the key demands of the CPDN to the negotiating parties had been to allow for maximum transparency during the talks. However, both parties decided to keep up a certain level of secrecy, which left the CPDN only the task of informing its constituency about the proceedings of the talks.

67 The influential CPDN march of 14 December 1991, with more than 100,000 participants (the CPDN claimed 200,000), was a response to mobilisations by the right-wing initiative *Unidad y Paz 91* and the death squad-related *Cruzada pro Paz y Trabajo*, which wanted to prevent a reduction of the armed forces and accused Cristiani of being a traitor (*Estudios Centroamericanos* Noviembre-Diciembre 1991, Vol. 46, No. 517-518, p. 1055; Interview with Héctor Córdova 1996).

68 Rubén Zamora and eight other delegates elected to the National Assembly in the March 1991 elections, decided to take their oaths of office before a massive first of May rally organised by the CPDN (Montgomery 1995: 223).

69 The *Grupo de los países amigos* was formed by Mexico, Venezuela, Colombia and Spain.

70 According to Palacios, UN mediator De Soto on several occasions admitted that proposals from the CPDN had been incorporated into the agreements. However, David Escobar Galindo, member of the negotiation team for the government, asserted that the influence of the CPDN had been marginal, also because the CPDN was considered to be an instrument of the FMLN, rather than a 'third party' (Interviews with Edgar Palacios 1996; David Escobar Galindo 1996).

71 Zamora became the principal leader of the Democratic Convergence after the previous leaders died: Héctor Oquelí was assassinated in Guatemala in January 1990 and Guillermo Ungo died in a Mexican hospital in March 1991.

72 A third institution that should be mentioned is the Human Rights Ombudsman, which took over the verification role of ONUSAL. Apart from these official institutions, a number of NGOs were created to work specifically on election monitoring and civic education (such as ISD, CAPAZ and ISED), which also took over key functions of the CPDN (Interview with Celina de Monterrosa 1995).

73 Which does not mean that the CPDN would have been able to press successfully for socio-economic reforms. As Rubén Zamora (1993: 146-7) noted: 'although political exclusion and material injustice were the origins of the war, it is clear that the negotiation process dealt with the first and postponed the second [...] because the political theme was a priority' (author's translation).

74 This was a unanimous opinion shared by the 'covert' FMLN members and others in the CPDN leadership (Interviews with Celina de Monterrosa 1995; Leonardo Hidalgo 1996; Héctor Córdova 1996; Víctor Rivera 1996).

75 This is also reflected in the documents of the CPDN, in which prior to 1992 it presented itself as 'the representative of social forces', and later as 'an important sector of civil society'. The most active sectors in the CPDN after 1992 were the churches, NGOs, and women's, slum dwellers' and peasant organisations (Morales 1994).

76 Palacios asserted that many activities of the CPDN simply would not have taken place without private foreign aid. Absence of aid would have affected the media and lobbying work, and to a lesser extent the public marches, as these were sometimes also financed by member organisations such as the UNTS (Interview with Edgar Palacios 1995b).

77 For example, a CPDN project from September 1991 in which it requested funding for activities scheduled for 1992 was only approved by ICCO in November 1992.

78 Even in 1996, one of the agency representatives was still quite positive about the role of the CPDN, an opinion largely based on observations from several CPDN member organisations. Possibly, the replacement of ICCO's desk officer responsible for the CPDN in early 1993 (a key moment for the CPDN) was a coincidence that influenced this perception (Interviews with Frans van Ballegooij 1995; Karel Roos 1996).

79 This was admitted by the independent evaluator to the author. His impression was that ICCO wanted to have a 'positive report' (Interview with Abelardo Morales 1995).

80 According to field representatives from ICCO and *Brot für die Welt* (Interviews with Henk Gilhuis 1995; Rolando Sierra 1996). Palacios not only was a leader of the Baptist Church, but also the secretary of the Salvadorean Council of Churches. An additional factor is a general dynamic within (private) aid agencies related to 'partnerism': once a partnership is established, strong arguments have to be presented to end this relationship, rather than providing arguments to continue it.

81 In relative terms, ICCO assumed that it was decreasing its contribution from over 50 percent of the income of the CPDN between 1990 and 1992 to 25 percent in 1993-94. However, the real income of the CPDN turned out to be only half of the proposed budget, which made ICCO still the largest funder, covering more than half of the budget of the CPDN (Interview with Karel Roos 1996).

82 Another reason for the existence of large reserves was the gap between planned activities and disbursements of agencies. Several activities had to be cancelled while agreed funding had not yet arrived at the CPDN. However, when these delayed funds were disbursed, they were allocated to other activities, thus creating a circulation of internal resources and the growth of a reserve fund.

83 For example, in 1995, priorities of the CPDN ranged from 'consolidating democracy', 'state reform' and 'economic bases for development' to 'social development', 'security of citizens' and 'environmental security' (CPDN 1995: 16-17).

84 The blame for overfunding cannot be attributed entirely to the funding agencies: the CPDN itself also inflated budgets and activities, knowing that the Salvadorean post-war democratic transition would attract foreign aid only for a short period of time. After the euphoria about peace had died down it was expected that external funds would become much more difficult to acquire, which proved to be true in hindsight.

85 According to an external evaluation led by Morales (1994) and confirmed by Edgar Palacios (Interview 1995b). The 'sectoral directorate' was reinstalled in 1995 but did not perform the representative role as it did in the period 1988-1992 (Interview with Leonardo Hidalgo 1996).

86 Interviews with Edgar Palacios (1996) and David Escobar Galindo (1996).

87 The use of the term Mayas to identify the indigenous population of Guatemala is contested, as not all indigenous peoples in Guatemala (such as the Xincas and Garífunas) have Mayan roots. The term was promoted in the late 1980s by several Indian organisations to stress their common identity and history. Instead of Mayas, I prefer to use the term 'Indian' and 'indigenous' to translate the word *indígena*, but stress that I am not referring to the term *indio*, which has a negative connotation in Central America (Barry 1992: 216; see also Carmack 1988; Le Bot 1992).

88 Among them PRODESSA, COINDI, SERJUS, CAPS, FUNDADESE and ALIANZA: all of them Guatemalan NGOs that had worked closely with indigenous communities at least since the 1980s and all of them members of the Guatemalan NGO coalition COINDE.

89 Interviews with Maribel Carrera (1995) and Santiago Bastos (1996). My attention was drawn to FUNDADESE by a case study for a TNI-PRISMA sponsored research project (1992-94) focusing on private aid and FUNDADESE's community development programme (Carrera 1994).

90 The origins of the current blossoming of indigenous organisations in Guatemala could even be traced back to the 'Guatemalan revolution' (1944-54), when indigenous people were first granted political rights. This initial phase of democratisation suddenly ended with the US-backed coup, followed by decades of military rule (see Chapter 4).

91 Financial support not only came from the Catholic Church, but also from the US-sponsored *Alliance for Progress* (Carmack 1988).

92 The emergence of CUC deserves much more attention, but in this framework it is unfortunately not possible to elaborate more on the development of this important peasant organisation. I refer to Le Bot (1992), Carmack (1988), Santos and Camus (1993) and to the testimony of one of its leaders and Nobel Peace Prize winner Rigoberta Menchú (Burgos 1983).

93 The oldest guerrilla force in Guatemala, the FAR, formed in 1962, was of Ladino origin and active on the eastern coast and in the capital. After FAR and other guerrilla groups were defeated in the late 1960s due to a failing *foco* strategy, they decided to rebuild forces in the 1970s based on broad popular support, particularly from *indígenas*. The strongest organisation became the EGP, set up in the mid-1970s in Ixcán, and adopting the mass-based 'prolonged people's war' strategy. CUC soon was closely related to the EGP. The other strong force, besides smaller factions of FAR and PGT, was ORPA. This organisation was formed in the early 1970s, and only publicly announced its existence in 1979. ORPA had its base in the highlands (particularly around Lake Atitlán) and on the southern coast (Jonas 1991; Le Bot 1992; Perera 1993).

94 The (unarmed) peasants of Panzós demanded property rights for land that they had been cultivating for decades. A meeting was called by the army to resolve the issue, but the peasants were killed upon arrival (Dunkerly 1988).

95 Carmack (1988) and Falla (1994) describe in detail how indigenous communities generally did not share the ideological goals of EGP or ORPA, but joined these Ladino-led movements as a way to protect themselves from selective repression and death squads. See also Bastos and Camus (1993).

96 A first alliance between ORPA, EGP, FAR and PGT was established in October 1980. Out of this the Guatemalan National Revolutionary Union (URNG) was formed in February 1982.

97 Still no agreement exists about the total number of victims, as it remained unclear how many 'disappeared' actually were killed or managed to flee to Mexico. Painter (1989: xiv) speaks of 30,000 victims, while Jonas (1991: 149), based on *Americas Watch*, reports 100,000 civilian victims. Here I use estimates given by Falla (1994: 8). More consensus exists over the number of widows (50,000) and orphans (250,000) (Bastos and Camus 1993).

98 The EGP established its base in the north-western part of Quiché together with thousands of refugees who had refused to be incorporated in model villages. These Popular Resistance Communities (CPR's) kept a low profile, but announced their existence publicly in 1991. ORPA was pushed back to the western San Marcos department and FAR to the Petén forest in the north (Dunkerly 1988).

99 Other new organisations included the peasant organisation CCDA, formed in 1982 and organising (predominantly Indian) peasants from the highlands, the Permanent Commissions CCPP (the organisation of refugees in Mexico) and the Popular Resistance Communities (CPR's) of the Sierra and the Ixcán. For a detailed analysis see Bastos and Camus (1993).

100 Two coordinating bodies served this purpose. One was the Labour and Popular Action Unity (UASP), an alliance of various popular sectors in which labour unions and the CUC also participated. UASP was created in 1987 and showed some 'mobilisation power' in 1988 and 1989, but was vulnerable to political repression and lacked coherence as an alliance (Barry 1992). The other was the Coalition of Sectors Resulting from Repression and Impunity, formally created in 1991, in

which organisations representing refugees, the displaced, widows and relatives of the disappeared were organised. It called for an independent investigation into the fate of the disappeared and punishment of those responsible for the genocide of the 1980s (Bastos and Camus 1993).

101 Another important event in 1990 was the massacre in December in Santiago Atitlán, an Indian town in the highlands that managed to chase the military troops out of town after a protest march was responded to by bullets. Eleven civilians were killed and 21 wounded. The withdrawal of the 600 troops from Santiago Atitlán received national and international admiration, and gave a new impulse to the discussion on 'Maya autonomy' (Perera 1993).

102 *Majawil Q'ij* means 'New Dawn'. Although for security reasons denied publicly, most of these organisations were directly linked to one of the tendencies of the URNG (see Le Bot 1992).

103 The idea of setting up a coalition of Maya organisations dates back to 1984, but only at the end of the Cerezo administration did COMG feel that the right conditions existed for making its existence public. COMG and the 15 institutions it assembled were run by young professional Indian leaders, who had broken with traditional political and cultural groups in Guatemala (Bastos and Camus 1993).

104 Interview with Alberto Mazariegos (1995), a leader of COMG in 1991.

105 During the first cycle of peace talks (from 1990 to 1992) several sectoral coalitions were formed to follow up conversations with the URNG in 1990. They have been named after the towns in which these talks took place: Ottawa (CACIF, entrepreneurial sector), El Escorial (political parties), Atlixco (universities, cooperatives and professional associations), Metepec (unions and popular sectors) and Quito (religious sector). From the talks in Metepec the Coalition of Civil Sectors (CSC) was formed; the Atlixco talks generated the Civilian Peace Council (COCIPAZ). These two coalitions later merged into the Civil Society Assembly (ASC), which was established in early 1994 (Ponciano 1995).

106 However, during the discussions new frictions emerged between *Majawil Q'ij* and COMG, which made the latter decide to stop participating in the *Mesa Maya*. The final proposal was published on 20 May 1993, five days before the *autogolpe* of President Serrano, which totally changed the political dynamic of the peace process. For a detailed treatment of these internal discussions, see Bastos and Camus (1995: 42-44).

107 Interview with Manolo García (1995a).

108 For a detailed analysis of the deadlock in the peace talks after the coup of May 1993, and the various positions of the two parties that were publicly discussed, see Aguilera and Ponciano (1994).

109 This Framework Agreement, signed on 10 January 1994 in Mexico, was in hindsight a break-through for the Guatemalan peace process. The main points of this agreement were: (i) that the agenda would be based on the Mexico agreement of 1991 (in which first 'substantive' issues would be discussed, before the operative issues on demobilisation and demilitarisation); (ii) that the UN would moderate the talks and verify the agreements; (iii) that a group of *países amigos* (Colombia, Spain, United States, Mexico, Norway and Venezuela) would accompany the process; (iv) that the ASC would be created to give input to the talks; and (v) that negotiations would in principle be concluded before the end of 1994 (which was of course far too optimistic). For details see Aguilera *et al.* (1996).

110 These issues were (1) human rights, (2) refugees and the displaced, (3) Indian rights and identity, (4) socio-economic and agrarian issues, (5) relationship of civilian and military power, (6) constitutional reforms. This was also the order in which the two parties negotiated their agreements between 1994 and 1996.

111 Present in the ASC were the following sectors: religious organisations, unions and popular sectors, political parties, women's organisations, research institutions, NGOs, Indian organisations, human rights organisations, the media and the Atlixco sector (a mixture of academic institutions,

cooperatives and small and medium enterprise). Every sector had five representatives in the ASC, and although they were appointed, the ASC was recognised by the two negotiating parties, the UN and the group of *países amigos* as a legitimate platform representing Guatemalan civil society (Palencia and Holiday 1996).

112   *Tukum Amam* ('Movement of the Grandfathers') was created in 1994 in Quetzaltenango and coordinated a dozen Indian organisations from the western highlands. Some of these organisations (such as FUNDADESE) had previously participated in COMG or in the *Mesa Maya*. UPMAG was formed in 1994 by several Indian peasant organisations that previously had been active in Majawil Q'ij (such as UNICAN and CCDA) and were now united in CONAMPRO (the umbrella organisation also part of ASOCODE, see 6.5). In UPMAG also some women's organisations and local community groups participated (Bastos and Camus 1995).

113   FUNDADESE started in 1985 as the Association for Socio-Economic and Educational Development (ADESE) and applied for legal registration as a 'foundation' in 1990, when it was renamed FUNDADESE. Formal legal status was only granted in 1992.

114   Rosalina Tuyuc, the leader of CONAVIGUA and in 1995 elected as member of Congress for the FDNG, would become part of the human rights sector of the ASC. Juan León, a leader of IUCM and co-founder of CUC, *Majawil Q'ij* and *Defensoría Maya*, was nominated by the FDNG as a vice-presidential candidate for the 1995 elections (Solano and Torres Escobar 1995).

115   Since 1991 Mazariegos tried to bring COMG and *Majawil Q'ij* (which was associated with the URNG-related 'popular Indian' current) closer together, although this move was rejected by 'Mayanist' leaders such as Demetrio Cojtí of ALMG. Publicly, Mazariegos never associated himself with the URNG (whose leadership was severely criticised within the Mayanist current as being Ladino-biased and alienated from daily Guatemalan reality), but close observers considered him to be a leader of the ORPA faction within the URNG (Interviews with Santiago Bastos 1996; Manolo García 1996b; Alberto Mazariegos 1996b).

116   Plans to form a coalition of Indian organisations in the area of Quetzaltenango date back to the large gathering of Indian organisations in 1991, when Mazariegos and others realised that few local Indian organisations of this region participated in national alliances. Mazariegos left COMG in late 1993 to prepare the foundation of *Tukum Amam*, although its formal existence was only announced in September 1994. In early 1995 *Tukum Amam* became officially part of COPMAGUA, as it first had to prove that it was an alliance of Indian organisations, rather than an individual organisation (Bastos and Camus 1995: 103). In a formal sense, Mazariegos did not represent any alliance in 1994, although *Tukum Amam* allowed him in March 1994 to become part of the 'Maya sector' of the ASC, after he was invited by Bishop Quezada (Interview with Alberto Mazariegos 1996a).

117   Riquiac, as a member of COMG, also was invited by the EC to represent the Guatemalan Indian organisations in a new Central American coalition of Indian organisations (CICA). But after a visit to Spain in 1993 (financed by FUNDADESE) she withdrew from this coalition because CICA appeared to be dominated by ALMG members (Interviews with María Riquiac 1995; Alberto Mazariegos 1996b).

118   *Wuqub' Noj* emerged during the quincentenary campaign in 1992 and was formally established in 1993 with support from FUNDADESE, which also provided a legal umbrella. Although initially a member of COMG, it switched to *Tukum Amam* when this alliance was set up in 1994 (Interviews with Félix Valerio 1996; Israel Sequén 1996).

119   A list of 14 specific rights was approved including the right to administer territories inhabited by Mayas, the right to participate in all political decisions of the state and the right to be educated in their own language (COPMAGUA 1995).

120   Participants of the ASC all agree that the period May-June 1994 was the most dynamic and productive phase of the ASC.

121 In June 1994 the parties signed the agreement for the establishment of a Commission for the Clarification of Human Rights Violations, a controversial issue that was left out of the Global Human Rights agreement of March 1994. Human rights organisations and other popular sectors from civil society strongly condemned the agreement as the investigations of the new Commission would not determine responsible perpetrators, nor would the report have legal consequences for those responsible for the genocide of the early 1980s (Palencia and Holiday 1996).

122 The Episcopal Conference decided in January 1995 to withdraw Quezada from the ASC. The formal reason was that Quezada's term was over, but most observers agree that he left because the URNG was getting too much influence in the ASC (Interview with Rolando Cabrera 1996). The ASC was seriously weakened by Quezada's departure; he had worked very efficiently and was the glue that held the ASC together. It would take eight months for the ASC to get organised again (a new secretariat was established only in September 1995) in which time it lost its momentum, but performed an important role as a discussion forum (Palencia and Holiday 1996).

123 Instead, the government of De León Carpio delegated its only Mayan cabinet member (vice-minister of Education Manuel Salazar) to participate in the talks (Bastos and Camus 1995: 75). The other demand of COPMAGUA, active participation in the verification process, was formally accepted.

124 Mazariegos and Sequén confirmed that since 1996 FUNDADESE (that is, the offices in Quetzaltenango and in Chimaltenango) had been providing technical support to the representatives of *Tukum Amam* in the working groups preparing the new *comisiones paritarias* (Interviews with Israel Sequén 1996; Alberto Mazariegos 1996a).

125 *N'ukuj Ajpop* ('exercise in popular government') did not consider itself a political party but rather a Maya forum active in the FDNG, in which three major Indian alliances (IUCM, UPMAG and *Tukum Amam*) took part, illustrating that these corresponded with the three major tendencies of the URNG: EGP, FAR and ORPA. The other two Indian alliances inside COPMAGUA (COMG and ALMG) refused to participate in *N'ukuj Ajpop*. COMG preferred to remain politically independent, and ALMG supported the development of a separate Mayan party (*K'amal B'e*, meaning 'pathfinder'), also advocated by Rigoberta Menchú (Interviews with Gabriel Aguilera 1995; Alberto Mazariegos 1996a; Vitalino Similox 1996. See also Bastos and Camus 1995: 154-8).

126 *Tzuk Kim-pop* was founded in August 1995 in Quetzaltenango as a coalition of existing local NGOs that had been rather isolated from international aid flows. Its priority areas are community development, organisation building and productive projects in agriculture and *artesanía*.

127 In addition, *Ibis* financed a Danish expert in public health to be based in Chichicastenango. From 1990 to 1992, *Ibis* supported FUNDADESE's activities in five communities in El Quiché and Totonicapan. In a second phase (1993-95), five communities were added to the programme by FUNDADESE. In this period *Ibis* contributed US$ 1 million (on average US$ 200,000 annually) (Interview with John Nielsen 1994).

128 NOVIB's annual contribution started in June 1993 and was on average US$ 100,000 (Interview with Ale Dijkstra 1996). The work of the Quetzaltenango office, which was opened in 1993 by Mazariegos to support returning refugees and the displaced, was financed by the ecumenical agencies of the *Project Counselling Service* (PCS).

129 Interview with John Nielsen (1994). Contacts with FUNDADESE came through recommendations by other Guatemalan NGOs working in the highlands. FUNDADESE was suggested to *Ibis* by a leader of CAPS, who knew the founders from earlier training programmes (Interview with Marco Azurdia 1995). NOVIB had already established contact in 1987 through its local consultant (Interview with Ale Dijkstra 1996).

130 Both *Ibis* and NOVIB simultaneously supported other Indian NGOs working with integrated rural development, such as the programme sponsored by COINDI in the nearby Sololá area. COINDI also was a founding member of COMG. However, COINDI and FUNDADESE were different:

COINDI was, more than FUNDADESE, a community-based organisation, because the local community councils were directly part of its formal structure. For a comparison see Vinding (1995).

131 According to the NOVIB desk officer in the Netherlands (Interview with Ale Dijkstra 1996).

132 Most of NOVIB's partners in Guatemala (such as GAM, *Tierra Viva*, CDRO, COINDI, COMG, INIAP, AVANCSO, UASP, UNSITRAGUA) were active players in at least five different sectors of the ASC.

133 Between July 1994 and July 1996 NOVIB funded Mazariegos's work in the ASC with approximately US$ 35,000 annually, consisting of salaries, travel, meetings and publication and distribution of the final Indian rights agreement to local organisations (Interview with Theo Bouma 1995).

134 External evaluations of this programme were executed by OXFAM-America (Méndez 1988), NOVIB (Puac and Ramírez 1995), and *Ibis* (Cabrera and Camposeco 1996). Independent studies include Carrera (1994), and Højrup Jensen (1995). My analysis is largely based on these documents, in addition to fieldwork in 1995-96.

135 Most communities have an *alcalde auxiliar* (assistant mayor) who relates to the municipality; a Civil Defence Patrol (PAC) and a military commissioner directly responsible to the armed forces; a *principal* (spiritual leader); the Catholic Church and several (up to nine) evangelical sects; seven or eight Maya priests and an improvement committee in which most of the leaders mentioned are participating. In addition, some popular organisations (such as CUC, GAM, CONAVIGUA and SERJ) have a covert presence in the communities (Carrera 1994; Højrup Jensen 1995).

136 Højrup Jensen (1995: 17) notes that the Ríos Montt regime used two political tools to disperse organisations and political mobilisation in indigenous communities: organised physical violence, followed by the installation of PAC's and the entrance of evangelical sects actively discouraging community participation.

137 A *comité pro-mejoramiento* (improvement committee) was set up in most communities during the Arévalo government of the 1940s. After the 1976 earthquake these committees were used for channelling relief from the governmental Committee for National Reconstruction (CRN). In the 1980s the armed forces used the committees for their civic action programmes, whereas FUNDA-DESE tried to transform them into a structure for political action.

138 The number of communities increased from 8 in 1988 to 28 communities in 1996, covering an area that included approximately 100,000 inhabitants (Méndez 1988; Carrera 1994).

139 FUNDADESE also was an active member of two NGO coalitions (COINDE and CONGCOOP) that were key fora for getting access to international aid agencies and for exchanging experiences with other development NGOs about how to deal with foreign aid. Based on that experience, Maza-riegos decided in 1995 to form his own NGO coalition *Tzuk Kim-pop* in Quetzaltenango, when the upcoming peace agreement was expected to attract a new influx of private foreign aid.

140 Many non-Mayan organisations and NGOs 'had not been created to unite but to disunite', he argued at the International Seminar of Indigenous People's, held in Guatemala, 4-7 December 1990.

141 Other key persons were the leaders Cojtí, Tuyuc and León. A crucial role also was played by Bishop Quezada, who was keen to prevent any exclusion of Maya sectors in the ASC (Interviews with several ASC-delegates: Enrique Alvarez 1995; Carmen Rosa de León 1995; Oscar Azmitia 1995; Edgar Cabnal 1995, 1996a; Vitalino Similox 1996; Rosalina Tuyuc 1996; Helmer Velásquez 1996).

142 The majority of elected FDNG deputies were prominent leaders of Indian organisations: Nineth Montenegro (GAM), Rosalina Tuyuc and José Antonio Móvil (CONAVIGUA), Amilcar Méndez (CERJ), Manuela Alvarado (Indian leader from Quetzaltenango) and Carlos Alfonso Barrios from San Marcos.

143 Interview with Roger Plant (1996), responsible for indigenous issues of MINUGUA.

144 For example, the peasant organisation *Kabawil*, a member of *Tukum Amam*, managed to give

input on ASC position papers through the national networks of human rights committees, peasant organisations and Indian organisations. However, leaders of *Kabawil* complained in 1996 about the delay in receiving final texts of the agreements. This was caused by Mazariegos withdrawal from the ASC, which had frustrated communication between the national and local level (Interview with Walter Castro 1996).

145 See in particular the studies by Junkov (1994), Vinding (1995) and Højrup Jensen (1995), and the external *Ibis* evaluation by Cabrera and Camposeco (1996).

146 The NOVIB consultant rarely visited the Chichicastenango office, although this was not considered a problem by director Riquiac (Interviews with Bo Rasmussen 1995; María Riquiac 1995). The *Ibis* consultant, who had known FUNDADESE from its early start, also rarely visited the communities. FUNDADESE complained that 'it was difficult to communicate with him as he never had time' (Cabrera and Camposeco 1996). Apparently, *Ibis* relied too much on the presence of its Danish expert and on the positive reports submitted by FUNDADESE (Interview with John Nielsen 1994).

147 Interestingly, the German agency *Brot für die Welt* (only supporting *Pop Wuj*) had been aware of FUNDADESE's problems through its Central American consultant. However, regardless of the fact that coordination with NOVIB was poor, *Brot für die Welt* did not take action: it considered the national activities of Mazariegos and Sequén to be crucial to creating broader political space for Indian organisations (Interview with Rolando Sierra 1996).

148 Interviews with Manolo García (1996a) and Mario Silvestre (1996).

149 The term is from the former CIPIE representative (Interview with Luisa Cabrera 1996). Also NOVIB and *Ibis* were aware that Mazariegos worked simultaneously for several organisations. As one person remarked: 'from the moment we started a meeting, he would tell us he already had to go to the next meeting' (Interview with John Nielsen 1996).

150 As alliances rapidly shifted inside COPMAGUA, NOVIB tried to spread its funding over the various Indian coalitions, relying on the advice from its local consultant. In that sense, NOVIB certainly was an active donor (Interview with Manolo García 1996b).

151 Interview with René Poitevin (1995). Some ASC members even complained that private aid agencies refused to support their organisations if they were not in some way active in the ASC (Interview with Rolando Cabrera 1996).

152 According to a leader of COMG and a coordinator of COPMAGUA (Interview with Mariano Cox 1996).

153 Similar critique was voiced in Bye *et al.* (1995: 23). *Ibis* started to support the ASC secretariat in early 1996, but this was delinked from support to any of its partners participating in the ASC.

154 If it is taken into account that FUNDADESE had been receiving private aid funding since 1987, it is reasonable to assess its achievements after almost ten years. Even if it is argued that results of the community development programme were hampered by severe political conditions up to the early 1990s, disarticulation was caused by the implementation of the organisation model in which community councils became dependent upon FUNDADESE.

155 Mazariegos was conscious of the fragile structure of these organisations and in 1995 began promoting (with the NGO coalition *Tzuk Kim-pop*) the incorporation of local communities in projects to strengthen municipal governments in the south-western highlands. A key purpose of these activities was to build up new leadership capacity, which would be essential to occupy the newly conquered political space (Interview with Alberto Mazariegos 1996a).

156 Agrarian cooperatives and small coffee producers were already organised at a Central American level in the 1980s. The Confederation of Cooperatives of the Caribbean and Central America (CCC-CA) was set up in 1980, and the Union of Small and Medium Coffee Producers (UPRO-CAFE) in 1989.

157 The Spanish *campesino* is generally translated as 'peasant', but the problematic nature of this

translation is acknowledged. In Central America, the *'campesino* sector' also includes (beside peasants) *parceleros* (smallholders) and medium-sized farmers (generally export crops). For a discussion of these categories see Baumeister (1994).

158 Since the 1987 Esquipulas agreement, peasant organisations from Costa Rica (who were first affected by structural adjustment policies) tried to set up a regional network of peasant organisations. But they encountered a number of obstacles, ranging from bad communication and governmental interference to mutual distrust and manipulation by political parties (ASO-CODE 1991b).

159 One of Costa Rica's representatives in ASOCODE's first Regional Commission, Jorge Hernández, was a trained sociologist. Wilson Campos, regional coordinator from 1991-95, completed two years of university before dropping out. It should be pointed out that ASOCODE's academics came exclusively from Costa Rica, which has an education system that is better than anywhere else in Central America.

160 The traditional perception of *campesinos* is still widespread, even in Europe. When ASOCODE's coordinator Wilson Campos visited a Dutch private aid agency in 1993, desk officers wondered whether he was a 'real peasant', as his appearance reminded them of a young successful entrepreneur, rather than a traditional peasant leader (Biekart and Jelsma 1994: 216).

161 Costa Rican *campesinos* were well organised, generally better educated and had suffered least from the repression of the 1980s. In the rest of Central America, Costa Ricans were often viewed with politically and culturally motivated suspicion; prejudices that can be traced to the colonial past. Costa Rica would provide the regional coordinator even though it was the smallest national alliance within ASOCODE, representing less than two percent of its regional membership.

162 UNAG was also viewed with some suspicion by organisations from other countries, as it often presented itself as *the* organisation for all Central American peasants. There was also jealousy about the broad funding base of UNAG. This created friction in the early years of ASOCODE, particularly because a Costa Rican and not a Nicaraguan was appointed as the first regional coordinator (although the Nicaraguans did receive the post of vice-coordinator). Tensions increased between UNAG and ASOCODE in late 1992, partly due to conflicts between personalities, almost leading to a split. The central office was transferred from Costa Rica to Nicaragua, and the dispute was finally settled in late 1993. After that, the Costa Ricans and the Nicaraguans became close allies in ASOCODE (Interviews with Wilson Campos 1993; Jorge Hernández 1994; Sinforiano Cáceres 1996).

163 As an early document stated: 'no governmental or non-governmental institution has the right to consider itself as the father or the facilitator of our process' (ASOCODE 1991b: 4).

164 The seminars were part of the food security programme (PFSA) of the Panama-based intergovernmental research programme CADESCA, run by Salvador Arias (who was Minister of Agriculture of El Salvador in the 1970s) and Eduardo Stein (who was appointed Minister of Foreign Affairs of Guatemala in 1996). Financed by the European Community, these seminars aimed to bring together peasant leaders from all over Central America to discuss possible alternative strategies for peasant organisations to respond to structural adjustment programmes. The technical advisers of the PFSA, in combination with agronomists from the French institute IRAM, were crucial in the early years for their contribution to ASOCODE's sophisticated political discourse. See Edelman (1995: 7-9); Stein and Arias (1992).

165 In July 1991 a large peasant conference was organised in Honduras with the participation of peasant organisations from six Central American countries (this time including Belize; only Guatemala was absent). At this occasion it was formally decided to found ASOCODE later that year (ASOCODE 1991b: 5).

166 The letter to the presidents was titled *'La urgencia del desarrollo exige concertar'* (The urgency of development requires concerted action). The 'productive strategy', ASOCODE's first policy

document, was drafted in April 1991 with close support from CADESCA advisers, and adapted and published in August 1991 (ASOCODE 1991a).

167 A major obstacle to the formation of ASOCODE was the different and often contrary political dynamics in the seven Central American countries. For some national associations the struggle against structural adjustment was the major issue, for others the roll-back of agrarian reform (Honduras) or military repression (El Salvador and Guatemala) (ASOCODE 1991b; Román 1994; Tangermann and Ríos 1994).

168 National alliances participating from the start in ASOCODE included UNAG (Nicaragua), CNA (Costa Rica), ADC (El Salvador), APEMEP (Panama), COCOCH (Honduras) and BFAC (Belize). See Hernández (1994).

169 The problem was that internal splits inside the Guatemalan armed opposition URNG in the early 1990s impeded unity among the Guatemalan peasant organisations. ASOCODE insisted that only a unified *instancia nacional* from Guatemala could be accepted as a member. However, when this national association (CONAMPRO) was finally founded in early 1993, two major peasant organisations (CUC and CONIC) left it for political reasons. Among other things, they felt that the leaders of CONAMPRO represented more the NGO sector than the (indigenous) peasants (Candanedo and Madrigal 1994: 41-2. Interviews with Juan Tiney 1994; Wilson Campos 1996c; Helmer Velásquez 1996).

170 In 1993 ASOCODE's member associations organised an estimated 1.5 million small and medium-sized farmers and peasants. The total number of economically active members in this sector in Central America is an estimated 5.5 million, corresponding to 45 percent of the economically active population (Baumeister 1994; Herrera 1995).

171 At the founding congress it was decided to send an ASOCODE delegation to the Earth Summit in Rio in 1992, and to participate in the foundation of the *Vía Campesina*, an international network of farmers' organisations (ASOCODE 1992; Blokland 1995).

172 This was decided for two reasons: some national associations were 'richer' than others, and the fear was that the 'richer' organisations would possibly impose their agenda; plus it was soon clear that private aid agencies from Canada and Europe were rather eager to finance a new regional coalition of peasant organisations. It was also decided that the Nicaraguans would raise 40 percent of the projected US$ 100,000 for 1991, and the Costa Ricans 60 percent. However, in the end all funding was raised by the Costa Ricans (Interview with Dineke van den Oudenalder 1996).

173 This was not entirely true, as the Costa Rican NGO *Nuestra Tierra* was the legal channel for funds received by *Justicia y Desarrollo*. Members of the provisional Regional Commission also mentioned their good relations with the Costa Rican NGO CECADE, whose director (William Reuben) at that time coordinated the Central American NGO coalition CCOD. In addition, their close relations with CADESCA contributed to getting the confidence of private aid agencies for the new proposal. The provisional Regional Commission initially presented itself as the Coalition of Small Agricultural Producers of the Central American Isthmus (COPIC) and requested funding for preparatory meetings in 1991, a small office in Costa Rica and for a round of consultations within all member organisations to discuss the proposal for the new coordinating body. The agencies were impressed by the broad participation of peasant organisations from all over Central America and by their open rejection of paternalism by NGOs who had been speaking in their name without serious consultation. The only doubt about COPIC (later ASOCODE) was the lack of reference in their documents to the position and participation of women in peasant organisations (Interviews with Dineke van den Oudenalder 1996; William Reuben 1996).

174 Other agencies that approved small funds were *Brot für die Welt*, *Diakonia*, OXFAM-UK/I, CUSO and PCS. Initially, it was tried to get all starting expenses financed by the four Dutch co-financing agencies, but CEBEMO and NOVIB were reluctant to do so. CEBEMO because it feared that regional networks would only create new bureaucratic layers; NOVIB because its policy was to

support intermediary NGOs, and not membership organisations (Interview with Dineke van den Oudenalder 1996).

175 It was a tactical move to criticise private aid agencies in public, when one agency representative had just expressed his honour and pride for being able to support ASOCODE; Campos very well understood that his criticism would be shared by most agencies. In his final declaration he even sharpened his point by saying that some agencies had been supporting peasant organisations indirectly with good intentions, but that he had had enough of good intentions and that 'full respect for popular processes' was needed (ASOCODE 1991b: 22).

176 Among the new private aid agencies that decided to support ASOCODE in 1992 were NOVIB (Netherlands) replacing ICCO's role, *Ibis* (Denmark) and *Horizons of Friendship* (Canada). The EC support was offered in April 1992, when Campos visited Europe to lobby the 8th San José ministerial conference between Europe and Central America. Through contacts of CADESCA, Campos was invited to meet top EC officials in Brussels.

177 This was, for example, the reason for the Protestant agencies ICCO and *Danchurchaid* to reject (new) requests from ASOCODE (Interviews with Lone Hogel 1993; Frans van Ballegooij 1993).

178 Some agencies even threatened to withdraw support from ASOCODE if its financial administration was not improved. This was a sensitive area as the major reason why peasant organisations had been supported indirectly through NGOs was their incapacity to administer foreign aid resources (see the example of CNTC in Chapter 5). Wilson Campos admitted that the unexpected acceleration of ASOCODE's 'process', combined with the lack of administrative experience of its leaders had caused this 'process of disorganisation' (ASOCODE 1993d: 86-89).

179 The office in Managua (Nicaragua) was opened in October 1992 (one block from the UNAG office), but the appointed executive director turned out to be incompetent. Besides that, regional coordinator Wilson Campos was most of the time outside Nicaragua. Only in late 1993 did the office start to function properly with a staff of five administrative workers, five technical advisors and a more regular presence of the coordinator.

180 At the First Regional Conference on Solidarity Aid in Panamá (17-19 March, 1993) representatives from nine private aid agencies from Europe and Canada attended; nine agencies were unable to attend and seven others requested to be involved in the future (ASOCODE 1993a: 39-40).

181 A HIVOS representative voiced concerns in the plenary that ASOCODE had been too much a coalition of leaders and that it was the task of national associations to increase participation from grassroots organisations (ASOCODE 1993d: 32).

182 In March 1993, national associations participating in ASOCODE jointly presented a large package of projects to foreign aid agencies, in which a total of more than US$ 15 million was requested.

183 According to ASOCODE's statutes (Article 38b) every national association is obliged to pay annually US$ 1,000 for ASOCODE's running costs. However, as Edelman (1995) correctly points out, the flow of resources has been exclusively in the other direction. As a result of the growing inflow of aid resources, in 1993 every national association received annually around US$ 15,000, growing to US$ 60,000 in 1995 and an estimated US$ 100,000 in 1996.

184 This was the main reason why the Dutch ministry for development cooperation had doubts about a US$ 1 million aid package for ASOCODE for 1993-94 which was requested by HIVOS. Only forty percent of this request was finally approved (Interview with Dineke van den Oudenalder 1996).

185 See ASOCODE (1993b). In 1995 ASOCODE received financial support from HIVOS, NOVIB, *Ibis*, *Diakonia*, OXFAM-UK/I, CCFD, OXFAM-Belgium, *ACSUR Las Segovias*, *Horizons of Friendship*, OXFAM-Canada, the *Ford Foundation* and the European Union. The two Dutch agencies covered about 45 percent of the US$ 1 million annual budget.

186 In Nicaragua UNAG and FENACOOP formed the national association, but the rural workers union ATC and smaller peasant organisations such as UNAPA and associations of the *Resistencia* did not participate (Candanedo and Madrigal 1994). In Belize, the organisations forming the *instancia*

nacional (BFAC and CCC-B) represented only a minority of Belize's rural workers. The language (Belize's national language is English), the different productive structure (for example, Belize has the second strongest fishermen's cooperatives in the world) and its orientation towards the Caribbean obstructed national unity for participation in ASOCODE (Candanedo and Madrigal 1994; Interview with Julián Avila 1993).

187 ASOCODE realised that it could only push for changes at this level if it managed to convene the broadest possible coalition of agricultural interests. Lobbying started a few months before the summit and was targeted at technical experts preparing the summit. As Campos noted, if lobbying was aimed at higher-level politicians in an early phase, the efforts would be counterproductive (ASOCODE 1994b: 4).

188 The reason that this fund was never established was that the ministers of agriculture, who were supposed to work out the proposal, delayed and frustrated the dialogue with ASOCODE (ASOCODE 1995b).

189 Belize was excluded, but was associated with SICA as part of the Central American Alliance for Sustainable Development (ALIDES). SICA was formally established by the Central American presidents in Tegucigalpa in December 1991, and the General Secretary (the Honduran Roberto Cáceres) formally started to function in February 1993, with headquarters in San Salvador.

190 Although the (elected) Central American parliament PARLACEN also is part of SICA, the fact that it was not lobbied by ASOCODE illustrates its symbolic function. In general, ASOCODE did not put any effort into lobbying politicians except those in power. According to Wilson Campos, political parties had lost their legitimacy as true representatives of the people, and ASOCODE at some point even considered setting up its own political 'peasant' parties. This idea, although still alive in Costa Rica, was not put into practice (Interview with Wilson Campos 1994b).

191 In June and September 1992 small ASOCODE delegations visited Europe. A large delegation of eight leaders made a one-month trip to nine European countries in April-May 1993. In March, May, August and September 1994, and March and June 1995 small delegations visited several European countries, generally invited by private aid agencies. Delegations visited Canada and the United States four times between 1993 and 1995. A delegation made a tour in the Caribbean (September 1994) and, as part of the *Vía Campesina*, several conferences were attended in Belgium, Peru, Mexico and the Philippines. See ASOCODE (1993b, 1995b).

192 Campos was invited as a coordinator of ICIC to address the International Conference on Peace and Development for Central America in Tegucigalpa (24-25 October 1994), where he severely criticised the presidents (who were also present) for promising more participation of civil society in their regional decision-making, but failing to put this into practice. His speech drew attention from several high-level representatives of international financial organisations who were open to more frequent dialogue and collaboration with ASOCODE and ICIC.

193 Unlike ASOCODE, FEDEPRICAP participated in technical commissions preparing the presidential summits, but its international contacts were less well-developed (Rivera 1995).

194 Edelman (1995) identified seven functions of ASOCODE's lobbying strategy: buffering national organisations against repression; providing information on policies; demonstrating the willingness to negotiate; contributing to democratisation; giving a presence to popular sectors in supranational bodies; widening the debate on credit, trade and agrarian reform; helping national platforms to win specific national demands. An important function should be added here: getting access to foreign aid.

195 During a visit to Canada in November 1994, ASOCODE mentioned the alarming human rights situation in Guatemala to Vice Minister of Foreign Affairs Stewart, who then personally undertook action in the UN (ASOCODE 1995b: 16). Similar requests were made to the European Union through the European network of private aid agencies CIFCA.

196 ASOCODE's leaders were afraid that a frontal attack on the Guatemalan president would harm

their good relations with him, particularly because the Guatemalan government at that time coordinated the regional presidential summits (Interview with Wilson Campos 1994a; Edelman 1995: 29-30).

197 This started in 1992 when COCENTRA and CTCA supported ASOCODE's proposal for alternative agricultural policies at the December Panama summit. During preparations at the Central American Peasant Forum, in which CCC-CA and UPROCAFE also took part, it was decided to present proposals to the summit in the name of a broad forum whose organisations presented 'another space in civil society'. From then on, these regional associations maintained close communications, and when CTCA learned that SICA was open to incorporate regional representatives from civil society into its Consultative Committee, a preparatory meeting was held in October 1993 in Costa Rica. At this occasion, funded by the *Friedrich Ebert Stiftung*, it was decided to found ICIC (Rivera 1995).

198 ICIC was founded in May 1994 in Costa Rica by ASOCODE, COCENTRA (labour unions), CTCA (labour unions), CCC-CA (cooperatives), UPROCAFE (coffee producers), CCOD (NGOs), FCOC (community organisations), and CONCAPE (small and medium private enterprise). In 1995 *Frente Solidario* (coffee producers) entered ICIC, and a year later CICA (organisations of indigenous people), CODEHUCA (human rights committees) and FOCAMI (women's organisations).

199 Wilson Campos pushed for a joint coordination role together with Ayax Irías (COCENTRA) and Roberto Ayerdi (CONAPE); however, Campos remained the public face of ICIC. ASOCODE allocated its own funds to ICIC that came from the European Union, OXFAM-UK/I, OXFAM-Canada and CUSO. The technical coordination was delegated to CCOD, which had a staff member permanently working for ICIC. In 1995 several European private aid agencies (*Ibis* and OXFAM-UK/I) financed part of ICIC's running costs. In 1996 the *Friedrich Ebert Stiftung* and HIVOS also contributed to ICIC (ICIC 1995a; 1996a). Not surprisingly, except for FES, all these donors also were funders of ASOCODE.

200 FEDEPRICAP, the federation of the Central American business associations, dominated this Committee as part of the Central American Inter-sectoral Coordination (CACI), a small coalition of regional associations (private universities and right-wing unions) all promoting a neoliberal agenda (Rivera 1995). As soon as ICIC was also admitted to the Committee it started negotiations with CACI's member organisations to isolate FEDEPRICAP (ICIC 1995a; Interview with Sinforiano Cáceres 1996).

201 Here the echo of ASOCODE's arguments within ICIC is evident. For an overview of ICIC's political position and organisational structure, see ICIC (1996a, 1996b).

202 Wilson Campos stated in an interview: 'We have forced them [the presidents] to recognise us as a legitimate force, but now, after two years, we have participated in four summits and over 20 regional fora. We are seeing that they have made a lot of promises that they have not kept' (Edelman 1994: 31).

203 Particularly the Salvadoreans had little confidence in diplomatic pressure and pushed for more systematic use of traditional forms of protest (Candanedo and Madrigal 1994).

204 The idea of *incidencia* ('incidence', or lobbying) was to search for common positions in contacts with governments and international organisations, but also with like-minded farmers' organisations and private aid agencies, without making any concessions and based on self-perceived strength. Its basic goal was to get political recognition and develop a basis for further collaboration. Later the word *cabildeo* (lobbying) started to enter ASOCODE's discourse. However, this was considered to be the next step after *incidencia*, a long-term process of trying to influence policies. To speak of 'lobbying' was probably a result of intensified relations with European and North American networks who are more used to pushing for changes without speaking in the name of a broad constituency. This difference became clear in a lobbying workshop organised by some European private aid agencies in Managua in May 1994 (ASOCODE 1994b).

205 According to Inés Fuentes, representative for Honduras in ASOCODE's Regional Coordination Commission between 1991 and 1994 (Interview with Inés Fuentes 1996).

206 However this accusation appeared to be untrue. Campos used some of ASOCODE's funds to finance activities of ICIC, including a small team of technical advisors that worked from ASOCODE's regional office. By not explicitly separating the expenses of ASOCODE and ICIC (which were often intertwined) he admitted to having created confusion. The advisory team had to be fired in March 1995 which seriously affected ICIC's performance that year. Behind this conflict was an effort by Salvadorean and Panamanian leaders to get control of ASOCODE, but they were voted out at the 3rd Congress in January 1996. Sinforiano Cáceres from Nicaragua was elected at this Congress to succeed Wilson Campos. He acknowledged that the crisis had harmed ASOCODE and that improved financial control and more transparency would prevent this confusion in the future (Interviews with Wilson Campos 1996c; Julio Bermúdez 1995; Eulogio Villalta 1996; Sinforiano Cáceres 1996; Wilber Zavala 1995).

207 Coordination among peasant organisations within the national associations worked best in Costa Rica, Nicaragua and (to a lesser extent) Honduras. In the other countries the *mesas nacionales* were often either weak, in a process of construction, or sometimes even artificial (Candanedo and Madrigal 1994: 82).

208 This was one of the conclusions of the external evaluation carried out in 1994 (financed by HIVOS). It concluded that internal disagreement existed about whether or not to prioritise the demand for agrarian reform, the participation of women or the participation of indigenous people; which organisations should be members and whether to prioritise political work or limit activities to productive issues (Candanedo and Madrigal 1994).

209 HIVOS considered ASOCODE to be one of its most important partners in the region and also the most 'flexible' (Interview with Chris Bransz 1996). ASOCODE, in turn, perceived that the open and critical attitude of private aid agencies had deepened and strengthened its relationships with funders (Interview with Wilson Campos 1996c).

210 This was one of the conclusions of an evaluation of *Ibis*'s regional programme. It was also concluded that agencies lacked adequate coordination, that partners often followed agency priorities instead of elaborating proper agendas, that agencies poorly coordinated local programmes with those of their regional networks and that they failed to prioritise exchange of information between member organisations in different countries (Morales and Cranshaw 1997: 55-6).

211 This position was shared by various funders, among them OXFAM-UK/I and *Brot für die Welt* (Interviews with Eduardo Klein 1995; Rolando Sierra 1996).

212 Interview with Wilson Campos (1996c). In the circles of the Central American presidents and their ministers it was commonly assumed that ASOCODE and other (regional) societal actors were a creation of foreign aid agencies, as these financed the large number of seminars in which lobbying issues were discussed (Interview with Sinforiano Cáceres 1996).

213 The first public statements about NGOs were made at the first Congress in December 1991 (ASOCODE 1991b), followed by interviews in *Pensamiento Propio* (No. 87, February 1992) and several European magazines (cf. Biekart and Jelsma 1994: 215-221).

214 It was worked out in a document prepared for the Earth Summit in Rio (ASOCODE 1992), but received only minor attention in the Strategic Plan of 1996 (ASOCODE 1996).

215 This was suggested by Candanedo and Madrigal (1994: 122-9), who concluded (after interviewing a number of leaders) that there was no consensus on this issue. One part did not see the need to have separate Indian organisation structures within ASOCODE, another part saw the need to give autonomous space to *indígenas* in the association, but more importantly to look for common problems. The problem was more or less resolved when CICA (the regional network of indigenous people's organisations) was accepted as a member of ICIC in 1995.

216 At the Panama conference on 'solidarity aid' (March 1993) private aid agencies urged ASOCODE to come up with concrete proposals about how to incorporate women in the regional coordination process. They warned that ASOCODE would face problems securing external support if these proposals remained vague.

217 See ASOCODE (1993d: 79). Campos also realised that gender balance was such a strong demand that it could have endangered funding relations. In fact, the acceptance of women in leading positions actually grew through the years. At the 2nd regional assembly of ICIC (in August 1996) Campos proposed a rule that ASOCODE had adopted in January 1996 to have a true fifty-fifty gender balance at all levels of the coalition; this was finally negotiated to the rule that every set of representative and alternate in the regional assembly would be shared by a man and a woman (ICIC 1996b).

218 See for example the intervention of HIVOS representative Dineke van den Oudenalder at ASOCODE's 2nd Regional Congress, in which she stressed that women were not equally integrated in the production process, and even less so in the organisational process (ASOCODE 1993d: 32). This was supported by conclusions of a survey conducted around that time showing that women accounted for 30 percent of the agricultural labour force, and not for the 8 percent that misleadingly appeared in official statistics (IICA 1993; Román 1994).

219 The 3rd Regional Congress in 1996 decided to elect a gender-balanced Regional Commission, although El Salvador and Belize refused to meet this requirement.

220 This was considered to be the most concrete result of a trip by the Regional Commission to Europe in 1993 (ASOCODE 1993b; 1993d).

221 With some jealousy colleagues from other regional networks observed that ASOCODE's leaders travelled by airplane and were often hosted in luxury hotels, where they (due to less financial resources) were used to travelling by buses and sleeping in cheap hostels (Edelman 1995). Overfunding also was a product of poor coordination among agencies, who often were not aware how funds of other private agencies were allocated.

222 The December 1993 Congress also decided that the members of the Regional Commission (representatives of the national associations) all would receive their salaries from ASOCODE in order to guarantee their commitment to the regional work.

223 This interpretation is based on conversations with several representatives of aid agencies. In the case of ASOCODE, HIVOS was very critical of ASOCODE's poor efforts to look for alternative sources of income. Despite that, HIVOS continued to be ASOCODE's largest funder, with an estimated donation of US$ 500,000 annually, more than one-third of ASOCODE's budget. It should be added that HIVOS receives 7.5 percent overhead on this annual sum from the Dutch ministry of development cooperation. This system thus encourages the allocation of large sums of aid, although this is contrary to the principles of both HIVOS and the Dutch ministry.

224 Interview with Guido Vargas (1996). Another regional representative for Costa Rica, Jorge Hernández, wrote in 1992 that he considered the acceptance of foreign aid as one of the 'original sins' of the organisation (Hernández 1992). These concerns about aid should be understood in the light of the prevailing 'poverty gap' between Costa Rica and the rest of Central America, and (related to that) the withdrawal of many private aid agencies from Costa Rica in the early 1990s.

225 Interview with Chris Bransz (1996). As an additional problem he mentioned that ASOCODE demonstrated a lack of ability to set clear priorities. One reason for this was, paradoxically, its democratic internal system of consultation. All longer term 'strategic plans' were substantially discussed by the national associations, leading to delays in planning and to a broad array of priorities – too broad and diverse to implement simultaneously, which made new priority-setting then necessary. But Bransz acknowledged that more authoritarian ways of decision-making also were not desirable.

226 Interview with Wilson Campos (1996c).

227 Members of the Guatemalan national association CONAMPRO discovered, for example, that ASOCODE leaders had easier access to governmental offices in Guatemala than its Guatemalan member organisations. As a result, ASOCODE negotiated agreements with the Guatemalan government and CONAMPRO did the follow-up (Candanedo and Madrigal 1994: 46).

228 Some argued that ICIC would not have existed without the organisational capacity and strategic vision of ASOCODE leader Wilson Campos, who coordinated ICIC until August 1996 (Interview with Combertty Rodríguez 1995).

Interviews

Aguilera, Gabriel. FLACSO Guatemala (Senior Researcher). Guatemala: 25 March 1991, 1 July 1993, 21 November 1995.

Albizurez, Miguel Angel. Former trade union leader. Guatemala: 6 July 1993.

Alegría, Rafael. CNTC (Secretary General). Tegucigalpa: 21 February 1991a, 27 February 1991b, 28 November 1995.

Alvarado, Luís. CODEH (Technical Coordinator). Tegucigalpa: 28 November 1995.

Alvarez, Carmen. FUNDE (Research Assistant). San Salvador: 8 July 1993.

Alvarez, Enrique. CIEP (Director). Guatemala: 14 November 1995.

Ardiz Smith, Daniel. European Union Delegation (Head of NGO Division). San José: 27 September 1996.

Ardon, Patricia. OXFAM-UK/I (Regional Director for Central America). Managua: 22 July 1993; Amsterdam: 26 November 1996.

Arias Peñate, Salvador. CADESCA (Director Food Security Programme); CRIES (Executive Director); FUNDESCA (Board Member). San José: 7 December 1995.

Avila, Julián. ASOCODE (Regional Representative for Belize). Amsterdam: 25 April 1993.

Avila, Oscar. CIIR (Representative for Honduras). Tegucigalpa: 28 February 1991.

Avirgan, Toni. Free-lance journalist. San José: 4 September 1991.

Azmitia, Oscar. PRODESSA (Director); ALOP (Secretary for Central America). Guatemala: 22 November 1995, 27 August 1996.

Azurdia, Marco Augusta. CAPS (Director). Guatemala: 20 March 1991, 13 November 1995.

Ballegooij, Frans van. ICCO (Central America Desk Officer). Zeist: 14 September 1990, 27 September 1993, 29 August 1995, 10 July 1996.

Barrera, Adolfo. ACEN-CIAG (Director). Guatemala: 24 March 1991, 5 July 1993.

Barry, Deborah. PREIS (Research Coordinator); PRISMA (Director). San Salvador: 7 March 1991, 26 October 1992, 23 November 1994, 8 November 1995.

Bastos, Santiago. Anthropologist. Guatemala: 21 August 1996.

Baumeister, Eduardo. Economist. Managua: 25 January 1993.

Bendaña, Alejandro. CEI (Director). Managua: 11 February 1991.

Bermúdez, Julio. APEMEP (Secretary General); ASOCODE (Regional Representative for Panamá). Brussels: 22 June 1995.

Beuningen, Cor van. CEBEMO (Policy and Evaluation Officer). Oegstgeest: 5 October 1993.

Bloemkolk, Eric. CEBEMO (Central America Desk Officer). Oegstgeest: 26 June 1996.

Boekraad, Edith. CEBEMO (Central America Desk Officer). Oegstgeest: 10 September 1993, 5 October 1993.

Bolton, Elaine. *Christian Aid* (Central America Desk Officer). London: 3 December 1993.

Bouma, Theo. NOVIB (Head of Central America Desk). Den Haag: 30 September 1993, 30 September 1995.

Bransz, Chris. HIVOS (Head of Latin America Department). Den Haag: 26 August 1993, 13 September 1995, 4 July 1996.

Bücher, Ernst. COSUDE (Representative for Honduras). Tegucigalpa: 22 February 1991.

Burbach, Roger. CENSA (Director). Amsterdam: 11 October 1990.

Burge, Alun. *Christian Aid* (Former Head of Central America Desk). Cardiff: 2 December 1993.

Buvollen, Hans Petter. *Norwegian People's Aid* (Representative for Central America). Guatemala: 2 November 1995.

Cabnal, Edgar. ASC (Excutive Secretary). Guatemala: 15 November 1995, 15 August 1996a, 22 August 1996b.

Cabrera, Luísa. CIPIE (Former Representative for Guatemala). Antigua: 26 August 1996.

Cabrera, Rolando. ASC (General Secretary in 1994); *Fundapazd* (Project Director). Guatemala: 28 August 1996.

Cáceres, Sinforiano. UNAG (Board Member); ASOCODE (Regional Coordinator 1996-98). Managua: 23 September 1996.

Campos, Napoleon. ASACS (Director). San Salvador: 5 March 1991.

Campos, Wilson. ASOCODE (Regional Coordinator 1991-95); ICIC (Coordinator 1993-96). Guatemala: 20 October 1993; San José: 3 January 1994a; Amsterdam: 24 March 1994b; San José: 6 December 1995; Guatemala: 21 August 1996a; San José: 25 September 1996b; Santa Barbara de Heredia: 29 September 1996c.

Carmelo García, Juan. IEPALA (Director). Madrid: 7 June 1994.

Carrera, Maribel. IDESAC (Head of Urban Department); COINDE (Researcher). Guatemala: 15 March 1991, 8 July 1992, 21 November 1995, 15 August 1996.

Cartín, Sandra. CEPAS (Director). San José: 7 February 1991.

Castillo, Rolando. UNDP (NGO Division Honduras). Tegucigalpa: 1 December 1995.

Castro, Walter. *Movimiento Campesino Kabawil* (Secretary General). San Cristobal Totonicapan: 18 August 1996.

Celada, Edgar. *Inforpress Centroamericana* (Director). Guatemala: 13 August 1996, 20 August 1996.

Chaves, Manuel. UNAH (Researcher at the Department of Anthropology). Tegucigalpa: 2 March 1991.

Cid, Rafael del. UNAH (Professor at the Postgraduate Economy Department). Tegucigalpa: 2 March 1991.

Contier, John. *Norwegian People's Aid* (Representative for Central America). Guatemala: 25 March 1991, 8 July 1992, 2 November 1995a, 16 November 1995b.

Contreras, Félix. CONAPRO (President). Managua: 13 September 1991.

Coolen, Anton. SNV Honduras (Director). Tegucigalpa: 22 July 1992.

Córdova, Héctor. FEDECACES (General Secretary). San Salvador: 5 September 1996.

Cornejo, Manuel. FMLN (Member of Political-Diplomatic Commission). Bonn: 13 November 1993.

Cox, Mariano. COPMAGUA (Coordinator). Guatemala: 21 August 1996.

Cruz, Margarita. FASTRAS (Head of Project Department). San Salvador: 6 March 1991.

Custodio, Ramón. CODEH (President). San Pedro Sula: 24 November 1995; Tegucigalpa: 11 September 1996a, 17 September 1996b.

Dada, Héctor. FLACSO El Salvador (Director). San Salvador: 10 July 1992, 9 July 1993.

Declerq, Stefan. OXFAM-Belgium (Representative for Central America). Managua: 14 February 1991; San Salvador: 17 July 1992, 31 January 1994.

Dejgaard, Hans Peter. *Ibis* (Representative for Central America). Managua: 12 February 1991, 17 July 1992; Copenhagen: 20 September 1993, 11 March 1996.

Deleon, Ariel. *Inforpress Centroamericana* (Director). Guatemala: 19 March 1991.

Delgado, Aníbal. *Frente Patriótico de Honduras* (FPH). San Pedro Sula: 25 February 1991.

Deveivere, Juan. AVANCSO (Head of the Documentation Centre). Guatemala: 21 August 1996.

Dielis, Henk. CEBEMO (Central America Desk Officer). Oegstgeest: 5 October 1993, 25 October 1995, 26 June 1996.

Dierckxsens, Wim. Development consultant. San José: 4 February 1991.

Dijkstra, Ale. NOVIB (Central America Desk Officer). Den Haag: 4 July 1996.

Dixon, Claire. CAFOD (Central America Desk Officer). London: 15 September 1995.

Dolores. FUNDADESE (Director of Quetzaltenango Office). Quetzaltenango: 19 August 1996.

Duarte, Pablo. FRG (Member of Parliament). Guatemala, 16 August 1996.

Dubois, Alfonso. HEGOA (Deputy Director); EC-NGO Liaison Committee (Representative for Spain). Madrid: 7 June 1994.

Dubon de Flores, Soña Martina. *Fiscalía de los Derechos Humanos* (Special Prosecuter for Human Rights at the Honduran Ministry of the Interior). Tegucigalpa: 17 September 1996.

Edinger, Kristian. *Ibis* (Head of Central America Desk). Copenhagen: 11 March 1996.

Ellehammer, Dorte. *Ibis* (Representative for El Salvador); *Danchurchaid* (Latin American Desk Officer). San Salvador: 15 October 1992; Copenhagen: 11 March 1996.

Enríquez, Alberto. FMLN (Commander in San Salvador during the 1989 offensive); FUNDE (Researcher). San Salvador: 6 September 1996.

Eriksson, Ina. *Diakonia* (Representative for Central America). San Salvador: 5 September 1996.

Es, Yvonne. NOVIB (Central America Desk Officer). Den Haag: 30 September 1993.

Escobar Galindo, David. *Universidad José Matías Delgado* (Rector). San Salvador: 20 September 1996.

Escoto, Jorge. AVANCSO (Researcher). Guatemala: 2 July 1993.

Espinal Irías, Rigoberto. Member of the Honduran Supreme Court of Justice. Tegucigalpa: 14 September 1996.

Espinoza, Noemi. CCD (Director). Tegucigalpa: 26 February 1991.

Evans, Traver. CRIES (Researcher). Berlin: 2 August 1990.

Fajardo Reina, Allan. CCOD (Executive Secretary). Managua: 16 July 1992.

Feldt, Heidi. Development consultant. San Salvador: 12 March 1991.

Flor Bonilla, Blanca. PROCOMES (Director). San Salvador: 7 November 1995.

Flores, Antonino. CODEH (Member of Directorate). Tegucigalpa: 12 September 1996.

Foley, Michael. Catholic University of America, Washington DC (Associate Professor). San Salvador: 10 November 1995.

Frenken, Rene. SNV Honduras (Volunteer). Tegucigalpa: 23 February 1991.

Fuentes, Inés. COCOCH (Former Secretary General). Tegucigalpa: 13 September 1996.

Ganzmann, Franz. EZE (Representative for Central America). San José: 27 September 1996.

García, Evaristo. FACS (Project Director). Managua: 14 July 1992.

García, Manolo. SERJUS (Director). Guatemala: 25 March 1991, 20 November 1995a, 22 November 1995b, 15 August 1996a, 26 August 1996b.

Garst, Rachel. COINDE (Researcher). Guatemala: 23 March 1991, 7 July 1992.

Gibson, Kate. *Christian Aid* (Central America Desk Officer). London: 3 December 1993.

Gilhuis, Henk. ICCO (Representative for Central America). San José: 6 December 1995.

Goitia, Alfonso. CINAS; FUNDE (Director). San Salvador: 11 March 1991, 10 November 1995, 5 September 1996.

González, Víctor. PREIS; PRISMA (Research Coordinator). San Salvador: 11 March 1991, 4 July 1992.

González Davidson, Fernando. *Revista Crónica* (Editor International Affairs). Guatemala: 24 March 1991.

Gómez, Inmaculada. *Solidaridad Internacional* (Central America Project Officer). Madrid: 8 June 1994.

Gorostiaga, Xabier. CRIES (Secretary General); UCA-Nicaragua (Rector). Managua: 30 June 1992.

Gottwald, Gaby. *Die Grünen* (Member of Parliament). Hamburg: 12 June 1990 (phone).

Granillo, Oscar Leonel. FMLN (Representative for the Netherlands). Amsterdam: 28 January 1991.

Guido Béjar, Rafael. UCA-El Salvador (Head of Sociology Department). San Salvador: 7 November 1995.

Gutiérrez, Edgar. *Fundación Myrna Mack* (Associate Director). Guatemala: 19 March 1991, 20 November 1995.

Hansen, Finn. *Ibis*; CRIES; ASOCODE; UNDP (Researcher). Managua: 1 December 1994; San José: 26 September 1996.

Hansen, Merete. *Ibis* (Representative for El Salvador). San Salvador: 7 March 1991.

Harnecker, Marta. Journalist. Amsterdam: 7 May 1990.

Hasboun, Franz Miguel. UCA-El Salvador (Head of International Cooperation Department); FUNDESCA (Project Officer). San Salvador: 6 September 1996.

Hayer, Elisabeth. Development consultant. San Salvador: 22 March 1993.

Helin, Kirsten. *Lutheran World Federation* (Representative for El Salvador). San Salvador: 17 October 1992.

Helmich, Henny. OECD Development Center (Head of NGO Department). Paris: 22 June 1995.

Hermansen, Gitte. *Ibis* (Central America Desk Officer). Copenhagen: 11 March 1996.

Hernández, Doris. CNTC (Head of Literacy Programme). Tegucigalpa: 27 February 1991.

Hernández, Jorge. UPANACIONAL (Executive Director); ASOCODE (Regional Representative for Costa Rica). Tibás: 7 February 1994.

Herrera Cáceres, Roberto. SICA (Secretary General). San Salvador: 20 September 1996.

Hidalgo, Leonardo. MCS (Board member); CPDN. San Salvador: 5 September 1996.

Hilhorst, Thea. SNV Honduras (Volunteer). Amsterdam: 10 November 1990.

Hoegen, Miguel van. ASIES (Director). Guatemala: 20 March 1991.

Hogel, Lone. *Danchurchaid* (Head of Central America Desk). Copenhagen: 21 September 1993.

Hollander, Gert den. COOPIBO (Representative for Costa Rica). San José: 6 February 1991.

Huezo Mixco, Miguel. *Primera Plana* (Editor). San Salvador: 7 July 1993.

Hutchinson, Gordon. PCS (Director). San José: 10 December 1995.

Irías, Jorge. CODEH (Vice-President). Tegucigalpa: 27 November 1995a, 29 November 1995b, 10 September 1996.

Jacinto. *Consejo Tukum Amam*. Quetzaltenango: 19 August 1996.

Jara, Oscar. *Alforja* (Secretary General). San José: 5 February 1991.

Jekke, Reinhard. *Heinrich Böll Stiftung* (Central America Desk Officer). Wuppertal: 19 November 1991.

Jiménez, Milton. Laywer. Tegucigalpa: 11 September 1996, 18 September 1996.

Jowett, Andrew. *Save the Children* (Representative for Honduras). Tegucigalpa: 1 December 1995.

Jungehülsing, Mechtilt. *Fundación Centroamericana* (Project Officer). Managua: 13 February 1991.

Kelly, Ana. CIPHES (Coordinator). San Salvador: 6 March 1991.

Kesper, Christina. *Friedrich Ebert Stiftung* (Representative in Brussels). Brussels: 29 September 1993.

Klein, Eduardo. OXFAM-UK/I (Head of Central America Regional Office). Managua: 4 December 1995.

Koudstaal, Willy. hivos (Desk Officer for Honduras and Guatemala). Den Haag: 25 July 1990, 19 September 1990.

Kuan, Elia Maria. cries (Researcher). Managua: 11 February 1991.

Lambregts, Ruud. novib (Desk Officer for Nicaragua and Mexico). Den Haag: 30 September 1993.

Lanza, Gladys. ccop (Member of Coordination Committee). Tegucigalpa: 16 September 1996.

LaRue, Frank. caldh (Director). Guatemala: 16 November 1995.

León, Carmen Rosa de. iepades (Project Director). Guatemala: 22 November 1995, 16 August 1996.

Linsenmeier, Klaus. *Buntstift* (Project Director). Göttingen: 1 August 1991.

Loohuis, Hans. icco (Representative for Central America). San José: 5 February 1991.

Luers, Richard Paolo. *Radio Venceremos* (Editor); *Primera Plana* (Managing Director). San Salvador: July 1992.

Madrid, Zaila. codemuh (General Secretary). Tegucigalpa: 21 February 1991.

Magnusson, Hans. *Diakonia* (Representative for Guatemala). San Salvador: 9 November 1995, 4 September 1996.

Marinello, Lili. gvc (Representative for Nicaragua). Managua: 15 February 1991.

Márquez, Iván. ciades (Director). San Pedro Sula: 25 February 1991.

Marroquin, Manfredo. avancso (Researcher). Guatemala: 2 July 1993.

Martell, Allan. crefac (Project Director). San Salvador: 23 March 1993.

Martin, Pauline. oxfam-uk/i (Head of Central America Desk). Oxford: 2 December 1993, 14 September 1995.

Martínez, Ana Guadalupe. fmln (Former *Comandante*; Member of Parliament). San Salvador: 17 October 1992.

Martínez, Edín. fundasal (Director). San Salvador: 3 November 1995a, 6 November 1995b.

Marx-Utzel, Beate. eze (Central America Desk Officer). Bonn: 5 September 1995.

Mazariegos, Alberto. fundadese (Board Member; Former Director). Chichicastenango: 17 November 1995; Guatemala: 15 August 1996a; Amsterdam: 11 October 1996b.

Mejía, Thelma. *Universidad de la Paz* (Project Officer). Tegucigalpa: 14 September 1996.

Méndez, César. *Arzobispado* (Officer at the Social Secretariat). Guatemala: 19 March 1991.

Méndez, María Elena. cem-h (Director). Tegucigalpa: 13 September 1996.

Meza, Víctor. cedoh (Director). Tegucigalpa: 22 February 1991, 18 September 1996.

Millán, Cecilia. *Christian Aid* (Head of Central America Desk). London: 15 September 1995.

Miranda, Roberto. acav. San José: 6 February 1991.

Möller, Alois. *Brot für die Welt* (Head of Central America Department). Stuttgart: 17 September 1993.

Monterrosa, Celina de. crefac (Director); cpdn (Member of Coordination Committee); isd (Director); ccod (Executive Secretary). San Salvador: 8 March 1991, 9 November 1995, 6 September 1996.

Morales, Abelardo. flacso Costa Rica (Researcher). San José: 4 February 1991, 5 September 1991, 20 July 1993, 6 December 1995.

Morales, Henri. *Movimiento Tzuk Kim-pop* (Coordinator International Relations and Projects). Quetzaltenango: 17 August 1996a; Amsterdam: 11 October 1996b.

Morales, Lesbia. *Ibis* (Representative for Nicaragua). Managua: 12 September 1991, 22 June 1992.

Muntingh, Monique. *European Commission* (Former Project Officer, dg i-ala). Brussels: 21 June 1995.

Murillo, José. *ACSUR Las Segovias* (Representative for Central America). San Salvador: 26 October 1993.

Murillo, Rafael. Dramaturge (Director and Author of *El Caso Riccy Mabel*). Tegucigalpa: 12 September 1996.

Nielsen, John. *Ibis* (Representative for Central America); COWI (Development consultant). San José: 22 June 1992, 22 January 1993a, 20 September 1993b, 8 February 1994; Copenhagen: 12 March 1996.
Nieto, Belisario. *Christian Aid* (Head of Central America Desk). London: 3 December 1993.
Nijland, Erik. SNV Honduras (Volunteer at CNTC). Tegucigalpa: 23 February 1991.
Noé Pino, Hugo. UNAH (Economist). Tegucigalpa: 1 March 1991, 22 July 1992.

O'Hara, Maritza. CODEH (Head of Education Section). Tegucigalpa: 28 November 1995.
O'Neill, Sally. *Trocaire* (Former Deputy Director; Representative for Central America). Brussels: 7 April 1994a; Tegucigalpa: 30 November 1994b, 30 November 1995, 13 September 1996.
Obregón, Pedro Félix. ASOCODE (Staff member Managua Office). Managua: 1 December 1994.
Öhlers, Heinz. *Misereor* (Central America Desk Officer). Aachen: 12 September 1995.
Oliva, Bertha. COFADEH (President). Tegucigalpa: 19 September 1996.
Orellano, Salvador. CORDES (Director). San Salvador: 12 March 1991, 9 July 1992, 8 November 1995.
Otero, Carmen. *ACSUR Las Segovias* (Central America Desk Officer). Madrid: 7 June 1994.
Oudenalder, Dineke van den. HIVOS (Central America Desk Officer). Den Haag: 27 October 1994, 4 July 1996.

Padilla, Luís Alberto, IRIPAZ (Director). Guatemala: 20 March 1991.
Palacios, Edgar. CPDN (Coordinator). Amsterdam: 3 June 1992; San Salvador, 6 November 1995a, 7 November 1995b, 2 September 1996.
Palacios, Rebecca. FMLN (Member of Political-Diplomatic Commission). Amsterdam: 20 November 1990.
Perla de Anaya, Mirna. CODEHUCA (Regional Coordinator). San José: 7 February 1991.
Petersen, Mogens. DANIDA (Head of Central America Department). Copenhagen: 11 March 1996.
Peña, Lazaro. CRIES (Researcher). Managua: 11 February 1991.
Pineda, Ana. CODEH (Legal Adviser). Tegucigalpa: 13 September 1996.
Pineda, Irma. *Comisonado de los Derechos Humanos* (Vice-President). Tegucigalpa: 11 September 1996.
Plant, Roger. MINUGUA (Head of Indigenous Department). Guatemala: 20 August 1996.
Poitevin, René. FLACSO Guatemala (Director). Guatemala: 21 November 1995.
Porras, Silvia. CODEHUCA (Regional Coordinator); ASOCODE (Researcher). Managua: 23 September 1996.

Quesada, Carlos. CODEHUCA (Researcher). San José: 25 September 1996.

Ramos, René. Development consultant. San Salvador: 2 December 1995, 2 September 1996.
Ramos, Carlos. FLACSO El Salvador (Researcher). San Salvador: 10 November 1995, 5 September 1996.
Rasmussen, Bo. *Ibis* (Volunteer at FUNDADESE). Chichicastenango: 18 November 1995.
Ravn, Jesper. *Ibis* (Volunteer at CCOD). Managua: 22 June 1992.
Regalado, María Luísa. CODEMUH (Board member). Tegucigalpa: 21 February 1991.
Reuben, William. CECADE (Director); CCOD (Coordinator); FOLADE (Director). San José: 1 February 1991, 27 September 1996.
Rheenen, Gerlof van. *Solidaridad* (Head of Latin America Desk). Utrecht: 25 September 1990.

Ríos, Gilberto. IDHER (Director). Tegucigalpa: 19 February 1991a, 28 February 1991b.

Riquiac, María. FUNDADESE (Director of Chichicastenango Office). Chichicastenango: 17 November 1995.

Rivas, Ramón. SNV Honduras (Deputy Field Director). Tegucigalpa: 29 November 1995.

Rivera, Gilda. CDM (Director). Tegucigalpa: 12 September 1996.

Rivera, Linda. Lawyer in Riccy Mabel case. Tegucigalpa: 11 September 1996.

Rivera, Victor. ADC; CPDN (Board member). San Salvador: 3 September 1996.

Rodas, Amanda. CONGCOOP (Policy Officer). Guatemala: 15 November 1995.

Rodrigo, Jean-Michel. CCFD (Information Department Officer). Amsterdam: 1 June 1990.

Rodríguez, Roberto. CADESCA (Researcher). San Salvador: 29 June 1992.

Rodríquez, Combertty. CEDAL. Santa Catalina: 10 December 1995.

Rojas, Jesús. FMLN (Member of Political-Diplomatic Commission). Amsterdam: 5 July 1990.

Rojas Bolaños, Manuel. CEPAS; FLACSO Costa Rica (Researcher). Amsterdam: 19 October 1990; San José: 7 February 1991.

Romero, Welvin. CRIES (Researcher). Managua: 4 December 1995.

Roos, Karel. ICCO (Desk Officer for El Salvador). Zeist: 10 July 1996, 2 September 1997.

Rueben, Ruurd. CDR (Development consultant). San José: 5 February 1991.

Ruiven, Nel. SNV Honduras. Tegucigalpa: 21 February 1991.

Ruminski, Hilmar. *Friedrich Ebert Stiftung* (Head of Central America Department). Bad Godesberg: 9 September 1993.

Sacher, Danuta. EZE (Representative for Guatemala); PCS. San José: 6 December 1995.

Saldomando, Angel. CRIES (Research Coordinator). Managua: 23 June 1992.

Salinas, Guadalupe. OXFAM-UK/I (Representative for Nicaragua). Managua: 12 February 1991.

Sanahuja, José Antonio. CIP (Researcher). Madrid: 31 October 1995.

Schulte, Christiane. CONSOC (Volunteer). Quetzaltenango: 18 August 1996.

Sequén, Israel. FUNDADESE / *Pop Wuj* (Director). Chimaltenango: 26 August 1996.

Sierra, Rolando. *Brot für die Welt* (Consultant). San José: 26 September 1996.

Silva, Héctor. *Convergencia Democratica* (Election Campaign Manager). Köln: 13 November 1993.

Silvestre, Mario. IDESAC (Director); COINDE (Coordinator); *Ibis* (Consultant). Guatemala: 20 March 1991, 7 July 1992, 14 November 1995, 22 August 1996.

Similox, Vitalino. CIEDEG (Director). Guatemala: 21 August 1996.

Skauen, Petter. *Norwegian Church Aid* (Representative for Guatemala). Guatemala: 20 November 1995.

Sojo, Carlos. FLACSO Costa Rica (Researcher). San José: 20 July 1993, 27 September 1996.

Solano, Luís. *Inforpress Centroamericana* (Journalist). Guatemala: 16 August 1996.

Soto, Hermilio. IDEPH. Tegucigalpa: 26 February 1991.

Sparre, Ulrik. *Ibis* (Policy Officer Central America Office). Copenhagen: 21 September 1993; San José: 6 December 1995; Guatemala: 24 August 1996.

Spjudvik, Rannveig. *Norwegian People's Aid* (Desk Officer for Central America). Guatemala: 2 November 1995.

Spray, Paul. *Christian Aid* (Head of Policy Department). London: 3 December 1993.

Straatsma, Corina. HIVOS (Central America Regional Representative). San José: 9 December 1995.

Sugranyes, Ana. IDESAC (Head of Urban Programme). Guatemala: 15 March 1991a, 21 March 1991b.

Swen, Herman. SNV Nicaragua (Deputy Director). Managua: 24 June 1992.

Tabora, Rocío. COMUNICA (Director). Tegucigalpa: 21 February 1991.

Talavera, Carlos. *Contecnica* (Director). Tegucigalpa: 30 November 1995.

Tangermann, Klaus-Dieter. *Buntstift* (Representative for Central America). Managua: 23 June 1992.

Téllez, Ramiro. ASOCODE (Consultant). Managua: 4 December 1995.

Thompson, Martha. OXFAM-UK/I (Consultant). Managua: 22 July 1993.

Thoresen, Beate. OXFAM- UK/I (Representative for Guatemala). Guatemala: 19 November 1995.

Ticehurst, Simon. OXFAM-UK/I (Representative for El Salvador). San Salvador: 20 October 1992.

Timossi, Gerardo. CRIES (Research Director). Managua: 20 July 1992.

Tiney, Juan. CONIC (Board member). Amsterdam: 31 October 1994.

Torras, Rosa María. *Intermón* (Representative for Guatemala). Guatemala: 21 March 1991.

Torres, Manuel. Journalist *El Heraldo*. Tegucigalpa: 12 September 1996.

Torres Rivas, Edelberto. FLACSO (Former Secretary General). Madrid: 30 October 1995.

Turcios, Roberto. *Tendencias* (Editor). San Salvador: 4 September 1996.

Tuyuc, Rosalina. CONAVIGUA (Coordinator), FDNG (Member of Parliament). Guatemala: 27 August 1996.

Tyndale, Wendy. *Christian Aid* (Representative for Central America). Guatemala: 21 November 1995.

Uitdenwilligen, Marjet. CODEHUCA (Policy Researcher); Royal Dutch Embassy (Project Officer). San José: 4 February 1991, 25 September 1996.

Urschel, Karin. *Buntstift* (Representative for Central America). San Salvador: 9 November 1995, 6 September 1996.

Valerio, Félix. *Wuqub N'oj* (Director). Quetzaltenango: 19 August 1996.

Valladares, Leo. *Comisonado de los Derechos Humanos* (President). Tegucigalpa: 11 September 1996.

Vanegas, Dimas. DIACONIA (Director). San Salvador: 8 March 1991.

Vargas, Guido. UPANACIONAL (General Secretary). San José: 26 September 1996.

Velásquez, Helmer. CONGCOOP (Director). San Salvador: 28 January 1994; Guatemala: 24 August 1996.

Ventura, Xiomara. FOPRIDEH (Consultant). Tegucigalpa: 27 February 1991, 28 November 1995.

Villalobos, Rafael. ASACS (Researcher). San Salvador: 7 March 1991.

Villalta, Eulogio. CONFRAS (Vice-President), ASOCODE (Regional Representative for El Salvador), ADC (Coordinator). Amsterdam: 26 September 1994; San Salvador: 3 September 1996.

Wehkamp, Andy. NOVIB (Representative for Nicaragua). Guatemala: 24 March 1991.

Weyersberg, Sabine. *Terre des Hommes* (Head of Central America Desk). Wuppertal: 19 November 1991.

Widén, Ewa. *Diakonia* (Representative for Central America). San José: 4 February 1991.

Wierema, Holke. CEBEMO (Head of Latin America Department). Oegstgeest: 22 September 1995, 26 June 1996.

Zamora, Ruben. *Convergencia Democrática* (Member of Parliament). San Salvador: 5 March 1991.

Zavala, Wilber. ASOCODE (Executive Director). Managua: 6 December 1995.

REFERENCES

Acevedo, Carlos (1988) 'Crónica del debate nacional'. *Estudios Centroamericanos*, Vol. 48, No. 478-479, pp. 767-779.

Achterhuis, Hans (1993) 'Als haaien mensen waren: Moralisme als internationalisme', in Achterhuis *et al.* (eds), *Het orkest van de Titanic*. (Brussel: Student Aid-vub Press), pp. 17-35.

Acuña, Víctor Hugo (1993) 'Clases subalternas y movimientos sociales en Centroamérica', in Acuña (ed.), *Historia general de Centroamérica* (Tomo IV). (Madrid-San José: CEE-FLACSO), pp. 255-323.

—— (1995) 'Autoritarismo y democracia en Centroamérica: La larga duración – siglo XIX y XX', in Tangermann (ed.), *Ilusiones y dilemas*. (San José: FLACSO), pp. 63-97.

African Rights (1994) 'Humanitarianism unbound?: Current dilemmas facing multi-mandate relief operations in political emergencies'. *Discussion Paper*, No. 5 (November). (London: African Rights).

Aguilera, Gabriel (1989) *El fusil y el olivo: La cuestión militar en Centroamérica*. (San José: DEI-FLACSO).

Aguilera, Gabriel; Abelardo Morales and Carlos Sojo (1991) *Centroamérica: de Reagan a Bush*. (San José: FLACSO).

Aguilera, Gabriel & Karen Ponciano (1994) 'El espejo sin reflejo: La negociación de paz en 1993'. *Cuaderno de debate*, No. 23. (Guatemala: FLACSO).

Aguilera, Gabriel; Rosalinda Bran and Claudienne Ogaldes (1996) 'Buscando la paz: El bienio 1994-1995'. *Cuaderno de debate*, No. 32. (Guatemala: FLACSO).

AIDAB (1995) 'NGO Programs Effectiveness Review'. Internal Working Document, March. (Canberra: *mimeo*).

Alecio, Rolando (1995) 'Uncovering the truth: Political violence and indigenous organizations', in Sinclair (ed.), *The New Politics of Survival*. (New York: Monthly Review Press), pp. 25-45.

Almond, Gabriel & Sidney Verba (1963) *The Civic Culture: Political Attitudes and Democracy in Five Nations*. (Princeton: Princeton University Press).

Altvater, Elmar *et al.* (Hrsg.) (1997) *Vernetzt und verstrickt: Nicht-Regierungs-Organisationen als gesellschaftliche Produktivkraft*. (Münster: Westfälisches Dampfboot).

Alvarez, Francisco & Pauline Martin (1992) 'The role of Salvadorean NGOs in post-war reconstruction'. *Development in Practice*, Vol. 2, No. 2, pp. 103-113.

Americas Watch (1991) *El Salvador's Decade of Terror: Human Rights since the Assassination of Archbishop Romero*. (New Haven and London: Yale University Press).

Anderson, Mary & Peter Woodrow (1989) *Rising from the Ashes: Development Strategies in Times of Disaster*. (Boulder and San Francisco: Westview Press).

Archer, Robert (1994) 'Markets and good government', in Clayton (ed.), *Governance, Democracy and Conditionality*. (Oxford: INTRAC), pp. 7-34.

Archibugi, Daniele & David Held (eds) (1995) *Cosmopolitan Democracy: An Agenda for a New World Order*. (Cambridge: Polity Press).

Arias, Salvador & Roberto Rodríguez (1994) 'Peasant agriculture and development alternatives in Central America', in Biekart and Jelsma (eds), *Peasants beyond Protest in Central America*. (Amsterdam: Transnational Institute), pp. 111-138.

Arias, Salvador & Roberto Rodríguez (1995) 'Reconversión productiva y ataque estructural a la pobreza rural en la globalización: Retos de Asocode hacia el 2000'. *Consultaría de apoyo de Fundesca a la planificación estratégica de Asocode*, Panamá, 21 de noviembre de 1995.

Arnson, Cynthia (1993) *Crossroads: Congress, the President, and Central America, 1976-1993* (2nd edition). (University Park, PA: The Pennsylvania State University Press).

Arrellano-López, Sonia & James Petras (1994) 'Non-governmental organisations and poverty alleviation in Bolivia'. *Development and Change*, Vol. 25, pp. 555-568.

Arruda, Marcos (1985) 'The Role of Latin American Non-Governmental Organizations in the Perspective of Participatory Democracy'. *Paper for Third International FFHC/AD Consultation* 3-6 September, pp. 1-18.

—— (1996) *Globalization and Civil Society: Rethinking Cooperativism in the Context of Active Citizenship.* (Rio de Janeiro: PACS).

ASOCODE (1991a) 'Estrategia productiva de los pequeños y medianos productores del istmo centroamericano', Agosto. (San José: *mimeo*).

—— (1991b) 'Memoria Primer Congreso Centroamericano de Pequeños y Medianos Productores'. Managua, 4-6 de diciembre de 1991. (*mimeo*).

—— (1992) 'Documento de posiciones ante la Conferencia Mundial de Naciones Unidas sobre Medio Ambiente y Desarrollo', abril de 1992. (*mimeo*).

—— (1993a) 'Memoria Primera Conferencia Regional Campesina sobre Cooperación Solidaria', Panamá, 17-19 de marzo de 1993. (*mimeo*).

—— (1993b) 'Gira a Europa: informe general', junio. (*mimeo*).

—— (1993c) 'Memoria IV Conferencia Regional Campesina', Panamá, 25-25 de septiembre de 1993. (Managua: *mimeo*).

—— (1993d) 'Memoria Segundo Congreso General de ASOCODE', 2-4 de diciembre. (Guatemala: *mimeo*).

—— (1994a) 'Bases y propuestas para una estrategia de incidencia de ASOCODE con respecto a la cooperación europea', marzo. (Managua: *mimeo*).

—— (1994b) 'Intervención de Wilson Campos, Coordinador General de ASOCODE, en el taller de cabildeo OXFAM-UK/I-Contrapartes', Managua, 30 de mayo al 1 de junio de 1994. (*mimeo*).

—— (1994c) 'Memoria del Primer Consejo Regional Campesino', Belize, septiembre de 1994. (*mimeo*).

—— (1995a) 'Conferencia El campesinado y la cooperación: Hacia una plataforma común contra la pobreza: Resumen ejecutivo'. San Salvador, 8 y 9 de febrero de 1995. (*mimeo*).

—— (1995b) 'Valoración del trabajo de incidencia de ASOCODE: Documento de insumo para el proceso de planificación de ASOCODE', octubre. (*mimeo*).

—— (1996) 'Plan estratégico (resumen ejecutivo)'. *Voz Campesina*, No. 9 (Junio).

Avina, Jeffrey (1993) The evolutionary cycle of non-governmental development organisations. *Public Administration and Development*, Vol. 13, No. 5, pp. 453-474.

Balletbò, Anna (ed.) (1994) *La consolidación democrática en América Latina.* (Barcelona: Editorial Hacer-Fundación Internacional Olof Palme).

Baloyra, Enrique (1987a) *Comparing New Democracies: Transition and Consolidations in Mediterranean Europe and the Southern Cone.* (Boulder, CO: Westview Press).

—— (1987b) *El Salvador en transición.* (San Salvador: UCA editores).

Baranyi, Stephen (1995) 'The challenge in Guatemala: Verifying human rights, strengthening national institutions and enhancing an integrated UN approach to peace'. *Research Paper*, No. 1. (London: Centre for the Study of Global Governance, LSE).

Barraclough, Solon *et al.* (1988) *Aid that Counts: The Western Contribution to Development and Survival in Nicaragua.* (Amsterdam: Transnational Institute-CRIES).

Barrez, Dirk (1993) 'De val der engelen: Waarom ontwikkelingsorganisaties falen', in Achterhuis *et al.*, *Het orkest van de Titanic*. (Brussel: VUB Press-Student Aid), pp. 35-117.

Barry, Deborah & Rodolfo Castro (1991) 'Negotiations, the war and Esquipulas II', in Sundaram and Gelber (eds), *A Decade of War*. (New York-London: Monthly Review Press-CIIR), pp. 102-127.

Barry, Deborah *et al.* (1989) 'Danish NGOs in Central America'. *CASA NGO Report*, No. 7 (June). (Copenhagen: DANIDA).

Barry, Tom (1987) *Roots of Rebellion: Land and Hunger in Central America*. (Boston: South End Press).

—— (1990) *El Salvador: A Country Guide*. (Albuquerque: The Inter-Hemispheric Education Resource Center).

—— (1992) *Inside Guatemala: The Essential Guide to its Politics, Economy, Society, and Environment*. (Albuquerque: The Inter-Hemispheric Education Resource Center).

Barry, Tom & Deb Preusch (1988) *The Soft War: The Uses and Abuses of US Economic Aid in Central America*. (New York: Grove Press).

Bastos, Santiago & Manuela Camus (1993) *Quebrando el silencio: Organizaciones del pueblo maya y sus demandas (1986-1992)*. (Guatemala: FLACSO).

—— (1995) *Abriendo caminos: Las organizaciones mayas desde el Nobel hasta el Acuerdo de Derechos Indígenas*. (Guatemala: FLACSO).

Baumeister, Eduardo (1994) 'Agrarian structures and small producers: Review and prospects', in Biekart and Jelsma (eds), *Peasants beyond Protest in Central America*. (Amsterdam: Transnational Institute), pp. 59-84.

Bayart, Jean-François (1986) 'Civil society in Africa', in Chabal (ed.), *Political Domination in Africa*. (Cambridge: Cambridge University Press), pp. 109-125.

Bayra, John-Jean (1993) 'The new political conditionalities of aid: An independent view from Africa'. *IDS Bulletin*, Vol. 24, No. 1, pp. 16-23.

Bebbington, Anthony (1997a) 'The Chile case study: NGO evaluation policies and practices', in Kruse *et al.* (eds), *Searching for Impacts and Methods*. (Helsinki: Ministry of Foreign Affairs of Finland), Appendix II.

—— (1997b) 'New states, new NGOs?: Crises and transitions among rural development NGOs in the Andean region'. *World Development*, Vol. 25, No. 11, pp. 1755-1765.

Bebbington, Anthony & Adalberto Kopp (1995) *Evaluation of the Swedish NGO Support Programme: Country Case Study Bolivia*. (London: Overseas Development Institute).

Beetham, David (1994) 'Key principles and indices for a democratic audit', in Beetham (ed.), *Defining and Measuring Democracy*. (London: Sage), pp. 25-43.

Bejar, Hector & Peter Oakley (1995) 'From accountability to shared responsibility: NGO evaluation in Latin America', in Edwards and Hulme (eds), *Non-Governmental Organisations – Performance and Accountability*. (London: Earthscan), pp. 73-81.

Bendaña, Alejandro (1991) *Una tragedia campesina: Testimonios de la resistencia*. (Managua: Edit-Arte, CEI).

Bennet, Jon (1995) *Meeting Needs: NGO Coordination in Practice*. (London: Earthscan).

Berg, Max van der & Bram van Ojik (1995) *Kostbaarder dan koralen: Beschouwingen over ontwikkelingssamenwerking*. (Den Haag: NOVIB/Van Gennep).

—— (1998) *De goede bedoelingen voorbij: Ontwikkelingssamenwerking van de toekomst*. (Amsterdam: NOVIB-Van Gennep).

Berg, Rob van den & Philip Quarles van Ufford (red.) (1995) *De toekomst van de Nederlandse ontwikkelingssamenwerking: Bijdragen aan een inhoudelijk debat*. (Woubrugge: Uitgeverij Jan Mets-Stichting AGORA).

Bering, Elna; Jacob Norvig Larsen, Sanne Olsen and Knud Vilby (1989) 'The Danish NGO

Evaluation: Non-Governmental Actions; A Necessary and Growing Option'. *CASA NGO Report*, No. 1 (November). (Copenhagen: DANIDA).

Berryman, Phillip (1984) *The Religious Roots of Rebellion: Christians in Central American Revolutions*. (Maryknoll: Orbis).

—— (1994) *Stubborn Hope: Religion, Politics and Revolution in Central America*. (New York: The New Press).

Biekart, Kees (1989) 'De invloed van West-Europa op het Latijnsamerikaanse democratiseringsproces: Een onderzoek naar de transnational politieke integratie van de Chileense centrumoppositie'. Doctoraalscriptie Internationale Betrekkingen. (Amsterdam: Faculteit PSCW-Universiteit van Amsterdam).

—— (1994) *La cooperación no-gubernamental europea hacia Centroamérica: La experiencia de los ochenta y las tendencias en los noventa*. (San Salvador: PRISMA).

—— (1995) 'European NGOs and democratisation in Central America: Assessing performance in the light of changing priorities', in Edwards and Hulme (eds), *Non-Governmental Organisations – Performance and Accountability*. (London: Earthscan), pp. 63-71.

—— (1996) 'Strengthening intermediary roles in civil society: Experiences from Central America', in Clayton (ed.), *NGOs, Civil Society and the State*. (Oxford: Intrac), pp. 141-156.

—— (1997) 'Regionalisation from below, funding from abroad: Central American civil society networks and private foreign aid'. Paper presented at the 12th ASERCCA Annual Conference, Portsmouth, 19-21 September. (*mimeo*).

Biekart, Kees & Alex Fernández Jilberto (eds) (1988) *Lente in het Zuiden: De Crisis van de Latijnsamerikaanse Dictaturen*. (Amsterdam: SUA).

Biekart, Kees & Martin Jelsma (eds) (1994) *Peasants Beyond Protest in Central America: Challenges for Asocode, Strategies towards Europe*. (Amsterdam: Transnational Institute).

Black, George (1981) *Triumph of the People: The Sandinista Revolution in Nicaragua*. (London: Zed Press).

Black, Maggie (1992) *A Cause for Our Times: Oxfam the First 50 Years*. (Oxford: OXFAM/Oxford University Press).

Blair, Harry (1997) 'Donors, democratisation and civil society: Relating theory to practice', in Hulme and Edwards (eds), *NGOs, States and Donors*. (London: MacMillan Press), pp. 23-42.

Blair, Harry *et al.* (1995) 'Civil society and democratic development in El Salvador', *CIDIE Assesment Report*. (Washington, DC: USAID).

Blankenberg, Floris (1995) *Oxfam UK/I and Novib methods of impact assessment research programme: Resource pack and discussion paper for the case studies phase*. (The Hague: NOVIB, Policy Support Desk).

Blokland, Kees (1992) *Participación campesina en el desarrollo económico: La Unión Nacional de Agricultores y Ganaderos de Nicaragua durante la Revolución Sandinista*. (Doetinchem: Paolo Freire Stichting).

—— (1995) 'Peasant alliances and 'concertacion' with society'. *Bulletin of Latin American Research*, Vol. 14, No. 2, pp. 159-170.

Bobbio, Norberto (1987) *La democracia socialista*. (Santiago de Chile: Ediciones Documentas).

—— (1988) 'Gramsci and the concept of civil society', in Keane (ed.), *Civil Society and the State*. (London: Verso), pp. 73-99.

Bolling, Landrum (1982) *Private Foreign Aid: US Philanthropy for Relief and Development*. (Boulder, CO: Westview Press).

Bonasso, Miguel & Ciro Gómez Leyva (1992) *El Salvador, cuatro minutos para las doce: Conversaciones con el comandante Shafick Hándal*. (Mexico: PAL).

Booth, John (1989) 'Elections and democracy in Central America: A framework for analysis', in

Booth and Seligson (eds), *Democracy in Central America*. (Chapell Hill and London: The University of North Carolina Press), pp. 7-39.

—— (1995) 'Central America and the United States: Cycles of containment and response', in Martz (ed.), *United States Policy in Latin America*. (Lincoln: University of Nebraska Press), pp. 184-214.

Booth, John & Thomas Walker (1993) *Understanding Central America* (2nd edition). (Boulder, CO: Westview Press).

Borgh, Chris van der (1997) 'Decision-making and participation in poverty alleviation pro-grammes in post-war Chalatenango, El Salvador'. *European Review of Latin American and Caribbean Studies*, No. 63, pp. 49-66.

Bossuyt, Jean (1993) 'De midlife crisis van de NGO-sector', in Achterhuis *et al.* (eds), *Het orkest van de Titanic*. (Brussel: Student Aid-VUB Press), pp. 201-216.

Boyce, James (1995) 'External assistance and the peace process in El Salvador'. *World Develop-ment*, Vol. 23, No. 12, pp. 2101-2116.

Boyce, James (ed.) (1996) *Economic Policy for Building Peace: The Lessons of El Salvador*. (Boulder, CO: Lynne Rienner Publishers).

Boye, Nancy (1992) 'The response of the churches and the NGOs to the challenge of peace'. *Paper presented at CIIR seminar 'A Negotiated Revolution: The Peace Accords and After'*, Heythrop College, London, 8 September 1992. (London: CIIR).

Bratton, Michael (1989) 'The politics of Government-NGO relations in Africa'. *World Develop-ment*, Vol. 17, No. 4, pp. 569-587.

—— (1990) 'Non-govermental organizations in Africa: Can they influence public policy?'. *Development and Change*, Vol. 21, pp. 87-118.

—— (1994) 'Civil society and political transitions in Africa', in Harbeson *et al.*, *Civil Society and the State in Africa*. (Boulder, CO: Lynne Rienner), pp. 51-81.

Brinkerhoff, Derick & Arthur Goldsmith (1992) 'Promoting sustainability of development institutions: A framework for strategy'. *World Development*, Vol. 20, No. 3, pp. 369-383.

Brockett, Charles (1988) *Land, Power, and Poverty: Agrarian Transformation and Political Conflict in Central America*. (Winchester, Ma.: Allen and Unwin).

Brockmann, Andreas & Martin Dabrowski (eds) (1996) *Mittelamerika und Deutschland: Das Potential einer guten Partnerschaft*. (Frankfurt am Main: Vervuert Verlag).

Brodhead, Tim; Brent Herbert-Copley and Anne-Marie Lambert (1988) *Bridges of Hope?: Canadian Voluntary Agencies and the Third World*. (Ottawa: North-South Institute).

Brown, David (1990) 'Rethoric or reality?: Assessing the role of NGOs as agencies of grassroots development'. *AERRD Bulletin*, No. 28, pp. 3-10.

Brown, David & Rajesh Tandon (1994) 'Institution development for strengthening civil society'. *IDR Reports*, Vol. 11, No. 9. (Boston, Ma.: Institute for Development Research).

Brunner, José Joaquín & Alicia Barrios (1987) *Inquisición, mercado y filantropía: Ciencias sociales y autoritarismo en Argentina, Brasil, Chile y Uruguay*. (Santiago de Chile: FLACSO).

Bulmer-Thomas, Victor (1987) *The Political Economy of Central America since 1920*. (Cambridge: Cambridge University Press).

Burbach, Roger & Orlando Núñez (1987) *Fire in the Americas: Forging a Revolutionary Agenda*. (London: Verso).

Burge, Alun (1995) 'Central America: NGO Coordination in El Salvador and Guatemala 1980-94', in Bennet (ed.), *Meeting Needs: NGO Coordination in Practice*. (London: Earthscan), pp. 145-165.

Burgos, Elisabeth (ed.) (1983) *Me llamo Rigoberta Menchú y así me nació la conciencia*. (Mexico: Siglo XXI).

Burnell, Peter (1991) *Charity, Politics and the Third World*. (Herfordshire: Harvester Wheatsheaf).

Burnell, Peter (1994) 'Good government and democratization: A sideways look at aid and political conditionality'. *Democratization*, Vol. 1, No. 3, pp. 485-503.

Bye, Vegard *et al.* (1995) 'A Time for Change: Programme Review Ibis Central America Programme', December. (Oslo: *mimeo*).

Byrne, Hugh (1996) *El Salvador's Civil War: A Study of Revolution.* (Boulder, CO: Lynne Rienner Publishers).

Caballero, Lily & Leticia Salomón (1996) 'Honduras: Estudio de contexto. Consulta para Oficina de Coordinación Regional (OCR)'. (Tegucigalpa: *mimeo*).

Cabarrús, Carlos Rafael (1983) *Génesis de una revolución: Análisis del surgimiento y desarrollo de la organización campesina en El Salvador.* (México: Ediciones de la Casa Chata).

Cabrera, Sayra & Manuel Camposeco (1996) 'Informe final de evaluación FUNDADESE-Ibis', Julio. (Guatemala: *mimeo*).

Callaghy, Thomas (1994) 'Civil society, democracy and economic change in Africa: A dissenting opinion about resurgent societies', in Harbeson *et al.*, *Civil Society and the State in Africa.* (Boulder, CO: Lynne Rienner), pp. 231-253.

Cammack, Paul (1994a) 'Democratization and citizenship in Latin America', in Parry and Moran (eds), *Democracy and Democratization.* (London: Routledge), pp. 174-195.

—— (1994b) 'Political development theory and the dissemination of democracy'. *Democratization*, Vol. 1, No. 3 (Autumn), pp. 353-374.

Campos, Andrés (1992) 'La cooperación no gubernamental de las paises nórdicos en Centroamérica, los dilemmas de la relación futura: Opiniones de las contrapartes centroamericanas'. *Conference 'Towards new models of Nordic cooperation with Central America'*, 9-10 April 1992. (San Salvador: CCOD).

Campos, Wilson (1994) 'ASOCODE: Our view on development', in Biekart and Jelsma (eds), *Peasants Beyond Protest in Central America.* (Amsterdam: Transnational Institute), pp. 27-31.

Candanedo, Diana & Víctor Julio Madrigal (1994) 'Informe final: Evaluación externa de ASOCODE, período julio 91-diciembre 93', Agosto. (*mimeo*).

Caouette, Dominique (1996) 'The Central American peace process: Possible lessons from El Salvador and Guatemala'. *Kasarinlan, Philippine Quarterly of Third World Studies*, Vol. 11, No. 3-4, pp. 67-92.

Cardenal, Rodolfo (1995) 'La iglesia en Centroamérica', in Dussel (ed.), *Resistencia y esperanza.* (San José: Editorial DEI), pp. 365-397.

Cardoso, Fernando Henrique & Enzo Faletto (1969) *Dependencia y desarrollo en América Latina.* (Mexico: Siglo XXI).

Carmack, Robert (1995) *Rebels of Highland Guatemala: The Quiché-Mayas of Momostenango.* (Norman: University of Oklahoma Press).

Carmack, Robert (ed.) (1988) *Harvest of Violence: The Mayan Indians and the Guatemalan Crisis.* (Norman: University of Oklahoma Press).

Carney, James (1983) *Metamorfosis de un revolucionario: Memorias de un sacerdote en Honduras.* (Managua: PRTC-H).

Carothers, Thomas (1991) *In the Name of Democracy: US Policy toward Latin America in the Reagan Years.* (Berkeley, CA: University of California Press).

—— (1995) 'Recent US experience with democracy promotion'. *IDS Bulletin*, Vol. 26, No. 2, pp. 62-69.

—— (1996) 'The resurgence of United States political development assistance to Latin America in the 1980s', in Whitehead (ed.), *The International Dimensions of Democratization.* (Oxford: Oxford University Press), pp. 125-145.

Carrera, Maribel (1994) 'Incidencia de la cooperación no gubernamental europea en el proceso político guatemalteco (1980-93)'. Proyecto TNI-PRISMA 'El impacto político de la cooperación no gubernamental europea en Centroamérica', Informe final, Octubre de 1994. (Guatemala: *mimeo*).

Carroll, Thomas F. (1992) *Intermediary NGOs: The Supporting Link in Grassroots Development*. (West Hartford: Kumarian Press).

Casaus, Marta (1995) *Guatemala: Linaje y racismo*. (San José: FLACSO).

Casley, Dennis & Krishna Kumar (1987) *Project Monitoring and Evaluation in Agriculture*. (Baltimore: Johns Hopkins University Press).

Cassen, Robert & Associates (1986) *Does Aid Work?* (New York and London: Oxford University Press).

Castañeda, Jorge G. (1993) *Utopia Unarmed: The Latin American Left after the Cold War*. (New York: Vintage Books).

Castañeda Sandoval, Gilberto (1993) 'Panorama después de la tempestad: El movimiento sindical y popular guatemalteco en la década de los ochenta', in Vilas (coord.), *Democracia emergente en Centroamérica*. (México: Universidad Nacional Autónoma de México), pp. 275-295.

Cauffield, Catherine (1997) *Masters of Illusion: The World Bank and the Poverty of Nations*. (London: Pan Books-MacMillan).

CCOD (1990) *Cooperación externa y desarrollo en Centroamérica: Documentos de la II consulta internacional de cooperación externa para Centroamérica*. (San José: CECADE).

—— (1991) *III consulta internacional sobre cooperación externa con Centroamérica: Memoria*. (Guatemala: CCOD-COINDE).

CEBEMO (1993) 'Documento básico Montevideo II'. (Oegstgeest: *mimeo*).

Cerdas, Rodolfo (1992) 'Colonial heritage, external domination, and political systems in Central America', in Goodman *et al.* (eds), *Political Parties and Democracy in Central America*. (Boulder, CO: Westview Press), pp. 17-31.

—— (1993) *El desencanto democrático: Crises de partidos y transición democrática en Centroamérica y Panamá*. (San José: REI)

—— (1996) 'Political parties and party systems', in Sieder (ed.), *Central America: Fragile Transition*. (London: MacMillan Press-ILAS), pp. 15-54.

Cernea, Michael (1988) 'Nongovernmental organisations and local development'. *Discussion Paper*, No. 40. (Washington: World Bank).

Chalmers, Douglas; Scott Martin and Kerianne Piester (1997) 'Associative networks: New structures of representation for the popular sectors?', in Chalmers *et al.* (eds), *The New Politics of Inequality in Latin America*. (Oxford: Oxford University Press), pp. 543-582.

Chambers, Robert (1983) *Rural Development: Putting the Last First*. (Harlow: Longman).

—— (1992) 'Spreading and self-improving: A strategy for scaling-up', in Edwards and Hulme (eds), *Making a Difference*. (London: Earthscan), pp. 40-47.

—— (1993) *Challenging the Professions: Frontiers for Rural Development*. (London: IT Publications).

—— (1997) *Whose Reality Counts?: Putting the First Last*. (London: IT Publications).

Charlton, Roger & Roy May (1995) 'NGOs, politics, projects and probity: A policy implementation perspective'. *Third World Quarterly*, Vol. 16, No. 2, pp. 237-255.

Chazan, Naomi (1992) 'Africa's democratic challenge'. *World Policy Journal*, Vol. 9, No. 2, pp. 279-307.

Child, Jack (1992) *The Central American Peace Process, 1983-1991: Sheathing Swords, Building Confidence*. (Boulder: Lynne Rienner).

Chomsky, Noam (1985) *Turning the Tide: US Intervention in Central America and the Struggle for Peace*. (Boston: South End Press).

Clark, John (1991) *Democratizing Development: The Role of Voluntary Agencies*. (London: Earthscan).

Clark, John (1992) 'Policy influence, lobbying and advocacy', in Edwards and Hulme (eds), *Making a Difference*. (London: Earthscan), pp. 191-202.

Clayton, Andrew (ed.) (1994) *Governance, Democracy and Conditionality: What Role for NGOs?* (Oxford: INTRAC).

—— (1996) *NGOs, Civil Society and the State: Building Democracy in Transitional Societies.* (Oxford: INTRAC).

Cleary, Seamus (1997) *The Role of NGOs under Authoritarian Political Systems.* (London: MacMillan Press).

Coate, Roger; Chadwick Alger and Ronnie Lipschutz (1996) 'The United Nations and civil society: Creative partnerships for sustainable development'. *Alternatives*, Vol. 21, No. 1, pp. 93-122.

CODEH (1993) 'Documento síntesis del encuentro nacional Militarismo y Sociedad', 31 de Marzo-1 de Abril. (Tegucigalpa: *mimeo*).

—— (1995a) *Estatutos de CODEH.* (Tegucigalpa: CODEH).

—— (1995b) *Informe narrativo y financiero del CODEH para 1994.* (Tegucigalpa: CODEH).

—— (1996) *Balance de los derechos humanos en Honduras 1996* (Tegucigalpa: CODEH).

Cohen, Jean & Andrew Arato (1992) *Civil Society and Political Theory.* (Cambridge: MIT Press).

COINDE (1991) *Perfil de la estrategia de incidencia del movimiento social guatemalteco en relación a la cooperación externa: Una aproximación.* (Guatemala: COINDE-SAT).

Cojtí, Demetrio (1994) *Políticas para la reivindicación de las Mayas de hoy: Fundamentos de los derechos específicos del Pueblo Maya.* (Guatemala: SPEM-Cholsamaj).

Comisionado Nacional de Protección de los Derechos Humanos (1994) *Los hechos hablan por sí mismos: Informe preliminar sobre los desaparecidos en Honduras, 1980-1993.* (Tegucigalpa: Editorial Guaymuras).

Comisión de la Verdad (1993) *De la locura a la esperanza: La guerra de 12 años en El Salvador. Informe de la Comisión de la Verdad, 1992-1993.* (San Salvador: Arcoiris).

Commission on Global Governance (1995) *Our Global Neighbourhood: The Report of the Commission on Global Governance.* (New York: Oxford University Press).

Coninck, Douglas de (1996) *Witte olifanten: De miljardenschandalen van de Belgische ontwikkelingssamenwerking.* (Leuven: Van Halewyck).

Coninck, John de (1992) 'Evaluating the Impact of NGOs in Rural Poverty Alleviation: Uganda Country Study'. *Working Paper*, No. 51, February. (London: Overseas Development Institute).

Conroy, Michael; Douglas Murray and Peter Rosset (1996) *A Cautionary Tale: Failed US Development Policy in Central America.* (Boulder-London: Lynne Rienner Publishers).

Constantino-David, Karina (1992) 'The Philippine experience in scaling-up', in Edwards and Hulme (eds), *Making a Difference*. (London: Earthscan), pp. 137-147.

COPMAGUA (1995) *Acuerdo sobre identidad y derechos de los pueblos indígenas: Punto 3 del Acuerdo de paz firme y duradera.* (Guatemala: COPMAGUA).

Couderé, Hugo (1994) *Van project tot beleid: Evaluatiemethodes voor niet-gouvernementele ontwikkelingssamenwerking.* (Brussel: NCOS).

Covey, Jane (1995) 'Accountability and effectiveness in NGO policy alliances', in Edwards and Hulme (eds), *Non-Governmental Organisations – Performance and Accountability*. (London: Earthscan), pp. 167-181.

Cox, Ronald W. (1994) *Power and Profits: US Policy in Central America.* (Lexington: University Press of Kentucky).

CPDN (1992) *Memoria 1992 Debate nacional por la paz en El Salvador.* (San Salvador: CPDN).

—— (1995) 'Propuestas de Agenda Nacional desde las fuerzas sociales: Un aporte para el debate y la concertación', diciembre. (San Salvador: *mimeo*).

Craig, Gary & Marjorie Mayo (eds) (1995) *Community Empowerment: A Reader in Participation and Development.* (London: Zed Books).

Crawford, Gordon (1995) 'Promoting Democracy, Human Rights and Good Governance Through Development Aid: A Comparative Study of Four Northern Donors'. *Working Papers on Democratization*. (Leeds: Leeds University Press).

Crombrugghe, Geneviève de; Howes, Mick; Nieuwkerk, Mark (1985) *An evaluation of CEC small development projects*. (Brussels: COTA).

Crombrugghe, Geneviève de; Francis Douxchamps and Nikita Stampa (1993) *Evaluation of EEC-NGO co-financing in relation to institutional support for grassroots organisations in developing countries*. Synthesis Report, March. (Brussels: COTA). Crosby, Benjamin (1990) 'Central America', in Lake (ed.), *After the Wars*. (New Brunswick: Transaction Publishers), pp. 103-138.

Curti, Merle (1963) *American Philanthropy Abroad: A History*. (New Brunswick, NJ: Rutgers University Press).

Custodio, Ramón (1986) 'The human rights crisis in Honduras', in Rosenberg and Shepherd (eds), *Honduras Confronts its Future*. (Boulder, CO: Lynne Rienner), pp. 65-74.

Dada, Héctor (1995) 'Los acuerdos de paz y la democratización'. *Estudios Centroamericanos*, Vol. 50, No. 558, pp. 367-376.

Dahl, Robert A. (1971) *Polyarchy: Participation and opposition*. (New Haven: Yale University Press).

—— (1989) *Democracy and Its Critics*. (New Haven: Yale University Press).

Declerq, Stefan (1994) 'Oxfam-België in Centraal Amerika en de Caraïben'. (San Salvador: mimeo).

De Feyter, Koen *et al.* (1995) *Development co-operation: A tool for the promotion of human rights and democratization*. (Antwerp: Institute for Development Policy and Management).

Delli Sante, Angela (1996) *Nightmare or Reality: Guatemala in the 1980s*. (Amsterdam: Thela Publishers).

Diamond, Larry (1994) 'Rethinking Civil Society: Towards democratic consolidation'. *Journal of Democracy*, Vol. 5, No. 3, pp. 4-17.

—— (1996) 'Is the third wave over?'. *Journal of Democracy*, Vol. 7, No. 3, pp. 20-37.

Diamond, Larry (ed.) (1992) *The Democratic Revolution: Struggles for Freedom and Pluralism in the Developing World*. (New York: Freedom House).

—— (1993) *Political Culture and Democracy in Developing Countries*. (Boulder: Lynne Rienner).

Diamond, Larry; Juan Linz and Seymour Martin Lipset (eds) (1989) *Democracy in Developing Countries: Latin America* (Volume Four). (Boulder: Lynne Rienner).

Diamond, Larry & Marc Plattner (eds) (1993) *The Global Resurgence of Democracy*. (Baltimore and London: The Johns Hopkins University Press).

—— (1995) *Economic Reform and Democracy*. (Baltimore: The Johns Hopkins University Press).

Dijk, Meine Pieter van (1992) 'Eindrapport Stuurgroep Impactstudie: Boekbespreking'. *International Spectator*, Vol. 46, No. 12, pp. 736-738.

—— (1994) 'The effectiveness of NGOs: Insights from the Danish, British and Dutch impact studies', in Hanisch und Wegner (Hrsg.), *Nichtregierungsorganisationen und Entwicklung*. (Hamburg: Deutsches Übersee Institut), pp. 27-42.

Dolan, Chris (1992) 'British development NGOs and advocacy in the 1990s', in Edwards and Hulme (eds), *Making a Difference*. (London: Earthscan), pp. 203-210.

Domínguez, Jorge (1997) 'Democratic transitions in Central America and Panama', in Domínguez and Lindenberg (eds), *Democratic Transitions in Central America*. (Gainesville, FL: University of Florida Press), pp. 1-31.

Domínguez, Jorge & Abraham Lowenthal (eds) (1996) *Constructing Democratic Governance: Latin America and the Caribbean in the 1990s*. (Baltimore and London: The Johns Hopkins University Press).

Douglas, James (1983) *Why Charity?: The Case for a Third Sector.* (Beverly Hill, CA: Sage).

Drake, Paul (1991) 'From good men to good neighbors: 1912-1932', in Lowenthal (ed.), *Exporting Democracy.* (Baltimore: The Johns Hopkins University Press), pp. 3-40.

Drake, Paul & Eduardo Silva (eds) (1986) *Elections and Democratization in Latin America, 1980-1985.* (San Diego: Center for Iberian and Latin American Studies).

Duffield, Mark (1993) 'NGOs, disaster relief and asset transfer in the Horn: Political survival in a permanent emergency'. *Development and Change,* Vol. 24, pp. 131-157.

—— (1995) 'Protracted political crises and the demise of developmentalism: From convergence to co-existence'. Paper presented to International Seminar 'Aid on Fire: Redefining Relief and Development Assistance in Unstable Situations', 7-9 April. (Wilton Park, Sussex: *mimeo*).

Duffield, Mark *et al.* (1994) 'Conclusion', in Macrae and Zwi (eds), *War and Hunger.* (London: Zed Books), pp. 222-232.

Dunkerly, James (1988) *Power in the Isthmus: A Political History of Modern Central America.* (London: Verso).

—— (1994) *The Pacification of Central America: Political Change in the Isthmus, 1987-1993.* (London: Verso).

Dunkerly, James & Rachel Sieder (1995) 'The Central American military: The challenge of transition'. Paper presented at the Congress of the Latin American Studies Association, September 28-30 (Washington: *mimeo*).

Edelman, Mark (1994) 'Three campesino activists'. *NACLA Report on the Americas,* Vol. 28, No. 3, pp. 30-33.

—— (1995) 'Organizing across the borders: The rise of a transnational peasant movement in Central America'. Paper presented at the Congress of the Latin American Studies Association, 28-30 September (Washington: *mimeo*).

Edwards, Beatrice & Gretta Tovar Siebentritt (1991) *Places of Origin: The Repopulation of Rural El Salvador.* (Boulder: Lynne Rienner).

Edwards, Michael (1993) 'Does the doormat influence the boot?': Critical thoughts on UK NGOs and international advocacy. *Development in Practice,* Vol. 3, No. 3, pp. 163-175.

—— (1996a) 'International development NGOs: Legitimacy, accountability, regulation and roles'. Paper prepared for TNI-workshop 'Re-inventing Solidarity: Private Aid Reconsidered', 5-6 June. (Amsterdam: *mimeo*).

—— (1996b) *NGO performance – what breeds success?* (London: Save the Children).

—— (1997) 'Organizational learning in non-governmental organizations: What have we learned?'. *Public Administration and Development,* Vol. 17, pp. 235-250.

Edwards, Michael & David Hulme (1994) 'NGOs and development: Performance and accountability in the new world order'. Background paper to the International Workshop on 'NGOs and Development', 27-29 June 1994. (Manchester: *mimeo*).

—— (1996) 'Too close for comfort?: The impact of official aid on nongovernmental organizations'. *World Development,* Vol. 24, No. 6, pp. 961-973.

Edwards, Michael & David Hulme (eds) (1992) *Making a Difference: NGOs and Development in a Changing World.* (London: Earthscan).

—— (1995) *Non-Governmental Organisations – Performance and Accountability: Beyond the Magic Bullet.* (London: Earthscan, Save the Children).

Eguizábal, Cristina *et al.* (eds) (1993) 'Humanitarian challenges in Central America: Learning the lessons of recent armed conflicts'. *Occasional Paper,* No. 14. (Providence RI: Watson Institute for International Studies).

Ekstermolengroep, De (1994) *Naakte keizers of volwaardige partners?: Rol en plaats van de NGO-beweging in de internationale samenwerking.* (Brussel: De Ekstermolengroep).

Ellacuría, Ignacio (1988) 'El significado del debate nacional'. *Estudios Centroamericanos*, Vol. 43, No. 478-479, pp. 713-729.

Elliott, Charles (1987a) 'Some aspects of relations between the North and the South in the NGO sector'. *World Development*, Vol. 15 (Supplement), pp. 57-68.

—— (1987b) *Comfortable Compassion?: Poverty, Power and the Church*. (London: Hodder and Stoughton).

Es, Yvonne; Jan Neggers and Floris Blankenberg (1996) 'Impact assessment: Making the most of what you've got'. Paper for the International Workshop on Evaluation of Social Development, 4-8 November. (Noordwijk: *mimeo*).

Escobar, Arturo & Sonia Alvarez (eds) (1992) *The Making of Social Movements in Latin America: Identity, Strategy, and Democracy*. (Boulder, CO: Westview Press).

Escoto, Jorge & Manfredo Marroquín (1992) *La AID en Guatemala: Poder y sector empresarial*. (Managua-Guatemala: CRIES-AVANCSO).

Esman, Milton & Norman Uphoff (1984) *Local Organizations: Intermediaries in Rural Development*. (New York: Cornell University Press).

Evans, Peter; Dietrich Rueschemeyer and Theda Skocpol (eds) (1985) *Bringing the State Back in*. (Cambridge: Cambridge University Press).

Evans, Trevor *et al.* (1995) *Structural Adjustment and the Public Sector in Central America and the Caribbean*. (Managua: CRIES).

Evers, Tilman (1982) 'European Social Democracy in Latin America: The case of Germany', in Pearce (ed.), *The European Challenge*. (London: Latin American Bureau), pp. 80-129.

Everts, Rob *et al.* (1996) 'Advocacy and negotiation: A process for changing institutional and governmental policies'. *Working paper*. (Silver Spring, MD: Center for Democratic Education).

EZE (1994) 'Promoting Democracy in Africa: The Role of Governmental and Church Development Cooperation'. *Report of Workshop*, 7-8 June. (Bonn: EZE).

Fagen, Richard (1987) *Forging Peace: The Challenge of Central America*. (New York: Basil Blackwell-PACCA).

Falk, Richard (1995a) *On Humane Governance: Toward a New Global Politics*. (University Park, PA: The Pennsylvania State University Press).

—— (1995b) 'The world order between inter-state law and the law of humanity: The role of civil society institutions', in Archibugi and Held (eds), *Cosmopolitan Democracy*. (Cambridge: Polity Press), pp. 163-179.

Falla, Ricardo (1994) *Massacres in the Jungle: Ixcán, Guatemala, 1975-1982*. (Boulder, CO: Westview Press).

Farrington, John; Anthony Bebbington, Kate Wellard and David Lewis (1993) *Reluctant Partners?: Non-Governmental Organizations, the State and Sustainable Agricultural Development*. (London: Routledge).

Ferraté, Luis (1995) 'El ciclo de los proyectos en el BID y la participación de las organizaciones de la sociedad civil'. Conferencia regional sobre el fortalecimiento de la sociedad civil en Centroamérica, Panamá, y República Dominicana, 27 al 29 de noviembre de 1995. (San José: *mimeo*).

Fine, Robert (1997) 'Civil society theory, enlightenment and critique'. *Democratization*, Vol. 4, No. 1, pp. 7-28.

Finsterbusch, Kurt & Warren Van Wicklin III (1987) 'The contribution of beneficiary participation to development project effectiveness'. *Public Administration and Development*, Vol. 7, No. 1, pp. 1-23.

Fisher, Julie (1993) *The Road from Rio: Sustainable Development and the Nongovernmental Movement in the Third World*. (Westport, CT: Praeger).

Fisher, Julie (1994) 'Is the iron law of oligarchy rusting away in the Third World?'. *World Development*, Vol. 22, No. 2, pp. 129-143.

—— (1998) *Nongovernments: NGOs and the Political Development of the Third World.* (West Hartfort, CT: Kumarian Press)

Foley, Michael (1995) 'Las ONGs y la sociedad civil en El Salvador', in Guido Béjar and Roggenbuck (eds), *Sociedad participativa en El Salvador.* (San Salvador: UCA-Fundación Konrad Adenauer), pp. 11-41.

—— (1996) 'Laying the groundwork: The struggle for civil society in El Salvador'. *Journal of Interamerican Studies and World Affairs*, Vol. 38, No. 1, pp. 67-103.

Foley, Michael & Bob Edwards (1996) 'The paradox of civil society'. *Journal of Democracy*, Vol. 7, No. 3, pp. 38-52.

Foley, Michael; Franzi Hasbún and Luis Córdova (1995) 'ONGs, desarrollo y democracia en El Salvador'. (San Salvador: *mimeo*).

Foweraker, Joe (1995) *Theorizing Social Movements.* (London: Pluto Press).

Fowler, Alan (1990) "Doing it better?: Where and how NGOs have a 'comparative advantage' in facilitating development". *AERDD Bulletin*, No. 28, pp. 11-20.

—— (1991) 'The role of NGOs in changing state-society relations: Perspectives from Eastern and Southern Africa'. *Development Policy Review*, Vol. 9, No. 1, pp. 53-84.

—— (1992) 'Distant obligations: Speculations on NGO funding and the global market'. *Review of African Political Economy*, No. 55, pp. 9-29.

—— (1993a) 'NGOs as agents of democratisation: An African perspective'. *Journal of International Development*, Vol. 5, No. 3, pp. 325-339.

—— (1993b) 'Non-governmental organisations and the promotion of democracy in Kenya'. *Unpublished dissertation*, (December). (Brighton: University of Sussex).

—— (1994) 'Capacity building and NGOs: Strengthening ladles for the global soup kitchen?'. *International Development*, Vol. 1, No. 1, pp. ????.

—— (1995) 'Assessing NGO performance: Difficulties, dilemmas and a way ahead', in Edwards and Hulme (eds), *Non-Governmental Organisations – Performance and Accountability.* (London: Earthscan), pp. 143-156.

—— (1996a) 'Authentic NGDO partnerships in the new policy agenda for international aid: Dead end or light ahead?'. Paper prepared for TNI-workshop 'Re-inventing Solidarity: Private Foreign Aid Reconsidered', 5-6 June 1996. (Amsterdam: *mimeo*).

—— (1996b) 'Strengthening civil society in transitional economies – From concept to strategy: Mapping an exit in a maze of mirrors', in Clayton (ed.), *NGOs, Civil Society and the State.* (Oxford: INTRAC), pp. 12-33.

—— (1997) *Striking a Balance: A Guide to Enhancing the Effectiveness of Non-Governmental Organisations in International Development.* (London: Earthscan).

Fowler, Alan & Kees Biekart (1996) 'Do private agencies really make a difference?', in Sogge *et al.* (eds), *Compassion and Calculation.* (London: Pluto Press), pp. 107-135.

Fowler, Alan & Rick James (1993) 'The role of southern NGOs in development co-operation', in DANIDA, *Strategi for Danidas NGO-samarbejde.* (Copenhagen: DANIDA-Udenrigsministeriet), pp. 82-107.

Fox, Jonathan (1992) 'Democratic rural development: Leadership accountability in regional peasant organizations'. *Development and Change*, Vol. 23, No. 2, pp. 1-36.

—— (1994) 'The difficult transition from clientelism to citizenship: Lessons from Mexico'. *World Politics*, Vol. 46, No. 2, pp. 151-184.

—— (1996) 'Assessing the impact of NGO advocacy campaigns on World Bank projects and policies: Analytical dilemmas'. Paper presented at the International Studies Association Convention, April 16-20 (*mimeo*).

Fox, Jonathan & David Brown (eds) (1998) *The Struggle for Accountability: The World Bank, NGOs, and Grassroots Movements*. (Cambridge, MA: MIT Press).

Frantz, Telmo Rudi (1987) 'The Role of NGOs in the strengthening of civil society'. *World Development*, Vol. 15 (Supplement), pp. 121-127.

Freire, Paulo (1972) *Pedagogy of the Oppressed*. (London: Sheed and Ward).

Freres, Christian (coord.) (1998) *La cooperación de las sociedades civiles de la Unión Europea con América Latina*. (Madrid: AIETI).

Freres, Christian & Jean Grugel (1994) 'Western European NGOs and political parties in the process of democratization and reconstruction in Central America'. Paper presented at the International Congress of the Latin American Studies Association, 10-12 March. (Atlanta: *mimeo*).

Freres, Christian; Alberto van Klaveren & Guadalupe Ruiz-Giménez (1992) 'Europa y América Latina: La busqueda de nuevas formas de cooperación'. *Síntesis*, No. 18, pp. 91-178.

Friedmann, John (1992) *Empowerment: The Politics of Alternative Development*. (Cambridge, MA: Blackwell).

—— (1996) 'Rethinking poverty: Empowerment and citizen rights'. *International Social Science Journal*, Vol. 14, No. 8, pp. 161-172.

Fukuyama, Francis (1989) 'The end of history?'. *The National Interest*, No. 16 (Summer), pp. 3-18.

—— (1995) *Trust: The Social Virtues and the Creation of Prosperity*. (New York: The Free Press).

Fundación Arias (1995) *Once enfoques de la cooperación internacional hacia Centroamérica*. (San José: Fundación Arias para la paz y el progreso humano).

Funes, Matías (1995) *Los deliberantes: El poder militar en Honduras*. (Tegucigalpa: Editorial Guaymuras).

Gálvez, Víctor & Evelyn Klüsmann (1992) 'Una nueva opción para el desarrollo: La articulación de las ONG's y los grupos de base en Guatemala'. (Guatemala: *mimeo*).

García, Evaristo *et al.* (1994) *Las migraciones forzadas en Centroamérica: Una visión actualizada de las ONG's*. (Managua: ARMIF).

Garoz, Byron *et al.* (1996) *Estudios base para una estratégia alternativa de desarrollo nacional*. (Guatemala: COINDE).

Garoz, Byron & Mandy Macdonald (1996) *La política de cooperación de la Unión Europea hacia Guatemala: Un análisis preliminar*, noviembre. (Guatemala-Aberdeen: ASC-CIFCA).

Garst, Rachel (1991) *Las ONGs centroamericanas ante la cooperación externa: Elementos para el diseño de una estrategia de incidencia en los espacios de acción y decisión*. (San José: CCOD).

—— (1993) *Ixcán: Colonización, desarraigo, y condiciones de retorNo*. (Guatemala: COINDE).

Garst, Rachel & Tom Barry (1990) *Feeding the Crisis: US Food Aid and Farm Policy in Central America*. (Lincoln: University of Nebraska Press).

Gellner, Ernest (1994) *Conditions of Liberty: Civil Society and its Rivals*. (London: Hamish Hamilton).

Ghai, Dharam & Jessica Vivian (eds) (1992) *Grassroots Environmental Action: People's Participation in Sustainable Development*. (London: Routledge).

Gills, Barry; Joel Rocamora and Richard Wilson (eds) (1993) *Low Intensity Democracy: Political Power in the New World Order*. (London: Pluto Press).

González, Víctor (1992) *Las organizaciones no-gubernamentales (ONGs): Una nueva expresión de la sociedad civil salvadoreña*. (San Salvador: PREIS).

Goodman, Louis; Johanna Mendelson and Juan Rial (eds) (1990) *The Military and Democracy: The Future of Civil-Military Relations in Latin America*. (Lexington, MA: Lexington Books).

Goodman, Louis; William Leogrande and Johanna Mendelson (eds) (1992) *Political Parties and Democracy in Central America*. (Boulder: Westview Press).

Gordenker, Leon & Thomas Weiss (1995) 'Pluralising global governance: Analytical approaches and dimensions'. *Third World Quarterly*, Vol. 16, No. 3, pp. 357-387.

Gorostiaga, Xabier (1988) 'Nordic initiatives for furthering regional peace and cooperation in Central America: A Central American perspective'. Presentation at the Nordic Seminar on Central America, 25-26 May. (Stockholm: *mimeo*).

—— (1993) 'An ambiguous democracy: Democratization in Latin America viewed from Central American standpoints'. *International Symposium 'Is Democracy taking Root in Latin America?'*, 27 January. (Tokyo: Latin American Association).

Graaf, Martin de; Sam Moyo and Ton Dietz (1991) 'Non-Governmental Organisations in Zimbabwe'. *NGO-landenstudie Zimbabwe/Impactstudie Medefinancieringsprogramma*, June. (Oegstgeest: GOM).

Grabendorff, Wolf (1984) 'West European perceptions of the crisis in Central America', in Grabendorff, Krumwiede and Todt (eds), *Political Change in Central America: Internal and External Dimensions*. (Boulder: Westview Press), pp. 285-297.

—— (1992) 'The party internationals and democracy in Central America', in Goodman *et al.* (eds), *Political Parties and Democracy in Central America*. (Boulder, CO: Westview Press), pp. 355-368.

—— (1996) 'International support for democracy in contemporary Latin America: The role of the party internationals', in Whitehead (ed.), *The International Dimensions of Democratization*. (Oxford: Oxford University Press), pp. 201-226.

Gramajo, Héctor (1997) 'Political transition in Guatemala, 1980-1990: A perspective from inside Guatemala's army', in Domínguez and Lindenberg (eds), *Democratic Transitions in Central America*. (Gainesville, FL: University of Florida Press), pp. 111-138.

Gramsci, Antonio (1971) *Selections from the Prison Notebooks*. (London: Lawrence and Wishart).

Grigsby, Arturo (1995) 'The free trade area of the Americas: Small boats on a rising tide'. *CIIR Conference Report, 'Central America in the New World Context'*, 10 January 1995. (London: CIIR).

Grugel, Jean (1996) 'Supporting democratisation: A European View — European political parties and Latin America'. *European Review of Latin American and Caribbean Studies*, No. 60 (June), pp. 87-104.

Guido Béjar, Rafael (1995) 'Reflexiones sobre movimientos sociales, la sociedad civil y los partidos políticos en El Salvador de post guerra', in Guido Béjar and Roggenbuck (eds), *Sociedad participativa en El Salvador*. (San Salvador: UCA-Fundación Konrad Adenauer), pp. 157-177.

Guido Béjar, Rafael & Stefan Roggenbuck (eds) (1995) *Sociedad participativa en El Salvador*. (San Salvador: UCA-Fundación Konrad Adenauer).

Gutiérrez, Edgar (1997) 'Derechos humanos y sociedad civil en la difícil transición guatemalteca', in Birk (ed.) *Guatemala: ¿Oprimida, pobre o princesa embrujada?*, (Guatemala: Friedrich Ebert Stiftung), pp. 19-87.

Hadenius, Axel & Fredrik Uggla (1996) 'Making civil society work, promoting development: What can states and donors do?'. *World Development*, Vol. 24, No. 10, pp. 1621-1639.

Halliday, Fred (1994) *Rethinking International Relations*. (London: MacMillan Press).

Hamelink, Cees (1997) 'Making moral choices in development cooperation: The agenda for ethics', in Hamelink (ed.), *Ethics and Development*. (Kampen: Kok), pp. 11-24.

Hanisch, Rolf & Rodger Wegner (Hrsg.) (1995) *Nichtregierungsorganisationen und Entwicklung: Auf dem Wege zur mehr Realismus*. (Hamburg: Deutsches Übersee-Institut).

Hansen, Finn (1995) 'Decentralization and local organizations in Central America'. *Report*, No. 2 (September). (Copenhagen: Ibis).

—— (1996) *Relaciones Europa-Centroamérica: Ayuda externa y comercio desfavorable*. (Managua: CRIES).

Hansen, Finn (1997) 'La cooperación de la Unión Europea hacia Centroamérica: Tendencias ante el nuevo milenio'. *Pensamiento Propio* (Nueva Epoca), Vol. 2, No. 5, pp. 3-18.

Hansen, Gary (1996) 'Constituencies for reform: Strategic approaches for donor funded civil advocacy programs'. *USAID Program and Operations Department Assessment Report*, No. 12 (Washington, DC: USAID-Center for Development Information and Evaluation).

Harbeson, John; Donald Rothchild and Naomi Chazan (eds) (1994) *Civil Society and the State in Africa*. (Boulder, CO: Lynne Rienner).

Hardeman, Jan *et al.* (1995) 'Se dice... exigimos créditos ágiles y oportunos: Evaluación programática de actividades generadores de ingresos de contrapartes de ICCO en El Salvador'. *DGIS programme evaluations of the co-financing programme*, No. 56. (The Hague: DGIS/ICCO).

Haynes, Jeff (1997) *Democracy and Civil Society in the Third World: Politics and New Political Movements*. (Cambridge: Polity Press).

Heijningen, Hans van (1994) *¿Una contrarrevolución campesina?: Análisis de las contradicciones entre el campesinado de la Región-V de Nicaragua y el gobierno Sandinista (1979-1990)*. (Nijmegen: Derde Wereld Centrum).

Held, David (1995) *Democracy and the Global Order: From the Modern State to Cosmopolitan Governance*. (London: Polity Press).

Held, David (ed.) (1993) *Prospects for Democracy: North, South, East, West*. (Cambridge: Polity Press).

Hellinger, Stephen; Douglas Hellinger and Fred O'Regan (1988) *Aid for Just Development: Report on the Future of Foreign Assistance*. (Boulder, CO: Lynne Rienner).

Hernández, Jorge (1992) 'Para la evaluación del Congreso Constitutivo de ASOCODE', 6 de enero de 1992. (San José: *mimeo*).

—— (1994) 'ASOCODE: Challenges and perspectives for the Central American peasant movement', in Biekart and Jelsma (eds), *Peasants beyond Protest in Central America*. (Amsterdam: Transnational Institute), pp. 85-110.

Hernández Pico, Juan (1995) 'El desafío centroamericano: Producir y participar'. *Envío*, No. 156 (Enero-Febrero), pp. 44-55.

Herrera, Vilma (ed.) (1995) *Centroamérica en cifras 1980-1992*. (San José: FLACSO).

Hertogs, Erik Jan (1985) 'Western European responses to revolutionary developments in the Caribbean Basin region', in Irvin and Gorostiaga (eds), *Towards an Alternative for Central America and the Caribbean*. (London: George Allen and Unwin), pp. 69-83.

Hewitt, Adrian (ed.) (1994) 'Crisis or transition in foreign aid'. *Special Report*. (London: Overseas Development Institute).

Hewitt, Adrian & Tony Killick (1996) 'Bilateral aid conditionality and policy leverage', in Stokke (ed.), *Foreign Aid Towards the Year 2000*. (London: Frank Cass), pp. 130-167.

Higley, John & Richard Gunther (eds) (1992) *Elites and Democratic Consolidation in Latin America and Southern Europe*. (Cambridge: Cambridge University Press).

Hippler, Jochen (1995) 'Democratisation of the Third World after the end of the Cold War', in Hippler (ed.), *The Democratisation of Disempowerment*. (London: Pluto Press), pp. 1-31.

Hirschman, Albert (1984) *Getting Ahead Collectively: Grassroots Experiences in Latin America*. (New York: Pergamon Press).

HIVOS (1991) Seminario 'Democratización en América Latina y el Caribe'. 3-7 de noviembre de 1991. (Heredia, Costa Rica: *mimeo*).

Hoebink, Paul (1994) 'De impact van de impactstudie: Medefinancierings-organisaties in verandering'. *Derde Wereld*, Vol. 12, No. 4, pp. 25-38.

—— (1995) 'De effectiviteit van de hulp: Een literatuuroverzicht van macro- naar micro-niveau's'. *Focus on Development*, No. 2, September. (The Hague: DGIS).

Holt, Eric (1988) 'Las ONG y la crisis en Centroamérica'. (Managua: *mimeo*).

Hook, Steven (ed.) (1996) *Foreign Aid toward the Milennium*. (Boulder: Lynne Rienner).

Howes, Mick (1992) 'Linking paradigms and practice: Key issues in the appraisal, monitoring and evaluation of British NGO projects'. *Journal of International Development*, Vol. 4, No. 4, pp. 375-396.

Howes, Mick & M. Sattar (1992) 'Bigger and better?: Scaling-up strategies pursued by BRAC 1972-1991', in Edwards and Hulme (eds), *Making a Difference*. (London: Earthscan), pp. 99-110.

Højrup Jensen, Malene (1995) 'Project study of FUNDADESE on local organisation and development'. *Working Paper*, No. 3 (June). (Copenhagen: Ibis).

Huber, Evelyne *et al.* (1997) 'The paradoxes of contemporary democracy: Formal, participatory and social dimensions'. *Comparative Politics*, Vol. 29, No. 3, (April), pp. 323-342.

Hulme, David & Michael Edwards (eds) (1997) *NGOs, States and Donors: Too Close for Comfort?*. (London: MacMillan Press).

Huntington, Samuel (1991) *The Third Wave: Democratization in the Late Twentieth Century*. (Norman: University of Oklahoma Press).

Hyden, Goran (1995) 'Assisting the growth of civil society: How might it be improved?'. Paper presented to the DAC-workshop 'Civil Society and Democracy', 12-13 June. (Uppsala: *mimeo*).

Hydén, Therese (1996) 'Implications of international human rights law in domestic legislation and practice in Central America: The cases of Costa Rica and Honduras'. *Thesis in International Law*, May. (Lund: Raoul Wallenberg Institute of Human Rights and International Law, Lund University).

Ibis (1995) 'Annual report Central America'. (Guatemala: *mimeo*).

ICIC (1994) 'Propuesta ante la Conferencia Internacional de Paz y Desarrollo en Centroamérica', 24-25 de octubre. (Tegucigalpa: *mimeo*).

—— (1995a) 'Perspectivas del proceso de San José'. Ponencia de Wilson Campos presentado al seminario de IRELA, Mayo. (San José: *mimeo*).

—— (1995b) 'Resumen del trabajo de la ICIC en el primer semestre de 1995', Agosto. (Managua: *mimeo*).

—— (1996a) 'Documento de consulta para el proceso previo a la Segunda Asamblea de la ICIC', Marzo. (Managua: *mimeo*).

—— (1996b) 'Segunda Asamblea General: Documento de propuestas', Agosto. (Guatemala: *mimeo*).

IICA (1993) *La política del sector agropecuario frente a la mujer productora de alimentos en Centroamérica y Panamá: Conclusiones y recomendaciones*. (San José: IICA-BID).

Ianni, Vanna (1998) 'El concepto de la sociedad civil en la cooperación internacional al desarrollo de los años 90: Una mirada particular a América Latina'. *Documento de Trabajo*, No. 1 (Madrid: AIETI).

Inforpress (1995) *Guatemala 1986-1994, Compendio del proceso de paz (Vol. 1): Cronologías, análisis, documentos, acuerdos*. (Guatemala: Inforpress Centroamericana).

—— (1996) *Guatemala 1995-1996, Compendio del proceso de paz (Vol. 2): Cronologías, análisis, documentos, acuerdos*. (Guatemala: Inforpress Centroamericana).

IRELA (1994a) *Diez años del proceso de San José: Un balance de la cooperación Unión Europea-América Central*. (Madrid: Comisión Europea-IRELA).

—— (1994b) 'La cooperación europea hacia América Latina en los 90: Una relación en transición'. *Dossier*, No. 51(Diciembre). (Madrid: IRELA).

Jäger, Johannes (1996) 'Macht- oder Gegenmachtstrategien in El Salvador?'. *Journal für Entwicklungspolitik*, Vol. 12, No. 3, pp. 317-330.

Jelin, Elizabeth & Eric Hershberg (eds) (1996) *Constructing Democracy: Human Rights, Citizenship, and Society in Latin America*. (Boulder, CO: Westview Press).

Jelsma, Martin & Edgar Celada (eds) (1997) *Centroamérica: Gobernabilidad y narcotráfico*. (Guatemala: Fundación Heinrich Böll-Transnational Institute).

Jelsma, Martin & Theo Roncken (coord.) (1998) *Democracias bajo fuego: Drogas y poder en América Latina*. (Montevideo: Ediciones Brecha-TNI-Acción Andina).

Jepma, Catrinus (1995) 'On the effectiveness of development aid'. *Focus on Development*, No. 1, September. (The Hague: DGIS).

Johnstone, Ian (1995) *Rights and Reconciliation: UN Strategies in El Salvador*. (Boulder, CO: Lynne Rienner Publishers).

Jonas, Susanne (1991) *The Battle for Guatemala: Rebels, Death Squads, and US Power*. (Boulder: Westview Press).

—— (1996) 'Dangerous liaisons: The US in Guatemala'. *Foreign Policy*, No. 103, pp. 144-160.

Jordan, Lisa & Peter van Tuijl (1997) 'Political responsibility in NGO advocacy: Exploring emerging shapes of global democracy'. June. (The Hague: *mimeo*).

Junkov, Micael (1994) 'Plan estratégico y de acción para la integración de conservación y desarrollo: Las ONG's de ADEP, FUNDAR y FUNDADESE'. Octubre. (San José: *mimeo*).

Kaimowitz, David (1993) 'NGOs, the state and agriculture in Central America', in Bebbington and Thiele (eds), *Non-Governmental Organizations and the State in Latin America*. (London: Routledge), pp. 178-198.

Kamsteeg, Frans (1996) 'NGO's en effectiviteit: Een Chileense case-studie'. *Derde Wereld*, Vol. 14, No. 3, pp. 324-338.

Kanter, Rosabeth Moss & David Summers (1987) 'Doing well while doing good: Dilemmas of performance measurement in non-profit organizations and the need for a multiple-constituency approach', in Powell (ed.), *The Nonprofit Sector: A Research Handbook*. (New Haven: Yale University Press), pp. 154-166.

Kaplan, Allan (1996) *The Development Practioners' Handbook*. (London: Pluto Press).

Karl, Terry Lynn (1990) 'Dilemmas of democratization in Latin America'. *Comparative Politics*, Vol. 23, No. 1, pp. 1-21.

—— (1992) 'El Salvador's negotiated revolution'. *Foreign Affairs*, Vol. 71, No. 2, pp. 147-164.

—— (1995) 'The hybrid regimes of Central America'. *Journal of Democracy*, Vol. 6, No. 3, pp. 72-86.

Keane, John (ed.) (1988) *Civil Society and the State: New European Perspectives*. (London: Verso).

Keck, Margaret & Kathryn Sikkink (1998) *Activists without Borders: Advocacy Networks in International Politics*. (Ithaca, NY: Cornell University Press).

Keogh, Dermot (ed.) (1990) *Church and Politics in Latin America*. (London: MacMillan).

Klare, Michael & Peter Kornbluh (eds) (1988) *Low-Intensity Warfare: Counterinsurgency, Proinsurgency and Antiterrorism in the Eighties*. (New York: Pantheon Books).

Klaveren, Alberto van (1986) 'Europa y la democratización de América Latina'. *Nueva Sociedad*, No. 85 (Sept-Oct), pp. 134-140.

Kolk, Ans (1996) *Forests in International Environmental Politics: International Organisations, NGOs and the Brazilian Amazon*. (Utrecht: International Books).

Koppel, Bruce (1993) 'The prospects for democratization in Southeast Asia: Local perspectives and international roles'. *Journal of Northeast Asian Studies*, Vol. 12, No. 3, pp. 4-33.

Kopsch, Uwe (1987) 'Grenzen und Möglichkeiten transnationaler Parteienkooperation am Beispiel der Sozialistischen Internationale in Lateinamerika'. *Zeitschrift für Lateinamerika Wien*, Jg. 1987, No. 33, pp. 51-64.

Korten, David (1986) 'Micro-policy reform: The role of private voluntary development agencies'. *NASPAA Working Paper*, No. 12. (Washington: NASPAA).

Korten, David (1987) 'Third generation NGO strategies: A key to people-centered development'. *World Development*, Vol. 15 (Supplement), pp. 145-159.

—— (1990) *Getting to the 21st Century: Voluntary Action and the Global Agenda*. (West Hartford, CT: Kumarian Press).

—— (1995) *When Corporations Rule the World*. (London: Earthscan).

Kruijt, Dirk (1992) 'Monopolios de filantropía: El caso de las llamadas "organizaciones no gubernamentales" en América Latina'. *Polémica* (San José), No. 16 (Enero-abril), pp. 41-47.

—— (1994) 'De private publieke sector'. *Derde Wereld*, Vol. 12, No. 4, pp. 97-105.

Kruse, Stein-Erik *et al.* (1997) 'Searching for impact and methods: NGO evaluation synthesis study' (Volume 1, Main Report): A report prepared for the OECD-DAC Expert Group on Evaluation. *Blue Series*, No. 8 (May). (Helsinki: Ministry of Foreign Affairs of Finland).

Krut, Riva (1997) 'Globalization and civil society: NGO influence in international decision-making'. *Discussion Paper*, No. 83 (April). (Geneva: UNRISD).

Krznaric, Roman (1997) 'Guatemalan returnees and the dilemma of political mobilisation'. *Journal of Refugee Studies*, Vol. 10, No. 1, pp. 61-78.

LaFeber, Walter (1993) *Inevitable Revolutions: The United States in Central America* (2nd edition). (New York: Norton and Company).

Lambregts, Ruud (1996) 'From "protesta" to "propuesta": NGOs in Latin America'. *NOVIB Network*, Vol. 2, No. 2, pp. 6-7.

Lapper, Richard & James Painter (1985) *Honduras: State for Sale*. (London: Latin America Bureau).

Le Bot, Yvon (1992) *La guerre en terre maya: Communauté, violence et modernité au Guatemala*. (Paris: Éditions Karthala).

Lechner, Norbert (1995) 'La problemática invocación de la sociedad civil'. *Espacios* (San José), No. 4, pp. 4-13.

Leftwich, Alan (ed.) (1996) *Democracy and Development*. (Cambridge: Polity Press).

Lehmann, David (1990) *Democracy and Development in Latin America: Economics, Politics and Religion in the Post-War Period*. (Cambridge: Polity Press).

Levy, Daniel (1996) *Building the Third Sector: Latin America's Private Research Centers and Non-Profit Development*. (Pittsburgh, PA: University of Pittsburgh Press).

Lewis, David (1990) 'NGOs and international aid in Central America: The development dialogue between North and South'. Paper presented at the CCIC consultation 'NGOs and North-South Dialogue in the 1990s', Quebec, Canada, 8-12 May 1990. (Managua: *mimeo*).

Lieten, Kristoffel & Fons van der Velden (red.) (1997) *Grenzen aan de hulp: Beleid en effecten van ontwikkelingssamenwerking*. (Amsterdam: Het Spinhuis).

Lindenberg, Marc (1997) 'Recent Central American transitions: Conclusions and policy implications', in Domínguez and Lindenberg (eds), *Democratic Transitions in Central America*. (Gainesville, FL: University of Florida Press), pp. 180-194.

Linz, Juan & Alfred Stepan (1996) *Problems of Democratic Transition and Consolidation: Southern Europe, South America, and Post-Communist Europe*. (Baltimore: The Johns Hopkins University Press).

Lipschutz, Ronnie (1992) 'Reconstructing world politics: The emergence of global civil society'. *Millenium: Journal of International Studies*, Vol. 21, No. 3, pp. 389-420.

Lissner, Jorgen (1977) *The Politics of Altruism: A study of the Political Behaviour of Voluntary Development Agencies*. (Geneva: Lutheran World Federation).

Lowenthal, Abraham (ed.) (1991) *Exporting Democracy: The United States and Latin America*. (Baltimore: The Johns Hopkins University Press).

Luckham, Robin & Gordon White (eds) (1996) *Democratization in the South: The Jagged Wave*. (Manchester: Manchester University Press).

Lungo, Mario (1990) *El Salvador en los 80: Contrainsurgencia y revolución*. (San José: EDUCA-FLACSO).

—— (1993) 'Los obstaculos a la democratización en El Salvador'. *El Salvador en construcción*, No. 11 (Agosto), pp. 21-32.

—— (1995) 'Building an alternative: The formation of a popular project', in Sinclair (ed.), *The New Politics of Survival*. (New York: Monthly Review Press), pp. 153-179.

MacDonald, Geraldine (1998) 'Alternative perspectives on building peace in Colombia and El Salvador'. Doctoral thesis University of Bradford. (Bradford: *mimeo*).

Macdonald, Laura (1994) 'Globalising civil society: Interpreting international NGOs in Central America'. *Millenium: Journal of International Studies*, Vol. 23, No. 2, pp. 267-285.

—— (1997) *Supporting Civil Society: The Political Role of Non-Governmental Organizations in Central America*. (London: MacMillan Press).

Macdonald, Mandy & Mike Gatehouse (1995) *In the Mountains of Morazan: Portrait of a Returned Refugee Community in El Salvador*. (London: Latin America Bureau).

Macdonald, Mandy *et al.* (1997) 'La cooperación de la Unión Europea hacia Guatemala: ¿Participación o paternalismo?'. *Informe de investigación*, Noviembre. (Guatemala: ASC-CIFCA).

Maghroori, Ray & Bennet Ramberg (eds) (1982) *Globalism versus Realism: International Relations' Third Debate*. (Boulder, CO: Westview Press).

Maihold, Günther (1994) 'Representación política y sociedad civil en Centroamérica', in Carballo y Maihold (comp.), *¿Qué será de Centroamérica?*. (San José: FES-CEDAL), pp. 203-223.

Mainwaring, Scott & Timothy Scully (eds) (1995) *Building Democratic Institutions: Party Systems in Latin America*. (Stanford: Stanford University Press).

Mainwaring, Scott; Guillermo O'Donnell and Samuel Valenzuela (eds) (1992) *Issues in Democratic Consolidation: The New South American Democracies in Comparative Perspective*. (South Bend: University of Notre Dame Press).

Mair, Stefan (1997) 'The role of the German "Stiftungen" in the process of democratisation'. *ECDPM Working Paper*, No. 32. (Maastricht: ECDPM).

Maldonado, Mario (1998) 'Centroamérica: Guerra después de la guerra', in Jelsma and Roncken (coord.), *Democracias bajo fuego*. (Montevideo: Ediciones Brecha-TNI-Acción Andina), pp. 153-170.

Malena, Carmen (1995) 'Relations between Northern and Southern non-governmental development organizations'. *Canadian Journal of Development Studies*, Vol. 16, No. 1, pp. 7-30.

Mangelschots, Daniela & Xiomara Ventura (1994) 'El impacto político de la cooperación no-gubernamental europea en Centroamérica: Caso de Honduras'. Informe de investigación PRISMA-TNI. (Tegucigalpa: *mimeo*).

Manor, James (ed.) (1991) *Rethinking Third World Politics*. (London: Longman).

Marcussen, Henrik Secher (1996) 'Comparative advantages of NGOs: Myths and realities', in Stokke (ed.), *Foreign Aid Towards the Year 2000*. (London: Frank Cass), pp. 259-285.

Maren, Michael (1997) *The Road to Hell: The Ravaging Effects of Foreign Aid and International Charity*. (New York: The Free Press).

Marsden, David & Peter Oakley (1990) *Evaluating Social Development Projects*. (Oxford: OXFAM).

Marsden, David; Peter Oakley and Brian Pratt (1994) *Measuring the Process: Guidelines for Evaluating Social Development*. (Oxford: INTRAC).

Martell, Allan (1994) 'El impacto político de la cooperación no-gubernamental europea en El Salvador (1981-1994)'. Informe de la investigación PRISMA-TNI. (San Salvador: *mimeo*).

Martin, Pauline (1991) 'La agenda de la cooperación externa para Centroamérica', in CCOD, *III consulta internacional sobre cooperación externa con Centroamérica*. (Guatemala: CCOD-COINDE), pp. 24-33.

Martinussen, John (1997) *Society, State and Market: A Guide to Competing Theories of Development*. (London: Zed Books).

McClintock, Michael (1985) *The American Connection, Volume II: State Terror and Popular Resistance in Guatemala*. (London: Zed Books).

Melrose, Dianna (1985) *Nicaragua: The Threat of a Good Example?*. (Oxford: OXFAM).

Méndez, Homero (1988) 'Análisis de la proyección de ADESE'. Evaluation report for OXFAM-America, Julio. (Guatemala: *mimeo*).

Méndez, María Elena & Leticia Salomón (1995) *El caso Riccy*, Agosto. (Tegucigalpa: CEM-H).

Menjívar, Rafael (1992) 'La concertación en la estrategia de desarrollo de Centroamérica', in Stein and Arias (coord.), *Democracia sin pobreza*. (San José: DEI-CADESCA), pp. 305-346.

Meyer, Carrie (1992) 'A step back as donors shift institution building from the public to the "private" sector'. *World Development*, Vol. 20, No. 8, pp. 1115-1126.

Middleton, Neil & Phil O'Keefe (1998) *Disaster and Development: The Politics of Humanitarian Aid*. (London: Pluto Press).

Molenaar, Klaas *et al.* (1997) ''El grupo meta somos nosotros...': Evaluación programática de actividades de generación de ingresos de las contrapartes de HIVOS en Centroamérica y Granada''. *DGIS programme evaluations of the co-financing programme*, No. 62. (The Hague: DGIS/HIVOS).

Montes, Segundo (1988) 'Clases y movimientos sociales en El Salvador: Caracterización, desarrollo e intervención'. *Realidad Económico-Social*, Vol. 1, No. 4, pp. 305-332.

Montgomery, Tommie Sue (1995) *Revolution in El Salvador: From Civil Strive to Civil Peace* (2nd ed.). (Boulder: Westview Press).

Moore, Barrington (1966) *The Social Origins of Dictatorship and Democracy*. (Harmondsworth: Penguin Books).

Moore, Mick (1995) 'Promoting good government by supporting institutional development?'. *IDS Bulletin*, Vol. 26, No. 2, pp. 89-96.

Morales, Abelardo (1994) 'Debate Nacional por la Paz en El Salvador: Informe de evaluación externa de los programas', Diciembre. (San Salvador: *mimeo*).

—— (1995a) *Oficios de paz y posguerra en Centroamérica*. (San José: FLACSO).

—— (1995b) 'Democracia y ONGs en Centroamérica'. *Papeles*, No. 55, pp. 29-36.

Morales, Abelardo & Martha Isabel Cranshaw (1997) *Regionalismo emergente: Redes de la sociedad civil e integración en Centroamérica*. (San José: FLACSO-Ibis).

Moreno, Dario (1994) *The Struggle for Peace in Central America*. (Gainesville, FL: University Press of Florida).

Moßmann, Peter (1995) 'Nicht-Regierungsorganisationen als quasi-föderale Stütze für Demokratie und relativ autonome Entwicklung?', in Hanisch and Wegner (Hrsg.), *Nichtregierungsorganisationen und Entwicklung*. (Hamburg: Deutsches Übersee-Institut), pp. 177-191.

Mujal-León, Eusebio (1987) 'Europa Occidental y los procesos de democratización en América Latina'. *Contribuciones* (Buenos Aires), Dossier '87, pp. 81-92.

—— (1989) *European Socialism and the Conflict in Central America*. (New York: Center for Strategic and International Studies-Praeger).

Munck, Gerardo (1994) 'Democratic transitions in comparative perspective'. *Comparative Politics*, Vol. 26, No. 3, pp. 355-375.

Munck, Ronaldo (1989) *Latin America: The Transition to Democracy*. (London: Zed Books).

—— (1993) 'Beyond electoralism in El Salvador: Conflict resolution through negotiated compromise'. *Third World Quarterly*, Vol. 14, No. 1, pp. 75-93.

Munting, Monique & Hans Peter Dejgaard (1994) 'Estrategia de cooperación con la región centroamericana'. Informe de consultaría para la Comisión Europea, Marzo. (Bruselas: *mimeo*).

Murray, Kevin (1995) *Inside El Salvador: The Essential Guide to its Politics, Economy, Society, and Environment*. (Albuquerque, NM: Resource Center Press).

Murray, Kevin *et al.* (1994) 'Rescuing reconstruction: The debate on post-war economic recovery in El Salvador'. *Hemisphere Initiatives Reports*, May 1994. (Cambridge, MA: Hemisphere Initiatives).

Najam, Adil (1996) 'NGO accountability: A conceptual framework'. *Development Policy Review*, Vol. 14, No. 4, pp. 339-353.

NAR (1992) 'Recommendation on private organisations and society building'. *NAR Advies*, No. 100. (The Hague: National Advisory Council for Development Cooperation).

Natsios, Andrew (1996) 'NGOs and the UN system in complex emergencies: Conflict or cooperation?', in Weiss and Gordenker (eds), *NGOs, the UN and Global Governance*. (Boulder: Lynne Rienner), pp. 67-81.

Ndegwa, Stephen N. (1996) *The Two Faces of Civil Society: NGOs and Politics in Africa*. (West Hartford, CT: Kumarian Press).

Nerfin, Marc (1992) 'The relationship NGOs, UN agencies, governments: Challenges, possibilities and prospects', in IBASE-UNDP, *Development, International Cooperation and the NGOs*. (Rio de Janeiro: IBASE-PNUD), pp. 79-96.

Niekerk, Nico van (1994) 'Desarrollo rural en los Andes: Un estudio sobre los programas de desarrollo de Organizaciones no Gubernamentales'. *Leiden Development Studies*, No. 13. (Leiden: Leiden University).

Noé Pino, Hugo & Mario Posas (1991) 'Honduras: Fuerzas sociales y sus proyectos'. *Cuadernos Cries*, No. 20, pp. 67-83.

Noël, Alain & Jean-Philippe Thérien (1995) 'From domestic to international justice: the welfare state and foreign aid'. *International Organization*, Vol. 49, No. 3, pp. 523-553.

Norsworthy, Kent & Tom Barry (1994) *Inside Honduras: The Essential Guide to its Politics, Economy, Society, and Environment*. (Albuquerque, NM: Resource Center Press).

Nunnenkamp, Peter (1995) 'What donors mean by good governance: Heroic ends, limited means, and traditional dilemmas of development cooperation'. *IDS Bulletin*, Vol. 26, No. 2, pp. 9-16.

Núñez Aguilar, Fidelina & María Consuelo Gámez (1994) 'El proyecto alternativo del movimiento popular de Honduras'. *Ciencias Sociales* (San José), No. 63 (Marzo), pp. 25-36.

O'Brien, David & Luciano Catenacci (1996) 'Towards a framework for local democracy in a war-torn society: The lessons of selected foreign assistance programmes in El Salvador'. *Democratization*, Vol. 3, No. 4 (Winter), pp. 435-458.

O'Connell, Helen & David Souter (eds) (1994) *Good Governance: Report of a One World Action Seminar*. (London: One World Action).

O'Donnell, Guillermo (1988) 'Challenges to democratization in Brazil'. *World Policy Journal*, Vol. 5, No. 2, pp. 281-300.

—— (1993) 'On the state, democratization and some conceptual problems: A Latin American view with glances at some postcommunist countries'. *World Development*, Vol. 21, No. 8, pp. 1355-1369.

O'Donnell, Guillermo & Philippe Schmitter (1986) 'Transitions from authoritarian rule: Tentative conclusions about uncertain democracies', in O'Donnell *et al.* (eds), *Transitions from Authoritarian Rule (Part 4)*. (Baltimore: The Johns Hopkins University Press).

O'Donnell, Guillermo; Philippe Schmitter and Laurence Whitehead (eds) (1986) *Transitions from Authoritarian Rule: Prospects for Democracy*. (Baltimore: The Johns Hopkins University Press).

Oakley, Peter (1996) 'Evaluating Social Development: Outcomes and Impact'. Background paper for the International Workshop on the Evaluation of Social Development, 4-8 November. (Noordwijk: *mimeo*).

Oakley, Peter; Brian Pratt and Andrew Clayton (1998) 'Outcomes and Impact: Evaluating Change in Social Development'. *NGO Management and Policy Series*, No. 6. (Oxford: INTRAC).

ODC and The Synergos Institute (1995) *Strengthening Civil Society's Contribution to Development: The Role of Official Development Assistance.* Report of Conference for Official Development Assistance Agencies, 26-28 September. (New York: Overseas Development Council and The Synergos Institute).

ODI (1995) '*NGOs* and official donors'. *Briefing Paper*, No. 4 (August). (London: Overseas Development Institute).

OECD (1988) *Voluntary Aid for Development: The role of Non-Governmental Organisations.* (Paris: OECD).

—— (1990) *Directory of Non-Governmental Organizations in OECD Member Countries.* (Paris: OECD).

—— (1993) *Human Rights, Refugees, Migrants and Development: Directory of NGOs in OECD Countries.* (Paris: OECD).

—— (1994) *Population and Development: Directory of Non-Governmental Organisations in OECD Countries.* (Paris: OECD).

—— (1995a) *Development Cooperation 1994 Report: Efforts and policies of the Members of the Development Assistance Committee.* (Paris: OECD).

—— (1995b) *Participatory Development and Good Government.* Development Cooperation Guidelines Series. (Paris: OECD).

—— (1996) *Directory of Non-Governmental Organisations Active in Sustainable Development; Part 1: Europe.* (Paris: OECD).

Ortega Carpio, Maria Luz (1994) *Las ONGD y la crisis del desarrollo: Un análisis de la cooperación con Centroamérica.* (Madrid: IEPALA).

Oxhorn, Philip (1995) *Organizing Civil Society: The Popular Sectors and the Struggle for Democracy in Chile.* (University Park, PA: The Pennsylvania State University Press).

Pacheco, Gilda & Carlos Sarti (1991) *Las migraciones forzadas en Centroamérica: Una visión regional.* (San José: ARMIF-CSUCA).

Padrón, Mario (1982) 'Cooperación al desarrollo y movimiento popular: Las asociaciones privadas de desarrollo'. *Leiden Development Studies*, No. 3. (Leiden: Institute of Cultural and Social Studies).

—— (1988) 'Desafíos de la cooperación al desarrollo no-gubernamental para los centros de promoción'. *Socialismo y participación*, No. 44 (Diciembre), pp. 17-32.

Paige, Jeffery (1997) *Coffee and Power: Revolution and the Rise of Democracy in Central America.* (Cambridge, MA: Harvard University Press).

Painter, James (1989) *Guatemala: False Hope, False Freedom* (Updated Edition). (London: Latin America Bureau).

Paiz-Andrade, Rodolfo (1997) 'Guatemala, 1978-1993: The incomplete process of the transition to democracy', in Domínguez and Lindenberg (eds), *Democratic Transitions in Central America.* (Gainesville, FL: University of Florida Press), pp. 139-164.

Palencia, Tania (1996) *Peace in the making: Civil groups in Guatemala.* CIIR Briefing, August 1996. (London: Catholic Institute for International Relations).

Palencia, Tania & David Holiday (1996) *Hacia un nuevo rol ciudadano para democratizar Guatemala.* (Montreal: International Center for Human Rights and Democratic Development).

Parry, Geraint & Michael Moran (eds) (1994) *Democracy and Democratization.* (London: Routledge).

Pearce, Jenny (1986) *Promised Land: Peasant Rebellion in Chalatenango, El Salvador*. (London: Latin America Bureau).

—— (1993) '*NGOs* and social change: Agents or facilitators?'. *Development in Practice*, Vol. 3, No. 3, pp. 222-227.

—— (1996a) 'Critical appreciation of the work and experience of the Project Counselling Service for Latin American refugees in Central America', September. (San José: *mimeo*).

—— (1996b) 'Chile: Democracy and development in a divided society', in Leftwich (ed.), *Democracy and Development*. (Cambridge: Polity Press), pp. 168-187.

—— (1997a) 'Civil society, the market and democracy in Latin America'. *Democratization*, Vol. 4, No. 2, pp. 57-83.

—— (1997b) 'Between co-option and irrelevance?: Latin American NGOs in the 1990s', in Hulme and Edwards (eds), *NGOs, States and Donors*. (London: MacMillan Press), pp. 257-274.

—— (1997c) 'Sustainable peace-building in the South: Experiences from Latin America'. *Development in Practice*, Vol. 7, No. 4, pp. 438-455.

—— (1998) 'From civil war to "civil society": Has the end of the Cold War brought peace to Central America?'. *International Affairs*, Vol. 74, No. 3, pp. 587-615.

Pereira, Anthony (1993) 'Economic underdevelopment, democracy and civil society: The North-East Brazilian case'. *Third World Quarterly*, Vol. 14, No. 2, pp. 365-380.

Perera, Jehan (1997) 'In unequal dialogue with donors: The experience of the Sarvodaya Shramadana movement', in Hulme and Edwards (eds), *NGOs, States and Donors*. (London: MacMillan Press), pp. 156-167.

Perera, Victor (1993) *Unfinished Conquest: The Guatemalan Tragedy*. (Berkeley: University of California Press).

Pérez-Brignoli, Héctor (1989) *A Brief History of Central America*. (Berkeley: University of California Press).

Pérez-Brignoli, Héctor (ed.) (1993) *Historia general de Centroamérica (Tomo V): De la posguerra a la crisis (1945-1979)*. (Madrid-San José: CEE-FLACSO).

Pinto-Duschinsky, Michael (1991) 'Foreign political aid: German political foundations and their US counterparts'. *International Affairs*, Vol. 67, No. 1, pp. 33-63.

—— (1996) 'International political finance: The Konrad Adenauer Foundation in Latin America', in Whitehead (ed.), *The International Dimensions of Democratization*. (Oxford: Oxford University Press), pp. 227-255.

Pinzón, Manuel (1989) *Las organizaciones no gubernamentales en Centroamérica: Contribución en las perspectivas de pacificación y desarrollo entre los pueblos*. (Managua: INIES).

Plant, Roger (1996) 'Hacia la reconstrucción de la sociedad civil: Las organizaciones de trabajadores rurales en Guatemala'. *Cuestiones de Desarrollo, Documento de discusión*, No. 5. (Geneva: Oficina Internacional del Trabajo).

Ponciano, Karen (1995) *Procesos de negociación comparados: El rol de la sociedad civil en Guatemala y El Salvador*. Tesis de licenciatura en relaciones internacionales, Octubre. (Guatemala: Universidad de San Carlos).

Posas, Mario (1989) *Modalidades del proceso de democratización en Honduras*. (Tegucigalpa: Editorial Universitario UNAH).

—— (1992) 'El movimiento campesino en Honduras: Poder político y concertación social'. (Tegucigalpa: *mimeo*).

Powell, Walter (ed.) (1987) *The Nonprofit Sector: A Research Handbook*. (New Haven: Yale University Press).

Prendergast, John (1997) *Crisis Response: Humanitarian Band-Aids in Sudan and Somalia*. (London: Pluto Press).

Pritchard, Diana (1996) 'The legacy of conflict: Refugee repatriation and reintegration in Central

America', in Sieder (ed.), *Central America, Fragile Transition.* (London: MacMillan Press-ILAS), pp. 103-134.

Przeworski, Adam (1991) *Democracy and the Market: Political and Economic Reforms in Eastern Europe and Latin America.* (Cambridge: Cambridge University Press).

Puac, Victor & Edgar Ramírez (1995) 'Informe evaluación externa FUNDADESE: Programa desarrollo comunal Chichicastenango, Quiché', Febrero. (Chichicastenango: *mimeo*).

Puryear, Jeffrey (1994) *Thinking Politics: Intellectuals and Democracy in Chile, 1973-1988.* (Baltimore: The Johns Hopkins University Press).

Put, Marcel (1998) *Innocent Farmers?: A comparative Evaluation into a Government and an NGO Project Located in Semi-arid Andrha Pradesh (India), Meant to Induce Farmers to Adopt Innovations for Dryland Agriculture.* (Amsterdam: Thela Publishers).

Putnam, Robert (1993) *Making Democracy Work: Civic Traditions in Modern Italy.* (Princeton: Princeton University Press).

Rabinowitz, Alan (1990) *Social Philantropy in America.* (New York: Quorum Books).

Raffer, Kunibert & H.W. Singer (1996) *The Foreign Aid Business: Economic Assistance and Development Cooperation.* (Cheltenham: Edward Elgar).

Ramos, René (1996) 'Informe final evaluación acompañada del plan estratégico 1994-96 (CODEH-Diakonia)', Junio. (San Salvador: *mimeo*).

Ramos González, Carlos (1993) *Solución político-negociada y fuerzas sociales mayoritarias en El Salvador (1984-1990).* Tésis de maestría del Programa de Estudios Postgrado en Sociología. (San José: Universidad de Costa Rica).

Randel, Judith & Tony German (eds) (1993) *The Reality of Aid: An Independent Review of International Aid.* (London: ICVA/Eurostep).

—— (1994) *The Reality of Aid 94: An Independent Review of International Aid.* (London: ICVA/Eurostep).

—— (1995) *The Reality of Aid 95: An Independent Review of International Aid.* (London: Earth-scan).

—— (1996) *The Reality of Aid 96: An Independent Review of International Aid.* (London: Earthscan).

Redclift, Michael (1992) 'Sustainable development and popular participation: A framework for analysis', in Ghai and Vivian (eds), *Grassroots Environmental Action.* (London: Routledge), pp. 23-49.

Reilly, Charles (ed.) (1995) *New Paths to Democratic Development in Latin America: The Rise of NGO-Municipal Collaboration.* (Boulder: Lynne Rienner).

Remmer, Karen (1991) *Military Rule in Latin America.* (Boulder: Westview Press).

—— (1995) 'New theoretical perspectives on democratization'. *Comparative Politics*, Vol. 28, No. 1, pp. 103-122.

Renshaw, Laura (1994) 'Strengthening civil society: The role of NGOs'. *Development*, No. 4, pp. 46-48.

Resource Center (1988a) *Private Organizations with US Connections: Honduras.* (Albuquerque: The Inter-Hemispheric Education Resource Center).

—— (1988b) *Private Organizations with US Connections: El Salvador.* (Albuquerque: The Inter-Hemispheric Education Resource Center).

Reuben, William (1991) 'El papel de las ONGs en la cooperación europea hacia Centroamérica', in Ruben and Van Oord (eds), *Más allá del ajuste: la contribución europea al desarrollo democrático y duradero de las economías centroamericanas.* (San José: Editorial DEI), pp. 337-69.

—— (1995) 'El financiamiento de las iniciativas de la sociedad civil'. Ponencia presentada a la Conferencia Regional sobre el Fortalecimiento de la Sociedad Civil en Centroamérica,

Panamá y República Dominicana, 27 al 29 de noviembre. (San José: *mimeo*).

Riddell, Roger (1987) *Foreign Aid Reconsidered*. (Baltimore: Johns Hopkins University Press).

—— (1990) 'Judging Success: Evaluating NGO Approaches to Alleviating Poverty in Developing Countries'. *Working Paper*, No. 37, May. (London: Overseas Development Institute).

—— (1993) 'Discerning the way together: Report on the work of Brot für die Welt, Christian Aid, EZE and ICCO', July. (London: *mimeo*).

Riddell, Roger & Anthony Bebbington (1995) *Developing Country NGOs and Donor Governments: Report to the Overseas Development Administration*. (London: ODI).

Riddell, Roger & Mark Robinson (1992) 'The Impact of NGO Poverty Alleviating Projects: Results of the Case Study Evaluations'. *Working Paper*, No. 68, November. (London: Overseas Development Institute).

—— (1995) *Non-Governmental Organisations and Rural Poverty Alleviation*. (London and Oxford: Overseas Development Institute and Clarendon Press).

Riddell, Roger; Anthony Bebbington, Märta Salokoski and Tuula Varis (1994) 'Strengthening the Partnership: Evaluation of the Finnish NGO Support Programme'. *Report 1994*, No. 1. (Helsinki: Finnish International Development Agency, FINNIDA).

Riddell, Roger; Anthony Bebbington and Lennart Peck (1995) 'Promoting Development by Proxy: An Evaluation of the Development Impact of Government Support to Swedish NGOs'. *SIDA Evaluation Report*, No. 1995/2. (Stockholm: Swedish International Development Authority).

Rivera, Linda (1994) 'El caso Riccy Mabel y la justicia en Honduras'. *Entre Amigas* (Tegucigalpa), Vol. 3, No. 16, pp. 3-5.

Rivera, Rolando (1995) 'Concertación social e integración regional: ¿Una nueva forma de participación social?', in Tangermann (ed.), *Ilusiones y dilemas*. (San José: FLACSO), pp. 207-261.

Robinson, Mark (1994) 'Governance, Democracy and Conditionality: NGOs and the New Policy Agenda', in Clayton (ed.), *Governance, Democracy and Conditionality*. (Oxford: INTRAC), pp. 35-51.

—— (1995a) 'Strengthening civil society in Africa: The role of foreign political aid'. *IDS Bulletin*, Vol. 26, No. 2, pp. 70-80.

—— (1995b) 'Political conditionality: Strategic implications for NGOs', in Stokke (ed.), *Aid and Political Conditionality*. (London: Frank Cass), pp. 360-376.

—— (1996a) 'The role of aid donors in strengthening civil society', in Clayton (ed.), *NGOs, Civil Society and the State*. (Oxford: INTRAC), pp. 204-218.

—— (1996b) 'Strengthening civil society through foreign political aid'. *ESCOR Research Report*, No. R 6234. (Brighton: Institute of Development Studies).

—— (1997) 'Privatising the voluntary sector: NGOs as public service contractors?', in Hulme and Edwards (eds), *NGOs, States and Donors*. (London: MacMillan Press), pp. 59-78.

Robinson, William (1996) *Promoting Polyarchy: Globalization, US Intervention, and Hegemony*. (Cambridge: Cambridge University Press).

Rojas, Manuel (1993) 'De la posguerra a la crisis (1945-1979): La política', in Pérez-Brignoli (ed.), *Historia general de Centroamérica (Tomo V)*. (Madrid-San José: CEE-FLACSO), pp. 85-163.

—— (1995) 'Consolidar la democracia en Centroamérica: Una ardua tarea', in Tangermann (ed.), *Ilusiones y dilemas*. (San José: FLACSO), pp. 99-155.

Román, Isabel (1994) 'Peasant organisation in Central America: Taking the path towards the future', in Biekart and Jelsma (eds), *Peasants beyond Protest in Central America*. (Amsterdam: Transnational Institute), pp. 33-37.

Rosa, Herman (1993) *AID y las transformaciones globales en El Salvador: El papel de la política de asistencia económica de los Estados Unidos desde 1980*. (Managua: CRIES).

Rosa, Herman & Deborah Barry (1993) '¿Hacia el desarrollo sostenible?: Buscando un papel para la AID en la post-guerra fría'. *Boletin de PRISMA*, No. 2 (Octubre), pp. 4-8.

Rosa Borjas, German (1995) 'La opción de la Iglesia frente a la sociedad civil y la política', in Guido Béjar and Roggenbuck (eds), *Sociedad participativa en El Salvador*. (San Salvador: UCA-Fundación Konrad Adenauer), pp. 101-153.

Rosada, Héctor (1997) Guatemala: 'El desafío de la paz'. *Nueva Sociedad*, No. 147 (enero-febrero), pp. 18-26.

Rosenberg, Justin (1994) *The Empire of Civil Society: A Critique of the Realist Theory of International Relations*. (London: Verso).

Rosenberg, Mark (1994) 'La experiencia democrática y los militares en Honduras'. *Polémica* (Tercera Epoca), No. 1 (enero-junio), pp. 41-59.

Rosenberg, Robin & Steve Stein (eds) (1995) *Advancing the Miami Process: Civil Society and the Summit of the Americas*. (Miami: North-South Center Press).

Rothchild, Donald & Naomi Chazan (eds) (1988) *The Precarious Balance: State and Society in Africa*. (Boulder: Westview Press).

Rouquié, Alain (1987) *The Military and the State in Latin America*. (Berkeley: University of California Press).

—— (1994) 'El Salvador', in Rouquié, Alain (coord.), *Las fuerzas políticas en América Central*. (Mexico: Fondo de cultura económica), pp. 59-108.

Roy, Joaquín (ed.) (1992) *The Reconstruction of Central America: The Role of the European Community*. (Miami: North-South Center).

Rueschemeyer, Dietrich; Evelyne Huber Stephens and John Stephens (1992) *Capitalist Development and Democracy*. (Cambridge: Polity Press).

Salamon, Lester (1994) 'The rise of the nonprofit sector'. *Foreign Affairs*, Vol. 73, No. 4, pp. 109-122.

Saldomando, Angel (1992) *El retorno de la AID: El caso de Nicaragua*. (Managua: CRIES).

Salom, Alberto (1991) *Los orígenes del Partido Liberación Nacional y la socialdemocracia*. (San José: Editorial Porvenir-CEDAL).

Samour, Héctor (1994) 'Movimientos sociales e iniciativas civiles en la construcción de un orden democrático en El Salvador'. *Cuadernos INSIDE*, No. 2. (San Salvador: Instituto de Investigación Social y Desarrollo).

Sanahuja. José Antonio (1992) 'Los EEUU en Centroamérica, 1980-1990: ¿Ayuda económica o seguridad nacional?'. *Cuaderno de trabajo de HEGOA*, No. 10. (Bilbao: HEGOA).

—— (1994) 'Las relaciones entre la Comunidad Europea y Centroamérica en los años noventa: ¿Continuidad, reactivación o cambio?'. *Documento de trabajo CRIES-TNI*, No. 94/1.

Sarti, Carlos (1991a) 'El nuevo momento regional', in CCOD, *III consulta internacional sobre cooperación externa con Centroamérica*. (Guatemala: CCOD-COINDE), pp. 11-24.

—— (1991b) 'Los refugiados centroamericanos y los espacios para la cooperación europea', in Ruben and van Oord (eds), *Más allá del ajuste: la contribución europea al desarrollo democrático y duradero de las economías centroamericanas*. (San José: Editorial DEI), pp. 307-35.

Saxby, John (1996) 'Who owns the private aid agencies?', in Sogge *et al.* (eds), *Compassion and Calculation*. (London: Pluto Press), pp. 36-67.

Schennink, Ben & Berma Klein Goldewijk (eds) (1993) *Liberation from Exclusion: Proceedings from a Conference on Liberation from Below in Latin America and Eastern Europe*. (Oegstgeest: Cebemo).

Schmitter, Philippe (1992) 'The consolidation of democracy and the representation of social groups'. *American Behavioral Scientist*, Vol. 35, Nos. 4-5, pp. 422-449.

—— (1994) 'La transitología: ¿ciencia o arte de la democratización?', in Balletbò (ed.), *La consolidación democrática en América Latina.* (Barcelona: Editorial Hacer-Fundación Internacional Olof Palme), pp. 31-52.

Schmitter, Philippe (1996) 'The influence of the international context upon the choice of national institutions and policies in neo-democracies', in Whitehead (ed.), *The International Dimensions of Democratization.* (Oxford: Oxford University Press), pp. 26-54.

Schmitter, Philippe & Terry Lynn Karl (1993) 'What democracy is... and is not', in Diamond and Plattner (eds), *The Global Resurgence of Democracy.* (Baltimore and London: The Johns Hopkins University Press), pp. 39-52.

Schneider, Benn Ross (1995) 'Democratic consolidations: Some broad comparisons and sweeping arguments'. *Latin America Research Review*, Vol. 30, No. 2, pp. 215-234.

Schori, Pierre (1982) *El desafío europeo en Centroamérica.* (San José: Editorial Universitaria Centroamericana).

Schulpen, Lau (1996) 'Democratisering en de rol van NGO's: Twee voorbeelden uit India'. *Derde Wereld*, Vol. 14, No. 3, pp. 308-323.

Schulte Nordholt, Nico (1991) 'Toegestaan, binnen smalle marges: De positie en rol van NGO's in de Nieuwe Orde van Indonesië'. NGO-landenstudie Indonesië. *Impactstudie Medefinancieringsprogramma*, maart. (Oegstgeest: GOM).

Schulz, Donald & Douglas Graham (eds) (1984) *Revolution and Counterrevolution in Central America and the Caribbean.* (Boulder, CO: Westview Press).

Schulz, Donald & Deborah Sundloff Schulz (1994) *The United States, Honduras, and the Crisis in Central America.* (Boulder: Westview Press).

Schumpeter, Joseph (1943) *Capitalism, Socialism and Democracy.* (London: Allen and Unwin).

Schuurman, Frans (1991) 'Niet-gouvernementele organisaties in Chili'. NGO-landenstudie Chili. *Impactstudie Medefinancieringsprogramma*, maart. (Oegstgeest: GOM).

Schuurman, Frans (ed.) (1993) *Beyond the Impasse: New Directions in Development Theory.* (London: Zed Books).

Schuurman, Frans & Ellen Heer (1992) 'Social movements and NGOs in Latin America: A case-study of the women's movement in Chile'. *Nijmegen Studies in Development and Cultural Change*, No. 11. (Saarbrücken: Verlag Breitenbach).

Scurrah, Martin (1996) 'NGOs, civil society and democracy in Peru: Ideas and experiences', in Clayton (ed.), *NGOs, Civil Society and the State.* (Oxford: INTRAC), pp. 157-171.

Shah, Ghanshyam (1991) 'Non-Governmental Organisations in India'. NGO Landenstudie India. *Impactstudie Medefinancieringsprogramma*, juni. (Oegstgeest: GOM).

Shapiro, Ian (1993) 'Democratic innovation: South Africa in comparative context'. *World Politics*, Vol. 46, No. 1, pp. 121-150.

Sharpe, Kenneth (1988) 'US policy towards Central America: The post-Vietnam formula under siege', in Hamilton *et al.* (eds), *Crisis in Central America.* (Boulder: Westview Press), pp. 15-34.

Shaw, Martin (1992) 'Global society and global responsibility: Historical and political limits of "international society"'. *Millenium: Journal of International Studies*, Vol. 21, No. 3, pp. 421-434.

—— (1994) *Global Society and International Relations.* (Cambridge: Polity Press).

—— (1996) *Civil Society and Media in Global Crisis: Representing Distant Violence.* (London: Pinter).

Shearer, Bruce (1995) *The Emerging Role of Civil Society in International Development: Challenges to Foreign Aid Programmes.* (New York: The Synergos Institute).

Shetty, Salil (1994) 'Development project in assessing empowerment'. *Occasional Paper Series*, No. 3. (New Delhi: Society for Participatory Research in Asia).

SICA (1993) *El sistema de la integración centroamericana.* (San Salvador: Secretaría General del SICA).

Sieder, Rachel (1996a) 'Conclusions', in Sieder (ed.), *Central America: Fragile Transition.* (London: MacMillan Press-ILAS), pp. 271-278.

—— (1996b) 'Elections and democratization in Honduras since 1980'. *Democratization*, Vol. 3, No. 2 (Summer), pp. 17-40.

Sikkink, Kathryn (1993) 'Human rights, principled issue-networks, and sovereignty in Latin America'. *International Organization*, Vol. 47, No. 3, pp. 411-441.

—— (1996) 'The effectiveness of US human rights policy, 1973-1980', in Whitehead (ed.), *The International Dimensions of Democratization.* (Oxford: Oxford University Press), pp. 93-124.

Sims, Beth (1990) *National Endowment for Democracy: A Foreign Policy Branch Gone Awry.* (Washington, DC: Council on Hemispheric Affairs and The Resource Center).

Sinclair, Minor (1995) 'Faith, community and resistance in the Guatemalan Highlands', in Sinclair (ed.), *The New Politics of Survival.* (New York: Monthly Review Press), pp. 75-106.

Skocpol, Theda (1994) *Social Revolutions in the Modern World.* (Cambridge: Cambridge University Press).

Slater, David (1991) 'New social movements and old political questions: Rethinking state-society relations in Latin American development'. *International Journal of Political Economy*, Vol. 21, No. 1.

Smillie, Ian (1993) 'Changing partners: Northern NGOs, Northern governments', in Smillie and Helmich (eds), *Non-Governmental Organisations and Governments.* (Paris: OECD), pp. 13-43.

—— (1995a) 'NGO learning, evaluation and results: Life in a three-ring circus'. (Paris: *mimeo*)

—— (1995b) *The Alms Bazaar: Altruism under fire – non-profit organizations and international development.* (London: IT Publications).

—— (1995c) 'Painting Canadian roses red', in Edwards and Hulme (eds), *Non-Governmental Organisations – Performance and Accountability.* (London: Earthscan), pp. 157-166.

—— (1997) 'NGOs and development assistance: A change in mind-set?'. *Third World Quarterly*, Vol. 18, No. 3, pp. 563-577.

Smillie, Ian & Henny Helmich (eds) (1993) *Non-Governmental Organisations and Governments: Stakeholders for Development.* (Paris: OECD).

Smith, Brian (1990) *More Than Altruism: The Politics of Private Foreign Aid.* (Princeton: Princeton University Press).

Smith, Hazel (1995) *European Union Foreign Policy and Central America.* (New York-London: St. Martin's Press-MacMillan Press).

Smith, Steven & Michael Lipsky (1993) *Nonprofits for Hire: The Welfare State in the Age of Contracting.* (Cambridge, MA: Harvard University Press).

Sogge, David & Kees Biekart (1996) 'Calculation, compassion ... and choices', in Sogge *et al.* (eds), *Compassion and Calculation.* (London: Pluto Press), pp. 198-206.

Sogge, David; Kees Biekart and John Saxby (eds) (1996) *Compassion and Calculation: The Business of Private Foreign Aid.* (London: Pluto Press).

Sogge, David & Simon Zadek (1996) '"Laws" of the market?', in Sogge *et al.* (eds), *Compassion and Calculation.* (London: Pluto Press), pp. 68-96.

Sojo, Carlos (1991) *La utopía del estado mínimo: Influencia de AID en Costa Rica en los años ochenta.* (Managua: CRIES).

Solano, Luís & Edelberto Torres Escobar (1995) *Guatemala, elecciones 1995.* Departamento de Estudios Especiales de Inforpress Centroamericana, Octubre. (Guatemala: Inforpress Centroamericana-Fundación Friedrich Ebert).

Solares, Jorge (1995) 'Derechos humanos desde la perspectiva indígena en Guatemala'. *Cuaderno de debate*, No. 29. (Guatemala: FLACSO).

Sollis, Peter (1992) 'Multilateral agencies, NGOs, and policy reform'. *Development in Practice*, Vol. 2, No. 3, pp. 163-178.

Sollis, Peter (1993) *Reluctant Reforms: The Christiani government and the international community in the process of Salvadoran post-war reconstruction.* June. (Washington, DC: Washington Office on Latin America).

—— (1995) 'Partners in development? The state, nongovernmental organisations and the UN in Central America'. *Third World Quarterly*, Vol. 16, No. 3, pp. 525-542.

—— (1996) 'Binding the wounds: Multilateral humanitarianism, peace and democracy in Central America'. Conference 'Peacemaking and Democratization in the Hemisphere, Multilateral Approaches', North-South Center, 11-13 April. (Miami: *mimeo*).

Sommer, John (1977) *Beyond Charity: US Voluntary Aid for a Changing Third World.* (Washington: Overseas Development Council).

Sørensen, Georg (1993) *Democracy and Democratization: Dilemmas in World Politics.* (Boulder, CO: Westview Press).

Sousa Santos, Boaventura de (1995) *Towards a New Common Sense: Law, Science and Politics in the Paradigmatic Transition.* (London: Routledge).

Sparre, Ulrik (1992) 'Cooperation Across the Ocean: The Nordic NGOs and Central America', February. (Copenhagen: *mimeo*).

—— (1996) 'Ibis in Central America: Programme document on Honduras'. (Guatemala: *mimeo*).

Spence, Jack *et al.* (1997) 'Chapúltepec: Five years later'. *Hemisphere Initiatives Reports*, January. (Cambridge, MA: Hemisphere Initiatives).

—— (1998) 'Promise and reality: Implementation of the Guatemalan peace accords'. *Hemisphere Initiatives Reports*, August. (Cambridge, MA: Hemisphere Initiatives).

Spoerer, Sergio (1987) 'La diplomacia informal: América Latina – Europa y los organismos no gubernamentales'. *Nueva Sociedad*, No. 90, pp. 45-51.

Stahler-Sholk, Richard (1994) 'El Salvador's negotiated revolution: From low-intensity conflict to low-intensity democracy'. *Journal of Interamerican Studies and World Affairs*, Vol. 36, No. 4, pp. 1-59.

Stein, Barry (1997) 'Reintegrating returning refugees in Central America', in Kumar (ed.), *Rebuilding Societies after Civil War.* (Boulder and London: Lynne Rienner Publishers), pp. 155-180.

Stein, Eduardo & Salvador Arias (eds) (1992) *Democracia sin pobreza: Alternativa de desarrollo para el istmo centroamericano.* (San José: DEI-CADESCA).

Stepan, Alfred (1988) *Rethinking Military Politics: Brazil and the Southern Cone.* (Princeton: Princeton University Press).

—— (1990) 'On the tasks of a democratic opposition'. *Journal of Democracy*, Vol. 1, No. 2, pp. 41-49.

Stokke, Olav (ed.) (1995) *Aid and Political Conditionality.* (London: Frank Cass).

—— (1996) *Foreign Aid Towards the Year 2000: Experiences and Challenges.* (London: Frank Cass).

Stuurgroep Impactstudie Medefinancieringsprogramma (1991) 'Betekenis van het Medefinancieringsprogramma: Een verkenning'. *Eindrapport Impactstudie Medefinancieringsprogramma*, september. (Oegstgeest: GOM).

Sugranyes, Ana & Edgar Gutiérrez (coord.) (1990) *ONGs, sociedad civil y estado en Guatemala: Elementos para el debate.* (Guatemala: AVANCSO-IDESAC).

Sullivan, Michael (1982) 'Transnationalism, power politics and the realities of the present system', in Maghroori and Ramberg (eds), *Globalism versus Realism.* (Boulder: Westview Press), pp. 195-221.

Sundaram, Anjali & George Gelber (eds) (1991) *A Decade of War: El Salvador Confronts the Future.* (New York-London: Monthly Review Press-CIIR).

Surr, Martin (1995) 'Evaluations of non government organisations (NGOs) development projects:

Synthesis report'. *Evaluation Report*, No. EV 554. (London: Overseas Development Administration).

Swaan, Abram de (1998) 'De sociale kwestie in de transnationale samenleving', in Gevers (ed.), *Uit de zevende*. (Amsterdam: Het Spinhuis), pp. 434-442.

Tandon, Rajesh (1995) 'Board games: Governance and accountability in NGOs', in Edwards and Hulme (eds), *Non-Governmental Organisations – Performance and Accountability*. (London: Earthscan), pp. 41-49.

—— (1996) 'Local governance, democratic transition and voluntary development organisations: Some lessons from South Asia', in Clayton (ed.), *NGOs, Civil Society and the State*. (Oxford: INTRAC), pp. 113-124.

Tandon, Yash (1991) 'Foreign NGOs, uses and abuses: An African perspective'. *IFDA Dossier*, No. 81, pp. 68-78.

Tangermann, Klaus-Dieter (1995) 'La democracia centroamericana en la discusión', in Tangermann (ed.), *Ilusiones y dilemas*. (San José: FLACSO), pp. 15-61.

Tangermann, Klaus-Dieter & Ivana Ríos (eds) (1994) *Alternativas campesinas: Modernización en el agro y movimiento campesino en Centroamérica*. (Managua: Latino editores).

Taraceno, Arturo (1993) 'Liberalismo y poder político en Centroamérica (1870-1929)', in Acuña (ed.), *Las repúblicas agroexportadoras (1970-1945) – Historia general de Centroamérica (Tomo IV)*. (Madrid-San Jose: CEE-FLACSO), pp. 167-253.

Tendler, Judith (1982) 'Turning Private Voluntary Organizations Into Development Agencies: Questions for Evaluation'. *AID Program Evaluation Discussion Paper*, No. 12, April.

Ten Haaft, Gonny et al. (1989) *Noodhulp, noodzakelijk, noodlottig*. (Nijmegen: Stichting Derde Wereld Publikaties-WEMOS).

Thérien, Jean-Philippe (1991) 'Non-governmental organizations and international development assistance'. *Canadian Journal of Development Studies*, Vol. 12, No. 2, pp. 263-280.

Theunis, Sjef (ed.) (1992) *Non-Governmental Development Organizations of Developing Countries: And the South Smiles*. (Dordrecht: Martinus Nijhoff).

Thompson, Martha (1995) 'Repopulated communities in El Salvador', in Sinclair (ed.), *The New Politics of Survival*. (New York: Monthly Review Press), pp. 109-151.

—— (1996) 'Empowerment and survival: Humanitarian work in civil conflict (Part one)'. *Development in Practice*, Vol. 6, No. 4, pp. 324-333.

—— (1997a) 'Empowerment and survival: Humanitarian work in civil conflict (Part two)'. *Development in Practice*, Vol. 7, No. 1, pp. 50-58.

—— (1997b) 'Transition in El Salvador: A multi-layered process'. *Development in Practice*, Vol. 7, No. 4, pp. 456-463.

—— (1997c) 'Conflict, reconstruction, and reconciliation: Reciprocal lessons for NGOs in Southern Africa and Central America'. *Development in Practice*, Vol. 7, No. 4, pp. 505-509.

TNI (1996) 'Re-inventing solidarity?: Private foreign aid reconsidered'. *Report of a TNI-workshop*, Amsterdam, 5-6 June 1996. (Amsterdam: Transnational Institute).

Torres, Miguel; Zulma Argueta and Eugenia Castellanos (1996) 'Resultados de la evaluación de Diakonia Acción Ecumenica Sueca sobre su trabajo en la región Centroamericana'. Informe de la evaluación externa de Diakonia, Agosto. (San Salvador: *mimeo*).

Torres Escobar, Edelberto (1994) 'Will Central America's farmers survive the export boom?'. *NACLA Report on the Americas*, Vol. 28, No. 3, pp. 28-33.

Torres Rivas, Edelberto (1971) *Interpretación del desarrollo social centroamericano: Procesos y estructuras de una sociedad dependiente*. (San José: EDUCA).

—— (1987) *Centroamérica: La democracia posible*. (San José: EDUCA-FLACSO).

—— (1989) *Repression and Resistance: The Struggle for Democracy in Central America*. (Boulder: Westview Press).

Torres Rivas, Edelberto (1992) *El tamaño de nuestra democracia.* (San Salvador: Istmo editores).

—— (1993) 'Personalities, ideologies and circumstances: Social democracy in Central America', in Vellinga (ed.), *Social Democracy in Latin America.* (Boulder: Westview Press), pp. 240-251.

—— (1994) 'Democracy and the peasants', in Biekart and Jelsma (eds), *Peasants beyond Protest in Central America.* (Amsterdam: Transnational Institute), pp. 39-57.

—— (1995) 'La gobernabilidad democrática y los partidos políticos en América Latina', in Perelli *et al.* (comp.), *Partidos y clase política en América Latina en los 90.* (San José (Costa Rica): IIDH-CAPEL), pp. 295-309.

—— (1996a) *Encrucijadas e incertezas en la izquierda centroamericana: Ensayo preliminar de interpretación.* (Guatemala: FLACSO).

—— (1996b) 'Guatemala: Democratic governability', in Domínguez and Lowenthal (eds), *Constructing Democratic Governance* (Vol. 3). (Baltimore and London: The Johns Hopkins University Press), pp. 50-63.

Torres Rivas, Edelberto & Mirta González Suárez (1994) 'Con tropiezos y esperanzas: Perspectivas de desarrollo democrático en El Salvador'. (San Salvador: *mimeo*).

Toye, John (1993) *Dilemmas of Development: Reflections on the Counter-Revolution in Development Economics* (2nd edition). (Oxford: Blackwell).

Trivedi, Roy & Jagabandhu Acharya (1996) 'Constructing the case for an alternative framework for understanding civil society, the state and the role of NGOs', in Clayton (ed.), *NGOs, Civil Society and the State.* (Oxford: INTRAC), pp. 55-64.

Trudeau, Robert (1993) *Guatemalan Politics: The Popular Struggle for Democracy.* (Boulder, CO: Lynne Rienner).

Ueltzen, Stefan (1994) *Conversatorio con los hijos del siglo: El Salvador de siglo XX... al siglo XXI.* (San Salvador: Editorial Tercer Milenio).

Umaña, Carlos *et al.* (1996) 'Fundamentos para el plan estratégico Guatemala 1997-2001'. Ayuda Popular Noruega, Julio. (Guatemala: *mimeo*).

UNDP (1992) *Directorio de Instituciones Privadas de Desarrollo de El Salvador.* (San Salvador: Programa de Naciones Unidas para el Desarrollo).

—— (1993) *Human Development Report 1993.* (Oxford: Oxford University Press).

United Nations (1995) 'The United Nations in El Salvador 1990-1995'. *Blue Books Series*, Vol. 4. (New York: United Nations, Dept. of Information).

Uphoff, Norman (1992) *Learning from Gal Oya: Possibilities for Participatory Development and Post-Newtonian Social Science.* (Ithaca: Cornell University Press).

—— (1993) 'Grassroots organizations and NGOs in rural development: Opportunities with diminishing states and expanding markets'. *World Development*, Vol. 21, No. 4, pp. 607-622.

—— (1995) 'Why NGOs are not a third sector: A sectoral analysis with some thoughts on accountability, sustainability and evaluation', in Edwards and Hulme (eds), *Non-Governmental Organisations – Performance and Accountability.* (London: Earthscan/Save the Children), pp. 17-30.

Urra, Pedro (1993) 'Los organismos no gubernamentales, ONGS, factores y protagonistas de desarrollo, reconstrucción y pacificación en El Salvador'. *Presencia*, Vol. 5, No. 18, pp. 33-53.

Valderrama, Mariano (1995) *Perú y América Latina en el nuevo panorama de la cooperación internacional.* (Lima: CEPES).

Vandepitte, Mark; Freddy Merckx, Pol de Vos and Dirk van Duppen (1994) *NGO's: Missionarissen van de nieuwe kolonisatie?.* (Berchem: EPO).

Van Rooy, Alison (1996) 'Civil Society: The Development Solution?'. Paper prepared for IDS-workshop on Civil Society Research, June. (Brighton: *mimeo*).

Van Rooy, Alison (1997) 'The frontiers of influence: NGO lobbying at the 1974 World Food Conference, the 1992 Earth Summit and beyond'. *World Development*, Vol. 25, No. 1, pp. 93-114.

Van Rooy, Alison (ed.) (1998) *Civil Society and the Aid Industry*. (London: Earthscan).

Velden, Fons van der (1994a) 'Particuliere ontwikkelingssamenwerking op de helling'. *Occasional Paper*, No. 43 (September). (Nijmegen: Derde Wereld Centrum).

—— (1994b) 'Tien dilemma's bij particuliere ontwikkelingssamenwerking'. *Derde Wereld*, Vol. 12, No. 4, pp. 4-23.

—— (1996) 'Private development cooperation in transition: The rise and fall of Northern NGDOs?', in Köhler *et al.* (eds), *Questioning Development*. (Marburg: Metropolis Verlag), pp. 403-425.

Vellinga, Menno (1993) 'The internationalization of politics and local response', in Vellinga (ed.), *Social Democracy In Latin America*. (Boulder: Westview Press), pp. 3-20.

VeneKlasen, Lisa (1996) 'The challenge of democracy-building: Practical lessons on NGO advocacy and political change', in Clayton (ed.), *NGOs, Civil Society and the State*. (Oxford: INTRAC), pp. 219-240.

Ventura, Xiomara (1990) 'Las organizaciones privadas de desarrollo en la economía hondureña y su relación con los sectores populares: Un enfoque teórico, histórica y de prospectiva'. *Tésis de maestría en economía y planificación del desarrollo*. (Tegucigalpa: UNAH).

Vergara, Raúl *et al.* (eds) (1989) *Centroamérica: La guerra de baja intensidad*. (San José: Editorial DEI-CRIES).

Verhagen, Koen (1987) *Self-help Promotion: A Challenge to the NGO Community*. (Amsterdam and Oegstgeest: Royal Tropical Institute-CEBEMO).

Vilas, Carlos (1995) *Between Earthquakes and Volcanoes: Market, State, and the Revolutions in Central America*. (New York: Monthly Review Press).

—— (1996) 'Prospects for democratization in a post-revolutionary setting: Central America'. *Kasarinlan, Philippine Quarterly of Third World Studies*, Vol. 11, No. 3-4, pp. 21-66.

—— (1997) 'Participation, inequality, and the whereabouts of democracy', in Chalmers *et al.* (eds), *The New Politics of Inequality in Latin America*. (Oxford: Oxford University Press), pp. 3-42.

Vinding, Diana (1995) 'The experience with integrated rural development programmes internationally and in Ibis projects in Central America'. Desk Study, August 1995. (Copenhagen: *mimeo*).

Visser, Evert & Cor Wattel (1991) 'Las relaciones de cooperación entre la Comunidad Europea y América Central', in Ruben and van Oord (eds), *Más allá del ajuste: la contribución europea al desarrollo democrático y duradero de las economías centroamericanas*. (San José: Editorial DEI), pp. 73-120.

Vivian, Jessica (1992) 'Foundations for sustainable development: Participation, empowerment and local resource management', in Ghai and Vivian (eds), *Grassroots Environmental Action*. (London: Routledge), pp. 50-77.

—— (1994) 'NGOs and sustainable development in Zimbabwe: No magic bullets'. *Development and Change*, Vol. 25, pp. 167-193.

VonDoepp, Peter (1996) 'Political transition and civil society: The cases of Kenya and Zambia'. *Studies in Comparative International Development*, Vol. 31, No. 1, pp. 24-47.

Waal, Alex de (1997) *Famine Crimes: Politics and the Disaster Relief Industry in Africa*. (Oxford: James Currey).

Wallace, Tina (1997) 'New development agendas: Changes in UK NGO policies and procedures'. *Review of African Political Economy*, No. 71, pp. 35-55.

Wapner, Paul (1995) 'Politics beyond the state: Environmental activism and world civic politics'. *World Politics*, Vol. 47, April, pp. 311-340.

—— (1996) *Environmental Activism and World Politics*. (Albany, NY: State University of New York Press).

Waterman, Peter (1996) 'A new world view: Globalization, civil society and solidarity', in Braman *et al*. (eds), *Globalization, Communication and Transnational Civil Society*. (Creskill: Hampton Press), pp. 37-61.

Watkins, Kevin (1995) *The Oxfam Poverty Report*. (Oxford: OXFAM-UK/I).

Wedin, Åke (1984) *International Trade Union Solidarity: ICFTU 1957-1965*. (Stockholm: Prisma).

Weffort, Francis (1993) *¿Cuál democracia?*. (San José: FLACSO).

Weiss, Thomas & Leon Gordenker (1996) 'Pluralizing global governance: Analytical approaches and dimensions', in Weiss and Gordenker (eds), *NGOs, the UN and Global Governance*. (Boulder: Lynne Rienner), pp. 17-47.

White, Gordon (1994) 'Civil society, democratization and development (I): Clearing the analytical ground'. *Democratization*, Vol. 1, No. 3 (Autumn), pp. 375-390.

—— (1995) 'Towards a democratic developmental state'. *IDS Bulletin*, Vol. 26, No. 2, pp. 27-36.

White, Sarah (1996) 'Depoliticising development: The uses and abuses of participation'. *Development in Practice*, Vol. 6, No. 1, pp. 7-15.

Whitehead, Laurence (1986) 'International aspects of democratization', in O'Donnell *et al*. (eds), *Transitions from Authoritarian Rule*. (Baltimore: The Johns Hopkins University Press), pp. 1-46 (Part 3).

—— (1991) 'The imposition of democracy', in Lowenthal (ed.), *Exporting Democracy*. (Baltimore: The Johns Hopkins University Press), pp. 216-242.

—— (1993) 'The alternatives to 'liberal democracy': A Latin American perspective', in Held (ed.), *Prospects for Democracy*. (Cambridge: Polity Press), pp. 313-329.

—— (1996a) 'Three international dimensions of democratization', in Whitehead (ed.), *The International Dimensions of Democratization*. (Oxford: Oxford University Press), pp. 3-25.

—— (1996b) 'Pacification and reconstruction in Central America: The international components', in Sieder (ed.), *Central America: Fragile Transition*. (London: MacMillan Press-ILAS), pp. 215-46.

—— (1997) 'Bowling in the Bronx: The uncivil interstices between civil and political society'. *Democratization*, Vol. 4, No. 1, pp. 94-114.

Whitfield, Teresa (1994) *Paying the Price: Ignacio Ellacuría and the Murdered Jesuits of El Salvador*. (Philadelphia: Temple University Press).

Wiarda, Howard (ed.) (1981) *Corporatism and National Development in Latin America*. (Boulder, CO: Westview Press).

Willetts, Peter (ed.) (1996) *'The Conscience of the World': The Influence of Non-Governmental Organisations in the UN System*. (London: Hurst and Company).

Williams, Maurice (1995) 'Report of conference proceedings', in ODC and The Synergos Institute, *Strengthening Civil Society's Contribution to Development*. (New York: Overseas Development Council and The Synergos Institute), pp. 2-8.

Wils, Frits (1991) 'NGOs and Development in Brazil: An overview and analysis'. NGO-landenstudie Brazil. *Impactstudie Medefinancieringsprogramma*, maart. (Oegstgeest: GOM).

—— (1995) 'NGOs in Latin America: Past strategies, current dilemmas, future challenges'. *Occasional Paper Series*, No. 8. (Oxford: INTRAC).

Wils, Frits *et al*. (1992) 'HIVOS and human rights in Central America: A programme evaluation'. *Programme Evaluations of the Cofinancing Programme*, No. 53. (The Hague: DGIS-HIVOS).

Wilson, Richard (1993) 'Continued counterinsurgency: Civilian rule in Guatemala', in Gills *et al*. (eds), *Low Intensity Democracy*. (London: Pluto Press), pp. 127-160.

Wilson, Richard (1995) *Maya Resurgence in Guatemala: Q'eqchi' Experiences.* (Norman: University of Oklahoma Press).

Wood, Ellen Meiksins (1990) 'The uses and abuses of "civil society"'. *Socialist Register 1990*, pp. 60-84.

Yariv, Danielle & Cynthia Curtis (1992) *After the war: A preliminary look at the role of US aid in post-war reconstruction of El Salvador*, December. (Washington, DC: The Foreign Aid Monitoring Project).

Yashar, Deborah (1997) 'The quetzal is red: Military states, popular movements, and political violence in Guatemala', in Chalmers *et al.* (eds), *The New Politics of Inequality in Latin America.* (Oxford: Oxford University Press), pp. 239-260.

Young, Crawford (1994) 'In search of civil society', in Harbeson *et al.* (eds), *Civil Society and the State in Africa.* (Boulder, CO: Lynne Rienner), pp. 35-50.

Zaal, Fred (1991) 'Politieke ruimte en ecologische beperking: Niet-gouvernementele organisaties in Burkina Faso'. NGO-landenstudie Burkina Faso. *Impactstudie Medefinancieringsprogramma*, juni. (Oegstgeest: GOM).

Zadek, Simon & Murdoch Gatward (1995) 'Transforming the transnational NGOs: Social auditing or bust?', in Edwards and Hulme (eds), *Non-Governmental Organisations: Performance and Accountability.* (London: Earthscan), pp. 194-205.

Zamora, Rubén (1991) 'The popular movement', in Sundaram and Gelber (eds), *A Decade of War.* (New York-London: Monthly Review Press-CIIR), pp. 182-195.

—— (1993) 'El Salvador 1993: Transformaciones y desafíos', in Cantor (comp.), *Visiones alternativas sobre la transición.* (San Salvador: Editorial Sombrero Azul), pp. 143-151.

—— (1997) 'Democratic transition or modernization?: The case of El Salvador since 1979', in Domínguez and Lindenberg (eds), *Democratic Transitions in Central America.* (Gainesville, FL: University Press of Florida), pp. 165-179.

Zarate, Juan Carlos (1994) *Forging Democracy: A Comparative Study of the Effects of US Foreign Policy on Central American Democratization.* (Lanham: University Press of America).

Zivetz, Laura *et al.* (1991) *Doing Good: The Australian NGO Community.* (Sydney: Allen and Unwin).

Acronyms and Abbreviations

ACASH	Asociación Campesina Social Cristiana de Honduras
ACAN	Asociación Campesina Nacional (Honduras)
ACAV	Asociación de Comunicación Alternativa Visión (Costa Rica)
ACEN-CIAG	Agencia Centroamericana de Noticias (Guatemala)
ACORDE	Asociación Costarricense de Organismos de Desarrollo (Costa Rica)
ACSUR	Asociación para la Cooperación con el Sur (Spain)
ADC	Alianza Democrática Campesina (El Salvador)
ADESE	Asociación de Desarrollo Educativo Social y Económico (Guatemala)
AFL-CIO	American Federation of Labor – Congress of Industrial Organizations (United States)
AID	Agency for International Development (United States; also USAID)
AIDAB	Australian International Development Assistance Bureau (Australia)
AIFLD	American Institute for Free Labor Development (United States)
AHPROCAFE	Asociación Hondureña de Productores de Café (Honduras)
ALIANZA	Alianza para el Desarrollo Juvenil Comunitario (Guatemala)
ALIDES	Alianza Centroamericana para el Desarrollo Sostenible
ALMG	Academia de Lenguas Mayas de Guatemala
ALOP	Asociación Latinoamericana de Organismos de Promoción
ANACH	Asociación Nacional de Campesinos de Honduras
ANDES	Asociación Nacional de Educadores Salvadoreños (El Salvador)
ANEP	Asociación Nacional de la Empresa Privada (El Salvador)
APEMEP	Asociación de Pequeños y Medianos Productores de Panamá
APM	Asamblea del Pueblo Maya (Guatemala)
APRODEV	Association of Protestant Development Organisations in Europe
APROSJU	Asociación Pro-Superación Juvenil (El Salvador)
ARDIGUA	Asociación de Refugiados Dispersos de Guatemala
ARENA	Alianza Republicana Nacionalista (El Salvador)
ARMIF	Asociación Regional para Migraciones Forzadas
ASACS	Asociación Salvadoreña de Cientistas Sociales (El Salvador)

ASC   Asamblea de la Sociedad Civil (Guatemala)
ASDI   Asociación Salvadoreña de Desarrollo Integral (El Salvador)
ASECSA   Asociación de Servicios Comunitarios de Salud (Guatemala)
ASEPAD   Asesores para el Desarrollo (Honduras)
ASIES   Asociación de Investigaciones y Estudios Sociales
           (Guatemala)
ASINDES   Asociación de Entidades de Desarrollo y de Servicio No
           Gubernamentales de Guatemala
ASOCODE   Asociación de Organizaciones Campesinas Centroamericanas
           para la Cooperación y el Desarrollo
ASTAC   Asociación Salvadoreña de Trabajadores del Arte y la Cultura
           (El Salvador)
ATC   Asociación de Trabajadores del Campo (Nicaragua)
AVANCE   Asociación de Promoción y Desarrollo Económico
           (Honduras)
AVANCSO   Asociación para el Avance de las Ciencias Sociales en
           Guatemala
BCIE   Banco Centroamericano de Integración Económica
BFAC   Belize Federation of Agrarian Cooperatives
BHN   Basic Human Needs
BPR   Bloque Popular Revolucionario (El Salvador)
CACI   Comité Centroamericano de Coordinación Intersectorial
CACIF   Comité Coordinador de Asociaciones Agrícolas,
           Comerciales, Industriales y Financieras (Guatemala)
CADERH   Consejo Asesor para el Desarrollo de Recursos Humanos de
           Honduras
CADESCA   Comité de Apoyo al Desarrollo Económico y Social de
           Centroamérica (Panamá)
CAEM   Cámara Empresarial (Guatemala)
CAFOD   Catholic Fund for Overseas Development (United
           Kingdom)
CALDH   Centro para la Acción Legal en Derechos Humanos
           (Guatemala)
CAM   Centro de Apoyo a la Microempresa (El Salvador)
CANSAVE   Canadian Save the Children Fund
CAO   Civil Advocacy Organisation
CAPAZ   Asociación 'Camino a la Paz' (El Salvador)
CAPS   Centro de Autoformación para Promotores Sociales
           (Guatemala)
CARE   Cooperative Assistance for Relief Everywhere (United States)
CASA   Center for Alternative Social Analysis (Denmark)
CCC-B   Confederation of Cooperatives and Credit Unions of Belize
CCC-CA   Confederación de Cooperativas del Caribe y Centroamérica

CCD	Comisión Cristiana de Desarrollo (Honduras)
CCDA	Comité Campesino del Altiplano (Guatemala)
CCFD	Comité Catholique contre la Faim et pour le Développement (France)
CCOD	Concertación Centroamericana de Organismos de Desarrollo
CCOP	Comité Coordinador de Organizaciones Populares (Honduras)
CCPP	Comisiones Permanentes de Refugiados y Retornados (Guatemala)
CCR	Coordinación de Comunidades de Repoblación de Chalatenango (El Salvador)
CCTEM	Consejo Coordinador de Trabajadores Estatales y Municipales (El Salvador)
CD	Convergencia Democrática (El Salvador)
CDH	Centro de Desarrollo Humano (Honduras)
CDIE	Center for Development Information and Evaluation (United States)
CDM	Centro de Derechos de Mujeres (Honduras)
CDR	Centro de Estudios para el Desarrollo Rural de la Universidad Libre de Amsterdam (Costa Rica; the Netherlands)
CDRO	Cooperación para el Desarrollo Rural del Occidente (Guatemala)
CEAAL	Consejo de Educación de Adultos de América Latina
CEB	Comunidad Eclesial de Base
CEBEMO	Centrale voor Bemiddeling bij Medefinanciering van Ontwikkelingsprogramma's (the Netherlands; renamed *Bilance* in 1996).
CECADE	Centro de Capacitación para el Desarrollo (Costa Rica)
CEDAL	Centro de Estudios Democráticos de América Latina (Costa Rica)
CEDLA	Center for Latin American Research and Documentation (the Netherlands)
CEDOH	Centro de Documentación de Honduras
CEI	Centro de Estudios Internacionales (Nicaragua)
CELADEC	Comisión Evangélica Latinoamericana de Educación Cristiana
CEM-H	Centro de Estudios de la Mujer (Honduras)
CENSA	Center for the Study of the Americas (United States)
CEPAD	Comité Evangélico Pro-Ayuda al Desarrollo (Nicaragua)
CEPAS	Centro de Estudios para la Acción Social (Costa Rica)
CEPROD	Centro de Estudios y Promoción del Desarrollo (Honduras)
CERJ	Consejo de Comunidades Etnicas Rujunel Junam (Guatemala)

CGT	Central General de Trabajadores (Honduras)
CGTC	Confederación General de Trabajadores Guatemaltecos (Guatemala)
CIA	Central Intelligence Agency (United States)
CIADES	Centro de Investigación y Acción para el Desarrollo (Honduras)
CICA	Consejo Indígena de Centroamérica
CIDSE	Cooperatión Internationale pour le Développement et la Solidarité
CIEDEG	Conferencia de Iglesias Evangélicas de Guatemala
CIEP	Centro de Investigación y Educación Popular (Guatemala)
CIEPRODH	Centro de Investigación, Estudios y Promoción de los Derechos Humanos (Guatemala)
CIF	Centro de Integración Familiar (Guatemala)
CIFCA	Copenhagen Initiative for Central America
CII	Coordinadora Interinstitucional (El Salvador)
CIIR	Catholic Institute for International Relations (United Kingdom)
CIMADE	Service Oecumenique d'Entraide (France)
CINAS	Centro de Investigación y Acción Social (El Salvador)
CIP	Centro de Investigación para la Paz (Spain)
CIPE	Center for International Private Enterprise (United States)
CIPHES	Consejo Coordinador de Instituciones Privadas de Promoción Humana de El Salvador
CIPIE	Centro de Investigaciones y Promoción Iberoamérica-Europa (Spain)
CIREFCA	Conferencia Internacional sobre Refugiados Centroamericanos
CLE	Cámara de la Libre Empresa (Guatemala)
CNA	Coordinadora Nacional Agraria (Costa Rica)
CNC	Consejo Nacional Campesino (Honduras)
CNR	Comisión Nacional de Reconciliación (Guatemala) Coordinadora Nacional de la Repoblación (El Salvador)
CNTC	Central Nacional de Trabajadores del Campo (Honduras)
COACES	Confederación de Asociaciones Cooperativas de El Salvador
COCADI	Coordinación Caqchikel de Desarrollo Integral (Guatemala)
COCENTRA	Coordinadora Centroamericana de Trabajadores
COCICA	Confederación Campesina del Istmo Centroamericano
COCIPAZ	Coordinadora Civil por la Paz (Guatemala)
COCOCH	Consejo Coordinador de Organizaciones Campesinas de Honduras
CODDERHH	Comités Regionales de Defensa de los Derechos Humanos de Honduras

CODEH	Comité para la Defensa de los Derechos Humanos de Honduras
CODEHUCA	Comisión para la Defensa de los Derechos Humanos en Centroamérica
CODEMUH	Colectiva de Mujeres Hondureñas
CODIMCA	Consejo de Desarrollo Integral de Mujeres Campesinas (Honduras)
COFADEH	Comité de Familiares de Desaparecidos de Honduras
COINDE	Consejo de Instituciones de Desarrollo (Guatemala)
COINDI	Cooperación Indígena para el Desarrollo Integral (Guatemala)
COMCORDE	Comité Coordinador para el Desarrollo Económico del Oriente (El Salvador)
COMG	Consejo de Organizaciones Mayas de Guatemala
COMUNICA	Centro de Comunicación y Capacitación para el Desarrollo (Honduras)
CONACADH	Coordinadora Nacional Campesina de Desarrollo de Honduras
CONADEHGUA	Coordinadora Nacional de Derechos Humanos en Guatemala
CONADES	Comisión Nacional de Atención a Desplazados (El Salvador)
CONAMPRO	Coordinadora Nacional de Medianos y Pequeños Productores (Guatemala)
CONAPRO	Federación Nicaragüense de Asociaciones Profesionales (Nicaragua)
CONARA	Comisión Nacional de Restauración de Areas (El Salvador)
CONAVIGUA	Coordinadora Nacional de Viudas de Guatemala
CONCAD	Consejo Cristiano de Agencias de Desarrollo (Guatemala)
CONCAPE	Confederación Centroamericana y el Caribe de la Pequeña y la Mediana Empresa
CONCORDE	Consejo Coordinador para el Desarrollo (Honduras)
CONDEG	Consejo Nacional de Desplazados de Guatemala
CONFRAS	Confederación de Federaciones de Cooperativas de la Reforma Agraria Salvadoreña
CONFREGUA	Confederación de Religiosos de Guatemala
CONGCOOP	Coordinación de Organizaciones No Gubernamentales y Cooperativas para el Acompañamiento de la Población Damnificada por el Conflicto Armado Interno (Guatemala)
CONIC	Coordinadora Nacional Indígena y Campesina (Guatemala)
CONSOC	Consultores Sociales (Guatemala)
COOPIBO	Coopération au Développement IBO (International Building Companions) (Belgium)
COPAZ	Comisión para la Consolidación de la Paz en El Salvador

COPIC	Coordinadora de Pequeños Productores Agrícolas del Istmo Centroamericano
COPMAGUA	Coordinadora de las Organizaciones de Pueblos Mayas de Guatemala
COPP	Coordinadora de Organismos de Promoción de Panamá
CORDES	Fundación para la Cooperación y el Desarrollo Comunal de El Salvador
CORECA	Consejo Regional de Cooperación Agrícola de Centroamérica
COSUDE	Cooperación Suiza para el Desarrollo (Switzerland)
COTA	Collectif d'Echanges pour la Téchnologie Appropiée (Belgium)
COWI	Consulting Engineers and Planners (Denmark)
CPDN	Comisión Permanente de Debate Nacional (El Salvador)
CPR	Comunidades de Población en Resistencia (Guatemala)
CRCC	Comité de Repobladores de Cuscatlán y Cabañas (El Salvador)
CREFAC	Centro de Reorientación Familiar y Comunitaria (El Salvador)
CRIES	Coordinadora Regional de Investigaciones Económicas y Sociales (Nicaragua)
CRIPDES	Comité Cristiano Pro Desplazados de El Salvador
CRN	Comité de Reconstrucción Nacional (Guatemala)
CRS	Catholic Relief Services (United States)
CSC	Coordinadora de Sectores Civiles (Guatemala)
CSO	Civil Society Organisation
CST	Coordinadora de Solidaridad con los Trabajadores (El Salvador)
CSUCA	Confederación Universitaria Centroamericana
CTCA	Confederación de Trabajadores de Centroamérica
CTH	Confederación de Trabajadores Hondureños
CTRC	Confederación de Trabajadores de Costa Rica
CTRN	Confederación de Trabajadores Rerum Novarum (Costa Rica)
CUC	Comité de Unidad Campesina (Guatemala)
CUSG	Confederación de Unidad Sindical de Guatemala
CUSO	Canadian University Service Overseas (Canada)
DAC	Development Assistance Committee
DANIDA	Department of International Development Cooperation (Denmark)
DCA	Danchurchaid (Denmark)
DCG	Democracia Cristiana Guatemalteca (Guatemala)
DEA	Drug Enforcement Administration (United States)

DIACONIA	Coordinación Ecuménica de Servicio y Ayuda Humanitaria de El Salvador
DNA	Deoxyribonucleic Acid
DNI	Dirección Nacional de Investigación (Honduras)
EC	European Community
EDUCSA	Educación Comunitaria para la Salud (Honduras)
EGP	Ejército Guerillero de los Pobres (Guatemala)
ERP	Ejército Revolucionario del Pueblo (El Salvador; after 1993: Expresión Renovadora del Pueblo)
ESIP	El Salvador Information Project
EU	European Union
EUROSTEP	European Solidarity Towards Equal Participation of People
EZE	Evangelische Zentralstelle für Entwicklungshilfe (Germany)
FACS	Fundación Augusto César Sandino (Nicaragua)
FAFIDESS	Fundación de Asesoría Financiera a Instituciones de Desarrollo y Servicio Social (Guatemala)
FAPU	Frente de Acción Popular Unificada (El Salvador)
FAO	Food and Agriculture Organization
	Frente Amplio Opositor (Nicaragua)
FAR	Fuerzas Armadas Revolucionarias (Guatemala)
FARN	Fuerzas Armadas de la Resistencia Nacional (El Salvador; also RN)
FASTRAS	Fundación para la Autogestión y Solidaridad de los Trabajadores Salvadoreños
FBI	Federal Bureau of Investigation (United States)
FCG	Federación Campesina de Guatemala
FCOC	Frente Continental de Organizaciones Comunales
FDNG	Frente Democrático Nueva Guatemala
FDR	Frente Democrático Revolucionario (El Salvador)
FECCAS	Federación Cristiana de Campesinos Salvadoreños (El Salvador)
FEDECACES	Federación de Cooperativas de Ahorro y Crédito de El Salvador
FEDECOAG	Federación de Cooperativas Agrícolas de Guatemala
FEDECOOPADES	Federación de Cooperativas de Producción Agropecuaria de El Salvador
FEDEPRICAP	Federación de Entidades de la Empresa Privada de Centroamérica
FEHMUC	Federación Hondureña de Mujeres Campesinas (Honduras)
FENACOOP	Federación Nacional de Cooperativas (Nicaragua)
FENASTRAS	Federación Nacional Sindical de Trabajadores Salvadoreños
FEPADE	Fundación Empresarial para el Desarrollo Educativo (El Salvador)

FER	Frente Estudiantil Revolucionario (Nicaragua)
FES	Fondo de Emergencia Social
	Friedrich Ebert Stiftung (Germany)
FFHC	Freedom From Hunger Campaign
FHIS	Fondo Hondureño de Inversión Social
FINNIDA	Finnish International Development Agency
FIPRO	Fundación Industrial para la Prevención de Riesgos Ocupacionales (El Salvador)
FIS	Fondo de Inversión Social (El Salvador; Guatemala)
FLACSO	Facultad Latinoamericana de Ciencias Sociales
FMLN	Frente Farabundo Martí para la Liberación Nacional (El Salvador)
FOCAMI	Foro Centroamericana de Mujeres Independientes
FOCES	Foro de Concertación Económico-Social (El Salvador)
FOLADE	Fondo Latinoamericano de Desarrollo
FONAPAZ	Fondo Nacional para la Paz (Guatemala)
FONG	Federación de ONGS de Nicaragua
FOPRIDEH	Federación de Organizaciones Privadas de Desarrollo de Honduras
FORTAS	Programa de Fortalecimiento de Asociaciones (El Salvador)
FOS	Fonds voor Ontwikkelingssamenwerking (Belgium)
FOV	Federación de Organizaciones Voluntarias (Costa Rica)
FPL	Fuerzas Populares de Liberación Farabundo Martí (El Salvador)
FRG	Frente Republicano Guatemalteco (Guatemala)
FRTS	Federación Regional de Trabajadores de El Salvador
FSLN	Frente Sandinista de Liberación Nacional (Nicaragua)
FTUI	Free Trade Union Institute (United States)
FUNC	Frente de Unidad Campesina (Honduras)
FUNDADESE	Fundación de Desarrollo Educativo Social y Económico (Guatemala)
FUNDAP	Fundación de Desarrollo de Programas Socioeconómicos (Guatemala)
FUNDASAL	Fundación Salvadoreña de Desarrollo y Vivienda Mínima (El Salvador)
FUNDASALVA	Fundación Antidrogas de El Salvador
FUNDE	Fundación Nacional para el Desarrollo (El Salvador)
FUNDESA	Fundación para el Desarrollo de Guatemala
FUNDESCA	Fundación para el Desarrollo Económico y Social de Centroamérica (Panamá, El Salvador)
FUNPROCOOP	Fundación Promotora de Cooperativas (El Salvador)
FUNSALPRODESE	Fundación Salvadoreña para la Promoción del Desarrollo Social y Económico (El Salvador)

FUNTEC	Fundación Tecnológica (Guatemala)
FUR	Frente Unido de la Revolución (Guatemala)
FUSADES	Fundación Salvadoreña para el Desarrollo Económico y Social (El Salvador)
FUSEP	Fuerza de Seguridad Pública (Honduras)
GAM	Grupo de Apoyo Mutuo (Guatemala)
GEXPORT	Gremial de Exportadores de Productos No Tradicionales (Guatemala)
GNP	Gross National Product
GRICAR	Grupo Internacional de Consulta y Apoyo al Retorno (Guatemala)
GRO	Grassroots Organisation
GSO	Grassroots Support Organisation
GVC	Gruppo di Volontariato Civile (Italy)
HEGOA	Centro de Documentación e Investigaciones sobre Países en Desarrollo (Spain)
HEKS	Hilfswerk der Evangelischen Kirchen der Schweiz (Switzerland)
HIVOS	Humanistisch Instituut voor Ontwikkelingssamenwerking (the Netherlands)
IAF	Inter-American Foundation (United States)
ICAL	Instituto Centroamericano de Asesoría Legal (Costa Rica)
ICCO	Interkerkelijke Coördinatie Commissie voor Ontwikkelingsprojecten (the Netherlands)
ICIC	Iniciativa Civil para la Integración Centroamericana
ICRC	International Committee of the Red Cross
ICVA	International Council for Voluntary Agencies
IDB	Inter-American Development Bank
IDEPH	Instituto de Educación Popular de Honduras
IDESAC	Instituto para el Desarrollo Económico Social de América Central (Guatemala)
IDHER	Instituto Hondureño de Desarrollo Rural (Honduras)
IDS	Institute of Development Studies (United Kingdom)
IEPADES	Instituto de Enseñanza para el Desarrollo Sostenido (Guatemala)
IEPALA	Instituto de Estudios Políticos para América Latina y Africa (Spain)
IESC	International Executive Service Corps (United States)
IICA	Instituto Interamericano de Cooperación para la Agricultura (Costa Rica)
IIDH	Instituto Interamericano de Derechos Humanos (Costa Rica)
ILO	International Labour Organisation

IMF	International Monetary Fund
INC	Instancia Nacional de Consenso (Guatemala)
INIAP	Instituto de Investigación y Autoformación Política (Guatemala)
INSSBI	Instituto Nicaragüense de Seguridad Social y Bienestar (Nicaragua)
INTRAC	International Non-governmental Organisation Training and Research Centre (United Kingdom)
IRAM	Institut de Récherches et d'Applications des Méthodes de Développement (France)
IRELA	Instituto de Relaciones Europeo-Latinoamericanas (Spain)
IRI	International Republican Institute (United States)
IRIPAZ	Instituto de Relaciones Internacionales y de Investigaciones para la Paz (Guatemala)
ISD	Iniciativa Social para la Democracia (El Salvador)
ISED	Instituto Salvadoreño de Estudios Democráticos (El Salvador)
IUCM	Instancia de Unidad y Consenso Maya (Guatemala)
KMU	Kilusang Mayo Uno (Philippines)
KZE	Katholische Zentralstelle für Entwicklungshilfe (Germany)
LIC	Low Intensity Conflict
LP-28	Ligas Populares 28 de febrero (El Salvador)
LWF	Lutheran World Federation
MAS	Movimiento de Acción Solidaria (Guatemala)
MCS	Movimiento Comunal Salvadoreño (El Salvador)
MEA	Municipalidades en Acción (El Salvador)
MINUGUA	Misión de Verificación de la Naciones Unidas para Guatemala
MLP	Movimiento de Liberación Popular (El Salvador)
MNR	Movimiento Nacional Revolucionario (El Salvador)
MPSC	Movimiento Popular Social Cristiano (El Salvador)
MPU	Movimiento Popular Unido (Nicaragua)
MR-13	Movimiento Revolucionario 13 de noviembre (Guatemala)
MSO	Membership Support Organisation
MUSYGES	Movimiento Unitario Sindical y Gremial de El Salvador
NED	National Endowment for Democracy (United States)
NDI	National Democratic Institute for International Affairs (United States)
NGDO	Non-Governmental Development Organisation
NGO	Non-Governmental Organisation
NORAD	Norwegian Agency for Development Cooperation (Norway)
NOVIB	Nederlandse Organisatie voor Internationale Bijstand (the Netherlands)

NPA	Norwegian People's Aid (Norway)
NRI	National Republican Institute for International Affairs (United States)
OAS	Organization of American States
OCR	Oficina de Coordinación Regional (Costa Rica, Guatemala)
ODA	Official Development Assistance Overseas Development Administration (United Kingdom)
ODCA	Organización Demócrata Cristiana de América
ODI	Overseas Development Institute (United Kingdom)
OECD	Organisation for Economic Cooperation and Development
ONUSAL	Organización de las Naciones Unidas en El Salvador
ORDEN	Organización Democrática Nacionalista (El Salvador)
ORIT	Organización Regional Interamericana del Trabajo
ORPA	Organización Revolucionaria del Pueblo en Armas (Guatemala)
OXFAM (UK/I)	Oxford Committee for Famine Relief (United Kingdom/ Ireland)
PAC	Patrulla de Autodefensa Civil (Guatemala)
PACT	Private Agencies Collaborating Together (United States)
PADECOMSM	Patronato para el Desarrollo de las Comunidades de Morazán y San Miguel (El Salvador)
PADF	Pan American Development Foundation (United States)
PAN	Partido de Avanzada Nacional (Guatemala)
PARLACEN	Parlamento Centroamericano
PCN	Partido Conciliación Nacional (El Salvador)
PCS	Partido Comunista Salvadoreño (El Salvador) Project Counseling Service (Costa Rica)
PD	Partido Democrático (El Salvador)
PDC	Partido Demócrata Cristiano (El Salvador)
PDCH	Partido Demócrata Cristiano Hondureño (Honduras)
PEC	Programa Especial de Cooperación Económica para Centroamérica
PFSA	Programa de Formación en Seguridad Alimentaria
PGT	Partido Guatemalteco del Trabajo (Guatemala)
PINU	Partido Innovación Nacional y Unidad (Honduras)
PLI	Partido Liberal Independiente (Nicaragua)
PLN	Partido de Liberación Nacional (Costa Rica)
PNC	Policia Nacional Civil (El Salvador)
PPM	Pan para el Mundo; *Brot für die Welt* (Germany)
PR	Partido Revolucionario (Guatemala)
PREIS	Programa Regional de Investigación sobre El Salvador
PRISMA	Programa Salvadoreño de Investigación sobre Desarrollo y Medio Ambiente (El Salvador)

PRN	Plan de Reconstrucción Nacional (El Salvador)
PROCOMES	Proyectos Comunitarios de El Salvador
PRODECA	Programa para la Democracia en Centroamérica (Denmark)
PRODERE	Programa para Desplazados, Repatriados y Refugiados en Centroamérica
PRODESSA	Proyecto de Desarrollo Santiago (Guatemala)
PRTC	Partido Revolucionario de Trabajadores Centroamericanos
PSC	Partido Social Cristiano (Nicaragua)
PSD	Partido Social Demócrata (El Salvador)
	Partido Socialista Democrático (Guatemala)
PUD	Partido Unificación Democrática (Honduras)
PUSC	Partido Unidad Social Cristiana (Costa Rica)
PVO	Private Voluntary Organisation
PVP	Partido de Vanguardia Popular (Costa Rica)
REDES	Fundación para la Reconstrucción y Desarrollo de El Salvador
RN	Resistencia Nacional (El Salvador)
SAT	Secretaría de Apoyo Técnico (Guatemala)
SERJUS	Servicios Jurídicos y Sociales (Guatemala)
SI	Socialist International
SICA	Sistema de la Integración Centroamericana
SIDA	Swedish International Development Authority (Sweden)
SIECA	Secretaría Permanente del Tratado General de Integración Económica Centroamericana
SNV	Stichting Nederlandse Vrijwilligers (the Netherlands)
SOH	Stichting Oecumenische Hulp (the Netherlands)
TANGO	Transnational Advocacy NGO
TEAG	Transnational Environmental Activist Group
TNC	Transnational Corporation
TNI	Transnational Institute (the Netherlands)
UASP	Unidad de Acción Sindical y Popular (Guatemala)
UDN	Unión Democrática Nacionalista (El Salvador)
UCA	Universidad Centroamericana (El Salvador, Nicaragua)
UCN	Unión del Centro Nacional (Guatemala)
UCS	Unión Comunal Salvadoreña
UDEL	Unión Democrática de Liberación (Nicaragua)
UK/I	United Kingdom/Ireland
UN	United Nations
UNAG	Unión Nacional de Agricultores y Ganaderos (Nicaragua)
UNAH	Universidad Nacional Autónoma de Honduras
UNAPA	Unión Nacional de Productores Agropecuarios Asociados (Nicaragua)

UNC	Unión Nacional de Campesinos (Honduras)
	Unión Nacional Campesina (El Salvador)
UNDP	United Nations Development Programme
UNEP	United Nations Environmental Programme
UNESCO	United Nations Educational, Scientific and Cultural Organization
UNHCR	United Nations High Commissioner for Refugees
UNICAN	Unión Indígena Campesina del Norte (Guatemala)
UNICEF	United Nations Children's Fund
UNO	Unión Nacional Opositora (El Salvador)
UNOC	Unión Nacional de Obreros Cristianos (El Salvador)
UNRISD	United Nations Research Institute for Social Development
UNSITRAGUA	Unión Sindical de Trabajadores de Guatemala
UNTS	Unión Nacional de Trabajadores Salvadoreños (El Salvador)
UPANACIONAL	Unión de Pequeños Agricultores Nacionales (Costa Rica)
UPMAG	Unión del Pueblo Maya de Guatemala
UPROCAFE	Unión de Pequeños y Medianos Productores de Café de México, Centroamérica y el Caribe
US	United States
USAID	United States Agency for International Development (also AID)
USIA	United States Information Agency
WHO	World Health Organization
WUS	World University Service (The Danish branch in 1992 was renamed *Ibis*)

Index

Accountability
  and civil society building 99
  and stakeholders 111
  definition of 305
  of private aid agencies 44,
    81-84
  strategic 82-84
  towards citizens 50
ACSUR Las Segovias 331, 349
Action Aid 67
Afghanistan 52
Africa 62, 75, 95
AID 39, 94, 102, 103, 112, 174, 175,
  185, 190, 200, 210, 218, 283, 313,
  324, 325, 327, 333
Aid chain
  analysis 128-130
  and civil society building
    93-103
  and impact evaluation 107-112
  complexity of 114
  dynamics 292-293
  tension in the 78-85
Alliance for Progress 144, 146, 149,
  153, 184, 307, 341
Alliances
  building of 44, 99-100
Altruism 60, 77
*American Friends Service Commit-
  tee* 64
Angola 52, 71
ARENA 162-165, 175, 215, 239, 252
Argentina 308, 322
Armed forces
  abolishment in Costa Rica 143
  and counter-insurgency
    149-150
  and drugs trade in Honduras
    160
  and oligarchy 137

Armed forces
  autonomy of 179
  in El Salvador 152
  in Guatemala 152
  in Honduras 156-159
ASC 169, 215, 216, 258-263, 297
ASOCODE 205, 213, 274-292, 297,
  298, 332
Assessing impact, *see* Impact
  studies
Associational life 30
Authoritarian rule
  and coffee oligarchy 137
  in Central America 136-154

Band Aid 70
Bangladesh 113, 309, 315
Baseline 110, 113, 116, 125, 128, 314
Basic Human Needs (BHN) 69
Belgium 68, 81, 309, 350
Belize 222, 277, 281, 316, 347-349,
  353
Bolivia 118, 315, 333
Brandt Commission 71
Brazil 139, 308, 315
Brot für die Welt 66, 186, 194,
  204, 226, 242-244, 248-253,
  263, 310, 331, 332, 337, 346, 348,
  352
Burkina Faso 315

CAFOD 67, 194, 331
Cambodia 52, 69, 71
Canada 68, 70, 81, 177, 185, 186,
  244, 309, 350
CANSAVE 186
CARE 66, 146, 186, 191, 327
Caribbean 27, 53, 313
Caritas 64, 66, 184, 325
Carter, Jimmy 152, 160, 162, 307,
  322

Case studies
  selection criteria for impact
    studies 114, 221-223
Catholic Church
  and anti-communism 144
  and authoritarian rule 26, 41,
    55-56, 137
  and historic NGOS 184-185
  and Southern NGOS 146
  changing doctrine 145-146
  in El Salvador 190, 326,
    238-240
  in Guatemala 254
  in Honduras 225
Catholic Relief Services 66, 191,
  214, 310, 325, 327
CCFD 67, 349
CEBEMO 67, 184, 186, 194,
  226-227, 233-237, 243, 310, 328,
  331, 332, 348
Central America
  and governance aid 313
  Federal Republic of 137
  natural disasters 9, 182
  reformist political opposition
    parties 147-148
  regional civil society networks
    204-206, 278-292
Charity market 59, 77, 81
Chile 15, 31, 71, 72, 100, 308, 315
Christian Aid 65, 186, 194, 226,
  310, 331, 333
Christian Base Communities
  (CEBS) 146
Christian Democracy
  European 325
  in Guatemala 165
Christian Democratic Inter-
  national 56
CIA 175, 321

CIDSE 309
CIMADE 65
CIPIE 263, 346
CIREFCA 198, 203, 205, 206, 211,
    213, 220, 329, 331
Citizenship
    building 46-47, 101
Civil advocacy organisations
    (CAOS) 305, 313
Civil rights 23
Civil society
    and democratic transition
        35-48
    dimensions of 32
    growth in Central America
        145-147
    meaning of 30-48
    means for strengthening 42-47
Civil society building
    and aid chains 93-103
    and democratic transition
        97-103, 193-220
    and service delivery 99
    evaluation results 120-125
    in Colombia 122-123
    in Costa Rica 123-124
    in Kenya 121-122
    in Nicaragua 123-124
    inclusive approach of 96
    strategies for 94-101, 192
    transnational 76
Civil society organisations (CSOS)
    39, 95
CODEH 211, 223-237, 292, 297
COPMAGUA 169, 202
Cold War
    and democracy 51
    civil society building during
        103
Colombia 316, 323, 342
Commission on Global Govern-
    ance 62
Compadrazgo 317
Compassion fatigue 13, 69, 73
Conditionality
    and new policy agenda 101
Costa Rica
    and democratic transition 136,
        142-143, 320

Costa Rica
    and Indian population 138
    and trade unions 139
    Communist Party 140
    peasant unions 276
    political society 153
    reformist parties 139
CPDN 199, 211, 237-253, 292, 297,
    326
Cuba 144, 149, 183, 307
CUSO 186, 348, 351

Danchurchaid (DCA) 194, 226, 331,
    335, 337, 349
Danish Refugee Council 309
Democracy
    and citizenship 23
    and middle classes 27
    construction of 136
    meaning of 22-24
    preconditions for 26
    promotion of 51-53
    see also Civil society; Demo-
        cratic transition; Elections;
        Political society
Democracy promotion
    and official aid 101-103
Democratic transition
    and civil society building
        97-103, 193-220
    and external actors in Central
        America 172-177
    and pacification 135
    and the international context
        49-57
    causes of 26
    hybrid character of 171
    in Costa Rica 142-143
    in El Salvador 160-165
    in Guatemala 165-170
    in Honduras 156-160
    meaning of 21-29
    modes of 28
    pacted 25
    stages of 28-29, 47-48, 154-156
Denmark 68, 81, 334
Development aid
    evaluation of 103-112

Development Assistance Commit-
    tee (DAC) 309
Development cooperation
    moral choices 13
Development education 60, 69,
    70
DIACONIA 242
Diakonia 66, 79, 186, 194, 204,
    226, 227, 233-237, 331, 348, 349
Direct funding
    and evaluation 105
    increase of 74, 89, 210
Dominican Republic 52, 307
Donor agencies, see Official
    donors; Multilateral donor
    agencies; Private aid agencies

Eastern Europe 52, 54, 62, 74, 75,
    95, 307
El Salvador
    1989 offensive 163
    CEBS in 146
    coup of 1979 152
    democratic transition in
        160-165
    historic NGOS 184-185, 196-200
    intermediary coalitions 100
    la matanza 139
    peace process 164, 237-242
    political parties 151
    private aid to 187-188, 196-200,
        213-215, 242-253
    private sector NGOS 190-191
    reformist parties 139, 141
    repression against popular
        organisations 160
    Truth Commission 159, 322
Elections
    fraud 148, 151, 152, 317
    low voter turn-out 165
Emergency relief
    and fund-raising 62, 70
    growth of 75
    in Central America 147
    to Central American refugees
        187-192
Empowerment 77, 86, 118, 125,
    206, 265, 314

Esquipulas peace agreement 173, 178, 193, 197, 219
Ethiopia 315
Europe
    and democracy promotion 52
European Community (EC) 173, 176, 198, 240, 282, 309, 324, 347
European NGOs, *see* Private aid agencies
European Union (EU) 203, 210, 211, 217, 226, 278, 283, 312, 313, 333, 349, 351
Evaluation
    and indicators 110-111
    inter-project 128, 316
    of successful projects 114, 127
    participatory methods 126
    problems of 103-112
    see also Impact; Impact studies
EZE 67, 194, 310, 331, 332

Family Foundation of America 327
Fastenopfer 66, 186, 194
Finland 309
FMLN 150, 160, 162-165, 168, 178, 189, 207, 213, 215, 218, 223, 237-242, 251-253, 319, 321, 323, 329, 333
Food aid
    and US private aid agencies 66
Ford Foundation 80, 226, 349
FOS 331
Foster Parents Plan 65, 327
France 176, 185, 309
Freedom from Hunger Campaign (FFHC) 66, 69
Freire, Paulo 59, 68, 87
Frères des Hommes 186
Friedrich Ebert Stiftung 67, 176, 194, 328, 331, 336, 351
Friedrich Naumann Stiftung 194
FSLN 145, 147, 150-154, 183, 207, 276, 318-320, 323
Fund-raising
    and child sponsorship 81
    large campaigns 70
FUNDADESE 202, 253-274, 298

Gender balance
    impact of private aid on 119
Germany 67, 68, 81, 162, 176, 185, 324, 334
Global civil society
    access to 101
    meaning of 54-57
    transnational advocacy in 124
    see also Transnational political space; Lobbying
Global state system 27, 49
Governmental aid, *see* Official donors
Good governance 95, 101
Gramsci, Antonio
    and civil society 30
    and political society 33
Grassroots organisations, *see* Popular organisations
Greece 65
Greenpeace 55
Grenada 52
GRICAR 330
Group of 77 68
Guatemala
    1976 earthquake 185
    1993 coup 169
    and Indian population 138
    democratic transition in 136, 165-170
    elections in 165
    historic NGOs 184-185, 200-204
    Indian organisations 150, 167, 322, 253-263
    intermediary coalitions 100
    peace process 167-170
    political parties 150-151
    private aid to 200-204, 215-217, 263-274
    private sector NGOs 191
    reformist parties 139
    reformist period 1944-54 141-142
    refugees 202-203
    revolutionary movements 147

Haiti 52, 295, 307, 308
HEKS 194, 226
Helvetas 186, 309
HIVOS 67, 186, 194, 278-280, 287-292, 331, 333
Honduras
    and banana enclaves 138
    and drugs trade 160
    and peasant unions 318, 319
    democratic transition 156-160
    historic NGOs 184-185, 193-196
    human rights organisations 223-237
    Liberal reforms 143
    private aid to 193-196, 211-213, 226-227, 233-237
    private sector NGOs 191-192
    trade unions 153
Horizons of Friendship 349
Human rights organisations 305
    in Guatemala 167, 256, 260
    in Honduras 223-237, 321
Hybrid transitions 29

Ibis 67, 194, 204, 263-264, 266, 270-274, 278-280, 287-292, 330, 331, 333
ICCO 67, 79, 186, 194, 242-244, 248-253, 278, 310, 313, 328, 331, 332, 349
ICIC 44, 205, 274, 283, 284-285, 287, 297, 350
ICVA 197, 309, 330
IDB 175, 185, 211, 217, 218, 278, 283, 332, 333
IEPALA 263, 331
Illich, Iván 68
Impact
    in relation to output and out-come 107-112
    of lobbying 124
    political 123
    role of context variables 107-109, 125, 128
Impact studies
    British ODA study 112, 116-118
    British ODI study 112-121
    Danish study 112-121

Impact studies
    Dutch study 112-121, 315
    Finnish study 112-121
    lessons from 125-128
    Swedish study 75, 112-121
    see also Evaluation
India 113, 315, 316
Indian organisations
    in Guatemala 150, 253-263
Indonesia 315
Information technology 54
Inter-American Foundation 112,
    192, 263, 314
Intermón 331
International Committee of the Red
    Cross (ICRC) 64, 187
International Rescue Committee
    327
Intervention strategies
    and evaluation 107-112
    compatibility with official aid
        101-103
    Elliot's framework 87
    Korten's framework 84-87
    of private aid agencies 77-91
    see also Civil society building
Ireland 309
Israel 71, 322
Italy 68, 185, 324

Kenya 315
Kindernothilfe 309
Knights of Malta 327
Konrad Adenauer Stiftung 67, 176,
    308
Korean War 66

Lobbying
    and civil society building 101
    by transnational alliances 124
    of private aid agencies 69
Lutheran World Federation (LWF)
    194, 242, 326

Manos Unidas 67, 331
Médecins sans Frontières (MSF) 309
Mexico 187, 188, 200, 303, 323,
    326, 341, 342, 350

Middle classes
    and democratic transition
        41
    in Central America 317
Misereor 66, 146, 184, 194, 310,
    328, 331, 332
Monitoring
    and impact evaluation 314
    new systems of 126
Moore, Barrington 27, 178
Multilateral donors
    and civil society building
        101-103
    see also Official donors
Myrdal, Alva 87

NED 102, 175
Neoliberalism
    and civil society building 96
    counter-revolution of 74
Nepal 315
Netherlands 67, 68, 81, 185, 324,
    334
NGO-EC Liaison Committee 309
NGOs, see Southern NGOs; Private
    sector NGOs, Aid chain
Nicaragua
    contras 154, 158, 173, 186, 191,
        275
    democratic transition 320
    political parties 151
    private aid to 183-187
    Sandinista revolution 71, 123,
        143, 153, 183, 315
Nigeria 309
Nobel Peace Prize 45
Northern NGOs, see Private aid
    agencies
Norway 68, 81, 323, 342
Norwegian Church Aid 331
Norwegian People's Aid 65, 80,
    186, 194, 204, 243, 331
NOVIB 14, 59, 67, 112, 186, 194,
    263-264, 270-274, 309, 312, 314,
    331, 348, 349

Official development assistance
    (ODA) 60

Official donors
    and Central America 173-176
    and civil society building
        101-103, 130-131
    and private aid 62, 68, 81,
        217-218
Ownership
    of evaluations 126
    of private aid agencies 82
    of Southern NGOs 40
OXFAM-America 263
OXFAM-Belgium 186, 194, 263,
    312, 331-333, 349
OXFAM-Canada 186, 349, 351
OXFAM-UK/I 65, 112, 124, 186,
    189, 194, 204, 226, 243, 314,
    316, 326, 329, 331, 348, 349, 351,
    352

PACT 192
PADF 192
Palestine 65, 295
Panama 52, 164, 207, 222, 277,
    316, 348
Paraguay 308
Participation
    evaluating the quality of
        118-121
    two dimensions of 120-121
Partnership
    with Southern recipients 84
    see also Aid chain
Peace Corps 67
Peasant organisations
    in Central America 274-278
    in Honduras 318
Peru 118, 350
Philippines 72, 100, 308, 313, 350
Plan International 109
    see also Foster Parents Plan
Plataforma de lucha 44, 159, 195,
    231
Pluralism
    and civil society 35
    and civil society building 96
Poland 308
Political impact, see Impact; Civil
    society building

Political parties
    and civil society 33, 47
    and peasant organisations 350
    Christian Democratic 147, 151
    during authoritarian rule 41
    in Costa Rica 142
    in Guatemala 318, 322
    in Nicaragua 318
    Social Democratic 147
    weakness of 100-101
Political rights 23
Political society
    and civil society building
        100-101
    in Central America 147-148,
        151-152
    meaning of 33-37
    strengthening of 43-48
Pope John Paul II 56, 308
Popular organisations
    and 'social movements' 306
    and civil society building
        97-99
    and Southern NGOs 39, 122
Portugal 52
Poverty relief
    impact of 115-121
Private aid agencies
    aid to regional civil society net-
        works 204-206, 278-292
    and impact evaluation 103-112
    and lobbying 186
    and official aid 217-218
    and reorganisations 74, 105
    and statistics 182, 308
    comparative advantage of 62
    competition among 75
    crisis of 59, 73-77
    difference Europe and US 63
    future perspectives 76-77
    growth of 60-63
    history of 64-73
    in El Salvador 187-188,
        196-200, 213-215, 242-253
    in Guatemala 200-204,
        215-217, 263-274
    in Honduras 193-196, 211-213,
        226-227, 233-237

Private aid agencies
    in Nicaragua 183-187
    income of 80-81
    social change oriented 18
    studies on Central America 181
    support to refugees 187-192
    transnational 83
    see also Aid chain; Civil society
        building; Fund-raising;
        Impact studies
Private sector NGOs
    and civil society building 102
    and neoliberalism in Central
        America 174
    in El Salvador 190-191
    in Guatemala 191
    in Honduras 191-192
PRODERE 203, 206, 211, 218, 329,
    331, 333
Project Hope 189, 191, 327
Puerto Rico 307

Rädda Barnen 331
Reagan, Ronald 158, 162, 173, 183,
    307, 320
Refugees
    in Central America 187-189
    repatriation of 197-198,
        202-203
Riccy Mabel case 229-230
Rockefeller Foundation 65

San José Dialogue 176
Save the Children 65, 83, 109, 112,
    327
Service delivery
    evaluation results of 115-121
SICA 316
SIDA 113
Sister Cities 327
Social audit 314
Social Democracy
    and trade unions in Central
        America 176
    European 162, 183-184
    in Costa Rica 317
    in Guatemala 322
Social Democratic governments
    71

Social energy 119
Social fabric 44
Social movements, see Popular
    organisations
Socialist International 56, 71, 176,
    324
Solidaridad Internacional 331
Solidarity 78, 83
Solidarity aid 18, 72, 186, 208,
    219, 297, 301, 326, 332
South Africa 72, 100, 295
South Korea 322
Southern NGOs
    and 'gap-filling' 122
    and civil society 38-40
    and democratic transition 53
    and direct funding 313
    and the new policy agenda 74
    emergence in Central America
        146-147
    growth of 62, 70
    historic 185
    in Colombia 122-123
    in Costa Rica 123-124
    in India 112, 305
    in Kenya 121-122
    in Nicaragua 123-124
    polarisation 190-193
Southern Europe 25, 307
Soviet Union 72, 173, 183, 186
Spain 52, 176, 185, 323, 324, 342
State
    counter-insurgency 149-150
    modernisation in Central
        America 144
    strengthening of the 43
Sustainability
    lack of 117-119
Sweden 68, 81, 176, 185, 313, 324,
    334
Switzerland 309

Taiwan 322, 333
Tanzania 315
Technoserve 327
Tenancingo 196
Terre des Hommes 186
Third sector 38

Trade unions
      in Central America 139, 146
      in Honduras 143
Transitologists 26, 36, 57
Transnational advocacy networks
      55
Transnational civil society, see
      Global civil society
Transnational party networks 57,
      308
Transnational political space
      providing access to 45, 101
      see also Lobbying; Global civil
         society
Trocaire 194, 331

Uganda 113, 315
UN Development Decade 309
UNDP 214, 217, 283, 329, 333
Ungo, Guillermo 160, 163, 240,
      321
UNICEF 309
United Fruit Company 140-142
United Kingdom 81, 309, 313, 334
United Nations
      in El Salvador 164
      in Guatemala 169
United States
      AID policies in Central
         America 149, 190-193
      aid to El Salvador 190-191
      aid to Guatemala 191
      aid to Honduras 191-192
      aid to Nicaragua 185
      ambiguous foreign policy 144,
         152-153
      and authoritarian rule in Cen-
         tral America 138-145
      and Central American armed
         forces 149
      and democracy promotion 52
      and governance aid 313
      and Honduras 156-159,
         223-224
      and private sector NGOs
         184-185
      intervention in Central
         America 172-175

United States
      involvement in Guatemalan
         coup of 1954 142
      military interventions 52
      Protestant sects 182
URNG 150, 151, 165, 167-169, 178,
      202, 203, 207, 255, 262, 322, 323
USAID, see AID

Venezuela 323, 342
Vietnam War 69, 174, 219

War on Want 186
Washington consensus 74
Women's organisations
      in Costa Rica 317
      in Guatemala 169, 273
      in Honduras 212, 230, 231, 317
World Bank 43, 45, 124, 175, 185,
      210, 216-218, 278, 283, 332, 333
World Council of Churches 66,
      197, 226, 242, 330
World Relief 189, 327
World Vision 309, 327
World Wildlife Fund 55

Zamora, Rubén 160, 163, 241,
      246, 321, 339
Zimbabwe 113, 315